Internet Firewalls
— and —
Network Security
Second Edition

Chris Hare

Karanjit Siyan

New Riders Publishing   **New Riders**   Indianapolis, Indiana

Internet Firewalls and Network Security, Second Edition

By Chris Hare and Karanjit Siyan

Published by:
New Riders Publishing
201 West 103rd Street
Indianapolis, IN 46290 USA

Printed in the United States of America 1 2 3 4 5 6 7 8 9 0

Library of Congress Cataloging-in-Publication Data

```
Hare, Chris, 1962-
     Internet firewalls and network security / Chris Hare, Karanjit
  Siyan. -- 2nd ed.
      p. cm.
   Siyan's name appears first on the earlier edition.
   Includes bibliographical references and index.
   ISBN 1-56205-632-8
   1. Computer networks--Security measures. 2. Internet (Computer
   network)--Security measures. I. Siyan, Karanjit, 1954-    .
   II. Title.
   TK5105.875.I57H36 1996
   005.8--dc20
                                                     96-28232
                                                     CIP
```

Warning and Disclaimer

This book is designed to provide information about the Internet. Every effort has been made to make this book as complete and as accurate as possible, but no warranty or fitness is implied.

The information is provided on an "as is" basis. The author(s) and New Riders Publishing shall have neither liability nor responsibility to any person or entity with respect to any loss or damages arising from the information contained in this book or from the use of the disks or programs that may accompany it.

PUBLISHER	*Don Fowley*
PUBLISHING MANAGER	*Emmett Dulaney*
MARKETING MANAGER	*Mary Foote*
MANAGING EDITOR	*Carla Hall*

ABOUT THE AUTHORS

Chris Hare is a senior network security analyst for the System Security Consulting Group at Northern Telecom Ltd. (Nortel), where his activities include policy development, consulting, and secure electronic commerce. He started working in computer-based technology in 1986, after studying health sciences. Since that time he has worked in programming, system administration, quality assurance, training, network management, consulting, and technical management positions.

Chris became the first SCO-authorized instructor in Canada in 1988 and has taught Unix courses all over the world. He also has taught system administration, shell and C programming, TCP/IP, and X Windows.

As a professional writer, Chris has authored almost twenty articles for *Sys Admin* magazine and coauthored several books for New Riders Publishing, including *Inside Unix, Internet Firewalls and Network Security, Building an Internet Server with Linux*, and the *Internet Security Professional Reference*.

Chris lives in Ottawa, Canada with his wife Terri and their children Meagan and Matthew.

Karanjit Siyan, Ph.D. is president of Kinetics Corporation. He has authored international seminars on Solaris & SunOS, TCP/IP networks, PC Network Integration, Novell networks, Windows NT, and Expert Systems using Fuzzy Logic. He teaches advanced technology seminars in the United States, Canada, Europe, and the Far East. Dr. Siyan has published articles in *Dr. Dobbs Journal, The C Users Journal*, and *Databased Advisor*, and is actively involved in Internet research. Dr. Siyan has been involved with Unix systems programming and administration since his graduate days at the University of California at Berkeley when BSD Unix was being developed. He holds a Ph.D. in computer science, and his dissertation topic was "Fuzzy Logic and Neural Networks for Computer Network Management." Before working as an independent consultant, Karanjit worked as a senior member of technical staff at ROLM Corporation. As part of his consulting work, Karanjit has written a number of custom compiler and operating system developmental tools. His other interests include Novell-based, Windows NT-based, and OS/2 networks. He holds an ECNE certification for Novell-based networks and Microsoft Certified Professional for Windows NT, and has written a number of books for Macmillan Computer Publishing. Karanjit Siyan is based in Montana where he lives with his wife, Dei.

TRADEMARK ACKNOWLEDGMENTS

All terms mentioned in this book that are known to be trademarks or service marks have been appropriately capitalized. New Riders Publishing cannot attest to the accuracy of this information. Use of a term in this book should not be regarded as affecting the validity of any trademark or service mark.

ACQUISITIONS EDITOR
Karen Scott

SENIOR EDITOR
Sarah Kearns

DEVELOPMENT EDITOR
Kristin Evan

PROJECT EDITOR
Lillian Duggan

COPY EDITOR
Susan Christopherson

TECHNICAL EDITOR
John Linn

ASSOCIATE MARKETING MANAGER
Tamara Apple

ACQUISITIONS COORDINATOR
Stacia Mellinger

PUBLISHER'S ASSISTANT
Karen Opal

COVER DESIGNERS
Jay Corpus, Aren Howell

BOOK DESIGNER
Sandra Schroeder

PRODUCTION MANAGER
Kelly Dobbs

PRODUCTION TEAM SUPERVISOR
Laurie Casey

GRAPHICS IMAGE SPECIALISTS
Stephen Adams, Dan Harris, Clint Lahnen, Laura Robbins

PRODUCTION ANALYSTS
Jason Hand, Bobbi Satterfield, SA Springer

PRODUCTION TEAM
Angela Calvert, Kim Cofer, Terrie Deemer, Tricia Flodder, Pamela Volk, Karen Walsh

INDEXER
Erika Millen

ACKNOWLEDGMENTS

From Chris Hare

I would like to acknowledge the assistance of several people who have contributed to this second edition. To Mike Martineau of iSTAR Internet for providing an ISDN connection and some computing equipment for the Internet connection; to David Cross and Frank Rosano of Milkyway Networks for providing the Black Hole software and hardware. A special thank you to Steve Bourgeois of Milkyway Networks who answered what seemed like an endless barrage of questions and provided general all-around moral and technical support.

And to my wife Terri for her love and patience while I worked through many nights—she only had to endure the grumpy mornings.

From Karanjit Siyan

One of the more pleasurable tasks of being an author is to thank the people responsible for the success of a book. My heartfelt thanks to my wife Dei for her love and support. I wish to thank my father Ahal Sing and my mother Tejinder, my brothers Harjee and Jagjit, and my sisters Kookie and Dolly. Thanks also to Margaret Cooper Scott, Cathryn and Bob Foley, Craig and Lydia Cooper, Robert and Janie Cooper, Heidi and Steve Bynum, Barbara and Edward L. Scott (Scotty), and Jacquelyn McGregor for their love and support. Special thanks to Mother, Saint Germain, El Morya, Babaji, and Bhagwan Krishna. Without their spiritual support, this book would not have been possible.

Others who deserve credit are Bob Sanregret and Anders Amundson, who initially got me interested in writing teaching materials on computer networks. I also wish to thank the many people at Learning Tree for their help and support and permission to use some viewgraphs from the courses I have authored for them. In particular I would like to thank John Moriarty, Rick Adamson, Dr. David Collins, and Eric Garen. I wish to thank John Rutkai for his advice in selecting server components that I needed for writing this book.

I wish to acknowledge the many people who have helped me along the way: Harpreet Sandhu, Bill Duby, Angela, Michael Anaast, and Janice Culliford; my students Lisa, Debi, Sheri, Rondi, and Linda; Edward and Mary Kramer, Daniel Gottsegen, David Stanfield, Dr. Wagner, Bill Joy, Professor Ramamoorthy, Professor G. S. Sanyal, Professor "M," Professor Kumar Subramaniam, Professor Mahabalipuram, Marti Lichtanski, Rex Cardinale, Dave Ford, mathematician D. R. Kaprekar, Mr. Gadre, Mr. Misra, and Mr. Hoffmann.

I also wish to thank the following individuals for their help in providing me with information on their firewall products: Maurius Nacht of CheckPoint Corporation; Rick Kuzuski and Bob Harvey of Internet Security Corporation for the FireWall-1 Gateway product; Robert M. Darden and Keith Ker of Trusted Information Systems, Inc. for the Gauntlet and TIS Firewall Toolkit; and Sarah Glinka of Advanced Network & Services (ANS), Inc. for the InterLock product.

Many thanks to the staff of Macmillan Computer Publishing. In particular, I wish to thank Emmett Dulaney and Jim LeValley for their encouragement throughout the development of this book. Thanks to the project editor, Lillian Duggan, for her editorial skills, and to Mary Foote, the Marketing Manager, for her patience and willingness to listen to my suggestions.

Contents at a Glance

TABLE OF CONTENTS

PART II ❖ SCREENING ROUTERS AND FIREWALLS

PART III ❖ **APPENDIXES**

INTRODUCTION

Internet Firewalls and Network Security, Second Edition is designed for system administrators and interested users who realize the risks involved in connecting a computer system to the Internet.

In days of old, brick walls were built between buildings in apartment complexes so that if a fire broke out, it would not spread from one building to another. Quite naturally, the walls were called "firewalls."

When you connect your LAN to the Internet, you are enabling your users to reach and communicate with the outside world. At the same time, however, you are enabling the outside world to reach and interact with your LAN. Firewalls, in their barest sense, are routers through which the data traffic flows. If intruders attempt unauthorized access to your network, you stop them at the firewall and do not allow them any further into the system.

WHO SHOULD READ THIS BOOK

Internet Firewalls and Network Security, Second Edition is designed for advanced users and system administrators. It contains information and procedures for the average networked site and represents many hours spent troubleshooting and administering that environment.

HOW THIS BOOK HELPS YOU

The information presented in Part I provides an overview of security and TCP/IP. Being the protocol of the Internet, it is important to understand how TCP/IP works and what utilities are available. It also is important to understand the concept of security and why it is necessary to limit access to resources.

Part II covers firewalls and screening routers. Not only are various theories and hypothetical examples discussed, but real-world examples are given. Over-the-counter products are discussed, as well as tool kits that enable you to build your own firewall from scratch.

Part III, the appendix section, offers a quick way to locate key information. Appendix A lists the sample worksheets contained in the chapters and where they can be found. Appendix B lists sources of more information. Appendix C provides a list of vendors. Appendix D provides the manual pages for OPIE and Log Daemon, two forms of the one-time password authentication system.

CONVENTIONS USED IN THIS BOOK

Throughout this book, certain conventions are used to help you distinguish the various elements of firewalls, system files, and sample data. Before you look ahead, you should spend a moment examining these conventions.

❖ Shortcut keys and key combinations are found in the text where appropriate. In most applications, for example, Shift+Ins is the shortcut key combination for the Paste command.

❖ Key combinations appear in the following formats:

KEY1+KEY2. When you see a plus sign (+) between key names, you should hold down the first key while pressing the second key. Then release both keys.

KEY1, KEY2. When a comma (,) appears between key names, you should press and release the first key and then press and release the second key.

❖ Information you type is in **bold**. This convention applies to individual letters and numbers, as well as words or phrases. It does not apply, however, to special keys, such as Enter, Esc, or Ctrl.

❖ New terms appear in *italic*.

❖ Text displayed on-screen but not as part of an application, such as system prompts and messages, appear in a special, `computer`, typeface.

SPECIAL TEXT USED IN THIS BOOK

Throughout this book you will find examples of special text. These passages have been given special treatment so you can instantly recognize their significance and easily find them for future reference.

NOTES, TIPS, AND WARNINGS

Internet Firewalls and Network Security, Second Edition features many special sidebars, which are set apart from the normal text by icons. The book includes three distinct types of sidebars: Notes, Tips, and Warnings.

A *note* includes "extra" information you should find useful, but which complements the discussion at hand instead of being a direct part of it. A note might describe special situations that arise when you use a firewall under certain circumstances, and tell you what steps to take when such situations arise. Notes also might explain ways to avoid problems with your software and hardware.

A *tip* provides quick instructions for getting the most from your firewall implementation as you follow the steps outlined in the general discussion. A tip might show you ways to conserve memory in some setups, speed up a procedure, or perform one of many timesaving and system-enhancing techniques.

WARNING

A *warning* tells you when a procedure might be dangerous, that is, when you run the risk of losing data, locking your system, or even damaging your hardware. Warnings generally explain ways to avoid such losses, or describe the steps you can take to remedy them.

NEW RIDERS PUBLISHING

The staff of New Riders Publishing is committed to bringing you the very best in computer reference material. Each New Riders book is the result of months of work by authors and staff who research and refine the information contained within its covers.

As part of this commitment to you, the NRP reader, New Riders invites your input. Please let us know whether you enjoy this book, if you have trouble with the information and examples presented, or if you have a suggestion for the next edition.

Please note, though, that New Riders' staff cannot serve as a technical resource for firewalls, security, or questions about software- or hardware-related problems. Please refer to the documentation that accompanies your product or to the application's Help systems.

If you have a question or comment about any New Riders book, there are several ways to contact New Riders Publishing. We will respond to as many readers as we can. Your name, address, or phone number never becomes part of a mailing list or is used for any purpose other than to help us continue to bring you the best books possible. You can write us at the following address:

New Riders Publishing
Attn: Associate Publisher
201 W. 103rd Street
Indianapolis, IN 46290

If you prefer, you can fax New Riders Publishing at (317)581-4670.

You can send electronic mail to New Riders at the following Internet address:

edulaney@newriders.mcp.com

NRP is an imprint of Macmillan Computer Publishing. To obtain a catalog of information, or to purchase any Macmillan Computer Publishing book, call (800)428-5331.

Thank you for selecting *Internet Firewalls and Network Security, Second Edition*!

PART I

NETWORK SECURITY BACKGROUND

## CHAPTER 1

UNDERSTANDING TCP/IP

T CP/IP IS A SET OF DATA communications protocols. These protocols allow for the routing of information from one machine to another, the delivery of e-mail and news, even the use of remote login capabilities.

The name TCP/IP refers to the two major protocols, Transmission Control Protocol and Internet Protocol. While there are many other protocols that provide services that operate over TCP/IP, these are the most common.

THE HISTORY OF **TCP/IP**

Internetworking with TCP/IP has been around for many years—almost as many years as Unix has been available. TCP/IP, or Transmission Control Protocol/Internet Protocol, grew out of the work that was done with the Defense Advanced Research Projects Agency, or DARPA. In 1969, DARPA sponsored a project that became known as the ARPANET. This network mainly provided high-bandwidth connectivity between the major computing sites in government, educational, and research laboratories.

The ARPANET provided those users with the ability to transfer e-mail and files from one site to another, while DARPA provided the research funding for the entire project. Through the evolution of the project, it became clear that a wide range of benefits and advantages were available, and that it was possible to provide cross-country network links.

During the 1970s, DARPA continued to fund and encourage research on the ARPANET, which consisted chiefly of point-to-point leased line interconnections. DARPA also started pushing for research into alternate forms of communication links, such as satellites and radio. It was during this time that the framework for a common set of networking technologies started to form. The result was TCP/IP. In an attempt to increase acceptance and use of these protocols, DARPA provided a low-cost implementation of them to the user community. This implementation was targeted chiefly at the University of California at Berkeley's BSD Unix implementation.

DARPA funded the creation of the company Bolt Beranek and Newman Inc. (BBN) to develop the implementation of TCP/IP on BSD Unix. This development project came at the time when many sites were in the process of adopting and developing local area network technologies, which were based closely on extensions of the previous single computer environments that were already in use. By January 1983, all the computers connected to the ARPANET were running the new TCP/IP protocols. In addition, many sites that were not connected to the ARPANET also were using the TCP/IP protocols.

Because the ARPANET generally was limited to a select group of government departments and agencies, the National Science Foundation created the NSFNet that also was using the successful ARPANET protocols. This network, which in some ways was an extension of the ARPANET, consisted of a backbone network connecting all the super-computer centers within the United States and a series of smaller networks that were then connected to the NSFNet backbone.

Because of the approaches taken with NSFNet, numerous network topologies are available, and TCP/IP is not restricted to any single one. This means that TCP/IP can run on token ring, Ethernet and other bus topologies, point-to-point leased lines, and more. However, TCP/IP has been closely linked with Ethernet—so much so that the two were used almost interchangeably.

Since that time, the use of TCP/IP has increased at a phenomenal rate, and the number of connections to the Internet, or this global network of networks, has also increased at an almost exponential rate. A countless number of people are making a living off the Internet, and with the current trends in information dissemination, it likely will touch the lives of every person in the developed world at some time.

TCP/IP, however, is not a single protocol. In fact, it consists of a number of protocols, each providing some very specific services. The remainder of this chapter examines how addressing is performed in TCP/IP, network configuration, the files controlling how TCP/IP can be used, and many of the various administrative commands and daemons.

> A daemon is a program that runs to perform a specific function. Unlike many commands that execute and exit, a daemon performs its work and waits for more. For example, sendmail is a daemon. It remains active even if there is no mail to be processed.

EXPLORING ADDRESSES, SUBNETS, AND HOST NAMES

Each machine on the Internet must have a distinctly different address, like your postal address, so that information destined for it can be successfully delivered. This address scheme is controlled by the Internet Protocol (IP).

> As of the time of this writing, the Internet Engineering Task Force (IETF) has almost completed the specification for the next version of IP, which will include a much larger address space. The larger address space is needed in response to the large number of computers that now are being connected to the Internet.

Each machine has its own IP Address, and that IP address consists of two parts: the network portion and the host portion. The network part of the address is used to describe the network on which the host resides, and the host portion is used to identify the particular host. To ensure that network addresses are unique, a central agency is responsible for the assignment of those addresses.

Because the original Internet designers did not know how the Internet would grow, they decided to design an address scheme flexible enough to handle a larger network with many hosts or a smaller network with only a few hosts. This addressing scheme introduces address classes, of which there are four.

IP addresses can be expressed in several different forms. First is the dotted decimal notation, which shows a decimal number with each byte separated by a period, as in 192.139.234.102. Alternatively, this address also can be expressed as a single hexadecimal number such as 0xC08BEA66. The most commonly used address format, however, is the dotted decimal notation.

ADDRESS CLASSES

As mentioned, there are four major address classes: class A, B, C, and D. Classes A, B, and C are used to identify the computers that share a common network. A class D, or multicast address, is used to identify a set of computers that all share a common protocol. Because the first three classes are more commonly used, this chapter focuses on them. Regardless of the address class, each address consists of 32 bits, or 4 bytes. Each byte is commonly referred to as an octet, so an IP address consists of four octets.

Each octet can have a value from 0 to 255. Certain values, however, have a special meaning that is shown in table 1.1 later in this chapter.

CLASS A ADDRESSES

In a class A address, the first octet represents the network portion, and the remaining three identify the host (see fig. 1.1).

FIGURE 1.1

The class A address format.

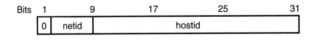

This address class means that this network can have millions of hosts because there are 24 bits available to specify the host address. In figure 1.1, you see that the first bit of the first octet is set to 0. This means that the network portion of the address must be less than 128. Actually, the network portion of a class A address ranges from 1 to 127.

CLASS B ADDRESSES

A class B address is similar in structure to a class A, with the exception that a class B address uses two octets for the network portion and two octets for the host portion (see fig. 1.2). This means that there can be more class B networks, each with thousands of hosts.

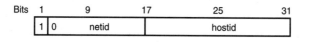

FIGURE 1.2

The class B address format.

As illustrated in figure 1.2, the configuration of the class B address is such that each portion shares the same amount of the address. The first two bits of the network address are set to 1 and 0, meaning that the network address ranges from 128 to 191. With this format, each network can have thousands of hosts.

CLASS C ADDRESSES

A class C address uses three octets for the network portion, and one octet for the host. The result is that there can be more class C networks, each with a small number of hosts. Because the maximum value of a single octet is 255, and there are two reserved values, there can be 253 hosts for a class C network. This network format is illustrated in figure 1.3.

FIGURE 1.3

The class C address format.

As illustrated in figure 1.3, the first two bits of the network address are set to one. This means that the network address for a class C network ranges from 192 to 223. The remaining values from 224 to 255 are used in the fourth address class.

SPECIAL ADDRESSES

It has been mentioned that there are several different addresses reserved for special purposes. These addresses are listed in table 1.1.

TABLE 1.1
Reserved Addresses

Dotted Decimal Address	Explanation
0.0.0.0	All hosts broadcast address for old Sun networks.
num.num.num.0	Identifies the entire network.
num.num.num.255	All hosts on the specified network. (Broadcast Address)
255.255.255.255	All hosts broadcast for current networks.

These reserved addresses cannot be used to address any host or network. They have been specifically reserved. There can be other reserved addresses depending upon other factors, which you will see later in this chapter.

SUBNETS

Each host on a network has a specific IP address to enable other hosts to communicate with it. Depending upon the class of network, there can be anywhere from 253 to millions of hosts on a network. It would not be practical, however, for a class A or class B address to be restricted to one network with thousands or millions of hosts. To solve this problem, subnets were developed to split the host portion of the address into additional networks.

Subnets work by taking the host portion of the address and splitting it through the use of a netmask. The netmask essentially moves the dividing line between the network and the hosts from one place to another within the address. This has the effect of increasing the number of available networks, but reduces the number of hosts that can be connected to each network.

The use of subnets does provide advantages. Many smaller organizations can only obtain a class C address, yet they have several distinct offices that must be linked together. If they only have one IP address, a router will not connect the two locations because the router requires that each network have a distinct address. By splitting the network into subnets, they can use a router to connect the two networks because they now have distinctly different network addresses.

The subnet is interpreted through the netmask, or subnet mask. If the bit is on in the netmask, that equivalent bit in the address is interpreted as a network bit. If the bit is off, it is considered part of the host address. It is important to note that the subnet is known only locally; to the rest of the Internet, the address looks like a standard IP address.

As noted in table 1.2, each class of IP addresses has a default netmask associated with it.

TABLE 1.2
Standard Netmasks

Address Class	Default Netmask
A	255.0.0.0
B	255.255.0.0
C	255.255.255.0

In order to understand fully and appreciate how this works, you need to consider an example. Assume that you have a network address of 198.53.64.0, and you want to break this up into subnets. To further subdivide this class C network, it is necessary for you to use some of the bits in the host portion, or last byte, of the address as part of the network portion. While this increases the number of networks you can have, it decreases the number of hosts that can be on each subnet.

The Internet RFC 950 also requires that the first and last division of each subnet be reserved. This means that the actual number of useable subnets is two less than the total number of divisions. For example, if you want to split your class C network into two divisions, you cannot connect any hosts! If you want to have six subnets, then you must split your network into eight divisions.

The following example illustrates how the bits in the last octet are set, and how many subnets and hosts can be created for each. The variable portion that represents the bits used for the host portion is identified by the letter V. The fixed portion of the address is identified by the letter F.

```
8  7  6  5  4  3  2  1  Divisions   Subnets   Hosts/Subnets
-------------------------------------------------------------
F  V  V  V  V  V  V  V     2           0           0
F  F  V  V  V  V  V  V     4           2           62
F  F  F  V  V  V  V  V     8           6           30
F  F  F  F  V  V  V  V     16          14          14
F  F  F  F  F  V  V  V     32          30          6
F  F  F  F  F  F  V  V     64          62          2
F  F  F  F  F  F  F  V     128         126         0
```

The preceding example shows that you can effectively only use a minimum division of four with two subnets and 62 hosts per net, or a maximum of 64 divisions which results in 62 subnets of two hosts each. The first example could be used for two separate ethernets, while the second could be used for a series of point-to-point protocol links.

However, the selection of the type of subnets that should be chosen is determined by the maximum number of users that will be required on any subnet, and the minimum number of subnets required.

The possible network portions formed in the development of your divisions are formed by evaluating the values of the fixed portion of the last byte. Looking back to the last example, you see that to split our class C address into eight divisions, or 6 subnets, you need to fix the first three bits in the last octet. The network portions are formed through the evaluation of the non-fixed portion of the last byte. Consider the following example, which lists the bit combinations and illustrates how the Class address is split into the subnets.

```
Network   Host
8  7  6 ¦ 5  4  3  2  1      Decimal Values
-----------------------------------------------
0  0  1 ¦ 0  0  0  0  0          32
0  1  0 ¦ 0  0  0  0  0          64
0  1  1 ¦ 0  0  0  0  0          96
1  0  0 ¦ 0  0  0  0  0         128
1  0  1 ¦ 0  0  0  0  0         160
1  1  0 ¦ 0  0  0  0  0         192
```

As shown in the preceding example, the top three bits—8, 7, and 6—are fixed in that they are used as part of the host address. This means that the available networks become the following, where N, O, and P represent the first three octets in the address respectively:

Network
N.O.P.32
N.O.P.64
N.O.P.96
N.O.P.128
N.O.P.160
N.O.P.192

The standard netmask for a class C address is 255.255.255.0. For our subnetted network, the first three bytes remain the same. The fourth byte is created by setting the network portion to 1s and the host portion to 0. Looking back at the preceding example, you see what the network addresses will be. You use the same format for determining the netmask. This means that the netmasks for these subnets are the following:

Network	Broadcast	Netmask
N.O.P.32	N.O.P.31	255.255.255.32
N.O.P.64	N.O.P.63	255.255.255.64
N.O.P.96	N.O.P.95	255.255.255.96
N.O.P.128	N.O.P.127	255.255.255.128
N.O.P.160	N.O.P.159	255.255.255.160
N.O.P.192	N.O.P.191	255.255.255.192

The end result is that you have split this class C address into six subnetworks, thereby increasing your available address space without having to apply for an additional network address.

When looking at the netmask, it is easy to see why many administrators stick with byte-oriented netmasks—they are much easier to understand. By using a bit-oriented approach to the netmask, however, many different configurations can be achieved. Using a netmask of 255.255.255.192 on a class C address, for example, creates four subnets. The same netmask on a class B address, however, creates more than a thousand subnets!

In an attempt to help control the assignment of IP Addresses to organizaitons that were not connected to the Internet, a series of Private Network Addresses were reserved. This was accomplished in RFC1597.

RFC1597, which is included on the CD-ROM that accompanies this book, provides for three network addresses to be reserved for the use of organizations that are not connected to the Internet or who will be installing a firewall. These networks are a Class A at 10.0.0.0 to 10.255.255.255, a Class B at 172.16.0.0 to 172.31.255.255, and a Class C. at 192.168.1.90 to 192.168.254.0. By using the Private Network Addresses, the available public address space can be used more effectively.

CLASSLESS ADDRESSES AND CIDR

With the rapid expansion of the Internet, and more and more organizations wanting to have a TCP/IP-based network, a problem has begun to emerge. Aside from the rapid use of available network address space, a more ominous problem is the size of the global routing tables for routing information throughout the world.

The problem with the global routing tables is that each network requires its own individual routing entry, which causes the routing tables to be very large, particularly in the backbone network. This problem is made even worse by the fact that many Internet Service Providers advertise the route to a PPP host whenever that host dials in. This causes the routes to change very quickly, which results in excessive load in the backbone.

Classless Inter-Domain Routing (CIDR) was introduced to solve this problem. The purpose of CIDR is to change our view of addresses from "classful" to "classless." This method of viewing network addresses also is known as *aggregation*. CIDR eliminates the concept of class A, B, and C networks and replaces this with a generalized IP prefix.

> The concept of CIDR was first presented back in 1992, at which time it was known as *Supernetting*. The name CIDR was adopted in 1993.

N O T E

The IP prefix refers to the number of bits of the network part of the IP address. A former class B address may appear as 172.50.0.0/16, which is the same as 256 class Cs, which can appear as 192.200.0.0/16. A single class C appears as 192.201.1.0/24. The IP prefix consists of an IP address and a mask length. The mask length specifies the number of leftmost contiguous significant bits in the corresponding IP address. Thus, an IP prefix with a prefix length of 15 (denoted /15) covers the address space of 128,000 IP addresses, and a /17 covers the address space of 32,000 IP addresses.

CIDR lessens the local administrative burden of updating external routing, saves routing table space in all backbone routers, and reduces route flapping (rapid changes in routes), and thus CPU load, in all backbone routers. The benefit of using aggregation in advertising network routes is felt by the entire Internet. Aggregation keeps the local routing changes local to the Internet Service Provider: the rest of the Internet does not see a new route go up or down. One Internet Service Provider was broadcasting approximately 12,000 routes before moving to aggregation. That provider is now advertising approximately 6,000 and expects to decrease this number even more. CIDR also allows delegation of pieces of what used to be called *network numbers* to customers, and therefore makes it possible to utilize available address space more efficiently.

Internet service providers are now responsible for assigning IP addresses or network numbers to their customers. These addresses are part of the CIDR block assigned to each individual provider.

There are a number of routing protocols in use on the Internet, including RIP, OSPF, IGRP, and EGRP. The only one that supports the use of CIDR, however, is BGP4. More information on CIDR can be obtained from the CIDR FAQ found at `http://www.rain.net/faqs/cidr.faq.html`.

HOST NAMES

Each device connected to the Internet must be assigned a unique IP address, but IP addresses can be difficult to remember. Consequently, each device is generally assigned a host name, which is used to access that device. The network does not require the use of names, but they do make the network easier to use.

For TCP/IP to work properly, the host name must be translated into the corresponding IP address. This can be accomplished through several different methods, including looking up the host name in a file called the host table or resolving it through the use of the Domain Name Service (DNS).

> Methods for translating the host name into the corresponding IP address and DNS are discussed later in this chapter.
>
> N O T E

Within each organization, the host name must be unique. The host name consists of two pieces: the actual host name and the TCP/IP domain. The domain is assigned by a central registry depending on the country you are in and the type of organization you are registering. The most commonly used domains are .com, .edu, and .gov for commercial, educational, and government institutions within the United States. While it is possible to obtain a domain using these outside the United States, it is best not to.

For organizations outside the United States, there may be other rules governing how domains are assigned. For example, a company in Canada named Widgets Inc. could apply for widgets.ca, where .ca denotes that the organization is in Canada. If the same company was in the United Kingdom, then the domain would likely be widgets.co.uk, indicating that it is a commercial organization within the United Kingdom.

Regarding the actual names for the given hosts, the Internet Request for Comments (RFC) number 1178 provides some excellent guidelines regarding how to name systems. Here are some guidelines you should remember:

❖ Use real words that are short, easy to spell, and easy to remember. The point of using host names instead of IP addresses is that they are easier to use. If host names are difficult to spell and remember, they defeat their own purpose.

❖ Use theme names. All hosts in a group could be named after human movements such as fall, jump, or hop, or cartoon characters, foods, or other groupings. Theme names are much easier to think up than unrestricted names.

❖ Avoid using project names, personal names, acronyms, or other such cryptic jargon. This type of host name typically is renamed in the future, which can sometimes be more difficult than it sounds.

> The only requirement is that the host name be unique within the domain. A well-chosen name, however, can save future work and make the user community happier.
>
> N O T E

The host name of your computer can be determined by using the hostname command, as shown in the following:

```
$ hostname
oreo.widgets.ca
$
```

17

On some TCP/IP implementations, the hostname command does not print the information as shown above, but only prints the actual name of the system. The output of hostname is the name of the system and the TCP/IP domain name.

WORKING WITH NETWORK INTERFACES

Each device that is to be connected to a network must have a network interface. This network interface must be consistent with the media on which the network is running. A network card for token ring, for example, cannot be connected to a thin coaxial cable network.

The following are the commonly used media types:

Token Ring

Thinnet (RG-58U coaxial cable)

Ethernet (RG-8U coaxial cable)

Twisted-pair cable

Fiber optics

Each network interface has a name for the device and an IP address. If there is more than one network interface in a device, each network interface must be part of a different network. That is, the IP addresses must be different, as shown in figure 1.4.

The exact name used for each device is vendor implemented, and often is different depending upon the type of interface that is in use. Table 1.3 lists some of the network interface names that are used, and on what systems those names are found.

TABLE 1.3
Network Interface Names

Interface Name	Operating System
le0, ie0	SunOS 4.1.3, 4.1.4
wdn0,e3a,sl0,ppp1	SCO Unix
du0	DEC Ultrix
le0	Linux
we0	BSD/OS Version 2.0
lan0	HP HP/UX 9.0

Bear in mind that these are only examples of a small collection of operating systems. There are many other network device names that are dependent upon the type of hardware installed on your system.

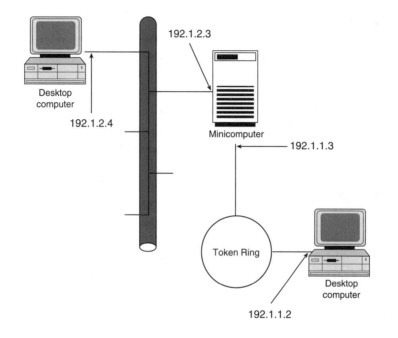

FIGURE 1.4

Network interfaces.

Consequently, as the system is configured, the network administrator must decide what the name of the device is, or must understand how to query the system to determine the name of the device. Having this information is essential to successfully configuring the network interface.

CONFIGURATION USING IFCONFIG

Except for Serial Line Internet Protocol (SLIP) and Point-to-Point Protocol (PPP) interfaces, the ifconfig command is used to configure the interface, including its IP address, broadcast address, netmask, and whether or not the interface is operational. There are some variations to this command, so it is wise to check out your system's documentation when setting up your interface.

Normally ifconfig is used at boot time to configure the interface. ifconfig also can be used after the system is running to change the IP address, or other interface configuration information.

The command syntax for ifconfig is the following:

```
ifconfig interface address-family address destination-address parameters
```

The interface value identifies the name of the interface that is being configured—wdn0, for example. The address family identifies the type of addressing used for this interface. Currently, the only value supported for this argument is inet.

The address value can consist of a host name that is found in /etc/hosts, or an Internet address expressed in dot notation. If the name form is used and the host name is not found in the /etc/hosts file, an error is returned.

Table 1.4 lists the commonly available parameters that can be configured with ifconfig. This list of options should by no means be considered exhaustive.

TABLE 1.4
ifconfig Commands

Command	Function
up	This marks the interface as being up, or operational. When the first address of the interface is configured, the interface is marked as up. It also can be used to reset an interface after it was previously marked down.
down	This marks an interface down. When the interface is marked down, the system does not attempt to transmit messages through that interface. If possible, the interface will be reset to prevent the reception of incoming packets as well. Use of this command does not automatically disable the routes that use this interface.
trailers	This requests the use of a trailer-link-level encapsulation when transmitting. If the interface is capable of supporting trailers, the system encapsulates the outgoing messages in a manner that minimizes the number of memory-to-memory copy operations performed by the receiver.
-trailers	Disables the use of trailer encapsulation.
arp	This enables the use of the Address Resolution Protocol in mapping between network-level addresses and link-level addresses.
-arp	This disables the use of the Address Resolution Protocol.

Command	Function
metric N	This sets the routing metric for this interface, which is by default 0. The routing metric is used by the route daemon, routed. The higher the metric, the less favorable the route is.
debug	This enables network-driver-level debugging.
-debug	This disables driver-dependent debugging code.
netmask MASK	This specifies how much of the address is used for the division of a network into subnets. The netmask contains 1s for the bit positions that are used for the network and subnet parts, and 0s for the host portion.
dest-address	This specifies the destination address of the correspondent on the other end of a point-to-point link.
broadcast	Specifies the address to use when sending a packet to all of the hosts on a network. The default value is the network portion and all 1s for the host portion. If the network portion is 192.139.234, for example, then the broadcast address is 192.139.234.255.

The following illustrates using ifconfig on an SCO system that has only one interface.

```
ifconfig lo0 localhost
ifconfig wdn0 198.73.138.2 -trailers netmask 255.255.255.0 broadcast
➡198.73.138.255
```

The preceding code has two lines. The first illustrates defining the localhost loopback interface, and the second defines an interface named wdn0 using an IP address of 198.73.138.2. The trailer encapsulation option is turned off (-trailers), the netmask is 255.255.255.0, and the broadcast address is the default, using all 1s for the host portion.

The following code illustrates using ifconfig on a SunOS 4.1.3 system.

```
ifconfig le0 198.73.138.6 -trailers netmask 0xffffff00 broadcast 198.73.138.255
```

The options used on the SunOS system are the same as with SCO systems, except that the netmask defined on the Sun system can use either a hexadecimal notation or the dot notation.

> The use of the ifconfig is restricted to the super-user when used to configure the interface. A normal user can use the ifconfig command to query the status of the interface.

NOTE

REVIEWING THE NETWORK CONFIGURATION FILES

A large number of files assist in the configuration and control of TCP/IP on the system. Next, this chapter examines those files, their use, and their formats. Understanding the services that are controlled from these files is essential to locate hidden security problems later. Some of these files also have inherent security problems, which will also be discussed.

THE /ETC/HOSTS FILE

The purpose of the /etc/hosts file is to provide simple host name to IP address resolution. Remember that TCP/IP only requires the use of IP addresses. The use of host names is for your convenience and ease of use. When a host name is used, TCP/IP examines the contents of the /etc/hosts file (assuming that Domain Name Service is not in use) to find the IP address for the host.

The format of an entry in the /etc/hosts file is as follows:

```
address      official name     alias ...
```

The columns refer to the IP address, the official or fully qualified domain name (FQDN), and any aliases for the machine. This is illustrated in the following sample hosts file:

```
# IP ADDRESS        FQDN                 ALIASES
127.0.0.1           localhost
192.139.234.50      gateway.widgets.ca      gateway
142.77.252.6        gateway.widgets.ca      router
142.77.17.1         nb.ottawa.uunet.ca
198.73.137.1        gateway.widgets.ca      ppp1
198.73.137.2        newton.widgets.ca       newton
198.73.137.50       gateway.widgets.ca      net2
```

Notice that the machine gateway has four IP addresses assigned to it. This implies that there are four network interfaces attached to this machine. The piece missing here is the netmask, making it reasonable to assume that two of the interfaces are on the same network.

The aliases include the short form of the host name, as well as any other names for the host. The routines that search this file skip text that follows a "#", which represents a comment, as well as blank lines.

> The network configuration files all support the use of comments with the "#" symbol. This allows the network administrator to document changes and notes.
>
> **N O T E**

THE /ETC/ETHERS FILE

After the IP address is known, TCP/IP converts this to the actual ethernet hardware address when the host is on the local network. This can be done by using the Address Resolution Protocol (ARP), or by creating a list of all of the ethernet addresses in the file /etc/ethers. The format of this file is the ethernet address followed by the official host name, as illustrated here:

```
# Ethernet Address       Host Name
8:0:20:0:fc:6f           laidbak
2:7:1:1:18:27            grinch
0:aa:0:2:30:55           slaid
e0:0:c0:1:85:23          lancelot
```

The information in this file actually is used by the Reverse Address Resolution Protocol daemon, rarpd, which is explained later in this chapter. The ethernet address notation used is x:x:x:x:x:x, where x is a hexadecimal number representing one byte in the address. The address bytes are always in network order, and there should be an entry in the hosts file for each device in this file.

THE /ETC/NETWORKS FILE

This file provides a list of IP addresses and names for networks on the Internet. Each line provides the information for a specific network, as follows:

```
# NETWORK NAME          IP ADDRESS
loopback                127
Ottawa.widgets.ca       192.139.234
Toronto.widgets.ca      192.139.235
WAN.widgets.ca          198.73.137
Lab.widgets.ca          198.73.138
Montreal.widgets.ca     198.73.139
```

Each entry in the file consists of the network IP address, the name for the network, any aliases, and comments.

THE ETC/PROTOCOLS FILE

The /etc/protocols file provides a list of known DARPA Internet protocols. This file should not be changed, as it gives the information provided by the DDN Network Information Center. As shown here, each line contains the protocol name, the protocol number, and any aliases for the protocol.

```
# Internet (IP) protocols
#
ip      0     IP      # internet protocol, pseudo protocol number
icmp    1     ICMP    # internet control message protocol
ggp     3     GGP     # gateway to gateway protocol
tcp     6     TCP     # transmission control protocol
egp     8     EGP     # Exterior Gateway Protocol
pup     12    PUP     # PARC universal packet protocol
udp     17    UDP     # user datagram protocol
hello   63    HELLO   # HELLO Routing Protocol
```

THE ETC/SERVICES FILE

The /etc/services file provides a list of the available services on the host. For each service, a line in the file should be present that provides the following information:

> Official service name
>
> Port number
>
> Protocol name
>
> Aliases

As with the other files, each entry is separated by a space or tab. The port number and protocol name are considered a single item, as a slash (/) is used to separate them. A portion of the /etc/services file is shown in the following:

```
#
# Network services, Internet style
#
echo      7/tcp
echo      7/udp
discard   9/tcp     sink      null
discard   9/udp     sink      null
systat    11/tcp    users
ftp       21/tcp
telnet    23/tcp
smtp      25/tcp    mail
time      37/tcp    timserver
time      37/udp    timserver
rlp       39/udp    resource        # resource location
```

```
whois        43/tcp     nicname
domain       53/tcp     nameserver      # name-domain server
domain       53/udp     nameserver
```

It's obvious that this file relies upon information from /etc/protocols to function. If the service is not available, or you want to remove support for a specific service, then the appropriate line can be commented out using the comment symbol. In many cases, however, the file /etc/inetd.conf also has to be updated to disable support for a given protocol.

THE ETC/INETD.CONF FILE

The inetd.conf file is used to provide the information to the inetd command. As discussed later in the chapter, inetd is the Internet super-server. It listens on a specified TCP/IP port and starts the appropriate command when a connection is requested on that port. This saves system resources by only starting the daemons when they are needed.

The following illustrates an inetd.conf file from an SCO system, along with the file format:

```
#
ftp          stream    tcp    nowait    NOLUID    /etc/ftpd -l -v    ftpd
telnet       stream    tcp    nowait    NOLUID    /etc/telnetd       telnetd
shell        stream    tcp    nowait    NOLUID    /etc/rshd          rshd
login        stream    tcp    nowait    NOLUID    /etc/rlogind       rlogind
exec         stream    tcp    nowait    NOLUID    /etc/rexecd        rexecd
# finger     stream    tcp    nowait    nouser    /etc/fingerd       fingerd
```

The SCO inetd.conf file differs from the format of most systems because of the C2 security components found in the SCO Unix operating system. Specifically, SCO requires the Login UID, or LUID, to be set for each user who accesses the system. Because setting the LUID should not be done until a user actually logs in, the LUID must not be set when the daemon starts up. This is accomplished by using the NOLUID parameter in the file.

The following illustrates the standard inetd.conf file that is found on most other Unix systems.

```
#
ftp          stream    tcp    nowait    root      /usr/etc/in.ftpd      in.ftpd
telnet       stream    tcp    nowait    root      /usr/etc/in.telnetd   in.telnetd
shell        stream    tcp    nowait    root      /usr/etc/in.rshd      in.rshd
login        stream    tcp    nowait    root      /usr/etc/in.rlogind   in.rlogind
exec         stream    tcp    nowait    root      /usr/etc/in.rexecd    in.rexecd
# finger     stream    tcp    nowait    nobody    /usr/etc/in.fingerd   in.fingerd
```

UNDERSTANDING THE NETWORK ACCESS FILES

Two files can have a significant impact on the security of your system. These files are the /etc/hosts.equiv and the .rhosts files.

THE /ETC/HOSTS.EQUIV FILE

The /etc/hosts.equiv file contains a list of trusted hosts. This file is used by the r* commands rlogin, rcp, rcmd, and rsh, and is discussed in detail later in this chapter. The format of this file consists of a list of machine names, one per line, as illustrated here:

```
localhost
oreo
wabbit.widgets.ca
chare
chelsea
widgets
pirate
```

It's a good habit to use a fully qualified name, but if the domain is omitted, TCP/IP adds it to the host name when validating the remote system.

THE .RHOSTS FILE

The .rhosts file that is used in the users HOME directory accomplishes a similar purpose to /etc/hosts.equiv. The file format is the same, with one notable exception. The hosts.equiv file is used to provide equivalence between hosts, while the .rhosts file is used to provide equivalence between users. The .rhosts file is appended to the information found in /etc/hosts.equiv when checking for equivalence.

The hosts.equiv file is not used for the root user. The only file processed in this case is /.rhosts.

USER AND HOST EQUIVALENCY

Host Equivalency, or Trusted Host Access, is configured by the system administrator by using the file /etc/hosts.equiv. This file consists of host names, one per line.

> It is a good idea to document in the file who the network administrator is, as comments can be included by using the comment symbol (#).

Each entry in the hosts.equiv file is trusted. That is, users on the named machine can access their equivalent accounts on this machine without a password. This is not applicable for root, however, as is explained later.

The two machines shown in figure 1.5, oreo and wabbit, both have a user named chare. If the user chare currently is logged into wabbit, and issues the command

```
$ rlogin oreo
```

with host equivalency established, then chare will be logged into oreo without being asked for his password. If host equivalency is not there, chare will be asked for his password on the remote machine.

The following must be considered with /etc/hosts.equiv:

   ✤ It assumes that you trust ALL the users on the remote machine.

   ✤ Root is never trusted through the use of this file.

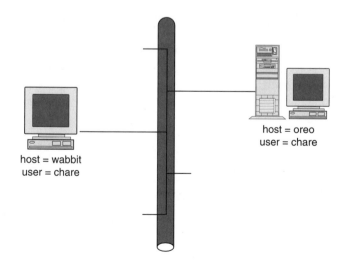

FIGURE 1.5

A sample network.

host = oreo
user = chare

host = wabbit
user = chare

There is a second format for the hosts.equiv file, known as .rhosts, which was shown previously. This format lists a system name and a user name. With the addition of the user name, the user is allowed to log in with any user name found in /etc/passwd.

User equivalence is a mechanism in which the same user is known to all of the machines in the network. This makes the network administrator's job easier in the long run. It should be considered absolutely necessary for environments where NFS is used or is planned.

To configure user equivalence, the user creates a file in his home directory called .rhosts. This file must be writeable only by the owner of the file. If it is not, then the file is ignored for validation purposes. As with the hosts.equiv file, this file contains a system name per line, but generally also includes the name of the user who is being equivalenced. The issue of host and user equivalence will be presented again in more detail in Chapter 2, "Security."

EXAMINING TCP/IP DAEMONS

Because of the varying implementations of TCP/IP that are available, a wide range of daemons can comprise the system. As many as possible are listed here along with a brief explanation of what they do. If they are operating system specific, the operating system version information also is included.

Many of the TCP/IP daemons are named with the name of the service they provide followed by the letter "d," as in bootpd. This convention is used to indicate that this command is a daemon.

THE SLINK DAEMON

The slink daemon provides the necessary components to link the STREAMS modules required for streams TCP/IP. When the system is started, a configuration file, typically /etc/strcf, is processed, thus establishing the links between STREAMS modules for each of the network devices present in the system.

This daemon is only found on versions of Unix that use STREAMS-based TCP/IP, such as most System V derivatives.

THE LDSOCKET DAEMON

The ldsocket command initializes the System V STREAMS TCP/IP Berkeley networking compatibility interface. This daemon also is found only on System V-based implementations of TCP/IP, as the BSD-based versions do not use a STREAMS-based implementation. As the ldsocket program is loaded, a file, generally /etc/sockcf, is processed, and the streams modules are loaded and configured to provide the socket style interface.

THE cpd DAEMON

This is a copy protection daemon that is specific to the Santa Cruz Operation versions of TCP/IP. When TCP/IP starts, it registers with the copy protection daemon. When the cpd receives a datagram from a remote system with the same serial number, a warning message is printed advising the system administrator of the problem. SCO is the only system with this feature.

THE LINE PRINTER DAEMON (LPD)

The lpd is the line printer daemon, or spool area handler, and is executed at boot time. It accepts incoming print jobs on a specific TCP/IP port, and queues the print job for printing on the local or remote system. The printer configuration information is stored in the file /etc/printcap, and the access control to the printer is maintained through the file /etc/hosts.lpd.

THE SNMP DAEMON (SNMPD)

The SNMP daemon is an implementation of the Internet Simple Network Management Protocol, as defined in RFCs 1155-1157, 1213, and 1227. While this daemon is capable of receiving information from SNMP agents on other systems, many systems do not include SNMP Management software.

THE RARP DAEMON (RARPD)

The RARP command is a daemon that responds to Reverse Address Resolution Protocol (RARP) requests. Other systems typically use RARP at boot time to discover their (32-bit) IP address given their (48-bit) Ethernet address. The booting machine sends its Ethernet address in an RARP request message. For the request to be answered, the system running rarpd must have the machine's name-to-IP-address entry in the /etc/hosts file or must be available from the domain name server and its name-to-Ethernet-address entry must exist in the /etc/ethers file. Using the above two sources, rarpd maps this Ethernet address into the corresponding IP address.

THE BOOTP DAEMON (BOOTPD)

The BOOTP daemon implements an Internet Boot Protocol server as defined in RFC 951 and RFC 1048. The bootpd daemon is started by the inetd super-server when a boot request arrives. If bootpd does not receive another boot request within 15 minutes of the last one it received, it exits to conserve system resources. The Internet Boot Protocol server is designed to provide network information to the client. This information can include, but is not restricted to, the client's IP address, netmask, broadcast address, domain server address, router address, etc.

THE ROUTE DAEMON (ROUTED)

The route daemon is invoked at boot time to manage the Internet Routing Tables. The routed daemon uses a variant of the Xerox NS Routing Information Protocol to maintain up-to-date kernel Routing Table entries. In normal operation, routed listens on the UDP socket 520 to provide the route service for routing information packets. If the host is an internetwork router, it periodically supplies copies of its routing tables to any directly connected hosts and networks.

The netstat command, which is discussed later in this chapter, is used to print the routing tables on a host. The netstat command is shown here:

```
$ netstat -r
Routing tables
Destination        Gateway            Flags  Refs  Use       Interface
nb.ottawa.uunet.   gateway            UH     0     1         du0
localhost.0.0.12   localhost.0.0.127. UH     3     0         lo0
topgun             gateway            UH     1     3218      du1
default            gateway            UG     1     669360    du0
Lab.widgets.ca     gateway            U      8     3340413   wdn0
Ottawa.widgets.ca  gateway            U      10    2083505   iat0
$
```

The list identifies the gateway that is used to reach a specific destination network, along with the status of the route (flags). It also includes how many connections are in use through that gateway, the number of packets through the gateway, and the name of the interface in this machine that connects the machine to the network.

Most systems are capable of handling dynamic and static routes. The dynamic routes are handled by the routed daemon. As the routes change, the routed daemon updates the tables and informs other hosts as needed. The static routes generally are manipulated by hand using the route command, and generally are not controlled by the routed daemon.

Bear in mind that routed can handle only the RIP protocol; it cannot handle CIDR. For enhanced routing protocol handling, the gated daemon is a better choice.

THE DOMAIN NAME SERVER (NAMED)

named is the Internet Domain Name Server, and it is the second mechanism available to provide host name to IP address resolution. The daemon can serve in a variety of roles, including primary, secondary, caching, and as a slave, depending upon the requirements of the network administrator. If the /etc/hosts file is not used, and domain name service (DNS) is configured, then the system makes requests to the DNS to provide the IP address for a host name. If the local DNS does not know the IP address for the specified host, it queries other name servers until it obtains the address.

The user command nslookup is used to query the DNS server for a given piece of information. The following illustrates using the nslookup command to find the IP address for the host name gatekeeper.dec.com.

```
$ nslookup gatekeeper.dec.com
Server:  gateway.widgets.ca
Address:  192.139.234.50
Non-authoritative answer:
Name:   gatekeeper.dec.com
Address:  16.1.0.2

$
```

In this output, the domain name server gateway.widgets.ca cannot provide an authoritative response because it is not the authoritative master for the dec.com domain. The end result is that you learn the IP address for gatekeeper.dec.com is, in fact, 16.1.0.2.

Systems that are not running a DNS server themselves must use a resolv.conf file to indicate where DNS queries should be addressed. The format of the resolv.conf file is as follows:

```
domain widgets.ca

nameserver 192.168.1.1
```

This format indicates the domain in which the current machine resides, which is used when only a hostname is provided, and the IP address of the server to which to send the request. Multiple nameservers can be specified by adding the additional IP addresses separated by commas.

THE SYSTEM LOGGER (SYSLOGD)

This daemon is responsible for logging various system messages in a set of files described by the syslogd configuration file /etc/syslog.conf. Each message is saved on a single line in the file and can contain a wide variety of information. The syslog daemon receives information sent to it and saves the messages in its log file. Information can consist of informational, error, status, and debug messages. Each message also can have a level of severity associated with it.

INETD—THE SUPER-SERVER

The inetd super-server listens on multiple TCP/IP ports for incoming connection requests. When the request is received, it spawns the appropriate server. The use of a super-server allows other servers to spawn only when needed, thereby saving system resources. When the connection is terminated, the spawned server terminates.

Typically, servers that are started through inetd include fingerd, ftpd, rexecd, rlogind, and others. inetd, however, cannot be used for servers like named, routed, rwhod, sendmail, or any RFS or NFS server.

THE RWHO DAEMON (RWHOD)

The RWHO daemon maintains the database used by the rwho and ruptime commands. Its operation is predicated by its capability to broadcast messages on a network. rwho operates by periodically querying the state of the system and broadcasting that information on the network. It also listens for rwho messages produced by other systems, so it can update its database of remote server information.

It is important to note that this service takes up more and more bandwidth as the number of hosts grows. For large networks, the cost in network traffic becomes prohibitive.

EXPLORING TCP/IP UTILITIES

TCP/IP commands can be split into three categories: those that are used to administer the TCP/IP network at one level or another, user commands that can be considered applications unto themselves, and third-party applications that have been implemented by using one or more of the services provided by TCP/IP, such as client-server databases.

ADMINISTRATION COMMANDS

This section examines some of the commands that are used to administer the TCP/IP services provided in a system. Many of the commands can be executed by either a regular user or the super-user, but some features are restricted due to the nature of the command. An understanding of the commands available to administer TCP/IP, however, is important for the administrator and helpful for the user.

THE PING COMMAND

The ping command is used to send Internet Control Message Protocol (ICMP) packets from one host to another. ping transmits packets using the ICMP ECHO_REQUEST command and expects to get an ICMP ECHO_REPLY in response to each transmitted packet. The name ping comes from the sonar detection device that uses a sound pulse resembling a ping to locate targets in the surrounding area. In this case, the sound pulses are ICMP packets to a target host.

ICMP is a protocol suite of its own that is used to report errors encountered in processing packets and to perform other Internet layer functions, such as supplying the protocol for the ping command.

ICMPv6 messages are grouped into two classes: error messages and informational messages. ICMP messages are described in table 1.5.

TABLE 1.5
ICMP Messages

Message	Type	Description
Destination Unreachable	Error	Normally generated by a router or by the IP layer in the originating node, in response to a packet that cannot be delivered to its destination address for reasons other than congestion.
Packet Too Big	Error	Sent by a router in response to a packet that it cannot forward because the packet is larger than the MTU of the outgoing link.
Time Exceeded	Error	If a router receives a packet with a hop limit of zero, or a router decrements a packet's hop limit to zero, the router discards the packet and sends an ICMP Time Exceeded message with Code 0 to the source of the packet. This message indicates either a routing loop or too small an initial hop limit value.
Parameter Problem	Error	If a node processing a packet finds a problem with a field in the IP header or extension headers such that it cannot

continues

TABLE 1.5, CONTINUED
ICMP Messages

Message	Type	Description
		completely process the packet, it discards the packet and sends an ICMP `Parameter Problem` message to the packet's source, indicating the type and location of the problem.
Echo Request	Information	Every node implements an ICMP Echo responder function that receives Echo Requests and sends corresponding Echo Replies. A node normally also implements an Application layer interface for sending Echo Requests and receiving Echo Replies for diagnostic purposes.
Echo Reply	Information	The response generated when an Echo Request packet is transmitted.
Group Membership Query, Group Membership Report, Group Membership Reduction	Information	The ICMP Group Membership messages are used to convey information about multicast group membership from nodes to their neighboring routers.

The following illustrates using ping with a responding host and using ping with a nonresponding host. Under normal circumstances, ping does not terminate, but broadcasts packets until the user stops it, typically through an interrupt signal such as Ctrl+C.

```
$ ping shylock
PING shylock (192.139.234.12): 56 data bytes
64 bytes from shylock (192.139.234.12): icmp_seq=0 ttl=254 time=10 ms
64 bytes from shylock (192.139.234.12): icmp_seq=1 ttl=254 time=10 ms
64 bytes from shylock (192.139.234.12): icmp_seq=2 ttl=254 time=10 ms
64 bytes from shylock (192.139.234.12): icmp_seq=3 ttl=254 time=10 ms

-- shylock ping statistics --
4 packets transmitted, 4 packets received, 0% packet loss
round-trip min/avg/max = 10/10/10 ms
$
```

The ping command has a wide variety of options that can be used to help locate potential problems in the connections. These options and their explanation are shown in table 1.6.

TABLE 1.6
ping Command Options

Option	Description
-c count	This instructs ping to continue sending packets until count requests have been sent and received.
-d	This option turns on the debug option for the socket being used.
-f	This is a flood ping. It causes ping to output packets as fast as they come back from the remote host or 100 times per second, whichever is faster. In this mode, each request is shown with a period, and for each response, a backspace is printed. Only the super-user can use this option. For obvious reasons, this can be very hard on a network and should be used with caution.
-i seconds	This option instructs ping to wait the specified number of seconds between transmitting each packet. This option cannot be used with the -f option.
-n	Numeric mode only. Normally ping attempts to resolve the IP address for a host name. This option instructs ping to print the IP addresses and not look up the symbolic names. This is important if for some reason the local name server is not available.
-p pattern	This enables the user to specify up to 16 pad bytes to be added to the packet. This is useful for diagnosing data-dependent problems in a network. Using -p ff, for example, causes the transmitted packet to be filled with all 1s.
-q	Normally, ping reports each response received. This option puts ping into quiet mode. The result is that it prints the summary information at startup and completion of the command.
-R	This adds the ICMP RECORD_ROUTE option to the ECHO_REQUEST packet. This asks for the route to be recorded in the packet, which ping then prints when the packet is returned. There is only room for nine routes in each packet, and many hosts ignore or discard this option.
-r	This causes ping to bypass the normal routing tables that would be used to transmit a packet. For this to work, the host must be on a directly attached network. If the target host is not, an error is printed by ping.

continues

Table 1.6, Continued
ping Command Options

Option	Description
-s packetsize	This enables the user to specify the number of data bytes that are to be sent. The default is 56 bytes, which translates into 64 ICMP data bytes when combined with the 8 bytes of ICMP header of data.
-v	This puts ping into verbose mode. It instructs ping to print all ICMP packets returned other than ECHO_RESPONSE packets.

The following demonstrates the -q option for ping. With this example, ping prints only the startup and summary information.

```
$ ping -q ftp.widgets.ca
PING chelsea.widgets.ca (198.73.138.6): 56 data bytes

-- chelsea.widgets.ca ping statistics --
7 packets transmitted, 7 packets received, 0% packet loss
round-trip min/avg/max = 0/0/0 ms
$
```

These examples are not representative of all implementations of ping. The following illustrates the output of ping on BSD versions of Unix:

```
% /usr/etc/ping gateway
gateway.widgets.ca is alive
%
```

For the BSD Unix users, the ping command generally does not print the information that was illustrated in preceding code. The preceding example serves to illustrate that even different versions of TCP/IP have been implemented differently.

When ping is used for fault isolation, it should first be run on the local host to ensure that the network interface is up and running. The ping program is intended for use in network testing, measurement, and management. Because of the load it can impose on the network, however, it is not wise to use ping during normal working hours or from automated test scripts.

THE RUPTIME AND RWHO COMMANDS

The ruptime command uses the facilities of the rwhod server to show the status of the local machines on the network. It prints a status line for each host in its database. This database is built by using broadcast rwho packets, once every one to three minutes. Machines that have not reported a status for five minutes are reported as down. The output of ruptime is shown as follows:

```
$ ruptime
chelsea       up 17+01:28,    0 users,   load 0.00, 0.00, 0.00
daffy         up 29+06:11,    0 users,   load 1.00, 1.00, 1.00
gateway       up 16+14:34,    1 user,    load 1.00, 1.05, 1.02
mallow        up  5+12:46,    0 users,   load 0.00, 0.00, 0.00
oreo          up 19+13:13,    1 user,    load 2.00, 2.00, 1.33
ovide         up  4+04:54,    1 user,    load 1.14, 1.16, 1.17
wabbit      down 107+01:33
$
```

If the rwhod server is not running on any of the hosts in your network, then ruptime reports the status message no hosts!!! and exits. In the preceding example, the system wabbit appears to be down. This might be accurate, but it also might be that the rwhod server has exited or is no longer running on the system.

Normally, the ruptime output is sorted by host name, but the following options alter the output format of ruptime.

TABLE 1.7
ruptime Options

Option	Description
-a	Includes all users in ruptime output. (Users idle for more than an hour are not usually counted in the user list.)
-l	Sorts the output by load average.
-t	Sorts the output by uptime.
-u	Sorts the output by the number of users.
-r	Reverses the sort order.

The rwho command lists the users who currently are logged in on each of the servers in the network. The rwho command reports the users who are logged in on hosts that are responding to and transmitting rwhod packets. The output of the rwho command is shown here:

```
$ rwho
chare     oreo:ttyp0    Oct  9 14:58 :01
root      ovide:tty08   Oct  4 18:05
topgun    gateway:tty2A Oct  9 13:54
$
```

In this output, the name of the user is shown as well as the system name, the port he is logged in on, and the date he logged in to the system. This looks like the output from the who command, except the system name is included in the port information.

THE IFCONFIG COMMAND

The ifconfig command has been presented in some detail, but this section illustrates some additional uses for it. By using ifconfig, for example, it is possible to query the interface to find out how it has been configured, as shown here:

```
$ /etc/ifconfig wdn0
wdn0: flags=23<UP,BROADCAST,NOTRAILERS>
inet 198.73.138.2 netmask ffffff00 broadcast 198.73.138.255
$
```

This output shows that the interface is up, it does not use trailer encapsulation, and it identifies the addresses and netmask currently used by the interface. Any interface that is configured on the system can be queried in this manner.

The following illustrates marking an interface down, verifying that information, and then marking the interface up:

```
# ifconfig du0
du0: flags=51<UP,POINTOPOINT,RUNNING>
        inet 142.77.252.6 --> 142.77.17.1 netmask ffff0000
# ifconfig du0 down
# ifconfig du0
du0: flags=50<POINTOPOINT,RUNNING>
        inet 142.77.252.6 --> 142.77.17.1 netmask ffff0000
# ping toradm
PING toradm.widgets.ca (142.77.253.13): 56 data bytes
ping: sendto: Network is unreachable
ping: wrote toradm.widgets.ca 64 chars, ret=-1
ping: sendto: Network is unreachable
ping: wrote toradm.widgets.ca 64 chars, ret=-1
ping: sendto: Network is unreachable
ping: wrote toradm.widgets.ca 64 chars, ret=-1

-- toradm.widgets.ca ping statistics --
3 packets transmitted, 0 packets received, 100% packet loss
# ifconfig du0 up
# ifconfig du0
du0: flags=51<UP,POINTOPOINT,RUNNING>
inet 142.77.252.6 --> 142.77.17.1 netmask ffff0000
# ping toradm
PING toradm.widgets.ca (142.77.253.13): 56 data bytes
64 bytes from toradm.widgets.ca (142.77.253.13): icmp_seq=0 ttl=251 time=610
➥ms
64 bytes from toradm.widgets.ca (142.77.253.13): icmp_seq=1 ttl=251 time=630
➥ms

-- toradm.widgets.ca ping statistics --
3 packets transmitted, 2 packets received, 33% packet loss
round-trip min/avg/max = 610/620/630 ms
#
```

In this example, the interface being affected is a point-to-point protocol link, which is illustrated in the output of ifconfig. When the interface is marked down, packets will not be transmitted on that link, as shown using ping. When the interface is later marked up, traffic once again flows on that link.

The use of ifconfig to configure an interface is restricted to the super-user. Any user on the system, however, can use ifconfig to query the interface for its current operating statistics.

THE FINGER COMMAND

By default, finger lists the login name, full name, terminal name and terminal write status (as a "*" before the terminal name if write permission is denied), idle time, login time, office location, and phone number (if known) for each current user.

> Idle time is minutes if it is a single integer, hours and minutes if a colon (:) is present, or days and hours if a "d" is present.

Longer format also exists and is used by finger whenever a list of names is given. (Account names as well as first and last names of users are accepted.) This is a multiline format; it includes all the information described earlier as well as the user's home directory, login shell, any plan the user has placed in the .plan file in her home directory, and the project on which she is working from the .project file that is also in her home directory. The output of finger is illustrated here:

```
$ finger chare
Login name: chare          (messages off)   In real life: Chris Hare
Directory: /u/chare                         Shell: /bin/ksh
On since Oct  8 22:06:31 on ttyp0
Project: Not assigned to one (yet).
Plan:
To complete the currently assigned tasks.
```

> Many people do not want the output of finger to be generally available; therefore it is either turned off, or restricted versions are implemented. The issue is that finger can provide the cracker with information about the users on the system, such as their login names, and some ideas about what their passwords might be.

In the preceding code, the output from this finger command is for a user who is currently logged into the system. Notice the (messages off) text. This indicates that any attempts to contact this user with the write command will fail because the user does not allow writes to her terminal. When the user is not logged in, the output is different, as shown here:

```
$ finger andrewg
Login name: andrewg                 In real life: Andrew Goodier
Directory: /u/andrewg               Shell: /bin/ksh
Last login Sun Sep 18 22:08
No Plan.
$
```

Table 1.8 lists the options that typically are available on the finger command.

TABLE 1.8
The Options for the finger Command

Option	Description
-b	Briefer output format
-f	Suppresses the printing of the header line (short format)
-i	Provides a quick list of users with idle times
-l	Forces long output format
-p	Suppresses printing of the .plan files
-q	Provides a quick list of users
-s	Forces short output format
-w	Forces narrow format list of specified users

It is important for you to recognize that the finger command allows the distribution of valuable user information, such as user names and home directories. For this reason, many sites choose to disable the finger daemon and remove the finger command entirely.

THE NETSTAT COMMAND

The netstat command is used to query the network subsystem regarding certain types of information. netstat, for example, can be used to print the routing tables, active connections, streams in use (on those systems that use streams), and more. netstat prints the information in a symbolic format that is easier for the user to understand. The options for netstat are listed in table 1.9.

TABLE 1.9
netstat Options

Option	Description
-A	Shows the addresses of any associated protocol control blocks. This option is primarily used for debugging only.
-a	Instructs netstat to show the status of all sockets. Normally, the sockets associated with server processes are not shown.
-i	Shows the state of the interfaces that have been auto-configured. Those interfaces that have been configured after the initial boot of the system are not shown in the output.
-m	Prints the network memory usage.
-n	Causes netstat to print the actual addresses instead of inter-preting them and displaying a symbol such as a host or network name.
-r	Prints the routing tables.
-f address-family	Causes netstat to print only the statistics and control block information for the named address family. Currently, the only address family supported is inet.
-I interface	Shows the interface state for only the named interface.
-p protocol-name	Limits the statistics and protocol control block information to the named protocol.
-s	Causes netstat to show the per protocol statistics.
-t	Replaces the queue length information with timer information in the output displays.

The output from netstat in the following code illustrates the retrieval of interface statistics from the interfaces on the system:

```
$ netstat -i
Name Mtu  Net/Dest     Address      Ipkts    Ierrs Opkts   Oerrs Collis Queue
le0  1500 198.73.138.0 chelsea      2608027  26    1421823 1     2632   0
lo0  1536 loopback     127.0.0.1    765364   0     765364  0     0      0
$ netstat -in
Name Mtu  Net/Dest     Address      Ipkts    Ierrs Opkts   Oerrs Collis Queue
le0  1500 198.73.138.0 198.73.138.6 2608082  26    1421862 1     2632   0
lo0  1536 127.0.0.0    127.0.0.1    765364   0     765364  0     0      0
$
```

41

In the second invocation of netstat in the preceding code, the use of the -n option is employed. This causes netstat to print the address instead of the symbolic name that was printed in the first invocation of netstat. This information is dependent upon the link level driver for the interface. If that driver does not attach itself to the ifstats structure in the kernel, then the phrase No Statistics Available is printed.

In the output of netstat shown in the preceding example, columns of information are shown. These columns and their meanings are listed in table 1.10.

TABLE 1.10
netstat Column Headings

Column	Description
Name	The name of the configured interface
Mtu	The maximum transmission unit for the interface
Net/Dest	The network that this interface serves
Address	The IP Address of the interface
Ipkts	The number of received packets
Ierrs	The number of packets that have been mangled when received
Opkts	The number of transmitted packets
Oerrs	The number of packets that were damaged when transmitted
Collisions	The number of collisions recorded by this interface on the network

Keep in mind that the notion of errors is somewhat ill-defined according to many of the manual pages for netstat, calling into question the validity of the values in the error columns. In addition, with the tables always being updated, the information presented is, like the output of ps, only a snapshot of the status at any given interval.

One of the common uses of netstat is to find out if there are any network memory allocation problems. This is achieved using the command netstat -m, as shown here:

```
$ netstat -m
streams allocation:
config    alloc    free    total    max     fail
streams            292     93      199   53882    112        0
queues             1424    452     972  122783    552        0
mblks              5067    279  478820190677      706        0
dblks              4054    279  377515804030      706        0
class 0,   4 bytes 652     55      597  475300    277        0
```

```
class 1,    16 bytes     652       8     644 2404108      62        0
class 2,    64 bytes     768      22     746 9964817     232        0
class 3,   128 bytes     872     138     734 1223784     386        0
class 4,   256 bytes     548      34     514  230688      75        0
class 5,   512 bytes     324      12     312   92565      76        0
class 6,  1024 bytes     107       0     107 1226009      49        0
class 7,  2048 bytes      90       0      90  182978      67        0
class 8,  4096 bytes      41      10      31    3781      13        0
total configured streams memory: 1166.73KB
streams memory in use: 98.44KB
maximum streams memory used: 409.22KB
$
```

This output is from an SCO Unix 3.2 version 4.2 system. If there are any non-zero values in the fail column, then it is important to readjust the number configured. When the configured number of data blocks is reached, a failure is generated. This means that a TCP/IP application or service could not get the needed resources. The only way to correct this problem in the short term is to reboot the machine. Over the long run, the only way to prevent these failures is to adjust the values and relink the kernel. The output of netstat -m on a SunOS system is similar in content to the SCO systems.

The netstat command also can be used to list all the sockets that are on the system using the -a option. This option is illustrated here:

```
$ netstat -a
Active Internet connections (including servers)
Proto Recv-Q Send-Q Local Address      Foreign Address       (state)
ip       0      0    *.*               *.*
tcp      0  28672    oreo.20           topgun.4450           ESTABLISHED
tcp      0    286    oreo.telnet       topgun.4449           ESTABLISHED
tcp      0      0    oreo.ftp          topgun.4438           ESTABLISHED
tcp      0      0    oreo.1725         gateway.telnet        ESTABLISHED
tcp      0      0    *.printer         *.*                   LISTEN
tcp      0      0    *.pop             *.*                   LISTEN
tcp      0      0    *.smtp            *.*                   LISTEN
tcp      0      0    *.finger          *.*                   LISTEN
tcp      0      0    *.exec            *.*                   LISTEN
tcp      0      0    *.login           *.*                   LISTEN
tcp      0      0    *.shell           *.*                   LISTEN
tcp      0      0    *.telnet          *.*                   LISTEN
tcp      0      0    *.ftp             *.*                   LISTEN
udp      0      0    *.snmp            *.*
udp      0      0    *.who             *.*
$
```

This output shows the status of the currently connected sockets and to what they are connected. For the TCP sockets, the status of the socket is reported in the output. The state is one of the following listed in table 1.11.

TABLE 1.11
TCP Socket Explanations

State	Meaning
CLOSED	The socket is not being used.
LISTEN	The socket is listening for an incoming connection.
SYN_SENT	The socket is actively trying to establish a connection.
SYN_RECEIVED	The initial synchronization of the connection is underway.
ESTABLISHED	The connection has been established.
CLOSE_WAIT	The remote has shut down: we are waiting for the socket to close.
FIN_WAIT_1	The socket is closed, and the connection is being shut down.
CLOSING	The socket is closed, and the remote is being shut down. The acknowledgment of the close is pending.
LAST_ACK	The remote has shut down and closed. They are waiting for us to acknowledge the close.
FIN_WAIT_2	The socket is closed, and we are waiting for the remote to shut down.
TIME_WAIT	The socket is waiting after the close for the remote shutdown transmission.

With this information, it is easy to tell what state the connection is in and how to trace the connection through the various stages of operation.

THE TRACEROUTE COMMAND

The traceroute command is used to trace the route that a packet must take to reach the destination machine. This command works by utilizing the time-to-live (TTL) field in the IP packet to elicit an ICMP TIME_EXCEEDED response from each gateway along the path to the remote host. The following code uses the traceroute command.

```
# traceroute toradm.widgets.ca
traceroute to toradm.widgets.ca (142.77.253.13), 30 hops max, 40 byte packets
 1  gateway (198.73.138.50)  10 ms  10 ms  10 ms
 2  nb.ottawa.uunet.ca (142.77.17.1)  260 ms  300 ms  270 ms
 3  gw.ottawa.uunet.ca (142.77.16.3)  240 ms  240 ms  270 ms
 4  wf.toronto.uunet.ca (142.77.59.1)  280 ms  260 ms  310 ms
```

```
 5  alternet-gw.toronto.uunet.ca (142.77.1.202)  250 ms  260 ms  250 ms
 6  nb1.toronto.uunet.ca (142.77.1.201)  260 ms  250 ms  260 ms
 7  toradm (142.77.253.13)  880 ms  720 ms  490 ms
#
```

As in the preceding example, the traceroute command attempts to trace the route that an IP packet would follow to some Internet host. The command works by sending probes until the maximum number of probes has been sent, or the remote responds with a DESTINATION UNREACHABLE message. The DESTINATION UNREACHABLE message is sent if the hop count to the remote site becomes zero, which implies that the TTL of the packet has been exceeded.

In the output of the traceroute command in the preceding example, the times following the host name are the round trip times for the probe. From this output, you can see that for a packet to travel from the originating host (oreo.widgets.ca), it must travel through seven hosts to reach the destination system, toradm.widgets.ca. The following illustrates another invocation of traceroute.

```
# traceroute gatekeeper.dec.com
traceroute to gatekeeper.dec.com (16.1.0.2), 30 hops max, 40 byte packets
 1  gateway (198.73.138.50)  10 ms  10 ms  10 ms
 2  nb.ottawa.uunet.ca (142.77.17.1)  250 ms  240 ms  240 ms
 3  gw.ottawa.uunet.ca (142.77.16.3)  270 ms  220 ms  240 ms
 4  wf.toronto.uunet.ca (142.77.59.1)  260 ms  270 ms  250 ms
 5  alternet-gw.toronto.uunet.ca (142.77.1.202)  250 ms  260 ms  260 ms
 6  Falls-Church1.VA.ALTER.NET (137.39.7.1)  470 ms  960 ms  810 ms
 7  Falls-Church4.VA.ALTER.NET (137.39.8.1)  760 ms  750 ms  830 ms
 8  Boone1.VA.ALTER.NET (137.39.43.66)  910 ms  810 ms  760 ms
 9  San-Jose3.CA.ALTER.NET (137.39.128.10)  930 ms  870 ms  850 ms
10  * * Palo-Alto1.CA.ALTER.NET (137.39.101.130)  930 ms
11  gatekeeper.dec.com (16.1.0.2)  830 ms  910 ms  830 ms
#
```

In this case, hop 10 did not report right away, but rather printed two asterisks before printing the gateway name and the round trip time. When traceroute does not receive a response within three seconds, it prints an asterisk. If no response from the gateway is received, then three asterisks are printed.

> Because of the apparent network load that traceroute can create, it should only be used for manual fault isolation or troubleshooting. This command should not be executed from cron or from within any automated test scripts.

N O T E

THE ARP COMMAND

The arp command displays and modifies the Internet-to-Ethernet address translation table, which normally is maintained by the address resolution protocol (ARP). When a host name is the only argument, arp displays the current ARP entry for that host. If the host is not in the current ARP table, then arp displays a message to that effect. The following illustrates using arp to find the Ethernet address for a specific host.

```
$ arp gateway
gateway (198.73.138.50) at 0:0:c0:11:57:4c
$ arp ovide
ovide (198.73.138.101) -- no entry
```

This illustrates the behavior of arp when no arguments are present. arp behaves a little differently, however, when options are combined. The available options for arp are defined in table 1.12.

TABLE 1.12
arp Command-Line Options

Option	Description
-a	Lists all the entries on the current ARP table.
-d host	Deletes the corresponding entry for host from the ARP table.
-s host address [temp] [pub] [trail]	Creates an entry in the ARP table for the named host, using an Ethernet address. If the keyword [temp] is included, the entry is temporary. Otherwise, the entry is permanent. The [pub] keyword indicates that the ARP entry will be published. Use of the [trail] keyword implies that trailer encapsulation is to be used.
-f file	Instructs arp to read the named file and create ARP table entries for each of the named hosts in the file.

The most commonly used option with arp is -a, which prints the entire ARP table, and is illustrated here:

```
$ arp -a
ovide.widgets.ca (198.73.138.101) at 0:0:c0:c6:4f:71
gateway.widgets.ca (198.73.138.50) at 0:0:c0:11:57:4c
chelsea.widgets.ca (198.73.138.6) at 8:0:20:2:94:bf
fremen.widgets.ca (198.73.138.54) at 0:0:3b:80:2:e5$
```

ARP is most commonly used to help debug and diagnose network connection problems. arp can help in that regard by assigning the Ethernet address for a given host. This is done by using the -s option, as shown here:

```
$ arp gateway
gateway (198.73.138.50) at 0:0:c0:11:57:4c
# arp -s ovide 0:0:c0:c6:4f:71
```

```
# arp -a
ovide.widgets.ca (198.73.138.101) at 0:0:c0:c6:4f:71 permanent
gateway.widgets.ca (198.73.138.50) at 0:0:c0:11:57:4c
#
```

This example illustrates adding an entry to the arp table. If you could not communicate with the remote host before the arp table entry was created, then you might have an addressing problem. If you still cannot communicate with the remote host after establishing the arp entry, then the problem is more likely to be hardware.

THE dig COMMAND

The Domain Information Groper, dig, is a flexible command line tool that can be used to gather information from the Domain Name System servers. The dig tool can operate in simple interactive mode, where it satisfies a single query, and a batch mode, in which multiple requests are satisfied.

The dig tool requires a slightly modified version of the BIND resolver library to gather count and time statistics. Otherwise, it is a straightforward effort of parsing arguments and setting appropriate parameters. The output of dig can be rather convoluted, as shown here:

```
# dig gatekeeper.dec.com
; <<>> DiG 2.0 <<>> gatekeeper.dec.com
;; ->>HEADER<<- opcode: QUERY , status: NOERROR, id: 6
;; flags: qr rd ra ; Ques: 1, Ans: 1, Auth: 2, Addit: 2
;; QUESTIONS:
;;      gatekeeper.dec.com, type = A, class = IN

;; ANSWERS:
gatekeeper.dec.com.     150369  A       16.1.0.2

;; AUTHORITY RECORDS:
DEC.com.        166848  NS      GATEKEEPER.DEC.COM.
DEC.com.        166848  NS      CRL.DEC.COM.

;; ADDITIONAL RECORDS:
GATEKEEPER.DEC.COM.     150369  A       16.1.0.2
CRL.DEC.COM.    166848  A       192.58.206.2

;; Sent 1 pkts, answer found in time: 400 msec
;; FROM: oreo.widgets.ca to SERVER: default -- 192.139.234.50
;; WHEN: Mon Oct 10 15:07:41 1994
;; MSG SIZE  sent: 36  rcvd: 141

#
```

In the output shown here, the dig command searches the Domain Name Server records looking for gatekeeper.dec.com. A DNS record is found and reported to the user. Consequently, the dig command can be used to help resolve difficult name server problems. When there is some suspicion about how the resolution is being performed when done from nslookup, dig can be used to examine the problem. If, for example, nslookup is pulling the answer from the nameserver cache, it will not be evident from nslookup itself. dig, however, would expose the source of the information.

USER COMMANDS

Just as there are a number of commands to assist the system administrator in the management of the system and network, there are a number of commands that are used by the users to get the information they want and to perform the tasks they need. While a user can execute some of the administration commands you have seen, the real work is done with commands you are about to examine: telnet, ftp, and the Berkeley r-commands.

THE BERKELEY R-COMMANDS

The first of the commands examined here fall into the set called the Berkeley r-commands. These are the rlogin, rcp, and rsh/rcmd commands. They are called the Berkeley r-commands because they all start with the letter r, and they originated from the University of California at Berkeley. The successful use of the command in this section is dependent upon user and host equivalency being properly configured. Most users have difficulty with these commands because their network administrators have not properly configured the host and user equivalency.

NOTE

> Host and user equivalency is accomplished with the /etc/hosts.equiv and .rhosts files, which were explained in the section "Understanding the Network Access Files," earlier in this chapter.

rlogin

The rlogin command connects your local session to a remote session on a different host. To initiate a remote terminal session, use the following command:

```
rlogin remote
```

This command starts a connection to the rlogind server on the remote host, as illustrated here:

```
$ rlogin gateway
Last    successful login for chare: Sun Oct 09 16:16:03 EDT 1994 on ttyp1
Last unsuccessful login for chare: Tue Sep 27 07:18:54 EDT 1994 on ttyp0
SCO UNIX System V/386 Release 3.2
```

```
Copyright (C) 1976-1989 UNIX System Laboratories, Inc.
Copyright (C) 1980-1989 Microsoft Corporation
Copyright (C) 1983-1992 The Santa Cruz Operation, Inc.
All Rights Reserved
gateway

Terminal type is dialup
$
```

The terminal type of the remote connection is the same as the terminal type that is in use for the current connections, unless modified by the user's shell startup files. All of the character echoing is done at the remote site, so except for delays, the use of the rlogin is transparent to the user. Termination of the connection is made either by logging out of the remote host, or through the termination character, which is ~. (tilde period).

rcp

The rcp, or remote copy, command enables the user to copy a file from one host to another. rcp copies files between two machines. Each file or directory argument is either a remote file name of the form "rhost:path", or a local file name (containing no ':' characters, or a '/' before any ':').

The syntax of the command is as follows:

```
rcp [ -p ] file1 file2
    rcp [ -p ] [ -r ] file ... directory
```

The remote file must be specified using the following syntax:

```
hostname:filename
```

The named file is copied to or from the remote system depending upon whether the source or destination file is remote. The following illustrates copying a file from the local host to the remote.

```
$ rcp test.new chelsea:test.new
$
```

When the filename, as illustrated in the preceding example, does not begin with a slash (/), the file is copied in a directory relative to your home directory on the remote system. The rcp command behaves like the cp command in that the file could be called by a different name on the remote system.

If the -r option is specified and any of the source files are directories, rcp copies each subtree rooted at that name; in this case, the destination must be a directory. By default, the mode and owner of file2 are preserved if the file already existed; otherwise, the mode of the source file modified by the umask on the destination host is used.

The -p option causes rcp to attempt to preserve (duplicate) in its copies the modification times and modes of the source files, ignoring the umask. The following illustrates using rcp with the -r option to copy a directory tree.

```
$ pwd
/u/chare
$ lc tmp
arp.ADMN      bootpd       dig.new      route.new
arp.new       bootpd.ADMN  rarpd.new    routed.new
$rcp -r chelsea:/tmp tmp
$ lf tmp
arp.ADMN      bootpd       dig.new      route.new    test.new
arp.new       bootpd.ADMN  rarpd.new    routed.new   tmp/
$
```

After executing the rcp command in the preceding example, a new directory is created called tmp in /u/chare/tmp. This directory contains the contents of the /tmp directory on host chelsea.

rsh, remsh, and rcmd

These three commands all perform a similar function, which is to execute a command on a remote system. Interactive commands are not good candidates for this type of execution.

The rsh implementation of remote execution is not to be confused with the restricted shell (rsh) that exists on System V Unix systems. Likewise, some System V Unixes use remsh instead of rsh also. Typically, the systems that use rsh for remote execution are BSD-based Unix systems. rsh works by connecting to the specified host name and executing the specified command. rsh copies its standard input to the remote command, the standard output of the remote command to its standard output, and the standard error of the remote command to its standard error. Interrupt, quit, and terminate signals are propagated to the remote command; rsh normally terminates when the remote command does.

The command syntax of rsh is as follows:

```
rsh [ -l username ] [ -n ] hostname [ command ]
rsh hostname [ -l username ] [ -n ] [ command ]
```

The execution of a command involves entering the name of the host where the command is to be executed and the name of the command. Running rsh with no command argument has the effect of logging you into the remote system by using rlogin. The following example illustrates using rsh to execute commands:

```
% rsh oreo date
Mon Oct 10 17:23:43 EDT 1994
% rsh oreo hostname
oreo.widgets.ca
%
```

There are only two options to rsh, as shown in table 1.13.

TABLE 1.13
rsh Command-Line Options

Option	Description
-l username	Use username as the remote username instead of your local username. In the absence of this option, the remote username is the same as your local username.
-n	Redirect the input of rsh to /dev/null. You sometimes need this option to avoid unfortunate interactions between rsh and the shell that invokes it. If, for example, you are running rsh and start an rsh in the background without redirecting its input away from the terminal, it will block even if no reads are posted by the remote command. The -n option prevents this.

Virtually any command on the remote system can be executed. Commands that rely upon terminal characteristics or a level of user interaction, however, are not good candidates for the use of rsh.

The rcmd command is virtually identical to the rsh except that it typically is found on System V systems. Actually, the rcmd has the same options and operates the same fashion as the rsh command under BSD Unix. The following illustrates rcmd accessing a remote system by not specifying a command when starting rcmd.

```
$ rcmd chelsea
Last login: Mon Oct 10 17:18:10 from oreo.widgets.ca
SunOS Release 4.1 (GENERIC) #1: Wed Mar 7 10:59:35 PST 1990
%
```

The use of rsh/rcmd can be of value when you want to run a command on the remote system without having to log into that system. Some system administrators use it to see what processes are running on a remote system, as shown here:

```
$ rcmd gateway ps -ef ¦ more
    UID   PID  PPID  C   STIME  TTY    TIME COMMAND
   root     0     0  0  Sep 22  ?      0:00 sched
   root     1     0  0  Sep 22  ?     23:36 /etc/init -a
   root     2     0  0  Sep 22  ?      0:00 vhand
   root   221     1  0  Sep 22  ?      0:00 strerr
   root   150     1  0  Sep 22  ?      7:51 /etc/cron
   root   212     1  0  Sep 22  ?      0:35 cpd
   root   156     1  0  Sep 22  ?      3:21 /usr/lib/lpsched
   root   214     1  0  Sep 22  ?      0:00 slink
```

```
   root   317   315   0  Sep 22    ?        0:00 nfsd 4
   root   256     1   0  Sep 22    ?        0:00 /usr/lib/lpd start
 topgun  5740     1   0  10:30:51  2A       0:19 /etc/pppd 198.73.137.101: log /u
sr/lib/ppp/ppp-users/topgun/log debug 2 nolqm
   root   306     1   0  Sep 22    ?        0:00 pcnfsd
   root 17008   234   0  Sep 29    ?        0:07 telnetd
   root 17009 17008   0  Sep 29    p0       0:02 -sh
   root   286     1   0  Sep 22    ?        0:05 snmpd
$
```

TERMINAL EMULATION USING TELNET

The rlogin command allows for a connection from one system to another. rlogin, however, requires the user to have an account on the remote machine and host equivalency to have been configured. telnet, on the other hand, does not need either of those things.

The telnet command uses the TELNET protocol to establish a connection from the client to a telnetd server on the remote system. Unlike rlogin, telnet has a host mode where it is connected to the remote system, and command mode where the user can enter commands and interact with the TELNET protocol to change how the connection is handled.

To create a telnet connection, the user enters the telnet command, with or without a host name. When telnet is started with a host name, a connection to the remote host is established. After the connection is established, the user must then provide a login name and password to access the remote system. This is illustrated in the following:

```
$ telnet chelsea
Trying 198.73.138.6...
Connected to chelsea.widgets.ca.
Escape character is '^]'.


SunOS Unix(chelsea.widgets.ca)

login: chare
Password:
Last login: Mon Oct 10 17:33:35 from oreo.widgets.ca
SunOS Release 4.1 (GENERIC) #1: Wed Mar 7 10:59:35 PST 1990
%
```

Command mode is entered either by starting telnet with no arguments, or by entering Ctrl+], which is the telnet 'escape' key. This control key instructs telnet to enter command mode, as shown here:

```
chelsea.widgets.ca%
telnet> ?
Commands may be abbreviated. Commands are:

close          close current connection
```

```
logout          forcibly logout remote user and close the connection
display         display operating parameters
mode            try to enter line or character mode ('mode ?' for more)
open            connect to a site
quit            exit telnet
send            transmit special characters ('send ?' for more)
set             set operating parameters ('set ?' for more)
unset           unset operating parameters ('unset ?' for more)
status          print status information
toggle          toggle operating parameters ('toggle ?' for more)
slc             change state of special characters ('slc ?' for more)
z               suspend telnet
!               invoke a subshell
environ         change environment variables ('environ ?' for more)
?               print help information
telnet>
```

In the preceding example, the switch to command mode is performed and is indicated by the telnet> prompt. Once in command mode, there are a number of commands that can be used to alter or reconfigure the current session. The actual number of commands available in command mode is far too numerous to be discussed here.

telnet, however, has another useful feature. It is to allow the connection to a specific TCP port on a system, which may or may not be remote. The following example illustrates a connection to the SMTP port, port 25, on the local system.

```
$ telnet localhost 25
Trying 127.0.0.1...
Connected to localhost.widgets.ca.
Escape character is '^]'.
220 oreo.widgets.ca Server SMTP (Complaints/bugs to:  postmaster)
helo
250 oreo.widgets.ca - you are a charlatan
help
214-The following commands are accepted:
214-helo noop mail data rcpt help quit rset expn vrfy
214-
214 Send complaints/bugs to:  postmaster
quit
221 oreo.widgets.ca says goodbye to localhost.0.0.127.in-addr.arpa at Mon Oct
➡10
20:35:24.
Connection closed by foreign host.
$
```

While this is a useful feature to have when debugging connection problems, it also enables a user to forge e-mail by giving it directly to the SMTP or sendmail daemon. Actually, most TCP/IP daemons can be connected to by using telnet with the port number, which might allow for other security mechanisms to be breached, particularly with sendmail.

53

FILE TRANSFERS WITH FTP

FTP is the ARPANET File Transfer Program that uses the File Transfer Protocol to allow for the verified transfer of a file from one PC to another. To reduce the chance of confusion, ftp usually refers to the program, while FTP refers to the protocol that is used to transfer the files.

The client host that ftp is to communicate with is normally provided on the command line. If so, ftp will immediately try to connect with the ftp server on that system. If a connection is established, then the user must log in to access the system. Logging in can be achieved either by having a valid account on the system, or through accessing a server that allows anonymous ftp access. Accessing an ftp server through anonymous mode is illustrated in the following:

```
$ ftp ftp.widgets.ca
Connected to chelsea.widgets.ca.
220 chelsea.widgets.ca FTP server (SunOS 4.1) ready.
Name (ftp.widgets.ca:chare): anonymous
331 Guest login ok, send ident as password.
Password:
230 Guest login ok, access restrictions apply.
ftp> quit
221 Goodbye.
$
```

N O T E

When configuring a server for anonymous ftp access, be sure to create the file /etc/ftpusers. This file contains a list of user names, one per line, who are not allowed to access the ftp server. On any ftp server that supports anonymous ftp, access to the server as the root user should not be permitted.

By not restricting access through certain accounts, anyone, once one machine is compromised, can gain access to the anonymous ftp server and complete the transaction shown in the following example:

```
$ ftp ftp.widgets.ca
Connected to chelsea.widgets.ca.
220 chelsea.widgets.ca FTP server (SunOS 4.1) ready.
Name (ftp.widgets.ca:chare): root
331 Password required for root.
Password:
230 User root logged in.
ftp> cd /etc
250 CWD command successful.
ftp> lcd /tmp
Local directory now /tmp
```

```
ftp> get passwd passwd.ccca
local: passwd.ccca remote: passwd
200 PORT command successful.
150 ASCII data connection for passwd (198.73.138.2,1138) (736 bytes).
226 ASCII Transfer complete.
753 bytes received in 0.01 seconds (74 Kbytes/s)
ftp> quit
221 Goodbye.
$
```

The user who made this connection now has your password file. This type of connection can be prevented by creating the /etc/ftpusers file, as shown in the following:

```
# cd /etc
# s -l ftpusers
-rw-r--r--  1 root            10 Oct 10 20:53 ftpusers
# cat ftpusers
root
uucp
#
```

Now when a user tries to access the system by using the root account, he does not get the chance to enter a root password because ftp informs him that root access through ftp is not allowed, as shown in the following:

```
$ ftp ftp.widgets.ca
Connected to chelsea.widgets.ca.
220 chelsea.widgets.ca FTP server (SunOS 4.1) ready.
Name (ftp.widgets.ca:chare): root
530 User root access denied.
Login failed.
ftp> quit
221 Goodbye.
$
```

Another problem with ftp is the .netrc file that enables users to automate a file transfer. The reason this file is a problem is because users can insert login and password information in the file. The ftp client aborts the use of the file if it finds that it is readable by anyone other than the owner, but even that is not enough as the file can still leave security holes wide open.

The .netrc file resides in the user's home directory and can contain information for accessing more than one system. Consider the sample .netrc file shown here:

```
$ cat .netrc
machine yosemite.widgets.ca login chare password yippee
default login anonymous password chare@widgets.ca
```

The file format of the .netrc file is to include the information for each machine on a single line. The first entry of this file, for example, shows the connection to a machine called yosemite.widgets.ca. When this machine name is provided as an argument to ftp, the .netrc file is checked, and the login information here is used to access the system. The second entry is used as the default. If the system is not found explicitly, then use the anonymous entry to allow for anonymous access to the ftp site.

As mentioned, the ftp command does perform a security check on the .netrc. If the file is readable by anyone other than the owner, the connection is not established. This is illustrated in the following:

```
$ ftp yosemite.widgets.ca
Connected to yosemite.widgets.ca.
220 yosemite.widgets.ca FTP server (Version 5.60 #1) ready.
Error - .netrc file not correct mode.
Remove password or correct mode.
Remote system type is Unix.
Using binary mode to transfer files.
ftp> quit
221 Goodbye.
$ ls -l .netrc
-rw-r--r--  1 chare     group          103 Oct 10 21:16 .netrc
$
```

In the preceding example, the connection to yosemite is not made because the permissions on the .netrc file are incorrect. After the permissions are changed, the connection can be established without incident, as shown in the following:

```
$ ls -l .netrc
-rw-r--r--  1 chare     group          103 Oct 10 21:16 .netrc
$ chmod 600 .netrc
$ ls -l .netrc
-rw-------  1 chare     group          103 Oct 10 21:16 .netrc
149$ ftp gateway.widgets.ca
Connected to gateway.widgets.ca.
220 gateway.widgets.ca FTP server (Version 5.60 #1) ready.
331 Password required for chare.
230 User chare logged in.
Remote system type is Unix.
Using binary mode to transfer files.
ftp>
```

N O T E

It's a good idea to teach users who want to use the .netrc file about security. By improperly setting the permissions on the file, users can prevent themselves from accessing the remote machine using the auto-login features, but can still allow someone else access by giving that person their login name and password.

SUMMARY

This chapter has introduced TCP/IP, addressing, the TCP/IP daemons, and user level commands. It has examined some of the commands that are available to both the user and the system administrator, and outlined how TCP/IP can be used to access and manipulate information.

Like anything else, the ability to utilize information presented here comes from experimenting and examining your own system. Keep in mind that most System V systems use STREAMS as their transport layer, while BSD systems use SOCKETS. TCP/IP provides a wide array of protocols and services to allow users to transport data from one place to another.

## CHAPTER 2

SECURITY

Unless the computer you are trying to protect is in a locked room where access is controlled and no connections to this computer from outside the room exist, then your computer is at risk. Break-ins and security violations occur almost daily around the world. These violators are not just Internet vandals, they include the employee down the hall who steals computer time or services for his own personal or malicious use.

This chapter examines computer security in some detail. You learn what computer security is, how you can protect yourself, and what is available to help you perform these security tasks. Because Unix is the predominant operating system on the Internet, this chapter focuses on Unix. This does not mean, however, that other operating systems do not have their security problems. Regardless of the manufacturer of your hardware and operating system, you must have a thorough understanding of the risks in your situation.

EXAMINING SECURITY LEVELS

According to the computer security standards developed by the United States Department of Defense, the Trusted Computer Standards Evaluation Criteria—the Orange Book, several levels of security are used to protect the hardware, software, and stored information from attack. These levels all describe different types of physical security, user authentication, trustedness of the operating system software, and user applications. These standards also impose limits on what types of other systems can be connected to your system.

NOTE

> The Orange Book has remained unchanged since it became a Department of Defense standard in 1985. It has been the primary method of evaluating the security of multi-user mainframe and mini operating systems for many years. Other subsystems, such as databases and networks, have been evaluated through interpretations of the Orange Book, such as the Trusted Database Interpretation and the Trusted Network Interpretation.

LEVEL D1

Level D1 is the lowest form of security available. This standard states that the entire system is untrusted. No protection is available for the hardware; the operating system is easily compromised; and there is no authentication regarding users and their rights to access information stored on the computer. This level of security typically refers to operating systems like MS-DOS, MS-Windows, and the Apple Macintosh System 7.*x*.

These operating systems do not distinguish between users and have no defined method of determining who is typing at the keyboard. These operating systems also do not have any controls regarding what information can be accessed on the hard drives in the computer.

LEVEL C1

Level C has two sublevels of security—C1 and C2. Level C1, or the Discretionary Security Protection system, describes the security available on a typical Unix system. Some level of protection exists for the hardware because it cannot be as easily compromised, although it is still possible. Users must identify themselves to the system through a user login name and password. This combination is used to determine what access rights to programs and information each user has.

These access rights are the file and directory permissions. These Discretionary Access Controls enable the owner of the file or directory, or the system administrator, to prevent certain people, or groups of people, from accessing those programs or information. However, the system administration account is not prevented from performing any activity. Consequently, an unscrupulous system administrator can easily compromise the security of the system without anyone's knowledge.

In addition, many of the day-to-day system administration tasks only can be performed by the user login known as *root*. With the decentralization of computer systems today, it is not uncommon to enter an organization and find more than two or three people who know the root password. This itself is a problem because no way exists to distinguish between the changes Doug or Mary made to the system yesterday.

LEVEL C2

The second sub-level, C2, was meant to help address these issues. Along with the features of C1, level C2 includes additional security features that create a controlled-access environment. This environment has the capability to further restrict users from executing certain commands or accessing certain files based not only upon the permissions, but upon authorization levels. In addition, this level of security requires that the system be audited. This involves writing an audit record for each event that occurs on the system.

Auditing is used to keep records of all security-related events, such as those activities performed by the system administrator. Auditing requires additional authentication because without it, how can you be sure that the person who executes the command really is that person. The disadvantage to auditing is that it requires additional processor and disk subsystem resources.

With the use of additional authorizations, it is possible for users on a C2 system to have the authority to perform system management tasks without having the root password. This enables improved tracking of system administration-related tasks because the individual user performs the work and not the system administrator.

These additional authorizations are not to be confused with the SGID and SUID permissions that can be applied to a program. Rather, they are specific authorizations that allow a user to execute specific commands or access certain kernel tables. Users who do not have the proper authority to view the process table, for example, see only their processes when they execute the ps command.

LEVEL B1

B-level security contains three levels. The B1 level, or Labeled Security Protection, is the first level that supports multilevel security, such as secret and top secret. This level states that an object under mandatory access control cannot have its permissions changed by the owner of the file.

LEVEL B2

The B2 level, known as Structured Protection, requires that every object be labeled. Devices such as disks, tapes, or terminals might have a single or multiple level of security assigned to them. This is the first level that starts to address the problem of an object at a higher level of security communicating with another object at a lower level of security.

LEVEL B3

The B3, or Security Domains level, enforces the domain with the installation of hardware. For example, memory management hardware is used to protect the security domain from unauthorized access or modification from objects in different security domains. This level also requires that the user's terminal be connected to the system through a trusted path.

LEVEL A

Level A, or the Verified Design level, is currently the highest level of security validated through the Orange Book. It includes a stringent design, control, and verification process. For this level of security to be achieved, all the components of the lower levels must be included; the design must be mathematically verified; and an analysis of covert channels and trusted distribution must be performed. *Trusted distribution* means that the hardware and software have been protected during shipment to prevent tampering with the security systems.

CANADIAN SECURITY

The Canadian government has undertaken its own design of trusted computing standards. These standards consist of two components: The Canadian Trusted Computer Product Evaluation Criteria (CTCPEC) and the Common Criteria.

The CTCPEC addresses both functionality and assurance of the product under development or evaluation. Functionality addresses the areas of confidentiality, integrity, availability, and accountability; and assurance focuses on the degree of confidence with which a product implements the organization's security policy.

The Common Criteria is a collaborative effort to pool the investigations and research of the United States, Canada, France, Germany, and the United Kingdom. This document contains the requirements for the selection of appropriate IT security measures.

There are seven levels of assurance within the Common Criteria: EAL-1 to EAL-7. These criteria are defined in the following sections.

LEVEL EAL-1

EAL-1 is the lowest level of assurance that is meaningful to the developer and the consumer. It defines the minimum level of assurance and is based on an analysis of the security functions of the product using the functional and interface designs, as presented by the developer, to understand the security behavior.

LEVEL EAL-2

EAL-2 is the highest level of assurance that can be granted without imposing on the developer of the product tasks additional to those required for EAL-1. An analysis of the functional and interface specifications is performed, along with a high-level design review of the subsystems of the product.

LEVEL EAL-3

EAL-3 describes a moderate level of independently assured security, meaning security validated by an outside source. This level permits maximum assurance from the design stage with few alterations to the testing process. Maximum assurance implies that the product has been designed with security in mind instead of security being implemented after design. The developer must provide evidence of testing including vulnerability analyses, which are then selectively verified. This is the first level to also include elements of configuration management evaluation.

LEVEL EAL-4

EAL-4 is the highest level of assurance that is feasible to retrofit an existing product line. An EAL-4-assured product is a methodically designed, tested, and reviewed product, which provides the consumer the highest level of security based on sound commercial software development practices. The use of these practices assist in eliminating the common software design problems that can plague a project.

Aside from the elements of Level EAL-3, EAL-4 also includes an independent search for vulnerabilities in the product.

LEVEL EAL-5

EAL-5 level is not easily achieved for existing products, as the product must be designed and built with the intention of achieving this rating. Here the developer must apply commercial software development practices as well as specialized security engineering techniques. This level is suited for those developers and users who require a high level of assurance through a rigorous development approach. At this level, the developer also must present the design specifications and how these specifications are implemented functionally in the product.

LEVEL EAL-6

Level EAL-6 consists of a semi-formal verified design and test component. This level includes all the elements of the Level EAL-5, with the requirement of a structured presentation of the implementation. Additionally, the product undergoes a high and low design review, and must ensure a high degree of resistance to attack. Level EAL-6 also assures that a structured development process, development controls, and configuration management controls are in place through the design cycle.

LEVEL EAL-7

Level EAL-7 is intended for only the highest level of security applications where high risks of security breaches justify the cost of development and, in turn, the price paid by the consumer. This level consists of a complete independent and formal design review, with a verified design and test stage. The developer must test every facet of the product, looking for obvious and non-obvious vulnerabilities, which are then completely verified by an independent source. This is an exhaustive process, and the evaluating agency must be involved from the conception of the idea to the completion of the product.

EXAMINING LOCAL SECURITY ISSUES

Aside from the security products or regulations developed outside your organization, you must work to resolve security issues that may be local or restricted to your organization or to a subgroup within your organization. These local security issues include security policies and password controls.

SECURITY POLICIES

Two major stances can be adopted when developing the policies that reflect security at your site. These major statements form the basis of all other security-related policies and regulate the procedures put into place to implement them.

That which is not expressly permitted is prohibited, is the first approach to security. This means that your organization provides a distinct and documented set of services, and anything else is prohibited. For example, if you decide to allow anonymous FTP transfers to and from a particular machine, but deny telnet services, then documenting support for FTP and not telnet illustrates this approach.

The alternative train of thought is *That which is not expressly prohibited is permitted*. This means that unless you expressly indicate that a service is not available, then all services are available. For example, if you do not expressly say that telnet sessions to a given host are prohibited, then they must be permitted. (You can still prevent the service, however, by not allowing a connection to the TCP/IP port.)

Regardless of which train of thought you follow, the reason behind defining a security policy is to determine what action should be taken in the event that the security of an organization is compromised. The policy is also intended to describe what actions will be tolerated and what will not.

THE PASSWORD FILE

The first line of defense against unauthorized access to the system is the /etc/password file. Unfortunately, it is also often the weakest link! The password file consists of lines or records in which each line is split into seven fields with a colon, as illustrated in the following example:

```
chare:u7mHuh5R4UmVo:105:100:Chris Hare:/u/chare:/bin/ksh
username:encrypted password:UID:GID:comment:home directory:login shell
```

Table 2.1 explains the contents and typical values for each file.

TABLE 2.1
The /etc/passwd File

Field Name	Description	Typical Values
username	This field identifies the user to the system. It is primarily for human benefit.	chare rceh brb

continues

Table 2.1, Continued
The /etc/passwd File

Field Name	Description	Typical Values
	They must be unique on a given machine and, ideally, unique within an organization.	markd
encrypted password	This field contains, or can contain, the encrypted password. How the passwords are encrypted is explained later in this chapter.	u7mHuh5R4UmVo x * NOLOGIN
UID	This is the numerical representation of the user on the system.	0—60,000
GID	This is the numerical representation of the login group to which the user belongs.	0—60,000
comment	This contains information regarding the user. It often lists a user's full name, phone number, or other information.	Chris Hare Ops Manager, x273
home directory	This is the directory where the user is placed upon login.	/u/chare /usr/lib/ppp /ppp-users
login shell	This is the login shell that is started for users to enable them to interact with the system. Remember, not all login shells are interactive.	/bin/sh /bin/csh /bin/ksh /bin/tcsh /usr/lib /uucp/uucico /usr/lib /ppp/ppd/

Table 2.1 provides some additional information worth mentioning. It is not necessary that the actual encrypted password be placed in the encrypted password field. This field can contain other values. For example, to prevent someone from logging in using a specific account, that password can be changed to a non-matchable value, such as NOLOGIN. This field, however, typically contains an x or an asterisk (*), indicating that the password is stored either in the Trusted Computing Base (TCB), which is explained later in this chapter, or in the shadow password file.

The permissions on the password file are read-only, which means that no one can edit the file. Similarly, the shadow password file and the files in the TCB are generally also read-only.

The password information in these files are updated by the password command. The permissions on the password command include the SUID (Set User ID) bit, which makes the user executing the program look like the owner of the program, or in this case, root. Because of the application of the SUID bit, the user can change the password even though he does not have the authority to edit the file.

THE SHADOW PASSWORD FILE

The versions of Unix that do not include the advanced security options from SecureWare can support the shadow password file. When you see the character x in the password field, then the user's actual password is stored in the shadow password file, /etc/shadow. Unlike the /etc/passwd file, the shadow password file must be readable only by root, as illustrated in the following example:

```
# ls -l /etc/shadow
-r--------   1 root      auth        861 Oct 24 11:46 /etc/shadow
#
```

> SecureWare is a software company specializing in network security, secure Web servers, and privacy-enhanced mail. SecureWare wrote the code for SCO needed to bring the SCO Unix operating system to C2 compliancy. More information on SecureWare can be found at the URL http://www. secureware.com.

The format of the /etc/shadow file is identical to the /etc/passwd file in that it also has seven colon-delimited fields. However, the /etc/shadow file only contains the user name, encrypted password, and password aging information, as illustrated in the following example:

```
# cat /etc/shadow
root:DYQC9rXCioAuo:8887:0:0::
daemon:*::0:0::
```

67

```
mmdf:MZ74AeYMs4sn6:8842:0:0::
ftp:b80lug/92lMeY:8363::::
anyone::8418::::
chare:7xqmj9fj3bVw2:9009::::
pppdemo:4QYrWsJEHc8IA:9062::::
#
```

The /etc/shadow file is created by the command pwconv on both SCO and SVR4 systems. Only the superuser can create the shadow password file. On SCO systems, the information in the /etc/passwd and the protected password database are used to create the shadow password files. On SVR4 systems, the information from /etc/passwd is used.

The primary advantage to using the shadow password file is that it puts the encrypted passwords in a file not accessible to normal users, thereby decreasing the chances that a vandal will be able to steal the encrypted password information.

THE DIALUP PASSWORD FILE

The issue of supporting dialup access directly on a Unix system is open to debate. Many people still do it, but it generally leads to problems. Allowing a vandal the opportunity to "hack" on the system might result in the system's compromise. Many Unix systems offer anonymous UUCP access, which could result in the loss of the password file and would be detrimental to the organization.

An alternative to offering dialup access on a Unix system is to provide access through a terminal server that supports authentication. In this manner, the user must validate to the terminal server before being permitted network access. Because there is no password file to steal from the terminal server, the job of attacking the terminal server becomes more difficult.

In those situations where you must provide dialup access on the Unix server, you can take some steps to better protect yourself from unauthorized network access.

The capability to install additional passwords on serial port lines is unfortunately not present in all versions of Unix. They have become most prominently found on SCO-based systems. The dialup password protection for these serial lines is controlled through two files: /etc/dialups and /etc/d_passwd. The /etc/dialups file contains a list of the serial ports protected by a dialup password. The file is illustrated in the following example:

```
# cat dialups
/dev/tty2A
#
```

The file /etc/d_passwd is used to identify the login shell that a given password is for. Unlike the regular password, which uses the user's login name, the dialup password is tied to the login shell that a given user is using. This means that every user who uses the Bourne shell has the same dialup password. The following example illustrates the typical dialup password.

```
# cat /etc/d_passwd
/bin/sh::
/usr/lib/uucp/uucico::
#
```

Each line or record in the file consists of two colon-delimited fields. The first field identifies the shell that the given password is for, and the second field lists the password. In the preceding example, neither shell has a password. This means that the user will not be prompted for a password when he logs in.

The dialup password is added through the use of the -m option on the passwd command. This option informs passwd that the password being collected is for a specific shell in the dialup passwords file. The syntax for this form of the command is as follows:

```
passwd -m shell_name
```

The execution of this command is illustrated in the following example:

```
# passwd -m /bin/s:
Setting modem password for login shell: /bin/sh
Please enter new password:
Modem password: testing
Re-enter password: testing
#
```

In the preceding example, the system administrator is adding a dialup password to the /bin/sh shell. This means that any users who log in to the system and have the Bourne shell as their login shell will be prompted for the dialup password. The password they must enter is shown in the preceding example as the system administrator would have typed it. Like the normal passwd command, the actual password is not displayed as it is typed. It is shown here only for illustration purposes. Note that only the system administrator can change the dialup password for a shell.

The passwd command modifies the contents of the d_passwd file to include the new password, as illustrated in the following example:

```
# cat d_passwd
/bin/sh:ORa691.Na1jjQ:
/usr/lib/uucp/uucico::
#
```

As shown in the preceding example, the Bourne shell users now have to provide the additional password when logging in on the terminal ports specified in the file /etc/dialups.

The following example illustrates the process that a user now experiences when he logs in with the dialup password:

```
gateway
gateway!login: chare
Password:
Dialup Password:
Last    successful login for chare: Fri Oct 28 22:52:02 EDT 1994 on tty2a
Last unsuccessful login for chare: Tue Oct 18 16:27:56 EDT 1994 on ttyp1
SCO Unix System V/386 Release 3.2
Copyright (C) 1976-1989 UNIX System Laboratories, Inc.
Copyright (C) 1980-1989 Microsoft Corporation
Copyright (C) 1983-1992 The Santa Cruz Operation, Inc.
All Rights Reserved
gateway
TERM = (ansi)
#
```

As illustrated, the user goes through the normal login procedure until he enters the user name and password. After these are validated, the dialup password control file, /etc/dialups, is checked. When the terminal on which the user is connecting is located in the file and the login shell is the Bourne shell, the user is prompted to enter the dialup password. If the dialup password is entered correctly, the user is granted access to the system, as illustrated in the preceding example. If the dialup password is incorrect, however, the login is aborted, and the user is forced to start over again. This is illustrated in the following example:

```
gateway
gateway!login: chare
Password:
Dialup Password:
Login incorrect
Wait for login retry: .
login: chare
Password:
Dialup Password:
Last    successful login for chare: Fri Oct 28 23:28:28 EDT 1994 on tty2a
       1 unsuccessful login for chare: Fri Oct 28 23:30:55 EDT 1994 on tty2a
SCO Unix System V/386 Release 3.2
Copyright (C) 1976-1989 UNIX System Laboratories, Inc.
Copyright (C) 1980-1989 Microsoft Corporation
Copyright (C) 1983-1992 The Santa Cruz Operation, Inc.
All Rights Reserved
gateway
TERM = (ansi)
$
```

THE GROUP FILE

The /etc/group file is used to control access to files not owned by the user. Recall how permissions work: If the user is not the owner of the file, then the group(s) to which the user belongs is checked to see if the user is a member of the group that owns the file. The group membership list is stored in /etc/group. The format of the file is shown in the following:

```
tech:*:103:andrewg,patc,chare,erict,lorrainel,lens
group name:password:GID:userlist
```

Table 2.2 explains each of the fields contained in the /etc/group file.

TABLE 2.2
The /etc/group File

Field Name	Description	Examples
group name	This is the name of the group. This name is primarily used for human purposes.	tech sales group
password	This is the password to use when switching to this group.	*
GID	This is the numerical group ID number stamped on all files.	0–30,000
userlist	This is a comma-separated list of users that are members of the group.	chare, andrewg

The password for the group file is not used, and no easy mechanisms are available to install a password in the file. If a user attempts to switch to a group that they are not a member of, then they are greeted by a prompt to enter a password, as illustrated in the following example:

```
$ newgrp tech
newgrp: Password
newgrp: Sorry
$ grep tech /etc/group
tech:*:103:andrewg,patc
$
```

If the user who executed this command had been a member of the group tech, then the newgrp command would have been successful. Many current versions of Unix, however, enable a user to be a member of more than one group at a time, thereby reducing or eliminating the need for the newgrp command.

It is important to consider that Berkeley Unix further protects the root account with the wheel group. Only the users who are also members of the wheel group can use the su command to become root.

> To provide access to the root login without providing the actual password, the system administrator should consider the use of the sudo command. More information on sudo, including configuration details, can be found at `http:/ /www.cs.colorado.edu/~millert/sudo/`.

PASSWORD AGING AND CONTROL

Many versions of Unix provide for password aging. This mechanism controls when users can change their passwords by inserting a value into the password file after the encrypted password. This value defines the minimum period of time that must pass before users can change their passwords, and the maximum period of time that can elapse before the password expires.

This explanation becomes clearer by thinking of a timeline, as shown in figure 2.1.

FIGURE 2.1

Password aging and lifetime.

The password aging control information is stored along with the encrypted password, as a series of printable characters. The controls are included after the password, preceded by a comma. Typically a number of characters after the comma represents the following information:

✧ The maximum number of weeks the password is valid

✧ The minimum number of weeks that must elapse before the user can change his or her password again

✧ When the password was most recently changed

The password aging values are defined in table 2.3.

TABLE 2.3
Password Aging Values

Character	Value in Weeks	Character	Value in Weeks
.	0	/	1
0	2	1	3

Character	Value in Weeks	Character	Value in Weeks
2	4	3	5
4	6	5	7
6	8	7	9
8	10	9	11
A	12	B	13
C	14	D	15
E	16	F	17
G	18	H	19
I	20	J	21
K	22	L	23
M	24	N	25
O	26	P	27
Q	28	R	29
S	30	T	31
U	32	V	33
W	34	X	35
Y	36	Z	37
a	38	b	39
c	40	d	41
e	42	f	43
g	44	h	45
i	46	j	47
k	48	l	49
m	50	n	51
o	52	p	53
q	54	r	55

continues

TABLE 2.3, CONTINUED
Password Aging Values

Character	Value in Weeks	Character	Value in Weeks
s	56	t	57
u	58	v	59
w	60	x	61
y	62	z	63

Using this information and looking at a password that has password aging in place, you can decipher the meaning of the following example:

```
chare:2eLNss48eJ/GY,C2:215:100:Chris Hare:/usr1/chare:/bin/sh
```

In the preceding example, the password has been set to age using the value of "C" to define the maximum number of weeks before the password expires, and "2" to define the minimum number of weeks that must pass before the user can change the password again. Each time the user logs in, the expiration time of his password is checked by comparing the last changed value with the maximum. If the user must change his password every three weeks, for example, and it was changed three weeks ago, then the user must change his password. When the user changes his password, the last changed value is updated to reflect when it was last changed.

Two special conditions are recognized by the aging control mechanisms: One forces a user to change his password on the next login, and one prevents a user from being able to change it.

To force a user to change his password, such as for a new user, the password field for that user would be modified to include a comma, followed by two periods for the maximum and minimum time periods. In this case, the user is forced to change his password on the next login. Once changed, the "force" control information is removed from the password entry. An example of the forced entry in the password is shown in the following:

```
chare:2eLNss48eJ/GY,./:215:100:Chris Hare:/usr1/chare:/bin/sh
```

The second special case prohibits a user from being able to change his password. This condition is established by setting the maximum value to be less than the minimum value (that is, first < second). In this case, the user is informed that his password cannot be changed and is illustrated in the following example:

```
chare:,..:215:100:Chris Hare:/usr1/chare:/bin/sh
```

With newer, more secure versions of Unix currently on the market, you may hear the term *password lifetime*. This is a grace period after the maximum time period in which the user can still log in to his account using the expired password. When the lifetime has been reached, the account is disabled. When the user attempts to log in to a system using a disabled account, he is informed that the account has been disabled and to see the system administrator.

The password aging mechanism doesn't prevent a user from changing his password and then changing it back to the old one later. Only a few Unix system versions keep track of what passwords a user has used. The actual process of implementing password aging is version-dependent. To implement it on your system, consult your system documentation.

The program in Listing 2.1, pwexp.pl, is a PERL language program that advises users when their passwords are going to expire so that they can be prepared for the day when the system informs them that their passwords have expired. Note, however, that this version of the program is for standard System V Unix in which a shadow password file is not used.

> PERL (Practical Extraction and Report Language) is a freely available and widely used programming language. It combines elements of many of the Unix commands into one neat package. Some of the features include pattern matching, arrays, conditional programming, and subroutines. PERL can be obtained from many anonymous FTP sites including uunet.uu.net and netlabs.com.

N O T E

This program addresses the aging mechanism implemented in versions of Unix up to System V Release 3.2. At this level, some variations took place in the interest of increasing system security. The AT&T/USL versions moved to using the /etc/shadow file for storing the password information, whereas the SCO implementations moved to using the Trusted Computing Base facilities from SecureWare. In SCO's Unix 3.2v4 product, the aging control information may be in one of /etc/passwd, /etc/shadow, or the Trusted Computing Base files, depending upon which level of security you configure. It also is important to note in SCO, that both the Protected Password Database and the /etc/shadow database might be in use simultaneously.

VANDALS AND PASSWORDS

The term *hacker* did not always have such a negative connotation. Rather, it was a term denoting someone who was persistent, who tried to break things and figure out how they worked. As a result of this reputation, and because most of the people doing hacking were computer science wizards, the term hacker developed a negative connotation. However, for the purpose of this discussion, and because I know "good" hackers, the bad guys are referred to as *vandals*.

A vandal wants to get access to your system for one reason or another. Some of those reasons can include the following:

- ✦ Just for the fun of it

- ✦ To look around

- ✦ To steal computer resources like CPU time

- ✦ To steal trade secrets or other proprietary information

Note that not every attempt to access your system is intended to do harm. However, in most cases they should be treated that way. Regardless of the reasons behind the attack, the piece of information most wanted by a vandal is the /etc/passwd file. When the vandal has a list of valid user account names, it is trivial to create a program to simply guess passwords. However, many modern login programs include a time delay between login prompts that gets longer with each unsuccessful attempt. They also might include program code to disable the access port should too many unsuccessful attempts be recorded.

The primary source of protection is to use /etc/shadow or the Protected Password Database because these files and directories require root access to view them. This makes it harder for the vandal to obtain encrypted password information. However, recall that the password information in /etc/passwd is encrypted. How can the vandal even hope to gain access when he cannot decrypt the passwords as they are stored?

UNDERSTANDING HOW VANDALS BREAK PASSWORDS

It is correct to say that after the password is encrypted it cannot be decrypted. But this doesn't mean that the password is still safe. A password *cracker* is a program used by a vandal that attempts to "guess" the passwords in the /etc/passwd file by comparing them to words in a dictionary. The success of the cracker program is dependent upon the CPU resources, the quality of the dictionary, and the fact that the user has a copy of /etc/passwd.

Password crackers are fairly easy to write. A simple, although less-effective one, can be written in approximately 60 lines of C code or 40 lines of PERL code. That's it. In attempting to provide for better passwords on your system, a system administrator may well give consideration to writing one. Be warned, however, that you might be inviting disaster. If the program is efficient enough, or detects some deficiencies in the passwords on your system, you may have further defeated the security of your machine! An efficient cracker program may be stolen and subsequently used to gain access to other machines. Other ways to better protect the system are available using the logical security tools.

Furthermore, because of the possibility that your cracking program could be stolen, other legal issues could be involved should damage be a direct result of the use of the program. This issue is not to be taken lightly; it is a serious example of how successful these types of programs can be.

For example, a system administrator once had the unfortunate circumstance of not knowing the root password of a machine and no distribution media to reinstall. In this case, he was a friendly vandal in that he owned the machine. He retrieved the /etc/passwd file through anonymous UUCP (Unix to Unix Copy). (So much for security.) After he had the file, he sent it to a contact who tried his password cracking program on it. With no success, he sent it to another machine where a supercomputer chewed on the file for about 18 hours before finally cracking the root password. The ironic part about it was that the password was the name of the company he was working for at the time! Sometimes the simple practice is so effective.

Over the last few years, several password cracking, or guessing, programs have been posted to the Internet. This does not mean that you should run out to get one. In fact, it may be the one program you do not want to have on your system. The authors of these programs clearly state in their documentation that they assume no responsibility for the use of these programs, yet they claim that the programs are highly efficient.

It is highly recommended that you have copies of any password cracking programs on a tightly secured machine and make use of them regularly. However, make sure that the company's security policy allows you, the system administrator, to use the files, and at the same time prohibits everyone else from doing so.

A number of password cracking tools are available; they are listed in Appendix B, "Sources of Information."

The moral of the story is to treat programs that try to guess passwords as dangerous and not worth the potential problems that they could be used to overcome.

WARNING

If you choose to have security programs available for auditing and other evaluations, it is essential that they are not contained on a network-accessible system. Making them available on a network may cause you more grief than you care to have.

C2 SECURITY AND THE TRUSTED COMPUTING BASE

The *Trusted Computing Base* (TCB) is part of the security system for C2-rated Unix systems. It adds a significant level of complexity to the operation of the system and to the administration of it. This system works by moving bits of the /etc/passwd file to other places, as well as adding additional information into the original information. The files that make up the databases for the trusted computing base are scattered in several different directory hierarchies. It is not a good idea to edit these files, however, because serious damage can result to your system.

On a system that uses the TCB, an asterisk is placed in the password field of /etc/passwd. This is because the actual user password is stored along with other user information in the Trusted Computing Base. Using the TCB doesn't change the operation of the system so much as how Unix provides the same services using TCB. On some versions of Unix, such as SCO Unix, even if you are not using C2 security, the Trusted Computing Base is still being used to provide the security services.

Table 2.4 shows the six components to the Trusted Computing Base.

TABLE 2.4
The Trusted Computing Base

Component	Description
/etc/passwd	The System Password File
/tcb/auth/files/	The Protected Password Database
/etc/auth/systems/ttys	The Terminal Control Database
/etc/auth/systems/files	The File Control Database
/etc/auth/subsystems/	The Protected Subsystem Database
/etc/auth/system/default	The System Defaults Database

When reference is made to the Trusted Computing Base, it points to all the components of table 2.4 collectively and not any single component.

The operation of a trusted system brings with it some concepts that must be understood to prevent putting the system in jeopardy.

The trusted computing base is comprised of a collection of software including the Unix kernel and the utilities that maintain the trusted computing base. These utilities include authck for verifying and correcting problems in the password database and integrity for verifying the accuracy of the system files. The trusted computing base implements the security policy on the system. This policy is a set of operating rules that governs the interaction between *subjects* such as processes, and *objects* such as files, devices, and interprocess communication objects.

Accountability for an action is defined only if the action can be traced back to a single person. On traditional Unix systems in which more than one person knows the root password, it is difficult, if not impossible, for the action to be traced to any single person. The pseudo-accounts like cron and lp run anonymously—their action can only be traced after the change of system information. This is corrected on a trusted Unix system because each account is associated with a real user, each action is audited, and every action is associated to a specific user.

Little Identification and Authentication (I&A) is performed on the traditional Unix system. On traditional Unix, the user logs in by providing a login name and password combination, which is validated by a search in the /etc/passwd file. If the login name and password are correct, then the user is allowed access to the system. In a trusted system, some additional rules are used to improve upon the standard I&A techniques. For example, new procedures for changing and generating passwords have been established, providing better protection for parts of the password database to prevent prying eyes from accessing it.

The following example illustrates a typical user entry in the trusted computing base on an SCO system that details the information for a specific user. This information should never be hand-edited because doing so could leave your system in a state of uselessness.

```
chare:u_name=chare:\          # Actual user name
    :u_id#1003:\              # User ID
    :u_pwd=MWUNe/9lrPqck:\    # Encrypted password
    :u_type=general:\         # User Type
    :u_succhg#746505937:\     # Last Successful Password Change
    :u_unsucchg#746506114:\   # Last Unsuccessful Password Change
    :u_pswduser=chare:\       #
    :u_suclog#747066756:\     # Last successful login
    :u_suctty=tty02:\         # Last successful login on tty
    :u_unsuclog#747150039:\   # Last unsuccessful login
    :u_unsuctty=tty04:\       # Last unsuccessful login on tty
    :u_numunsuclog#1:\        # Number of unsuccessful logins
    :u_lock@:\                # Lock Status
    :chkent:                  #
```

The preceding example has been modified to insert the comments on the entry. The "# text" does NOT appear in the file. This example is included here to illustrate that in the TCB, other information is, in fact, being tracked. This is not all of the information, but that which is contained in one file. For each user, a file named with the user name is stored and contains the information shown in the preceding example.

In the preceding illustration, the entry for u_succhg shows a value of 746505937. This is how Unix keeps track of time. The value is the number of seconds since January 1, 1970. The value can be given to a function in the Unix kernel that can convert it to the actual date and time.

Traditional Unix systems keep a limited amount of information regarding system activity, and in some cases, only when they have been configured to do so. In trusted Unix, auditing is a major element to ensure that the actions taken are associated with a specific user. The audit system writes a series of records for each action to generate an audit trail of the events that have occurred on a system. This trail consists of every action between a subject and an object that is either successful or unsuccessful in regards to object access, changes made to subject or object, and system characteristics. Consequently, the audit system provides the audit administrator with an extensive history of system actions. This helps the administrator determine what happened, who did it, and when it occurred.

UNDERSTANDING NETWORK EQUIVALENCY

The two primary types of network equivalency are trusted host access and trusted user access. Throughout this discussion, keep in mind that many network administrators prefer to use these facilities to deliver services throughout their organizations without understanding how they operate and what impact these facilities have on host and network security.

HOST EQUIVALENCY

Host equivalency, or *trusted access*, enables the users of a system to access their accounts on remote systems without having to use their login names and passwords. Through the use of the /etc/hosts.equiv file, the system administrator can list all the trusted systems. If no user names are identified for the machine entry, then all the users are trusted. Similarly, if the system administrator does not specify a particular machine for all users, each individual user can use the.rhosts file in their home directory to list machines to which they want trusted access.

Each entry in the hosts.equiv file is trusted. This means that users on the specified machine can access their equivalent accounts on the local machine without a password. This is not applicable for root because this would be a major security problem. For root, and for the user who wants to provide access to systems not included in the system-wide list, use of the .rhosts file in the user's home directory is required.

Consider the following sample /etc/hosts.equiv file:

```
# cat /etc/hosts.equiv
macintosh.mydomain.com
delicious.mydomain.com
#
```

In the preceding example, the entries enable any user on these machines to log into the local system using the same account name without using a password. However, as the following example shows, it is possible to list account names in this file.

```
# cat /etc/hosts.equiv
macintosh.mydomain.com andrewg
delicious.mydomain.com
#
```

As the preceding example illustrates, the user andrewg on that system can log in using any account name other than root on the local system. Consequently, this creates the potential for problems because andrewg's account may be compromised, and then a vandal can access the local system from that machine. As a result, use of account names in the /etc/hosts.equiv and .rhosts files is discouraged.

The security issues regarding host equivalency include root equivalency and file permissions. It is very dangerous to allow root equivalency between systems. Although root equivalency makes the administration tasks easier to complete, it also makes vandalization of the network easier. If security is compromised on one node that has root equivalency with other nodes, it takes the vandal seconds to determine this and access the other machines. Consequently, it is the author's recommendation not to allow root equivalency in your network environment.

Another problem is the permissions on the network access files /etc/hosts.equiv and .rhosts. The /etc/hosts.equiv file must only be writable by root, although other users can read the file. The .rhosts file must only be writable by the owner of the file. Having the file world writable—and even world readable—can create problems such as enabling users to edit the file and add in other systems.

Some implementations of the Berkeley r-commands that use the .rhosts and /etc/host.equiv files check the permissions on them and refuse to use them if the permissions are set inappropriately. However, it wouldn't take too much effort to write a shell program to look for inappropriately authorized .rhosts files.

USER EQUIVALENCY

Trusted user access is much easier to configure but can be very difficult if it is being installed after a list of users has already been configured. User equivalence is a simple concept that is quite different from trusted host access. Trusted host access is not required for user equivalence to work. For NFS (Network File System) use, user equivalence becomes mandatory to prevent access problems.

User equivalence is configured by giving each user on your network, not just the machine, a unique user name and numerical UID (User ID). This means that on each machine, the user has an account with the same UID. If you do not want to allow a user to access a specific machine, then you do not have to provide an account. Another way to explain this is to say that all the /.etc/passwd and /etc/group files on the machines in the network will be the same.

As you will see, not using user equivalence in your networks can put your file systems and data at risk by allowing unauthorized access to them. Consider the following user list:

Username	UID
chare	003
janicec	1009
terrih	1009
andrewg	1004

The users in the preceding list each have a unique user name, but their UID numbers are not unique. In figure 2.2, you see that janicec has her account on `macintosh.mydomain.com`, and terrih has her account on `delicious.mydomain.com`.

FIGURE 2.2

A user equivalence example.

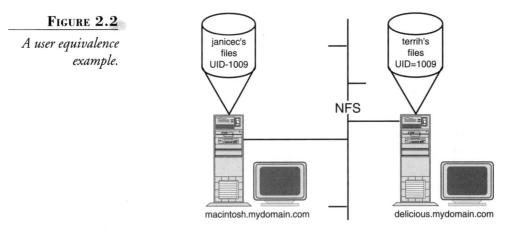

The file system on which terrih has her account is part of an exported file system to the users working on macintosh.mydomain.com. When janicec accesses the files in terrih's directory and lists them, the ls -l command lists janicec as the owner of the files because the UID numbers are the same. This means that janicec can erase or modify the information in those files as if she were the rightful owner. In this case, it does not matter that the user names are different. The key with NFS and user equivalence is the UID.

Another type of problem can occur when user equivalence is not properly configured. Consider the following user list:

Username	Home System
efudd (Elmer)	delicious
efudd (Elizabeth)	macintosh

In the preceding list, two users named efudd exist. The user efudd on the system named delicious is Elmer Fudd, whereas Elizabeth Fudd uses the account name efudd on the system known as macintosh. In an effort to make things easier, the system administrator on delicious has configured trusted host access, or host equivalency, for all the other systems in the network. One day Elizabeth uses the rlogin command to access macintosh and finds that she can log in without having to provide a password. She can see all the files that belong to Elmer, and she has access to all of them. That is because as far as macintosh is concerned, Elizabeth is really Elmer. In this situation, the user name is the determining factor—not the UID.

As you can see, both types of network equivalency, although creating a more productive and user-friendly environment, can actually create a list of security problems that are difficult to track down and correct.

DEFINING USERS AND GROUPS

As you saw in the preceding discussion on network equivalency, placing some forethought into how you will handle the addition of users in your network is essential to your defense. The comment that your /etc/passwd and /etc/group files will be the same across all the systems is an accurate one. However, a strategy for assigning UID numbers and ensuring their uniqueness is more the issue.

This can be done in many ways. You can assign them in sequential order, allocate number blocks to departments or categories of users, or allocate number blocks to offices. Regardless of the method, it is critical that it be the standard for adding users.

UNDERSTANDING PERMISSIONS

The permissions that Unix uses on each file determine how access to the files and directories is controlled. Many situations can be prevented through the correct application of this simple, yet powerful mechanism. The next section reviews how permissions are handled in the Unix environment.

A REVIEW OF STANDARD PERMISSIONS

The permissions applied to a file are based upon the UID and GID (Group ID) stamped on the file and the UID or GID of the user trying to access the file. The three sets of permissions are as follows:

❖ Those applicable to the owner of the file

❖ The users who have the same GID as that on the file

❖ All other users

For each category of users, there are three permission bits: read, write, and execute. This means that for each file or directory there are nine permission bits. These bits are represented in the following example:

```
$ ls -l output
-rw-r--r-- 1 chare    users        236 Aug 24 20:13 output
$
```

In the output in the preceding example, the permissions are as follows:

```
-rw-r--r--
```

The first hyphen represents the file type, which can be one of the types listed in table 2.5, and the remaining characters represent the permissions.

TABLE 2.5
Unix File Types

Symbol	Description	Explanation
-	Regular file	A file that contains a program, data, or text
d	Directory	A special type of file that contains a list of files and the index to their location on the disk
b	Block device file	A file that allows access to devices such as disk drives

Symbol	Description	Explanation
c	Character device file	A file that allows access to devices such as terminals and modems
l	Symbolic link	A pointer to another file that can be on this or another filesystem
p	Named pipe	A method of communicating between two processes

In the permissions, the symbols r, w, and x represent the read, write, and execute permissions respectively. Read permission means that the requesting user can view the contents of the file or directory. Write permission grants the user the authority to modify files or create new files in a directory. Finally, execute permission allows the file to be executed like a command. Table 2.6 summarizes these permissions and their impact on a file or directory.

TABLE 2.6
File and Directory Permissions

Permissions Symbol	Meaning	Impact on Files	Impact on Directories
r	read	View the file with cat or more	List the directory with ls
w	write	Modify the file with vi	Create or delete files
x	execute	Run the file as a command	Search the directory looking for a file; use the cd command

When the permissions on files or directories are not set appropriately, it creates pathways into the system for vandals and also offers the potential for any user to make a mistake and invite disaster. The following example shows some problems involving permissions.

This example illustrates a directory that has no write permission, thereby meaning that file cannot be removed with rm.

```
$ id
uid=1009(terrih)  gid=101(users)
$ ls -l
total 4
dr--r--r--  2 chare    users         48 Aug 24 21:09 a
dr-xr-xr-x  2 chare    users         48 Aug 24 21:12 a2
drwxr--xr--x  2 chare    users         32 Aug 24 21:08 micro_light
$ ls -ld a2
dr-xr-xr-x  2 chare    users         48 Aug 24 21:12 a2
$ls a2
output
$ rm a2/output
rm: a2/output not removed. Permission denied
$ ls -l a2
total 1
-rw-rw-r--  1 chare    users        133 Aug 24 21:12 output
$ date > a2/output
$ ls -l a2
total 1
-rw-rw-r--  1 chare    users         29 Aug 24 21:14 output
```

As the user finds out, he cannot remove the file with the rm command because the directory does not have write permission. Remember, a directory is only a special type of file. As the user checks the permission on the file output itself, he sees that the file has its group write permission turned on. This means that the contents of the file can be changed, as shown, by redirecting the output of the date command into the file.

What has not been mentioned yet is the fact that the user executing these commands is not the owner of the file. Here, through a common error, chare didn't protect his files from terrih because the contents of output could be erased even though he thought he had taken the needed precautions.

Such are the woes of the system administrator. Many attacks are successful not because the system administrator isn't doing his job, but because despite the best of intentions, the users leave these types of holes around. Often users change the value of their umask, for example, without understanding it properly. Some facilities, such as ftp and the r-commands, check the permissions on the files used by these commands and prevent their use if the file permissions are not correct.

NOTE

> The umask is a bit pattern that is applied against the default permissions to achieve the permissions assigned to a file. Say, for example, the default permissions are 777. When a umask of 022 is applied, the resulting permissions are 755, or rwxr-xr-x.

The Set User ID (SUID) and Set Group ID (SGID) are a major part of the security on a Unix system. The SUID and SGID bits allow a user to assume another identity while executing the program. For example, the passwd command uses the SUID bit to allow users to become root in order to change the contents of the password file.

In the case of the SUID bit, the user who executes the program assumes the identity of the owner of the program. For SGID, the user who executes the program becomes a member of the same group that owns the program.

ROOT AND NFS

When you think about root, you think of uncontrolled access to the files, directories, programs, and devices on a system. However, when root attempts to access files on a remote system through NFS, the root user has little or no permission. This is due to the security features built into NFS. This security feature looks for a UID value of zero. When it finds that value, it knows that this is root, and it remaps the UID value to 65534, or -2. This means that over NFS, root falls into the other category of user.

The advantage here is that if you have no root equivalency between your network machines and one becomes compromised, it becomes harder for the vandal to propagate through your filesystems.

EXPLORING DATA ENCRYPTION METHODS

The opportunity to encrypt information to provide a higher level of security for your system and its data is of interest to users and system administrators everywhere. However, even encrypted data can be at risk without the proper monitoring and training for the users who want to use these facilities.

HOW PASSWORDS ARE ENCRYPTED

At one time, the passwords were stored in a plain text format, and only the administrator and system software had access to the file. However, numerous problems occurred when the password file /etc/passwd was being edited. Most editors create a temporary file, which is the file actually edited. At this point, the file would be world readable, giving away the passwords for all the accounts.

As a result, a method of encrypting the passwords using a one-way encryption algorithm was developed. The encrypted values were then stored instead of the clear text. However, the security of the system is only as good as the encryption method chosen.

When a user logs in to a Unix system, the getty program prompts the user for his user name and then executes the login program. The login program prompts for the password but does not decrypt it. In fact, the login program encrypts the password and then compares the newly encrypted value to the one stored in /etc/passwd. If they match, then the user supplied the correct one.

The Unix encryption method for password encryption is accessed through a kernel mechanism named *crypt(3)*. Because of United States Federal licensing issues, the crypt routines might not be available on your machine. The issue is that while the needed routines to encrypt information are available, those programs that decrypt information are not available outside the United States.

The actual password value stored in /etc/passwd is the result of using the user's password to encrypt a 64-bit block of zeroes using the crypt(3) call. The *clear text* is the user's password, which is the key to the encryption operation. The text being encrypted is 64 bits of zeroes, and the resulting *cipher text* is the encrypted password.

This crypt(3) algorithm is based upon the Data Encryption Standard (DES) developed by the National Institute of Standards and Technology or NIST. In normal operation according to the DES standard, a 56-bit key, such as eight 7-bit characters, is used to encrypt the original text, which is commonly called clear text. This clear text is typically 64 bits in length. The resulting cipher text cannot easily be decrypted without knowledge of the original key.

The Unix crypt(3) call uses a modified version of this method by stating that the clear text is encrypted in a block of zeroes. The process is complicated by taking the resulting cipher text and encrypting it again with the user's password as the key. This process in performed 25 times! When complete, the resulting 64 bits are split into 11 printable characters and then saved in the password file.

Despite the fact that the source for crypt can be obtained from many vendors, although the commercial distribution of this is limited outside the United States (you can find public versions of the code on the Internet), no known method is available to translate the cipher text or encrypted value back to its original clear text.

Robert Morris, Sr. and Ken Thompson, who originally implemented the Unix crypt(3) technology, were afraid that with the advent of hardware DES chips, the security of the Unix system could be easily bypassed. By using a "grain of salt," they managed to bypass this threat.

The "grain of salt," which has become known as salt, is a 12-bit number that is used to modify the result of the DES function. The value of this 12-bit number ranges from 0 to

4,095. So for each possible password, 4,096 ways exist that each password could be encrypted and stored in the password file. It is possible for multiple users on the same machine to use the same password, and no one, including the system manager, would be the wiser.

When a user runs the /bin/passwd program to establish a new password, the /bin/passwd program picks a salt based upon the time of day. This salt is used to modify the user's password.

The problem comes later in encrypting the password the next time the user logs in. It is possible, but unlikely, that the user will log in and the salt will be the same. For things to work correctly, Unix stores the salt in /etc/passwd as well. It, in fact, makes up the first two characters of the encrypted password. The following is a sample encrypted value.

```
2eLNss48eJ/GY
```

In the preceding example, the initial two characters—2e—are the salt for this password. When the user logs in to the system, the login program collects the salt from the stored password and uses it to encrypt the password provided by the user. If the newly encrypted password and the stored password match, then the password entered by the user is correct, and the user is logged in to the system. If the values do not match, then the user is greeted by a Login incorrect message, and the user must try to login again.

ENCRYPTING FILES

As you have seen, the encryption of passwords using a mechanism that is not easily decrypted provides a relatively secure method of preventing unauthorized users from having access to the system. But how can users prevent unauthorized access to their files? This can be accomplished through the use of the command crypt(1). This is a relatively unsecured method of encryption, however. Interestingly enough, some Unix commands support the direct manipulation of these encrypted files without having to decrypt them first.

Encrypting files using the crypt command is relatively simple. If no arguments are provided on the command line, crypt prompts for the key, reads the data to encrypt from standard input, and prints the encrypted information on standard output. Ideally however, the information to use is provided on the command line, as illustrated in the following example:

```
crypt key < clear > cipher
```

The preceding command reads from the file clear, encrypts the test using the password key, and saves the resulting encrypted text in the file cipher. Encrypted files can be viewed or decrypted by using a similar command line, as shown in the following:

```
crypt key < cipher > clear
crypt key < cipher ¦ pr ¦ lp
```

In the first command of the preceding example, the encrypted text in cipher is decrypted using key and saved in the file called clear. The second command-line example uses crypt to decrypt the text and sends the resulting clear text to pr for formatting and then to lp to be printed. The files generated by crypt can be edited by ed or vi, provided the version of ed or vi you have on your system supports editing encrypted files.

The exact mechanism used by crypt is well documented, and many versions of this command are publicly available on the Internet. crypt(1) does not use the same encryption routines as crypt(3), which is used for password encryption. The mechanism is a one-rotor encryption machine designed along the lines of the German Enigma, but using a 256-element rotor. Although the methods of attack on such types of encryption machines are known, the amount of work required may be large.

The encryption key used is the limiting factor to determine the level of effort to decrypt the data. The longer the password, the more complex the encryption pattern, and the longer it takes to transform the key to the internal settings used by the machine. For example, the transformation process is meant to take close to a second, but if the key is restricted to three lowercase letters, encrypted files can be read by expending only a substantial fraction of five minutes of real machine time!

Because the key given to crypt might be seen by prying eyes using ps, crypt destroys any record of the actual key immediately upon entry. Consequently, like any other security system, the password used to encrypt the data is the most critical component—and the most suspect.

NOTE

> This encryption mechanism is not unbreakable and can be figured out given enough time. One method of improving your chances of protecting your data is to compress the file prior to encrypting it.

EXAMINING KERBEROS AUTHENTICATION

The Kerberos Authentication system was developed by the Massachusetts Institute of Technology's Project Athena. Since that time, Kerberos has been adopted by other organizations for their own purposes. Many third-party application developers include support for the Kerberos Authentication system in their products.

UNDERSTANDING KERBEROS

Kerberos is an authentication system. Simply put, it is a system that validates a principal's identity. A *principal* can be either a user or a service. In either case, the principal is defined by the following three components:

❖ Primary name

❖ Instance

❖ Realm

In Kerberos terminology, this is called a three-tuple and is illustrated by the following example:

```
<primaryname, instance, realm>
```

The *primaryname*, in the case of a genuine person, is the login identifier. The *instance* is either null or contains particular information regarding the user. For a service, the primaryname is the name of the service, and the machine name is used as the instance, as in rlogin.mymachine. In either case, the *realm* is used to distinguish between different authentication domains. By using the realm, it is possible to have a different Kerberos server for each small unit within an organization instead of a single large one. The latter situation would be a prime target for vandals because it would have to be universally trusted throughout the organization. Consequently, it is not the best configuration choice.

Kerberos principals obtain tickets for services from a special server known as a *ticket-granting server*. Each ticket consists of assorted information identifying the principal that is encrypted in the private key for that service. Because only Kerberos and the service know the private key, it is considered to be authentic. The ticket granted by the ticket-granting server contains a new private session key that is known to the client as well. This key is often used to encrypt the transactions that occur during the session.

The major advantage to the Kerberos approach is that each ticket has a specific lifetime. After the lifetime is reached, a new ticket must be applied for and issued from the ticket-granting server.

DISADVANTAGES OF KERBEROS

As mentioned earlier, the Kerberos system was originally developed at MIT during the development of Project Athena. The disadvantage here is that the configuration of the environment at MIT is unlike any other organization. Simply speaking, Kerberos is designed to authenticate the end user—the human being sitting at the keyboard—to some number of servers. Kerberos is not a peer-to-peer system, nor was it meant for one computer system's daemons to contact another computer.

Several major issues concern the Kerberos authentication system. First and foremost, the majority of computer systems do not have a secure area in which to save the keys. Because a plain text key must be stored in the initial dialog to obtain a ticket-granting ticket, there must be a secure place to save this information. In the event that this plain text key is obtained by an unauthorized user, the Kerberos authentication server in that realm can be easily compromised.

The next problem is how Kerberos handles keys on multiuser computers. In this case, the cached keys can be obtained by other users logged into the system. In a single-user workstation environment, only the current user has access to system resources, so there is little or no need to enable remote access to the workstation. However, if the workstation supports multiple users, then it is possible for another user on the system to obtain the keys.

Other weaknesses also exist in the Kerberos protocol, but these are difficult to discuss without a thorough understanding of how the protocol works and is implemented.

UNDERSTANDING IP SPOOFING

IP Spoofing is a potentially dangerous threat to any network connected to the Internet. On a network, a host allows other "trusted" hosts to communicate with it without requiring authentication. This is accomplished by setting up the .rhost and other files. Any communications coming from sources other than those defined as trusted must provide authentication before they are allowed to establish communication links.

With IP Spoofing, a host not connected to the network connects and makes it look as if they are one of the trusted hosts on the network. This is accomplished by changing their IP number to one of those on the network. In essence, the intruding host impersonates a local system's IP address and fools other hosts into not prompting for authentication.

Security measures to avoid being hit by IP Spoofing include avoiding any IP address based authentication. Require passwords every way you can, and implement encryption based authentication. Many firewalls are also capable of checking the IP source address against the physical location of origin and ascertaining whether or not the data is coming from a real host.

SUMMARY

This chapter examined some of the areas that both the user and system administrator must be concerned with to protect the system. It is vitally important that all users on a machine understand that the security of the machine is not up to the system administrator alone, but also to the users.

For example, the use of good-quality passwords helps to make the system less accessible. The fact of the matter is, though, that few users choose good passwords. Consequently, the system administrator can help achieve a higher level of security through the following mechanisms:

✤ Periodic examination of the system for common problems

✤ Use of a security probing tool like COPS (Computer Oracle and Password System) or TAMU (Texas A&M University)

✤ Education of system users that they each hold a key to the front door of the system

Acknowledgments

Some of the text and examples in this chapter originally appeared in *Sys Admin Magazine*, Volume 1, No 1, "How Unix Password Controls Work" by Chris Hare; Volume 2, No 4, "More Network Security: Equivalency;" Volume 2, No. 6, "C2 Security: Is Big Brother Watching?". *Sys Admin Magazine* is published bimonthly by R&D Publications.

A Sample Program

The sample program pwexp.pl reports the number of days until the user's current password expires. This program could be called from the /etc/profile file and if password aging is enabled for that user, it will report the number of days before the password expires.

Worth noting about this program is that the getpwuid command provides more fields than are actually in the /etc/passwd file. This is because the command puts the password aging information into a separate variable instead of having the programmer split the aging data from the password.

Listing 2.1—pwexp.pl

```
#! perl
eval '(exit $?0)' && eval 'exec perl -S $0 ${1+"$@"}'
& eval 'exec perl -S $0 $argv:q'
if 0;
#
# pwexp.pl - PERL program to check for password expiration times
#
#
#
# get the passwd file entry for this account. $< is the numerical
# representation of our REAL UID
#
```

```
  ( $username, $passwd, $uid, $gid, $pwage,
    $comment, $gcos, $dir, $shell ) = getpwuid($<);
#
# If passwd aging value is defined
#
if ( $pwage ne "" )
    {
    #
    # extract the maxweeks value
    #
    $maxweeks = &a64l( substr( $pwage, 0, 1 ) );
    #
    # extract the minweeks value
    #
    $minweeks = &a64l( substr( $pwage, 1, 1 ) );
    #
    # extract the last changed value
    #
    $lastchange = &a64l( substr( $pwage, 2 ) );
    #
    # what is NOW?
    #
    $now = time / 604800;
    #
    # If maxweeks < minweeks, the user can't change his passwd
    #
    if ( $maxweeks < $minweeks )
            {
            printf "You cannot change your password. Ever. \n";
            }
    #
    # The special case where the password must be changed
    #
    elsif ( ( $minweeks == 0 ) && ( $maxweeks == 0 ) )
            {
            printf "You must change your password. Now.\n";
            }
    #
    # if lastchanged is > now, then expired
    # if now > lastchanged + maxweeks, then expired
    #
    elsif ( $lastchange > $now ||
                    ( $now > $lastchange + $maxweeks ) &&
                    ( $maxweeks > $minweeks ) )
            {
            printf "Your password has expired.\n";
            }
    #
    # tell the user when his password expires
    #
    else
```

```
                {
                printf "Your password expires in %d weeks.\n",
                        $lastchange + $maxweeks - $now;
                printf "Please start thinking of a new one.\n";
                }
        }
else
        {
        printf "Password aging is not enabled.\n";
        }
exit(0);
#
# the a64l routine was written by Randall Schwartz after a call for help
# in the comp.lng.perl newsgroup. Thanks Randall!
#
sub a64l {
        local($_) = @_; # arg into $_
        die "a64l: illegal value: $_" unless m#^[./0-9A-Za-z]{0,6}$#;
        unless (defined %a64map) {
                @a64map{'.','/',0..9,'A'..'Z','a'..'z'} = 0..63;
        }
        local($result) = 0;
        for (reverse split(//)) {
                $result *= 64;
                $result += $a64map{$_};
        }
        $result;
}
```

## CHAPTER 3

DESIGNING A NETWORK POLICY

Bᴇꜰᴏʀᴇ ʙᴜɪʟᴅɪɴɢ ᴀ ꜰɪʀᴇᴡᴀʟʟ in preparation for connecting your network to the rest of the Internet, it is important to understand exactly what network resources and services you want to protect. The *Network Policy* is a document that describes an organization's network security concerns. This document becomes the first step in building effective firewalls.

This chapter discusses this first step of designing a Network Policy for your Internet. Among the issues explored are overall network security planning, site security policy, and risk analysis. This chapter discusses identification of resources and threats, network use and responsibilities, and action plans when the security policy is violated. It helps you monitor system use, mechanisms, and schedules; it also covers account and configuration management procedures and recovery procedures. Finally, this chapter discusses using encryption to protect the network, using authentication systems, and using Kerberos, mailing lists, newsgroups, and security response teams.

Network Security Planning

It is important to have a well-conceived and effective network security policy that can guard the investment and information resources of your company. A network security policy is worth implementing if the resources and information your organization has on its networks are worth protecting. Most organizations have sensitive information and competitive secrets on their networks; these should be protected against vandalism in the same manner as other valuable assets such as corporate property and office buildings.

Most network designers commonly begin implementing firewall solutions before a particular network security problem has been properly identified. Perhaps one reason for this is that coming up with an effective network security policy means asking some difficult questions about what types of Internetwork services and resources you are going to allow your users to access, and which ones you will have to restrict because of security risks.

If your users currently enjoy unrestricted access to the network, it can be difficult to enforce a policy that restricts their access. You should also keep in mind that the network policy that you should use is such that it will not impair the functioning of your organization. A network security policy that prevents network users from effectively implementing their tasks can have an unwanted consequence: network users may find means of bypassing your network policy, rendering it ineffective.

An effective network security policy is something that all network users and network administrators can accept and are willing to enforce.

Site Security Policy

An organization can have multiple sites with each site having its own networks. If the organization is large, it is quite probable that the sites have differing network administrations with different goals and objectives. If these sites are not connected through an internal network, each of these sites may have their own network security policies. However, if the sites are connected through an internal network, the network policy should encompass the goals of all the interconnected sites.

In general a site is any part of an organization that owns computers and network-related resources. Such resources include, but are not restricted to, the following:

❖ Workstations

❖ Host computers and servers

❖ Interconnection devices: gateways, routers, bridges, repeaters

❖ Terminal servers

❖ Networking and applications software

❖ Network cables

❖ Information in files and databases

The site security policy should take into account the protection of these resources. Because the site is connected to other networks, the site security policy should consider the security needs and requirements of all of the interconnected networks. This is an important point because it is possible to come up with a network security policy that safeguards your interests but can be harmful to others. An example of this could be a deliberate use of IP addresses, behind the firewall gateway, that are already used by someone else. In this case, attacks made against your network by spoofing your network's IP addresses will be deflected to the organization whose IP addresses you are using. This situation should be avoided, because it is in your own interests to be a "good citizen" of the Internet.

> RFC 1244 discusses site security policy in considerable detail. Many of the security policy issues in this chapter are based on the issues raised in this RFC.
>
> N O T E

APPROACH TO SECURITY POLICY

Defining a network security policy means developing procedures and plans that safeguard your network resources against loss and damage. One possible approach to developing this policy is to examine the following:

❖ What resources are you are trying to protect?

❖ Which people do you need to protect the resources from?

❖ How likely are the threats?

❖ How important is the resource?

❖ What measures can you implement to protect your assets in a cost-effective manner and timely manner?

❖ Periodically examine your network security policy to see if your objectives and network circumstances have changed.

Figure 3.1 shows a worksheet that can be used to help you direct your thinking along these lines.

- ✤ The "Network Resources Number" column is an internal identification network number of the resources to be protected (if applicable).

- ✤ The "Network Resources Name" column is an English description of the resources. The importance of the resource can be on a numeric scale of 0 to 10, or in "fuzzy" natural-language expressions such as low, high, medium, very high, and so on.

- ✤ The "Type of users to protect resource from" column can have designations such as internal, external, guest, or group names such as accounting users, corporate assistants, and so on.

- ✤ The "Likelihood of a threat" column can be on a numeric scale of 0 to 10, or in "fuzzy" natural language expressions such as low, high, medium, very high, and so on.

- ✤ The "Measures to be implemented to protect network resource" column can have values such as "operating system permissions" for files and directories; "audit trail/alerts" for network services; "screening routers" and "firewall" for hosts and networking devices; or any other description of the type of security control.

In general, the cost of protecting your networks against a threat should be less than the cost of recovering should you be affected by the security threat. If you do not have sufficient knowledge of what you are protecting and the sources of the threat, reaching an acceptable level of security can be difficult. Don't hesitate to enlist the help of others with specialized knowledge concerning your network's assets and possible threats aginst it.

It is important to get the right type of people involved in the design of the network security policy. You might already have user groups who would consider implementation of a network security policy to be their specialty. These groups could include those that are involved with auditing/control, campus information systems groups, and organizations that deal with physical security. If you want universal support of the network security policy, it is important to involve these groups so that you can have their cooperation and acceptance of the network security policy.

Worksheet for Developing Security Approach

Network Resources		Type of users to protect resource from	Likelihood of a threat	Measures to be implemented to protect network resource
Number	Name	Importance of resource			

FIGURE 3.1 *A worksheet for developing a security approach.*

ENSURING RESPONSIBILITY FOR THE SECURITY POLICY

An important aspect of network security policy is ensuring that everyone knows their own responsibility for maintaining security. It is difficult for a network security policy to anticipate all possible threats. The policy can, however ensure that each type of problem does have someone who can deal with it in a responsible manner. There may be many levels of responsibility associated with a network security policy. Each network user, for example, should be responsible for guarding their password. A user who allows their account to be compromised increases the likelihood of compromising other accounts and resources. On the other hand, network administrators and system managers are responsible for maintaining the overall security of the network.

RISK ANALYSIS

When you create the network security policy, it is important to understand that the reason for creating a policy in the first place is to ensure that efforts spent on security are cost-effective. This means that you should understand which network resources are worth protecting, and that some resources are more important than others. You also should identify the threat source that you are protecting the network resource from. Despite the amount of publicity about external intruders breaking into a network, many surveys indicate that for most organizations, the actual loss from "insiders" is much greater.

Risk analysis involves determining the following:

✦ What you need to protect

✦ What you need to protect it from

✦ How to protect it

The risks should be ranked by the level of importance and severity of loss. You should not end up with a situation where you spend more to protect that which is of less value to you. Risk analysis involves determining the following two factors:

1. Estimating the risk of losing the resource *(Ri)*

2. Estimating the importance of the resource *(Wi)*

As a step towards quantifying the risk of losing a resource, a numeric value can be assigned. For example, the risk *(Ri)* of losing a resource can be assigned a value from 0 to 10, where 0 represents no risk, and 10 represents the highest risk. Similarly, the importance of a resource *(Wi)* can be assigned a value from 0 to 10, where 0 means no importance and 10 means highest importance. The overall weighted risk for the resource is then, the numeric product of the risk value and its importance (also, called the weight). This can be written as the following:

```
     WRi = Ri*Wi
WRi = Weighted risk of resource "i"
Ri = Risk of resource "i"
Wi = Weight (importance) of resource "i"
```

Consider figure 3.2, a simplified network with a router, a server, and a bridge. Assume that the network and system administrators have come up with the following estimates for the risk and importance of the network devices.

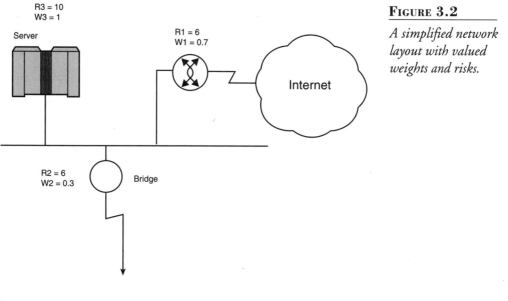

FIGURE 3.2

A simplified network layout with valued weights and risks.

Router:

$R1 = 6$

$W1 = .7$

Bridge:

$R2 = 6$

$W2 = .3$

Server:

$$R3 = 10$$

$$W3 = 1$$

The computation of the weighted risks of these devices is shown next:

Router:

$$WR1 = R1 * W1 = 6 * 0.7 = 4.2$$

Bridge:

$$WR2 = R2 * W2 = 6 * 0.3 = 1.8$$

Server:

$$WR3 = R3 * W3 = 10 * 1 = 10$$

Figure 3.3 shows a worksheet that you can use for recording the previous calculations.

❖ The "Network Resources Number" column is an internal identification network number of the resource (if applicable).

❖ The "Network Resources Name" column is an English description of the resources.

❖ The "Risk to Network Resources (Ri)" column can be on a numeric scale of 0 to 10, or in "fuzzy" natural language expressions such as low, medium, high, very high, and so on.

❖ Similarly, the "Weight (Importance)of Resource (Wi)" column can be on a numeric scale of 0 to 10, or in "fuzzy" natural language expressions such as "low," "high," "medium," "very high," and so on. If you are using numerical values for the risk and weight columns, you can compute the value in the "Weighted Risk ($Ri * Wi$)" column as the product of the Risk and Weight values.

One can compute the overall risk of the resources on the network by using the following formula:

```
WR = (R1*W1 + R2*W2 + .... + Rn*Wn)/(W1 + W2 + ... + Wn)
```

For the network in figure 3.2, the overall network risk would be as follows:

```
WR = (R1*W1 + R2*W2 + R3*W3)/(W1 + W2 + W3)
   = (4.2 + 1.2 + 10)/(0.7 + 0.3 + 1)
   = 15.4/2
   = 7.7
```

Worksheet for Network Security Risk Analysis

Network Resources		Risk to Network Resources (Ri)	Weight (Importance) of Resource (Wi)	Weighted Risk (Ri * Wi)
Number	Name			

FIGURE 3.3 *A sample worksheet for a network security analysis.*

NOTE

> A threat and risk assessment should not be a one-time activity; it should be carried out regularly, as defined in the site security policy. The United States Fish and Wildlife Service has documented the issues involved in performing a threat and risk assessment. The VRL for the threat and risk assessment document is `http://www.fws.gov/~pullenl/security/rpamp.html`.

Other factors to consider in estimating the risk to a network resource are its availability, integrity, and confidentiality. Availability of a resource is a measure of how important it is to have the resource available all the time. Integrity of a resource is a measure of how important it is that the resource or the resource's data be consistent. This is particularly important for database resources. Confidentiality applies to resources such as data files to which you wish to restrict access.

IDENTIFYING RESOURCES

In performing a risk analysis, you should identify all the resources that are at risk of a possible security breach. Resources such as hardware are fairly obvious to list in this estimate, but resources such as the people who actually use the systems are often overlooked. It is important to identify *all* network resources that could be affected by a security problem.

RFC 1244 lists the following network resources that should be considered in estimating threats to overall security:

1. **HARDWARE:** processors, boards, keyboards, terminals, workstations, personal computers, printers, disk drives, communication lines, terminal servers, routers.

2. **SOFTWARE:** source programs, object programs, utilities, diagnostic programs, operating systems, communication programs.

3. **DATA:** during execution, stored on-line, archived off-line, backups, audit logs, databases, in transit over communication media.

4. **PEOPLE:** users, people needed to run systems.

5. **DOCUMENTATION:** on programs, hardware, systems, local administrative procedures.

6. **SUPPLIES:** paper, forms, ribbons, magnetic media.

IDENTIFYING THE THREATS

Once the network resources requiring protection are identified, you should identify the threats to these resources. The threats can then be examined to determine what potential for loss exists. You should also identify from what threats you are trying to protect your resources.

The following sections describe a few of the possible threats.

DEFINING UNAUTHORIZED ACCESS

Access to network resources should only be permitted to authorized users. This is called *authorized access*. A common threat that concerns many sites is unauthorized access to computing facilities. This access can take many forms, such as use of another user's account to gain access to the network and its resources. In general, the use of any network resource without prior permission is considered to be *unauthorized access*.

The seriousness of an unauthorized access depends on the site and the nature of the potential loss. For some sites, the mere act of granting access to an unauthorized user may cause irreparable harm by negative media coverage.

> Some sites, because of their size and visibility, may be more frequent targets than others. The Computer Emergency Response Team (CERT) has made the observation that in general, well-known universities, government sites, and military sites seem to attract more intruders. More information on CERT, as well as other similar organizations, can be found in the section, "Security Response Teams," later in this chapter.

RISK OF DISCLOSURE OF INFORMATION

Disclosure of information, whether it is voluntary or involuntary, is another type of threat. You should determine the value or sensitivity of the information stored on your computers. In the case of hardware and software vendors, source code, design details, diagrams, and product-specific information represent a competitive edge. Hospitals, insurance companies, and financial institutions maintain confidential information, the disclosure of which can be damaging to the clients and to the reputation of the company. Pharmaceutical labs may have patent applications and cannot risk loss due to theft.

At a systems level, disclosure of a password file on a Unix system may make you vulnerable to unauthorized access at a future date. For many organizations, a glimpse of a proposal or research project containing many years of research may give a competitor an unfair advantage.

> People often make the assumption that network and computer break-ins are made by individuals working independently. This is not always so. The dangers of systematic industrial and governmental espionage are unfortunate realities of life.
>
> In addition, when a break-in is achieved, the information typically flows through the Internet in very short order. There are newsgroups and Internet Relay Chat (IRC) channels where users share break-in information.

DENIAL OF SERVICE

Networks link valuable resources such as computers and databases, and provide services that an organization depends on. Most users on such networks rely on these services for performing their jobs efficiently. If these services are not available, there is a corresponding loss in productivity. A classic example of this was the Internet Worm incident that took place on November 2–3, 1988, where a large number of computers on the network were rendered unusable.

It is difficult to predict the form in which the denial of service may come. The following are some examples of how a denial of service can affect a network.

❖ A network may be rendered unusable by a rogue packet.

❖ A network may be rendered useless by traffic flooding.

❖ A network may be partitioned by disabling a critical network component such as a router joining the network segments.

❖ A virus might slow down or cripple a computer system by consuming system resources.

❖ The actual devices that protect the network may be subverted.

NOTE

> You should determine which services are absolutely essential, and for each of these services determine the effect of loss of this service. You should also have contingency policies on how you can recover from such losses.

NETWORK USE AND RESPONSIBILITIES

There are a number of issues that must be addressed when developing a security policy:

1. Who is allowed to use the resources?

2. What is the proper use of the resources?

3. Who is authorized to grant access and approve usage?

4. Who may have system administration privileges?

5. What are the user's rights and responsibilities?

6. What are the rights and responsibilities of the system administrator vs. those of the user?

7. What do you do with sensitive information?

These issues are discussed in the sections that follow.

IDENTIFYING WHO IS ALLOWED USE OF NETWORK RESOURCES

You must make a list of users who need access to network resources. It is not necessary to list every user on the network. Most network users fall into groups such as accounting users, corporate lawyers, engineers, and so on. You must also include a class of users called the external users. These are users who can access your network from elsewhere, such as stand-alone workstations or other networks. These external users can be users who are not employees, or who are employees accessing the network from their homes or while traveling.

IDENTIFYING THE PROPER USE OF A RESOURCE

After you determine which users are allowed access to network resources, you should provide guidelines for the acceptable use of these resources. The guidelines will depend on the class of user, such as software developers, students, faculty, external users, and so on. For each of these user classes, you should have separate guidelines. The policy should state what types of network usage are acceptable and unacceptable, and what type of usage is restricted. The policy that you develop is called the Acceptable Use Policy (AUP) for your network. If access to a network resource is restricted, you should consider the level of access the different user classes will have.

> Your AUP may clearly state that individual users are responsible for their actions. Each user's responsibility exists regardless of the security mechanisms that are in place. It makes no sense building expensive firewall security mechanisms if a user can disclose the information by copying files on disk or tape and making data available to unauthorized individuals.

NOTE

Though it may seem obvious, the AUP should clearly state that breaking into accounts or bypassing security is not permitted. This can help avoid legal issues raised by employees who bypass network security and later claim they were not properly informed or trained about network policy. The following is a guideline of issues that should be covered when developing an AUP:

✦ Is breaking into accounts permitted?

✦ Is cracking passwords permitted?

✦ Is disrupting service permitted?

✦ Should users assume that a file being world-readable grants them the authorization to read it?

✦ Should users be permitted to modify files that are not their own, even if they happen to have write permission?

✦ Should users share accounts?

Unless you have unusual requirements, the answer to most of these questions for most organizations will be *No*.

Additionally, you may want to incorporate a statement in your policies concerning copyrighted and licensed software. In general, your network usage procedures should be such that it should be difficult for employees to download unauthorized software from the network. Copying software illegally is punishable by law in most countries in the West. Large organizations often have very strict policies concerning licensing because of the risk of lawsuits and damage caused by publicity of incidents.

NOTE

Many licensed software products for networks determine their usage and restrict the number of users that can access the network. However, some licensing agreements may require that you monitor the license usage so that the license agreement is not violated.

You may want to include information concerning copyrighted or licensed software in your AUP. Examples of the points that you may want to address are the following:

✦ Copyrighted and licensed software may not be duplicated unless it is explicitly stated.

✦ Indicate methods of conveying information on the copyright/licensed status of software.

✦ Err on the side of caution. When in doubt, do not copy.

An AUP that does not clearly state what is prohibited can make it difficult to prove that a user has violated the policy. Exemptions to your policy could be members of so-called *tiger teams*, charged with the responsibility of probing the security weakness of your networks. The users comprising these tiger teams must be clearly identified. On occasion you may have to deal with users who are self-appointed members of the tiger team and want to probe the security weakness for research purposes or to make a point. Your AUP should address the following issues about security probing:

❖ Is user-level hacking permitted at all?

❖ What type of security probing activities are permitted?

❖ What controls must be in place to ensure that the security probing does not get out of control?

❖ What controls must be in place to protect other network users from being victims of security probing activities?

❖ Who should have the permission to do security probing, and what is the process for obtaining permission to conduct these tests?

If you want to permit legitimate security probing, you should have separate network segments and hosts on your network for these tests. In general, it is very dangerous to test worms and viruses. If you must perform these tests, it would be foolish to conduct them on a live network. You should, instead, physically isolate the hosts and network segments that are used for the test, and do a complete and careful reload of all the software at the end of each test.

Assessing the security weaknesses and taking proper measures can be effective in repelling hacker attacks. Some organizations use outside consultants to evaluate the security of their services. As part of this evaluation, they may legitimately perform "hacking." Your policy should make allowances for these situations.

DETERMINING WHO IS AUTHORIZED TO GRANT ACCESS AND APPROVE USAGE

The network security policy should identify who is authorized to grant access to your services. You also should determine what type of access these individuals can grant. If you cannot control who is granted access to your system, it is difficult to control who is using your network. If you can identify the persons who are charged with granting access to the network, you can trace what type of access or control has been granted. This is helpful in identifying the cause of security holes as a result of users being granted excessive privileges.

You may want to consider the following factors in determining who will grant access to services on your networks:

❖ Will access to services be granted from a central point?

❖ What methods will you use for creating accounts and terminating access?

If the organization is large and decentralized, you may have several central points, one for each department, that is responsible for the security of its departmental network. In this case you must have global guidelines on what types of services are to be permitted for each class of user. In general, the more centralized the network administration is, the easier it is to maintain security. On the other hand, centralized administration can create problems when departments want greater control over their network resources. The correct amount of centralization or decentralization will depend on factors that are beyond the scope of this discussion.

The system administrators will, of course, need special access to the network, but other users may need certain privileges as well. The network security policy should address this issue. A universal policy restricting all special privileges, while being more secure, may prevent legitimate users from performing their work. A more balanced approach is needed.

The challenge is to balance restricted access to special privileges in order to make the network more secure, versus giving people who need these privileges access so that they can perform their tasks. In general you should grant only enough privilege to accomplish the necessary tasks.

Some system administrators take the easy way out and assign more privileges than the user needs, so the users will not bother them again. Also, the system administrator may not properly understand the fine points in assigning security and may err on the side of giving more privileges. Training and education can help avoid these types of problems.

People holding special privileges should be responsible and also accountable to some authority identified within the security policy. Some systems may have custom audit trails that can be used so that privileged users cannot abuse their trust.

WARNING

If the people you grant privileges to are not accountable and responsible, you run the risk of creating security holes in the system and inconsistent granting of permissions to users. Such systems are invariably difficult to manage.

If there are a large number of network and system administrators, it is difficult to keep track of what permissions have been granted to network resources. A formalized way of granting requests can be used. After the user makes the request and the request is authorized by the user's supervisor, the system administrator must document the security restrictions or access the user has been granted.

Figure 3.4 shows a worksheet that can be used to keep a paper trail of what permissions have been granted to a user. The following is a description of the columns used in this worksheet.

- ❖ The network resource number column is an internal identification network number of each resource (if applicable).

- ❖ The resource name column is an English description of the resources.

- ❖ The type of access column can be used for a description of the resource, such as "read and execute access to directory."

- ❖ The operating system permissions column contains the operating system flags used to implement the security access. For Unix systems, these are the read(r), write(w), execute(x) flags. Other operating systems will use their own sets of flags.

You also should examine the procedure that you will be using to create user accounts and assign permissions. In the least restrictive case, the people who are authorized to grant access would be able to go into the system directly and create an account by hand or through vendor-supplied mechanisms. These mechanisms place a great deal of trust in the person running them, and the person running them usually has a large amount of privileges, such as the root user in Unix. Under these circumstances, you need to select someone who is trustworthy to perform this task.

You should develop specific procedures for the creation of accounts. Under Unix, there are several methods that can be used for creating accounts. Regardless of which procedure you decide to use, it should be well documented to prevent confusion and reduce mistakes.

Security vulnerabilities can easily occur as a result of mistakes made by the system administrator. If you have well-documented procedures, this will help ensure fewer mistakes.

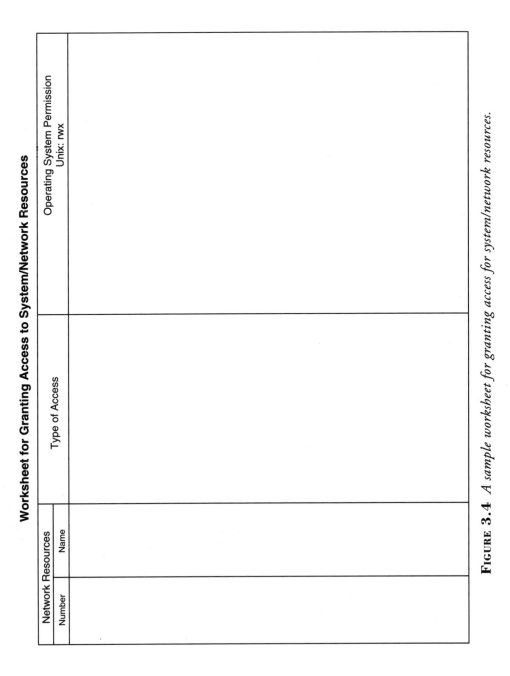

Worksheet for Granting Access to System/Network Resources

Network Resources		Type of Access	Operating System Permission Unix: rwx
Number	Name		

FIGURE 3.4 *A sample worksheet for granting access for system/network resources.*

These procedures also enable future system administrators to be easily trained on the peculiarities of a particular system. Another issue to consider is to select a user account creation procedure that is the simplest and most easily understood. This ensures that fewer mistakes will be made, and that the system administrators are most likely to follow them (as they normally should).

You also should have a policy on the selection of an initial password. The granting of an initial password is a vulnerable time for the user account. Policies such as the initial password being the same as the user name, or being left blank, can leave the accounts wide open. Also, avoid setting the initial password as a function of the user name, or part of the user name, or some algorithmically generated password that can easily be guessed. The selection of an initial password should not be obvious.

CERT estimates that 80 percent of all network security problems are created by insecure passwords.

N O T E

Some users do not use their account for a considerable period of time after their account is created; others never log in. In these circumstances, if the initial password is not secure, the account and the system are vulnerable. For this reason, you should have a policy for disabling accounts that have never been accessed for a period of time. The user is then forced into asking for enabling of their user account.

It is also a mistake to allow users to continue to use the initial password indefinitely. If the system permits, you should force users to change their password on their first login. Many systems have a password aging policy. This can be helpful in protecting the passwords. There are also Unix utilities such as password+ and npasswd that can be used to test the security of the password.

passwdt is an application for analyzing passwords. It can be found at `ftp://ftp.dartmouth.edu/pub/security/passwd+.tar`.

npasswd is plug-compatible replacement for the passwd command. It incorporates a password-checking system that disallows simple passwords. npasswd can be found at `ftp://ftp.uga.edu/pub/security/npasswd.tar.gz`.

N O T E

DETERMINING USER RESPONSIBILITIES

The network security policy should define the users rights and responsibilities for using the network resources and services. The following is a list of issues that you may want to address concerning user responsibilities:

✧ Guidelines regarding network resource usage such as whether users are restricted and what the restrictions are.

✧ What constitutes abuse in terms of using network resources and affecting system and network performance.

✧ Are users permitted to share accounts or let others use their accounts?

✧ Should users reveal their passwords on a temporary basis to allow others working on a project to access their accounts?

✧ User password policy—How frequently should users change their passwords and any other password restrictions or requirements?

✧ Are users responsible for providing backups of their data, or is this the system administrator's responsibilities?

✧ Consequences for users disclosing information that may be proprietary. What legal action or other punishment may be implemented?

✧ Statement on electronic mail privacy (Electronic Communications Privacy Act).

✧ A policy concerning controversial mailing or postings to mailing lists or discussion groups.

✧ A policy on electronic communications such as mail forging.

The Electronic Mail Association (EMA) recommends that every site have a policy on the protection of employee privacy. Organizations should establish privacy policies that are not limited to electronic mail, but which encompass other media such as disks, tapes, and paper documents. The EMA suggests five criteria for evaluating any policy:

1. Does the policy comply with law and with duties to third parties?

2. Does the policy unnecessarily compromise the interest of the employee, the employer, or third parties?

3. Is the policy workable as a practical matter and likely to be enforced?

4. Does the policy deal appropriately with all different forms of communications and record keeping with the office?

5. Has the policy been announced in advance and agreed to by all concerned?

Determining the Responsibilities of System Administrators

The system administrator often needs to gather information from files in users' private directories to diagnose system problems. The users, on the other hand, have a right to maintain their privacy. There is, therefore, a tradeoff between a user's right to privacy and the needs of the system administrators. When threats to the network security occur, the system administrator may have greater need to gather information on files on the system, including the users' home directories.

The network security policy should specify the extent to which system administrators can examine users' private directories and files for diagnosing system problems and for investigating security violations. If the network security is at risk, the policy should allow a greater flexibility for the system administrators to correct the security problems. Other related questions that you should address are the following:

    ✣ Can the system administrator monitor or read a user's files for any reason?

    ✣ Do network administrators have the right to examine network or host traffic?

    ✣ What are the users', system administrators', and organization's liabilities for gaining unauthorized access to other people's private data?

What to Do with Sensitive Information

You must determine what types of sensitive data can be stored on a specific system. From a security standpoint, extremely sensitive data such as payroll and future plans should be restricted to few hosts and few system administrators. Before granting users access to a service on a host, you should consider what other services and information are provided that a user can gain access to. If the user has no need to deal with sensitive data, the user should not have an account on a system containing such material.

You also should consider if adequate security exists on the system to protect sensitive data. In general, you do not want users to store very sensitive information on a system that you do not plan to secure very well. On the other hand, securing a system can involve additional hardware, software, and system administration cost, and it might not be cost-effective to secure data on a host that is not very important to the organization or the users.

The policy also should take into account the fact that you need to tell users who might store sensitive information what services are appropriate for the storage of this sensitive information.

PLAN OF ACTION WHEN SECURITY POLICY IS VIOLATED

Each time the security policy is violated, the system is open to security threats. If no change to the network security occurs when the security policy is violated, then the security policy should be modified to remove those elements that do not have security.

> A security policy and its implementation should be as non-obtrusive as possible. If the security policy is too restrictive, or improperly explained, it is quite likely to be violated.

Regardless of what type of policy is implemented, there is a tendency for some users to violate the security policy. Sometimes it is obvious when a security policy is broken; other times these infractions can go undetected. The security procedures that you implement should minimize the possibility of a security infraction going undetected.

When you detect a security policy violation, you should classify if the violation occurred due to an individual's negligence, an accident or mistake, ignorance about the current policy, or deliberate ignoring of the policy. In the latter case, the violation may be performed not by just one individual, but by a group of individuals who knowingly perform an act that is in direct violation of the security policy. In each of these circumstances, the security policy should provide guidelines on the immediate course of action.

> An investigation should be performed to determine the circumstances surrounding the security violation, and how or why the violation occurred. The security policy should provide guidelines on the corrective action for a security breach. It is reasonable to expect that the type and severity of action will depend on the severity of the violation.

RESPONSE TO POLICY VIOLATIONS

When a violation takes place, the response can depend on the type of user responsible for the violation. Violations to policy may be committed by a wide variety of users. Some of these users may be local users and others may be external users. Local users are often called insiders and external users and called outsiders. The distinction between the two is usually based on network, administrative, legal, or political boundaries. The type of boundary determines what the response should be to the security violation. Examples of responses can range from a verbal reprimand or warning, a formal letter, or the pressing of legal charges.

You need to define actions based on the type of violation. These actions need to be clearly defined, based on the kind of user violating your computer security policy. The internal and external users of your network should be aware of your security policy. If you have outsiders who are using your computer network legally, it is your responsibility to verify that these individuals have a general awareness of the policies that you have set. This is particularly important if you need to take legal action against the offending parties. If a significant amount of loss was incurred, you may want to take more drastic action. If adverse publicity is involved, you may prefer to fix the security hole and not pursue legal action.

The security policy document also should include procedures for handling each security violation incident. A proper log of such security violations should be maintained, and should be periodically reviewed to observe trends and perhaps adjust security policy to take into account any new types of threats.

RESPONSE TO POLICY VIOLATIONS BY LOCAL USERS

You could have a security policy violation in which an internal user violates the security policy. This could occur in the following situations:

✦ A local user violates the local site security policy.

✦ A local user violates a remote site security policy.

In the first case, because your internal security policy is violated, you may have more control over the type of response to this security violation. In the second case, a local user has violated another organization's security policy. This could happen through a connection such as the Internet. This situation is complicated by the fact that another organization is involved, and any response you take will have to be discussed with the organization whose security policy your local user has violated. You also should consult your corporate attorneys or attorneys who specialize in computer legal security.

RESPONSE STRATEGIES

There are two types of response strategies to security incidents:

✦ Protect and Proceed

✦ Pursue and Prosecute

If the administrators of the security policy feel that the company is sufficiently vulnerable, they may choose the Protect and Proceed strategy. The goal of this policy is to immediately protect the network and restore it to its normal status so that the users can continue using the network. In order to do this, you may have to actively interfere with the intruder's actions and prevent further access. This should be followed with an analysis of the amount of damage done.

Sometimes it may not be possible to immediately restore the network to its normal operation; you may have to isolate network segments and shut down systems, with the objective of preventing further unauthorized access to the system. A disadvantage to this approach is that the intruders know that they have been detected and will take actions to avoid being traced. Also, the intruder could react to your protection strategy by attacking the site using a different strategy; at the very least, the intruder likely will live to pursue their hacking against another site.

The second approach—Pursue and Prosecute—adopts the strategy that the major goal is to allow the intruders to pursue their actions while monitoring their activities. This should be done as unobtrusively as possible so that the intruders are not aware of the fact that they are being monitored. The intruders' activities should be logged, so proof will be available in the Prosecute phase of the strategy. This approach is the one recommended by law enforcement agencies and prosecutors, because it yields proof these agencies can use in prosecuting the intruders. The disadvantage of this approach is that the intruder will continue stealing information or doing other damage, and you are still vulnerable to lawsuits resulting from damage to the system and loss of information.

One possible way of monitoring the intruders without causing damage to the system is to construct a "jail." A *jail*, in this case, defines a simulated environment for the intruders to use, so that their activities can be monitored. The simulated environment presents fake data, but the system is set up in such a way that the intruders' keystrokes and activities are monitored.

Figure 3.5 shows the general idea behind constructing a jail. To construct a jail, you need access to the source code for the operating system and in-house programming talent who can simulate this environment. It is safest to construct the jail using a sacrificial machine on an isolated network segment to minimize the risk of pollution of other network segments and systems by the intruders' activities. It is also possible to construct the jail using a software-simulated environment; however this approach is more difficult to set up.

On a Unix system the chroot mechanism can be very handy in setting up a jail. The chroot mechanism irrevocably confines a process to a single branch of the file system. For all practical purposes, the root of this branch of the file system appears as the root of the file system to the process. This mechanism prevents access to device files and the real password file (/etc/passwd).

If you do not want other users logged into the sacrificial machine, you will have to periodically update the utmp file that contains a log of the users logged in so that the Jail looks realistic. You should also remove access to utilities that can reveal that the jail is a simulated environment. Examples of these utilities are netstat, ps, who, w. Alternatively, you can provide fake versions of these utilities to make the simulated environment appear like a real one.

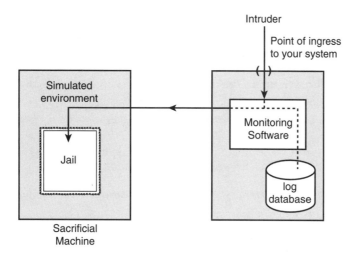

FIGURE 3.5

The general architecture of a jail.

Once you have sufficient evidence against the intruder, you may want to prosecute. However, prosecution is not always the best possible outcome. If the intruder is an internal user or a guest user such as a student, proper disciplinary actions can be equally effective without the additional cost of legal prosecution and the ensuing publicity. The network security policy should list these choices and provide guidelines on when they should be exercised.

> The following can be used as a guideline to help determine when the site should use a policy of Protect and Proceed or Pursue and Prosecute.

N O T E

The Protect and Proceed strategy can be used under the following conditions:

❖ If network resources are not well-protected against intruders.

❖ If continued intruder activity could result in great damage and financial risk.

❖ If the cost of prosecution is deemed too costly, or the possibility or willingness to prosecute is not present.

❖ If there is considerable risk to the existing users on the network.

❖ If the types of users for a large internal network are not known at the time of attack.

❖ If the site is vulnerable to lawsuits from users. This is true for insurance companies, banks, security forms, network providers, and so on.

121

The Pursue and Prosecute strategy can be used under the following conditions:

✦ If network resources and systems are well protected.

✦ If the risk to the network is outweighed by the disruption caused by present and potentially future intrusions.

✦ If this is a concentrated attack and has occurred before.

✦ If the site is highly visible and has been a target of past attacks.

✦ If not pursuing and prosecuting will invite further intrusions.

✦ If the site is willing to incur the risk to network resources by allowing the intruder to continue.

✦ If intruder access can be controlled.

✦ If the monitoring tools are sufficiently well-developed to create proper logs and gather evidence for prosecution.

✦ If you have in-house programming talent to construct specialized tools quickly.

✦ If the programmers, system and network administrators are sufficiently clever and knowledgeable about the operating system, system utilities, and systems to make the pursuit worthwhile.

✦ If there is willingness on the part of management to prosecute.

✦ If the system administrators know what kind of evidence would lead to prosecution, and can create proper logs of the intruders activities.

✦ If there is established contact with knowledgeable law enforcement.

✦ If there is a site representative versed in the relevant legal issues.

✦ If the site is prepared for possible legal action from its own users if their data or systems become compromised during the pursuit.

✦ If good backups are available.

DEFINING RESPONSIBILITIES OF BEING A GOOD CITIZEN ON THE INTERNET

The Internet is a cooperative venture, and the sites that have networks connected to it should be expected to follow rules of good behavior to other sites. This is similar to the workings of a successful modern society. Your security policy should include a statement that deliberate attempts at violating another site's networks is a violation of the company policy.

You should also define what types of information should be released. It may be more economical for you to publish documents about your organization on an FTP server. In this case, you should decide what type of information and how much should be released.

Contacts and Responsibilities to External Organizations

The network security policy should define procedures for interacting with external organizations. External organizations could include law enforcement agencies, legal experts, other sites affected by the security violation incident, external response team organizations such as the CERT (Computer Emergency Response Team), CIAC (Computer Incident Advisory Capability), and if necessary, press agencies.

The people who are authorized to contact these organizations should be identified. You should identify more than one person for each area, to cover situations when the designated individuals may not be reachable. Issues that you should address can include the following:

❖ Identify "public relation types" who are versed in talking to the press.

❖ When should you contact local and federal law enforcement and investigative agencies?

❖ What type of information can be released?

During an investigation, certain rules regarding evidence handling must be followed. Failure to follow these rules might result in the loss of your case. Consequently, it is essential that you contact the authorities in your country responsible for computer crime and have them assist you in planning your investigation. Many law-enforcement agencies offer training in evidence-handling procedures, and there are companies that offer services in the investigation arena.

Interpreting and Publicizing the Security Policy

It is important to identify the individuals who will interpret the policy. It is usually not a good idea to have only one individual involved, in case that person would be unreachable at the time of crisis. One can identify a committee, but it is also not a good idea to have too many members of such a committee. From time to time, the security policy committee will be called upon to interpret, review, and revise the document.

Once the site security policy has been written and agreed upon, the site must ensure that the policy statement is widely disseminated and discussed. Mailing lists can be used. The new policy can also be reinforced by internal education such as training seminars, group briefings, workshops, one-on-one meetings with administrators, or all of these depending on the size of the institution and the needs at hand.

Implementing an effective security policy is a collective effort. Therefore, the network users should be allowed to comment on the policy for a period of time. You may want to hold meetings to elicit comments and to ensure that the policy is correctly understood. This also will help you in clarifying the language of the policy and avoid ambiguities and inconsistencies in the policy.

The meetings should be open to all network users and higher-level management who may be needed to make global decisions when important questions come up. User participation and interest further ensures that the policy will be better understood and more likely to be followed.

> If users perceive that the policy reduces their productivity, they should be allowed to respond. If necessary, additional resources may have to be added to the network to ensure that the users can continue performing their jobs without loss in productivity. To create an effective network policy, you need to find a fine balance between protection and productivity.

Sometimes new programs are met with enthusiasm initially, when everyone is aware of the policy. Over a period of time, though, there is a tendency to forget the contents of the policy. Users need periodic reminders. Also, as new users are added to the network, they need to understand the security policy.

Periodic reminders (properly timed) and continual education on the policy, will increase the chances that the users will follow the security policy. New users should have the policy included as part of their network user information packet. Some organizations require a signed statement from every network user that they have read and understood the policy. If users later require legal action for serious security violations, the signed statement can help you pursue the legal action successfully.

IDENTIFYING AND PREVENTING SECURITY PROBLEMS

The security policy defines what needs to be protected, but the policy may not explicitly spell out how the resources should be protected and the general approach to handling security problems. A separate section on the security policy should discuss the general procedures to be implemented to prevent security problems. The security policy may refer to the site's system administrator's guide for additional details on implementing the security procedures.

Before establishing the security procedures, you must assess the level of importance of network resources and their degree of security risk. The earlier discussion in this chapter on "Approach to Security Policy" and "Risk Analysis," and the worksheets in figures 3.1 and 3.3 can be used as a guide in focusing attention on the more important network resources.

> It is often tempting to start implementing procedures such as the following without first defining the network security policy:
>
> "Our site needs to provide users with telnet access to internal hosts and external hosts, prevent NFS access to internal hosts but deny this to external users, have smart cards for logging in from the outside, have dial-back modems ..."
>
> Without a proper understanding of the most important resources and those that are at the greatest risk, the previous approach could lead to some areas having more protection than they need, and other more important areas that do not have sufficient protection.

NOTE

Developing an effective security policy requires considerable effort. It takes a determined effort to consider all the issues and a willingness to set the policies in paper and do what it takes to see that the policy is properly understood by network users.

Besides performing a risk analysis of the network resources, you must identify other vulnerabilities. The following list is an attempt to describe some of the more common problem areas. This list can point you in the right direction, but is by no means complete, because your site is likely to have a few unique vulnerabilities.

- ❖ Access points
- ❖ Improperly configured systems
- ❖ Software bugs
- ❖ Insider threats
- ❖ Physical security

A discussion of these issues is next.

ACCESS POINTS

Access points are points of entry (also called *ingress*) by unauthorized users. Having many access points will increase the security risks to the network.

125

Figure 3.6 shows a simplified network for an organization in which there exists several points of ingress to the network. The access points are the terminal server and router on network segment A. The workstation on segment A has a private modem which is used for dial-out connections. Host B on network segment B is also an access point to this network segment. Because a router joins the two network segments, an intruder can use any of the access points on each network segment to reach the entire network.

FIGURE 3.6

Identifying access points in a network.

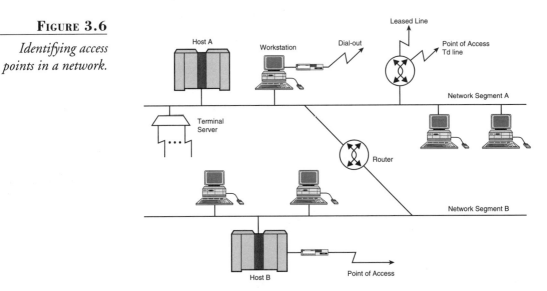

You may secure the listed access points in figure 3.6, but it is easy to forget the workstation on segment A which was going to be used for dial-out connections, perhaps to simple computer bulletin boards.

Consider the following situation: The user of the workstation on segment A may have an account with an Internet Access Provider. Suppose this user uses a SLIP (Serial Line Interface Protocol) or PPP connection to access this Internet Access Provider. If the TCP/IP software that the user is running on the workstation is also configured as a router, it is possible for an intruder to access the entire network. Also, if a routing protocol such as RIP (Routing Information Protocol) or OSPF (Open Shortest Path First) is enabled at the workstation, the workstation can expose the internal network to routing protocol-based attacks.

Note that the user may not deliberately enable the workstation as a router. The workstation operating system might be by default enabled as a router. This is true for many Unix systems as well as DOS/Windows TCP/IP packages. Even the workstation is properly configured by the networking staff, the user could plug in their laptop computer to the network and use a modem to dial out to the Internet Access Provider. If the user was using a dial-up (also called a shell account) where the user is running terminal emulation software at the workstation and not TCP/IP software, perhaps no harm can be done. However, if the user is using SLIP or PPP connection, the user has inadvertently created another access point which the network administration staff may not be aware of. This could represent a security risk to the entire network.

The situation in figure 3.6 can be prevented if the network security policy informs the user that private connections through individual workstations are prohibited. This situation also underscores the importance of having a network security policy that clearly delineates the AUP for the network.

If you want to connect to the Internet, you must have at least one network link to networks outside the organization. A network link can make available a large number of network services, both inside the network and outside the network, and each service has a potential to be compromised.

> Terminal servers can represent a security risk if not properly protected. Many terminal servers on the market do not require any kind of authentication. Check with your vendor about authentication capabilities of your terminal server. Intruders can use terminal servers to disguise their actions, dialing in to the terminal server and accessing your internal network.
>
> If the terminal server permits this, an intruder can access the internal network from the terminal server, and then use telnet to go out again, making it difficult to trace them. Also, if the intruder uses this to attack another network, it may appear that the attack originated from your network.

N O T E

Dialup lines, depending on their configuration, may provide access merely to a login port of a single system. If connected to a terminal server, the dialup line may give access to the entire network. As mentioned in the discussion in figure 3.6, a dialup line at a workstation running TCP/IP software can give access to the entire network.

IMPROPERLY CONFIGURED SYSTEMS

If intruders penetrate the network, they usually try to subvert the hosts on the system. Hosts that act as telnet servers are popular targets. If the host is improperly configured, the system can be easily subverted. Misconfigured systems account for a large number of security problems on networks.

Modern operating systems and their associated software have become so complex that under-standing how the system works is not only a full-time job, but often requires specialized knowledge. Vendors may also be responsible for misconfigured systems. Many vendors ship systems with wide-open security. Passwords to critical accounts may not be set, or they use easily guessable login name and password combinations. The book *The Cuckoo's Egg*, by Cliff Stoll, which tells the true story of the global hunt for a computer spy, mentions how an intruder obtained access to systems by using login name/password combinations such as "system/manager," "field/service," and so on.

SOFTWARE BUGS

As the complexity of software increases, so does the number and complexity of bugs in any given system. Perhaps software will never be bug free unless revolutionary ways of creating software are developed. Publicly known security bugs are common methods of unauthorized entry. If a system's implementation is open and widely known (such as with Unix), an in-truder can use weaknesses in the software code that runs in a privileged mode to gain privi-leged access to the system.

The system administrators must be aware of security weaknesses in their operating systems and be responsible for obtaining updates and implementing fixes when these problems are discovered. You also should have a policy to report bugs (when found) to the vendor so that a solution to the problem can be implemented and distributed.

INSIDER THREATS

Insiders usually have more direct access to the computer and network software than to the actual hardware. If an insider decides to subvert the network, he can represent a considerable threat to the security of the network. If you have physical access to the components of a system, the system is easier to subvert. For example, many workstations easily can be ma-nipulated to grant privileged access. One can easily run protocol decode and capture software to analyze protocol traffic. Most standard TCP/IP application services such as telnet, rlogin, and ftp have very weak authentication mechanisms where passwords are sent in the clear. Access to these services using privileged accounts should be avoided because it can easily compromise the passwords for these accounts.

PHYSICAL SECURITY

If the computer itself is not physically secure, software security mechanisms easily can be bypassed. In the case of DOS/Windows workstations, there is not even a password level of protection. If a Unix workstation is left unattended, its physical disks can be swapped out, or if the workstation is left in a privileged mode, the workstation is wide open. Alternatively, the intruder can halt the machine and bring it back up in privileged mode, and then plant Trojan-horse programs or take any number of actions that can leave the system wide open to future attacks.

All critical network resources such as backbones, communications links, hosts, important servers, and key machines should be located in physically secure areas. The Kerberos authentication mechanism, for example, requires that the Kerberos server be physically secure. *Physically secure* means that the machine is locked in a room or placed in such a manner that restricts physical access to the data on the machine.

Sometimes it is not always easy to physically secure machines. In this case care should be taken not to trust those machines too much. You should limit access from non-secure machines to more secure machines. In particular, you should not allow access to hosts using trusted access mechanisms such as the Berkeley-r* utilities (rsh, rlogin, rcp, rwho, ruptime, rexec).

Even when the machine is physically secure, care should be taken about who has access to these machines. Using electronic "smart" cards to access the room in which the machines are secured can limit the number of people with access and also provide a log of the identity and time-of-day individuals accessed the room. You should also have a policy for your employees that other persons cannot tag along when the door to the secure room is opened, even when the identity of the individual is known. If you allow people to tag along, you will not have a proper log of who entered the room and when.

> Also remember that maintenance and building staff may have access to the secure rooms. Make sure you take this into account when designing your system security.

CONFIDENTIALITY

Confidentiality can be defined as the act of keeping things hidden or secret. This is an important consideration for many types of sensitive data.

Some of the situations in which information is vulnerable to disclosure are the following:

❖ When the information is stored on a computer system

❖ When the information is in transit to another system on the network

❖ When the information is stored on backup tapes

129

Access to information that is stored on a computer is controlled by file permissions, access control lists (ACLs), and other similar mechanisms. Information that is in transit can be protected by encryption or by firewall gateways. Encryption can be used to protect all three situations. Access to information stored on tapes can be controlled by physical security such as by locking them in a safe, or an inaccessible area.

IMPLEMENTING COST-EFFECTIVE POLICY CONTROLS

Controls and protection mechanisms should be selected so that they can adequately counter the threats found during risk assessment. These controls should be implemented in a cost-effective manner. It makes little sense to spend large sums of money, and over-protect and restrict the use of a resource if the risk of exposure is very small.

Common sense is often a very effective tool to use to establish your security policy. While elaborate security schemes and mechanisms are impressive, they can be quite expensive. Sometimes the costs of these implementations are hidden. For example, you might implement a freely available software security solution but not take into account the cost of administering such a system and keeping it updated. Also if the security solution is very elaborate, it may be difficult to implement and administer. If the administration is a one-time installation experience, the commands to administer such a system can be easily forgotten.

> You should also maintain a sense of perspective that no matter how elaborate is the solution, a weak password or stolen password can compromise the system.

The following are some guidelines for implementing cost-effective policy controls.

SELECTING THE POLICY CONTROL

The controls that you select are the first line of defense in the protection of your network. These controls should accurately represent what you intend to protect as outlined in the security policy. If a major threat to your system is external intrusions, it may not be cost-effective to use biometric devices to authenticate your internal users. If the major threat to your systems is unauthorized use of computing resources by internal users, you may want to establish good automated accounting procedures. If the major threat to your network is external users, you may want to build screening routers and firewall solutions.

USING FALLBACK STRATEGIES

If the risk analysis indicates that protecting a resource is critical to the security of the network, you may want to use multiple strategies to protect your network. Using multiple strategies gives you the assurance that if one strategy fails or is subverted, another strategy can come into play and continue protecting the network resource.

It might be more cost-effective and simpler to use several simple-to-implement, but nevertheless effective, strategies rather than use a single elaborate and sophisticated strategy. The latter is an all-or-nothing approach. If the elaborate mechanism is circumvented, there is no fallback mechanism to protect the network resource.

> Examples of simpler controls are dial-back modems that can be used in conjunction with traditional logon mechanisms. These can be augmented with smart cards or one-time hand-held authenticators.

DETECTING AND MONITORING UNAUTHORIZED ACTIVITY

If a break-in or attempted break-in takes place, it should be detected as soon as possible. You can implement several simple procedures to detect unauthorized uses of a computer system. Some procedures rely on tools provided with the operating system by the vendor. There are also tools that are publicly available on the Internet.

MONITORING SYSTEM USE

System monitoring can be done periodically by the system administrator. Alternatively, software written for the purposes of monitoring the system can be used. Monitoring a system involves looking at several parts of the system and searching for anything unusual. A few of the ways this can be done are outlined in this section.

Monitoring must be done on a regular basis. It is not sufficient to do this on a monthly or weekly basis, because this could leave a security breach undetected for a long time. Some security breaches may be detected a few hours after the fact by other means, in which case monitoring on a weekly or monthly basis will do little good. The goal of monitoring is to detect the security breach in a timely manner so that you can respond to it appropriately.

If you are using monitoring tools, you should regularly examine the output of these tools. If the logs are voluminous, you may want to use awk or perl scripts to analyze the output. These tools are also available for non-Unix systems.

MONITORING MECHANISMS

Many operating systems store information about logins in special log files. The system administrator should examine these log files on a regular basis to detect unauthorized use of the system. The following is a list of methods that can be used at your site.

❖ You can compare lists of currently logged-in users with past login histories. Most network users have regular working hours and log in and log out at about the same time every day. An account that shows login activity outside the "normal" hours for the user should be closely monitored. Perhaps this account is in use by an intruder. Users can also be alerted to watch for the last login message that appears when they first log in. If they see some unusual times, they should alert the system administrator.

❖ Many operating systems can use accounting records for billing purposes. These records can also be examined for any unusual usage patterns for the system. Such unusual accounting records may indicate illegal penetration of the system.

❖ The operating system may have system logging facilities, such as the syslog used in Unix. The logs produced by such tools should be checked for unusual error messages from system software. For instance, a large number of failed login attempts in a short period of time may indicate someone trying to guess passwords. You should also monitor the number of attempts at logging into sensitive accounts such as root, sysadm, and so on.

❖ Many operating systems have commands, such as the ps command under Unix, to list currently executing processes. These can be used to detect users running programs they are not authorized to use, as well as to detect unauthorized programs which have been started by an intruder.

❖ Firewall gateways can be used to produce a log of the network access. These should be monitored regularly. Firewalls are discussed in detail later in the book.

❖ If you have special resources that you want to monitor, you can construct your own monitoring tools using standard operating system utilities. For example, you can combine the Unix ls and find commands in a shell script to check for privileged file ownerships and permission settings. You can store the output of your monitoring activity in lists that can be compared and analyzed using ordinary Unix tools such as diff, awk, or perl. Differences in file permissions of critical files can indicate unauthorized modifications to the system.

MONITORING SCHEDULE

Regular and frequent monitoring should be done by system administrators throughout the day. If the monitoring is done at fixed times, it can become very irksome, but monitoring commands can be run at any time of the day during idle moments, such as when you're conducting business over the phone.

By running monitoring commands frequently, you quickly will become aware of the normal output of the monitoring tools. This can help in detecting unusual monitoring outputs. One can try to automate this process by running search tools on the output, and one can look for certain set patterns, but it is generally difficult to anticipate all the unusual outputs caused by an intrusion into the system. The human brain is still better than most programs in detecting subtle differences in the monitor log.

If you run various monitoring commands at different times throughout the day, it is difficult for an intruder to predict your actions. The intruder cannot guess when a system administrator might run the monitor command to display logged in users, and thus runs a greater risk of detection. On the other hand, if the intruder knows that at 6:00 p.m. daily the system is checked to see that everyone has logged off, they will wait for the system check to be completed before logging in.

W A R N I N G

> Monitoring is useful, but the monitoring process can itself be subverted. Some intruders may be aware of the standard logging mechanisms in use on your system, and may attempt to disable these monitoring mechanisms. Regular monitoring can detect intruders, but does not provide any guarantee that your system is secure. It is not an infallible method of detecting intruders.

REPORTING PROCEDURES

In the event that unauthorized access is detected, you should have procedures on how this access will be reported and to whom it will be reported. In addition, your security policy should cover the following:

❖ Account management procedures

❖ Configuration management procedures

❖ Recovery procedures

❖ Problem reporting procedures for system administrators

ACCOUNT MANAGEMENT PROCEDURES

When creating user accounts, you must exercise care that you do not leave any security holes. If the operating system is being installed from the distribution media, the password file should be examined for privileged accounts that you do not need.

WARNING

Some operating system vendors provide accounts for their field service and system services engineers. These accounts either have no password or they may be common knowledge. If you need these accounts, you should give them new passwords, or else disable or delete them. There is generally no good reason to allow accounts that do not have a password set.

Accounts without passwords are dangerous even if they do not execute a command interpreter, such as accounts that exist only to see who is logged in to the system. If these are not set up correctly, system security can be compromised. For example, if the anonymous user account used by FTP (File Transfer Protocol) is not set up correctly, you could allow any users to access your system to retrieve files. If mistakes are made in setting up this account and write access to the file system is inadvertently granted, an intruder can change the password file or destroy the system.

TIP

Some operating systems such as Unix System V provide a special /etc/shadow password file that is used for storing passwords. This file is accessible only to privileged users. If your system supports this facility, you should use it.

The shadow password facility was first introduced with System V, but other Unix systems such as SunOS 4.0 and above, and 4.3BSD Unix Tahoe, provide this feature. The shadow password file permits the encrypted form of the passwords to be hidden from non-privileged users. The intruder, therefore, cannot copy the password file and attempt to guess passwords.

Your policy also should include procedures for keeping track of who has privileged user accounts, such as root on Unix, and MAINT under VMS. Under Unix, if you know the root password you can use the su command to assume root privileges. If the password is inadvertently discovered, the user can log in with his own personal accounts and assume root privileges. You must therefore implement a policy that forces change of passwords for privileged user accounts at periodic intervals.

W A R N I N G

> Also, when a privileged user leaves the organization, you should be alerted and the passwords for the privileged accounts should be changed. In addition the user accounts for those who have left the company should be changed.

Network services should undergo a close scrutiny. Many vendors provide default network permission files which implies that all outside hosts are to be trusted. This is not the case when connected to a network such as the Internet.

Intruders themselves collect information on the vulnerabilities of particular system versions. Sometimes they circulate their findings in underground magazines such as the following:

2600 Magazine
Phrack
Computer Underground Digest

Some system administrators subscribe to these journals to keep abreast of the intruders.

CONFIGURATION MANAGEMENT PROCEDURES

You should keep updated versions of the operating system and critical utilities. The security weaknesses of older systems are usually well known, and it is likely that the intruder is aware of the security problems. Unfortunately, new releases of software, while fixing old security problems, often introduce new ones. For this reason, it is important to weigh the risks of not upgrading to a new operating system release and leaving security holes unplugged, against the cost of upgrading to the new software.

Although most vendors can be trusted when shipping updates, many organizations rely on the wealth of publicly developed software for some activity within their company. Many software projects are shipping their software with PGP or other digital signatures to signify that the software has not been tampered with.

Tripwire is a tool that aids system administrators and users in monitoring a designated set of files for any changes. Used with system files on a regular (that is, daily) basis, Tripwire can notify system administrators of corrupted or tampered files so damage control measures can be taken in a timely manner.

Tripwire can be found at URL `ftp://ftp/nordu.net/networking/security/tools/tripwire/tripwire-1.2.tar.gz`.

Generally, most vendors can be trusted so that the new releases of software are more likely to fix old problems and not create bigger security problems. Another complication is that the new release may break existing application software that your users depend upon. You may have to coordinate your upgrade efforts with more than one vendor.

You also can receive fixes through network mailing lists. You must have competent personnel who can examine these bug fixes carefully and only implement them if they are safe.

As a rule, you should not install a bug fix unless you know the consequences of a fix. It is always possible that the authors of the fix may have non-obvious code to allow them unauthorized access to your system.

RECOVERY PROCEDURES

Whenever you install a new version of the operating system, you should not only take a backup of the binary image of the operating system kernel but also the files that are used to compile and configure the operating system. The same also applies to all other applications and networking software.

File system backups are like an insurance policy. They not only protect you in the event of disk or other hardware failures, but also against accidental deletions and as a fallback measure if your system has been penetrated. If you suspect your system has been broken into, you might have to restore the system from a backup to protect yourself against changes made by the intruder. If you cannot detect when the unauthorized changes took place, you have to examine several backups. If you do not have a good copy of your system software, it is hard to determine what your system data and files are supposed to be.

Daily backups, such as incremental backups, can be useful in providing a history of the intruder's activities. By examining older backups, you can determine when the system was first penetrated. Even though the intruder's files have been deleted, you can see them on the backup tapes.

> When examining traces for intruders files, you should check for file names that normally would not show up in a directory listing. On Unix systems, some intruders like to save data in files beginning with a period (.), or files containing non-displayable characters. These files are harder to detect.

You must decide on a backup strategy. Backup strategies usually involve the combination of the following methods:

- ✤ Full backup
- ✤ Level 1 backup
- ✤ Level 2 backup
- ✤ Custom backup

In Unix systems a full backup is also called a level 0 backup. In Unix systems, a *level 1 backup* backs up all files that have been modified since the last level 0 backup. In general, a level N *backup* backs up all files modified since the last *N-1 backup*. In the case of backup utilities such as dump, a level N *backup* backs up all files modified since the last *N-1 backup* or lower.

One can use an arbitrary number of levels, but generally this does not make sense because it becomes difficult to keep track of the backups. The numeric backup levels are supported in BSD-style backup commands from levels 0 to 9, but the concept can be used on any system, and you may have to do some manual bookkeeping. On BSD Unix the backup program is dump, and the files that were backed up at a specific level are kept in the /etc/dumpdates file.

In *full backup* (level 0), all data is backed up, regardless of when it was last modified, or whether it has not been modified at all. An example of this is all directories and files in a file system. After the data is backed up, the archive bit is cleared for all files that are backed up.

N O T E

> The full backup strategy is the most comprehensive of all backup strategies, because it backs up all files regardless of the fact that they have been modified since the last back up or not. Because of the large volume of data that may need to get backed up, however, it is the slowest of the backup strategies.

A level 1 backup backs up all files that have been modified since the last full backup (level 0). This means that all files that were backed up in the first level 1 backup are also backed up in the second level 1 backup, together with any files that have been modified since the first level 1 backup. This process continues with each level 1 backup, and more files can be expected to be backed up with each level 1 backup.

There is an unfortunate confusion of terms to describe the level 1 backup. On Unix systems, the level 1 backup is called an *incremental* backup. On many non-Unix systems (DOS/Windows/PC LAN operations systems), the level 1 backup is called a *differential* backup. The term incremental backup on many non-Unix systems means something entirely different. To avoid confusion, your policy must state which definition you are using.

To obtain a complete record of the most updated versions of the files, you would have to start with the most recent full backup (level 1), and add to it the files in the most recent level 1 backup. That is,

$$\text{Most Recent Backup} = \text{Last Full Backup} + \Delta d$$

where Δd is the most recent level 1 backup.

Because the last level 1 backup contains all files that have been modified since the last full backup, you can restore data with just two tape backup sets: the backup set for the full backup and the backup set for the last level 1 backup.

If the data on one of the last level 1 backups is corrupt, you have to fall back on the next-to-the-last differential backup. On the other hand, if any data in another level 1 backup tape is corrupt, it does not matter as long as the data in the most recent differential backup is good.

If a full backup has not been done for some time, and there have been many changes to the file, the size of the data that needs to be backed up tends to grow, with each level 1 backup. If all files have been modified, the level 1 backup session is the same as the full backup sessions. This tends not to be the case, because most file systems contain a mix of programs and data, and program files are not usually modified.

In many non-Unix systems the term *incremental backup* is used to describe a backup of all files that have been modified since the last backup (level 0 or level 1). This is like a level 2 backup on Unix systems. Files that have not been modified are not backed up. To obtain a complete record of the most update versions of the files, you would have to start with the most recent full backup and add all the incremental changes recorded in each incremental backup session. That is,

Most Recent Backup = Last Full Backup + $\Delta 1$ + $\Delta 2$ + Δn

= Last Full Backup + Δi (i =1 to n)

where each Δi is an incremental backup.

The incremental backup contains a sequential history of the files that have been modified. This means that to restore data, you need the last full backup and every incremental backup after it. If the data on one of the backup tapes is corrupt, you might not be able to restore data. The exception to this is situations in which later incremental backups have the files that were inaccessible on the corrupted tape. In this case, you could restore the data from a later tape.

Custom backup gives you complete control over what files to backup or not to backup. You can include or exclude parts of the directory structure to be backed up or select different type of data items to be backed up. Custom backups are useful if you want to selectively back up a few files and directories and not wait for a scheduled backup.

PROBLEM REPORTING PROCEDURES FOR SYSTEM ADMINISTRATORS

Earlier in this chapter, problem reporting procedures for users was discussed. System administrators should have a defined procedure for reporting security problems. In large network installations, this can be done by creating an electronic mailing list that contains the e-mail addresses of all system administrators in the organization. Some organizations set up a response team that provides a hotline service.

PROTECTING NETWORK CONNECTIONS

If the intruder attack is likely to take place through an externally connected network such as the Internet, you may want to protect your connections to the external network.

A firewall device can be used to provide a point of resistance to the entry of flames (intruders) into the network. Besides firewalls, screening routers can be used. These topics are the subject of discussion in the following chapters.

Some organizations' sites need to connect to other sites in the same organization and are prohibited from connecting to external networks. These networks are less susceptible to threats from outside the organizations' network. Unexpected intrusions can still occur through dial-up modems at users' desktop workstations.

An organization may require connections to their other sites through larger networks such as the Internet. If the protocols they are using are different from the Internet protocols, a technique called IP tunneling can be used. These sites are susceptible to external threats.

Many organizations require connections to the Internet because of the services it offers. The security risks of connecting to outside networks must be weighed against the benefits. You should limit the number of access points to the network. Moreover, you should connect to external networks through hosts that do not store sensitive material. Such hosts should also have removed software development tools and other privileged tools that could be used to probe your network. The idea is to provide a degree of isolation or a firewall between your network and the external network. Important services needed by the organization can be kept behind the isolated network segment.

You should seriously consider restricting the access to an external network through a single system. If all access to an external network is provided through a single host, this host acts as a firewall between you and the external network. The firewall system should be strictly controlled and password-protected. External users who need access to your internal network will have to pass through the firewall. The firewall host can properly screen the incoming calls.

> The firewall system is not a guarantee against a successful intruder attack. If the intruder succeeds in compromising the security of the firewall, the intruder can gain access to your internal network behind the firewall.

USING ENCRYPTION TO PROTECT THE NETWORK

Encryption can be used to protect data in transit as well as data in storage. Some vendors provide hardware encryption devices that can be used to encrypt and decrypt data on point-to-point connections.

Encryption can be defined as the process of taking information that exists in some readable form and converting it into a form so that it cannot be understood by others.

If the receiver of the encrypted data wants to read the original data, the receiver must convert it back to the original through a process called *decryption*. Decryption is the inverse of the encryption process. In order to perform the decryption, the receiver must be in possession of a special piece of data called the key. The key should be guarded and distributed carefully.

> The advantage of using encryption is that, even if other methods of protecting your data (Access Control Lists, file permissions, passwords, and so on) are overcome by an intruder, the data is still meaningless to the intruder.

There are several types of encryption packages in both hardware and software forms. The software encryption packages are available either commercially or as free software. Hardware encryption engines are usually built around dedicated processors and are much faster than the software equivalent. On the other hand, if the intruder has access to hardware, they can build hardware-based decryption schemes that can be used for a brute-force attack on your encrypted information.

Data in transit over a network may be vulnerable to interception. Some sites prefer to encrypt the entire file as a separate step before sending it. This is sometimes called end-to-end encryption. Others prefer encrypting the data dynamically as it reaches the network using hardware encryption engines creating a secure link.

If the entire packet is encrypted before being sent, as in the case of hardware encryption engines, the IP protcol routers that do not understand the encrypted packet will reject it. The Internet routers do not understand encrypted packets and will reject it. If you want to use encryption over the Internet, you must encrypt the data in a separate step and pass it to the application process.

The following is a brief discussion on the different types of encryption methods. In your network security policy, you must specify which, if any, of these encryption techniques should be used.

DATA ENCRYPTION STANDARD (DES)

DES is a very widely used data encryption mechanism. There are many hardware and software implementations of DES. DES transforms plain text information into encrypted data called *ciphertext* by means of a special algorithm and *seed* value called a key. If the key is known to the receiver, it can be used to convert from the ciphertext the original data.

A potential weakness of all encryption systems is the need to remember the key under which any data was encrypted. In this regard, it is similar to the problem of remembering the password. If the key is written and becomes known to an unauthorized party, they can read your original data. If the key is forgotten, then you are unable to recover the original data.

Many systems support a DES command, or utilities and code libraries that can be used for DES.

CRYPT

On Unix systems the crypt command also can be used to encrypt data. The algorithm used by crypt based on the World War II *Enigma* device and is very insecure. Files encrypted with crypt can be decrypted easily by brute-force approach in a matter of a few hours. For this reason, the crypt command should be avoided for sensitive data. It can be used for trivial encryption tasks. Chapter 2, "Security," discusses the use of the crypt command.

PRIVACY ENHANCED MAIL (PEM)

E-mail is usually sent on the Internet using SMTP (Simple Mail Transfer Protocol). This protocol is very simple and transmits data in the clear. Moreover, it can be used for transmitting ASCII text data only. If you want to send an encrypted message you have to use indirect means. You have to first encrypt the message. This converts the message into a binary file. Because SMTP cannot be used to transmit binary data—it transmits text data only—you have to encode the binary data as text.

A popular way of doing this on the Internet is to use a utility called uuencode. The recipient of the e-mail has to use a utility called uudecode to convert the text message back to the original encrypted binary form. If the recipient knows the key, he can decrypt the message. While it is possible to secure mail by using the method just outlined, it is cumbersome and laborious. Also, there is the problem of distributing the key to the recipients of the message. You should consider whether this should be done through the Internet, or by some other distribution methods.

Another approach that has attracted a great deal of interest is Privacy Enhanced Mail (PEM). PEM provides a means to automatically encrypt e-mail messages before sending. There are no separate procedures one has to invoke to encrypt the mail message. Therefore, even if the mail is intercepted at a mail distribution host, the interceptor cannot read the encrypted mail.

PRETTY GOOD PRIVACY

Pretty Good Privacy, or PGP, was written by Phil Zimmerman to address the issue of public-key, or asymmetric, file encryption and digital signatures. PGP provides a strong form of cryptographic protection not previously available. PGP is used to protect e-mail, files, and digitally signed documents and is available in commercial and non-commercial forms.

Residents of the U.S. and Canada can obtain PGP through MIT: `http://web.mit.edu/network/pgp-form.html`. It also can be found in other places on the Internet.

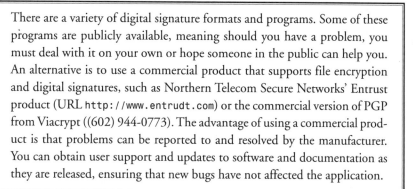

There are a variety of digital signature formats and programs. Some of these programs are publicly available, meaning should you have a problem, you must deal with it on your own or hope someone in the public can help you. An alternative is to use a commercial product that supports file encryption and digital signatures, such as Northern Telecom Secure Networks' Entrust product (URL http://www.entrudt.com) or the commercial version of PGP from Viacrypt ((602) 944-0773). The advantage of using a commercial product is that problems can be reported to and resolved by the manufacturer. You can obtain user support and updates to software and documentation as they are released, ensuring that new bugs have not affected the application.

N O T E

ORIGIN AUTHENTICATION

When an e-mail is received, the header of the e-mail indicates the originator of the message. Most users of Internet mail take it for granted that the header of the e-mail message truly indicates the sender of the message. It is possible, if one is clever enough, to forge the header so that it indicates a message sent from another e-mail address. This is called e-mail address *spoofing*. To prevent this type of forgery, a technique called origin authentication can be used.

Origin authentication provides a means to ascertain that the originator of a message is indeed who he claims to be. You might think of origin authentication as an electronic notary service similar to the human notary public who verifies signatures on legal documents. Origin authentication is commonly implemented by a public key cryptosystem.

A *cryptosystem* uses two keys. The keys are independent in the sense that one key cannot be derived from the other key using any mathematical or algorithmic procedures. One of the keys is a *public key*, which means that it can be easily found out by anyone and there is no attempt made to hide it. The other key is called a *private key* which means that this key is known only to the party who owns the key. The private key must be guarded very carefully.

In a public key cryptosystem, the originator uses a private key to encrypt the message. The recipient uses a public key obtained from the originator of the message to decrypt the message. The public key is used to authenticate that only the originator could have used their private key. There are several public cryptosystems that are available.

The most widely known implementation of the public key cryptosystem is the RSA (Rivest Shamir Adleman) system. The Internet standard for privacy enhanced mail makes use of the RSA system.

N O T E

INFORMATION INTEGRITY

When a file or document is sent on the network, you should have some means of verifying that the file or document has not been altered. This is called information integrity, and it refers to the process of verifying that the information that was sent is complete and unchanged from the last time it was verified. Information integrity is important for military, government, and financial institutions. It may also be important that classified information be undisclosed, whether it is modified or not modified. Information that is maliciously modified can create misunderstandings, confusion, and conflict.

If the information is sent in electronic form across the network, one way of ensuring that the information is not modified is to use *checksums*. Any form of encryption also provides information integrity, because an interceptor would have to first decrypt the message before modifying it.

USING CHECKSUMS

Checksums are a very simple and effective mechanism to verify the integrity of a file. A simple checksum procedure can be used to compute a value for a file and then compare it with the previous value. If the checksums match, the file is probably unchanged. If the checksums do not match, the file has been altered. Many compression and decompression utilities that can be used to conserve disk space and reduce transmission costs for files generate internal checksums to verify their compression/decompression algorithms.

Arithmetic checksums are simple to implement. They are formed by adding up 16-bit or 32-bit elements of a file to arrive at the checksum number. Though simple to implement, arithmetic checksums are weak from a security point of view. A determined attacker can modify and add data to the file so that the arithmetic checksum computes to the correct value.

The CRC (Cyclic Redundancy Checksum), also called the *polynomial checksum*, is more secure than the arithmetic checksum. Its implementation is fairly simple. However, like the arithmetic checksum, it too can be compromised by a determined interceptor.

N O T E

Checksums make it difficult for the interceptor to alter the information and be undetected. They cannot, however, guard against changes being made. You may want to use other mechanisms such as the operating system access controls and encryption. The operating system access controls can only guard the data when it is stored in a file system. It cannot protect data while it is being transmitted in a network.

Cryptographic checksums provide improvements over arithmetic checksums and CRC checksums. This type of checksum is discussed next.

CRYPTOGRAPHIC CHECKSUMS

In cryptographic checksums, also called *cryptosealing*, the data is divided into smaller sets and a CRC checksum is calculated for each data set. The CRCs of all the data sets are then added together.

This method makes it difficult to alter the data, because the interceptor does not know the sizes of the data sets that are used. The data set size can be variable and computed using pseudo-random techniques, thus making it extremely difficult for the interceptor to alter the data. A disadvantage of this mechanism is that it is sometimes computationally intensive.

Another method, called the *Manipulation Detection Code* (MDC) or one-way hash function, can be used to detect modifications to a file. The one-way hash function is so called because no two inputs can produce the same value. The data in the file is used as the input to the one-way hash function to produce a hash value. If the data in the file is modified, it will have a different hash value. One-way hash functions can be implemented quite efficiently and they make unbreakable integrity checks possible. Examples of a one-way hash function are the MD2 (Message Digest 2) and MD5 (Message Digest 5) functions, described in RFC 1319 and RFC 1321, respectively.

USING AUTHENTICATION SYSTEMS

Authentication can be defined as the process of proving a claimed identity to the satisfaction of some permission-granting authority.

On most systems, the user has to specify a password to their user account before they are allowed to log in. The purpose of the password is to verify that the user is who they claim to be. In other words, the password acts as a mechanism that authenticates the user. However, passwords can be stolen, and someone else can impersonate the user. Because adequate measures are not taken as often as they should be, stolen passwords are the cause of a large number of security breaches on the Internet.

Authentication systems are a combination of hardware, software, and procedural mechanisms that enable a user to obtain access to computing resources. Your site policy must state what type of authentication mechanism you should adopt. If users are to log in to their accounts from an external site, you should use stronger authentication mechanisms than passwords.

NOTE

> Authentication mechanisms range from smart cards to biometric devices such as fingerprint readers, voice print readers, and retina scan devices.

Authentication mechanisms can be augmented by challenge/response mechanisms. Challenge/response mechanisms ask the user to supply some piece of information shared by both the computer and the user, such as the user's mother's maiden name or some special information known to the user and the system.

USING SMART CARDS

A smart card is a hand-held portable (HHP) device that has a microprocessor, input-output ports, and a few kilobytes of non-volatile memory. The user must have one of these devices in their possession to be able to log on to the system. This authentication is based on "something you know." The host computer prompts the user for a value obtained from a smart card when asked for a password by the computer. Sometimes, the host machine gives the user some piece of information that the user has to enter into the smart card. The smart card then displays a response that must then be entered into the computer. If the response is accepted, the session will be established. Some smart cards display a number that changes over time, but is synchronized with the authentication software on the computer.

USING KERBEROS

Many systems can be modified to use the Kerberos authentication mechanism. Kerberos, named after the dog who in Greek mythology is said to stand at the gates of Hades, is a collection of software used in a large network to establish a user's claimed identity. Developed at the Massachusetts Institute of Technology (MIT), it uses a combination of encryption and distributed databases so that a user at a campus facility can log in and start a session from any computer located on the campus.

This mechanism was briefly discussed in Chapter 2.

KEEPING UP-TO-DATE

Your security policy, besides identifying the agencies with which you should establish contact in case of security incidents, should also designate individuals who should keep up-to-date with security issues and problems.

If your organization is connected to the Internet, you might want to join mailing lists or newsgroups that discuss security topics of interest to you.

> Remember that it takes time to keep up with the information in mailing lists and newsgroups. Unless you identify the individuals who should keep up with this information, and make it part of their job description, your system administrators will probably not find any time to do so.
>
> **N O T E**

MAILING LISTS

Mailing lists are maintained by list servers on the Internet. When you join a mailing list, you can communicate with users in this mailing list through electronic mail. To send your response or views on a topic, you can send e-mail to the mailing list. Everyone who is on the mailing list will receive your message. The request to join a mailing list is sent to another e-mail address. This address is *different* from the list e-mail address. You should send your subscription request to the e-mail request address and not the e-mail address of the list. The members of a list, which may number in the thousands, will not appreciate receiving requests to join the mailing list! Some mailing list administrators compile a special list of Frequently Asked Questions (FAQs). FAQs are often a good place to begin finding more information.

Mailing lists can be moderated or unmoderated. In moderated mailing lists, the list owner usually acts as a moderator and screens out mail responses that are not in keeping with the objectives of the mailing list.

> A variety of mailing list managers are available. Some are automatic, and some are processed by hand. If you have any doubts about how to subscribe to or unsubscribe from a list, send the following command, where *listname* is the name of the list about which you want information:
>
> INFO <*listname*>
>
> **N O T E**

In unmoderated mailing lists, there is no screening process. Consequently, the signal-to-noise ratio can be very low. If you decide that the mailing list is not for you send an "unsubscribe" request to the e-mail request address for the mailing list (and not the mailing list itself!). This request should include the following in the mail body:

UNSUBSCRIBE *listname*

147

> The e-mail term *signal-to-noise ratio* borrows its meaning from the audio usage. *Signal* represents actual, relevant e-mail messages. *Noise* represents useless messages, such as subscribe and test messages, that hinder normal communications among others using the mailing list.

UNIX SECURITY MAILING LISTS

The goal of the Unix security mailing list is to notify system administrators of security problems before they become common knowledge, and to provide information on security related topics. Because this kind of information can be damaging if it falls into the wrong hands, the Unix security mailing list is a restricted-access list. This list is open only to people who can be verified as being principal system administrators of a site.

In order to join this list, the requests must originate from the site contact listed in the Defense Data Network's Network Information Center's (DDN NIC) WHOIS database, or from the root account on one of the major site machines. You must include the destination e-mail address you want on the list. You should also indicate if you want to be on the mail reflector list or receive weekly digests. You should also include the e-mail address and voice mail telephone number of the site contact.

The e-mail address to send the subscription request is as follows:

```
security-request@cpd.com
```

THE RISKS FORUM LIST

The Risks forum is a component of the ACM Committee on Computers and Public Policy. This is a moderated list and discusses risks to the public in computers and related systems. It also discusses security issues of topical interest, major international computer-related security incidents, problems in air and railroad traffic control systems, software engineering, and so on.

To join the mailing list, send an e-mail subscribe message to the following address:

```
risks-request@csl.sri.com
```

In the body of the list include the following line:

```
subscribe risks Firstname Lastname
```

If you want to receive a digest version, rather than individual e-mail responses, include the following line:

```
set risks digest
```

This Risks list is also available through the Usenet newsgroup by the following name:

```
comp.risks
```

THE VIRUS-L LIST

The VIRUS-L list discusses computer virus experiences, protection software, and related topics. The list is open to the public and is implemented as a moderated digest. Most of the information is related to personal computers, although some of it may be applicable to larger systems. To subscribe, send e-mail to the following address:

```
listserv%lehiibm1.bitnet@mitvma.mit.edu
```

or

```
listserv@lehiibm1.bitnet
```

In the body of the list include the following line:

```
subscribe virus-L Firstname Lastname
```

If you want to receive a digest version, rather than individual e-mail responses, include the following line:

```
set virus-L digest
```

This list is also available through the Usenet newsgroup by the following name:

```
comp.virus
```

THE BUGTRAQ LIST

The Bugtraq list discusses software bugs and security holes. This can be used to assess the security risk to your system. It also discusses how these security holes can be fixed, so that you can use this information to fix security holes in your system.

To subscribe, send e-mail to the following address:

```
bugtraq-request@crimelab.com
```

In the body of the list include the following line:

```
subscribe bugtraq-list Firstname Lastname
```

149

If you want to receive a digest version, rather than individual e-mail responses, include the following line:

```
set bugtraq-list digest
```

THE COMPUTER UNDERGROUND DIGEST

The Computer Underground Digest states its goal as "an open forum dedicated to sharing information among computerists and to the presentation and debate of diverse views."

The Computer Underground Digest contains discussions about privacy and other security-related topics. It can be reached at the following URL:

```
http://sun.soci.nui.edu/~cudigest/
```

To subscribe, send e-mail to the following address:

```
cu-digest-request@weber.ucsd.edu
```

In the body of the list include the following line:

```
SUB CuD
```

Also include the subject SUB CuD in your message.

This list is also available through the Usenet newsgroup by the following name:

```
comp.society.cu-digest
```

THE CERT MAILING LIST

The CERT (Computer Emergency Response Team) puts out advisories. CERT is discussed in this chapter in an earlier section on organizations you can contact for security-related help.

To subscribe, send e-mail to the following address:

```
cert-request@cert.sei.cmu.edu
```

In the body of the list include the following line:

```
subscribe cert Firstname Lastname
```

If you want to receive a digest version, rather than individual e-mail responses, include the following line:

```
set cert digest
```

THE **CERT-TOOLS** MAILING LIST

The CERT also maintains a CERT-TOOLS list for the purposes of exchanging of information on tools and techniques that increase the secure operation of Internet systems. The CERT/CC does not review or endorse the tools described on the list.

To subscribe, send e-mail to the following address:

`cert-tools-request@cert.sei.cmu.edu`

In the body of the list include the following line:

`subscribe cert-tools `*`Firstname Lastname`*

If you want to receive a digest version, rather than individual e-mail responses, include the following line:

`set cert-tools digest`

CERT's Web site contains a wealth of security information, including all of the CERT advisories. You can reach it at `http://www.cert.org`.

THE **TCP/IP** MAILING LIST

The TCP/IP mailing list is a discussion forum for developers and maintainers of implementations of the TCP/IP protocol suite. However, many of the questions that are received on the list are from users of various TCP/IP packages, or those seeking help on TCP/IP applications. This list also discusses network security problems.

To subscribe, send e-mail to the following address:

`tcp-ip-request@nisc.sri.com`

In the body of the list include the following line:

`subscribe tcp-ip `*`Firstname Lastname`*

If you want to receive a digest version, rather than individual e-mail responses, include the following line:

`set tcp-ip digest`

This list is also available through the Usenet newsgroup by the following name:

`comp.protocols.tcp-ip`

THE **SUN-NETS** MAILING LIST

The SUN-NETS list discusses issues related to networking on SUN Microsystems workstation systems. The discussion centers around networking and security issues dealing with NFS, NIS, and name servers.

151

To subscribe, send e-mail to the following address:

`sun-nets-request@umiacs.umd.edu`

In the body of the list include the following line:

`subscribe sun-nets `*`Firstname Lastname`*

If you want to receive a digest version, rather than individual e-mail responses, include the following line:

`set sun-nets digest`

NEWSGROUPS

Newsgroups are discussion groups that exchange information through special news reader programs. To join a newsgroup, you must use a special news reader program. These are programs such as nn and tin for Unix systems. DOS/Windows systems have many commercial shareware/freeware packages. Using a news reader, you have greater flexibility in handling messages.

Like mailing lists, newsgroups can be moderated or unmoderated.

The Usenet groups dealing with security-related issues are:

> misc.security
>
> alt.security
>
> comp.security.announce

The misc.security is a moderated group and also includes discussions of physical security and locks. The alt.security is unmoderated. The comp.security.announce newsgroup contains mailings sent to the CERT mailing list.

Some of the mailing lists are also available via newsgroups. These were mentioned in the section on mailing lists and are listed here for your reference.

> comp.risks
>
> comp.virus
>
> alt.society.cu-digest
>
> comp.protocols.tcp-ip

SECURITY RESPONSE TEAMS

Some organizations have formed a group of security experts that deal with computer security problems. These teams gather information about possible security holes in systems. They disseminate this information and report it to the appropriate people. They can help in tracking intruders, and provide help and guidance in recovering from security violations. The teams may have electronic mail distribution lists and special telephone numbers that you can call for information or to report a problem. Some of the teams are members of the CERT System.

COMPUTER EMERGENCY RESPONSE TEAM

The Computer Emergency Response Team/Coordination Center (CERT/CC) was established in December 1988 by the Defense Advanced Research Projects Agency (DARPA). The goal of this team was to address computer security concerns of research users of the Internet. The CERT is coordinated by the U.S. National Institute of Standards and Technology (NIST), and exists to facilitate exchange of information between the various teams.

> A major motivation for the promotion of the CERT/CC team was to prevent and handle incidents such as the Internet Worm. This incident was mentioned earlier in this chapter.

N O T E

CERT is operated by the Software Engineering Institute (SEI) at Carnegie Mellon University (CMU). The CERT team has the ability to immediately confer with experts to diagnose and solve security problems. They can also assist in establishing and maintaining communications with your site and government authorities.

When not responding to emergencies, the CERT/CC serves as a clearinghouse for identifying and repairing security vulnerabilities in major operating systems. They can also provide informal assessments of existing systems and guide you in improving your emergency-response capability. Because of this, they can help you indirectly in formulating an effective network security policy. The team has also been known to work with vendors of software systems in order to coordinate the fixes for security problems.

CERT operates a 24-hour hotline that you can call to report security problems such as someone breaking into your system. You can also call this number to obtain current information about rumored security problems. This 24-hour hotline number for CERT is (412)268-7090.

The CERT/CC sends out security advisories to the CERT-ADVISORY mailing list whenever appropriate. To join the CERT-ADVISORY mailing list, send a message to:

`cert-request@cert.sei.cmu.edu`

Security information that is sent to this list also appears in the following Usenet newsgroup:

`comp.security.announce`

Past security advisories are available for anonymous FTP from the host cert.sei.cmu.edu. The FTP server on the host cert.sei.cmu.edu maintains other useful information on security issues. The README file on this server can inform you on what is available. For more information, contact:

CERT
Software Engineering Institute
Carnegie Mellon University
Pittsburgh, PA 15213-3890
(412)268-7090
`cert@cert.sei.cmu.edu`
`http://www.cert.org`

DDN SECURITY COORDINATION CENTER

For Defense Data Network (DDN) users, the Security Coordination Center (SCC) serves as a clearinghouse for host/user security problems and fixes, and works with the DDN Network Security Officer. In this regard, the DDN SCC provides a function similar to CERT.

The SCC publishes the DDN Security Bulletin. This bulletin discusses issues that relate to network and host security, security fixes, and concerns to security and management personnel at DDN facilities. The DDN Security Bulletin is available on-line, via Kermit downloads or anonymous FTP, from the host NIC.DDN.MIL. The security bulletins are in files with the following format:

`SCC:DDN-SECURITY-yy-nn.TXT`

The *yy* is the year and *nn* is the bulletin number.

The SCC provides assistance on DDN-related host security problems through the hotline number (800)235-3155 (6 a.m. to 5 p.m. Pacific Time).

To reach the SCC by e-mail, send a message to:

`SCC@NIC.DDN.MIL.`

For 24-hour coverage, you can call the MILNET Trouble Desk at (800)451-7413.

NIST Computer Security Resource and Response Clearinghouse

The National Institute of Standards and Technology (NIST), besides dealing with standards issues, also has responsibility within the U.S. government for computer science and technology activities. The NIST has played a major role in organizing the CERT System, and serves as the CERT System Secretariat.

NIST operates a Computer Security Resource and Response Clearinghouse (CSRC) that provides help and information regarding computer security events and incidents. They are also interested in raising awareness about computer security vulnerabilities. The CSRC team operates a 24-hour hotline at (301)975-5200.

The NIST provides on-line publications and computer security information that can be downloaded using anonymous FTP from the host csrc.nist.gov. The information also is available via the World Wide Web at the URL http://crsc.nist.gov.

In addition to the FTP server, NIST operates a personal computer bulletin board that contains information regarding computer viruses as well as other aspects of computer security. To access this bulletin board, use the following information:

> Bulletin Board line: 301-948-5717
>
> 8 bits, no parity, 1 stop bit

When you first log in to the bulletin board, you must register your user name and address.

NIST also produces special publications related to computer security and computer viruses. These can be downloaded through the bulletin board or the FTP server. For additional information, you can contact NIST at the following address:

Computer Security Resource and Response Center
A-216 Technology
Gaithersburg, MD 20899
(301)975-3359
csrc@nist.gov
http://csrc.nist.gov

DOE COMPUTER INCIDENT ADVISORY CAPABILITY (CIAC)

The CIAC is the Department of Energy's Computer Incident Advisory Capability. CIAC was formed to provide a centralized response capability and technical assistance center for the DOE sites.

CIAC consists of a four-person team of computer scientists from Lawrence Livermore National Laboratory (LLNL). This group's primary responsibility is to assist DOE sites faced with computer security incidents such as intruder attacks, virus infections, worm attacks, and so on. CIAC keeps sites informed of current security-related events, and maintains liaisons with other response teams and agencies.

CIAC assists sites through direct technical assistance, by providing information, or referring inquiries to other technical experts. It also serves as a clearinghouse for information about security threats, known security incidents, and vulnerabilities. Additionally, it develops guidelines for security incident handling and develops software for responding to security incidents.

CIAC analyzes security events and trends, and conducts training and awareness activities to alert and advise sites about vulnerabilities and potential attacks.

The following are CIAC's phone number, e-mail address, and URL:

(415)422-8193
```
ciac@tiger.llnl.gov
http://ciac.llnl.gov
```

NASA AMES COMPUTER NETWORK SECURITY RESPONSE TEAM

The Computer Network Security Response Team (CNSRT) was formed by NASA Ames Research Center in August 1989. The team's primary goal is to provide help to Ames users, but it is also involved in assisting other NASA Centers and federal agencies.

The CNSRT is NASA's equivalent of CERT. The CNSRT maintains liaisons with the DOE's CIAC team and the DARPA CERT, and it is a charter member of the CERT System.

The CNSRT can be reached through 24-hour pager at (415)694-0571. CNSRT's e-mail address is:

cnsrt@ames.arc.nasa.gov

SUMMARY

This chapter discussed the factors and issues you need to take into account when designing a secure network. These factors are formalized into a Network Policy that helps you identify security threats, perform risk analysis, and determine how you are going to protect your network resources.

You need to formulate an effective network security policy before building a firewall for connecting your network to the rest of the Internet. It is important to understand exactly what resources and services that you want to protect on the network.

The Network Policy is a document that describes an organization's network security concerns. This document becomes the first step in building effective firewalls.

THE ONE-TIME PASSWORD AUTHENTICATION SYSTEM

As is well known in the security community, two of the most common forms of attack on computing systems connected to the Internet are through the theft of the system password file and through eavesdropping on network connections to obtain user IDs and passwords of legitimate users. The captured user ID and password are, at a later time, used to gain access to the system; or in the case of the suitable password file, the encrypted passwords are converted to plain text through the use of a password cracker. Some systems no longer store the encrypted passwords in the typical password file for this reason. With the theft of a suitable password file, it is likely that a good password-cracking program will crack at least five percent of the passwords!

Alternatively, "sniffer" type systems that analyze the packets on the network looking for TCP connections can sniff out the first 100 bytes of user data, which will easily catch the user ID and associated password. However, if such a system is found on your network, it is likely that more than only passwords have been violated.

The one-time password system is designed to counter these types of attack and force a user to use a different password each time he or she logs in. This is accomplished by providing the user with a password that is different for each login, whether the login attempt is successful or not. As a result, it is not possible for the passwords to be re-used in a replay attack.

One-time passwords work by providing the user with a challenge. The *challenge* is a predetermined string of text, to which there is only one possible response. In this chapter, several implementations of one-time passwords are discussed.

What Is OTP?

In general, the one-time password system, hereafter referred to as OTP, protects the secured system from external attacks on its authentication subsystem. OTP does not prevent the wily cracker from eavesdropping on your network and gaining access to sensitive information, however. This cannot even be achieved solely with the use of a firewall. Network eavesdropping can be prevented only by eliminating the ability to sniff packets where sensitive data passes. (For more information on firewalls, see Chapter 8, "Firewall Architecture and Theory.") OTP also does not protect the organization from "inside jobs" or against active attacks in which the potential intruder is able to intercept and modify the packet stream.

OTP is available in a number of different forms: Bellcore's S/KEY Version 1.0, Bellcore's Commercial S/KEY Version 2.0, the United States Naval Research Laboratory's (NRL) One Time Passwords In Everything (OPIE), and Wietse Venema's LogDaemon.

Before continuing the discussion of OTP, consider the authentication, or login, process for the typical Unix system. The typical Unix system presents an unsecured login prompt where the user enters a password. If the combination of user ID and password match, the user is allowed access to the system. An example of an unsecured login is shown in figure 4.1.

In this configuration, the user enters his user name and password. The password is sent in clear text across the local- or wide-area network, thereby making it easier for the cracker to steal the password. In this example, the user has a multi-use password: one that is used over and over again.

When the OTP system is in operation, only a single-use password (one that is used once, and not again) ever crosses the network. Furthermore, this one-time password consists of six

English words and therefore is not discernible from an ordinary Unix cleartext password. When using either the multi-use or single-use password, the text is sent in the clear across the network. This means that the text is not private.

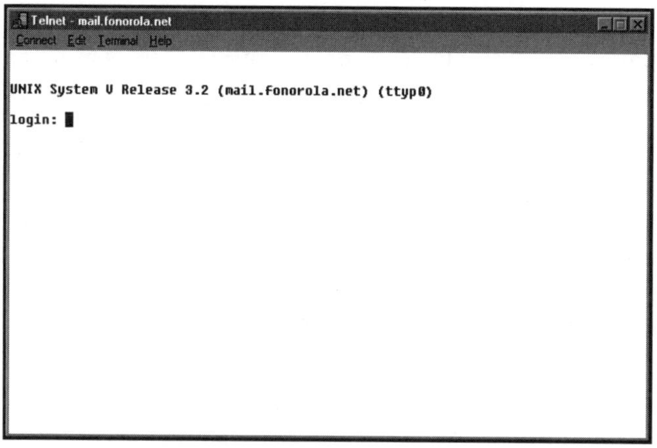

FIGURE 4.1

Unsecured login.

When using OTP, the user is prompted with a challenge: she must provide the answer to a question that only she can know. OTP makes use of a seed value, an iteration value, and a secret pass phrase that is known only to the user. The challenge is composed of the seed value and the iteration value. The response to the challenge is generated using a special program called a *calculator* on the user's workstation. Using the seed and iteration values, along with the user's secret pass phrase, the response to the challenge is generated. The user's secret pass phrase never crosses the network at any time, including during login or when executing other commands requiring authentication, such as the Unix commands passwd or su. This interaction with the OTP-protected system is illustrated in figure 4.2.

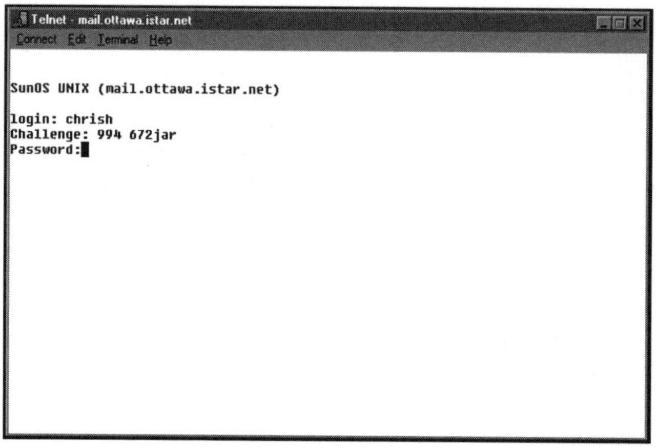

FIGURE 4.2

OTP-protected login.

161

The OTP-protected system responds to the user with a challenge. This challenge consists of the iteration, which is 994 in this case, and the seed, which is 672jar. These values are specific to each user and were configured when the user was added to the OTP database. Worth noting is that even if two users use the same iteration and seed value, their generated passwords will not be the same if they have chosen different pass phrases. The combination of these values and the user's secret pass phrase is passed through a hashing algorithm in the OTP calculator to derive the single-use password. Consequently, OTP is not vulnerable to either eavesdropping or password replay, or to theft or password file attacks.

The operation of the OTP one-time password system involves two sides: the client and the host. On the client side, the appropriate one-time password must be generated. On the host side, the server must verify the one-time password and permit the secure changing of the user's secret pass phrase. This chapter addresses the history of OTP, where to obtain the source and compile it, how to implement the server side, and how to put all the pieces together.

THE HISTORY OF OTP

The idea of using hash functions to generate one-time passwords is not new, having first been presented by Leslie Lamport in the early 1980s. Developed by the Bell Communications Research Center, commonly known as Bellcore, in 1991, S/KEY was the first implementation of a one-time password system. It was first proposed by Phil Karn with contributions from Neil Haller and John Walden.

Through activities involving TCP/IP and amateur radio, Phil Karn saw the problem of password eavesdropping that would be facing network users. To address this problem, Mr. Karn proposed using a one-time password scheme to provide a higher level of access security and to reduce, if not eliminate, the likelihood of password eavesdropping. A description of S/KEY can be found in RFC 1760, an HTML version of which is included on the CD-ROM that accompanies this book.

S/KEY is a one-time password authentication initially implemented using DES as the hashing algorithm. This process was slow on the 8088 systems available at that time, and an encrypted file of one-time passwords was used instead of computing them as needed. Using this encrypted file introduced other potential security problems, which were addressed by moving to a system based on the MD4 Message Digest algorithm, as documented in RFC 1320.

The MD4 algorithm takes as input a message of arbitrary length and produces as output a 128-bit "fingerprint" or "message digest" of the input. To produce two messages having the same message digest, or to produce any message having a given prespecified target message digest, is conjectured to be computationally unfeasible.

Since the initial development of S/KEY, a newer form of digest algorithm, known as *Message Digest 5*, or MD5, has been developed. The MD5 algorithm is documented as RFC 1321 and is an extension of the MD4 algorithm. The Bellcore S/KEY Version 1.0 is currently considered to be a reference implementation, and ongoing development of it is nonexistent. Bellcore is putting its efforts behind the commercial implementation. Recognizing the security limitations placed upon the MD4 implementation, several other OTP implementations have been developed using the MD5 hash algorithm.

> Both the client and the server must be using the same algorithm, either MD4 or MD5. An MD4 client cannot interact with an MD5 server.

N O T E

This chapter does not cover the mathematics discussed in RFC 1320 and RFC 1321; suffice it to say that MD5 was written to address some concerns in the MD4 design and the haste with which it had been adopted. Because MD4 was considered exceptionally fast, designers had concerns about the risks associated with successful cryptoanalytic attack. MD5 designers addressed this concern by making MD5 somewhat slower in computation and also by making some fundamental changes to those computations. The end result is that, unlike MD4, people consider MD5 to be sufficient for use in high and very high security applications.

Starting in April 1995, the Internet Engineering Task Force, known as the IETF, undertook an effort to write a standard for one-time passwords. Neil Haller became one of the cochairs of this working committee, which chose *One Time Password System* (OTP) as the name of the system. This name was chosen because of concern over the use of the name S/KEY, which is a trademark of Bellcore. The current plan of the IETF is to have an RFC assigned and OTP declared a standard in 1996. Ongoing information about and status of the Internet draft and the working group can be found at `ftp.bellcore.com:/pub/ietf-otp/archive`.

Now that you have an overview of why and how OTP developed and matured, you can turn your focus to implementing OTP in your environment.

IMPLEMENTING OTP

OTP works by combining publicly available information, the *challenge*, with a secret known only to the user to produce the proper response. This means that OTP is implemented using one of the major security concepts, Something You Know (SYK). The secret is called a *pass phrase*, and when it is combined with the challenge in either the MD4 or MD5 algorithm, it produces the *password* or response. The challenge is in the form of an iteration number and a string of characters called a *seed*. Your seed is not considered a secret, but having all your seeds be unique between systems is important. If you choose your dog's name as a seed on one system, you should not reuse this seed on another system. Your secret (your password) can be the same on all systems, provided that your seed is different.

Different hardware architectures and OS versions have a variety of OTP implementations. When you connect to a system running OTP, you are prompted for your user name. The system responds with an iteration number and your seed. You must then calculate the required response by typing the iteration number, your seed, and your secret password at a trusted piece of hardware, such as a calculator that supports MD4/MD5 or a piece of calculator software.

N O T E

> You can access the system running OTP without being challenged. This can occur on service ports such as SMTP and POP. It is permitted so that new clients are not required.

The calculator computes the required response, and you type that response as your password. The challenge and required response change every time you successfully log in. This mechanism is demonstrated in figure 4.3.

FIGURE 4.3

An OTP login.

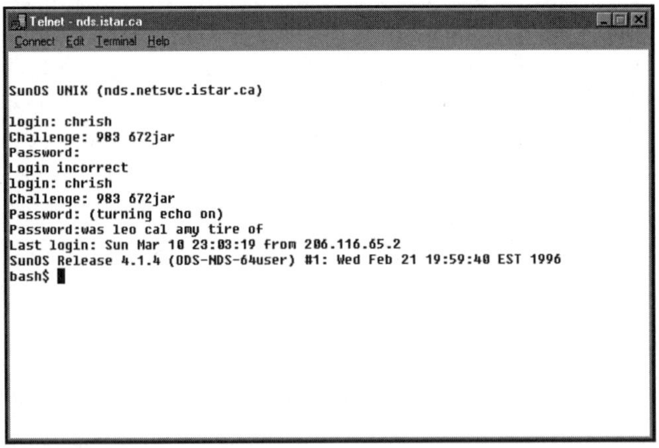

```
Telnet - nds.istar.ca
Connect  Edit  Terminal  Help

SunOS UNIX (nds.netsvc.istar.ca)

login: chrish
Challenge: 983 672jar
Password:
Login incorrect
login: chrish
Challenge: 983 672jar
Password: (turning echo on)
Password:was leo cal amy tire of
Last login: Sun Mar 10 23:03:19 from 206.116.65.2
SunOS Release 4.1.4 (ODS-NDS-64user) #1: Wed Feb 21 19:59:40 EST 1996
bash$ ▇
```

Figure 4.3 shows a sample login to a system protected by OTP. When the user connects to the remote system, the login program provides the iteration number and seed for this user. Using the seed and iteration value supplied in the challenge, the user must then calculate his or her one-time password and log in. In this example, password echoing was enabled so that the password that was provided could be seen.

You must take several actions in order to secure a system with OTP. These are the following:

❖ Get the OTP code for the system.

❖ Get the needed calculators for the clients.

❖ Compile and install the OTP components.

❖ Have users initialize their keys.

❖ Enable OTP.

Now you can turn your focus to the steps involved in installing OTP.

DECIDING WHICH VERSION OF OTP TO USE

A number of free and commercial versions of OTP are available on the market. These versions are listed in table 4.1.

TABLE 4.1
OTP Implementations

Version	Developed By	Status	FTP Site	Notes
S/KEY 1.0	Bellcore	Free	`ftp.bellcore.com`	This version is more of a reference and is outdated at this point. It is based on MD4.
S/KEY	Bellcore	Commercial		This is a commercial implementation. It supports both MD4 and MD5.

continues

TABLE 4.1, CONTINUED
OTP Implementations

Version	Developed By	Status	FTP Site	Notes
OPIE	NRL	Free	ftp.nrl.navy.mil	Version 2.1 is in production, and 2.2 is in Beta (as of March 22, 1996). OPIE favors MD5 but does support MD4.
LogDaemon	Wietse	Free	ftp.win.tue.nl	The current version is 5.3 and it supports both MD4 and MD5.

Unfortunately, choosing one version or the other can be a difficult task. Each of these versions has its own strengths and weaknesses (such as installation issues, support for only one algorithm, ease of ongoing administration, or operating system support) and differing implementations. The result is that not one of these implementations has everything that the user wants. Consequently, you might see security administrators mix components from all the freely available tool sets.

How S/KEY and OPIE Work

The S/KEY system derives its strength from the interdependence of several parts. These parts consist of the server application, the encryption system, and the calculator. The server application is the component that resides on the server system and prompts the user to authenticate using S/KEY. For example, the /bin/login program, when appropriately modified, constitutes a server program.

The encryption mechanism is the component that performs the encryption and one-time password generation. Combined with the calculator, this mechanism results in a password that is provided by the user to the server program and, if the generated password is correct, results in successful authentication.

THE ITERATION, SEED, AND PASS PHRASE

The initialization of a user ID to authenticate through S/KEY involves several parts. These are the iteration value, the seed, and the pass phrase. The *iteration value* is a counter that is decreased each time the user authenticates off a given server. The *seed* is a phrase that is provided to the server; the seed is given to the user on each authentication attempt. For example, consider the output of figure 4.3.

In figure 4.3, the iteration value is 983, and the seed is 672jar. As you will see later in this chapter, these values were initially provided when the user account was configured to authenticate through OTP.

The pass phrase is the one piece of information that the user must know. The iteration and seed values are provided by the system. With these values and the appropriate pass phrase, users can generate the correct challenge password/response with their calculators. This process is illustrated in figure 4.4.

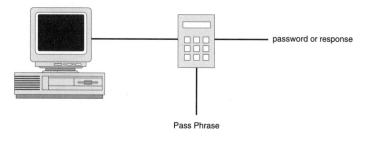

password or response

Pass Phrase

FIGURE 4.4

OTP calculation.

On each successful login, the iteration value is decreased by one. This is how a different password is used on each login attempt. The iteration value should not fall below a value of five because those last five logins will occur very quickly and, when users reach zero, they have no way of logging in to reinitialize their OTP passwords. At that point, only the system administrator can restore access to the system for them.

BELLCORE S/KEY VERSION 1.0

The Bellcore S/KEY distribution, which is available free of charge, is for reference purposes only, according to Bellcore. It no longer receives any real development cycles because S/KEY is also a commercial product. As noted previously, the use of S/KEY for the newly undertaken versions of this software is a violation of the trademark held by Bellcore. If you desire, however, you can use the Bellcore S/KEY distribution without compromising security, considering that this implementation is based on MD4, which is not rated for high security applications.

Bearing in mind the lack of ongoing development of the Bellcore S/KEY distribution, the focus of this chapter is on the two other major development efforts to date: OPIE and LogDaemon.

167

U. S. NAVAL RESEARCH LABORATORIES OPIE

The United States Naval Research Laboratories produced the One-Time Passwords in Everything (OPIE) Version 2.1 software distribution. OPIE provides a one-time password system for POSIX-compliant Unix-like operating systems. The system should be secure against the passive attacks that are now commonplace on the Internet, as described in RFC 1704, which is included on the accompanying CD-ROM. Despite the use of OPIE, and OTP in general, the system is vulnerable to active dictionary attacks, although these are not widespread at present and can be detected through proper use of system audit software. The NRL OPIE software is derived in part from and is backward-compatible with the Bell Communications Research (Bellcore) S/KEY Version 1 software distribution.

Although the OPIE Version 2 code is backward-compatible with Bellcore S/KEY Version 1.0, it is more tightly based upon the Internet Draft standard for OTP than on S/KEY. Consequently, anyone who has seen or worked with S/KEY Version 1.0 will find the presentation of OPIE somewhat different.

> During the preparation of this book, the U.S. Naval Research Laboratories released OPIE 2.2. This release incorporates minor bug fixes and adds support for the development of OTP clients using the OPIE library. You can find OPIE 2.2 at the following URL:
>
> `ftp://ftp.nrl.navy.mil/pub/security/nrl-opie/opie-2.22.tar.gz.`

OBTAINING THE OPIE SOURCE CODE

The location of the OPIE source code is defined in table 4.1, earlier in this chapter. To obtain the source code, select the site for the version you want to download and then retrieve that version via FTP. When you attempt to contact the United States Naval Research Laboratory, you might experience a rough ride. Because it is a busy site during work hours, anonymous access can be difficult to achieve. The best time to get this code is during off-peak hours.

After you have recovered the most recent code, which, at the time of this writing is opie-2.11, you must extract the source code from the tar image. This creates a new subdirectory named opie-2.11, which is where the source code is extracted.

Reading the README and INSTALL files included with the software distribution in the order mentioned is essential. Those documents are supplemented with further explanation in this text. The README file lists all the changes made from the last release to the current and identifies the systems that have been evaluated for properly running OPIE. The list of platforms tested for the 2.11 release is shown in table 4.2.

Table 4.2
Tested OPIE Platforms

Hardware	Software	Referred To As	System
Sun SPARCStation 20	Solaris 2.4+SunPro C	Solaris	solaris
Sun 4/300	SunOS 4.1.3+GNU C	SunOS	sunos
Sun SPARCStation 2	4.4BSD-Encumbered	4.4BSD	44bsd
486/66 PC	BSDI BSD/OS 1.1 & 2.0	BSD/OS	bsdos
486/66 PC	Slackware Linux 2.1	Linux	linux
SGI Indigo^2	IRIX 5.2	IRIX	irix
HP 9000/750	HP-UX 9.01+GCC	HP-UX9	hpux9
HP 9000/755	HP-UX 10.0+GCC	HP-UX10	hpux10
IBM RS/6000 550	AIX 3.2.5	AIX	aix

Additionally, information provided to NRL from beta testers suggests that OPIE will work on the platforms listed in table 4.3:

Table 4.3
Operating Systems Reported to Support OPIE

Hardware	Software	Referred To As	System
486 PC	FreeBSD	FreeBSD	freebsd
486 PC	NetBSD	NetBSD	netbsd
Macintosh IIfx	A/UX 3.0	A/UX	aux
Sun 3/50	SunOS 4.1	SunOS	sunos

If the Unix system you use appears on either of these tables, you stand a good chance of putting OPIE into operation with little extra effort.

COMPILING THE OPIE CODE

Compiling the OPIE code involves running the autoconfigure script and building the executables for your particular system. If your system is listed in either table 4.2 or 4.3, then you should not have a problem when you compile OPIE for your system. The OPIE developers caution that if you experience a problem when using OPIE, you should defer to the full installation as listed in the INSTALL file. Regardless of which path you choose, most of the steps are still the same.

If you choose to run the autoconfigure script, you will see output similar to that shown in listing 4.1. This example was generated from a Linux Slackware 1.2 system.

LISTING 4.1—SAMPLE AUTOCONFIGURE SCRIPT

```
reliant:/home/opie-2.11# sh configure
creating cache ./config.cache
checking for gcc... gcc
checking whether we are using GNU C... yes
checking whether gcc accepts -g... yes
checking how to run the C preprocessor... gcc -E
checking whether ln -s works... yes
checking for ranlib... ranlib
checking for bison... bison -y
checking for AIX... no
checking for POSIXized ISC... no
checking for minix/config.h... no
checking for chown... /bin/chown
checking for su... /bin/su
checking for su... no
checking for scheme... no
checking for login... /bin/login
checking for ftpd... no
checking for in.ftpd... no
checking for default PATH entries... /usr/bin:/bin:/usr/sbin:/sbin
checking for test -e flag... yes
checking for mkdir -p flag... yes
checking for /etc/default/login... no
checking for /etc/securetty... yes
checking for /etc/logindevperm... no
checking for /etc/fbtab... no
checking mail spool location... /usr/spool/mail
checking whether the system profile displays the motd... no
checking whether the system profile checks for mail... no
checking for -lcrypt... no
checking for -lnsl... no
checking for -lposix... no
checking for -lsocket... no
```

```
checking for dirent.h that defines DIR... yes
checking for -ldir... no
checking for sys/wait.h that is POSIX.1 compatible... yes
checking for crypt.h... no
checking for sigemptyset... yes
checking for sigaddset... yes
checking for sigprocmask... yes
checking for getspent... no
checking for endspent... no
updating cache ./config.cache
creating ./config.status
creating configure.munger
creating Makefile.munge
creating config.h

Binaries are going to be installed into /usr/local/bin
Manual pages are going to be installed into /usr/local/man.

creating Makefile

Have you read the README file?
reliant:/home/opie-2.11#
```

If you choose not to use the autoconfigure script, you must edit the Makefile by hand to suit the configuration of your system. After the Makefile is generated, you can run a "make" to build the executables. The make process builds each of the executables and, upon completion, the OPIE system is ready to be tested before being placed into operation.

The Makefile has several command-line arguments. These options select the system for which the commands will be built, and what those commands are. The command used to build the programs is as follows:

```
make system target
```

The system options are listed in table 4.2 earlier in this chapter, and the target options are shown in table 4.4.

WARNING

The make command is a powerful command generator that is used to build a sequence of commands to be executed by the Unix shell. If you are experienced at using make, then you should use the supplied Makefile or one generated by autoconfigure.

TABLE 4.4
Makefile Target Options

Option	Action
client	Builds the opiekey(1) client only
client-install	Builds the opiekey(1) client; installs it and the associated man pages
server	Builds the server programs only
server-install	Builds the server programs and installs the programs and associated man pages
all	Builds everything
install	Builds both the client and server programs; also installs them, opiekey's aliases, and the associated man pages

WARNING

Do not attempt to install the newly compiled programs until they have been tested. Furthermore, unless you are an experienced system administrator, do not install them at all. Installing programs to replace the operating system versions could render the system unusable.

Typing the command **make system** is the same as using the command **make system all**. The authors of the Makefile have written it so that if you simply type **make**, the Makefile asks you whether you know what you are doing. It is recommended that you build all the programs and then install one after you verify that they are functioning properly.

TESTING THE COMPILED PROGRAMS

Before putting OPIE into production, you should perform some very thorough testing to validate the compile. This testing is important; if you do not do it, and you place these untested programs into production, you could end up with an unusable machine. Also, before you do anything else, back up your system and make sure you have a set of emergency boot disks to restart. To do this, you need two accounts on the system: one with superuser access privileges and one ordinary user account.

Log into the system as root on the system console. The installation cannot be done from any other device than the system console. You must not log out during this testing and installation process because, if the OPIE software is not working properly, logging out might leave your system in a state that prevents you from logging in again. You also must have a non-root account that can access the newly compiled OPIE programs.

Run the opiepasswd command to set the test user's OPIE password. To do this, run the following command:

```
./opiepasswd -c <username>
```

The *<username>* parameter specifies the name of the normal account that you will use to test OPIE. The following list shows the execution of this command:

```
reliant:/home/opie-2.11# ./opiepasswd -c chrish
Adding chrish:
Reminder - Only use this method from the console; NEVER from remote. If you
are using telnet, xterm, or a dial-in, type ^C now or exit with no password.
Then run opiepasswd without the -c parameter.
Adding chrish:
Using MD5 to compute responses.
Enter new secret pass phrase:  <pass phrase typed here>
Again new secret pass phrase:  <pass phrase typed here>
ID chrish OTP key is 499 re1192
HEBE FORD VAN BEAR BEAK LEND
reliant:/home/opie-2.11#
```

The -c option tells opiepasswd that this work is being done on the console.

WARNING

> The warning notice printed by opiepasswd tells you to abort the command if you are using telnet, xterm, or a dial-in session. The same is true if your connection is through rlogin, even though it is not explicitly listed here.

If you don't use the -c option, users must enter their pass phrase through an OPIE-compatible calculator. Because you are testing the code at this point, you do not have to use a calculator. The pass phrase must be between 10 and 127 characters long.

The output of opiepasswd consists of the user identification information (ID chrish), the type of authentication (OTP), and the iteration and seed value. The iteration and seed value are used by the OPIE calculator to generate the password. The group of six words that follow the iteration and seed value is the password that is to be used to access the system. From the previous example showing the use of opiepasswd, the output generated is illustrated here:

```
ID chrish OTP key is 499 re1192
HEBE FORD VAN BEAR BEAK LEND
```

The output is the ID (chrish), the iteration (499), and the seed (rel192). The second line is the actual password used to access the remote system.

The next step is to test the output generated by the opiepasswd command. You perform this test using the opiekey command. To use opiekey, you must supply the iteration number and seed that were provided by opiepasswd. Using the information from the previous example, the execution of opiekey would appear as follows:

```
reliant:/home/opie-2.11# ./opiekey 499 re1192
Using MD5 algorithm to compute response.
Reminder: don't use opiekey from telnet or dial-in session.
Enter secret pass phrase: <pass phrase typed here>
HEBE FORD VAN BEAR BEAK LEND
reliant:/home/opie-2.11#
```

When opiekey prompts for the secret pass phrase, you must use the same one that was used for opiepasswd. If the generated six-word response is the same as the one generated by opiepasswd, then the OPIE software is working properly, and you can continue your testing. If they do not match, you might have misconfigured some piece of software.

N O T E

> The typical problem with the software is the byte ordering in the MD4/5 calculations. The OPIE software is supposed to take care of this, but you should check out the generated Makefile if you think there is a problem.
>
> Another, more common, problem is an inconsistent use of the MD4 or MD5 algorithm for the client and server sides. To check, find the lines in the Makefile that read
>
> ```
> MDX=5
> ```
>
> ```
> #MDX=4
> ```
>
> If you decide to use MD4, then set the value of MDX to MD4 and recompile the OPIE programs. If this doesn't fix the problem, then contact one of the OTP mailing lists to discuss your situation. Information on the various OTP mailing lists is found at the end of this chapter.

At this point, you have reason to have confidence in the compile of the OPIE software. Now you need to run the make system-test command to install the OPIE software into your local directories. When you perform this test, the system binaries for login, su, and ftpd are not yet replaced. That replacement occurs later, after you are sure that everything is working as it should. The following is the output of your make:

```
reliant:/home/opie-2.11# make linux-test
make CHOWN="/bin/chown" EXISTS="-e" MKDIR="mkdir -p" RANLIB="ranlib"
➥LOCALBIN="/usr/local/bin"
LOCALMAN="/usr/local/man" SU="/usr/bin/su" LOGIN="/bin/login" DEFAULT_PATH=
➥"/usr/bin:/bin"
FTPD="/usr/sbin/in.ftpd" OPTIONS="-DDOSECURETTY=1" YACC="yacc" test
```

```
make[1]: Entering directory '/home/opie-2.11'
Installing OPIE server software...
Copying OPIE user programs
Changing ownership
Changing file permissions
Preparing opiesu and opielogin for testing
make[1]: Leaving directory '/home/opie-2.11'
reliant:/home/opie-2.11#
```

At this point, you can continue testing your OPIE software. The make output shows that the OPIE binaries have been placed in /usr/local/bin.

You should now run a test to ensure that, with the files in the correct directories, everything still works properly. You perform this test by running opiekey from the newly installed directory. If you receive a message indicating that the opiekey command could not be found, check to make sure that the directory where it was installed is in the PATH. When you run opiekey at this point, an additional option is used because you will need some slightly different information to continue testing. Use the command

opiekey -n 7 499 <seed>

in which *<seed>* is the same as the seed you used previously. The -n 7 option instructs opiekey to generate seven passwords. The output follows:

```
reliant:/home/opie-2.11# opiekey -n 7 re1192
Using MD5 algorithm to compute response.
Reminder: don't use opiekey from telnet or dial-in session.
Enter secret pass phrase: <pass phrase typed here>
493: GLOM IO OLGA HASH BAH LILY
494: DEAF DUEL SUM MY FOLD ANN
495: GREG ROY BIDE DEAD DAM LOIS
496: FLO BONN SON SKEW GLIB FOLD
497: LUSH OWNS TOOK YALE AFRO HIKE
498: BOP SELL MAYO ORB MID TEN
499: HEBE FORD VAN BEAR BEAK LEND
reliant:/home/opie-2.11#
```

Here, opiekey provides seven different passwords. In this manner, opiekey can be used to generate lists of passwords for future use. However, you should omit the leading ./ from the opiekey command at this stage to make sure that the copy from the binary directory is used. Write down the output from opiekey; you need it to complete the installation and testing instructions.

Type *./opiesu <username>*, where *<username>* is the same user name you used when you ran opiepasswd. You are not asked for a password at this point. Again, type the command *./opiesu <username>*. opiesu should now ask you for a password. Press Enter once. You should receive a message saying (echo on) and asking you for a password again. This message is shown in the following example:

```
reliant:/home/opie-2.11# ./opiesu chrish
reliant:/home/opie-2.11$ ./opiesu chrish
otp-md5 498 re1192
(OTP response required)
chrish's password:  (echo on)
chrish's password: BOP SELL MAYO ORB MID TEN
reliant:/home/opie-2.11$ id
uid=502(chrish) gid=100(users) groups=100(users)
reliant:/home/opie-2.11$
```

Notice that opiesu prompts with the iteration number and seed value. The seed value is the same as in the previous examples, but the iteration value has decreased from 499 to 498. Remember, for each successful login attempt, the iteration value is decremented by one. You must be aware of this value to provide the correct password in response to the challenge.

When you press Enter once and turn on the password echo feature, you can easily see the six words as you type them, thereby reducing your chances of making a mistake. To turn password echo on, simply press Enter when asked for your password. When password echo is turned on, you will see the words echo on, and your text will start on a new line.

NOTE

> Having a password visible on the screen is not a common practice because common sense tells us to keep our passwords secret. However, so long as the pass phrase is divulged, the passwords themselves can be echoed. This enables the user to see the words he is typing and eliminates the likelihood of a typing error.

Enter the six words (and only the six words) on the line starting with 498 that you got when you ran the opiekey command. If you receive the message Sorry, verify that you are using the correct password and repeat the password once. If the message is still Sorry, the OPIE software is not working properly on your machine.

You now need to use the opieinfo command to verify the seed that OPIE thinks is to be used. The output provided by opieinfo, as follows, indicates the iteration number and the current seed:

```
reliant:/home/opie-2.11$ opieinfo
497 re1192
reliant:/home/opie-2.11$
```

The final step in the testing process is to test the operation of the replacement login command. Type the command

./opielogin <username>

where *<username>* is the user name that you have been using. The program should now ask you for a password. Press Enter once. You should see the message (echo on), along with a request for a password again. Enter the six words (and only the six words) on the line starting with 497 that you received from the opiekey command earlier. The following list shows this sequence:

```
reliant:/home/opie-2.11$ ./opielogin chrish
otp-md5 497 re1192
Password:
Linux 1.1.18. (POSIX).
Welcom to Reliant
reliant:~$
```

If opielong responds with Login incorrect, repeat the preceding sequence once. If the message is still Login incorrect, the problem is related to either byte-ordering or an inconsistency in the MD4/MD5 algorithm specification between the calculator and the server.

If the software works but displays your message of the day twice, you need to change the setting for -DDOMOTD to zero in the Makefile and start over. If everything seems to be functioning properly, then it is safe to install OPIE and start using it.

INSTALLING OPIE

Installing OPIE involves replacing some of your system binaries and reevaluating your system. Remember to make sure you have a backup or some way of restarting and reinstalling your system. To complete the installation of the programs, use the following command:

make install

This command installs the OPIE replacements for login, su, and ftpd. The installation process will try to rename your old programs to their original names with the extension opie.old.

W A R N I N G

> If programs or files with the same name (that is filename.opie.old) already exist, then your old programs will not be backed up.

Listing 4.2 shows the installation being run.

Listing 4.2—Installing the OPIE Software

```
reliant:/home/opie-2.11# make linux-install
make CHOWN="/bin/chown" EXISTS="-e" MKDIR="mkdir -p" RANLIB="ranlib"
➥LOCALBIN="/usr/local/bin"
LOCALMAN="/usr/local/man" SU="/usr/bin/su" LOGIN="/bin/login" DEFAULT_PATH=
➥"/usr/bin:/bin"
FTPD="/usr/sbin/in.ftpd" OPTIONS="-DDOSECURETTY=1" YACC="yacc" install
make[1]: Entering directory '/home/ftp/security/opie-2.11'
Installing OPIE client software...
Copying OPIE key-related files
Changing file permissions
Symlinking aliases to opiekey
Installing manual pages
Installing OPIE server software...
Copying OPIE user programs
Changing ownership
Changing file permissions
Preparing opiesu and opielogin for testing
Clearing testing permissions on opiesu and opielogin
Installing OPIE system programs...
Renaming existing /bin/login to /bin/login.opie.old
Clearing permissions on old /bin/login
Copying opielogin to /bin/login
Changing ownership of /bin/login
Changing file permissions of /bin/login
Renaming existing su to su.opie.old
Clearing permissions on old su
Copying opiesu to su
Changing ownership of su
Changing file permissions of su
Renaming existing ftp daemon to /usr/sbin/in.ftpd.opie.old
Clearing permissions on old ftp daemon
Copying OPIE ftp daemon
Changing ownership of ftpd
Changing file permissions of ftpd
Creating OPIE key file
Changing permissions of OPIE key file
Changing ownership of OPIE key file
Installing manual pages
REMEMBER to run opiepasswd on your users immediately.
make[1]: Leaving directory '/home/ftp/security/opie-2.11'
reliant:/home/opie-2.11#
```

Checking the operation of some components before exiting and restarting the system is important. First, evaluate the operation of the replacement FTP daemon. Type **ftp localhost**. At the prompt, enter the user name you have been using. You should receive an OTP challenge. Log in using the user that you configured earlier in this process, and use the correct password for the current iteration. This is illustrated in the following example:

```
reliant:/home/opie-2.11#ftp localhost
Connected to reliant.unilabs.org.
```

```
220 reliant FTP server ready.
User (reliant.unilabs.org:(none)): chrish
331 OTP response otp-md5 496 re1192 required for chrish.
Password:
230 User chrish logged in.
ftp>
```

If you do not see a line that starts with 331 OTP response..., then you either did not install the OPIE replacement program in the proper directory (in which case you need to change the value in the Makefile and start over), or you are using a client program that will not allow users to see challenges, in which case you need to contact the author of your client for an updated version that fixes this deficiency.

> The default configuration of the OPIE FTP Server is not to allow anonymous connections. To allow anonymous connections, add the DDOANONYMOUS option to your system's options entry and rebuild. This is further explained in the later section entitled "opieftpd."

The last step is to test the operation of the telnet program. To test the program, execute the command **telnet localhost** and log in using the previously defined non-root user and the appropriate challenge response, as follows:

```
reliant:/home/opie-2.11# telnet localhost
Trying 127.0.0.1 ].
Connected to localhost
Escape character is "^]"
Linux 1.1.18 (reliant.unilabs.org) (ttyp1)
login: chrish
otp-md5 494 re1192
(OTP response required)
Password: (echo on)
Password:DEAF DUEL SUM MY FOLD ANN
Linux 1.1.18. (POSIX).
reliant:~$
```

If the connection is configured correctly and responds as it should, then your system is operational and successfully OPIE-ized. You must now configure the users by running opiekey for each account. At this point, you should reboot your system to make sure it comes up as it should. If you experience any problems, you might need to reinstall and recover your system from a backup taken prior to the OPIE configuration.

THE OPIE COMPONENTS

The OPIE implementation of OTP consists of several components, or programs. These programs are as follows:

- ✤ opieftpd
- ✤ opieinfo
- ✤ opiekey
- ✤ opielogin
- ✤ opiepasswd
- ✤ opiesu

OPIEFTPD

This FTP server daemon is a full-featured FTPD implementation. It is not a stripped-down version, yet it does not have all the functionality of the Washington University Archive FTP server. If you did not choose to install the FTP server during the initial installation of OPIE, then you can do so by changing the name of the existing FTP server and copying the OPIE FTP server into the same directory.

The opieftp daemon does not, by default, support anonymous FTP logins. Anonymous access would allow access to the server through one of the most attacked points—not to mention the fact that anonymous FTP sites often are used to store pirated applications. If you require the use of anonymous FTP, however, then you must set it up according to the following instructions.

Look in the Makefile for the OPIE software to find the configuration options. This section is shown in listing 4.3:

LISTING 4.3—MAKEFILE OPTIONS SECTION

```
# * Vendor-compatible "features"
#
# -DDOUTMPX=1            If your system uses a utmpx file along with a utmp
# -DDOSECURETTY=1        If you want to use an /etc/securetty file to control
#                        which terminals root can log in from
# -DPERMSFILE="<file>"   Change the permissions of certain devices on login,
#                             as specified in <file>
# -DDOWHEEL=1            Implement the BSD "wheel group" su restriction
#                             (only members of group 0 can su)
```

```
# -DDOTITLE=1          Change the process info of ftpd so that ps listings
#                         will show status information
# -DDOMOTD=0           If your system's login program *doesn't* display
#                      /etc/motd and check for mail (i.e., it is done in
#                      shell scripts like /etc/profile and /etc/.login)
#
# * Miscellaneous
#
# -DDOANONYMOUS=1      If you want ftpd to support anonymous logins
#                      whenever an "ftp" account exists in /etc/passwd.
#
# -DSYS_FCNTL_H=1      Use <sys/fcntl.h> instead of <fcntl.h>.
# -DMJR=1              Support Marcus J. Ranum's scheme to prevent
```

To allow for anonymous user access, find the OPTIONS line that corresponds to your system and add the -DDOANONYMOUS option, as shown here:

```
# Linux
OPTIONS=-DDOANONYMOUS=1
```

The operating-system-specific OPTION lines are found in the Makefile following the text shown in the listing 4.3. You must then recompile the FTPD server and install that version. In addition, the standard configuration issues for anonymous logins to the FTPD server must be observed. In this situation, however, performing those configuration steps is very important; without them, you might be invalidating the OPIE configuration steps you have just taken.

OPIEINFO

opieinfo retrieves and prints the current iteration and seed from the OPIE database, either for the current user or for the specified user. opieinfo will retrieve the next iteration value and the seed for the user. If no user is specified on the command line, then opieinfo looks for the information on the user who is running the program. The following example shows the output of opieinfo:

```
reliant:/home/ftp/security/opie-2.11$ opieinfo
488 re1192
reliant:/home/ftp/security/opie-2.11$ opieinfo chrish
488 re1192
reliant:/home/ftp/security/opie-2.11$ opieinfo terrih
terrih not found in database.
reliant:/home/ftp/security/opie-2.11$
```

In this example, chrish is found in the OPIE database, so his information is printed by opieinfo. When chrish attempts to look up the iteration and seed for terrih, he is told that terrih is not in the database. This means that terrih has not been initialized with opiepasswd yet. That initialization is demonstrated later in this chapter.

OPIEKEY

opiekey is just one of many names used for the same program. opiekey is also known as opie-md4, opie-md5, otp-md4, otp-md5, and opie-des. opiekey takes the optional count of the number of responses to print along with a (maximum) sequence number and seed as command-line arguments. It prompts for the user's secret password twice and produces an OPIE response as six words. Using this, you can generate a list of OPIE passwords in advance, so if you are away from a calculator, you still have some means of logging in. This could be rather dangerous, though, because you could lose the paper and unintentionally allow someone to gain access to your systems.

The operation of opiekey is illustrated in listing 4.4:

LISTING 4.4—SAMPLE OPIEKEY EXECUTION

```
reliant:/home/ftp/security/opie-2.11$ opieinfo
488 re1192
reliant:/home/ftp/security/opie-2.11$ opiekey -n 10 488 re1192
Using MD5 algorithm to compute response.
Reminder: Don't use opiekey from telnet or dial-in sessions.
Enter secret pass phrase:
479: MAD EM SELF TOTE FORD SLAY
480: HUFF VEAL RUST DAYS FEAR GIL
481: BUSY FEAR LAY MONA SINK CROW
482: YELL RANT HIDE KENT HE PO
483: TAB ITEM COAL BROW HAAG FUR
484: PUP SKID HALF BALD TELL HASH
485: INN AT LARK KEN LONG KEEN
486: HILL REAR ADAM MESS FOUL EWE
487: BANG ANA NEWT MADE OMAN OTTO
488: LOS RAYS NAME VASE FOOT RIFT
reliant:/home/ftp/security/opie-2.11$
```

This example shows how to use opieinfo to obtain the current iteration and seed, which are required by opiekey. In this example, 10 passwords are printed for future use. As already mentioned, this is valuable information and must be handled with care. Anyone who obtains this information and your user name will be able to access your account.

OPIELOGIN

The opielogin command is a straight replacement for the standard login command. This command is used to authenticate users when they want to access the system. Most people see the output of login as the login prompt. In fact, the login command is also responsible for authenticating users before their admittance to the system.

To have the data it needs to authenticate the user, opielogin uses the file /etc/opiekeys, which contains the user authentication information. If you choose to live dangerously, you might also use the ./opiealways file to determine which users can log in with clear text and which ones must have the OTP challenge. This is a major security hole and should be used only if the site security administrator determines that no other way exists.

OPIEPASSWD

opiepasswd is the command that initializes the user into the OPIE database, /etc/opiekeys. Before this initialization, the user will not be able to log in to an OPIE-secured system. The initialization of the user can take place in one of several ways.

First, the opiepasswd command can be executed from a secure terminal or console, which allows users to provide their own secret pass phrase. If opiepasswd is not executed from a secure terminal, users must have access to an OPIE-capable calculator. Finally, users on the console, perhaps root, can assign the initial iteration and seed value for each user.

opiepasswd can generate a default number of iterations, which is 499, or a user-specified value. Furthermore, opiepasswd can generate a random seed value or use one provided by the user.

OPIESU

opiesu is a replacement program for the su command. This application is used to switch to another userid, with the appropriate OTP challenge being issued. If the correct response is provided, then the request is granted, and the user identity is changed. Otherwise, the failure is logged and reviewed later.

LOGDAEMON 5.0

The LogDaemon 5.0 tools are a project of Wietse Venema of Eindhoven University of Technology in the Netherlands. Venema is well known for his TCP Wrapper and SATAN projects. The LogDaemon programs were originally developed in 1990 after Eindhoven University experienced a case of severe hacking after it was connected to the Internet. Wietse immediately wrote an early version of the TCP Wrapper programs in an attempt to gain control over the hacking problem. At that time, Wietse was preparing for the worst possibility: an intruder penetrating one of the university's systems. The resulting LogDaemon programs were intended to be direct plug-in replacement programs with built-in keystroke logging. The official distribution does not have keystroke logging, however, so don't look for it in the downloaded implementation. Wietse added OTP support to LogDaemon during the SA-TAN development project with Dan Farmer because he did not want to type his password over an unsecured link from San Francisco. This project resulted in the current implementation of the LogDaemon tools that exist today.

The LogDaemon kits are a variation of the Bellcore S/KEY package and include not only support for MD4 and MD5 but also a large array of server-side daemons that were modified to include support for OTP. These server daemons, whose transformation occurred over a number of years, are based on the BSD sources.

The rsh and rlogin daemons log the remote user name and perform logging and access control in TCP/IP wrapper style. To improve the level of security that is generally lacking in the r* commands, these daemons, by default, do not accept wild cards in either the hosts.equiv or .rhosts files. Both daemons have an '-l' option to disable user .rhosts files. The rshd command has a compile time that will cause it to log the user command.

The ftpd, rexecd, and login software supports considerable login failure logging, with optional support for S/KEY one-time passwords. The rexecd daemon disallows root logins, which is a popular back door for the interloper. The support for S/KEY one-time passwords is optional and completely invisible to users that do not need it. Unix passwords are still permitted by default. Like rshd, the rexecd command can be compiled to log executions of the user command.

For those network administrators who want an S/KEY login shell but, for whatever reason, cannot replace the standard login program, the S/KEY shell is provided. The user first logs in to a dummy account that does not require a password. The S/KEY login shell prompts for the user's real account name and presents the corresponding S/KEY challenge.

With Wietse's knowledge and visibility in the network security field, this code is very popular and is often used in conjunction with applications from other packages.

OBTAINING THE LOGDAEMON CODE

The LogDaemon code can be found at `ftp.win.tue.nl` in the /pub/security directory, or through the URL `ftp://ftp.win.tue.nl/pub/security/logdaemon-5.3.tar.gz`. To get the code, download the file logdaemon-5.3.tar.gz (or later) from this directory. In fact, if you are looking for security-related code, you will find some good packages here, including TCP Wrapper, Portmap, Crack, COPS, Tiger, and SATAN.

If you plan to build the rsh and rlogin programs, you might as well download the latest release of the TCP Wrapper code in addition to the LogDaemon code. The rshd and rlogind compiles depend on a library in the TCP Wrapper package.

N O T E

The LogDaemon and TCP Wrapper sources as downloaded are GNU gzip compressed files, so you must have GNU gzip to decompress them. After they are decompressed, untar the images, which results in the creation of a directory called logdaemon-5.0 and the installation of the source files installed under it.

You can find many other high-quality, interesting security programs here that are also worth investigating. Some of them have been discussed in *Actually Useful Internet Security Techniques* (ISBN: 1-56205-508-9) and the *Internet Security Professional Reference* (ISBN: 1-56205-557-7), both of which were published by New Riders.

N O T E

COMPILING THE LOGDAEMON CODE

With the source code now unpacked on your system, you must configure and compile it. The sources are based on the original BSD Unix sources and have been tested on a number of different platforms. These platforms are as follows:

Sun OS 4.1*x*, 5

Sunsoft Solaris 1.1.2, 2.4

DEC Ultrix 4.*x*

IRIX 5.*x*

HP/UX 9.*x*

DEC OSF 1.*x*

Sony NewsOS 4.*x*

These are the only currently supported platforms. The LogDaemon code was evaluated also on Linux, but only parts of the tools could be compiled. Therefore, if you are not running one of these versions of the Unix operating system, you can expect to have some porting problems.

The LogDaemon programs require the libwrap.a library from the TCP Wrapper 7.3 distribution. Consequently, you must compile the TCP Wrapper distribution first. You do this by simply running the make command identifying the named target. The available targets for TCP Wrapper are identified in the following list:

generic	386bsd
aix	alpha
apollo	convex-ultranet
dell-gcc	dgux dgux543
dynix	epix
esix	freebsd
hpux	irix4 irix5
isc (untested)	iunix
linux	machten
mips (untested)	ncrsvr4
netbsd	next
osf	ptx-2.x ptx-generic
pyramid	sco sco-nis sco-od2 sco-os5
sunos4 sunos40 sunos5	sysv4
ultrix	unicos (untested)
unixware1 unixware2	uxp

To compile TCP Wrapper, you need only to set the value of REAL_DAEMON_DIR in the Makefile. You can do this on the make command line, as follows:

```
$ make REAL_DAEMON_DIR='pwd' sunos4
```

In this example, the REAL_DAEMON_DIR is set to the current directory. Normally, it would be set to the location in which the daemons are actually installed. In this case, however, all you want is the libwrap.a library, so the actual value of the REAL_DAEMON_DIR is less important.

After the TCP Wrapper libwrap.a library archive is built, the location of this library must be saved in the user environment to be used when you are compiling the actual LogDaemon tools. You save the location of this library in the user environment by using one of the following commands:

For C-shell:

```
setenv LOG_TCP path to librwap.a file
```

For Bourne and Korn shells:

export LOG_TCP=path to libwrap.a file

Now go back to the logdaemon directory and run the command

make *target*

where *target* is one of the supported platforms previously listed.

> Your success with nonsupported platforms might be very limited. The author attempted to compile the LogDaemon tools under Linux, but found considerable problems with some of the tools—most notably the FTP daemon.

N O T E

With the LogDaemon programs successfully compiled, it is necessary to test them before placing them into operation.

TESTING THE COMPILED PROGRAMS

The test procedures for the LogDaemon tools are not as well defined as for the OPIE tools. Bear in mind, however, that this tool set, like OPIE, replaces a number of system programs. You must be ready to and capable of recovering your system should these new replacement programs not function properly. The compiled programs are best tested before moving them into their target locations.

First, test the creation of users in the OTP database. Remember, although the term *OTP* is used, the LogDaemon programs use a modified version of the S/KEY Version 1.0 implementation. Creation of users in the OTP database is performed with keyinit, which is illustrated here:

```
reliant:/home/ftp/security/logdaemon-5.0/skey# pwd
/home/ftp/security/logdaemon-5.0/skey
reliant:/home/ftp/security/logdaemon-5.0/skey# ./keyinit terri
Adding terri:
Reminder - Only use this method if you are directly connected.
If you are using telnet or rlogin exit with no password and use keyinit -s.
Enter secret password: <type pass phrase here>
Again secret password: <type pass phrase here>
ID terri s/key is 99 re21065
LID HILL LOIS AX HILT KIN
reliant:/home/ftp/security/logdaemon-5.0/skey#
```

The preceding example uses the keyinit command to add the user terri to the OTP database, which is in /etc/skeykeys. You can verify this key by testing it against another calculator that also is configured appropriately. For example, you can test it with the Windows calculator, WinKey, as shown in figure 4.5.

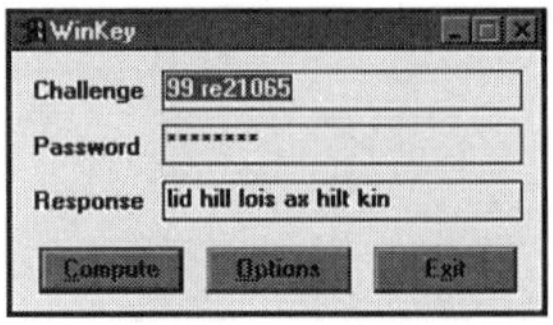

FIGURE 4.5

The Microsoft Windows OTP calculator.

In figure 4.6, the WinKey calculator has two different answers for the same challenge and pass phrase, but only one is correct. You know from the previous calculation that the answer shown on the left is the correct one. This is a common problem when you set up the LogDaemon tools, however, because they understand both MD4 and MD5. Incidentally, the WinKey on the left in figure 4.6 is MD4, and the one on the right is MD5.

As you can see, the calculated response in WinKey is the same as that shown in the same execution of keyinit. During testing, bear in mind that it is possible to confuse the encryption types. For example, if you expect to be using MD5, and the answer doesn't match in an MD5 calculation, try the MD4 method.

The only difference between the two generated passwords is that one will work and one will not. Both the MD4 and MD5 algorithms generate a six-word password, but because the algorithm is different, the series of words will not be the same. Often the case is that the algorithm does not match, as shown in figure 4.6.

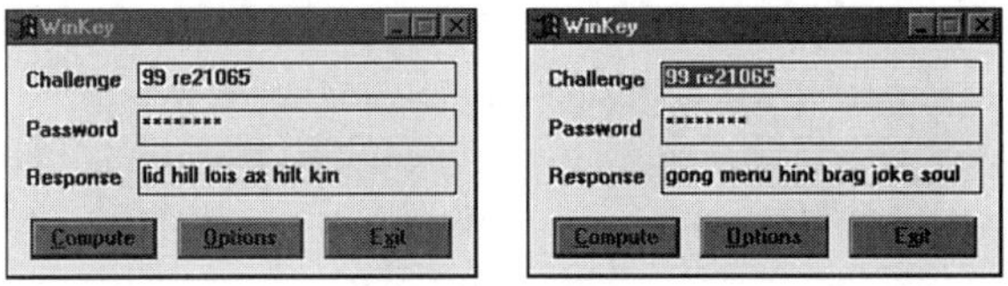

FIGURE 4.6

MD4 and MD5 generated password differences.

In figure 4.6, the WinKey calculator has two different answers for the same challenge and pass phrase, but only one is correct. You know from the previous calculation that the answer shown on the left is the correct one. This is a common problem when you set up the LogDaemon tools, however, because they understand both MD4 and MD5. Incidentally, the WinKey on the left in figure 4.6 is MD4, and the one on the right is MD5.

If you want to use the MD5 algorithm but got MD4 instead, now is the time to change it. To make the correction, edit Makefile in the skey directory and then change the following lines to read MD5:

```
CFLAGS  = -O $(XFLAGS) -DPERMIT_CONSOLE -DKEYACCESS=\"$(KEYACCESS)\" \
          -DKEYFILE=\"$(KEYFILE)\" -DMD4
```

You then change to the top-level directory, type **make**, and rebuild the components. You must rebuild the entire structure because the libskey.a archive will be rebuilt, and some of the other components rely upon this library.

Having proven the operation of the keyinit program by using an external calculator, you can test the key program to make sure that the local calculator can generate the correct response. The key command will print the password for the supplied iteration and seed value. The user is asked to enter his secret pass phrase, and the password is then generated, as shown here:

```
reliant:/home/ftp/security/logdaemon-5.0/skey# ./key 99 re21065
Reminder - Do not use this program while logged in via telnet or rlogin.
Enter secret password: <enter secret pass phrase>
LID HILL LOIS AX HILT KIN
reliant:/home/ftp/security/logdaemon-5.0/skey#
```

As illustrated, the generated password is the same as that previously shown. Consequently, you can assume that the keyinit and key programs are functioning properly.

Now that you have tested the basic OTP functionality, you need to examine the other tools. You don't necessarily have to use any of these other tools. Some people have retrieved the tools for only part of the package's functionality. In fact, although the LogDaemon tools include the BSD r* commands, many sites disable these commands because of their inherent dangers. The purpose of these tools, however, is to allow users the freedom of using these facilities.

INSTALLING LOGDAEMON

The LogDaemon tools are installed by simply copying the newly compiled programs into the same places as their existing versions. Remember to save the system-provided implementation in case the newly compiled version has a problem.

> Before you install any of these tools over system-provided copies, make a backup of the existing system so that you can recover it in the event of a disaster.

After the new programs have been installed into the proper directories, your system is ready to have its users configured with keyinit. Putting OTP into practice is discussed in a later section of this chapter.

THE LOGDAEMON COMPONENTS

As mentioned previously, the LogDaemon package consists of a collection of commands to replace the operating system versions and to provide additional support. This section provides a brief overview of each of the components in the LogDaemon package.

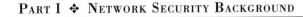

FTPD

The ftpd program is a direct plug-in replacement for the system implementation. It is, however, a much less impressive version than the wu-ftpd from Washington University, or even the implementation provided with OPIE. It does support extensive failure logging, one-time passwords, and the SecurID card, however.

LOGIN

The login program is a direct replacement with extensive logging and support for one-time passwords. You should note that support for OTP is not a requirement. Those sites that cannot or will not replace the login program can create a generic access account and then use skeysh to authenticate a specific user. Creating this account is illustrated in the later section "Putting OTP into Practice."

REXECD

The rexecd program is the server program for the rcmd command. To place this program into operation, review the /etc/inetd.conf file for an entry for rexecd. Check this line to make sure it is not commented out, as it is in the following example:

```
#exec   stream tcp      nowait  root /usr/sbin/in.rexecd
```

Replace the named program (in.rexecd) with the newly compiled rexecd. This new command supports OTP and extensive logging. By default, the logging records are written using the syslog facility LOG_AUTH. This can be changed by altering the following line in the rexecd/Makefile and building the executable again:

```
CFLAGS = -I$(UTIL) -O -DFACILITY=LOG_AUTH $(XFLAGS) # -DLOG_COMMANDS
```

RLOGIND

The rlogind program is the server side of the rlogin program. It supports extensive logging and access control capability. It logs regular access using the syslog priority DAEMON.INFO and other messages using DAEMON.WARN.

RSHD

The rshd program is the server program for the rcmd and rsh client programs. It supports OTP, and extensive logging Regular access is logged (by default) with priority DAEMON.INFO.

SKEYSH

The skeysh program is a login shell that understands S/KEY for those sites that cannot replace the login program. The solution is to create a dummy account with skeysh as the login shell, because skeysh is nothing but a stripped-down skey-only login program. The solution to the problem using skeysh is to first have users log in to a dummy user account. Doing so drops them into skeysh, which prompts them for their real account name and presents the corresponding S/KEY challenge.

USING THE S/KEY AND OPIE
CALCULATORS

As you have seen thus far, a calculator or list of pregenerated passwords is required before a user can access the OTP-protected system. The calculator can take a number of forms. It can be an application that runs on an OTP-protected system to allow access to other remote OTP systems. It can be an application that runs on the user's desktop system for use when needed. It can be a list of printed pregenerated passwords, or even an external calculator. This section covers the available hardware calculators and the software calculators available for different operating systems.

The critically important point to understand here is that you use only a calculator that you trust to be secure. This can be in the form of a hand-held calculator, an application running on your Mac or PC, or a bit of paper having some precomputed pass phrases. You should never type your secret password over the network.

UNIX

Each of the OTP systems comes with its own OTP password program for the Unix operating system. The names of these programs and the relevant package are listed in table 4.5.

TABLE 4.5
Unix OTP Calculators

Package	Key Generator Name
S/KEY	key
OPIE	opiekey
LogDaemon	winkey

These programs run on the Unix host itself. They do not allow access to the individual host where they are executed, because it is likely to be OTP-protected also. To use these calculators, the user must execute them with the iteration and seed information so that a key can be generated. Figure 4.7 illustrates using the LogDaemon implementation, winkey, to generate a password for a specific iteration and seed value.

Figure 4.7

*The LogDaemon
S/KEY calculator.*

```
s/key                                    _ □ X
Challenge: 977 672jar
Reminder - Do not use this program while
logged in via telnet or rlogin.
Enter secret password;
TILT DAVE PHI SINK ARID GIST
Challenge: █
```

This example illustrates using the winkey program that is part of the LogDaemon package. winkey is an S/KEY calculator that runs in an X Window and generates the required keys.

Figure 4.7 illustrates the LogDaemon version. The OPIE implementation, opiekey, appeared in earlier examples.

MACINTOSH

The most popular Macintosh calculator is found at `ftp.nrl.navy.mil` in /pub/security/nrl-opie/OPIEcalc.sit.hqx. Like the other calculators, it is used to calculate the response to the OTP challenge provided by the remote system. The calculator computes a response based on the iteration and seed value provided by the remote system, and on the user's secret pass phrase. Figure 4.8 illustrates the most popular Macintosh calculator.

Figure 4.8

*The NRL OPIE
calculator for the
Macintosh.*

```
               OPIE Calculator
 Challenge String [                        ]
 Password         [                        ]
 Reply (chars)    [                        ]
 Reply (hex)      [                        ]

        Hash algorithm  [ MD5 ▼ ]
        Information Technology Division  [ Compute ]
        Naval Research Laboratory
```

This file is a self-extracting archive and contains a fat binary, meaning it will run on both the 68-KB and Power Macintosh systems. It supports both S/KEY and OPIE using MD4 or MD5.

192

MICROSOFT WINDOWS

The Microsoft Windows calculator for Windows 3.1 and Windows 95 can be found at either ftp.nrl.navy.mil in /pub/security/nrl-opie/opie.contrib/winkey11.zip, or at ftp.tlogic.com/pub/skey. This is a DOS zip file that requires you to have an unzip program to extract the files. The contents of the archive include the compiled application winkey.exe and all the source code. Figure 4.9 illustrates the WinKey application.

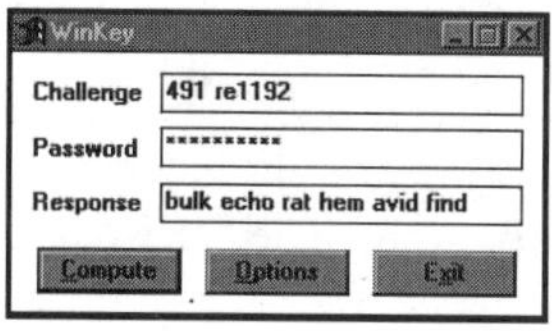

FIGURE 4.9

Generating passwords with WinKey.

WinKey has a number of options that increase its usability. For example, it can be configured to read the challenge from the Clipboard and to paste the computed value back into the Clipboard. It generates both S/KEY MD4 and OPIE MD5 passwords. Generating both passwords is important because the application keyapp.exe, which is part of the Bellcore S/KEY reference set, can generate only MD4 passwords.

If you use WinKey on Windows 95 and find that the application is not visible on-screen when you start it, the problem is the winkey.ini file in the Windows directory. You can either remove the winkey.ini file, or edit it and change the X and Y values to 0. This will start WinKey in the top left corner of the screen. It is a nonissue for the author of WinKey, who will one day get around to fixing it.

EXTERNAL CALCULATORS

You can use external calculators that hold the necessary program code. For example, the Hewlett-Packard HP48 series hand-held calculator has the capability to accept a downloaded program, and it will generate a key given the iteration, seed, and password for the user. This is a highly trusted method, because a cracker cannot gain access to your external calculator and therefore your password unless he or she is sitting right beside you. If you choose this route, note that the G, GX, S, and SX versions of the HP48 all can run this code. It requires 16 KB of memory, so the low-end versions might need memory upgrades.

To use an external calculator, you must type the iteration, seed, and then your password into the calculator. The calculator performs the computation, and you must then type the generated pass phrase into the remote system in order to complete the authentication. The downside is that users can make an error when they type the authenticated pass phrase, thereby delaying the login and raising the users' frustration level.

193

PUTTING OTP INTO PRACTICE

With your OTP software installed, you need to look at how to put OTP into practice. Your system is protected by OTP; now you need to configure the users. You accomplish this configuration with the keyinit/opieinit program. If the command is being run from a secure console, then you will not require the use of an OTP calculator in the process of configuring OTP for each user. If the configuration cannot be done over a secure terminal, then an OTP calculator will be required to generate a password to be sent across the network.

The first step is to initialize the OTP password for the user, which is illustrated as follows using the command keyinit. Keyinit asks you for the sequence number or iteration value, the key (or seed), and an S/KEY access password. The S/KEY password is generated using the same iteration and seed value, and a pass phrase.

```
host.mycorp.com >    keyinit
Adding chrish:
Reminder you need the 6 english words from the skey command.
Enter sequence count from 1 to 9999: 1000
Enter new key [default nd12043]: heather
s/key 1000 heather
s/key access password: ORB HURD LENT CRAM MELD HOSE
ID chrish s/key is 1000 heather
ORB HURD LENT CRAM MELD HOSE
```

In this example, the keyinit program informs you that the six English words from the skey program, from the OTP calculator, are required. This is because the keyinit program was not started with the -s flag indicating that it is being executed from a secure terminal. Had keyinit been started with the -s flag, it would have assumed that it was being executed on a secure terminal, and your pass phrase would have been requested rather than the S/KEY password.

This means that in order to complete the process, the skey command will have been run previously from a secure terminal, or the user will have access to an OTP calculator on the local machine. This instance is illustrated in figure 4.10.

Figure 4.10 illustrates using the OPIE commands to initialize the user chrish. Notice that the local WinKey calculator was available to provide the six English words.

WARNING

> As the administrator of the OTP service, you must inform your users that they should not let their iteration value drop below five. Doing so could lock them out of the system. Getting locked out normally occurs when the iteration value reaches zero, and that value can be reset only by the super user.

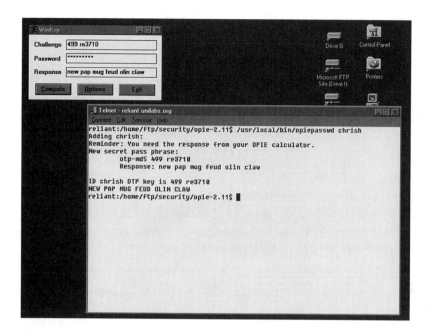

FIGURE 4.10

Initializing a user with opiepasswd.

Regardless of how good your password is, you should assume that it is known. Do not use the same Unix login password as your OTP password. Change your Unix password after you initialize your OTP passwords to completely eradicate any possibility that a compromised password exists.

Select the number of one-time passwords that you would like to set up, and use your calculator to predetermine the Nth corresponding response. This is illustrated in figure 4.10, which shows the opiepasswd program prompting with the iteration and seed. These values can be user configurable. In this example, however, the opiepasswd program was permitted to use its default values of 499 and a randomly generated seed value.

> It is imperative to note that none of the current OTP calculators detect any typing mistake that you might make. Consequently, it is recommended that, at this state, you calculate the six English words twice to ensure that the value you provided as your pass phrase is correct.

In the example in figure 4.10, opiepasswd initialized an iteration value of 499. Before users reach that limit, they must reinitialize their OTP configuration using a different and unique seed. They can keep the same password, however, if they want. In an earlier example, "heather"

195

was used as the seed; whereas, as figure 4.10 illustrates, using the opiepasswd provided a random seed. Bear in mind that a disadvantage of using system-generated seeds is that they can be difficult to type, creating a higher login failure rate.

SECURITY NOTES REGARDING /BIN/ LOGIN

Although an intruder can log into a system, then log in again by running the login command from a shell, most people remain unaware of this almost universal "feature." Because the second login is from the local host, the utmp entry will not show a remote login host any more. This technique is used by hackers to trick the system administrator into thinking the hacker is a local user, when in fact he is logged in from another site.

The OPIE replacement for /bin/login currently carries on this behavior for compatibility reasons. To prevent this from happening, change the permissions of /bin/login from 4511 to 0100, thus preventing unprivileged users from executing it. This fix should work on non-OPIE /bin/login programs as well. This does not restrict access to the system, nor prevent users from logging in. It only means that once they have logged in, they cannot run the login program.

USING OTP AND X WINDOWS

The major concern for users of the X Window environments is how to integrate OTP into their environments. The typical X Display Manager does not know how to interact with the OTP challenge/response format during the login session. An implementation of XDM with the OTP capability has been produced, however. The complete source code for the Release 6/Fix 13 version of XDM with S/KEY capability is available from the following location:

`ftp://cs.anu.edu.au/pub/people/Hugh.Fisher/skey-xdm.tar.Z`

Figure 4.11 illustrates how this implementation of XDM looks when it is in operation.

The implementation is robust and, like the login program, it supports password echoing. When you press the Enter key, you activate character echoing, which enables you to see the password as it is typed. This implementation was produced by Hugh Fisher of the Computer Science Department, Australian National University, and is freely available.

FIGURE 4.11

Adding OTP to the XDM login process.

GETTING MORE INFORMATION

Other sources of ongoing information and mailing lists that discuss S/KEY and its continuing development are available. One mailing list is sponsored directly by Bellcore. Bellcore uses this mailing list to announce its own changes to the S/KEY code, as well as for bug reporting and any general discussions related to S/KEY authentication.

If you want to be added or deleted from this list, send mail to the following address:

`skey-users-request@thumper.bellcore.com`

To send a message to the mailing list, send mail to the following address:

`skey-users@thumper.bellcore.com`

This mailing list is manually administered. You will not find a listserv or majordomo on the receiving end of your message. This means that the traditional listserv or majordomo command such as SUBSCRIBE does not work with this list. The list itself is for implementation issues and general discussion surrounding S/KEY.

Another mailing list, `Ietf-otp@bellcore.com`, is used for following the discussions of the IETF group working on one-time passwords. If you want to be added to or removed from the list, send a message to the following address:

`ietf-otp-request@bellcore.com`

To send a message to the list, use this address:

`ietf-otp@bellcore.com`.

SUMMARY

The development of OTP and the ongoing maintenance and support for a freely available product of this nature has made a difference in network security. After OTP is implemented, it is virtually impossible for a hacker to attack through the password security system. In fact, one company that uses OTP has field personnel access equipment using a one-time password that is generated for them from the central site. The field personnel do not know the pass phrase. In this situation, the field personnel contact their central office, at which time the OTP password is given to them.

The OTP-secured system is considered safe for high-security applications according to the current Internet Drafts and the RFC documents on the MD4 and MD5 encryption methods. Implementing OTP is a wise practice, and the success of the implementation might be dependent upon the use of tools from the several different tool sets that have been presented in this chapter.

PART II

SCREENING ROUTERS AND FIREWALLS

AN INTRODUCTION TO SCREENING ROUTERS

MANY COMMERCIAL routers provide the capability to screen packets based on criteria such as the type of protocol, the source address and destination address fields for a particular type of protocol, and control fields that are part of the protocol. Such routers are called *screening routers*. Screening routers can provide a powerful mechanism to control the type of network traffic that can exist on any network segment. By controlling the type of network traffic that can exist on a network segment, the screening routers can control the type of services that can exist on a network segment. Services that can compromise the network security can therefore be restricted.

This chapter examines how devices such as screening routers can be used to improve network security.

CLARIFYING DEFINITIONS

Screening routers can discriminate between network traffic based on the protocol type and the values of the protocol fields in the packet. The router's capability to discriminate between packets and restrict packets on its ports based on protocol-specific criteria is called *packet filtering*. For this reason, screening routers also are called *packet filter routers*.

ZONES OF RISK

An example of a packet filtering service implemented by a screening router is shown in figure 5.1. This figure shows an enterprise network connected to the Internet through a router that performs packet filtering.

FIGURE 5.1

A screening router forming a security perimeter.

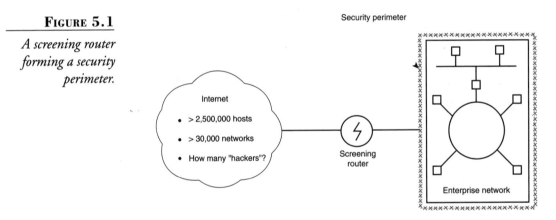

The latest statistics on the Internet indicate that it consists of over 30,000 networks with a total of over 2.5 million hosts. With so many network users on the Internet, there is, unfortunately, a small segment of users who are malicious hackers. This situation is similar to moving to a large city that has its share of criminals. In this case, it is wise to protect your abode using locked doors. Prudence on your part also demands that if someone knocks on your door, you should have the ability to examine the person before allowing them entrance into your abode. Persons who appear to be harmful or look dangerous (high-security risks) should not be allowed entrance. In a similar manner, the screening router examines incoming packets to determine which of them could be potentially harmful.

In the network in figure 5.1, the enterprise network's boundary is called the *security perimeter*. Because malicious hackers abound on the Internet, it is useful to define a zone of risk. The *zone of risk* includes all TCP/IP-capable networks that are directly accessible through the Internet. *TCP/IP-capable* means that the host supports the TCP/IP protocol and its support protocols. *Directly accessible* means that there are no strong security measures (no "locked doors") between the Internet and hosts on your enterprise network.

From your point of view, the Internet's regional, national, and backbone networks represent a zone of risk. Hosts within the zone of risk are vulnerable to attacks. Placing your networks and hosts outside the zone of risk is highly desirable. However, without a device that can block attacks made against your network, the zone of risk will extend to your network. The screening router is one such device that can reduce the zone of risk so that it does not penetrate your network's security perimeter.

Not all hosts in your enterprise network may be TCP/IP-capable. Even so, these non-TCP/IP hosts can become vulnerable despite the fact that they are not technically part of the zone of risk. This can occur if the non-TCP/IP host is connected to the TCP/IP host. The intruder can use a protocol common to both the TCP/IP host and the non-TCP/IP host to access the non-TCP/IP host from the TCP/IP host (see fig. 5.2). If the hosts are on the same Ethernet segment, for example, the intruder can reach the non-TCP/IP host through the Ethernet protocol.

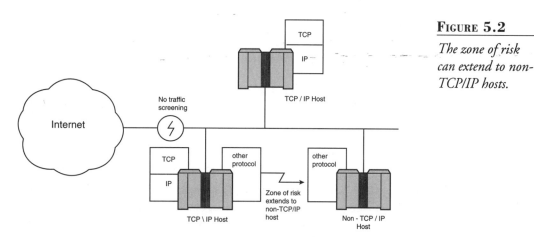

FIGURE 5.2

The zone of risk can extend to non-TCP/IP hosts.

Screening routers by themselves might not be able to eliminate the zone of risk. They can, however, be extremely effective in reducing the zone of risk.

THE OSI REFERENCE MODEL AND SCREENING ROUTERS

The term *router* in *screening router* implies a level of functionality dealing with routing issues. Understanding the overall role of the router in providing network communications helps you understand what types of filtering actions are provided by such routers. The preeminent model for understanding communication functions is the OSI Reference Model. This model can be used to describe the functionality of a router, and it helps explain the extent of the packet filtering capability of a screening router and its limitations.

The OSI Reference Model was developed in 1978 by the International Organization of Standards (ISO) to specify a standard that could be used for the development of open systems and as a yardstick to compare different communication systems. Network systems designed according to OSI framework and specifications speak the same language; that is, they use similar or compatible methods of communication. This type of network system enables systems from different vendors to interoperate.

In the early days of computer networks (prior to the OSI model), the proprietary computer network architecture reigned supreme. In those days, an organization interested in installing a computer network examined the choices available from vendors such as IBM, DEC, HP, Honeywell, and Sperry and Burroughs (now UNISYS). Each of those choices had its own proprietary architecture; the capability to interconnect networks from different vendors was almost nonexistent.

NOTE

Despite the fact that OSI is a documented standard, TCP/IP is the de facto standard. OSI was largely unaccepted and even ridiculed by the IP community. While OSI was being evaluated and developed into a suite of protocols, TCP/IP was already accumulating momentum in the academic marketplace. Few applications today can actually use OSI—even X.400 e-mail can run on TCP/IP.

Once committed to buying equipment from a specific vendor, the organization was virtually locked in. Updates or modifications to the system were provided by the vendor, and because the vendor had a closed proprietary architecture, no one could compete with that vendor in supplying equivalent services. Prices were determined based on what the customer could bear without complaining too much!

Today's users probably realize that in many areas of the computer industry, this picture has not changed much. Proprietary architecture history is still around, but the OSI model can, at the very least, provide you with a clearer picture of how the different components of a network relate to each other.

LAYERS OF THE OSI MODEL

The OSI model has seven layers, as shown in figure 5.3. The layers, working from the bottom up, are as follows:

Physical

Data link

Network

Transport

Session

Presentation

Application

The OSI Reference Model

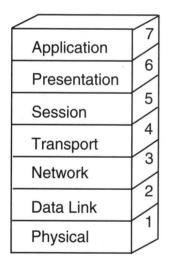

- Applications-specific services (API)

- Provides data representation

- Session services: checkpointing, activity management

- End-to-end data integrity

- Switches and router information

- Transmits information as groups of bits

- Transmits bit stream over physical medium

FIGURE 5.3

The OSI Reference Model (graphic courtesy of Learning Tree International).

API = application program interface

The ISO applied five principles when structuring the layers of the model:

1. A layer should be created only when a different level of abstraction is needed.

2. Each layer should provide a well-defined function.

3. The function of each layer should define internationally standardized protocols.

4. The layer boundaries should minimize the information flow across layer interfaces.

5. Distinct functions should be defined in separate layers, but the number of layers should be small enough that the architecture does not become unwieldy.

205

The following is a summary of the functions of the seven layers.

PHYSICAL LAYER

The *physical layer* deals with the mechanical, electrical, and procedural interfaces over the physical medium. The physical layer transmits bits over a communication channel. The bits might represent database records or file transfers; the physical layer is oblivious to what those bits represent. The bits can be encoded as digital 1s and 0s or in analog form.

In the case of the enterprise network of figure 5.1, the physical layer represents the cabling, physical ports, and attachments of the enterprise network. The physical connection of the screening router to the Internet, such as a leased line of the T1-link, also is part of the physical layer.

DATA LINK LAYER

The *data link layer* builds on the transmission capability of the physical layer. The bits that are transmitted/received are grouped in logical units called a *frame*. In the context of LANs, a frame could be a token ring or Ethernet frame.

The bits in a frame have special meanings. The beginning and ending of a frame can be marked by special bit patterns. Additionally, the bits in a frame are divided into an address field, control field, data field, and error-control field. Figure 5.4 shows a typical data link frame.

FIGURE 5.4

A typical data link layer frame.

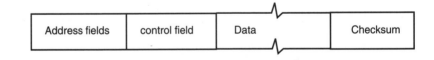

The *address field(s)* contains the sender and receiving node address. The *control field* is used to indicate the different types of data link frames, which include data frames and frames used for managing the data link channel. The *data field* contains the actual data being transmitted by the frame. The error control field usually detects errors in the data link frame. The data link layer also is the first layer in which you see error control concerns. The error control field usually is a hardware-generated checksum that is used to detect errors in the data link frame.

In figure 5.1, the screening router's Ethernet or token ring connection to the internal network is part of the data link layer. On the Internet port, the protocol used for the data link layer of the screening router could be SLIP, PPP, X.25, Frame Relay, and so on.

Network Layer

The *network layer* builds on the node-to-node connection provided by the data link layer by extending the node-to-node data link services across a network. An additional service provided by the network layer is how to route *packets* (units of information at the network layer) between nodes connected through an arbitrarily complex network.

Besides routing, the network layer helps eliminate congestion and regulate flow of data. The network layer also makes it possible for two networks to be interconnected by implementing a uniform addressing mechanism. Token ring or Ethernet LANs, for instance, have different types of data link addresses. To interconnect these two networks, you need a uniform addressing mechanism that can be understood by both token ring and Ethernet. For TCP/IP-based networks, this capability is provided by the Internet Protocol (IP).

The primary function of a router (including a screening router) resides in the network layer. When this router sees an IP packet, it examines the destination IP address in the packet. As discussed in Chapter 1, "Understanding TCP/IP," an IP address consists of a network number (also called netid) and a host number (also called hostid). The router examines the network number portion of the destination IP address in the IP packet and compares it to the entries in its routing table. If there is a match, the router forwards the IP packet as indicated in the routing table. If there is no match and there is no default route, the IP packet is rejected.

Screening routers can use criteria in addition to the routing table to forward the packet or reject it. The screening router can perform filtering at the network layer based upon the Source IP address, the Target IP address, and IP options (source routing or loose source routing). Figure 5.5 shows the fields within the IP packet on which the screening router can perform filtering, and figure 5.6 shows some of the IP options that can be used for filtering.

Transport Layer

The *transport layer* provides enhancements to the services of the network layer. This layer helps ensure reliable data delivery and end-to-end data integrity. To ensure reliable delivery, the transport layer builds on the error-control mechanisms provided by the lower layers. If the lower layers do not do a good enough job, the transport layer has to work harder. For this reason, this layer is also called the "last chance for error recovery" layer. In fact, when it comes to providing error-free delivery, you could say "The buck stops here" at the transport layer.

FIGURE 5.5

IP packet fields used by screening routers (graphic courtesy of Learnimg Tree International).

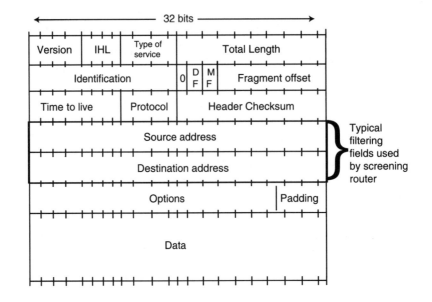

FIGURE 5.6

IP options used by screening routers (graphic courtesy of Learning Tree International).

IP Options Reference

Option Type	Option Length	Option Value
0	N/A	End of option list.
1	N/A	No operation.
2	11	Security. As required by DoD compartment, user group, handling restriction, label events.
3	variable	Loose source routing. Permits sender to specify *general* route followed by datagram.
4	variable	Timestamp. Permits a time trace of a datagram's *route* through the internet specified by sender.
7	variable	Record route. Traces path taken.
8	4	Stream ID. Permits routers to handle collections of IP datagrams in a similar way. Provides a tailored virtual circuit service.
9	variable	Strict source routing. Packet must *strictly* follow path.

The transport layer is the middle layer of the OSI model. The three lower layers constitute the network, and the three upper layers usually are implemented by networking software on the node. The transport layer usually is implemented on the node also; its job is to convert an unreliable subnet into a more reliable network.

The transport layer also can be responsible for creating several logical connections over the same network connection, a process called *multiplexing*. Multiplexing occurs when a number of transport connections share the same network connection.

Because of multiplexing, several software elements share the same network layer address. To uniquely identify the software elements within the transport layer, a more general form of addressing is necessary. These addresses, called *transport addresses,* usually are a combination of the network layer address and a transport Service Access Point (SAP) number. In TCP/IP, the term *port numbers* is used to identify transport addresses.

Routers normally do not perform processing at the transport layer. Screening routers, however, can examine port number fields in the TCP header. They can perform filtering decisions based on the port number values in the TCP header.

The source and destination port number fields used by screening routers are highlighted in the TCP header shown in figure 5.7. Many TCP/IP application services have standard port number values; for example, the FTP server uses port numbers 20 and 21. If you want to identify FTP sessions for the purposes of performing filtering, you can do so based on the port number values of 20 and 21. The source and destination port number are 16-bits, and can have values that range from 0 to 65535. The lower port numbers are assigned to Well Known Services (WKS) such as FTP, TELNET, and so on. The port numbers from 512 to 1024 usually are reserved for Unix-specific TCP/IP applications.

The port numbers are defined in an Internet Request for Comments (RFC) document that is updated on a frequent basis. As of the printing of this book, the current RFC for assigned numbers is RFC 1700. Most of the RFC documents are available on the World Wide Web at `http://www.cis.ohio-state.edu/htbin/rfc/rfc-index.html`.

Table 5.1 shows a few of the well-known port number assignments.

FIGURE 5.7

TCP fields used by screening routers (graphic courtesy of Learning Tree International).

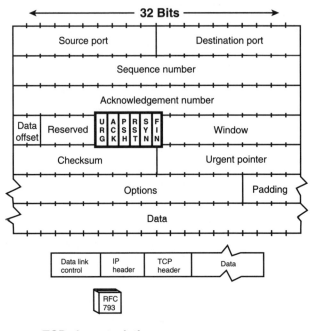

- **TCP characteristics**
  - Virtual circuits
  - Full duplex
  - Octet-stream orientation
  - Every octet numbered
  - Graceful close
  - Window flow control

TABLE 5.1
Some Well-Known TCP Port Numbers

Port Number	Description
0	Reserved
5	Remote Job Entry
7	Echo
9	Discard
11	Systat
13	Daytime
15	Netstat

Port Number	Description
17	Quotd (Quote of the day)
20	ftp_data
21	ftp (Control)
23	telnet
25	smtp (mail)
37	time
53	name server
70	Gopher protocol
79	Finger protocol
80	World Wide Web HTTP
88	Kerberos
102	ISO-TSAP
103	X.400
104	X.400 sending service
111	Sun RPC
123	Network Time Protocol (NTP)
139	NetBIOS session source
144	News
179	Border Gateway Protocol
512	exec
513	rlogin
514	rexec
515	lpd (line printer daemon)
517	talk
518	ntalk
2000	Open Windows (SUN)
X11	6000–6999

Besides port numbers, the screening routers are be able to filter packets based on the TCP flags. The TCP flags are used to indicate the type of TCP packet, such as the following:

❖ Open connection

❖ Acknowledgment of open connection

❖ Acknowledgment packet or data packet

The meanings of the TCP flags are shown in table 5.2. The most important TCP flags are the SYN and ACK flags. When the SYN flag is set to 1, it indicates that a TCP connection is being processed. This information is vital for designing proper filter rules for screening routers. If you want to prevent a TCP connection to an FTP service, for example, the screening router can reject packets to the FTP control port 21 that has the SYN flag set. The advantage of this is that the FTP connection is cut off before the client has the opportunity to reach a server.

TABLE 5.2
TCP Flags

TCP Flag	Description
URG	This flag is used to send out-of-band data without waiting for the receiver to process octets already in the stream. When the URG flag is set, the urgent pointer field is valid. RFC 1122 states that the urgent pointer points to the sequence number of the LAST octet (not LAST+1) in a sequence of urgent data, and that RFC 793 describes it incorrectly as LAST + 1. A TCP implementation must support a sequence of urgent data of any length. A TCP layer must inform the application layer asynchronously whenever the TCP layer receives an Urgent pointer with no previous pending urgent data, or whenever the urgent pointer advances in the data stream. There must be a way for the application to learn how much urgent data remains to be read from the connection, or at least to determine whether more urgent data remains to be read. Although the urgent mechanism can be used for any application, it normally is used to send interrupt-type commands to a Telnet program. The asynchronous, or `out-of-band`, notification enables the application to go into urgent mode, reading data from the TCP connection. This enables control commands to be sent to an application whose normal input buffers are full of unprocessed data.
ACK	The ACK flag indicates that the acknowledgment number field is valid.

TCP Flag	Description
PSH	This flag tells TCP to deliver data for this message immediately to the upper-layer process. When an application issues a series of send calls without setting the PSH flag, the TCP may aggregate the data internally without sending it. Similarly, when a series of segments is received without the PSH bit, a TCP may queue the data internally without passing it to the receiving application. The PSH bit is not a record marker and is independent of segment boundaries. Some implementations incorrectly think of the PSH as a record marker, however. The transmitter should collapse successive PSH bits when it packetizes data to send the largest possible segment. TCP can implement PSH flags on send calls. If PSH flags are not implemented, then the sending TCP must not buffer data indefinitely and must set the PSH bit in the last buffered segment (for example, when no more queued data is to be sent). RFC 793 erroneously implies that a received PSH flag must be passed to the application layer. Passing a received PSH flag to the application layer is optional. An application program is logically required to set the PSH flag in a send call whenever it needs to force delivery of the data to avoid a communication deadlock. A TCP should send a maximum-size segment whenever possible to improve performance, however. This means that on the sender side, a PSH may not result in the segment being immediately transmitted. When the PSH flag is not implemented on send TCP calls (or when the application/TCP interface uses a pure streaming model), responsibility for aggregating any tiny data fragments to form reasonable-size segments is partially borne by the application layer. Generally, an interactive application protocol must set the PSH flag at least in the last send call in each command or response sequence. A bulk transfer protocol like FTP should set the PSH flag on the last segment of a file, or when necessary to prevent buffer deadlock. At the receiver, the PSH bit forces buffered data to be delivered to the application (even if less than a full buffer is received). Conversely, the lack of a PSH can be used to avoid unnecessary wake-up calls to the application process; this can be an important performance optimization for large time-sharing hosts.
RST	The RST bit resets the virtual circuit due to unrecoverable errors. The reason could be a host crash or delayed duplicate SYN packets.

continues

213

TABLE 5.2, CONTINUED
TCP Flags

TCP Flag	Description
SYN	This flag indicates the opening of a virtual-circuit connection. TCP connections are opened using the three-way handshake procedure.
FIN	The FIN flag terminates the connection. Connection termination in TCP is accomplished by using a graceful close mechanism. Both sides must agree to terminate by sending a FIN = 1 flag before connection termination can occur; doing this ensures that data is not unexpectedly lost by either side by an abrupt connection termination.

When the SYN flag is set to 1, the ACK flag can be set to either 0 or 1. The settings of the ACK flag indicate whether the TCP packet is a connection or connection acknowledgment packet. If the SYN flag is set to 1 and the ACK flag is set to 1, the TCP packet is a connection acknowledgment packet. You can see this in figure 5.8 where a connection is made by a client on the Internet to a server on a local network. The server has a passive open connection and is waiting for a connection packet on a specified port. When the TCP connection packet is received by the server, it sends an open connection acknowledgment packet. The open connection packet has the following flag settings:

SYN = 1

ACK = 0

The open connection acknowledgment packet has the following settings:

SYN = 1

ACK = 1

When the client receives the open connection acknowledgment packet, it acknowledges this packet, completing the three-way handshake. The acknowledgment of the open connection acknowledgment packet has the following TCP flag settings:

SYN = 0

ACK = 1

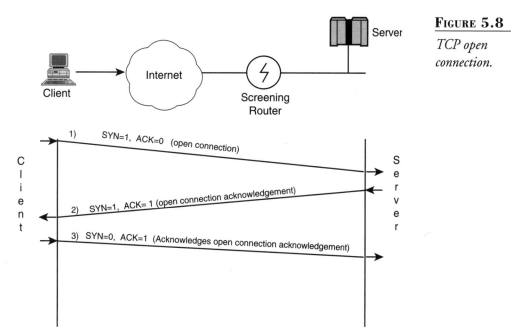

FIGURE 5.8

*TCP open
connection.*

The three major combinations of SYN and ACK flag settings are summarized in table 5.3.

TABLE 5.3
SYN and ACK Flag Combinations

SYN Flag	ACK Flag	Meaning
1	0	Open connection TCP packet
1	1	Open connection acknowledgment
0	1	Acknowledgment packet or data packet

Figures 5.9 through 5.11 show the establishment of a TCP connection as previously described. They illustrate the SYN and ACK flags in a protocol decode of a TCP connection three-way handshake taken from a live TELNET connection. Figure 5.9 shows the open connection packet to the server, figure 5.10 shows the open connection acknowledgment, and figure 5.11 shows the acknowledgment to this open connection acknowledgment packet. Figure 5.11 shows that besides acknowledging the server connection acknowledgment, the client also sends application data that is part of the telnet protocol (option negotiation).

Thus, screening routers can perform packet filtering based upon the following:

- ✦ Source port number
- ✦ Destination port number
- ✦ TCP flags

Although screening routers can filter on any of the TCP flag settings, the flags that are most frequently used are the SYN and ACK flags. Not all router software has the capability to access the TCP flags. Consequently, such software has limited sensitivity to the SYN and ACK flags.

Besides TCP, another transport protocol that can be used is UDP (User Datagram Protocol). The User Datagram Protocol is a simpler transport protocol than TCP. It is popular in many LAN-oriented applications and is a connectionless transport protocol, meaning that it does not use a preestablished connection to transmit data.

Whereas the TCP protocol is responsible for reliable, simultaneous, full-duplex connections, the UDP protocol provides unreliable connectionless transport services. The term *reliable* means that TCP takes care of transmission errors by resending the portion of data that was in error. Any application that uses TCP does not have to be concerned with reliability of data transmission because this is handled by TCP. TCP provides for simultaneous connections. This means that several TCP connections could be established at a host over which data could be sent simultaneously independent of data on other connections. TCP provides full-duplex connections, which means that data can be sent and received on a single connection.

On the other hand, the UDP protocol is not as robust as TCP and can be used by applications that do not require the reliability of TCP at the host-to-host layer. It is called an *unreliable protocol* because the protocol does not guarantee the reliable delivery of a packet. It makes the best efforts it can to deliver the packet. Although the UDP protocol does provide an optional checksum for data integrity, unlike TCP it does not guarantee the sequenced delivery of the packets. *Sequenced delivery* means that packets are received in the order in which they are sent. UDP cannot guarantee sequenced delivery because it has no provision for keeping track of sequence numbers for packets. UDP has less overhead compared to TCP. If additional reliability such as data being received in the order in which it was sent (sequenced delivery) is required, the application that uses UDP has to provide for it.

```
┌─────────────────────────────────────────────────────────────────┬──┐
│  ▭          LANalyzer for Windows - [Capture Buffer]        ▼ │▲│
│ ▭ File  Monitor  Alarms  Capture  Decode  Window  Help        │▼│
│ ┌────┬──────────────┬──────────────┬───────┬───────────────────┐│▲│
│ │No. │ Source       │ Destination  │ Layer │ Summary           ││ │
│ ├────┼──────────────┼──────────────┼───────┼───────────────────┤│ │
│ │  1 │0000C0DD145C  │0000C0664E19  │ arp   │Reply 199.245.180.15=0000C0DD145C││ │
│ │  2 │0000C0664E19  │0000C0DD145C  │ tcp   │Port:11806 ---> TELNET SYN││ │
│ │  3 │0000C0DD145C  │0000C0664E19  │ tcp   │Port:TELNET ---> 11806 ACK SYN││ │
│ │  4 │0000C0664E19  │0000C0DD145C  │ telnt │Cmd=Do; Code=Echo; Cmd=Do; Code=Supp││ │
│ │  5 │0000C0DD145C  │0000C0664E19  │ telnt │Cmd=Do; Code=Terminal Type; Cmd=Do;││ │
│ │  6 │0000C0664E19  │0000C0DD145C  │ telnt │Cmd=Won't; Code=Terminal Type; Cmd=W││ │
│ │  7 │0000C0DD145C  │0000C0664E19  │ telnt │Cmd=Will; Code=Echo; Cmd=Will; Code=▼││▼│
│ │◄│                                                           │►││ │
│ ├───────────────────────────────────────────────────────────────┤│▲│
│ │tcp: ================ Transmission Control Protocol ============ ││ │
│ │     Source Port: 11806                                        ││ │
│ │     Destination Port: TELNET                                  ││ │
│ │     Sequence Number: 48357376                                 ││ │
│ │     Acknowledgement Number: 0                                 ││ │
│ │     Data Offset (32-bit words): 6                             ││ │
│ │     Window: 512                                               ││ │
│ │     Control Bits: Synchronize Sequence Numbers (SYN)          ││ │
│ │     Checksum: 0x90C7(Valid)                                   ││ │
│ │     Urgent Pointer: 0                                         ││▼│
│ ├───────────────────────────────────────────────────────────────┤│ │
│ │ 0: 00 00 C0 DD 14 5C 00 00 C0 66 4E 19 08 00 45 00 │.....\...fN...E. ││ │
│ │10: 00 2C 00 01 00 00 64 06 5E CF C7 F5 B4 01 C7 F5 │.,....d.^.....'. ││ │
│ │20: B4 0F 2E 1E 00 17 02 E1 E0 00 00 00 00 00 60 02 │...............'. ││ │
│ │30: 02 00 90 C7 00 00 02 04 02 00 FC 22             │..........."    ││ │
│ │                                                               ││ │
│ └───────────────────────────────────────────────────────────────┘│ │
│            ┌───────────────┐ ┌─────────────────┐ ┌──────────┐     │ │
│            │ Packet:  2    │ │ Unfiltered: 293 │ │          │     │ │
│            └───────────────┘ └─────────────────┘ └──────────┘     │ │
└─────────────────────────────────────────────────────────────────┴──┘
```

FIGURE 5.9

Three-way handshake: open connection TCP packet with SYN=1, ACK=0.

```
┌─────────────────────────────────────────────────────────────────┬──┐
│  ▭          LANalyzer for Windows - [Capture Buffer]        ▼ │▲│
│ ▭ File  Monitor  Alarms  Capture  Decode  Window  Help        │▼│
│ ┌────┬──────────────┬──────────────┬───────┬───────────────────┐│▲│
│ │No. │ Source       │ Destination  │ Layer │ Summary           ││ │
│ ├────┼──────────────┼──────────────┼───────┼───────────────────┤│ │
│ │  1 │0000C0DD145C  │0000C0664E19  │ arp   │Reply 199.245.180.15=0000C0DD145C││ │
│ │  2 │0000C0664E19  │0000C0DD145C  │ tcp   │Port:11806 ---> TELNET SYN││ │
│ │  3 │0000C0DD145C  │0000C0664E19  │ tcp   │Port:TELNET ---> 11806 ACK SYN││ │
│ │  4 │0000C0664E19  │0000C0DD145C  │ telnt │Cmd=Do; Code=Echo; Cmd=Do; Code=Supp││ │
│ │  5 │0000C0DD145C  │0000C0664E19  │ telnt │Cmd=Do; Code=Terminal Type; Cmd=Do;││ │
│ │  6 │0000C0664E19  │0000C0DD145C  │ telnt │Cmd=Won't; Code=Terminal Type; Cmd=W││ │
│ │  7 │0000C0DD145C  │0000C0664E19  │ telnt │Cmd=Will; Code=Echo; Cmd=Will; Code=▼││▼│
│ │◄│                                                           │►││ │
│ ├───────────────────────────────────────────────────────────────┤│▲│
│ │tcp: ================ Transmission Control Protocol ============ ││ │
│ │     Source Port: TELNET                                       ││ │
│ │     Destination Port: 11806                                   ││ │
│ │     Sequence Number: 3825856001                               ││ │
│ │     Acknowledgement Number: 48357377                          ││ │
│ │     Data Offset (32-bit words): 6                             ││ │
│ │     Window: 4096                                              ││ │
│ │     Control Bits: Acknowledgement Field is Valid (ACK)        ││ │
│ │              Synchronize Sequence Numbers (SYN)               ││ │
│ │     Checksum: 0xAEAA(Valid)                                   ││▼│
│ ├───────────────────────────────────────────────────────────────┤│ │
│ │ 0: 00 00 C0 66 4E 19 00 00 C0 DD 14 5C 08 00 45 00 │...fN......\..E. ││ │
│ │10: 00 2C 12 3D 00 00 3C 06 74 93 C7 F5 B4 0F C7 F5 │.,.=..<.t...... ││ │
│ │20: B4 01 00 17 2E 1E E4 09 EE 01 02 E1 E0 01 60 12 │.............`. ││ │
│ │30: 10 00 AE AA 00 00 02 04 04 00 FC 22             │..........."    ││ │
│ │                                                               ││ │
│ └───────────────────────────────────────────────────────────────┘│ │
│            ┌───────────────┐ ┌─────────────────┐ ┌──────────┐     │ │
│            │ Packet:  3    │ │ Unfiltered: 293 │ │          │     │ │
│            └───────────────┘ └─────────────────┘ └──────────┘     │ │
└─────────────────────────────────────────────────────────────────┴──┘
```

FIGURE 5.10

Three-way handshake: open connection acknowledgment TCP packet with SYN=1, ACK=1.

FIGURE 5.11

Three-way hand-shake: acknowledgment of open connection acknowledgment packet with SYN=0, ACK=1.

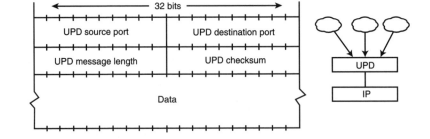

Figure 5.12 shows a UDP header. Notice that like the TCP packet in figure 5.7, the UDP header has source and port numbers. Because these port numbers refer to the UDP protocol that is distinct from the TCP protocol, these port numbers are in a different address space than the TCP port numbers. Some application services are available through both the TCP and UDP protocols, in which case they have port numbers defined for both TCP and UDP. Table 5.4 shows some of the examples for the UDP port numbers.

FIGURE 5.12

A UDP packet header (graphic courtesy of Learning Tree International).

- **Notable points**
  - No sequence or acknowledgment numbers
  - No flow control
  - Messages can be duplicated or arrive out of order
  - Checksum includes pseudoheader

TABLE 5.4
Example UDP Port Numbers

UDP Port Number	Description
0	Reserved
2	Management Utility
3	Compression Process
5	Remote Job Entry
7	Echo
9	Discard
11	Active Users (systat)
13	Daytime
17	Quote of the Day (QUOTD)
35	Any private printer server
37	Time
39	Resource Location Protocol
42	Host name server (nameserver)
43	Who Is (nicname)
49	Login Host Protocol (login)
52	XNS Time Protocol
53	Domain Name Server (domain)
54	XNS clearing house
66	Oracle SQL*NET (sql*net)
67	Bootstrap Protocol Server (bootps)
68	Bootstrap Protocol Client (bootpc)
69	Trivial Transfer Protocol (tftp)
80	World Wide Web HTTP

continues

TABLE 5.4, CONTINUED
Example UDP Port Numbers

UDP Port Number	Description
88	Kerberos
94	Trivoli Object Dispatcher (objcall)
95	SUPDUP
108	SNA Gateway Access Server (snagas)
110	Post Office Protocol - Version 3 (POP3)
111	Sun Remote Procedure Call (sunrpc)
119	Network News Transfer Protocol (NNTP)
123	Network Time Protocol (NTP)
134	INGRES-NET Service
137	NETBIOS Naming Service (netbios-ns)
138	NETBIOS Datagram Service (netbios-dgm)
139	NETBIOS Session Service (netbios-ssn)
142	Britton-Lee IDM
161	SNMP
162	SNMP Traps
191	Prospero
194	Internet Relay Chat Protocol (irc)
201	AppleTalk Routing Maintenance (at-rtmp)
202	AppleTalk Name Binding (at-nbp)
213	IPX (used for IP tunneling)
215	Insignia (Soft PC)
217	dBASE Unix
372	Unix Listserv
513	Maintains database on who is logged on to machines on a local net and the load average of the machine (who)

UDP Port Number	Description
517	talk
518	ntalk
519	unixtime
525	Time Server (timed)
533	Emergency broadcasts (netwall)
556	RFS server (remoterfs)
565	Who Am I (whoami)
749	Kerberos Administration (kerberos-adm)
767	Phone (phonebook)
1025	Network Blackjack (blackjack)
1352	Lotus Notes (lotusnote)
2000	Open Windows
2049	Network File System (NFS)
6000 to 6999	X11
7000 to 7009	Used by Andrew File System (AFS)
17007	ISODE Directory User Agent (isode-dua)

The term *connectionless,* when applied to a protocol, means that the data can be sent without requiring that an IP data circuit be established. Each data unit is sent with complete source and destination IP addresses and port numbers that identify the application level processes that are involved in the data exchange. Connectionless IP focuses on its relationship with routing rather than the applications involved per se. This means that although the application port numbers are included in the packet, the application itself does not concern itself with routing—only with the exchange and processing of the data in the packet. UDP is similar to ordinary postal services in that complete addressing information is sent with each UDP message.

A big advantage that UDP has over TCP is that UDP is more suited for applications that require broadcast data. A single datagram can be broadcast on the network by specifying a broadcast address on the destination address. UDP is popular in many LAN-based applications that are broadcast-based and do not require the complexity of TCP.

N O T E

Examples of applications that use UDP are NFS (Network File System), DNS (Domain Name System), SNMP (Simple Network Management Protocol), and TFTP (Trivial File Transfer Protocol). UDP also is used for IP tunneling.

SESSION LAYER

The *session layer* of the OSI model makes use of the transport layer to provide enhanced session services. Examples of a session include a user being logged in to a host across a network, or a session being established for the purpose of transferring files.

The session layer can provide some of the following enhancements:

> Dialog control
>
> Token management
>
> Activity management

A session, in general, enables two-way communications (full duplex) across a connection. Some applications might require alternate one-way communications (half duplex). The session layer has the option of providing two-way or one-way communications, an option called *dialog control.*

For some protocols, it is essential that only one side attempt a critical operation at a time. To prevent both sides from attempting the same operation, a control mechanism, such as the use of tokens, can be implemented. When using the token method, only the side holding a token is permitted to perform the operation. Determining which side has the token and how it is transferred between the two sides is known as *token management.*

N O T E

The use of the word *token* here should not be confused with token ring operation. Token management is a much higher level concept than token ring operation, residing at layer five of the OSI model. IBM's Token-Ring operation belongs to layers two and one of the OSI model.

If you are performing a one-hour file transfer between two machines, and network crashes occur approximately every 30 minutes, you might never be able to complete the file transfer. After each transfer aborts, you have to start all over again. To avoid this problem, you can treat the entire file transfer as a single activity with checkpoints inserted into the datastream. That way, if a crash occurs the session layer can synchronize to a previous checkpoint. This operation of managing an entire activity is called *activity management.*

In the TCP/IP world, the RPC (Remote Procedure Call) protocol used by NFS (Network File System) can be considered an example of a session layer protocol.

NOTE

PRESENTATION LAYER

The *presentation layer* manages the way data is represented. Many ways of representing data exist, such as ASCII and EBCDIC for text files, and 1s or 2s complement representation for numbers. If the two sides involved in communication use different data representations, they will not be able to understand each other. The presentation layer represents data with a common syntax and semantics. If all the nodes used and understood this common language, misunderstanding in data representation could be eliminated.

An example of this common language is Abstract Syntax Notation, Rev 1 (ASN.1), an OSI recommendation. In the TCP/IP world, the ASN.1 is used for encoding SNMP messages. Another example of a protocol that corresponds to this layer is the External Data Representation (XDR) protocol that is used in the NFS.

NOTE

APPLICATION LAYER

The *application layer* contains the protocols and functions needed by user applications to perform communication tasks. Examples of common functions include the following:

❖ Protocols for providing remote file services, such as open, close, read, write, and shared access to files

❖ File transfer services and remote database access

❖ Message handling services for e-mail applications

❖ Global directory services to locate resources on a network

❖ A uniform way of handling a variety of system monitors and devices

❖ Remote job execution

Many of these services are called application programming interfaces (APIs). *APIs* are programming libraries that an application writer can use to write network applications.

N O T E

> For TCP/IP, examples of application layer protocols are FTP, SMTP, TELNET, SNMP, NFS, and X Windows.

Firewalls used for protecting networks operate at the application layer of the OSI model. Because firewalls operate at the highest level of the OSI model, they have access to more information than screening routers and can be programmed to operate more intelligently than screening routers.

SCREENING ROUTERS AND FIREWALLS IN RELATIONSHIP TO THE OSI MODEL

Figure 5.13 compares screening routers and firewalls in relationship to the OSI model. This figure shows that the screening router functions primarily correspond to the network (IP protocol) and transport (TCP protocol) layers of the OSI model. Screening routers also can include the data link and physical layers, however, because most filtering systems apply to the type of interface, the network media in use, and even the MAC address itself. Firewalls often are described as gateways. Gateways can perform processing at all the seven layers of the OSI model. Typically, gateways perform processing at the seventh (application) layer of the OSI model. This is true for most firewall gateways.

FIGURE 5.13

Screening routers, firewalls, and the OSI model.

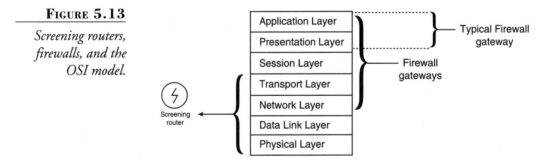

Figure 5.13 also shows that because firewalls cover the network and transport layers, they can perform packet filtering functions. Some vendors, for marketing reasons perhaps, blur the distinction between a screening router and a firewall, to the extent that they call their screening router products firewall products. For the sake of clarity, this book makes the distinction between screening routers and firewalls based on the OSI model.

Sometimes screening routers are also called packet filter *gateways*. Perhaps one justification of the use of the term gateway for the packet filter device is that filtering based on the TCP flags done at the transport layer is not a function of the router that operates at the network layer of the OSI model. Devices that operate above the network layer also are called gateways.

You will learn in Chapter 8, "Firewall Architecture and Theory," how screening routers and firewall gateways can be combined to provide robust network security.

UNDERSTANDING PACKET FILTERING

Screening routers can use packet filtering as a means to enhance network security. The screening function also can be performed by many commercial firewall products and by software-based products such as the Karlbridge PC-Based Filters. However, many commercial routers can be programmed to perform filtering. Router vendors such as Cisco, Wellfleet, 3COM, Digital, Newbridge, ACC, and many others provide routers that can be programmed to perform packet filtering functions.

PACKET FILTERING AND NETWORK POLICY

Packet filtering can be used to implement a wide variety of network security policies. As discussed in Chapter 3, the network security policy must clearly state the types of resources and services that are being protected, their level of importance, and the people from whom the services are being protected.

Generally the network security policy guidelines are focused more in keeping outsiders out, than trying to police insiders. For example, it is more important to prevent outsiders from breaking in and intentionally exposing sensitive data or disrupting services than preventing insiders from using external network services. This type of network security policy determines where screening routers should be placed and how they should be programmed to perform packet filtering. Good network security implementations also should make it difficult for insiders to harm the network security. This usually is not the major thrust of security efforts.

One of the goals of a network security policy is to provide a transparent mechanism so that the policy is not a hindrance to the users. Because packet filtering operates at the network and transport layers of the OSI model, and not at the application layer, this approach generally tends to be more transparent than the firewall approach. Recall that firewalls operate at the application layer of the OSI model, and security implementations at this layer tend not to be as transparent.

A SIMPLE MODEL FOR PACKET FILTERING

A packet filter usually is placed between one or more network segments, as shown in figure 5.14. The network segments are classified as either an external or internal network segment. *External network segments* connect your network to outside networks such as the Internet. *Internal network segments* are used to connect the enterprise's hosts and other network resources.

FIGURE 5.14

A packet filter placed between multiple segments.

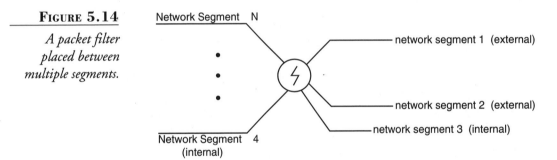

Each of the ports of the packet filter device can be used to implement network policies that describe the type of network service that is accessible through the port. If the number of network segments that connect with the packet filter device is large, the policies that the packet filter device implements can become complex. In general, complex solutions to security problems should be avoided because of the following reasons:

❖ They are harder to maintain.

❖ It is easy to make mistakes in configuring packet filtering.

❖ They have an adverse effect on the performance of the device on which they are implemented.

Sheer economics, however, often dictate that a router with extra ports is purchased rather than several smaller routers. The advantages of a router that has several ports are scalability and the processing capacity of its CPU interface. Furthermore, because the packet filtering rules often are bound to one interface, a multiport router can be a manageable solution if designed properly.

In many instances, the simple model shown in figure 5.15 can be used to implement the network security policy. This model shows that the packet filter device has only two network segments connected to it. Typically, one of these network segments is an external network segment and the other is an internal network segment. Packet filtering is done to restrict the network traffic for the services that are to be denied. Because the network policy is written to favor insiders contacting external hosts, the filter on each side of the screening router's ports must behave differently. In other words, the filters are asymmetric.

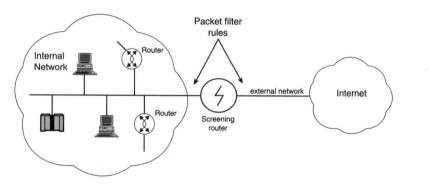

FIGURE 5.15

A packet filter placed between two network segments.

PACKET FILTER OPERATIONS

Almost all current packet filter devices (screening routers or packet filter gateways) operate in the following manner:

1. Packet filter criteria must be stored for the ports of the packet filter device. The packet filter criteria are called *packet filter rules.*

2. When the packet arrives at the port, the packet headers are parsed. Most packet filter devices examine the fields in only the IP, TCP, or UDP headers.

3. The packet filter rules are stored in a specific order. Each rule is applied to the packet in the order in which the packet filter rule is stored.

4. If a rule blocks the transmission or reception of a packet, the packet is not allowed.

5. If a rule allows the transmission or reception of a packet, the packet is allowed to proceed.

6. If a packet does not satisfy any rule, it is blocked.

These rules are expressed as a flowchart in figure 5.16.

FIGURE 5.16

*A flowchart of
packet filter
operation.*

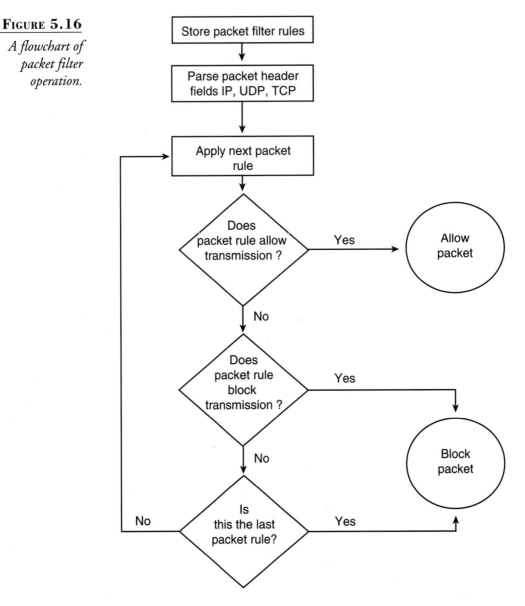

From rules 4 and 5, you should realize that it is important to place the rules in the correct order. A common mistake in configuring packet filter rules is to place the rules in the wrong order. If the packet filter rules are placed in the wrong order, you might end up denying valid services, while permitting services that you wanted to deny.

Rule number 6 follows this philosophy:

> *That which is not expressly permitted is prohibited.*

This is a fail-safe philosophy that you should follow when designing secure networks. It is the opposite of a permissive philosophy that says:

> *That which is not expressly prohibited is permitted.*

If the latter philosophy were used for designing packet filters, you would have to think of every possible case not covered by the packet filter rules to make the network secure. And as new services are added, you easily can end up with situations in which no rule is matched. Rather than block this service and hear complaints from users if you have blocked a legitimate service (at which time you can unblock the service), you may end up allowing a service that can be a security risk to the network.

PACKET FILTER DESIGN

Consider the network in figure 5.17 for which the screening router is used as the first line of defense between the internal protected network and an external untrusted network.

Network 199.245.180.0

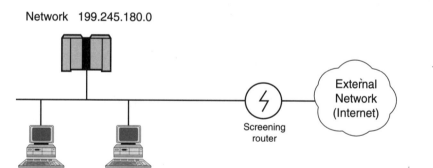

FIGURE 5.17

Sample network for packet filter design.

Assume that the network security policy requires that Internet mail be received from external hosts on a specific gateway, and you want to deny network traffic originating from the host named CREEPHOST that you do not trust. (Perhaps one reason for this could be that they have a tendency to send large messages that your mail cannot handle. Another could be that you suspect security threats originating from this host.)

In this example, the network security policy on SMTP use must be translated into packet filter rules. You could translate the network security rules into the following English language rules:

[Filter Rule 1]

We do not trust connections from host CREEPHOST.

[Filter Rule 2]

We wish to allow connections to our mail gateway.

These rules can be encoded into the table of rules shown in figure 5.18. The asterisk (*) symbol is used to match any values for that column.

For filter rule 1 (in figure 5.18) there is an entry for the External Host column, and all other columns have the asterisk symbol. The action is to block the connection. This translates to the following:

Block any connection from CREEPHOST originating from *any* (asterisk) of its ports to *any* (asterisk) of our ports on *any* (asterisk) of our hosts.

For filter rule 2 there is an entry for the Our Host and the Port on Our Host columns. All other columns have the asterisk symbol. The action is to allow the connection. This translates to the following:

Allow any connection from *any* (asterisk) external host originating from *any* (asterisk) of its ports to port 25 of on our MAIL-GW host.

Port 25 is used because this TCP port is reserved for SMTP (refer to table 5.1).

FIGURE 5.18

An attempt to encode packet filter rules.

Filter Rule Number	Action	Our Host	Portion on Our Host	External Host	Port on External Router	Description
1	Block	*	*	CREEPHOST	*	Block traffic from CREEPHOST
2	Allow	Mail-GW	25	2	*	Allow connection to our mail gateway
3	Allow	*	*	3	25	Allow outgoing SMTP traffic to remote mail gateway

Legend: * = Matches all values

The rules are applied in the order of their number in the table. If a packet does not match any of the rules, it is rejected.

A problem with the way the rules are specified in figure 5.18 is that it allows any external machine to originate a call from port 25. Port 25 should be reserved for SMTP, as per RFC 1700 (Assigned Numbers), but an external host could use this for other purposes. The third rule illustrates how an internal host would be able to send SMTP mail to an external host's port 25. This enables the internal host to send mail to external sites. If the external site is not using port 25 for SMTP, the SMTP-sender process will not be able to send mail. This is equivalent to mail not being supported on the external host.

As mentioned before, a TCP connection is a full duplex connection and information flows in both directions. The packet filter rules in figure 5.18 do not explicitly specify in which direction the information in the packet is being sent: from our host to the external site, or from an external site to our host.

When a TCP packet is sent in any direction, it must be acknowledged by the receiver. The receiver sends the acknowledgment by setting the ACK flag. Figure 5.8 shows the use of the ACK flag in acknowledging the TCP open connection requests. However, ACK flags are used in normal TCP transmission as illustrated in figure 5.19. In this figure, the sender sends a TCP segment (data sent by TCP is called a *segment*) whose starting byte number (SEQ#) is 1001 and length is 100 bytes. The receiver sends back a TCP acknowledgment packet indicated by the ACK flag set to 1, and the acknowledgment number (ACK#) set to 1001+100 = 1101. The sender then sends two TCP segment numbers that are 200 bytes each. These are acknowledged by a single acknowledgment packet that has the ACK flag set to 1, and acknowledgment number indicating the starting byte number of the next TCP data segment (1101 + 200 + 200 = 1501).

From figure 5.19, you can see that ACK packets will be sent on all TCP connections. When the ACK packet is sent, the sending direction is reversed, and the packet filter rules should take into account the ACK packets that are sent in response to control or data packets.

Based on the previous discussion, the modified set of packet rules can be written as indicated in figure 5.20.

For filter rule 1 (in figure 5.20) there is an entry for the Source Host/Net column of 199.245.180.0, and an entry in the Destination Host Port column of 25. All other columns have the asterisk symbol.

The action in filter rule 1 is to allow a connection. This translates to the following:

> Allow any connection from network 199.245.180.0 originating from *any* (asterisk) of its ports to port 25 on any (asterisk) destination host with any TCP flags or IP options set (including source routing).

Note that because 199.245.180 is a class C network number (also called the *netid*), the 0 in the host number (also called *hostid*) field refers to any host on the class C network 199.245.180.

For filter rule 2 there is an entry for the Source Host Port column of 25, an entry in the Destination Host column, and a TCP ACK entry in the TCP flags/IP options column. All other columns have the asterisk symbol.

231

FIGURE 5.19

Use of acknowledgments in TCP data transfer (graphic courtesy of Learning Tree International).

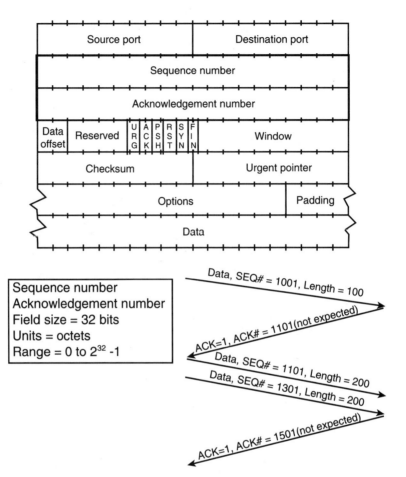

FIGURE 5.20

Packet filter rules for SMTP.

Filter Rule Number	Action	Source Host/Net	Source Host Port	Destination Host/Net	Destination Host Port	TCP Flags/ IP Optional	Description
1	Allow	199.245.180.0	*	*	25	*	Allow packet from network 199.245.180.0 to any destination host port 25
2	Allow	Mail-GW	25	199.245.180.0	*	ACK	Allow return acknowledgement

The action in filter rule 2 is to allow a connection. This translates to the following:

Allow any connection to continue to be set up from *any* network originating from port 25 and which has the TCP ACK flag set to *any* (asterisk) port on any (asterisk) host on our network (199.245.180.0).

The combined effects of filter rules 1 and 2 of figure 5.20 is to allow TCP packets between the network 199.245.180.0 to the SMTP port on any external host.

Because the packet filter examines only layers 2 and 3 in the OSI model, there is no way to absolutely guarantee that the return TCP acknowledgments are part of the same connection. In actual practice, the scheme works well because TCP connections maintain state information on each side. They know what sequence numbers and acknowledgments to expect. Also, the upper layer application services, such as TELNET and SMTP, can accept only those packets that follow the application protocol rules. It is very difficult (though theoretically possible) to forge return replies that contain the correct ACK packets. For a higher level of security, one can use application-level gateways such as firewalls.

PACKET FILTER RULES AND FULL ASSOCIATIONS

Figure 5.21 shows a worksheet that can be used for designing packet filter rules. Screening routers, in general, can filter based upon any of the field values in the TCP or IP protocol headers. For most network security policies that can be implemented by screening routers, you need to specify only the TCP flags, IP options, and source and destination address values.

Filter Rule Number	Direction	Action	Source	Source Port	Destination	Dest. Port	Protocol Flags Options	Description
1								
2								
3								
4								
5								
6								
7								
8								

FIGURE 5.21

A worksheet for designing packet rules.

If you examine each row in the worksheet, you will notice that it completely describes the TCP connection. Formally, a complete description of a connection is called a *full association*.

When designing packet filter rules it is helpful to keep in mind the definitions of full association, half association, and endpoints. This helps you better understand the packet filtering rules.

233

A *full association* is illustrated in figure 5.22, which shows that a TCP connection between two hosts can be described by the following information:

❖ Protocol type

❖ Local IP address

❖ Local TCP port number

❖ Remote IP address

❖ Remote TCP port number

Process Addressing

Association **describes a connection in terms of**

- Protocol
- Local address
- Local port number
- Remote address
- Remote port number
- Example: (tcp, 199.21.32.2, 1400, 196.62.132.1, 21)

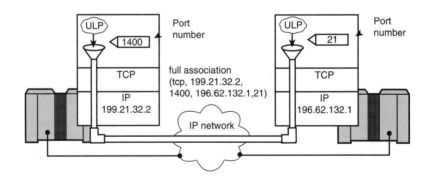

In figure 5.22, the protocol type is TCP, the local IP address is 199.21.32.2, the local TCP port number is 1400, the remote IP address is 196.62.132.1, and the remote TCP port number is port 21. The full association for this circuit is represented as a 5-tuple. In the example in figure 5.22, this 5-tuple is:

(TCP, 199.21.32.2, 1400, 196.62.132.1, 21)

Comparing this 5-tuple with the entries in worksheet 5.21, you can see that each worksheet describes the full association between hosts. The worksheet also contains the following additional information:

❖ Action

❖ TCP and IP options

❖ Order in which the rule should be executed

Each side of the connection can be described by a half association. A *half association* describes only one end of the connection and consists of the following:

❖ Protocol type

❖ IP address

❖ TCP port number

Thus, the two half associations that form the TCP connection of figure 5.22 are the following:

(TCP, 199.21.32.2, 1400)

(TCP, 196.62.132.1, 21)

The *endpoint,* also called the *transport address,* consists of the following:

❖ IP address

❖ TCP port number

The endpoints for the TCP connection in figure 5.22 are the following:

(199.21.32.2, 1400)

(196.62.132.1, 21)

Because each rule in the worksheet of figure 5.21 can have a range of values for any of the values in the fields that describe a full association, a number of different types of TCP circuits can be described by the packet filter rule. This enables a packet filter rule to implement a network security policy by describing a variety of different types of TCP connections.

SUMMARY

This chapter introduced the concepts necessary to understand screening routers and packet filtering. The role of the packet filter was described in reference to the OSI model. You also learned about the typical protocol flags on which routing decisions are made. The next chapter follows this logic and discusses how packet filter rules are implemented and applied.

PACKET FILTERS

THE LAST CHAPTER introduced packet filtering after explaining the information necessary to understand the process. This chapter continues that topic and discusses implementing packet filter rules, protocol-specific issues in packet filtering, and examples of screening router configurations.

To make the screening router configuration examples more practical, these discussions are done in the context of Cisco routers. These examples include defining access lists, using standard access lists, using extended access lists, filtering on incoming/outgoing calls, and IP security options for Cisco routers. You will learn about packet filter placement and filtering on input and output ports. This chapter discusses examples of filtering FTP network traffic and problems in filtering an FTP session.

IMPLEMENTING PACKET FILTER RULES

Once you have designed the packet filter rules and described them in the packet filter rule worksheet (shown in figure 5.21 of the preceding chapter), you have to implement them on the screening router or firewall (if it allows packet filter rules to be specified).

Each type of packet filter device has its own set of rules and syntax on how to program the packet filter rules. Therefore, one must read the packet filter device documentation and learn the peculiarities of the packet filter rules syntax for that device. If you change the vendor of the packet filter device, you will have to learn a different set of syntax rules.

NOTE

One of the goals of this book is to give you practical advice on building Internet firewalls and improving network security. Because of this, the author believes that it is important to show some practical examples of how packet filter rules can be specified. This will be done in relationship to the screening routers from the router vendor Cisco, Inc.

A word or two about the selection of the vendor is perhaps in order. Selection of the Cisco routers in the packet filtering examples is by no means an endorsement of the product. The author would be equally happy discussing another router vendor's product. On the other hand, Cisco dominates the router market and implements many of the packet filter capabilities discussed in this book. The packet filter rules for other vendors' routers are similar in principle to the ones used by Cisco routers, but are syntactically different.

DEFINING ACCESS LISTS

Cisco routers define *access lists* as a sequential collection of permit-and-deny conditions that apply to Internet addresses. These access-list conditions are used to implement the packet filter rules.

When the screening router is programmed with access lists, it tests the packets against the conditions in the access list one by one. The first match determines if the router accepts or rejects the packet. Because the screening router stops testing conditions in the access lists after the first match, the order of the conditions is critical. If no conditions are matched, the packet is rejected.

The Cisco routers have two types of access lists:

- ✤ Standard access lists
- ✤ Extended access lists

The standard access lists have a single address for matching operations, and the extended access lists have two addresses with optional protocol-type information for matching operations. For many practical filtering operations, you need both the standard and extended access lists.

USING STANDARD ACCESS LISTS

The syntax for the standard access lists is as follows:

```
access-list list {permit | deny} address wildcard-mask
no access-list list
```

The *list* is an integer ranging from 1 to 99 and is used to identify one or more permit/deny conditions. The filter rules as defined in figure 5.21 of Chapter 5 are assigned to an access list. It is possible to assign each rule to its own access list, but this is highly inefficient and prone to errors. Each access list is associated with an interface on the router, such as a network interface, or the console. Access list 0 is predefined; it is the default list for all interfaces, and the only restrictions placed on the interface are what the router operating system will support.

The use of the keywords "permit" and "deny" corresponds to the words "allow" and "block" in the packet filter rules discussed earlier. The IP source address in the packet is compared to the *address* value specified in the access-list command. If the keyword "permit" is used, a match causes the packet to be accepted. If the keyword "deny" is used, a match causes the packet to be rejected.

The *address* and the *wildcard-mask* are 32-bit values and are written using the dotted-decimal notation. The *wildcard-mask* should not be confused with subnet masks that are used to subdivide an IP network number assignment. Address bits corresponding to a 1 in the *wildcard-mask* are ignored in the comparison. Address bits corresponding to a 0 in the *wildcard-mask* are used in the comparison. Consider the following example:

```
access-list 1 permit 199.245.180.0  0.0.0.255
access-list 1 permit 132.23.0.0  0.0.255.255
```

In this example, two address/wildcard-mask values are specified, and they both apply to the access-list number 1. The first access-list command permits access from hosts on the class C network 199.245.180.0, and the second access-list command permits access from hosts on the class B network 132.23.0.0.

If the wildcard-mask value is not specified, it is assumed to be 0.0.0.0; that is, all the bits in the address are compared. Thus, the following two access-list commands have an identical effect:

```
access-list 2 permit 132.23.1.3  0.0.0.0
access-list 2 permit 132.23.1.3
```

Both of the previous commands allow packets for the host with IP address 132.23.1.3 only. If the wildcard-mask value is non-zero, it can specify a range of IP addresses. Therefore, this should be done with care.

Perhaps another example of the use of standard access lists will clarify its use. Assume a class A network 67.0.0.0 connected to a screening router that is using a subnet mask of 255.255.0.0. Consider the following access-list commands:

```
access-list 3 permit 67.23.2.5  0.0.0.0
access-list 3 deny 67.23.0.0  0.0.255.255
access-list 3 permit 67.0.0.0  0.255.255.255
```

The first rule of the access list permits traffic for a single host with IP address 67.23.2.5 on subnet 23 of the class A network. The second access list blocks all traffic to subnet 23. Because this follows the rule that permits traffic to host 67.23.2.5, it does not affect traffic sent to that host. The third rule permits traffic sent to the entire class A 63.0.0.0 network. Therefore, the access lists implement the following network policy:

> "Block all traffic to subnet 0.23.0.0 for class A network 67.0.0.0, with the exception of allowing traffic to host 67.23.2.5 on this network. Allow traffic for all other subnets of 67.0.0.0."

You can use the "no access-list list" command to delete the entire access list, but use it with caution. If an incorrect access list is specified, you might be deleting something you want to keep. In fact, because of how access lists are entered into the router, if you want to make a change to a rule in the middle of the list, you must re-enter the entire list. Consequently, if you have to deal with a large set of access lists, it is easier to test them and then save them in a file so that later edits can be performed and then uploaded to the router.

WARNING

> Access lists take effect immediately. If care is not taken, you can lock yourself out of the router, thereby making configuration and operation impossible.

USING EXTENDED ACCESS LISTS

The extended access lists enable you to filter interface traffic based on source and destination IP addresses and protocol information.

The syntax for the extended access lists is as follows:

```
access-list list {permit | deny} protocol source source-mask destination
destination-mask [operator operand]
```

The *list* is an integer ranging from 100 to 199 and is used to identify one or more extended permit/deny conditions. The numbers 100 to 199 are reserved for extended access lists and are outside the range of the numbers 1 to 99 used for standard access lists.

If the keyword "permit" is used, a match with the condition causes the packet to be accepted. This is equivalent to the "allow" rule used in packet filter design rules. If the keyword "deny" is used, a match causes the packet to be rejected. This is equivalent to the "block" rule used in packet filter design rules. The rest of the extended list is not processed after a match occurs.

The *protocol* can represent any of the following values corresponding to the IP, TCP, UDP, and ICMP protocols:

✦ ip

✦ tcp

✦ udp

✦ icmp

Because IP encapsulates TCP, UDP, and ICMP packets, it can be used to match any of these protocols.

The *source* and the *source-mask* are 32-bit values and are written using the dotted-decimal notation. These are used to identify the source IP address. The *source-mask* should not be confused with subnet masks that are used to subdivide an IP network number assignment. Address bits corresponding to a 1 in the *source-mask* are ignored in the comparison. Address bits corresponding to a 0 in the *source-mask* are used in the comparison.

The *destination* and *destination-mask* are used for matching the destination IP address. These also are written using the dotted-decimal notation, and the *destination-mask* is used in the same way as the *source-mask* for *source* addresses.

The *operator* and *operand* are used to compare port numbers, service access points, or contact names. These values are meaningful for the TCP and UDP protocols. For the tcp and udp protocol key values, the *operator* can be any of the following values:

✦ lt (less than)

✦ eq (equal to)

✦ gt (greater than)

✦ neq (not equal to)

The *operand* is either a keyword or the decimal value of the destination port for the specified protocol. It also can consist of a range of values, enabling the access list rule to be effective over a range of ports. The following are examples of the use of access-list commands.

EXAMPLE 1

Suppose network policy requires that you deny incoming SMTP connections from host 132.124.23.55 to your network 199.245.180.0. You can implement this policy by the following extended access list:

```
no access-list  101
access-list 101 any any
access-list 101 deny  tcp 132.124.23.55 0.0.0.0 199.245.180.0 0.0.0.255 eq 25
```

The first command deletes any prior extended access-list 101. The second command accepts any packet from any host. Without this command, the default action would be to deny all packets. The third command denies a TCP packet coming from host 132.124.23.55 to network 199.245.180.0 with a destination port of 25 (SMTP).

EXAMPLE 2

In this example, the internal network is 133.34.0.0.

```
no access-list 101
access-list 101 permit tcp 0.0.0.0 255.255.255.255 133.34.0.0 0.0.255.255 gt
➡1023
access-list 101 permit tcp 0.0.0.0 255.255.255.255 133.34.12.3 0.0.0.0 eq 25
access-list 101 permit icmp 0.0.0.0 255.255.255.255 133.34.0.0 255.255.255.255
interface ethernet 0 out
ip access-group 101
```

The first access-list command deletes any existing access-list 101. The second access-list command permits any incoming TCP connections with destination ports greater than 1023. The second access-list command permits incoming TCP connections to the SMTP port of host 133.34.12.3. The last access-list command permits incoming ICMP messages for error feedback.

Note that the extended access-list command must be used with the access-group interface command that can take an extended access list number (100 to 199) as an argument. The access-group command is used to apply the access-list definitions to the interface. The syntax of the access-group command is as follows:

```
ip access-group list
```

where *list* is a number from 1 to 199 and specifies the access list to be applied to the interface.

EXAMPLE 3

In this example, assume that you have a network (181.12.0.0) connected to the Internet. Your network security policy requires any host on the internal network to be able to form TCP connections to any host on the Internet. However, you do not want Internet hosts to be able to form TCP connections to hosts on the internal network, except to the mail (SMTP) port of a dedicated mail host (181.12.34.12).

The keyword "established" can be used for the TCP protocol to indicate an established connection. A match occurs if the TCP datagram has the ACK or RST bits set, which indicates that the packet belongs to an existing connection.

```
access-list 102 permit tcp 0.0.0.0 255.255.255.255 181.12.0.0 0.0.255.255
➥established
access-list 102 permit tcp 0.0.0.0 255.255.255.255 181.12.34.12 0.0.0.0 eq 25
interface ethernet 0
ip access-group 102
```

FILTERING ON INCOMING AND OUTGOING TERMINAL CALLS

To restrict incoming and outgoing connections between a line into the Cisco router and the addresses in an access list, you can use the access-class line configuration command.

```
access-class list {in ¦ out}
```

The *list* is the number of the access list. Using the value "in" at the end of the command restricts incoming traffic between the Cisco device and the addresses in the access list. Using the value "out" at the end of the command restricts outgoing traffic between the Cisco device and the addresses in the access list. To remove access restrictions for a specified access list, use the following command:

```
no access-class access-list-number {in ¦ out}
```

The following example defines an access list that permits only hosts on network 199.245.75.0 to connect to the virtual terminal ports 1 to 5 on the router:

```
access-list 18 permit 199.245.75.0 0.0.0.255
line 1 5
access-class 18 in
```

The following example blocks connections to networks other than network 156.233.0.0 on terminal lines 1 through 3:

```
access-list 19 permit 156.233.0.0 0.0.255.255
line 1 3
access-class 19 out
```

243

EXAMINING PACKET FILTER PLACEMENT AND ADDRESS SPOOFING

When designing packet filter rules, you must specify whether to perform packet filtering on incoming or outgoing packets. A related issue is determining where to place a packet filter. Packet filter rules should also be written in a manner that prevents address spoofing. These issues are examined in the sections that follow.

PACKET FILTER PLACEMENT

Consider the screening router of figure 6.1. The router can examine packets at any one of its interfaces. In the case of figure 6.1, the router can examine the packet traffic at either the inside port or outside port. Another factor to consider is the fact that packets can be either incoming or outgoing at any of the router's interfaces. The packet filtering, therefore, can be done on either incoming packets, outgoing packets, or both.

FIGURE 6.1

The placement of a packet filter.

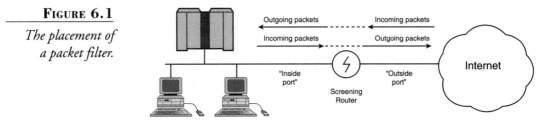

Many router vendors implement packet filtering on outgoing packets for efficiency reasons. For outgoing packets, the filter rules can be applied when the router consults its tables to determine the destination of the packet. If the packet is not routable, or there is no match of the filter rules, the packet is rejected, and an ICMP destination unreachable message is sent.

If routers filter packets at the time the packets are being sent out of a router port, some information is lost. The router does not know which interface the packet arrived on. This can leave your network vulnerable to a type of attack known as *address spoofing*.

Consider the network in figure 6.2. A class B network 135.12.0.0 is connected to the Internet using a screening router. This class B internal network is using subnetting. The subnet mask is 255.255.255.0 for both subnets 10 and 11. An outside TCP/IP host sends a packet claiming to originate from the IP address 135.12.10.201. This packet is received by the screening router in its outside port. If the router was filtering incoming packets, it could quickly catch this pretender packet because it knows that the network 135.12.10.0 is connected to a different (inside) port, and therefore the packet could not have originated on its outside port. However, if the packet filtering is done on outgoing packets, the router does not check to see that this packet that was received on an outside port could not have originated from the internal network.

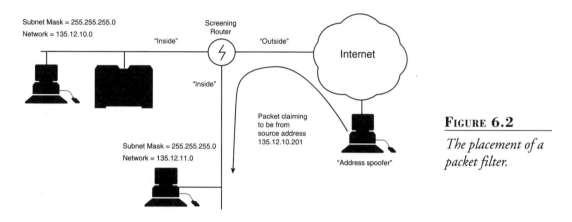

FIGURE 6.2

The placement of a packet filter.

Therefore, filtering on incoming packets can prevent a class of attack called address spoofing. In general, you should perform filtering as quickly as possible.

In figure 6.2, there are two inside ports and one outside port to the router. If all packets that are exchanged with the outside world are through this single access point, then the screening router can effectively act as a discriminating "choke" between the outside world (screening routers are also referred to as *chokes*) and the internal network.

Also in figure 6.2, if you wrote packet filter rules at the inside port for screening traffic between the internal network and the Internet, you would have to write a set of rules at each of the inside ports.

If the screening router has only two ports—one connecting to the external network and the other connecting to the internal network (see fig. 6.1)—then the packet filter rules are symmetric whether they are written for the inside or outside port. This is because the incoming packets on one port will appear, if not rejected by the router's routing table, as outgoing packets on the other port.

FILTERING ON INPUT AND OUTPUT PORTS

Not all routers can filter on both source and destination ports. Many routers filter on the destination port alone. The reason is that because TCP connections require data flow in both directions, the port on which you want to place the filter will appear as a destination port either when data is sent, or when the acknowledgment is received. However, because you are not able to supply source and destination ports simultaneously, this can cause problems.

Consider that your network security policy allows TCP connections for a custom application between an internal and external host. Assume that this custom service uses TCP port number 5555 on both sides. This situation is shown in figure 6.3. You can design the packet filter rule using the worksheet of figure 5.21 in the preceding chapter. This packet filter design table is shown in figure 6.4.

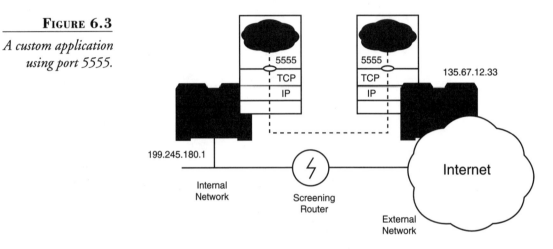

FIGURE 6.3

A custom application using port 5555.

FIGURE 6.4

The packet filter rule design for custom application when source and destination ports can be specified.

Filter Rule Number	Action	Source	Source Port	Destination	Dest. Port	Protocol Flags Options	Description
1	allow	199.245.180.1	5555	135.67.12.33	5555	TCP	Allow TCP session at port 5555 on specified hosts
2							
3							

The table in figure 6.4 shows that only one packet filter rule is needed. However, if the screening router permits only the destination port to be specified, the single filter rule in the table in figure 6.4 has to be written as two rules as shown in figure 6.5.

If you examine figure 6.6, you can see that although the new rules encompass the rule specified in figure 6.5, they are a lot more permissive. The new rules allow a set of full associations that includes the single full association specified in figure 6.4. This is because the rules allow the following types of connections:

1. Connection from any of the internal hosts' ports to port 5555 on the external host

2. Connection from *any port on the external host* to port 5555 on the internal host

Filter Rule Number	Action	Source	Source Port	Destination	Dest. Port	Protocol Flags Options	Description
1	allow	199.245.180.1	*	135.67.12.33	5555	TCP	Allow TCP session to external host port 5555 from internal hosts
2	allow	135.67.12.33	*	199.245.180.1	5555	TCP	Allow TCP session to internal host port 5555 from external hosts
3							

FIGURE 6.5

The packet filter rule design for custom application when only destination port can be specified.

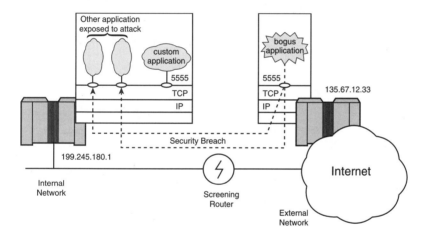

FIGURE 6.6

A bogus program invading an internal machine as a consequence of rules specified in figure 6.5.

Rule 1 in figure 6.5 is probably not very damaging because you usually can trust an internal host. Rule 2 in figure 6.5, however, can be a breach in network security. Consider the situation in figure 6.6, where a bogus program on the host can connect to any port on the internal host. This type of connection was not intended in the network security policy but is allowed from rule 2 of figure 6.6.

This is one example where it is not possible to achieve 100-percent security. If all of the security checks pass, then there is no way of knowing that the program is bogus. Consequently, the security policy and the router did their jobs. The end result, however, is that the programmer who wrote the program knew how to circumvent the policy and make it work to his or her advantage.

Therefore, to write packet filter rules effectively, screening routers should allow both source and destination ports to be specified in a single matched rule.

EXAMINING PROTOCOL-SPECIFIC ISSUES IN PACKET FILTERING

When you design packet filter rules, you should understand the behavior of the application service that you are trying to filter. Some of the application services, such as FTP, require a call-back mechanism, in which an external host might need to initiate a connection to the internal host on a port that is not known at the time of specifying the packet filter rules.

The X11 protocol used in Unix X-Windows applications also requires an "incoming" call to an internal host from an external host. The internal hosts should be protected from these types of incoming calls. The sections that follow discuss the application services in relationship to packet filtering.

FILTERING FTP NETWORK TRAFFIC

The following section discusses the normal behavior of FTP and points out the problem this behavior poses for screening routers. Solutions to solve packet filtering for FTP sessions are discussed.

UNDERSTANDING THE *FTP* PROTOCOL

Figure 6.7 shows the FTP model. The FTP client makes a connection to the FTP server on the well-known Port 21 that is assigned to the FTP server. This connection is called the *control* connection. The control connection is used for sending FTP commands and receiving replies from the FTP server.

When a file is retrieved or stored on the FTP server, a separate data connection is established. This data connection is established on well-known Port 20 on the FTP server. The data connection exists only for the duration of the data transfer. It is destroyed at the end of the data transfer.

The different phases of an FTP transfer are discussed next for a live FTP session captured using a protocol analyzer. In this file transfer, the FTP client and FTP server have the following IP addresses and were connected on an Ethernet LAN:

FTP client: 199.245.180.1

FTP server: 199.245.180.15

FIGURE 6.7

The FTP model (graphic courtesy of Learning Tree International).

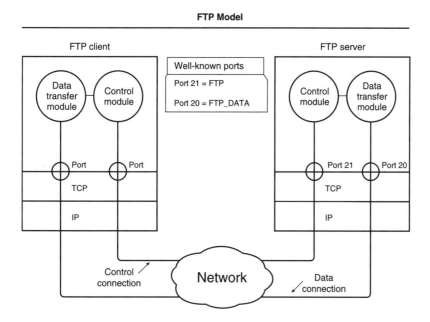

FTP Model

- **Control connection**
  - Created when connection to FTP server is established
  - Used for FTP commands/replies only

- **Data transfer connection**
  - Created on demand for each data transfer
  - Destroyed on end of each data transfer

Figures 6.8 and 6.9 show that the FTP session had 43 packets. Figure 6.8 shows packets 1 through 27, and figure 6.9 shows packets 17 through 43. All references to packet numbers in the discussion that follows is to the first column in these figures.

Packets 1-3:

> Packet 1 is the FTP client (199.245.180.1) doing an ARP broadcast announcing its hardware address and IP address association.

> Packet 2 is the FTP client doing an ARP request broadcast to discover the FTP server's hardware address.

> Packet 3 is the ARP reply from the FTP server. This ARP reply contains the server's hardware address (shown as 0000C0DD145C in figure 6.8).

Packets 4-6:

> Packet 4 is the FTP client making an FTP control connection to the FTP server. The FTP client local-port number is 15676 and the FTP server port number is 21.

249

FIGURE 6.8

The FTP session packets (screen 1 of 2).

```
━━━━━━━━━━━━━ LANalyzer for Windows - [Capture Buffer] ━━━━━━━▼━┫
▢  File  Monitor  Alarms  Capture  Decode  Window  Help                   ┃
 No.   │ Source      │ Destination │ Layer │ Summary
    1  │ 6801142CA201│ Broadcast   │ arp   │ Req by 199.245.180.1 for 199.245.180
    2  │ 6801142CA201│ Broadcast   │ arp   │ Req by 199.245.180.1 for 199.245.180
    3  │ 0000C0DD145C│ 6801142CA201│ arp   │ Reply 199.245.180.15=0000C0DD145C
    4  │ 6801142CA201│ 0000C0DD145C│ tcp   │ Port:15676 ----> FTP SYN
    5  │ 0000C0DD145C│ 6801142CA201│ tcp   │ Port:FTP ----> 15676 ACK SYN
    6  │ 6801142CA201│ 0000C0DD145C│ tcp   │ Port:15676 ----> FTP ACK
    7  │ 0000C0DD145C│ 6801142CA201│ ftp   │ Reply:(Service ready for new user.)
    8  │ 6801142CA201│ 0000C0DD145C│ tcp   │ Port:15676 ----> FTP ACK
    9  │ 6801142CA201│ 0000C0DD145C│ ftp   │ Command=USER(User Name)
   10  │ 0000C0DD145C│ 6801142CA201│ ftp   │ Reply:(User name okay, need password
   11  │ 0000C0DD145C│ 6801142CA201│ tcp   │ Port:15676 ----> FTP ACK PUSH
   12  │ 6801142CA201│ 0000C0DD145C│ ftp   │ Command=PASS(Password)
   13  │ 0000C0DD145C│ 6801142CA201│ tcp   │ Port:FTP ----> 15676 ACK
   14  │ 0000C0DD145C│ 6801142CA201│ tcp   │ Port:15676 ----> FTP ACK PUSH
   15  │ 0000C0DD145C│ 6801142CA201│ ftp   │ Reply:(User logged in, proceed.)
   16  │ 6801142CA201│ 0000C0DD145C│ ftp   │ Port:15676 ----> FTP ACK PUSH
   17  │ 6801142CA201│ 0000C0DD145C│ ftp   │ Command=PORT(Data Port)
   18  │ 0000C0DD145C│ 6801142CA201│ ftp   │ Reply:(Command okay.)
   19  │ 6801142CA201│ 0000C0DD145C│ ftp   │ Command=RETR(Retrieve File)
   20  │ 0000C0DD145C│ 6801142CA201│ tcp   │ Port:FTP-DATA ----> 55814 SYN
   21  │ 6801142CA201│ 0000C0DD145C│ tcp   │ Port:55814 ----> FTP-DATA ACK SYN
   22  │ 0000C0DD145C│ 6801142CA201│ tcp   │ Port:FTP-DATA ----> 55814 ACK
   23  │ 0000C0DD145C│ 6801142CA201│ ftp   │ Reply:(File status okay; about to op
   24  │ 6801142CA201│ 0000C0DD145C│ tcp   │ Port:15676 ----> FTP ACK PUSH
   25  │ 0000C0DD145C│ 6801142CA201│ tcp   │ Port:FTP-DATA ----> 55814 ACK
   26  │ 0000C0DD145C│ 6801142CA201│ ftp   │ Reply:(Closing data connection; Requ
   27  │ 6801142CA201│ 0000C0DD145C│ tcp   │ Port:15676 ----> FTP ACK PUSH
                                    Packet:  44    Unfiltered:  44
```

FIGURE 6.9

The FTP session packets (screen 2 of 2).

```
━━━━━━━━━━━━━ LANalyzer for Windows - [Capture Buffer] ━━━━━━━▼━┫
▢  File  Monitor  Alarms  Capture  Decode  Window  Help                   ┃
 No.   │ Source      │ Destination │ Layer │ Summary
   17  │ 6801142CA201│ 0000C0DD145C│ ftp   │ Command=PORT(Data Port)
   18  │ 0000C0DD145C│ 6801142CA201│ ftp   │ Reply:(Command okay.)
   19  │ 6801142CA201│ 0000C0DD145C│ ftp   │ Command=RETR(Retrieve File)
   20  │ 0000C0DD145C│ 6801142CA201│ tcp   │ Port:FTP-DATA ----> 55814 SYN
   21  │ 6801142CA201│ 0000C0DD145C│ tcp   │ Port:55814 ----> FTP-DATA ACK SYN
   22  │ 0000C0DD145C│ 6801142CA201│ tcp   │ Port:FTP-DATA ----> 55814 ACK
   23  │ 0000C0DD145C│ 6801142CA201│ ftp   │ Reply:(File status okay; about to op
   24  │ 6801142CA201│ 0000C0DD145C│ tcp   │ Port:15676 ----> FTP ACK PUSH
   25  │ 0000C0DD145C│ 6801142CA201│ tcp   │ Port:FTP-DATA ----> 55814 ACK
   26  │ 0000C0DD145C│ 6801142CA201│ ftp   │ Reply:(Closing data connection; Requ
   27  │ 6801142CA201│ 0000C0DD145C│ tcp   │ Port:15676 ----> FTP ACK PUSH
   28  │ 6801142CA201│ 0000C0DD145C│ tcp   │ Port:55814 ----> FTP-DATA ACK
   29  │ 0000C0DD145C│ 6801142CA201│ tcp   │ Port:FTP-DATA ----> 55814 ACK
   30  │ 6801142CA201│ 0000C0DD145C│ tcp   │ Port:55814 ----> FTP-DATA ACK
   31  │ 0000C0DD145C│ 6801142CA201│ tcp   │ Port:FTP-DATA ----> 55814 ACK
   32  │ 6801142CA201│ 0000C0DD145C│ tcp   │ Port:55814 ----> FTP-DATA ACK
   33  │ 0000C0DD145C│ 6801142CA201│ tcp   │ Port:FTP-DATA ----> 55814 ACK PUSH FI
   34  │ 6801142CA201│ 0000C0DD145C│ tcp   │ Port:55814 ----> FTP-DATA ACK FIN
   35  │ 0000C0DD145C│ 6801142CA201│ tcp   │ Port:FTP-DATA ----> 55814 ACK
   36  │ 6801142CA201│ 0000C0DD145C│ ftp   │ Command=QUIT(Logout)
   37  │ 0000C0DD145C│ 6801142CA201│ ftp   │ Reply:(Service closing control conne
   38  │ 0000C0DD145C│ 6801142CA201│ tcp   │ Port:FTP ----> 15676 ACK FIN
   39  │ 6801142CA201│ 0000C0DD145C│ tcp   │ Port:15676 ----> FTP ACK FIN
   40  │ 6801142CA201│ 0000C0DD145C│ tcp   │ Port:15676 ----> FTP ACK PUSH
   41  │ 0000C0DD145C│ 6801142CA201│ tcp   │ Port:FTP ----> 15676 ACK FIN
   42  │ 0000C0DD145C│ 6801142CA201│ tcp   │ Port:FTP ----> 15676 ACK FIN
   43  │ 6801142CA201│ 0000C0DD145C│ tcp   │ Port:15676 ----> FTP ACK PUSH
                                    Packet:  44    Unfiltered:  44
```

The protocol analyzer has translated this port number to the symbolic representation of "21" to "FTP" (see fig. 6.10). You can decode the hexadecimal dump of the packet, showing that the destination port has a value of 15(hex) or 21 decimal.

Packets 4 and 5 are useful when setting up packet filters. If your router supports creating filters to detect an open FTP connection request (Cisco does not), you can filter for the following conditions:

Destination port = 21.

TCP SYN flag is set.

TCP ACK flag is set in open-connection acknowledgment.

Packet 6 completes the three-way handshake. It is the acknowledgment packet that is sent in response to the open-connection acknowledgment packet.

FIGURE 6.10

An FTP Open Control connection packet.

```
  ┌─                  LANalyzer for Windows - [Capture Buffer]           ▼ ▲
  ─  File   Monitor   Alarms   Capture   Decode   Window   Help              ▲
     ip: ======================= Internet Protocol =======================  ▲
         Station:199.245.180.1 ----->199.245.180.15
         Protocol: TCP
         Version: 4
         Header Length (32 bit words): 5
         Precedence: Routine
                 Normal Delay, Normal Throughput, Normal Reliability
         Total length: 44
         Identification:         1
         Fragmentation allowed, Last fragment
         Fragment Offset: 0
         Time to Live: 100 seconds
         Checksum: 0x5ECF(Valid)
    tcp: ================= Transmission Control Protocol =================
         Source Port: 15676
         Destination Port: FTP
         Sequence Number: 64208896
         Acknowledgement Number: 0
         Data Offset (32-bit words): 6
         Window: 512
         Control Bits: Synchronize Sequence Numbers (SYN)
         Checksum: 0xA0B9(Valid)
         Urgent Pointer: 0
         Option:MAXIMUM SEGMENT SIZE                                         ▼
  ─  0: 00 00 C0 DD 14 5C 68 01 14 2C A2 01 08 00 45 00   .....\h..,....E.
    10: 00 2C 00 01 00 00 64 06 5E CF C7 F5 B4 01 C7 F5   .,....d.^.......
    20: B4 0F 3D 3C 00 15 03 D3 C0 00 00 00 00 00 60 02   ..=<.........`.
    30: 02 00 A0 B9 00 00 02 04 02 00 0D 0A               ............

                          Packet:  4    Unfiltered:  44
```

Packets 7-8:

Packet 7 is the reply from the FTP server. The FTP commands are sent using a four-character ASCII text command followed by parameters. The FTP reply is a three-digit decimal status code followed by an optional text message.

The FTP command and FTP reply syntax are shown in figure 6.11. This figure also summarizes the FTP session activities that have taken place so far. Figure 6.12 shows packet number 7 that contains the FTP reply code 220 that means "Service ready for new user." The text message that is sent for displaying at the FTP client console is ucs FTP server (Version 5.60) ready.

Packet 8 sent from the FTP client to the server acknowledges the server reply.

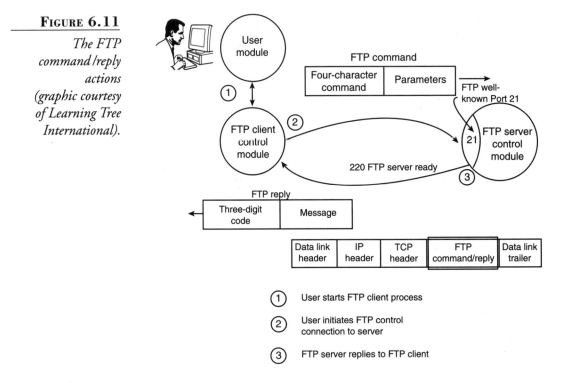

FIGURE 6.11

The FTP command/reply actions (graphic courtesy of Learning Tree International).

Packets 9-11:

Packet 9 is an FTP command USER sent from the FTP client to the FTP server. Figure 6.13 shows the protocol decode for packet 9. This decode shows that the user requesting the FTP session is user1.

Packet 10 is the FTP server's reply to the FTP client's USER command. Figure 6.14 shows the protocol decode for packet 10. This decode shows that the reply code sent back is 331, which means that the user name is fine, but a password is needed.

Packet 11 sent from the FTP client to the server acknowledges the server's response.

```
┌─────────────────────────────────────────────────────────────────────────────┐
│─                    LANalyzer for Windows - [Capture Buffer]            ▼ ▲│
│  File  Monitor  Alarms  Capture  Decode  Window  Help                      ▲│
│├───────────────────────────────────────────────────────────────────────────┤│
│         Total length: 82                                                  ▲ │
│         Identification:  8195                                               │
│         Fragmentation allowed, Last fragment                               │
│         Fragment Offset: 0                                                  │
│         Time to Live: 60  seconds                                          │
│         Checksum: 0x6697(Valid)                                            │
│   tcp: ================= Transmission Control Protocol =================    │
│         Source Port: FTP                                                    │
│         Destination Port: 15676                                            │
│         Sequence Number: 24602114                                          │
│         Acknowledgement Number: 64208897                                    │
│         Data Offset (32-bit words): 5                                       │
│         Window: 4096                                                        │
│         Control Bits: Acknowledgement Field is Valid (ACK)                  │
│                 Push Function Requested (PSH)                               │
│         Checksum: 0x635C(Valid)                                            │
│         Urgent Pointer: 0                                                   │
│   ftp: ===================== File Transfer Protocol =====================   │
│         Reply: 220 (Service ready for new user.)                           │
│         Text:  ucs FTP server (Version 5.60) ready.                        │
│  Data:                                                                      │
│     0: 0D 0A                                    |..                      ▼ │
│├───────────────────────────────────────────────────────────────────────────┤│
│     0: 68 01 14 2C A2 01 00 00 C0 DD 14 5C 08 00 45 10  h.........\...E.    │
│    10: 00 52 20 03 00 00 3C 06 66 97 C7 F5 B4 0F C7 F5  .R ...<.f......     │
│    20: B4 01 00 15 3D 3C 01 77 66 02 03 D3 C0 01 50 18  ....=<.wf.....P.    │
│    30: 10 00 63 5C 00 00 32 32 30 20 75 63 73 20 46 54  ..c\..220 ucs FT   │
│    40: 50 20 73 65 72 76 65 72 20 28 56 65 72 73 69 6F  P server (Versio   │
│    50: 6E 20 35 2E 36 30 29 20 72 65 61 64 79 2E 0D 0A  n 5.60) ready...   │
│├───────────────────────────────────────────────────────────────────────────┤│
│                        │ Packet:  7 │ Unfiltered:  44 │                    │
└─────────────────────────────────────────────────────────────────────────────┘
```

FIGURE 6.12

An FTP server reply-ready packet.

```
┌─────────────────────────────────────────────────────────────────────────────┐
│─                    LANalyzer for Windows - [Capture Buffer]            ▼ ▲│
│  File  Monitor  Alarms  Capture  Decode  Window  Help                      ▲│
│├───────────────────────────────────────────────────────────────────────────┤│
│ ether: =================== Ethernet Datalink Layer ==================     ▲ │
│         Station: 68-01-14-2C-A2-01 ----> 00-00-C0-DD-14-5C                  │
│         Type: 0x0800 (IP)                                                   │
│    ip: ===================== Internet Protocol =====================       │
│         Station:199.245.180.1 ---->199.245.180.15                          │
│         Protocol: TCP                                                       │
│         Version: 4                                                          │
│         Header Length (32 bit words): 5                                     │
│         Precedence: Routine                                                 │
│                 Normal Delay, Normal Throughput, Normal Reliability         │
│         Total length: 52                                                    │
│         Identification:    4                                                │
│         Fragmentation allowed, Last fragment                                │
│         Fragment Offset: 0                                                  │
│         Time to Live: 100 seconds                                           │
│         Checksum: 0x5EC4(Valid)                                             │
│   tcp: ================= Transmission Control Protocol =================    │
│         Source Port: 15676                                                  │
│         Destination Port: FTP                                               │
│         Sequence Number: 64208897                                           │
│         Acknowledgement Number: 24602156                                    │
│         Data Offset (32-bit words): 5                                       │
│         Window: 512                                                         │
│         Control Bits: Acknowledgement Field is Valid (ACK)                  │
│                 Push Function Requested (PSH)                               │
│         Checksum: 0x9F3F(ERROR:Correct checksum=0xBF3F)                     │
│         Urgent Pointer: 0                                                   │
│   ftp: ===================== File Transfer Protocol =====================   │
│         Command: USER(User Name)                                            │
│         User Name: user1                                                  ▼ │
│├───────────────────────────────────────────────────────────────────────────┤│
│                        │ Packet:  9 │ Unfiltered:  44 │                    │
└─────────────────────────────────────────────────────────────────────────────┘
```

FIGURE 6.13

The FTP USER command.

253

FIGURE 6.14

*The FTP server's
response to the
USER command.*

```
─                     LANalyzer for Windows - [Capture Buffer]          ▼ ▲
═ File   Monitor   Alarms   Capture   Decode   Window   Help                ▲
ether: =================== Ethernet Datalink Layer ===================       ▲
        Station: 00-00-C0-DD-14-5C -----> 68-01-14-2C-A2-01
        Type: 0x0800 (IP)
  ip:   ====================== Internet Protocol ======================
        Station:199.245.180.15 ---->199.245.180.1
        Protocol: TCP
        Version: 4
        Header Length (32 bit words): 5
        Precedence: Routine
                Low Delay, Normal Throughput, Normal Reliability
        Total length: 74
        Identification:  8196
        Fragmentation allowed, Last fragment
        Fragment Offset: 0
        Time to Live: 60  seconds
        Checksum: 0x669E(Valid)
  tcp:  ================= Transmission Control Protocol =================
        Source Port: FTP
        Destination Port: 15676
        Sequence Number: 24602156
        Acknowledgement Number: 64208909
        Data Offset (32-bit words): 5
        Window: 4096
        Control Bits: Acknowledgement Field is Valid (ACK)
                Push Function Requested (PSH)
        Checksum: 0x695C(Valid)
        Urgent Pointer: 0
  ftp:  ====================== File Transfer Protocol ==================
        Reply: 331 (User name okay, need password.)
        Text:  Password required for user1.                              ▼

                          ┌──────────┬─────────────┐
                          │ Packet: 10 │ Unfiltered: 44 │
                          └──────────┴─────────────┘
```

Packets 12-14:

Packet 12 is an FTP command PASS sent from the FTP client to the FTP server.
Figure 6.15 shows the protocol decode for packet 12. This decode shows that the
user's password is user1pw.

Please note that the FTP command sends the password in the clear. Any protocol
analyzer, such as the one used in this study, can be used to discover the FTP
password. For this reason, a stronger authentication mechanism is needed if you
want to access an FTP server using your user account over an untrusted network.

Packet 13 is the server's acknowledgment that it received the user password command.

Packet 14, sent from the client to the server, acknowledges this acknowledgment and
sets the PSH flag, indicating that for the time being, there are no commands from
the FTP client. Figure 6.16 summarizes the actions performed by packets 7 to 14.

Packets 15-16:

Packet 15 is the FTP server's reply to the user password. Figure 6.17 shows the
protocol decode for packet 15. This decode shows that the user has logged in
successfully.

Packet 16 sent from the FTP client to the server acknowledges the server's response.

FIGURE 6.15

The FTP PASS command.

```
LANalyzer for Windows - [Capture Buffer]
File   Monitor   Alarms   Capture   Decode   Window   Help
ether: ==================== Ethernet Datalink Layer ====================
       Station: 68-01-14-2C-A2-01 ----> 00-00-C0-DD-14-5C
       Type: 0x0800 (IP)
   ip: ====================== Internet Protocol ======================
       Station:199.245.180.1 ---->199.245.180.15
       Protocol: TCP
       Version: 4
       Header Length (32 bit words): 5
       Precedence: Routine
               Normal Delay, Normal Throughput, Normal Reliability
       Total length: 54
       Identification:      6
       Fragmentation allowed, Last fragment
       Fragment Offset: 0
       Time to Live: 100 seconds
       Checksum: 0x5EC0(Valid)
  tcp: ================= Transmission Control Protocol =================
       Source Port: 15676
       Destination Port: FTP
       Sequence Number: 64208909
       Acknowledgement Number: 24602190
       Data Offset (32-bit words): 5
       Window: 512
       Control Bits: Acknowledgement Field is Valid (ACK)
               Push Function Requested (PSH)
       Checksum: 0x25A9(ERROR:Correct checksum=0x45A9)
       Urgent Pointer: 0
  ftp: ==================== File Transfer Protocol ====================
       Command: PASS(Password)
       Password: user1pw

                          Packet: 12    Unfiltered: 44
```

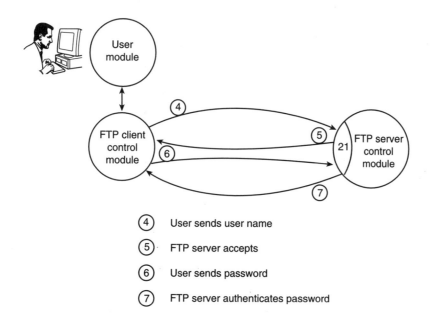

FIGURE 6.16

The FTP client user name authentication (Graphic Courtesy of Learning Tree International).

④ User sends user name

⑤ FTP server accepts

⑥ User sends password

⑦ FTP server authenticates password

At this point, the user has entered the following command from the FTP client console in order to retrieve the file "netstart:"

```
get netstart
```

255

```
                                LANalyzer for Windows - [Capture Buffer]
  File   Monitor   Alarms   Capture   Decode   Window   Help
ether: ================= Ethernet Datalink Layer ====================
       Station: 00-00-C0-DD-14-5C -----> 68-01-14-2C-A2-01
       Type: 0x0800 (IP)
    ip: ===================== Internet Protocol ======================
       Station:199.245.180.15 ---->199.245.180.1
       Protocol: TCP
       Version: 4
       Header Length (32 bit words): 5
       Precedence: Routine
              Low Delay, Normal Throughput, Normal Reliability
       Total length: 67
       Identification:  8198
       Fragmentation allowed, Last fragment
       Fragment Offset: 0
       Time to Live: 60  seconds
       Checksum: 0x66A3(Valid)
   tcp: ================= Transmission Control Protocol ==============
       Source Port: FTP
       Destination Port: 15676
       Sequence Number: 24602190
       Acknowledgement Number: 64208923
       Data Offset (32-bit words): 5
       Window: 4096
       Control Bits: Acknowledgement Field is Valid (ACK)
                     Push Function Requested (PSH)
       Checksum: 0x1E96(Valid)
       Urgent Pointer: 0
   ftp: ===================== File Transfer Protocol =================
       Reply: 230 (User logged in, proceed.)
       Text:  User user1 logged in.

                               Packet:  15    Unfiltered:  44
```

As mentioned before, files are retrieved and stored using a separate data connection originating from the server's FTP port 20. However, the FTP server does not know the FTP client's local port to connect to. The FTP protocol solves this problem by having the FTP client send the local end-point address (IP address and port number) to the FTP server. The FTP server then knows the destination port number to open the connection. The FTP client sends its local port number using the PORT command.

Packets 17-18:

Packet 17 is the FTP command PORT sent by the FTP client to the server. Table 6.1 shows the FTP commands and their meanings. This table contains the definition of the PORT command. The last two numbers, p1 and p2, are the dotted decimal representation of the 16-bit port number. The FTP client selects a dynamic value (greater than 1024) that can be used by the server to make a data connection to the FTP client. Suppose the FTP selects the port number 55814, which is not in use. The PORT command sent by the FTP client with IP address 199.245.180.1 will be

PORT 199,245,180,1,218,6

The first four numbers represent the FTP client's IP address 199.245.180.1. The numbers 218 and 6 are the most significant and least significant bytes of the port number. If you were to convert this to a decimal port number, you could do so using the following calculations:

218*256 + 6

= 55808 + 6

= 55814

This value equals the port number that was selected by the FTP client.

Packet 18, sent from the FTP server to the client, acknowledges the client's PORT command.

TABLE 6.1
FTP Commands

FTP Command	Description
USER	Used to identify user for authentication.
PASS	Specifies user's password.
PORT	Specifies FTP client's Internet address and TCP port address as a series of 8-bit decimal numbers: PORT i1,i2,i3,i4,p1,p2. p1 and p2 represent the most significant and least significant bytes of the 16-bit port number.
TYPE	Data type used in file transfer: A = ASCII, E = EBCDIC, I = IMAGE, L = Logical byte size.
STRU	File structure of file to be transferred. F = Unstructured, R = Record, P = Page.
MODE	Transfer mode. S = Stream, B = Block, C = Compressed.
RETR	Gets a file from FTP server.
STOR	Stores a file on the FTP server.
QUIT	Logs user out.
PASV	Specifies that receiver should do a passive TCP open.
NOOP	No operation.

Packet 19:

Packet 19, sent from the FTP client to the FTP server, contains the RETR (Retrieve) command used to download this file. Figure 6.18 shows a protocol decode of this packet. This shows that the name of the file that is retrieved is netstart.

The events described by packets 17-19 are summarized in figure 6.19.

FIGURE 6.18

The FTP RETR command.

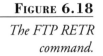

```
                            LANalyzer for Windows
File   Monitor   Alarms   Capture   Decode   Window   Help
                            C:\LZFW\FTP.TR1
  ip: ===================== Internet Protocol =====================
      Station:199.245.180.1 ---->199.245.180.15
      Protocol: TCP
      Version: 4
      Header Length (32 bit words): 5
      Precedence: Routine
               Normal Delay, Normal Throughput, Normal Reliability
      Total length: 55
      Identification:      10
      Fragmentation allowed, Last fragment
      Fragment Offset: 0
      Time to Live: 100 seconds
      Checksum: 0x5EBB(Valid)
 tcp: ================= Transmission Control Protocol =================
      Source Port: 15676
      Destination Port: FTP
      Sequence Number: 64208949
      Acknowledgement Number: 24602247
      Data Offset (32-bit words): 5
      Window: 512
      Control Bits: Acknowledgement Field is Valid (ACK)
                    Push Function Requested (PSH)
      Checksum: 0xCCFA(ERROR:Correct checksum=0xECFA)
      Urgent Pointer: 0
 ftp: ===================== File Transfer Protocol =====================
      Command: RETR(Retrieve File)
      Pathname:netstart

                              Packet:  19   Unfiltered:  44
```

FIGURE 6.19

The use of the PORT and RETR commands (graphic courtesy of Learning Tree International).

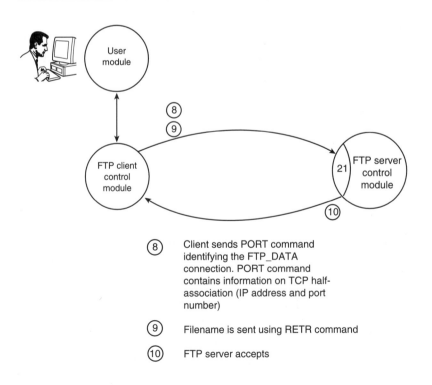

⑧ Client sends PORT command identifying the FTP_DATA connection. PORT command contains information on TCP half-association (IP address and port number)

⑨ Filename is sent using RETR command

⑩ FTP server accepts

Packets 20-22:

In reply to the RETR command, the FTP server opens a data connection to the FTP client.

Packet 20 shows an incoming TCP connection request from the FTP server to the FTP client. The destination port in the connection request is the one that was specified by the FTP client in the PORT command. Figure 6.20 shows a protocol decode of packet 20. This shows that the source port is port number FTP_DATA (port 20), and the destination port is 55814, specified in the PORT command.

Packets 21 and 22 complete the open connection handshake.

Packets 20 to 22 are very important from a packet filtering standpoint. These packets represent an incoming call from the FTP server. If the FTP server resides on an untrusted network, you must place a filter to allow this connection. The problem is that one does not know beforehand what the port number used by the client is going to be. Because of this, it is difficult to set a proper filter for the incoming call.

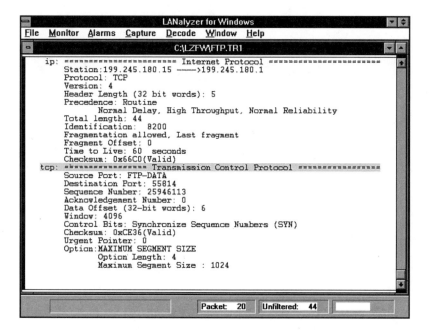

FIGURE 6.20

An FTP data connection from FTP server to FTP client.

Packets 23-24:

In packet 23, the FTP server replies with a status on the file to be retrieved. Figure 6.21 shows a protocol decode of packet 23.

Packet 24 is sent from the FTP client to the FTP server to acknowledge the server's status of file reply. Figure 6.22 summarizes the events in packets 20-24.

FIGURE 6.21

*The status of
file reply sent
by FTP server.*

```
┌──────────────────────────────────────────────────────────────────────┐
│ ─                          LANalyzer for Windows                   ▼ ▲ │
│ File   Monitor   Alarms   Capture   Decode   Window   Help             │
│ ┌──────────────────────────────────────────────────────────────── ▼ ▲ │
│ │ ─                         C:\LZFW\FTP.TR1                        │   │
│ │    Header Length (32 bit words): 5                             ↑ │   │
│ │    Precedence: Routine                                          │   │
│ │         Low Delay, Normal Throughput, Normal Reliability        │   │
│ │    Total length: 107                                            │   │
│ │    Identification:  8202                                        │   │
│ │    Fragmentation allowed, Last fragment                         │   │
│ │    Fragment Offset: 0                                           │   │
│ │    Time to Live: 60  seconds                                    │   │
│ │    Checksum: 0x6677(Valid)                                      │   │
│ │ tcp: ================= Transmission Control Protocol =========== │   │
│ │    Source Port: FTP                                             │   │
│ │    Destination Port: 15676                                      │   │
│ │    Sequence Number: 24602247                                    │   │
│ │    Acknowledgement Number: 64208964                             │   │
│ │    Data Offset (32-bit words): 5                                │   │
│ │    Window: 4096                                                 │   │
│ │    Control Bits: Acknowledgement Field is Valid (ACK)           │   │
│ │               Push Function Requested (PSH)                     │   │
│ │    Checksum: 0x4060(Valid)                                      │   │
│ │    Urgent Pointer: 0                                            │   │
│ │ ftp: ==================== File Transfer Protocol =============== │   │
│ │    Reply: 150 (File status okay; about to open data connection.)│   │
│ │    Text:  Opening ASCII mode data connection for netstart (1967 bytes).│
│ │ Data:                                                           │   │
│ │    0: 0D 0A                                     |..             │   │
│ │ ◄ ───                                                         ► │   │
│ ├────────────────────────────┬──────────────┬──────────────────┤   │
│ │                            │ Packet:  23  │ Unfiltered:  44  │   │
└──────────────────────────────────────────────────────────────────────┘
```

Packet 25:

Packet 25 commences the transfer of the data in the file to be retrieved. Figure 6.23 shows the data packet containing the contents of the file.

Packet 26:

The FTP server has sent the entire file as a TCP message segment for transmission to the TCP layer. The FTP server then server-announces its intention to break the data connection when file transfer is completed. Figure 6.24 shows a reply code of 226, which indicates that the data connection will close at end of file transfer.

Packets 27-32:

Data is transferred and acknowledged. This phase of the FTP session is illustrated by figure 6.25.

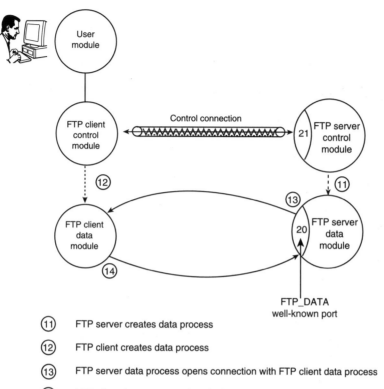

FIGURE 6.22

The FTP data connection creation (graphic courtesy of Learning Tree International).

(11)   FTP server creates data process

(12)   FTP client creates data process

(13)   FTP server data process opens connection with FTP client data process

(14)   FTP client data process acknowledges connection

Packet 33:

Packet 33 is the last data packet. The FIN flag is set in this packet indicating that the FTP server wants to close the connection (see fig. 6.26).

Packets 34-35:

TCP uses a graceful close mechanism, in which both sides have to agree to break the connection. Packet 34, sent from the FTP client to the FTP server with the FIN flag set, indicates that the FTP client agrees to close the connection (see fig. 6.27). Figure 6.28 summarizes the events described by packets 33 to 35.

Packet 35 is sent from the FTP server to the FTP client to acknowledge the client's agreement in the previous message to break the data connection.

FIGURE 6.23

An FTP data transfer packet.

```
┌─────────────────── LANalyzer for Windows - [C:\LZFW\FTP.TR1] ──────────▼│▲│
│ □  File  Monitor  Alarms  Capture  Decode  Window  Help                    ▲│
│       ip: ===================== Internet Protocol =====================    ▲│
│           Station:199.245.180.15 ---->199.245.180.1                          │
│           Protocol: TCP                                                       │
│           Version: 4                                                         │
│           Header Length (32 bit words): 5                                    │
│           Precedence: Routine                                                │
│                   Normal Delay, High Throughput, Normal Reliability          │
│           Total length: 552                                                  │
│           Identification:  8203                                              │
│           Fragmentation allowed, Last fragment                               │
│           Fragment Offset: 0                                                 │
│           Time to Live: 60  seconds                                          │
│           Checksum: 0x64C1(Valid)                                            │
│      tcp: ================= Transmission Control Protocol =================  │
│           Source Port: FTP-DATA                                              │
│           Destination Port: 55814   .                                        │
│           Sequence Number: 25946114                                          │
│           Acknowledgement Number: 64954369                                   │
│           Data Offset (32-bit words): 5                                      │
│           Window: 4096                                                       │
│           Control Bits: Acknowledgement Field is Valid (ACK)                 │
│           Checksum: 0xB74F(Valid)                                            │
│           Urgent Pointer: 0                                                  │
│    Data:                                                                     │
│       0: 23 21 2F 62 69 6E 2F 73 68 20 2D 0D 0A 23 0D 0A |#!/bin/sh -..#..   │
│      10: 23 09 40 28 23 29 6E 65 74 73 74 61 72 74 09 35 |#.@(#)netstart.5   │
│      20: 2E 39 20 28 42 65 72 6B 65 6C 65 79 29 20 33 2F |.9 (Berkeley) 3/   │
│      30: 33 30 2F 39 31 0D 0A 23 0D 0A 23 20 54 68 65 73 |30/91..#..# Thes   │
│      40: 65 20 66 6C 61 67 73 20 73 70 65 63 69 66 79 20 |e flags specify    │
│      50: 77 68 65 74 68 65 72 20 6F 72 20 6E 6F 74 20 74 |whether or not t   │
│ ┌─────────────────────────┐  ┌────────────┐ ┌────────────┐ ┌──────────┐  ▼│
│ └─────────────────────────┘  │ Packet: 25 │ │Unfiltered: 44│ └──────────┘   │
└──────────────────────────────────────────────────────────────────────────────┘
```

FIGURE 6.24

The FTP server announces intention to break data connection.

```
┌─────────────────── LANalyzer for Windows - [C:\LZFW\FTP.TR1] ──────────▼│▲│
│ □  File  Monitor  Alarms  Capture  Decode  Window  Help                    ▲│
│    ether: ================== Ethernet Datalink Layer ==================      ▲│
│           Station: 00-00-C0-DD-14-5C ----> 68-01-14-2C-A2-01                 │
│           Type: 0x0800 (IP)                                                  │
│       ip: ===================== Internet Protocol =====================      │
│           Station:199.245.180.15 ---->199.245.180.1                          │
│           Protocol: TCP                                                       │
│           Version: 4                                                         │
│           Header Length (32 bit words): 5                                    │
│           Precedence: Routine                                                │
│                   Low Delay, Normal Throughput, Normal Reliability           │
│           Total length: 64                                                   │
│           Identification:  8204                                              │
│           Fragmentation allowed, Last fragment                               │
│           Fragment Offset: 0                                                 │
│           Time to Live: 60  seconds                                          │
│           Checksum: 0x66A0(Valid)                                            │
│      tcp: ================= Transmission Control Protocol =================  │
│           Source Port: FTP                                                   │
│           Destination Port: 15676                                           │
│           Sequence Number: 24602314                                          │
│           Acknowledgement Number: 64208964                                   │
│           Data Offset (32-bit words): 5                                      │
│           Window: 4096                                                       │
│           Control Bits: Acknowledgement Field is Valid (ACK)                 │
│                   Push Function Requested (PSH)                              │
│           Checksum: 0x6F18(Valid)                                            │
│           Urgent Pointer: 0                                                  │
│      ftp: ===================== File Transfer Protocol ==================== ▼│
│           Reply: 226 (Closing data connection; Requested file action successful│
│ ←│ ├─────────────────────────────────────────────────────────────────────→│ │
│ ┌─────────────────────────┐  ┌────────────┐ ┌────────────┐ ┌──────────┐     │
│ └─────────────────────────┘  │ Packet: 26 │ │Unfiltered: 44│ └──────────┘   │
└──────────────────────────────────────────────────────────────────────────────┘
```

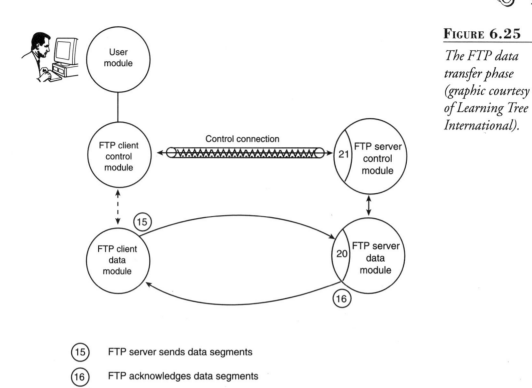

FIGURE 6.25

The FTP data transfer phase (graphic courtesy of Learning Tree International).

(15) FTP server sends data segments

(16) FTP acknowledges data segments

```
┌─────────────────────────────────────────────────────────────┐┌─┐
│■            LANalyzer for Windows - [C:\LZFW\FTP.TR1]       ▼│┤▲│
├─────────────────────────────────────────────────────────────┤├─┤
│□ File  Monitor  Alarms  Capture  Decode  Window  Help       │┤ │
├─────────────────────────────────────────────────────────────┤├─┤
│  tcp: ================ Transmission Control Protocol ========││▲│
│        Source Port: FTP-DATA                                 ││ │
│        Destination Port: 55814                               ││ │
│        Sequence Number: 25947650                             ││ │
│        Acknowledgement Number: 64954369                      ││ │
│        Data Offset (32-bit words): 5                         ││ │
│        Window: 4096                                          ││ │
│        Control Bits: Acknowledgement Field is Valid (ACK)    ││ │
│                      Push Function Requested (PSH)           ││ │
│                      No More Data from Sender (FIN)          ││ │
│        Checksum: 0x363A(Valid)                               ││ │
│        Urgent Pointer: 0                                     ││ │
│  Data:                                                       ││ │
│    0: 6E 73 20 63 6F 6D 70 72 65 73 73 20 54 43 50 20 │ns compress TCP│
│   10: 74 72 61 66 66 69 63 0D 0A 23 20 20 20 20 20 6C │traffic..#    l│
│   20: 69 6E 6B 31 20 6D 65 61 6E 73 20 73 75 70 70 72 │ink1 means suppr│
│   30: 65 73 73 20 49 43 4D 50 20 74 72 61 66 66 69 63 │ess ICMP traffic│
│   40: 0D 0A 23 20 20 20 20 20 6C 69 6E 6B 32 20 6D 65 │..#     link2 me│
│   50: 61 6E 73 20 61 75 74 6F 2D 65 6E 62 6C 65 20 │ans auto-enable│
│   60: 54 43 50 20 63 6F 6D 70 72 65 73 73 69 6F 6E 0D │TCP compression.│
│   70: 0A 23 69 66 63 6F 6E 66 69 67 20 73 6C 30 20 24 │.#ifconfig sl0 $│
│   80: 68 6F 73 74 6E 61 6D 65 20 5F 5F 72 65 6D 6F 74 │hostname __remot│
│   90: 65 68 6F 73 74 5F 5F 20 6C 69 6E 6B 32 20 75 70 │ehost__ link2 up│
│   A0: 0D 0A 23 74 74 79 20 2D 66 20 2F 64 65 76 2F │..#stty -f /dev/│
│   B0: 74 74 79 30 30 20 63 6C 6F 63 61 6C 0D 0A 23 73 │tty00 clocal..#s│
│   C0: 6C 61 74 74 61 63 68 20 2F 64 65 76 2F 74 74 79 │lattach /dev/tty│
│   D0: 30 30 20 39 36 30 30 0D 0A 0D 0A 23 20 73 65 74 │00 9600....# set│
│   E0: 20 74 68 65 20 61 64 64 72 65 73 73 20 66 6F 72 │ the address for│
│   F0: 20 74 68 65 20 6C 6F 6F 70 62 61 63 6B 20 69 6E │ the loopback in│
│  100: 74 65 72 66 61 63 65 0D 0A 69 66 63 6F 6E 66 69 │terface..ifconfi│
├─────────────────────────────────────────────────────────────┤├─┤
│                    │ Packet:  33 │ Unfiltered:  44 │        │┤▼│
└─────────────────────────────────────────────────────────────┘└─┘
```

FIGURE 6.26

The TCP layer in FTP sends the FIN flag to break data connection.

263

FIGURE 6.27

The TCP layer in FTP client sends a reciprocating FIN flag to break data connection.

```
▭                    LANalyzer for Windows - [C:\LZFW\FTP.TR1]              ▼ ◆
▭  File  Monitor  Alarms  Capture  Decode  Window  Help                       ◆
Packet Number : 34                    1:18:18 PM                              ◆
Length : 64 bytes
ether: ==================== Ethernet Datalink Layer ====================
        Station: 68-01-14-2C-A2-01 ----> 00-00-C0-DD-14-5C
        Type: 0x0800 (IP)
    ip: ==================== Internet Protocol ====================
        Station:199.245.180.1 ---->199.245.180.15
        Protocol: TCP
        Version: 4
        Header Length (32 bit words): 5
        Precedence: Routine
              Normal Delay, Normal Throughput, Normal Reliability
        Total length: 40
        Identification:    17
        Fragmentation allowed, Last fragment
        Fragment Offset: 0
        Time to Live: 100 seconds
        Checksum: 0x5EC3(Valid)
   tcp: ================== Transmission Control Protocol ==================
        Source Port: 55814
        Destination Port: FTP-DATA
        Sequence Number: 64954369
        Acknowledgement Number: 25948139
        Data Offset (32-bit words): 5
        Window: 0
        Control Bits: Acknowledgement Field is Valid (ACK)
              No More Data from Sender (FIN)
        Checksum: 0xC865(Valid)
        Urgent Pointer: 0
                                                                             ◆
┌───────────────────┐            ┌──────────┐ ┌────────────┐ ┌───────────┐
                                 │ Packet:  34 │ │ Unfiltered:  44 │
```

Packets 36-37:

> The user enters the QUIT or BYE command to end the FTP session. In packet 36, the FTP client issues the QUIT command to the FTP server (see fig. 6.29).
>
> In packet 37, the FTP server replies that it is ready to close the connection (see fig. 6.30).

Packets 38-43:

> The FTP server initiates a termination of the FTP connection with FIN flag set, and the FTP client agrees to it with FIN flag set. Additional packets are sent to acknowledge the termination, but the breaking of the control connection is similar to the breaking of the data connection, and therefore, protocol decodes are not shown.

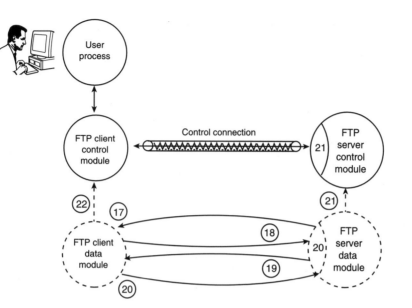

FIGURE 6.28

The breaking of the FTP data connection (graphic courtesy of Learning Tree International).

(17)   FTP server sends last data segment

(18)   FTP client acknowledges last data segment

(19)   FTP server closes data connection

(20)   FTP client acknowledges close data connection request

(21)   FTP server data process terminates

(22)   FTP client data process terminates

FIGURE 6.29

The QUIT command from the FTP client.

```
┌─────────────────────────────────────────────────────────────────────────┐
│ ═    LANalyzer for Windows - [C:\LZFW\FTP.TR1]          ▼ ‖ │
│ ═  File  Monitor  Alarms  Capture  Decode  Window  Help         ‖ │
│ ┌───────────────────────────────────────────────────────────────────┬─┐ │
│ │ether: ================= Ethernet Datalink Layer ===================│▲│ │
│ │       Station: 68-01-14-2C-A2-01 -----> 00-00-C0-DD-14-5C         │ │ │
│ │       Type: 0x0800 (IP)                                           │ │ │
│ │   ip: ==================== Internet Protocol =====================│ │ │
│ │       Station:199.245.180.1 ---->199.245.180.15                   │ │ │
│ │       Protocol: TCP                                               │ │ │
│ │       Version: 4                                                  │ │ │
│ │       Header Length (32 bit words): 5                             │ │ │
│ │       Precedence: Routine                                         │ │ │
│ │             Normal Delay, Normal Throughput, Normal Reliability   │ │ │
│ │       Total length: 46                                            │ │ │
│ │       Identification:      18                                     │ │ │
│ │       Fragmentation allowed, Last fragment                        │ │ │
│ │       Fragment Offset: 0                                          │ │ │
│ │       Time to Live: 100 seconds                                   │ │ │
│ │       Checksum: 0x5EBC(Valid)                                     │ │ │
│ │  tcp: ================= Transmission Control Protocol =============│ │ │
│ │       Source Port: 15676                                          │ │ │
│ │       Destination Port: FTP                                       │ │ │
│ │       Sequence Number: 64208964                                   │ │ │
│ │       Acknowledgement Number: 24602338                            │ │ │
│ │       Data Offset (32-bit words): 5                               │ │ │
│ │       Window: 512                                                 │ │ │
│ │       Control Bits: Acknowledgement Field is Valid (ACK)          │ │ │
│ │             Push Function Requested (PSH)                         │ │ │
│ │       Checksum: 0xA454(Valid)                                     │ │ │
│ │       Urgent Pointer: 0                                           │ │ │
│ │  ftp: ==================== File Transfer Protocol =================│ │ │
│ │       Command: QUIT(Logout)                                       │▼│ │
│ └───────────────────────────────────────────────────────────────────┴─┘ │
│        ┌──────────────────┐  ┌─────────────┐ ┌────────────┐ ┌────────┐  │
│        │                  │  │ Packet:  36 │ │Unfiltered: 44│ │       │  │
│        └──────────────────┘  └─────────────┘ └────────────┘ └────────┘  │
└─────────────────────────────────────────────────────────────────────────┘
```

FIGURE 6.30

The FTP server's response to the client's QUIT command.

```
┌─────────────────────────────────────────────────────────────────────────┐
│ ═    LANalyzer for Windows - [C:\LZFW\FTP.TR1]          ▼ ‖ │
│ ═  File  Monitor  Alarms  Capture  Decode  Window  Help         ‖ │
│ ┌───────────────────────────────────────────────────────────────────┬─┐ │
│ │ether: ================= Ethernet Datalink Layer ===================│▲│ │
│ │       Station: 00-00-C0-DD-14-5C ----> 68-01-14-2C-A2-01         │ │ │
│ │       Type: 0x0800 (IP)                                           │ │ │
│ │   ip: ==================== Internet Protocol =====================│ │ │
│ │       Station:199.245.180.15 ---->199.245.180.1                   │ │ │
│ │       Protocol: TCP                                               │ │ │
│ │       Version: 4                                                  │ │ │
│ │       Header Length (32 bit words): 5                             │ │ │
│ │       Precedence: Routine                                         │ │ │
│ │             Low Delay, Normal Throughput, Normal Reliability      │ │ │
│ │       Total length: 54                                            │ │ │
│ │       Identification:  8209                                       │ │ │
│ │       Fragmentation allowed, Last fragment                        │ │ │
│ │       Fragment Offset: 0                                          │ │ │
│ │       Time to Live: 60  seconds                                   │ │ │
│ │       Checksum: 0x66A5(Valid)                                     │ │ │
│ │  tcp: ================= Transmission Control Protocol =============│ │ │
│ │       Source Port: FTP                                            │ │ │
│ │       Destination Port: 15676                                     │ │ │
│ │       Sequence Number: 24602338                                   │ │ │
│ │       Acknowledgement Number: 64208970                            │ │ │
│ │       Data Offset (32-bit words): 5                               │ │ │
│ │       Window: 4096                                                │ │ │
│ │       Control Bits: Acknowledgement Field is Valid (ACK)          │ │ │
│ │             Push Function Requested (PSH)                         │ │ │
│ │       Checksum: 0x4F22(Valid)                                     │ │ │
│ │       Urgent Pointer: 0                                           │ │ │
│ │  ftp: ==================== File Transfer Protocol =================│ │ │
│ │       Reply: 221 (Service closing control connection.)            │ │ │
│ │       Text:  Goodbye.                                             │▼│ │
│ └───────────────────────────────────────────────────────────────────┴─┘ │
│        ┌──────────────────┐  ┌─────────────┐ ┌────────────┐ ┌────────┐  │
│        │                  │  │ Packet:  37 │ │Unfiltered: 44│ │       │  │
│        └──────────────────┘  └─────────────┘ └────────────┘ └────────┘  │
└─────────────────────────────────────────────────────────────────────────┘
```

PROBLEMS IN FILTERING AN FTP SESSION

The previous section showed the detailed behavior of an FTP session. Consider figure 6.31, in which a screening router is set up between an FTP client on an internal network and an FTP server on an external network. Assume that the network security policy allows internal hosts to initiate FTP sessions with external hosts. Figure 6.32 shows an attempt to set up packet filter rules to implement this policy. From figure 6.32, you can see that you do not know the destination port number for rule 2 because this is set dynamically by the FTP protocol. If you allow the host to call any one of the ports for the FTP "call back" from the server, a program written with evil intent can probe any of the internal network hosts if it originates a call from port 20. This is clearly undesirable.

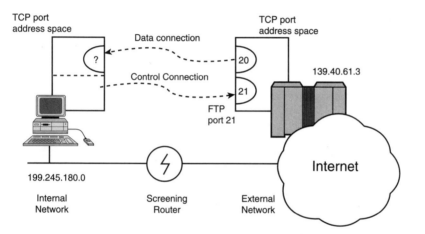

FIGURE 6.31

An FTP session to an external host through a screening router.

Filter Rule Number	Action	Source	Source Port	Destination	Dest. Port	Protocol Flags Options	Description
1	allow	199.245.180.0	*	*	*	TCP	Permit outgoing TCP connection.
2	allow	*	20	199.245.180.0	*	TCP	Destination port not known.
3							

FIGURE 6.32

An attempt to set up an FTP connection filter.

267

FTP PACKET FILTERING USING PORT RANGE RULES AND TCP FLAGS

One way to solve the problem is to use the TCP ACK flag to identify legitimate incoming connections and to block connections to the internal host's standard service ports (usually less than 1024).

Figure 6.33 shows the redesigned packet filter rules for an FTP session. Filter rule 1 allows calls to the external host from any port from the internal network. Filter rule 2 blocks calls to ports less than 1024. This is safe for FTP operation because the local call-back port is greater than 1024 in standard FTP. Filter rule 3 only allows ACK packets from port 20 on the external host.

FIGURE 6.33

The redesigned packet filter rules using the ACK flag.

Filter Rule Number	Action	Source	Source Port	Destination	Dest. Port	Protocol Flags Options	Description
1	allow	199.245.180.0	*	139.40.61.3	21	TCP	Permit outgoing TCP connection
2	block	139.40.61.3	20	199.245.180.0	< 1024	TCP	Block connections to standard services
3	allow	139.40.61.3	20	199.245.180.0	*	TCP ACK=1	Allow ACK packets to any port on internal machine from port 20

A determined intruder could, however, still originate calls from port 20 and probe the port addresses above 1024. Because the ACK flag is on, this attack would require a degree of skill.

FTP PACKET FILTERING USING THE PASV COMMAND

RFC 1579 on "Firewall-Friendly FTP" proposed the use of an FTP command PASV (passive open) that does not require a modification to the FTP protocol, but a modification to the FTP clients. The FTP protocol says that, by default, all data transfers should be over a single data connection. The FTP server does an active open from TCP port 20 to a local dynamic port on the FTP client, which does a passive open on this local port.

Most current FTP clients do not behave that way; they assign a new local port for each transfer and announce this through the PORT command.

If the FTP client sends a PASV command to the FTP server, the server does a passive TCP open on a random port and informs the client of the port number. The client can initiate an active open to establish the connection using a random local port. This mechanism avoids the FTP server call-back to a service port on the FTP client. The FTP client initiates an active open to an external host, and this is usually not a problem with most organizations' network security policies.

If the FTP server does not implement the PASV command, this scheme does not work. PASV is required by STD 3 (RFC 1123); however, not all FTP servers implement it. You usually can detect this problem when you receive a reply code of `500 Command not under-stood`.

When a PASV command is sent, the server can respond to it with the following:

`227 Passive i1,i2,i3,i4,p1,p2`

The *i1*, *i2*, *i3*, and *i4* are the decimal numbers of the server's IP address in dotted decimal notation. The *p1* and *p2* represent a random port assigned by the server. The FTP client can issue an active TCP open with destination port of $256*p1 + p2$ to the server FTP. This mechanism is shown in figure 6.34.

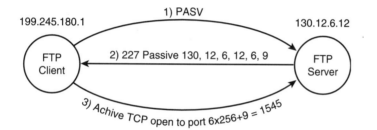

FIGURE 6.34

The use of PASV in Firewall-Friendly FTP.

FILTERING TELNET NETWORK TRAFFIC

TELNET traffic does not require any call-back mechanisms to an unprotected port on the TELNET client, so filtering TELNET sessions on standard port 23 is relatively straightforward.

TELNET can be used as a general mechanism to connect to any port using the following command:

`telnet host [portnumber]`

If *portnumber* is not specified, the default TELNET port of 23 is used. If your site security policy does not want internal users to contact services such as Gopher, WWW, or the Weather Underground, these actions are difficult to control if a non-standard port number is used.

TELNET also can be used by external users to probe what special services, if any, you are providing on TCP ports on your internal machines. You should protect all such services using screening routers or firewall gateway solutions.

FILTERING X-WINDOWS SESSIONS

The X11 protocol uses TCP. Like FTP, the X11 protocol requires an incoming call to the X11 server. The X-server here is the user's display (X-terminal or X-workstation). If internal users want to run an X11 application at an external site (see fig. 6.35), the X11 application needs to make an incoming call to the X11 server. The X11 servers usually use port numbers in the range 6000-6999. You should at a minimum protect the port range 6000-6100.

FIGURE 6.35

The X11 across a screening router.

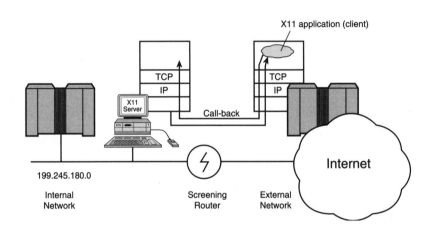

Consider the network security policy specifying that X-access from the external site 128.23.0.0 should be allowed, but all other external access should be blocked. If the internal X11-servers use port numbers 6000-6100, you can use the filter design table in figure 6.36 as a start.

FIGURE 6.36

An example of X11 packet filter rules.

Filter Rule Number	Action	Source	Source Port	Destination	Dest. Port	Protocol Flags Options	Description
1	allow	199.245.180.0	*	*	*	TCP	Permit outgoing TCP connections.
2	block	128.23.0.0	*	199.245.180.0	6000-6100	TCP	Block access to X11 services from 128.23.0.0
3	allow	*	*	199.245.180.0	6000-6100	TCP	Allow X11 access to all other sites.

PACKET FILTERING AND THE UDP TRANSPORT PROTOCOL

The application services you have examined so far have used TCP. TCP is a connection-oriented protocol. It uses virtual circuits where each side maintains state information, such as sequence and acknowledgment numbers, to determine what data is expected next. This state information specifies a context in which the next packet should occur. This context information is very useful in packet filtering. You can use the TCP ACK flag, for example, to associate a packet as part of an existing TCP session. The ACK flag can be used to distinguish between an incoming or return packet, and the SYN flag can be used to indicate if the packet is part of an open-connection request.

UDP sessions are connectionless. UDP does not use virtual circuits, so it does not retain any state information. There are no sequence and acknowledgment numbers to determine the next packet. Because of this, one has to rely on filtering UDP based on port numbers.

Consider the situation (see fig. 6.37) where host 190.245.180.9 wants to poll an SNMP agent on an external machine at 157.23.13.44, and the network security policy permits such an operation. The SNMP agents use well-known UDP port number of 161. You could write this as a filter rule shown in figure 6.38. Filter rule 1 allows outgoing SNMP polls, and filter rule 2 allows incoming SNMP replies.

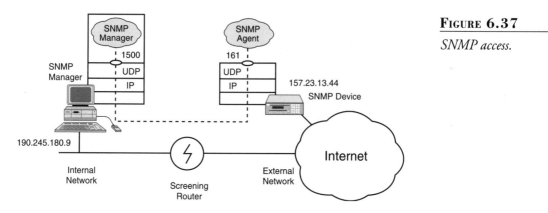

FIGURE 6.37

SNMP access.

271

FIGURE 6.38

The implemention of SNMP access security policy.

Filter Rule Number	Action	Source	Source Port	Destination	Dest. Port	Protocol Flags Options	Description
1	allow	190.245.180.9	1500	157.23.13.44	161	UDP	Permit outgoing SNMP polls
2	allow	157.23.1.3.44	161	190.245.180.9	1500	UDP	Allow SNMP replies

Assume the local port used by the SNMP Manager is 1500. The SNMP poll packet consists of the following:

> Source IP address = 190.245.180.9
>
> Source port = 1500
>
> Destination IP address = 157.23.13.44
>
> Destination port = 161

The SNMP reply would be the following:

> Source IP address = 157.23.13.44
>
> Source port = 161
>
> Destination IP address = 190.245.180.9
>
> Destination port = 1500

What if the following reply was received?

> Source IP address = 157.23.13.44
>
> Source port = 161
>
> Destination IP address = 190.245.180.9
>
> Destination port = 1352

Because the source port is 161, by filter rule 2 in figure 6.38, you would allow this packet access. But what if someone has forged a UDP packet with a source port of 161? They could, then, use this to attack port 1352 on the local machine, which is assigned to Lotus Notes.

One way to solve this problem is to explicitly specify rules preventing access to Well-Known Services (WKS) running on internal hosts. The problem here is that it may be hard to keep the packet filter rules updated as new UDP services are added to the network.

> **TIP**
>
> A generally accepted practice is to deny all UDP traffic with the exception of DNS traffic, which is UDP-based for name resolution.

Many of the UDP applications such as NFS, TFTP, and SNMP are LAN-oriented. There-fore, you may consider blocking these UDP services entirely. An exception to this is DNS, which uses UDP, and is definitely not confined to LANs. In this case, you might want to block all UDP traffic from external sites, except DNS. One possible set of filter rules for doing this is shown in figure 6.39. However, as explained earlier, someone can still do address spoofing by impersonating DNS port number 53, and packet filter rule 2 of figure 6.39 will permit this type of packet to reach the internal network 190.245.180.0.

Filter Rule Number	Action	Source	Source Port	Destination	Dest. Port	Protocol Flags Options	Description
1	allow	190.245.180.0	**	*	*	UDP	Allow outgoing UDP packets
2	allow		*	190.245.180.0	53	UDP	Allow DNS queries
3							

FIGURE 6.39

Blocking UDP services with the exception of DNS.

PACKET FILTERING ICMP

The Internet Control Message Protocol (ICMP) is part of the Internet Layer and is described in RFC 792. ICMP must be implemented in all IP protocol modules. This means that all TCP/IP hosts have ICMP support.

ICMP is used to report errors on the IP datagrams. It does not make the IP protocol layer more reliable. It reports errors on the Internet layer, and it is up to an upper-layer protocol such as TCP to make the Internet layer more reliable. ICMP reports information on network parameters and errors on the network; it can also be used to diagnose the network. The following ICMP services are defined:

❖ Echo test—used to test the availability of a TCP/IP host (ping).

❖ Time stamp messages for measuring network delay.

❖ Time to Live expired messages.

❖ Destination network or host is unreachable messages.

❖ Errors in IP parameters in the IP header messages.

❖ Redirect messages for determining better routes.

❖ Determining subnet address mask of network to which host is attached.

❖ Source quench messages to inform source to slow down sending of packets. This is an attempt to provide flow control.

ICMP redirect messages generally are sent by routers to other devices, informing them about new routes. If ICMP redirect messages are allowed to filter into the internal network, an external site can send bogus ICMP redirect messages to internal hosts and cause havoc with the internal network's routing tables. This is an example of a "denial of service" attack because it disrupts normal operations. There generally is no good reason for an internal network to listen to ICMP redirect messages from an external network, especially if these originate from an untrusted network. For this reason, you might consider filtering out ICMP redirect packets coming from an external network.

Some hosts are susceptible to ICMP subnet reply messages, even when they have not made an ICMP subnet request. This is obviously a bug in the TCP/IP implementation, and should be identified and eliminated to prevent your network from responding to false ICMP subnet reply messages.

Although the ICMP echo service (popularly implemented by the ping utility) is useful for verifying connections, if you allow external sites to ping your internal network, they can obtain a logical map of your internal network. If this is an important security issue, you might consider denying ICMP requests to the internal network.

PACKET FILTERING RIP

RIP (Routing Information Protocol) is used by many internal networks. RIP exchanges "hop count" information about network and host destinations at periodic intervals (30 seconds). These RIP exchanges are based on trust between the routers. There is no authentication of RIP messages. If a router is mistaken about a route, this error can easily propagate to other routers, producing such ills as routing loops, inefficient routes, and unreachable destinations.

WARNING

> Because of RIP's trustedness between the hosts, it is wise to use an access list to establish trusted hosts or to avoid RIP and use static routes.

It does not take a great deal of imagination to see what can happen if false routing information is deliberately leaked to an internal network. Someone could change the default route information on hosts, for example, so that internal network traffic is diverted to an attacker's host.

You also should disable source routing at the screening router. An intruder can use source routing to force the sending and receiving of packets through the screening router. If you are using Cisco routers, for example, you can disable source routing by using the following command:

```
no ip source-route
```

EXAMPLE SCREENING ROUTER CONFIGURATIONS

This section discusses a few screen routing configuration scenarios to provide you with additional guidance on designing and implementing packet filter rules.

CASE STUDY 1

Figure 6.40 shows a network that has the following security policy:

1. All hosts on internal network 131.44.0.0 can access any TCP service on the Internet.

2. External hosts cannot connect to the internal network except through the mail gateway at 131.44.1.1 where they can access the SMTP mail service only.

3. ICMP messages to the Internet should be blocked.

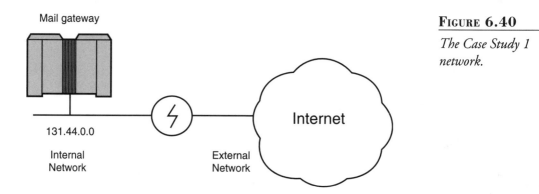

Mail gateway

131.44.0.0

Internal Network

External Network

Internet

FIGURE 6.40

The Case Study 1 network.

You can express this security policy as filter rules for the Internal (see fig. 6.41) and External port (see fig. 6.42) of the screening router.

Filter Rule Number	Action	Source	Source Port	Destination	Dest. Port	Protocol Flags Options	Description
1	allow	131.44.0.0	*	*	*	TCP	Allow outgoing TCP connections
2	block		NA	*	NA	ICMP	Block ICMP messages to external network
3							

NA = Not Applicable

FIGURE 6.41

Case Study 1: Filter rules for external port.

275

FIGURE 6.42

*Case Study 1:
Filter rules for
internal port.*

Filter Rule Number	Action	Source	Source Port	Destination	Dest. Port	Protocol Flags Options	Description
1	allow	131.44.0.0	*	*	*	TCP	Allow incoming TCP connections
2	block	131.44.0.0	*	*	*	TCP	Block ICMP from reaching the Internet

Using Cisco routers, the packet filter rules for the external port (see fig. 6.41) can be implemented as shown in the following.

Packet filter rule 1 for external port:

```
access-list 101 permit tcp 131.44.0.0 0.0.255.255 0.0.0.0 255.255.255.255
```

Packet filter rule 2 for external port:

```
access-list 101 deny icmp 131.44.0.0 0.0.255.255 0.0.0.0 255.255.255.255
```

Using Cisco routers, the packet filter rules for the internal port (see fig. 6.42) can be implemented as shown in the following.

Packet filter rule 1 for internal port:

```
access-list 102 permit tcp 0.0.0.0 255.255.255.255 131.44.1.1  0.0.0.0 eq 25
```

Packet filter rule 2 for internal port:

```
access-list 102 deny tcp 0.0.0.0 255.255.255.255 131.44.0.0 0.0 0.0.255.255
```

CASE STUDY 2

Figure 6.43 shows a network that has the following security policy:

1. Incoming e-mail and news are permitted to hosts 144.19.74.200, 144.19.74.201.

2. DNS access to gateway server 144.19.74.202 is allowed.

3. Access to NFS services on internal network is not allowed from external hosts.

4. Internal hosts are allowed all TCP access to external networks, except to Gopher and WWW.

You can express this security policy as filter rules for the External (see fig. 6.44) and Internal port (see fig. 6.45) of the screening router.

Using Cisco routers, the packet filter rules for the external port (see fig. 6.44) can be implemented as shown in the following.

144.19.0.0

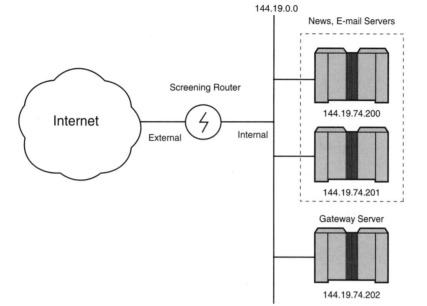

FIGURE 6.43

The Case Study 2 network.

Filter Rule Number	Action	Source	Source Port	Destination	Dest. Port	Protocol Flags Options	Description
1	block	144.19.0.0	*	*	70	TCP	Block outgoing access to Gopher
2	block	144.19.0.0	*	*	80	TCP	Block outgoing access to WWW
3	allow	144.19.0.0	*	*	*	TCP	Allows all other TCP access

FIGURE 6.44

Case Study 2: Filter rules for external port.

Filter Rule Number	Action	Source	Source Port	Destination	Dest. Port	Protocol Flags Options	Description
1	allow	*	*	144.19.0.0	*	TCP ACK=1 TCP SYN=1	Permit incoming packets that are part of an established TCP connection
2	allow	*	*	144.19.74.200	25	TCP	Allow e-mail access per security policy
3	allow	*	*	144.19.74.201	25	TCP	Allow e-mail access per security policy
4	allow	*	*	144.19.74.200	119	UDP	Allow NNTP access per security policy
5	allow	*	*	144.19.74.201	119	UDP	Allow NNTP access per security policy
6	allow	*	*	144.19.74.202	53	UDP	Allow DNS access per security policy

FIGURE 6.45

Case Study 2: Filter rules for internal port.

277

Packet filter rule 1 for external port:

```
access-list 101 deny tcp 144.19.0.0 0.0.255.255 0.0.0.0 255.255.255.255 eq 70
```

Packet filter rule 2 for external port:

```
access-list 101 deny tcp 144.19.0.0 0.0.255.255 0.0.0.0 255.255.255.255 eq 80
```

Packet filter rule 3 for external port:

```
access-list 101 permit tcp 144.19.0.0 0.0.255.255 0.0.0.0 255.255.255.255
```

Using Cisco routers, the packet filter rules for the internal port (see fig. 6.45) can be implemented as shown in the following.

Packet filter rule 1 for internal port:

```
access-list 102 permit tcp 0.0.0.0 255.255.255.255 144.19.0.0  0.0.255.255
➥established
```

Packet filter rule 2 for internal port:

```
access-list 102 permit tcp 0.0.0.0 255.255.255.255 144.19.74.200 0.0.0.0  eq
➥25
```

Packet filter rule 3 for internal port:

```
access-list 102 permit tcp 0.0.0.0 255.255.255.255 144.19.74.201 0.0.0.0  eq
➥25
```

Packet filter rule 4 for internal port:

```
access-list 102 permit tcp 0.0.0.0 255.255.255.255 144.19.74.200 0.0.0.0  eq
➥119
```

Packet filter rule 5 for internal port:

```
access-list 102 permit tcp 0.0.0.0 255.255.255.255 144.19.74.201 0.0.0.0  eq
➥119
```

Packet filter rule 6 for internal port:

```
access-list 102 permit udp 0.0.0.0 255.255.255.255 144.19.74.202 0.0.0.0  eq
➥53
```

Case Study 3

Figure 6.46 shows a network 144.19.0.0 that is using two subnets. The subnet 1 acts as a demilitarized zone (DMZ) between the internal and external networks. The DMZ is on subnet 15, and the internal protected network is on subnet 16. A firewall gateway, 144.19.15.1 exists in the DMZ. The mail router is on the subnet 16 and has an IP address of 144.19.16.1. The ports of the internal router connecting subnets 15 and 16 has IP address assignments of

144.19.16.81 and 144.19.16.82. The network has the following security policy for the internal router:

1. IP Source routing not permitted.

2. Services originating from subnet 16 are permitted to the firewall gateway on DMZ (subnet 15).

3. Allow all internal traffic to DMZ, except e-mail access to the DMZ (subnet 15).

4. Allow traffic from firewall gateway to internal network.

5. Allow connections from DMZ that show source ports in the range 1024 to 5000. The reason for this could be to allow FTP callbacks (another reason is to show you how to filter on port ranges).

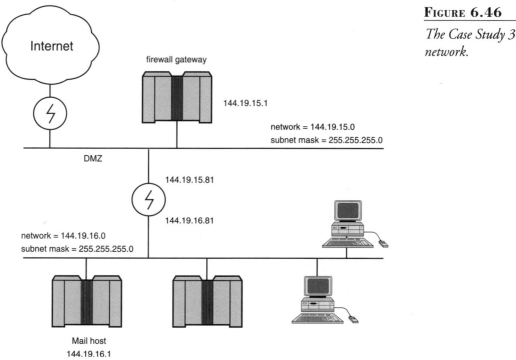

FIGURE 6.46

The Case Study 3 network.

You can express this security policy as filter rules for Ethernet interface connections subnet 15 (see fig. 6.47) and subnet 16 (see fig. 6.48) of the router.

FIGURE 6.47

Case Study 3: Filter rules for Ethernet interface on subnet "15."

Filter Rule Number	Action	Source	Source Port	Destination	Dest. Port	Protocol Flags Options	Description
1	allow	144.19.16.0	NA	*	NA	IP	Allow packets from internal network to firewall gateway
2	block	144.19.15.0	*	*	25	TCP	Block e-mail access to DMZ per security policy
3	allow	144.19.15.0	*	*	*	TCP	Allow all other access to DMZ

NA = Not Applicable

FIGURE 6.48

Case Study 3: Filter rules for Ethernet interface on subnet "16."

Filter rule number	Action	Source	Source Port	Destination	Dest. Port	Protocol Flags Options	Description
1	allow	144.19.15.1	NA	144.19.0.0	NA	IP	Allow traffic to internal network from firewall gateway
2	block	144.19.0.0	*	*	25	TCP	Block E-mail access to DMZ per security policy
3	allow	144.19.0.0	*	*	*	TCP	Allow all other access to DMZ

NA = Not Applicable

The following example shows a more complete procedure on configuring the router interfaces. To configure the router Ethernet interface on subnet 15, you can use the following:

```
no ip source-route      ! Disable source routing for router
interface ethernet 0    ! Identify physical interface
ip address 144.19.15.81 255.255.255.0 ! Assign IP address and subnet mask
ip group access 150     ! Extended access list 150 will apply to this
                          interface
```

To configure the router Ethernet interface on subnet 16, you can use the following:

```
! You do not need to disable source routing as it was done before
interface ethernet 1    ! Identify physical interface
ip address 144.19.16.81 255.255.255.0 ! Assign IP address and subnet mask
ip group access 160     ! Extended access list 160 will apply to this
                          interface
```

The packet filter rules for subnet 15 (see fig. 6.47) can be implemented as shown in the following.

Packet filter rule 1 for Ethernet 0 interface:

```
access-list 150 permit ip 144.19.16.0 0.0.255.255 144.19.15.1 0.0.0.0
```

Packet filter rule 2 for Ethernet 0 interface:

```
access-list 150 deny tcp 144.19.15.0 0.0.255.255  0.0.0.0 255.255.255.255 eq
➡25
```

Packet filter rule 3 for Ethernet 0 interface:

```
access-list 150 permit tcp 144.19.15.0 0.0.255.255  0.0.0.0 255.255.255.255
```

The packet filter rules for the Ethernet interface on subnet 16 (see fig. 5.48) can be implemented as shown in the following.

Packet filter rule 1 for Ethernet 1 interface:

```
access-list 160 permit ip 144.19.15.1 0.0.255.255 144.19.15.0 0.0.255.255
```

Packet filter rule 2 for Ethernet 1 interface:

```
access-list 160 deny tcp 0.0.0.0  255.255.255.255  144.19.15.0 0.0.255.255 lt
➡1024
access-list 160 deny tcp 0.0.0.0  255.255.255.255  144.19.15.0 0.0.255.255 gt
➡5000
access-list 160 permit tcp 0.0.0.0  255.255.255.255  0.0.0.0 255.255.255.255
➡lt 1025
```

SUMMARY

This chapter discussed the implementing of packet filter rules. The packet filter rules were implemented using examples of a commercially available router product. The problems of designing packet filter rules when a "call-back" connection is made from an external network were discussed. Call-back connections are required by most FTP and X11 implementations. Several case studies showing the design and implementation of packet filter rules were discussed.

PC PACKET FILTERING

PACKET FILTERING CAN BE applied to the PC world as well as to Unix towers and work-stations. PC-based products are popular because of their relatively low cost compared to RJSC-based Unix platforms or special router products. This chapter explores the ways in which that is possible—in particular, by carefully examining some popular PC-based products that serve as examples.

PC-BASED PACKET FILTER

Packet filtering software packages can be run on IBM-PCs. The IBM-PC, then, becomes a packet filter device. Two popular examples of such devices are:

❖ KarlBridge

❖ Drawbridge

THE KARLBRIDGE PACKET FILTER

The *KarlBridge* is a program written by Doug Karl of Ohio State University that runs on a 286/386/486 clone. The KarlBridge provides an inexpensive two-port Ethernet-to-Ethernet bridge that performs protocol filtering.

The KarlBridge filters packets based on any specified Ethernet protocol such as IP, XNS (Xerox Network System), DECNET (Digital Equipment Corporation Network), LAT (Local Area Transport), AppleTalk, NetBEUI (Net BIOS Extended User Interface), and Novell IPX (Internetwork Packet Exchange). As KarlBridge has evolved, some of its features resemble a firewall gateway more than a packet filter device.

KarlBridge can provide filtering of IP packets based upon IP address, network, and subnet combinations and port number values. Besides IP, it can also filter the following protocol types:

❖ DECNET packets based upon DECNET address, area, object number, and object name

❖ AppleTalk Phase 1 & 2 NBP packets based upon file server name, printer name, and/or zone name

❖ NetWare SAP packets based upon IPX network number, server name, and socket service number

The shareware working demo of KarlBridge V2.0 is available through anonymous ftp from `ftp://ftp.net.ohio-state.edu/pub/kbridge`.

The KarlBridge is also a commercial bridge or brouter product. The commercial products are based on the commercial version of the KarlBridge or KarlBRouter code. The Ethernet version of the commercial KarlBridge version comes with AUI/10BASE2 or AUI/10BASE-T connectors. It is implemented in a specially configured PC workstation with two Ethernet cards, a special boot ROM, and a floppy drive.

The KarlBridge Shareware/Demo is a limited-function, free version of the commercially available KarlBridge and KarlBRouter. Even though it is a demo version, it is very functional and, for many situations, has just the right features to be very useful.

REQUIREMENTS FOR KARLBRIDGE

To build your own KarlBridge, you need the following:

❖ 286, 386SX, 386DX, 486, or Pentium PC computer (keyboard and monitor are optional)

❖ Two SMC Elite 16 Ethernet cards 8013EPC

❖ KarlBridge software

The PC must be a good, reliable clone. The following lists typical hardware specifications for the KarlBridge:

❖ 16 MHz, 0 wait state 286 or 386SX motherboard or 386DX motherboard with AMI BIOS, 1 MB of RAM, floppy drive and controller; it must be able to boot with no monitor and no keyboard.

❖ The speaker connection must be modified to power a front panel LED that signifies LAN traffic. Different motherboards need different types of modification. Without this modification, the speaker clicks for each packet forwarded.

❖ The floppy drive must be capable of withstanding a dusty environment so that if the system is operating for months at a time and then a power failure causes a reboot, the floppy drive will still work. This usually requires a modification to the case so that the air does not flow through the floppy drive itself.

❖ For additional reliability, the entire system can be burned in for a minimum of two weeks with cycling temperature with full Ethernet load.

❖ Two SMC Elite 16 boards can be configured with either of the following configurations:

Configuration 1:

First board: IRQ 3 I/O Addr 280, Shared RAM D000 (Remote Port)

Second board: IRQ 5 I/O Addr 2A0, Shared RAM D400 (Local Port)

Configuration 2:

First board: IRQ 3 I/O Addr 280, Shared RAM E000 (Remote Port)

Second board: IRQ 5 I/O Addr 2A0, Shared RAM E400 (Local Port)

If you chose to construct your own PC clone, be aware that the designers of KarlBridge have not tested the program with hardware other than a 16 MHz, 0 wait state 286-16, 386SX-16, and 386DX40 with the I/O bus running at 8 MHz. The SMC cards may not function properly in some 486 machines.

The software is configured in a PC. The configuration produces a disk that contains properly configured software.

OVERVIEW OF SETTING UP KARLBRIDGE

After you obtain a copy of KarlBridge software, you must configure it on an MS-DOS PC. The current release is compressed ("zipped"), so you must use a tool such as PKUNZIP to extract the files. The distribution software comes with a program called KBRIDGE that you can use to configure the KarlBridge software. The KarlBridge distribution should contain the programs shown in table 7.1.

TABLE 7.1
KarlBridge Distribution Software

Program Name	Description
kbconfig.exe	KarlBridge configuration program
kbc.exe	KarlBridge configuration support program
kbc.sun4	Sun 4 Sparc version of kbc.exe program
kbconfig.cfg	File that contains IP address, mask, and so on
kbhelp.hlp	Help file for the KBCONFIG.EXE program
kbridge.exe	Executable image of KarlBridge for 2 SMC Elite 16 boards with the WD83C690 chip

The following is an outline of the steps to configure KarlBridge:

1. From the DOS prompt, change to the directory that has the KarlBridge software. Issue the following command on your PC:

```
KBCONFIG KBRIDGE.EXE
```

You should see the KarlBridge configuration program. Set up the KarlBridge configuration. The configuration procedure is quite lengthy and can be quite involved. Details of this procedure are presented in the next section.

2. The KBCONFIG program modifies the actual bridge program file KBRIDGE.EXE.

3. Create a bootable floppy. You can do this from the DOS prompt by issuing the following command:

   FORMAT A: /S

4. Create an AUTOEXEC.BAT file on the floppy disk that contains the following single command:

   KBRIDGE

5. Copy the KBRIDGE.EXE file and the AUTOEXEC.BAT to the bootable floppy:

   COPY KBRIDGE.EXE A:

6. You now have a bootable KarlBridge floppy.

7. After setting up the hardware for the KarlBridge, boot with this floppy.

KARLBRIDGE CONFIGURATION

The KarlBridge configuration is done by KBCONFIG.EXE. This is a menu-driven program that modifies the KBRIDGE.EXE program. The KarlBridge provides a great deal of flexibility. This section guides you in configuring the more important capabilities of KarlBridge. The shareware product is a bridge that can be configured to perform protocol filtering. If your network requires that the filter device be a router, you must purchase the router version of this product.

The term *remote* in the KBCONFIG program refers to machines connected to the bridge's Port 0. This is the SMC Ethernet board with the I/O address 280. The term *local* refers to machines connected to the bridge's Port 1. This is the SMC Ethernet board with the I/O address 2A0.

The rest of this section illustrates the different configuration options for KarlBridge. Start the configuration by issuing the following command:

KBCONFIG KBRIDGE.EXE

You should see the opening screen similar to figure 7.1. Select OK.

FIGURE 7.1

The KarlBridge opening screen.

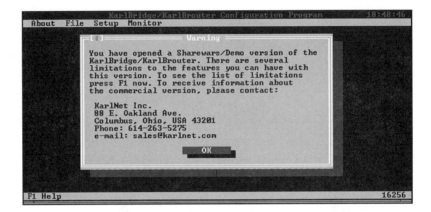

Press Alt+S to invoke the setup menu. You should see a screen showing you the setup options (see fig. 7.2). Select the General Setup option (see fig. 7.3).

FIGURE 7.2

The KarlBridge Setup menu.

FIGURE 7.3

The KarlBridge General Setup screen.

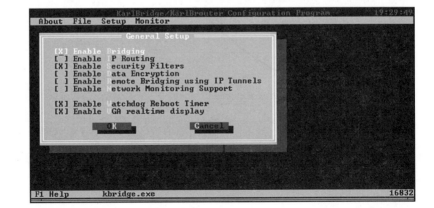

The following options are enabled by default:

Enable Bridging

Enable Security Filters

Enable Watchdog Reboot Timer

Enable VGA real-time display

Select OK after making your selections. Use the spacebar to select/deselect. The meaning of the options in figure 7.3 are described next:

❖ **ENABLE BRIDGING.** The transparent bridging function will be enabled. The device acts as a bridge (examining the data-link layer addresses only), transferring packets between local and remote ports. If you want the Bridge/Router to perform the bridging function, then you must enable this. When bridging is enabled, the Bridge Menu can be used.

❖ **ENABLE IP ROUTING.** If you have purchased the IP Routing option with the KarlBridge, you can enable it with this button. The routing works properly only if the routes are set up in the IP Route menu.

❖ **ENABLE SECURITY FILTERS.** Enabling security filters causes the KarlBridge/KarlBRouter to analyze each of the network layer headers in a packet to determine if it should be passed or dropped. If the KarlBridge or KarlBRouter is to be used as a simple, standard transparent bridge or simple IP Router with no advanced filtering, then this feature should be disabled. If you want to use the advanced filtering, firewall, and security features, then you must enable security filters. Note that the default settings for UDP/TCP, Novell, AppleTalk, and DECNET is to drop the packets (*That which is not explicitly permitted is prohibited.*). After enabling security filters, you then must enable the appropriate protocol-specific security filter.

❖ **ENABLE DATA ENCRYPTION.** The Data Encryption option can be used either to encrypt tunneled data that flows between KarlBridge tunnel partners or to encrypt UDP/TCP packets that flow between KarlBridge/KarlBRouters. Because only the UDP/TCP data portion of the packet is encrypted, the packet is routed correctly by standard IP routers.

❖ **ENABLE REMOTE BRIDGING USING IP TUNNELS.** The KarlBridge/KarlBRouter supports a special feature that enables Ethernet packets of any protocol type to be encapsulated in IP and then sent to other KarlBridges for decapsulation. This tunneling behavior is described in RFCs 1226, 1234, and 1241. This method can be used to set up "virtual" Ethernet LANs between several points on an IP network.

289

❖ **ENABLE WATCHDOG REBOOT TIMER.** The KarlBridge/KarlBRouter contains a watchdog timer reboot feature. If no packets are seen on the network for more than 10 minutes (a very rare occurrence), the KarlBridge/KarlBRouter reboots itself. After it reboots, the 10-minute reboot timer does not activate again until a packet is seen on one of the ports. This ensures that only one reboot occurs if the entire network is truly shut down.

❖ **ENABLE REAL-TIME DISPLAY.** Some KarlBridges and KarlBRouters contain a CGA, EGA, or VGA controller board and display. You can enable the displaying of real-time bridge/router statistics with this option. If you do not have a display, it is recommended that you disable this function.

The next step is to configure the network interfaces. For Ethernet, no special hardware setup is required because these settings are fixed in the hardware requirements discussed earlier. If Bridging is enabled, select Bridge Setup (press Alt+S to see the options). You should see a screen showing you the setup options (see fig. 7.4).

FIGURE 7.4

The KarlBridge Setup screen.

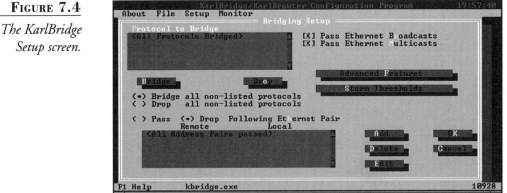

This is the main screen for configuring the bridge. The different configuration options are described next:

❖ **PROTOCOL TO BRIDGE/TUNNEL.** This menu specifies the Ethernet protocols to bridge, drop, or tunnel. Each protocol can be bridged or dropped by selecting the Bridge or Drop button.

All other protocols not specified in the menu are then either bridged or dropped depending upon the mode selected by radio buttons labeled Bridge all non-listed protocols or Drop all non-listed protocols.

It is recommended that you bridge only the protocols that you absolutely need and drop all non-listed protocols. This follows from implementing the security policy

That which is not explicitly permitted is prohibited. If you bridge IP, DECNET, Novell, or AppleTalk, you have the opportunity to set up additional filters under the Security Setup options. At this step, you can specify in more detail the types of services you want to allow or block in accordance with the security policy.

✤ **BRIDGE/DROP ALL NON-LISTED PROTOCOLS.** This setting determines whether the packets not listed in the Protocol to Bridge or Tunnel menu should be bridged or dropped.

✤ **PASS ETHERNET BROADCAST.** Standard Ethernet bridges always forward broadcast packets. Although many protocols do not use broadcasts, many do. For example, the IP, UDP, and ARP protocols use broadcasts. If you do not use IP or any other protocol that requires broadcasts, then you can drop them. Blocking broadcast packets reduces the traffic on your network and the number of interrupts that each computer connected to your network experiences. Networks with a high number of broadcasts slow down the processing of each attached computer even if it is not using the network.

✤ **PASS ETHERNET MULTICASTS.** Standard Ethernet bridges always forward multicast packets. Some protocols, such as IP and Novell IPX, do not use multicasts. Other protocols, such as OSPF, require multicasts. If you do not use protocols that use multicasts, then you can drop them by shutting off multicasts on the KarlBridge. Shutting off multicast packets reduces the traffic on your network as well as the number of interrupts that each computer connected to your network experiences.

✤ **PASS/DROP FOLLOWING ADDRESS PAIR.** This menu specifies the Ethernet addresses that should be either allowed or blocked. Both source and destination data-link address are checked against this filter. An entire 6-byte Ethernet address can be filtered or just portions of it. This menu can be used to inhibit or promote communication with several particular Ethernet addresses or groups of Ethernet addresses. Because the first 3-bytes of an Ethernet packet (or any IEEE LAN) represent the manufacturer's code, you can filter packets based on the make of the host's Ethernet board. This approach of specifying Ethernet addresses is similar to a standard bridge that supports Ethernet address filtering.

For example, if the menu is set to Drop following Pair and an address pair of 00-00-C0-00-1A-7B and 00-00-00-4F-XX-XX-XX is specified, then data packets from the address 00-00-C0-00-1A-7A to any addresses that start with 00-00-4F are dropped.

✤ **ADVANCED FEATURES.** This menu contains advanced bridging options. These options are described in figure 7.5.

FIGURE 7.5

*KarlBridge
Advanced Features
Bridging options.*

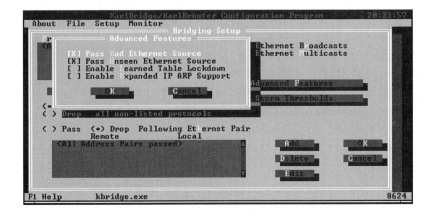

The advanced options are as follows:

❖ **ADVANCED FEATURES—PASS BAD ETHERNET SOURCE.** Most Ethernet bridges pass Ethernet packets with a broadcast or multicast address as their source (when the first bit is set to 1). The Ethernet specification for Non-Source Routing bridges does not allow these types of packets. These types of packets can be considered "bad" packets. A common failure mode of many Ethernet interfaces and networking software is to transmit packets that have broadcast or multicast addresses in their source address fields. If you do not need the KarlBridge to pass Source Routing packets, you can configure KarlBridge to drop these packets. The default is to pass bad packets.

❖ **ADVANCED FEATURES—PASS UNSEEN ETHERNET SOURCE.** Ethernet bridges always forward packets with destination addresses that have not been *learned* (addresses that have not been seen as a source address in a packet). This characteristic is essential for the proper operation of an Ethernet bridge. However, failure mode of many Ethernet interface cards is to send out erroneous packets with good CRCs but with random Ethernet destination and source addresses. Standard bridges pass these erroneous packets because they have not learned the random destination address, and they add this packet's random source address to their finite learned table. This situation can hinder the operation of standard bridges. If you chose to drop unlearned packets, the KarlBridge does not forward unicast packets to an Ethernet address that has not already been seen as a source address. This scheme works for most protocols because it relies on the characteristics of most upper-layer protocols to transmit ARP requests or Hello packets. The default is to pass packets with unseen source addresses.

❖ **ADVANCED FEATURES—ENABLE LEARNED TABLE LOCKDOWN.** A standard bridge watches the source addresses of each packet it receives on any of its ports. As new addresses are seen, entries are added in the bridge table. These entries contain the source address and the port number on which that address was received. If that source address is later seen on a different port, the bridge changes the port number in the learned table entry. This condition could happen in a correctly functioning network if someone moved the computer to a different part of the network. This also could happen if someone was trying to capture network packets by spoofing the bridge. Enabling learned table lockdown prevents the port number from being changed after the source address has been seen.

A standard bridge also times-out the learned table records. If learned table lockdown is enabled, then these records are not be timed out; once a record is learned, it cannot be changed or deleted until either the bridge reboots or the learned table becomes completely filled and needs to be reset. A typical KarlBridge learned table can contain over 10,000 records. The default is for this option to be disabled.

❖ **ADVANCED FEATURES—ENABLE EXPANDED IP ARP SUPPORT.** Enabling this feature causes the bridge to also watch the IP/ARP packets that occur on the network. No action is taken in response to an IP/ARP packet because that is the role of an IP router. However, the bridge adds the IP address to its IP/ARP table. This feature is helpful on an IP network because it builds a database of MAC layer addresses to IP address pairs. An SNMP monitoring program such as KBCONFIG (Monitor menu) can be used to extract this information. Note that the IP/ARP table is never timed-out in this mode, and this feature is not available if the KarlBRouter is routing IP. The default is that this feature is disabled.

❖ **STORM THRESHOLDS.** One of the features of the KarlBridge/KarlBRouter is its capability to keep Broadcast and Multicast storms from spreading across a network. Network storms are common and can cause bridges, routers, workstations, servers, and PCs to slow down or crash. Storms occur if network equipment is configured incorrectly, network software is not functioning correctly, or programs, such as network games, are not designed correctly.

When you select the Storm Thresholds option in the Bridging Setup menu, you see something similar to figure 7.6.

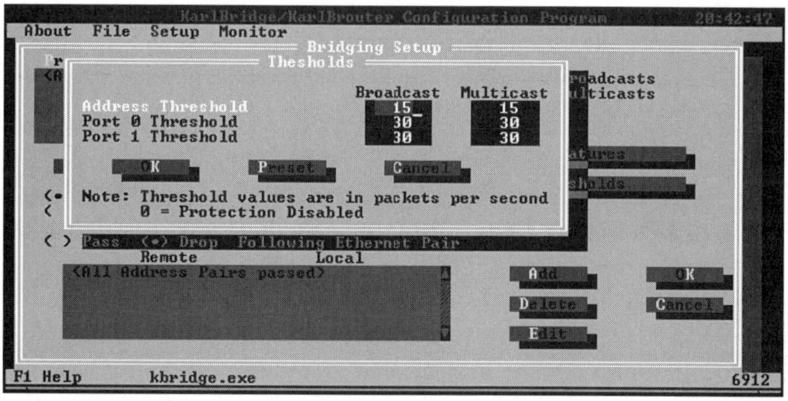

FIGURE 7.6

KarlBridge Storm Thresholds options.

The options in this screen are explained next:

✦ **Storm Thresholds—Address Threshold—Broadcast.** This is the number of broadcast packets that can occur in each one-second period before a storm condition is declared for a particular address (host). When a storm is declared, then any additional broadcast packets from that host address are dropped until the storm is determined to be over. The storm is determined to be over when 30 seconds has passed in which every one-second period has less than the stated threshold in broadcast packets.

✦ **Storm Thresholds—Address Threshold—Multicast.** This is the number of multicast packets that can occur in each one-second period before a storm condition is declared for a particular address. When a storm is declared, then any additional multicast packets from that host address are dropped until the storm is determined to be over. The storm is determined to be over when 30 seconds has passed in which every one-second period has less than the stated threshold in multicast packets.

✦ **Storm Thresholds—Port Threshold—Broadcast.** This is the number of broadcast packets that can occur in each one-second period before a storm condition is declared for a particular port. When a storm is declared, then any additional broadcast packets received on that port are dropped until the storm is determined to be over. The storm is determined to be over when a one-second period has occurred with no broadcast packets received on that port.

✦ **Storm Thresholds—Port Threshold—Multicast.** This is the number of multicast packets that can occur in each one-second period before a storm condition is declared for a particular port. When a storm is declared, any additional multicast packets received on that port are dropped until the storm is determined to be over. The storm is determined to be over when a one-second period has occurred with no multicast packets received on that port.

✦ **Storm Thresholds—Preset.** This button sets the Broadcast and Multicast storm thresholds to the recommended values (see fig. 7.6). These values have been determined to offer good protection without interfering with the operation of the typical network. These values may need to be tuned for your particular network.

If in the General Setup menu the Remote Bridging using IP Tunnels is enabled, then tunnel partners can be set up. The Tunnel Partners menu specifies the IP addresses of each of the KarlBridges set up to participate in the tunnel group. Only specify the other bridges; do not specify the IP address of this bridge.

Some KarlBridges and KarlBRouters contain a special software encryption algorithm that is distinct from the optional WaveLAN DES encryption chip. If Data Encryption is enabled on the General Setup menu and if an Encryption Key is set up in the Data Encryption menu, then enabling encryption here causes all packets transmitted to tunnel partners to be encrypted and any packets received from tunnel partners to be decrypted.

Select IP Hosts Setup (press Alt+S to see the options). You should see a screen showing you the setup options (see fig. 7.7). This screen is used to set up the IP address of the KarlBridge.

FIGURE 7.7

IP Host settings.

The fields that you may need for bridges are described next:

❖ **OUR IP ADDRESS.** This is the IP address of the KarlBridge itself. If you want to configure or monitor your KarlBridge or if your network supports IP and you want to enable the Ping support and IP/SNMP support, set this to a valid IP address. Setting this address to 0.0.0.0 disables Ping and IP/SNMP support. The KarlBridge is not an IP router. It has only one IP address, and that address applies to both the remote and local networks (both sides of the bridge). Having two Ethernet interfaces with the same IP address is different from a standard IP host, but is appropriate for a transparent bridge.

❖ **OUR SUBNET MASK.** This is the subnet mask assigned to the IP address. The value is expressed as a hexadecimal pattern. Select a value that is compatible with your subnet.

If you want the KarlBridge to be monitored from an SNMP Manager station, select SNMP Setup (press Alt+S to see the options). You should see a screen showing the setup options (see fig. 7.8). This screen is used to set up the IP address of the KarlBridge.

FIGURE 7.8

SNMP Setup.

The fields that you may need for bridges are described next:

✥ **READ PASSWORD.** This is the read-only password used for SNMP I support. It is the SNMP password needed to read the MIB variables. The string *public* is the common password used by most SNMP monitors.

✥ **READ/WRITE PASSWORD.** This is the read/write password used for SNMP support. It is the SNMP password needed to write the MIB variables. The string should be set to a value known only by you. The factory default value for this variable is the string *public* and should be changed to a string known only to you.

✥ **SYSTEM CONTACT.** This defines the value of the MIB variable, *sysContact*, for system contact. This could be the name of a person or a telephone number.

✥ **SYSTEM NAME.** This defines the value of the MIB variable, *sysName*, for system name. This is a description of the system.

✥ **SYSTEM LOCATION.** This defines the value of the MIB variable, *sysLocation*, for system location. This is a description of the system.

✥ **TRAP HOST IP ADDRESS.** This is the address of the host to which the KarlBridge's trap messages are sent. The host must be set to run an SNMP trap logger that can log these traps. Typically, this is the IP address of the SNMP manager.

✥ **TRAP HOST PASSWORD.** Only hosts that have this password set for trap messages can receive this trap message. The string *public* is the common password used to receive SNMP trap receivers.

✥ **ENABLE SNMP COLD/WARM START TRAP.** When enabled, SNMP trap messages are sent for cold and warm boot of the SNMP agent in the KarlBridge. If you have an SNMP manager that can log these events, you should enable these messages in case an intruder causes a shutdown of the KarlBridge.

296

❖ **ENABLE SNMP AUTHENTICATION TRAPS.** If an SNMP manager uses an incorrect password when trying to poll the bridge, it could represent an intruder trying to probe the KarlBridge. In this case, an SNMP authentication failure trap message is sent if this option is enabled.

❖ **SNMP IP ACCESS LIST.** This identifies the SNMP managers that can poll the KarlBridge.

If you want the KarlBridge to be used as a screening router, select Security (Firewall) Setup (press Alt+S to see the options). You should see a screen showing the protocol options for which you set filters (see fig. 7.9). The protocol options are TCP/UDP, AppleTalk, DECNET, and Novell's IPX. If you select the TCP/UDP option, you should see a screen for programming the filter (see fig. 7.10).

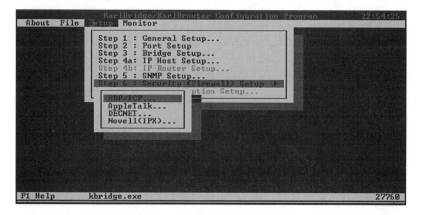

FIGURE 7.9

Protocol options for setting filters.

FIGURE 7.10

Protocol configuration options.

These fields are described next:

❖ **REMOTE AND LOCAL SERVERS.** These menus specify up to 10 IP networks, subnets, host IP address combinations, and server port numbers (referred to as sockets in the interface) that are to be passed or dropped. These two menus must be used together and will be combined into one menu in a future release of the software (see fig. 7.11).

FIGURE 7.11

Remote and local servers.

```
                    KarlBridge/KarlBrouter Configuration Program        23:24:25
  About   File   Setup   Monitor
 ┌────────────────────────── UDP/TCP Security Filter ──────────────────────┐
 │┌──────────────────── UDP/TCP Security Filter for Connection ────────────┐│
 ││       129.12.0.0 FFFF0000  and  199.245.180.10 FFFFFFFF                 ││
 ││ (•) Pass   ( ) Drop      ( ) Pass  (•) Drop      ( ) Pass  (•) Drop     ││
 ││Following Remote Servers  Following Local Servers  Following > 1024 Servers││
 ││<All will be dropped>  ▲  <All will be passed>  ▲  <All will be passed> ▲││
 ││                       █                        █                       ██││
 ││                       █                        █                        ││
 ││                       █                        █                        ││
 ││                       ▼                        ▼                       ▼││
 ││ [ ] Enable Data Encryption on Packets          ┌─Add─┐ ┌Delete┐ ┌Edit─┐││
 ││ [X] Pass IP/ICMP Packets (including PING)       └─────┘ └──────┘ └─────┘││
 ││ [X] Pass IP Packets that are not TCP/UDP        ┌──OK──┐   ┌Cancel─┐    ││
 ││                                                 └──────┘   └───────┘    ││
 │└────────────────────────────────────────────────────────────────────────┘│
 └──────────────────────────────────────────────────────────────────────────┘
 F1 Help        kbridge.exe                                           10880
```

Each IP packet that passes through the bridge is checked against the filter entry consisting of an IP Address and an IP Mask. If a packet matches the Remote IP network then the corresponding entry in the Local menu is checked for a match. If a match is found in the Local IP network, the port number conditions set for this entry are matched.

Each IP packet source and destination address is checked against each entry in the list to determine if the packet is to be allowed or blocked. Blocked packets are dropped. Matching is performed on the first entry first and then goes down the list. When a match is found, the action specified on that line is performed immediately. A bit-wise AND operation is performed between the packet's IP addresses and the Mask values. The same is done for the addresses specified in the entry. The two results are then compared. If they are the same, a match has occurred.

Note that the KarlBridge is not an IP Router. This menu specifies the IP networks, IP subnets, and IP hosts on the remote network that hosts on the local network can communicate with.

The following examples can clarify the use of these filter specifications:

Example 1

IP Address	IP Mask	Action Performed
128.146.0.0	FFFF0000	Pass packets to Network 128.146.x.x
128.150.0.0	FFFF0000	Pass packets to Network 128.150.x.x
Drop All Others		Drop packets to all other networks

Example 2

IP Address	IP Mask	Action Performed
128.146.10.8	FFFFFFFF	Pass packets to 128.146.10.8
128.146.10.9	FFFFFFFF	Pass packets to 128.146.10.9
128.146.10.0	FFFFFF00	Drop packets to Subnet 128.146.10.x
128.150.25.0	FFFFFF00	Drop packets to Subnet 128.146.25.x
128.146.0.0	FFFF0000	Pass packets to Network 128.146.x.x
128.150.0.0	FFFF0000	Pass packets to Network 128.150.x.x
Drop All Others		Drop packets to all other networks

❖ **LOCAL IP ADDRESS/MASK MENU.** This menu specifies the local IP subnets and hosts that are to be allowed or blocked. Each entry consists of an IP address and an IP mask. A packet that matches is then either passed or dropped as indicated. Each IP packet's source or destination address is checked against each entry in the list to determine if the packet is to be passed or dropped. Matching is performed on the first entry first and then goes down the list. When a match is found, the action specified on that line is performed immediately. A bit-wise AND operation is performed between the packet's IP addresses and the Mask values. The same is done for the addresses specified in the entry. The two results are then compared. If they are the same, a match has occurred.

This option is similar in function to that configured in the Remote IP Address/Mask Menu discussed previously, with the exception that it applies to IP hosts, IP subnets, and IP network on the local network (connected to the local port of the KarlBridge).

❖ **PASS/DROP IP REMOTE SERVERS MENU.** This menu specifies the remote IP/UDP and IP/TCP server sockets to be passed or dropped. In this context, *server sockets* are sockets assigned numbers less than 1,024, such as the Telnet daemon, the FTP daemon, the SMTP daemon, and many others. *Remote server sockets* are servers located on the remote network. For example, if ftp and Telnet are passed and all other sockets are dropped in this menu, then machines on the local network can initiate an ftp or Telnet session to remote machines, but no other outgoing connections can be initiated.

If the Sockets button is selected (see fig. 7.12), you can specify the port numbers to be used for filtering.

FIGURE 7.12

Selecting service port numbers.

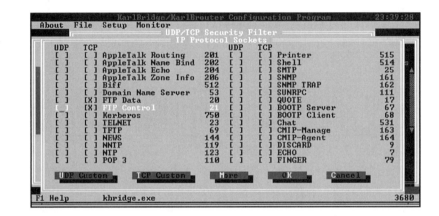

❖ **PASS/DROP IP LOCAL SERVERS MENU.** This menu specifies the local IP/UDP and IP/TCP server port numbers to be allowed or blocked. In this context, *server sockets* are sockets assigned numbers less than 1,024, such as the Telnet daemon, the FTP daemon, the SMTP daemon, and many others. *Local server sockets* are servers located on the local network. For example, if ftp and telnet are dropped and all other sockets are passed in this menu, then machines on the remote network cannot initiate an ftp or telnet session on local machines.

❖ **PASS/DROP IP SOCKETS > 1023 MENU.** This menu specifies the remote and local IP/UDP and IP/TCP sockets greater than 1,023 to be passed or dropped. X11, Multiuser Dungeons (MUD), NFS, and other nonprivileged sockets are in this range. No distinction is made between *local* and *remote* for this menu. You can drop MUD sockets, for example, either by specifying them individually or by setting the menu to pass nothing and Drop All Others. This causes the KarlBridge to drop all packets to or from server sockets > 1,023, which includes MUD, X11, NFS, and all other server port numbers in this range.

You can add a port filter specification by selecting the Add button. Figure 7.12 showed the flexibility available for adding port numbers.

When done setting up security filter, save your changes by pressing Alt+S and selecting Save. Exit the KBCONFIG program by pressing Alt+F and selecting Exit. The options that you have configured are stored in the KBRIDGE.EXE program.

KARLBRIDGE IMPLEMENTATION CONSIDERATIONS

The SMC Elite 16 Ethernet card-based KarlBridge is a general-purpose PC card and is not as fast at forwarding packets as some commercial bridges. At times, extra speed might be needed, such as in situations of network congestion or high network traffic. Commercial versions of KarlBridge are based upon special, ultra-fast Ethernet cards that boost the forwarding rate up to full Ethernet speed.

A commercial clone, such as 286/386/486/Pentium, provides adequate performance for most small networks. If additional performance and reliability are needed to withstand larger extremes of heat, dust, and restarting after power failures, you might want to use the commercial version of KarlBridge.

Currently, if you are using the shareware version of KarlBridge, you must use SMC Elite 16 cards with the 83C690 chip. The SMC Ultra card is expected to be supported in future versions of the shareware/demo KarlBridge.

Other enhancements planned for KarlBridge include the following:

✤ Drives for:

> COM Port with 16650 UART (SLIP and PPP)
>
> Aggregation of multiple ports, which means making multiple 56K/T1 or multiple V.Fast modem lines work together to provide faster remote Ethernet bridging and routing
>
> CATV card for an Ethernet to CATV bridge/router

✤ Support for:

> Additional wireless card to add to the existing WaveLAN support
>
> FDDI support
>
> Token Ring support
>
> ATM card support

❖ Adding RIP to the IP router module of KarlBRouter

❖ Support for spanning tree and source routing

❖ Filter and firewall enhancements for IP and support for Windows NT server filters

USES OF THE KARLBRIDGE

The KarlBridge designers estimate that over 7,000 people worldwide use the shareware and commercial versions of the KarlBridge. The following paragraphs provide some examples that may benefit you in using KarlBridge.

A wireless KarlBridge with the CellWave algorithm was used at Interop, Las Vegas (Spring 1994) to provide a 2 Megabit/sec Internet connection from the Las Vegas Convention center to the MGM Grand hotel (2.5 miles away) and the Bally's hotel (2.0 miles away). Each location had over 25 diskless X terminals. The convention center was configured as a Wireless KarlBridge base station, and the hotels were satellite stations. The CellWave algorithm provides lossless connectivity and takes care of base station repeat and hidden node problems both normally associated with wireless networks.

The Ohio State University network uses over 150 KarlBridges. This network consists of an FDDI ring connecting five hub sites. Each hub has one or more Cisco 7000 Routers with an FDDI interface and several Ethernet interfaces. Each Ethernet network connects through fiber to one or more buildings. A KarlBridge is set up at the entrance to each building to filter out unwanted protocols and to provide firewall and broadcast storm protection and SNMP monitoring. Many of the university buildings have several departments, each with a KarlBridge that can be used to isolate unwanted network traffic between departments. The departments run a combination of AppleTalk, NetWare-based, and TCP/IP-based networks. Protocol problems characteristic for each type of network can be prevented from propagating to other networks. Thus traffic caused by zone name problems need not appear on NetWare networks, and network number collisions on NetWare networks can be prevented from appearing on other networks.

COMMERCIAL VERSION OF KARLBRIDGE

The commercial version of KarlBridge supports additional features, such as the following:

❖ Expanded firewall filters

❖ Logging of break-in attempts

❖ Broadcast storm detection and suppression

❖ Logging of all TCP establish packets

❖ A new SNMP management, monitoring, and configuration program

❖ Encryption

❖ IP Routing

❖ Supports for high-speed Ethernet cards that enable the KarlBridge/KarlBRouter to forward at full Ethernet speeds

❖ Support for WAN links such as a dual 56 KB/64 KB card with T1/E1 speeds, ATT/NCR/DEC WaveLAN wireless card, and standard 16550 UART and modem support for dial-up SLIP links

❖ PPP over the synchronous and asynchronous lines with support for channel aggregation

❖ RIP for the IP router module

❖ Intelligent firewall filters that enable the Karlbridge to function like an application level gateway

The commercial version of KarlBridge is also licensed to OEMs by KarlNet, Inc. KarlNet, Inc. is the main commercial supplier of the KarlBridge hardware and software in the United States. KarlBridges and KarlBrouters are manufactured and sold in the United Kingdom by Sherwood Data Systems, Ltd., and other resellers exist worldwide.

KarlNet, Inc. sells the Ethernet-to-Ethernet KarlBridge box for approximately $1,200 (prices vary). KarlBridge models that come with Flash ROM kits cost more.

KarlBridge/Brouter can be obtained with different networking options, such as the following:

❖ Ethernet-to-wireless bridging and routing using the ATT/NCR/DEC WaveLAN card

❖ Ethernet-to-56 KB/64 KB/T1/E1 bridging and routing, Ethernet-to-Async SLIP line

❖ A standard Hayes AT command set compatible modem (supports V.Fast modems, auto dial, dial on demand, and secure lines)

You can obtain additional information on KarlBridge from the following sources:

For the commercial version:

In the United States:

> KarlNet, Inc.
> 614-263-5275
> sales@KarlNet.com
> URL: http://www.karlbridge.com

303

In the United Kingdom:

> Sherwood Data Systems, Ltd. UK
> 44- (0) 494 464 264

For the shareware version:

> Doug Karl
> Senior Computer Specialist
> Networking Engineering Group
> Ohio State University
> kbridge@osu.edu

THE DRAWBRIDGE PACKET FILTER

The Texas AMU security tools include a package for implementing screening routers called *Drawbridge*. Drawbridge can be found at many security-related sites, so it might be best to research using WWW or Archie to find the closest and latest version. This package is available at the URL `ftp://net.tamu/edu/pub/security/TAMU`.

Version 1.1 of Drawbridge is available in drawbridge-1.1.tar.Z and drawbridge-1.1-des.tar.Z. The drawbridge-1.1.tar.Z package is the Drawbridge base package without DES support. The drawbridge-1.1-des.tar.Z package is a supplemental package that contains the DES support. This package is installed in addition to the drawbridge-1.1.tar.Z package; just extract it on top of the regular package. This adds a few source files and new makefiles to the filter and fm directories. Note that the DES package is not required to operate Drawbridge; it only allows you to manage Drawbridge in a secure manner.

Because of United States export restrictions, only U.S. domestic sites can download the DES package. The package can function without any encryption package, but with reduced security on filter updates across the network.

Drawbridge is a copyrighted but freely distributed bridging filter. It uses a PC with two Ethernet cards to perform the filtering. It is composed of the following three tools:

> ✤ Filter
>
> ✤ Filter Compiler
>
> ✤ Filter Manager

Drawbridge was designed and programmed by David K. Hess, Douglas Lee Schales, and David R. Safford of Texas A&M University. You can send comments and suggestions about their package to drawbridge@sc.tamu.edu

OVERVIEW OF DRAWBRIDGE

Drawbridge is a bridging filter that has filtering at the center of the design. It uses custom, table-driven software called the Filter that can run on a dedicated PC. The authors recommend a 33-MHz 486 or better PC. The PC requires two Ethernet cards. Only 16-bit SMC cards are currently supported. The Filter Manager and Filter Compiler both run on Sun workstations.

The Filter Manager communicates and manages Filter (running on a PC) using SUN's NIT support. The Filter Compiler generates filtering tables that are loaded into Filter through the Filter Manager.

The Filter program filters TCP/IP on an incoming and outgoing basis and UDP/IP on an incoming basis. All other protocols are transparently bridged.

EXTRACTING THE DRAWBRIDGE SOFTWARE

The file is a Unix "GNU zipped" tar file. After you download this file, you must use the Unix gunzip and tar utilities on the downloaded file. The following commands are listed as a guideline to performing these steps:

```
mkdir /usr/tamu       # Create a working directory
#Retrieve archive into this directory. The following
#commands assume that the name of the archive is
#drawbridge.tar.Z
gunzip drawbridge.tar.Z             # This unzips the file
tar -xvBf drawbridge.tar            # On BSD UNIX. Your UNIX command
                                    # may differ.
```

The following subdirectories and files are created relative to your working directory:

```
drawbridge-1.1/
drawbridge-1.1/drawbridge.README
drawbridge-1.1/fm/
drawbridge-1.1/fm/Makefile
drawbridge-1.1/fm/comm.c
drawbridge-1.1/fm/crypt.c
drawbridge-1.1/fm/fm.8
drawbridge-1.1/fm/fm.c
drawbridge-1.1/fm/fm.h
drawbridge-1.1/fm/lex.h
drawbridge-1.1/fm/lex.l
drawbridge-1.1/fm/nit.c
```

```
drawbridge-1.1/fm/util.c
drawbridge-1.1/doc/
drawbridge-1.1/doc/OVERVIEW
drawbridge-1.1/doc/MANAGER
drawbridge-1.1/doc/FILTER
drawbridge-1.1/doc/COMPILER
drawbridge-1.1/doc/filtering.ps.Z
drawbridge-1.1/doc/DES
drawbridge-1.1/doc/firewall.ps.Z
drawbridge-1.1/COPYING
drawbridge-1.1/filter/
drawbridge-1.1/filter/crypt.c
drawbridge-1.1/filter/filter.8
drawbridge-1.1/filter/filter.c
drawbridge-1.1/filter/message.c
drawbridge-1.1/filter/wd.c
drawbridge-1.1/filter/filter.h
drawbridge-1.1/filter/wd.h
drawbridge-1.1/filter/filter.exe
drawbridge-1.1/filter/makefile.mak
drawbridge-1.1/fc/
drawbridge-1.1/fc/Makefile
drawbridge-1.1/fc/chario.c
drawbridge-1.1/fc/chario.h
drawbridge-1.1/fc/classes.c
drawbridge-1.1/fc/classes.h
drawbridge-1.1/fc/fc.8
drawbridge-1.1/fc/fc.c
drawbridge-1.1/fc/grammar.y
drawbridge-1.1/fc/groups.c
drawbridge-1.1/fc/groups.h
drawbridge-1.1/fc/hosts.c
drawbridge-1.1/fc/hosts.h
drawbridge-1.1/fc/lex.c
drawbridge-1.1/fc/macros.h
drawbridge-1.1/fc/ports.h
drawbridge-1.1/fc/protocols.h
drawbridge-1.1/fc/services.c
drawbridge-1.1/fc/services.h
drawbridge-1.1/fc/Sample
```

The directories fm, doc, filter, and fc are created under the drawbridge directory. In the preceding example, this directory is drawbridge-1.1. This name might change as newer versions of the drawbridge program are released.

The doc directory contains the documentation about Drawbridge. The fm directory contains the source code for the Filter Manager. The fc directory contains the source code for the Filter Compiler. The filter directory contains the source code for the Filter. The Filter program runs under DOS on a PC configured with two network interfaces.

The Filter Compiler (fc) and Filter Manager (fm) both require an ANSI C compiler. The GNU C Compiler (gcc) is recommended by the authors. The Filter requires Borland's Turbo C++ 3.0. An executable version of Filter is provided in case you do not have access to Turbo C++.

To build Filter Compiler and Filter Manager, just go into the respective directories and type the following command:

```
make
```

The preceding command builds the executables. To install the Filter Compiler and Filter Manager, edit the makefiles to set the destination directory, login as root user, and type the following:

```
make install
```

If you have the DES portion of the package, make sure to install that before typing **make**.

To build Filter, copy all of the filter directory to a PC and type **make**.

DRAWBRIDGE DESIGN

Drawbridge compares best to a filtering router firewall configuration as shown in figure 7.13. In a filtering router firewall, a router that has packet filtering support is used to filter packets to an internal network.

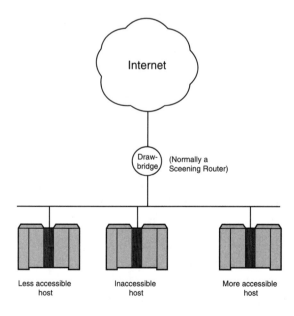

FIGURE 7.13

Drawbridge as filtering router firewall.

307

In figure 7.13, instead of using a screening router (firewall router), the filtering function is moved from the router into Drawbridge, which acts as a bridging filter.

One problem with packet filtering implementations is that they are difficult to configure. The simple syntax is designed so that a router can efficiently implement it, and not for a network administrator to remember the filter. In Drawbridge, the filter programming is off-loaded. Filter tables are specified using a rich and powerful language. The compiled tables are used for the dedicated filter. This allows Drawbridge to filter in terms of connections, rather than at the level of a packet.

This table design enables arbitrarily complex filters to be defined. In most conventional filtering routers, as filters are added, the performance begins to quickly drop due to how they implement the filtering rules. In Drawbridge, arbitrary numbers of complex filters can be set up, and the performance remains almost constant because simple look ups are performed and only connection establishment packets are filtered for TCP.

Drawbridge enables the testing of the configuration by enabling the administrator to see the results of a compiled configuration file, and to see if the correct filtering rules have been applied.

Drawbridge, unlike many screening routers, provides support for TCP source port filtering. Because source port filtering does allow the possibility of tunneling, Drawbridge does add the restriction that the destination port must be greater than 900. The authors selected 800 because of "broken" FTP implementations that happen to use FTP data ports beginning at around 900 rather than 1,024.

Figure 7.14 shows the steps involved in developing a filter specification. A source file containing filtering specifications in a special language is generated and maintained by an administrator. This file is then passed through the filter compiler, which generates the tables used by Filter. These tables can be loaded using a Filter Manager or by floppy disk.

FIGURE 7.14

Developing a Filter Specification.

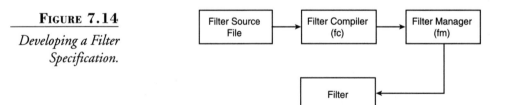

The Filter Compiler generates four types of tables. The first is a network table, which has an entry for each host in the network. The host portion of an address determines the index into the table. The value in the table defines the "class" that is applied to a host when a TCP connection attempt or UDP packet is directed at that host. Currently, only class B and C networks are supported because class A tables would consume 16 MB of memory, and Filter does not have the capability to use any memory above 1 MB. The tables are defined in terms of *internal hosts* (hosts on the inside of Filter). No filtering is done based on the address of the host outside of the filter, except on a global basis. Filter only controls which inside host services are open, not which outside hosts may access an inside host services.

The *host class* is used as an index into the classes table. This table is composed of four subtables: TCP in, TCP out, TCP source, and UDP in. These subtables are in turn composed of lists that contain port number ranges. A *class* specifies a list out of each subtable that defines a host's filtering. TCP filtering only occurs when packets with SYN=1 and ACK=0 flags (connection initiation) are detected in a TCP header. All other packets of a TCP session are not filtered. Also, all UDP packets are filtered on an incoming basis only.

The last two tables are the allow and reject tables. The *allow table* globally allows packets out from any machine on the inside of the filter to the list of addresses in the allow table. The *reject table* globally rejects packets coming in from any machine on the outside of the filter with an address corresponding to an address in the reject table.

Figure 7.15 shows the algorithm used for filtering outgoing packets, and figure 7.16 shows the algorithm used for filtering incoming packets.

The language used by the Filter Compiler contains constructs for creating the various tables used by the filter. Constructs exist for specifying the network access on a per host basis or a network or subnetwork basis. The language enables groups of services to be created. These groups can be used in cases of related services or to group related machines.

The basic element of the language is a service specification. The service specification contains the following four pieces of information:

- ✧ The service
- ✧ The protocol
- ✧ The source or destination
- ✧ The traffic direction

The service can be either an entry from /etc/services or a numeric port. A range of port numbers also can be used. The protocol specifies the protocol that the service uses. The source or destination indicates whether the filter should use the source port or the destination port. The traffic direction indicates whether this is for outbound packets or inbound packets, or both.

FIGURE 7.15

Filtering of outgoing packets in Drawbridge.

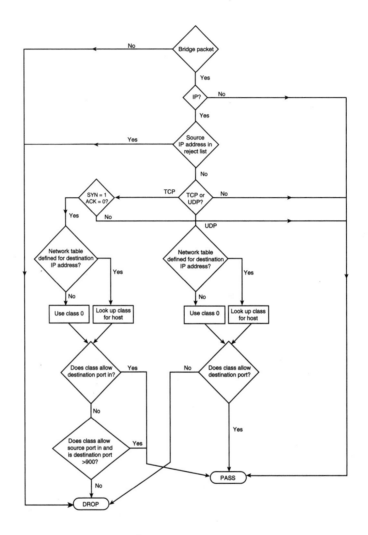

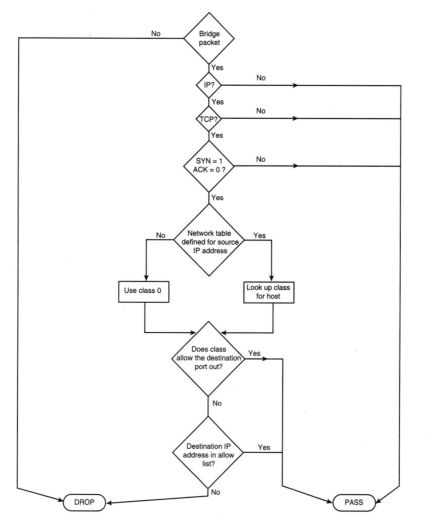

FIGURE 7.16

Filtering of incoming packets in Drawbridge.

A *group* is a list of comma-separated service specifications or other previously defined groups. Groups can be used to relate services or to categorize machines, enabling quick global changes to a category of machines. Hosts and networks can be granted network access using service specifications or group names.

DRAWBRIDGE FILTER LANGUAGE

The basic element of the language is a service specification. The service specification was described in the preceding section. The following are some sample specifications of the filter language.

Example 1 allows SMTP connections in either direction:

```
<smtp in-out>
```

Example 2 allows all outbound connections:

```
<1-65535 out>
```

Example 3 allows UDP-based network time protocol (NTP):

```
<ntp/udp in>
```

Example 4 allows data connect for ftp callback:

```
<src=ftp-data in>
```

Prefacing the service specification with an exclamation mark (!), indicates that this service is not allowed.

Example 5 does not allow TFTP:

```
<!tftp/udp in>
```

Example 6 does not permit rlogin:

```
<!login in>
```

Example 7 does not allow call to an internal NFS server:

```
<!2049/udp in>
```

Groups of service specifications can be used to repeatedly enter the same data. Groups also can be used to quickly change the access characteristics of an entire set of machines.

A *group* is a list of comma-separated service specifications or other previously defined groups, terminated by a semicolon (;).

Example 8 allows incoming mail and gopher connections.

```
define normal <smtp in>, <gopher in>;
```

The preceding example creates a group called normal that includes inbound smtp and inbound gopher. This group can be used in other groups to build up larger groups.

Example 9:

```
define server normal, <telnet in>;
```

In the preceding example, the new group server includes smtp, gopher, and telnet in.

The special group "default" is used to define access class #0, which is the default access for any machine not explicitly defined in the configuration file:

Example 10:

```
define default <1-65535 out>, <src=ftp-data in>, <smtp in>;
```

The preceding example allows all outbound connections, e-mail in, and ftp's data connections in for all machines that do not appear in the configuration file. Normally, all machines want the default services as well; therefore, group default should be added to the machines in the configuration file.

To define the access for a particular host, simply give the hostname and a comma-separated list of service specifications and group names.

Consider the following host services in Example 11:

```
host myhost default, normal;
host newshost default, <nntp in>;
```

Using the preceding definitions for normal and default, host myhost defines the following service definition.

```
<1-65535 out>, <src=ftp-data in>, <smtp in>,
<gopher in>, <telnet in>;
```

And host newshost defines the following service definition:

```
<1-65535 out>, <src=ftp-data in>, <smtp in>,
<gopher in>, <nntp in>;
```

If you want to specify access for an entire range of addresses, you can use the *network* command, which is similar to the host command.

Example 12:

```
network 123.45.67.0-123.45.68.255 255.255.255.0 <!1-65535 in-out>;

network 123.45.69.0 255.255.255.0 <!1-65535 in>;
```

The first entry allows no TCP connections "in" or "out" for 123.45.67.* and 123.45.68.*. The second allows no incoming connections for 123.45.69.*. Notice that the second example is an implicit range of 123.45.69.0–123.45.69.255. In the first example, you must fully specify the full range. For example, the range 123.45.67.0–123.45.68.0 would not include the hosts 123.45.68.1–123.45.68.255.

When multiple service specifications appear in a group definition or host/network command, they are merged. Service specifications are merged by doing an OR on the allowed services and keeping those explicitly disallowed, as shown in the following example:

```
define group1 <telnet in>, <!login in>, <!tftp/udp in>;
define group2 <telnet out>, <smtp in>, <login in>;
define group3 group1 group2 <tftp/udp in>;
group3 will have <telnet in-out>, <smtp in>.
```

Note that even though group2 allows <login in>, it is not possible to override the <!login in> specified in group1. Similarly it is not possible to override the <!tftp/udp in> from group1. group3 inherits the <!login in>. In other words, the actual value of group3 is as follows:

```
<telnet in-out>, <smtp in>, <!login in>, <!tftp/udp in>
```

The <telnet in> and <telnet out> in the combined group are equivalent to <telnet in-out>.

As a host's access capability is specified, either by use of a host or network command, classes of hosts are generated. All the members of a specific class have the same access allowed to them. There can be up to 256 different classes, with class 0 reserved for those hosts not specified in the configuration file. Class 0's capabilities are defined by the special group default. Each class can have up to 32 port ranges for each of incoming TCP, outgoing TCP, incoming TCP srcport, and incoming UDP.

You can break up the configuration file and include the separate files to create the filter control files, as shown in the following example:

```
include file1;
include file2;
```

Nesting of include statements is permitted.

```
reject address netmask
```

You can use the reject command to reject all incoming packets coming from a network address, as in the following example:

```
reject 18.23.0.0 255.255.255.0;
```

You can use the allow command to permit outbound packets from this destination, even if the access for the source host does not allow it. The expected use of the allow subcommand is in situations in which a restricted machine is being granted a network service. For example, if a workstation normally does not have access to the Internet, the allow subcommand can allow these machines to access a service on a specific machine/network. The syntax of the allow command is as follows:

```
allow address netmask [service-specification list];
```

After the rules are specified, you can use the compiler fc to generate the filter control tables from the source configuration file, as in the following example:

```
fc configuration-file
```

The following is a sample configuration file adapted from the Drawbridge documentation:

```
# Example config file
#------------------------------------------------------------------------
#
# Defaults for any machine not listed in this file.
#
define tcpdefault <1-65535 out>, <src=ftp-data in>, <smtp in>, <auth in>,
                <gopher in>;
define udpdefault <1-65535/udp in>, <!tftp/udp in>, <!2049/udp in>,
        <!sunrpc/udp in>;
define default tcpdefault, udpdefault;
# Include 'default' in telftp since most will need defaults as well.
define telftp default, <telnet in>, <ftp in>;
# Admin requested no access in/out for these subnets
network 123.45.58.0 255.255.255.0 <!1-65535 in-out>;
network 123.45.39.0 255.255.255.0 <!1-65535 in-out>;
network 123.45.40.0 255.255.255.0 <!1-65535 in-out>;
#------------------------------------------------------------------------
#
host m1.dt.tamu.edu                     telftp, <domain in>;
#------------------------------------------------------------------------
# NNTP host and CSO phonebook server
host mailnews.tamu.edu                  telftp,
                                        <nntp in>, <time in>,
                                        <csnet-ns in>, <domain in>,
                                        <finger in>;
host slow.tamu.edu                      telftp;
host previous.tamu.edu                  telftp, <domain in>;
host mvt.tamu.edu                       telftp;
# IRC server on here...
host ick.tamu.edu                       <1-65535 out>, <6667 in>, <smtp in>,
<auth in>,udpdefaults;

#
# Machine (PC) in library which use tftp to do document transfers
host sender.tamu.edu                    <1-65535/udp in>;
#------------------------------------------------------------------------
host h1.tamu.edu                        default, telftp;
#------------------------------------------------------------------------
# These are all the VMS machines which have been cleared for telnet/ftp.
host h2.tamu.edu                        telftp;
```

```
host h3.tamu.edu                    telftp;
host h4.tamu.edu                    telftp, <domain in>; # zone transfers
host h5.tamu.edu                    telftp;
host h6.tamu.edu                    telftp;
host h7.tamu.edu                    telftp;
host h8.tamu.edu                    telftp;
host h9.tamu.edu                    telftp;
host h10.tamu.edu                   telftp;
# Research group using port 4211
host h11.tamu.edu                   telftp, <4211 in>;
host h12.tamu.edu                   telftp;
host h13.tamu.edu                   telftp;
host h14.tamu.edu                   telftp;
# NTP time server
host h15.tamu.edu                   telftp, <ntp in>,
                                    <time in>;

#--------------------------------------------------------------------
host s1.tamu.edu                    telftp;
host fast.tamu.edu                  telftp;
host dunno.tamu.edu                 telftp;
host meat.tamu.edu                  telftp, <finger in>;
# A PC FTP server
host somepc.tamu.edu                default, <ftp in>;
# Has to have X11
host arrow.tamu.edu                 default, <ftp in>, <6000 in>;
host d2.tamu.edu                    default, <ftp in>;
host trouble.tamu.edu               default, telftp;
#
host td.tamu.edu                    default,
                                    <ftp in>, <auth in>, <domain in>;
# No access in/out
host bee.tamu.edu                   <!1-65535 in-out>;
host g1.tamu.edu                    <!1-65535 in-out>;
host see.tamu.edu                   <!1-65535 in-out>;
host bam.tamu.edu                   <!1-65535 in-out>;
# NTP server
host bird.tamu.edu                  default, <ntp in>, <time in>;
#--------------------------------------------------------------------
# Gotta have X...
host gotta.tamu.edu                 default, <6000 in>;
host be.tamu.edu                    default, <6000 in>;
host very.tamu.edu                  default, <6000 in>;
host slow.tamu.edu                  default, <6000 in>;
#--------------------------------------------------------------------
# More name servers for subdomains
host add.tamu.edu                   default, <domain in>;
host bigadd.math.tamu.edu           default, <domain in>;
#
host dead.tamu.edu                  telftp;
#
host someone.tamu.edu               default, <ftp in>;
```

```
# Nuclear Engineering
host hot.tamu.edu                          default, <ftp in>;
#
# Robotics Lab.  For demo. until 12/19?
host sp1.dt.tamu.edu                       telftp,
                                           <2650 in>, <2655 in>, <2700-2702 in>,
                                           <3200-3202 in>, <3300-3302 in>,
<3500-3502 in>;
# Local MUD's
host someklingon.tamu.edu                  default, <2000 in>;
host hmmmmm.tamu.edu                       default, <2000 in>;
```

DRAWBRIDGE FILTER

Filter is an executable program file called FILTER.EXE and should run on most compatibles. The FILTER.EXE is the software component of Drawbridge that runs on a 286/386/486/ Pentium PC and performs packet filtering. This module takes full control of the PC and converts it into a dedicated packet filter device. You can place a line containing the FILTER command in the AUTOEXEC.BAT file of the PC. This implies that the system should be DOS-bootable. DOS versions of 5.0 or higher can be used. By placing the Filter program in the AUTOEXEC.BAT you can ensure that the system boots automatically on power failures of system reboots initiated by the Filter Manager.

The Filter program is written using ANSI C. In its current distribution, Filter is compiled with Borland's Turbo C++ 3.0. No special settings are needed for the CONFIG.SYS file, so you can delete the CONFIG.SYS file or leave it empty. If you are using the Filter on a test PC, you may need to eliminate any device drivers that can cause conflicts. As usual with the PC world, these conflicts are hard to predict because of the many varieties of BIOS systems and device drivers.

The PC on which Filter runs should have 1 MB of memory and 5 MB of hard disk space. A 486 PC is recommended for good performance. Any memory over 1 MB is not used by the filter program because it runs in the DOS-real mode. If you are using the same PC to do the compilation, you will need more memory to modify and recompile the program with Turbo C++.

The Filter program is currently hard-coded to use only the Elite16 (8013) series of Ethernet cards from SMC. Future versions might add support for more cards. Because the PC acts as a bridge, two cards are needed for Filter. One Ethernet interface card is used for the internal network, and the other interfaces to the external network.

For those who do not intend to compile or modify Filter, an executable version of Filter is supplied with the source code. The make files (called *project files* in Borland C++) are included for those who want to examine, modify, or compile the code themselves. Except for two warnings about an unused parameter in a function definition, which can be safely ignored, the compilation process should go smoothly.

The two Ethernet boards must be set as follows:

> Ethernet Card 1 [Inside (Internal) Network]
>
>> Memory Base Address: 0xD000
>>
>> I/O port address: 0x280
>
> Ethernet Card 2 [Outside (External) Network]
>
>> Memory Base Address: 0xCC00
>>
>> I/O port address: 0x300

Other considerations in setting up the hardware are as follows:

❖ Configure the cards properly for either AUI, Thin Wire, or 10BASE-T cabling.

❖ Interrupt settings are not so critical because the Filter program always polls.

❖ Depending on the model of 8013 card, you may need to set these configurations with jumpers, with the ezsetup program, or both.

For a system to be used in a production environment, you should "burn-in" a PC configuration for a week before you start using it. Other considerations are to ensure proper cooling and power regulation and protection from high humidity and dusty environments.

The Filter takes one argument, which determines which Ethernet interface is used for listening for remote Filter Manager commands. You can use the following syntax for invoking the Filter program:

```
filter [-l (inside¦outside¦both)]
```

The "inside" should be used if the commands are to be received on the internal network Ethernet interface. The "outside" should be used if the commands are to be received on the external network Ethernet interface. The "both" should be used if the commands are to be received on either internal or external network Ethernet interfaces. If no arguments are specified, the Filter does not respond to any Filter Manager commands.

A typical sample AUTOEXEC.BAT file includes the following:

```
rem Change to the "filter" directory
cd \FILTER
filter -1 inside
```

In the preceding example, the FILTER.EXE has been copied to a special directory called FILTER. You can, of course, use any other directory name.

After the Filter program is loaded, all management activity occurs on the Filter Manager host. If you do not want to use the management software, you need to take the output files from Filter Compiler (using the byte reversal switch), and then copy them to the same directory on the PC on which FILTER.EXE is located.

To halt a running Filter program, type the $ character at the PC Filter's keyboard. This causes Filter to exit and return you to the DOS prompt. If you never intend to access the Filter PC physically after it is installed, you can remove the monitor, monitor card, and keyboard, provided that you can disable the use of these devices from the BIOS so that your system does not generate errors on rebooting. If you have a keyboard attached to the system, your security policy should consider locking the keyboard or physically securing the Filter PC against accidental or intentional damage.

If you are using the Filter in conjunction with DES and lose your DES key on the Filter Manger host, you must disable the existing key. You can do this by halting the Filter program and then deleting (or replacing) the DES.KEY file in the Filter directory. This puts the Filter in a non-secure mode. You can then install a new DES key.

DRAWBRIDGE FILTER MANAGER

The Filter Manager is the tool used for managing a PC running the Filter program. The Filter Manager enables you to load new tables into the Filter and inspect them.

Currently, the Filter Manager can only run on Sun4 systems running SunOS 4.1.*x* with a kernel that has the Network Interface Tap (NIT) driver properly configured. Attempts to compile on other systems using the make files that come with the distribution produce error messages about missing critical "include" files.

If you do not have access to the hardware platform required for the Filter Manager, you can use the "sneaker-net" for distributing the filter tables to the Filter PC. You can do this by using a floppy disk to copy the output files of the Filter Compilation rules to the Filter PC.

You can build the Filter Manager by running the make program in the fm distribution directory. A binary image of the program also exists in the fm distributing directory, so you can copy it to the Filter Manager platform. The Filter Manager is written using ANSI C. The GNU C compiler is recommended.

The executable can be installed anywhere and does not need any support files. However, the Filter Manager program must be installed with SUID set for root. The Filter Manager uses root privilege only long enough to open the network interface and then changes its SUID to the real user.

The Filter Manager is an interactive program modeled after lpc. It provides more feedback and help than your typical Unix tool. The following is the syntax for using the Filter Manager:

```
fm [-i interface ]
```

If the network interface is not specified, the Filter Manager picks a likely device. You can use the following command to determine which interface to use.

```
netstat -i
```

To manage the Filter PC, you must select an interface on the same physical network to which the PC running Filter is attached. If Filter Manager's standard input is not a tty device, it does not print out any information on standard output. Instead, it sends an error message to the standard error (stderr) device.

After the Filter Manager starts, you can use commands such as help or ? to get additional help information. The commands supported include the following:

```
set (verbose¦target¦key) <args>
load (network¦classes¦allow¦reject) <filename>
show (host¦class¦allow¦reject¦target¦verbose¦key) [<args>]
query (host¦class¦allow¦reject¦stats) [<args>]
upload (networks¦classes¦allow¦reject)
write
release (classes¦allow¦reject¦network) [<args>]
ping
reboot
clear
reset
newkey <name>
genkey <name>
quit
```

A "#" at the beginning of a line comments the entire line. You can use the "!" to "escape" to the shell. The following command gives you additional information on using a specified command:

```
help command
```

To communicate with Filter PC, you need to tell the Filter Manager the Ethernet address of the Ethernet card on the PC that is connected to the same physical network. This is done using the set target command. You must specify the correct hardware address, or you cannot communicate with Filter. Filter Manager uses a nonroutable protocol to communicate with the Filter PC, so that it is not susceptible to remote attacks on routed, gated, or routing tables.

The Filter program must be started with the correct switches to enable communication with the Filter Manager. The following are examples of commands that can be used to start the Filter and enable communication with the Filter Manager:

```
filter -l inside
filter -l outside
filter -l both
```

When Filter is first started, it does not have any tables loaded (unless you used a floppy to copy the tables to the Filter PC). In this case, the default rules apply for all packet filtering. You must build a filter configuration file and use Filter Compiler to generate the filtering tables.

By default, Filter also does not use DES. You can use the newkey command in the Filter Manager to install a key in Filter to enable DES. To enable DES support, you must add additional files from a separate DES-enabled version of Drawbridge and then generate an executable using make.

When you run the newkey command, a ~/.fmkey.[name] file is created. This file holds your DES key. In this first case, the key is transmitted to the Filter PC on the network in an unencrypted form. All subsequent newkey generated keys are encrypted with the previous key. If you are extremely concerned about security, you can use the genkey command and copy the first DES key to the Filter PC using a floppy disk.

DES is only used for authentication, and it is not used to encrypt every packet. The authentication mechanism is used to prevent spoofing of the Filter Manager host or the Filter. The filter data goes across the network unencrypted, except for sequence numbers used for the authentication. Changes made to the DES key are sent with the new key encrypted with the current DES key.

The filtering tables created by the Filter Compiler are loaded into Filter Manager, using the Filter Manager load commands. Each table is loaded with separate load commands. These tables can be inspected with the show command. After the tables are loaded into the Filter Manager, you can load the information into the Filter PC using the upload command.

For example, the following command:

```
upload networks
```

uploads all the networks. When the uploaded information is successfully transferred, it is used immediately by the Filter PC. However, the uploaded information is made permanent until you issue a write command that tells Filter to write its currently loaded tables to disk.

You can inspect the currently loaded tables in the Filter PC with the query command. The use of the query command is similar to the show command for examining the tables loaded at the Filter Manager. The query command, however, queries the loaded tables in Filter PC and not the Filter Manager.

If you want to delete tables loaded into the Filter PC, you can use the release command. This command takes effect immediately and also deletes the tables from disk. The Filter PC reverts to default behavior for the deleted tables until new ones are loaded.

When the Filter Manager is started, it reads the file ~/.fmrc on startup and executes all commands in this file. Typically, the .fmrc file contains a set target command so that the Filter Manager can communicate with the Filter PC on startup, as in the following example:

```
set target 00:00:C0:04:AC:89
```

If you are using DES for authentication, you can add a set key command to the .fmrc file to avoid manually entering this command every time the Filter Manager is started.

The ~/.fmkey.* files contain DES keys so that you can manage Filter PC in a secure manner. The machine running the Filter Manager must be secured against attacks, otherwise, the key can be stolen from this machine and the Filter PC accessed by intruders. The ~/.fmrc and ~/.fmkey.* files must be set with the permission mode of 400 or the Filter Manager will complain about excessive permissions granted for these files.

You can use the Filter Manager ping command to determine if you can communicate with the Filter PC. The reboot command can be used to cause Filter PC to cold boot the PC. Therefore, the AUTOEXEC.BAT file on the PC must be configured to correctly restart the Filter PC on rebooting.

The reset and clear commands can be used to reset the Filter Manager. The reset command completely resets the Filter Manager and causes the .fmrc file to be reread. The clear command only causes the currently loaded tables to be unloaded.

SUMMARY

This chapter discussed examples of PC-based packet filters. Packet filtering enables the rejection of "suspect" packets based upon protocol information corresponding to the network and transport layers of the OSI model. The "suspect" packets are those in violation of the network security policy.

By controlling the type of network traffic that can exist on a network segment, the PC-based packet filters can control the type of services that can exist on a network segment. Services that can compromise the network security can be, therefore, restricted.

This chapter also discussed some practical tips in designing and configuring the KarlBridge and Drawbridge filters. A number of examples of packet filter specifications for Drawbridge were presented. Because screening routers operate with limited information from the network and transport layers, they are not as effective as firewall gateway solutions for controlling network traffic. However, they can be combined with firewall gateway solutions to provide a first line of defense. These solutions are discussed in the next chapter.

CHAPTER 8

FIREWALL ARCHITECTURE AND THEORY

IN CHAPTER 5, "An Introduction to Screening Routers," you learned about screening routers and how you can use them to secure a network against intrusions. Screening routers are often used as the first level of defense against an untrusted network.

The packet-filtering technologies that are used in screening routers provide an efficient and general way to control network traffic. They have the advantage that no changes are required to client and host applications because they operate at the IP and TCP layers, and these layers are independent of application-level issues. On the other hand, packet-filtering approaches have not addressed many security requirements because they have incomplete information with which to work. Only network and transport layer (OSI model) information, such as IP addresses, port numbers, and TCP flags, is available for filtering decisions. In many packet filter implementations, the number of rules may be limited. Additionally, as the number of rules increases, there is a high performance penalty because of the extra processing needed for the additional rules.

Because of lack of context information, certain protocols such as UDP and RPC are more difficult to filter effectively. Also, in many packet-filtering implementations, auditing and alerting mechanisms are missing. To ensure their successful implementation, the implemention of packet filters often requires a high level of understanding of communication protocols and their behavior when used by different applications.

Packet-filtering devices such as screening routers are often augmented by other devices called firewalls. *Firewalls*, because they operate at the upper layers of the OSI model, have complete information on the application functions on which to base their decisions. In this chapter, you learn the different types of firewalls that can be deployed.

There are several approaches to building a firewall. Organizations that have programming talent and financial resources often prefer to use a "roll your own" approach. This involves building custom firewall solutions to protect the organization's network. If implemented properly, this is perhaps the most effective (and also the more expensive) approach.

Other organizations prefer to use existing off-the-shelf products, and customize and configure them to meet the organization's network security policy. To make the discussion on firewalls more practical, several commercial and noncommercial firewall products are discussed in the next chapter.

EXAMINING FIREWALL COMPONENTS

The major objective of a firewall is to protect one network from another. Usually, the network that is being protected belongs to you (or is your responsibility), and the network that you are protecting against is an external network that cannot be trusted and from which security intrusions can originate. Protecting your network involves preventing unauthorized users from having access to sensitive data, while allowing legitimate users to have unencumbered access to the network resources.

Chapter 3, "Designing a Network Policy," introduced the OSI model as a means of making the distinction between screening routers and firewalls. Though the OSI model is a time-honored way of making distinctions between communication architectures and capabilities, not everyone is aware of it or makes use of it. The term firewall is used by many as a generic term that describes a wide range of functions and the architecture of devices that protect the network. Some, in fact, use the term firewall to describe almost any network security device, such as a hardware encryption device, a screening router, or an application-level gateway.

In general, a firewall is placed between the internal trusted network and the external untrusted network. The firewall acts as a choke-point that monitors and rejects application-level network traffic (see fig. 8.1). Firewalls also can operate at the network and transport layers, in which case they examine the IP and TCP headers of incoming and outgoing packets, and reject or pass packets based on the programmed packet filter rules.

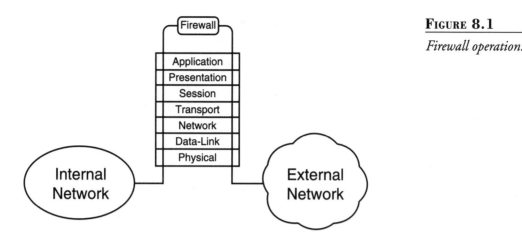

FIGURE 8.1

Firewall operation.

> The firewall is the chief instrument used to implement an organization's network security policy. In many cases, authentication, security, and privacy enhancement techniques are needed to enhance the network security or implement other aspects of the network security policy.
>
> N o t e

The following sections describe the different types of firewalls that can be used.

DUAL-HOMED HOST

In TCP/IP networks, the term *multi-homed host* describes a host that has multiple network interface boards (see fig. 8.2). Usually, each network interface board is connected to a network. Historically, this multi-homed host also could route traffic between the network segments. The term *gateway* was used to describe the routing function performed by these multi-homed hosts. Today, the term *router* is used to describe this routing function, whereas the term gateway is reserved for those functions that correspond to the upper layers of the OSI model.

If the routing function in the multi-homed host is disabled, the host can provide network traffic isolation between the networks it connects to, and yet each network will be able to process applications on the multi-homed hosts. Furthermore, if the applications permit, the networks can also share data. A dual-homed host is a special example of a multi-homed host that has two network interfaces and has the routing functions disabled. Figure 8.3 shows an example of a dual-homed host with the routing functions disabled. Host A on Network 1 can access Application A on the dual-homed host. Similarly, Host B can access Application B on the dual-homed host. The two applications on the dual-homed hosts can even share data. It is possible for the hosts A and B to exchange information through the shared data on the dual-homed hosts, and yet there is no exchange of network traffic between the two network segments connected to the dual-homed host.

327

FIGURE 8.2

A classic multi-homed host.

FIGURE 8.3

A dual-homed host.

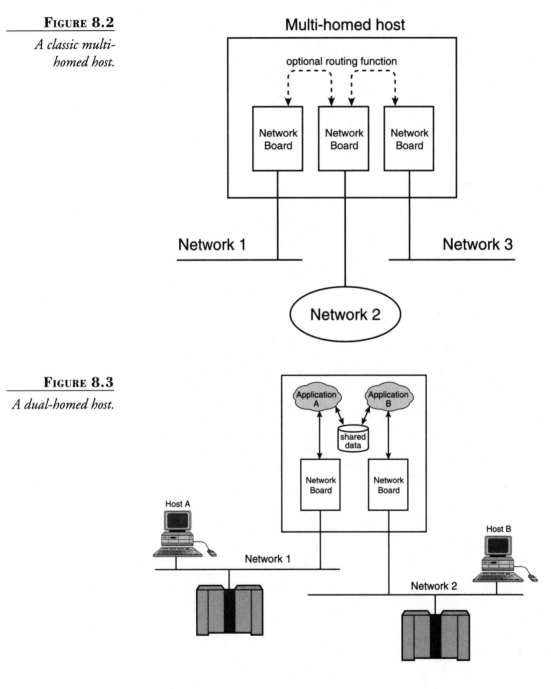

DUAL-HOMED HOST AS A FIREWALL

The dual-homed host can be used to isolate an internal network from an external untrusted network (see fig. 8.4). Because the dual-homed host does not forward any TCP/IP traffic, it completely blocks any IP traffic between the internal and external untrusted network.

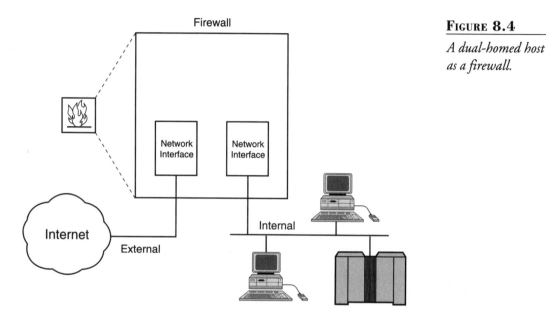

FIGURE 8.4

A dual-homed host as a firewall.

Internet services such as mail and news are essentially store-and-forward services. The World Wide Web also can be considered store and forward, but the terms "caching" and "proxy" are more commonly used in Web vocabulary. If these services run on the dual-homed host, they can be configured to transmit application services from one network to the other. If application data must cross the firewall, application forwarder agents can be set up to run on the dual-homed host (see fig. 8.5). Application forwarder agents are special software used to forward application requests between two connected networks. Another approach is to allow the users to log in to the dual-homed host, and then access external services from the external network interface of the dual-homed host (see fig. 8.6).

If application forwarders are used, the application traffic cannot cross the dual-homed firewall unless the application forwarder is running and configured on the firewall machine. This is an implementation of the policy "That which is not expressly permitted is prohibited." If users are allowed to log in to the firewall directly (see fig. 8.6), the firewall security can be compromised. This is because the dual-homed firewall is a central point of connection between the external network and the internal network. By definition, the dual-homed firewall is in the zone of risk. If the user selects a weak password, or allows his user account to be compromised (such as by giving away passwords), the zone of risk could extend to the internal network, thus defeating the purpose of the dual-homed firewall.

329

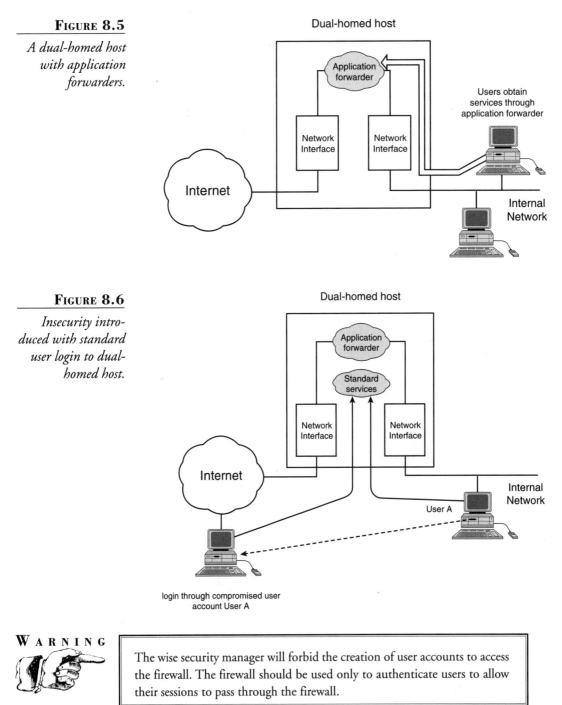

FIGURE 8.5

A dual-homed host with application forwarders.

Dual-homed host

Application forwarder

Users obtain services through application forwarder

Network Interface

Network Interface

Internet

Internal Network

FIGURE 8.6

Insecurity introduced with standard user login to dual-homed host.

Dual-homed host

Application forwarder

Standard services

Network Interface

Network Interface

Internet

Internal Network

User A

login through compromised user account User A

WARNING

The wise security manager will forbid the creation of user accounts to access the firewall. The firewall should be used only to authenticate users to allow their sessions to pass through the firewall.

If proper logs are kept of user logins, it is possible to trace unauthorized logins to the firewall when a security breach is discovered. If users are not permitted direct login to the dual-homed firewall, however, any attempt at a direct user login will be registered as a noteworthy event and a potential security breach.

Examples of store-and-forward services are SMTP (mail) and NNTP (news). Figure 8.7 shows a situation where the dual-homed host is configured to provide discretionary forwarding of mail messages between an external untrusted network and an internal network. Figure 8.8 shows a situation where the dual-homed host is configured to provide discretionary forwarding of news messages between news servers on the external untrusted network and the internal network.

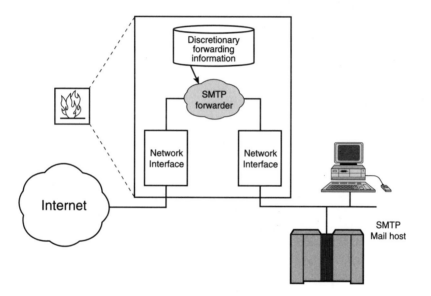

FIGURE 8.7

A dual-homed host as a mail forwarder.

The dual-homed host is the basic configuration used in firewalls. The critical aspect of dual-homed firewall hosts is that routing is disabled, and that the only path between the network segments is through an application layer function. If the routing is accidentally (or by design) misconfigured so IP forwarding is enabled, it is possible that the application layer functions of the dual-homed firewalls are bypassed (see fig. 8.9).

Most firewalls are built around Unix machines. On some Unix implementations, the routing functions are enabled by default. It is therefore important to verify that the routing functions in the dual-homed firewall are disabled, and if they are not, you should know how to disable them.

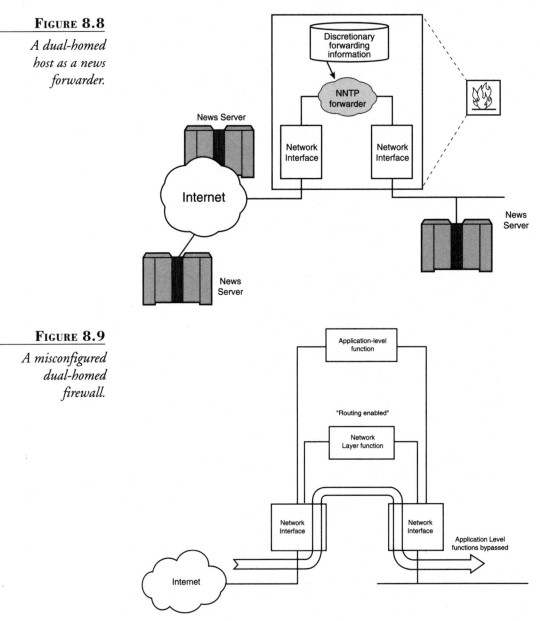

FIGURE 8.8

A dual-homed host as a news forwarder.

FIGURE 8.9

A misconfigured dual-homed firewall.

DISABLING ROUTING IN A DUAL-HOMED FIREWALL

Disabling routing functions in a dual-homed host based on Unix requires reconfiguring and rebuilding the kernel. This section describes that process for BSD Unix.

The Unix kernel is compiled using the make command. A command called config is used to read the kernel configuring file and generate the files that are needed to build the kernel. The kernel configuration file is in /usr/sys/conf or /usr/src/sys. In BSDI (Berkeley Systems Design, Inc.) Unix for the Intel platform, the configuration file is in /usr/src/sys/i386/conf directory.

To check to see which kernel configuration you are using, you can use the strings command on the kernel image file and look for the name of your operating system. The following shows an example of how you can check the kernel version.

```
% strings  /bsd ¦ grep BSD
BSDI $Id: if_pe.c,v 1.4 1993/02/21 20:35:01 karels Exp $
BSDI $Id: if_petbl.c,v 1.2 1993/02/21 20:36:09 karels Exp $
BSD/386
@(#)BSDI BSD/386 1.0 Kernel #0: Wed Mar 24 17:23:44 MST 1993
    polk@hilltop.BSDI.COM:/home/hilltop/polk/sys.clean/compile/GENERIC
```

The last line reveals that the current configuration is GENERIC.

You should change to the configuration directory (/usr/src/sys/i386/conf) and copy this GENERIC file into a new file suggestive of the new configuration. You can call this new file FIREWALL or LOCAL, for example.

```
cd /usr/src/sys/i386/conf
cp GENERIC FIREWALL
```

Next, edit the options parameter IPFORWARDING in the file FIREWALL and change it to −1 to represent "never forward IP datagrams." This variable has the affect of setting the *ipforwarding* kernel variable so that IP forwarding is disabled.

```
options IPFORWARDING=-1
```

On some systems, instead of the IPFORWARDING parameter, you might see the following statement in the configuration file.

```
options  GATEWAY
```

To disable forwarding of IP packets, comment this line out by placing a # as the first character in the line.

```
#options  GATEWAY
```

Also, verify that the following kernel configuration statements for TCP/IP exist.

```
options      INET          # Internet Protocol support is to be included
pseudo-device   loop       # The loop back device is to be defined
                             (127.0.0.1)
pseudo-device   ether      # Generic Ethernet support such as ARP
                             functions
pseudo-device   pty        # Pseudo teletypes for telnet/rlogin access
device we0 at isa? port 0x280 # Could be different for your Ethernet
                             interface
```

Run the config command to build the LOCAL directory and go to the directory shown in the following example:

```
config LOCAL
cd ../../compile/LOCAL
```

Next, run the make commands to create the necessary dependencies and build the kernel.

```
make depend
make
```

Copy the kernel image to the root directory, and then reboot.

```
cp /bsd /bsd.old
cp bsd /bsd
reboot
```

After rebooting, the machine can be set up as a dual-homed firewall.

COMPROMISING THE SECURITY OF A DUAL-HOMED FIREWALL

You should understand how the integrity of a dual-homed firewall can be compromised. With this understanding, then, you can take steps to prevent such an occurrence.

The biggest threat is if an intruder obtains direct login access to the dual-homed host. Login should always occur through an application proxy on the dual-homed host. Logins from external untrusted networks should require a strong authentication.

WARNING

> The only access to the firewall itself should be either through the console or secure remote access. To prevent the circumvention of the firewall, no user accounts should be permitted on the system.

If the user obtains login access to the dual-homed host, the internal network is subject to intrusions. These intrusions can come through any of the following sources:

❖ Weak permissions on the file system

❖ Internal network NFS-mounted volumes

❖ Permissions granted to Berkeley r*-utilities through host equivalent files, such as .rhosts, in users home directories for user accounts that have been compromised

❖ Network backup programs that could restore excessive permissions

❖ The use of administrative shell scripts that have not been properly secured

❖ Learning about the system from older software revision levels and release notes that have not been properly secured

❖ Installing older operating system kernels that have IP forwarding enabled, or installing versions of older operating system kernels with known security problems

❖ The use of sniffing programs such as tcpdump or etherfind to "sniff" the internal network looking for user name and password information.

If the dual-homed host fails, the internal network is wide-open for future intruders, unless the problem is detected and corrected quickly.

As mentioned previously, the Unix kernel variable *ipforwarding* controls whether IP routing is performed. If the intruder gains sufficient system privileges, the intruder can change the value of this kernel variable and enable IP forwarding. With IP forwarding enabled, the firewall mechanism is bypassed.

SERVICES ON A DUAL-HOMED FIREWALL

Besides disabling IP forwarding, you should remove from the dual-homed firewall all programs, utilities, and services that could be dangerous in the hands of an intruder. The following is a partial list of some useful checkpoints for Unix dual-homed firewalls:

❖ Remove programming tools: compilers, linkers, and so forth.

❖ Remove programs with SUID and SGID permissions that you do not need or do not understand (see Chapter 2, "Security"). If things do not work, you can always put back essential programs. If you have the experience, build a disk space monitor that will shut down the dual-homed host should a critical disk partition become full.

❖ Use disk partitions so that an intrusion to fill all disk space on the partition will be confined to that partition.

❖ Remove unneeded system and special accounts.

❖ Delete network services that are not needed. Use the netstat -a command to verify that you only have network services that you need. Edit the /etc/inetd.conf and /etc/ services files and remove unneeded service definitions.

❖ Alter the system startup scripts to prevent the initialization of unneeded programs such as routed/gated and any routing support programs.

BASTION HOSTS

A *bastion host* is any firewall host that is critical to the network security. The bastion host is the central host in an organization's network security. Because the bastion host is critical to network security, it must be well-fortified. This means that the bastion host is closely monitored by the network administrators. The bastion host software and system security should undergo regular audits. The access logs should be examined for any potential security breaches and any attempts to assault the bastion host.

The dual-homed host discussed earlier is an example of a bastion host because it is critical to the security of the network.

335

Simplest Deployment of a Bastion Host

Because bastion hosts act as an interface point to an external untrusted network, they are often subject to intrusion. The simplest deployment of a bastion host is as the first and only point of entry for external network traffic (see fig. 8.10).

Figure 8.10

The simplest deployment of a bastion host (B2 configuration).

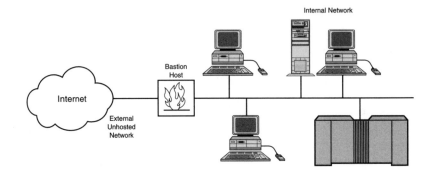

Notation Used to Describe Bastion Configurations

The author has devised a notation that can simplify the description of a firewall configuration. In this notation, symbols are used to have the following meanings:

Symbol	Description
S	Screening router
R	Ordinary router
F1	Firewall with single network connection to the network
F2	Firewall with two network connections
B1	Bastion host with single network connection to the network
B2	Bastion host with two network connections

Using these symbols, you can describe the network configuration in figure 8.10. You can follow the path of the network traffic from the external to the internal networks:

B2

So the network in figure 8.10 is a B2 configuration.

Screened Host Gateway

Because the bastion host is critical to the security of the internal network, another first line of defense is often introduced between the external untrusted network and the internal network. This first line of defense is usually provided by a screening router. Figure 8.11 shows the use of a bastion host with a screening router as the first line of defense. In this example, only the network interface of the bastion host is configured, and this network interface is connected to the internal network. One of the ports of the screening router is connected to the internal network, and the other port is connected to the Internet. This type of configuration is called the *screened host gateway.*

Using the notation defined in this chapter, the screened host gateway configuration shown in figure 8.11 can be described as the S-B1 configuration or just "SB1."

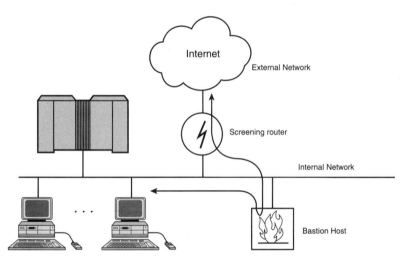

FIGURE 8.11

A bastion host with single network interface and screening router as the first line of defense (SB1 configuration).

You must configure the screening router so that it sends all traffic received from the external networks for the internal network to the bastion host first. Before it forwards traffic to the bastion host, the screening router will apply its filter rules to the packet traffic. Only network traffic that passes the filter rules is diverted to the bastion host; all other network traffic is rejected. This architecture gives a level of confidence in the network security that is missing in figure 8.10. An intruder must first penetrate the screening router. If the intruder manages to penetrate the screening router, he must contend with the bastion host.

The bastion host uses application-level functions to determine if requests to and from the external network are permitted or denied. If the request passes the scrutiny of the bastion host, it is forwarded to the internal network for incoming traffic. For outgoing traffic (traffic to the external network), the requests are forwarded to the screening router. Figure 8.12 shows the path of network traffic between the external and internal networks.

OFF-LOADING PACKET FILTERING TO THE IAP

Some organizations prefer to have their Internet Access Provider (IAP) provide packet filter rules for network traffic sent to the organization's network (see fig. 8.13). The packet filter

337

still acts as the first line of defense, but you have to rely on your IAP for the correct maintenance of the packet filter rules.

FIGURE 8.12

The path of network traffic for network with screening router and bastion host.

FIGURE 8.13

The IAP provides packet filtering to the internal network.

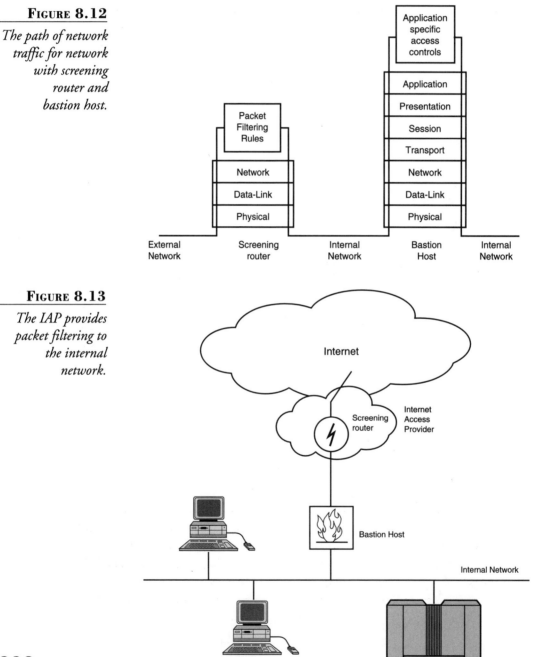

ROUTING CONFIGURATION FOR SCREENED HOST GATEWAY NETWORKS

The routing tables of the screening routers must be configured so that external traffic is forwarded to the bastion host. The routing tables in the screening router should be protected from intrusion and unauthorized change. If the routing table entry is changed so that the traffic is not forwarded to the bastion host but sent directly to the locally connected network, the bastion host is bypassed.

Figure 8.14 shows a situation where the screening router's routing table points to the bastion host. The internal network number is 199.245.180.0, and the bastion hosts IP address is 199.245.180.10. The screening router has the following entry in its routing table.

> Destination = 199.245.180.0
>
> Forward to = 199.245.180.10

All network traffic for network 199.245.180.0 is forwarded to the bastion host's IP address of 199.245.180.10.

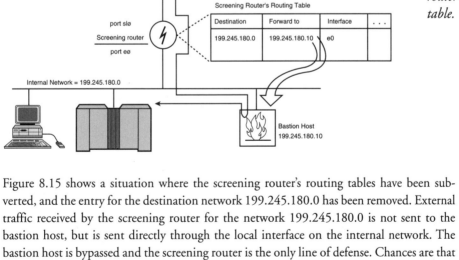

FIGURE 8.14

The normal setting of the screening router's routing table.

Figure 8.15 shows a situation where the screening router's routing tables have been subverted, and the entry for the destination network 199.245.180.0 has been removed. External traffic received by the screening router for the network 199.245.180.0 is not sent to the bastion host, but is sent directly through the local interface on the internal network. The bastion host is bypassed and the screening router is the only line of defense. Chances are that if the screening router has been subverted, other functions of the router could also be subverted, and the zone of risk will encompass the internal network.

FIGURE 8.15

The screening router's routing table is subverted.

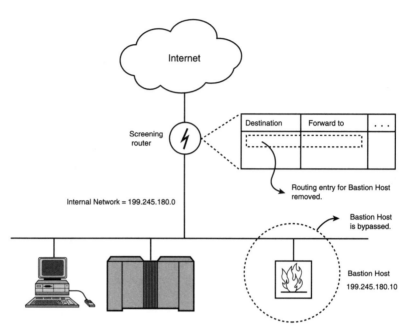

If the screening router responds to ICMP (Internet Control Message Protocol) redirect messages, it is vulnerable to false ICMP messages sent by the intruder. For this reason, response to ICMP redirect messages should be disabled.

> If the screening router is based on Unix-derived software, you should configure the kernel to disable directed broadcasts so that broadcast packets from the internal network are not forwarded to the external network. Otherwise, information on the internal network can leak to the outside world. You can configure the kernel to disable directed broadcasts by setting the following in the configuration file:
>
> ```
> options DIRECTED_BROADCAST=0
> ```
>
> Next, you must run config on the configuration file. After this, you must run the make commands as follows:
>
> config *nameoffile*
>
> make depend
>
> make

> You should also remove unneeded network services and use static routing. Especially ensure that "routed" or "gated" daemons are not running, otherwise routes will be advertised to the external world.
>
> Also, make permanent entries in the ARP cache table to point to the bastion host. Use the following command to make permanent entries in the ARP cache.
>
> ```
> arp -s ipaddress hardware-address
> ```
>
> For example, to specify that the hardware address of the bastion host 199.245.180.10 is 0000C005564A, use the following command:
>
> ```
> arp -s 199.245.180.10 0000C004564A
> ```

You should configure the screening routers to use static routing. Static routes are not expired and changed by routing protocols. This protects the static routes from false route advertisements.

You also should disable the processing of the following at the router: ARP, ICMP redirects, proxy ARP, and ICMP unreachable messages. You can use the following configuration statements, for example, on a Cisco router.

  no ip redirects

  no ip route-cache

  no ip proxy-arp

  no ip unreachables

  no service finger

If your screening router supports TELNET access, you should disable it. On a Cisco router, you can set access control lists on virtual terminals to prevent remote access through TELNET.

In normal ARP operation, ARP table entries are built dynamically and are expired after a predetermined time interval. You should manually initialize the ARP cache table for the router and the bastion host. ARP entries that are made manually are never expired and act as "static" entries. With ARP processing disabled at the router, the router will not give out its hardware address.

In BSD Unix, static routes are set up using the route command. The general syntax of this command is shown in the following example.

```
route [-n] [-q] [-v] command [-net ¦ -host] destination forward_to
[count]
```

The flags in this example have the following meanings:

-n	Prevents attempts to print symbolic names when reporting actions
-v	(verbose) Prints additional details
-q	Suppresses all output

The *command* can have the following values:

add	Adds a route
flush	Removes all routes
delete	Deletes a specific route
change	Changes aspects of a route (such as its gateway)
get	Looks up and displays the route for a destination
monitor	Continuously reports any changes to the routing information base, routing lookup misses, or suspected network partionings

To forward network traffic for the network 199.245.180.0 to the bastion host 199.245.180.10, for example, you would use the following command.

```
route add -net 199.245.180.0  199.245.180.10
```

It is best to specify all four numeric values of the dotted decimal IP address, unless you understand how partial IP addresses are interpreted. Here are some examples:

Using 130.33 without the -host or -net is interpreted as:

-host 130.0.0.33

The address 130.33.5 is interpreted as:

-host 130.33.0.5

The address -net 130.33 is interpreted as:

130.33.0.0

The address -net 130.33.5 is interpreted as:

130.33..5

The *count* keyword, which is optional on some systems and required on others, is used to indicate whether the host is local or remote. If the count is 1 or more, then the forward to is a remote system. If the value is 0, then the forward to is another interface on the same system.

BASTION HOST WITH BOTH NETWORK INTERFACES CONFIGURED

Figure 8.16 shows the use of a bastion host with a screening router, but both network interfaces of the bastion host are configured. One network interface is connected to the "outside" network and the other network interface is connected to the "inside" network. One of the ports of the screening router is connected to the "inside" network and the other port is connected to the Internet. Using the notation defined in this chapter, figure 8.16 can be described as the S-B2 configuration or just as "SB2."

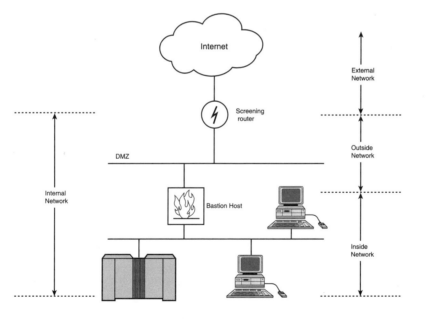

FIGURE 8.16

A bastion host with two network interfaces and a screening router as the first line of defense (SB2 configuration).

The screening router must be configured so that it sends all traffic received from the external networks for the internal network to the "inside" network interface of the bastion host. Before it forwards traffic to the bastion host, the screening router will apply its filter rules to the packet traffic. Only network traffic that passes the filter rules is diverted to the bastion host; all other network traffic is rejected. An intruder must first penetrate the screening router. If the intruder manages to penetrate the screening router, he must contend with the bastion host.

There are no hosts on the outside network, other than the screening router and one of the network interfaces of the bastion host. The outside network forms a Demilitarized Zone (DMZ). Because the DMZ has only two network connections, it can be replaced by a dedicated point-to-point link. This makes it more difficult to tap into this link using protocol analyzers. If an Ethernet or token ring network is used for the DMZ, a workstation that places its network interface in the promiscuous mode can capture network traffic and access sensitive data. Normally, network interfaces only read the packet directly addressed to it. In the promiscuous mode, however, network interfaces read all packets seen by the network interface. All the organization's hosts (except for the bastion host) are connected to the inside network.

The network configuration in figure 8.16 has another advantage over the network configuration in which only one network interface of the bastion host was used (refer to fig. 8.11). This advantage is that the bastion host cannot be bypassed by attacking the screening routers routing tables. Network traffic must pass through the bastion host to reach the inside network.

USES OF TWO BASTION HOSTS AND TWO DMZS

Figure 8.17 shows the use of two bastion hosts with a screening router. Both network interfaces of the two bastion hosts are configured. Three network zones are formed in the internal network: the outside network, the private network, and the inside network. Using the notation defined in this chapter, figure 8.17 can be described as the S-B2-B2 configuration, or just "SB2B2."

FIGURE 8.17

Two bastion hosts with both network interface cards configured (SB2B2 configuration).

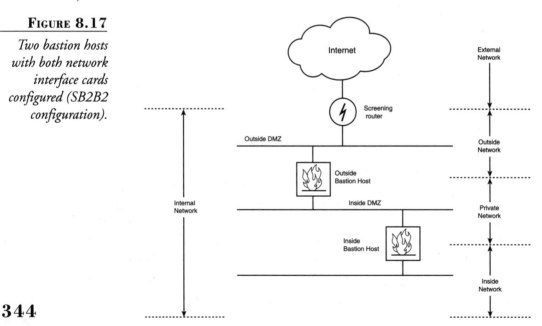

The screening router and the outside bastion host are the only two network interfaces on the outside network. The outside network forms the outside DMZ.

A private network exists between the inside and outside bastions. The private network provides a level of protection similar to that in figure 8.18. An organization could place some of its hosts on the private network and keep the more sensitive hosts behind the inside bastion host. Alternatively, an organization may want maximum security and use the private network as a second buffer zone or inside DMZ, and keep all of the hosts on the inside network.

If an organization wants to provide full access to a wide array of services, such as anonymous FTP (File Transfer Protocol), Gopher, and WWW (World Wide Web) services, it can provide certain sacrificial hosts on the outside DMZ (see fig. 8.18). The bastion hosts should not trust any traffic originating from these sacrificial hosts.

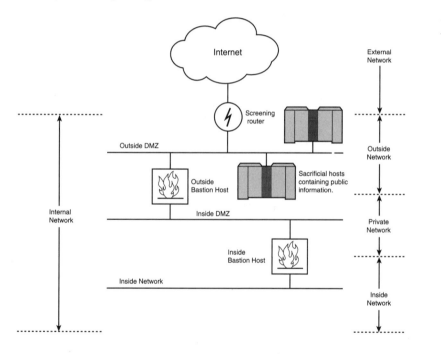

FIGURE 8.18

Sacrificial hosts on the outside DMZ.

The screening router must be configured so that it sends all traffic received from the external networks for the internal network to the inside bastion host. Before it forwards traffic to the bastion host, the screening router will apply its filter rules to the packet traffic. Only network traffic that passes the filter rules is diverted to the outside bastion host; all other network traffic is rejected. An intruder must first penetrate the screening router. If the intruder manages to penetrate the screening router, he must contend with the outside bastion host.

Even if the defenses of the outside network are breached, the intruder must penetrate the inside bastion host. If resources permit, you might want to make each bastion host the responsibility of a different administrative group. This ensures that the mistakes committed by one set of administrators will not be repeated by the other administrators. You also should ensure that the two groups share information about discovered weaknesses in the bastion hosts. Figure 8.19 shows the path that the network traffic has to take between the external and internal networks.

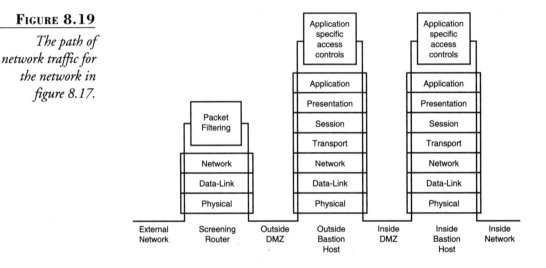

Another type of network configuration is to use two bastion hosts but only one network interface of each bastion host (see fig. 8.20). A second router called the *choke* is added between the DMZ and the inside networks. Figure 8.21 shows the path taken by network traffic between the external and internal networks.

With the network configuration of figure 8.20, you should ensure that the bastion hosts are not bypassed. You should ensure that the screening routers are using static routes. Using the notation defined in this chapter, figure 8.20 can be described as the S-B1-S-B1 configuration, or just "SB1SB1."

Other possible combinations are shown in figures 8.22 and 8.23. Whenever only a single network interface of the bastion is used, you should use static routes at the routers and properly configure the routing table entries to ensure that the bastion hosts are not bypassed. Using the notation defined in this chapter, figure 8.22 can be described as the S-B2-B1 configuration, or just "SB2B1;" figure 8.23 can be described as the S-B1-B2, or just "SB1B2."

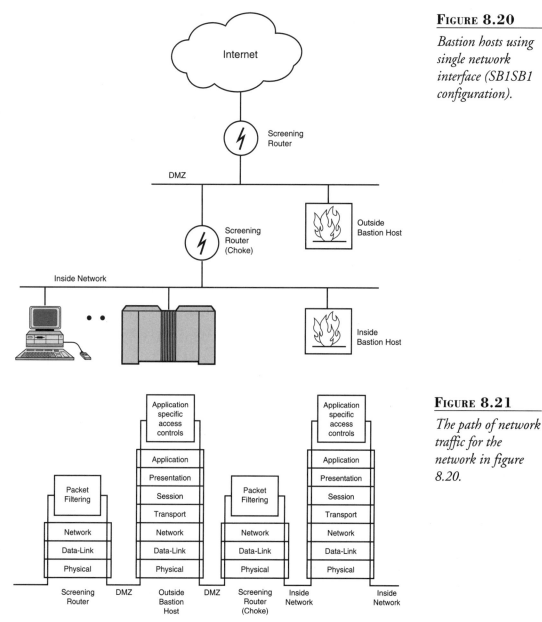

FIGURE 8.21

The path of network traffic for the network in figure 8.20.

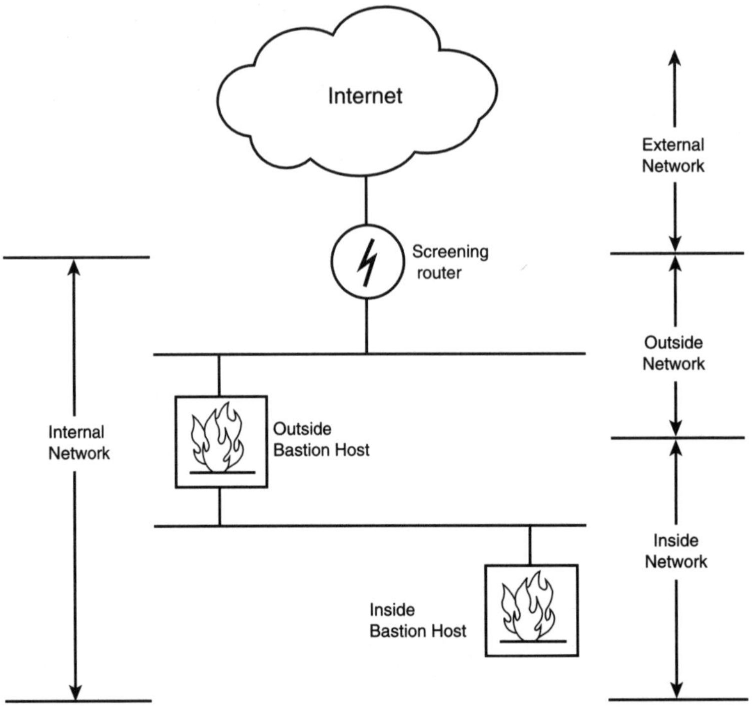

FIGURE 8.22

A double-ended/ single-ended bastion configuration (SB2B1 configuration).

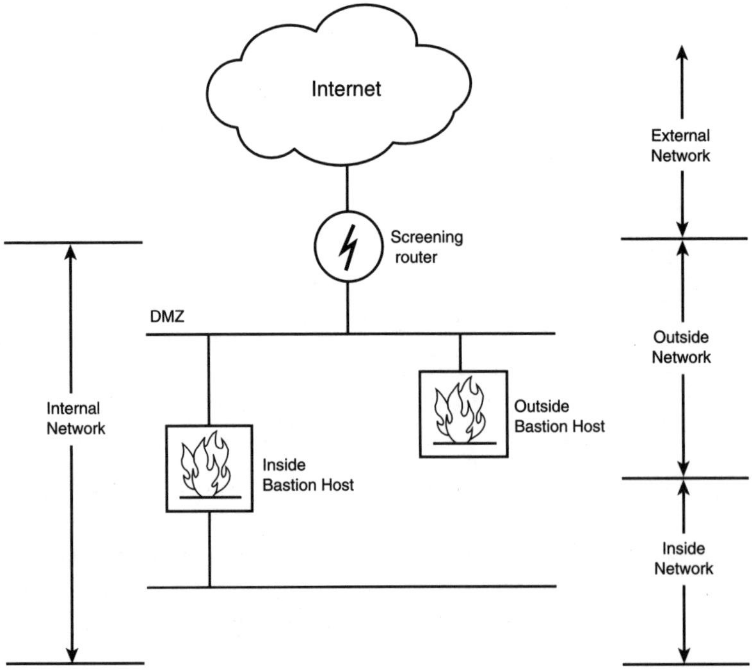

Internet

Screening router

External Network

Outside Network

Internal Network

Outside Bastion Host

Inside Network

Inside Bastion Host

FIGURE 8.23

A single-ended/ double-ended bastion configuration (SB1B2 configuration).

Internet

Screening router

External Network

DMZ

Outside Network

Internal Network

Outside Bastion Host

Inside Bastion Host

Inside Network

SCREENED SUBNETS

In some firewall configurations, an isolated network of the type shown in figure 8.24 can be created. In this network, both the untrusted external network and the internal network can access the isolated network. However, no network traffic can flow between the untrusted external network and the internal network *through the isolated network*. The isolation of the network is performed using a combination of screening routers that are properly configured (see fig. 8.25). Such an isolated network is called a screened subnet.

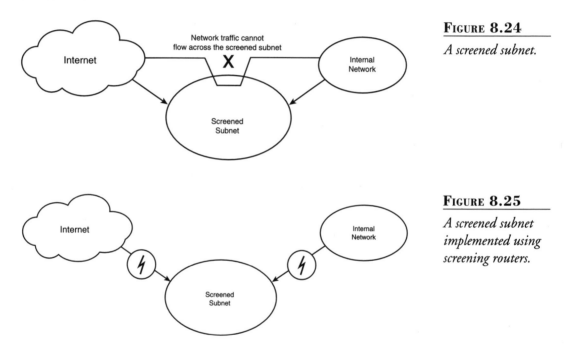

FIGURE 8.24

A screened subnet.

FIGURE 8.25

A screened subnet implemented using screening routers.

Some screened subnets may have application-level gateways on them that act as bastion hosts and provide interactive access to outside services (see fig. 8.26).

Figure 8.27 shows a screened subnet configured with a bastion host as the central access point to the screened subnet. This type of configuration is the S-B1-S, or "SB1S" configuration. Screening routers are used to connect the Internet and the internal network. The bastion host is an application gateway and denies all traffic that is not expressly permitted.

Because the only access to the screened subnet is through the bastion host, it is very difficult for an intruder to breach the screened subnet. If the intrusion comes through the Internet, the intruder would have to reconfigure the routing on the Internet, the screened subnet, and the internal network to have free access (which is made difficult if the screening routers allow access to only specific hosts). Even if the bastion host is breached, the intruder would have to break into one of the hosts on the internal network and then back into the screening router to access the screened subnet. This type of island-hopping intrusion is difficult to do without disconnecting oneself or tripping over an alarm.

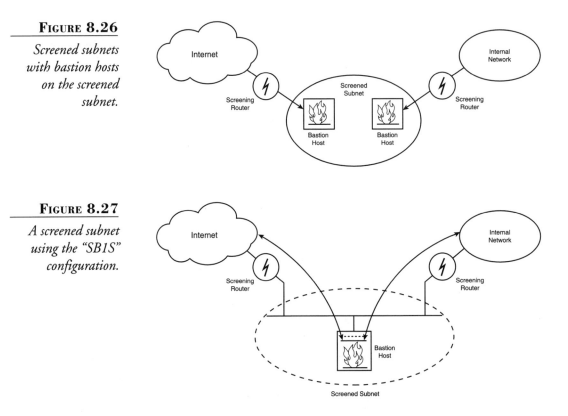

FIGURE 8.26

Screened subnets with bastion hosts on the screened subnet.

FIGURE 8.27

A screened subnet using the "SB1S" configuration.

Because screened subnets do not allow network traffic to flow between the Internet and internal network, the IP addresses of the hosts on these networks are hidden from each other. This allows an organization that has not converted over to officially assigned network numbers from the NIC (Network Information Center) to access the Internet through application gateway services provided by the bastion host on the screened subnet. If these services through the application gateway are restrictive, these restrictions can act as a spur to convert the internal network to officially assigned network numbers.

APPLICATION-LEVEL GATEWAYS

Application-level gateways can handle store-and-forward traffic as well as some interactive traffic (see fig. 8.28). Application-level gateways are programmed to understand the traffic at the user application level (layer 7 of the OSI model). They can therefore provide access controls at a user level and application protocol level. Moreover, they can be used to maintain an intelligent log of all usage of the applications. The ability to log and control all incoming and outgoing traffic is one of the main advantages of having an application-level gateway. The gateways themselves can have additional security built into them as needed.

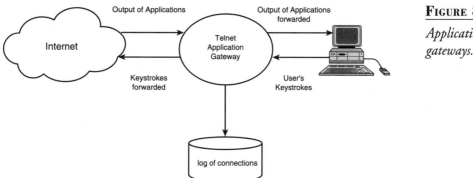

FIGURE 8.28

Application-level gateways.

For each application that is relayed, application-level gateways use a special-purpose code. Because of this special-purpose code, application gateways provide a high level of security. For each new type of application that is added to the network and that requires protection, new special-purpose code has to be written. Therefore, most application-level gateways provide a limited subset of basic applications and services.

To use application-level gateways, users must log in to the application gateway machine, or implement a specific client application service on every host that will utilize this service. Each application-specific gateway module can have its own set of management tools and command language.

> Some applications will have trouble interacting with the application gateway. If your application, such as a WWW browser, is capable of handling the challenge that will be presented to you, then your connection will succeed. If your application does not have support to deal with the challenge, then you will need to either use a special client application or authenticate your session through alternate means.

N O T E

A disadvantage of application-level gateways is that a custom program often has to be written for each application. This fact is also an advantage from a security view point, though, because you cannot go through the firewall unless an explicit application-level gateway has been provided. This is an implementation of the philosophy, *That which is not expressly permitted is prohibited.*

351

The custom application program acts a "proxy" that accepts incoming calls and checks them against an access list of what types of requests are permitted. The proxy in this case is an application server proxy. On receiving the call—and after verifying that the call is permitted—the proxy forwards the request to the requested server. The proxy, therefore, acts as both a server and a client (see fig 8.29). It acts as a server to receive the incoming request and as a client when forwarding the request. After the session is established, the application proxy acts as a relay and copies data between the client that initiated the application and the server. Because all data between the client and server is intercepted by the application proxy, it has full control over the session and can perform as detailed a log as needed. In figure 8.29, the proxy is shown as a client and server for the purposes of explaining its behavior. In most implementations, this is implemented by a single application module.

FIGURE 8.29

An application proxy as a client and server.

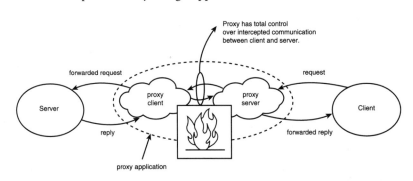

To connect to a proxy application, many application-level gateways require that you run a custom client application on your internal machines. Alternatively, you can use the telnet command to specify the port at which the proxy application service is available. If the proxy application was on host gatekeeper.kinetics.com and on port 63, for example, you would use the following command.

```
telnet gatekeeper.kinetics.com  63
```

After you connect to the port at which the proxy service runs, you should see a special prompt that identifies the proxy application. You have to run custom commands to specify the destination server. Regardless of which approach is used, the user interface to the standard application changes. If a custom client is used, the client is usually modified so that it always connects to your proxy machine and tells the proxy machine where to connect. The proxy machine then connects to the ultimate destination and passes the data through.

Some proxy application services are written so that they behave like the standard application. When the user specifies a connection target that is in a different network, the proxy application is invoked.

If you are using a custom client with the proxy application, you must install the custom client on all your internal machines that access a network through the application-level gateway. Depending on the size of the network, this can be a difficult task. If some of your users use DOS/Windows and Macintosh clients, it is usually the case that proxy versions of your client programs are not available. If you do not have the source code to these client applications (which is usually the case for Macintosh and PC client programs), you cannot modify them.

If the proxy client knows about only one application gateway server, and if this server is down, then you are vulnerable to a single point of failure. If the proxy client can be changed by the administrator to point to an alternate application gateway, the single point of failure problem can be avoided.

Because of the problems of configuring proxy clients, some sites prefer to use packet filtering for those applications such as FTP and TELNET that can be secured by proper filter rules. These sites use the proxy client approach for more complex applications, such as DNS, SMTP, NFS, HTTP, Gopher, and so forth.

If a custom client application is needed to communicate with the proxy server, some standard system calls such as connect() have to be replaced by a proxy version of these system calls. You must then compile and link the client application with the proxy versions of the system calls. A freely available library called *socks* contains nearly compatible replacements of the standard system calls such as socket(), bind(), connect(), and so on. This is available at the URL (Uniform Resource Locator) of ftp://ftp.inoc.dl.nec.com/pub/security/socks.cstc.

The proxy servers should be written in such a way as to provide a 'fail-safe' mode of operation if the properly modified client is not used. If a standard client is used to contact the proxy server, for example, then the communication should be prohibited and not cause undesirable and unpredictable behavior of the firewall and the screening routers.

Another type of application-level gateway is called the *circuit-gateway*. In circuit-level gateways, the packets are addressed to a user-application level process. A circuit-gateway is used to relay packets between the two communication end-points. The circuit-gateway simply copies the bytes back and forth between the two end points (see fig. 8.30).

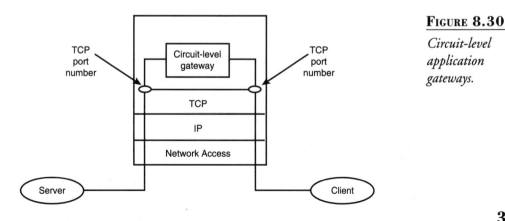

FIGURE 8.30

Circuit-level application gateways.

353

Circuit-level gateways are a more flexible and general approach to build application gateways. Although they may include code to support some specific TCP/IP application, this is usually limited. If they support an application, it is likely to be a TCP/IP application.

In circuit-level gateways, special client software might have to be installed, and the users might have to interact with an altered user interface or change their work habits. Installing and configuring special applications on each internal host can be time consuming and error prone for large heterogeneous networks because of the difference in hardware platforms and operating systems.

Because each packet is processed by software running at the application layer, the host performance is affected. Each packet is processed twice by all the communication layers and requires user-level processing and context switching. The application-level gateway (either a bastion-host or dual-homed host) remains exposed to the network. Other means such as packet filtering can be used to protect the application gateway host.

SUMMARY

In this chapter, you learned about different network configurations that use firewalls and screening routers to provide enhanced network security. The advantages and disadvantages of the different network configurations were discussed.

Chapter 9, "Firewall Implementations," discusses practical implementations of firewall solutions. Some of these examples are taken from commercial firewall products and others are freely available software.

FIREWALL IMPLEMENTATIONS

THE PREVIOUS CHAPTER addressed firewall architecture and theory. This chapter completes the section by showing how those principles are implemented in the real world.

Several commercially available packages are discussed, as well as a shareware toolkit which allows you to construct your own firewall from scratch.

THE TCP WRAPPER

The TCP Wrapper is a freely available access control software for Unix systems. It is not a program that is run on a firewall. Rather it is used to protect the systems in the public network outside the firewall. The TCP Wrapper performs the following basic functions:

✤ Logs request for internet service made through the /etc/inetd.conf file

✤ Provides an access control mechanism to control access to the services

Both of these capabilities can be used to construct a simple firewall solution. The solution is simple because the TCP Wrapper does not provide an application or circuit-level gateway. It does provide, however, a series of tools intended to improve the level of auditing and security for the commonly available network utilities.

The current version of the TCP Wrapper program is 7.4 and is available at the following URL:

```
ftp://cert.sei.cmu.edu/pub/network_tools/tcp_wrapper*.shar
```

or

```
ftp://ftp.win.tue.nl/pub/network_tools/tcp_wrapper*.shar.Z
```

The file contains a shell archive. You must first uncompress and unarchive the files:

```
gunzip tcp_wrappers_6.3.shar.Z    # You can also use the Unix uncompress
sh tcp_wrappers_6.3.shar
make                              # You will see instructions on what to do
                                  # for building the binaries
```

The TCP Wrapper program is created in a file called *tcpd*. Place this file in a directory such as /usr/local/bin. Next, edit the /etc/inetd.conf file and place under the control of tcpd the services that you want to log and control. Suppose that you want to log and control telnet sessions to the host. The entry for telnet in the inetd.conf file should be similar to the following:

```
telnet    stream    tcp    nowait    root    /usr/libexec/telnetd    telnetd
```

To monitor access to telnet, replace the sixth field by the /usr/local/bin/tcpd program, as shown:

```
telnet    stream    tcp    nowait    root    /usr/local/bin/tcpd    telnetd
```

You can make similar changes to monitor any other services such as ftpd, tftpd, rlogind, rexecd, rshd, fingerd, and so forth.

After making the changes, restart inetd:

```
ucs# ps -aux ¦ grep inetd
root       82  0.0  0.0   652  124 ??  Is   3:17AM    0:00.27 inetd
ucs# kill -HUP 82
```

When the inetd program receives a request for the telnet service, the program tcpd is started, instead of the normal program telnetd. The tcpd program logs the request and checks the access control information in two files:

/etc/hosts.allow

/etc/hosts.deny

The hosts.allow file contains a list of hosts that are allowed access to the service. The hosts.deny file contains a list of hosts that are denied access. If these files do not exist, tcpd logs the request and allows all hosts access to the service. The tcpd program first checks the file hosts.allow, then the file hosts.deny. If a match is found for a service, it stops further examination of these files. This means that access granted through the hosts.allow cannot be overridden by the hosts.deny file.

The format of the entries for each file is as follows:

`service-list: host-list [:shell-cmd]`

The *service-list* is a comma-separated list of services defined in the /etc/services file.

The *host-list* is a comma-separated list of host names, IP addresses, network names, network numbers, domain names or NIS netgroups.

If a match occurs in the hosts.allow file, the listed systems are allowed access, and if a match occurs in the hosts.deny file, the listed systems are denied access.

Consider the following examples:

EXAMPLE 1

Take following entry in the hosts.allow file:

`fingerd, telnetd: 144.19.74.1, 144.20`

This means that hosts 144.19.74.1 and all hosts on class B network 144.20.0.0 are allowed access to telnet and finger services.

EXAMPLE 2

In the following entry in the hosts.deny file, all hosts in the domain HACKER.ORG are denied access to telnet and finger services:

`fingerd, telnetd: .hacker.org`

EXAMPLE 3

The keyword ALL can be used to match any service or any host. The keyword LOCAL can be used to match any host on the locally connected network:

Note the following entry in the hosts.allow file:

```
ALL: LOCAL, .KINETICS.COM
```

This means that all hosts on the locally connected network that are in the domain KINETICS.COM are allowed access to *all* services.

EXAMPLE 4

Consider the following entry in the hosts.deny file:

```
ALL: ALL
```

This means that all hosts on the network are denied access to all services, if there are no matching entries in the hosts.allow file. Remember that hosts.allows is processed before hosts.deny.

The definition of ALL is limited to those services that are invoked through inetd and are under the control of the tcpd wrapper program.

THE FIREWALL-1 GATEWAY

The FireWall-1 is a commercial gateway product, available from Internet Security Corporation. The product currently runs on SUN SparcStations.

The FireWall-1 uses the following two methods to establish network security.

❖ Application gateway

❖ Packet filtering

The configuration of the FireWall-1 gateway is done using graphical interfaces such as OpenLook for SunOS operating systems. The FireWall-1 gateway provides the following features:

❖ Secure packet filtering

❖ Adding context information to stateless connections

❖ Auditing and alerting

❖ Ability to define and add new protocols and services

❖ Authenticated telnet and FTP sessions

❖ Creating encrypted channels

A unique aspect of FireWall-1 is that, although it uses packet filtering as its basic mechanism, the packet filtering is done at layers 2 to 7 of the OSI model. Protocols that lack context information, such as UDP, are handled by building context information within the FireWall-1 gateway.

RESOURCE REQUIREMENTS FOR FIREWALL-1

Before investing resources in evaluating a product to see if it is suitable for your network environment, it is helpful to know details such as the hardware and software and training resources needed to implement the product. This information is provided for your reference. The FireWall-1 can currently run on the following platform/operating systems:

Hardware platform: Sun Sparc-based systems

                          Intel running Solaris 2.4 or higher

Operating System: SunOS 4.1.3 or Solaris

                          NetWare server platforms

Graphical Interface: X11R5/Open Look

                          (Open Windows 3)

Disk space requirements: 5 MB

Memory requirements: 16 MB control module

Network Interface: Standard SUN workstation interfaces

                          Access List support for Cisco routers (version 9.1 or higher) and Wellfleet routers (version 8.0 or higher)

OVERVIEW OF FIREWALL-1 ARCHITECTURE

The FireWall-1 gateway acts as a secure router between an organization's internal network and an external network (see fig. 9.1). All the network traffic between the organization's network and an external, untrusted network is sent through the FireWall-1 gateway. Each packet exchanged between the external network and internal networks thus can be verified to comply with the organization's internal security.

359

FIGURE 9.1

*The FireWall-1
gateway.*

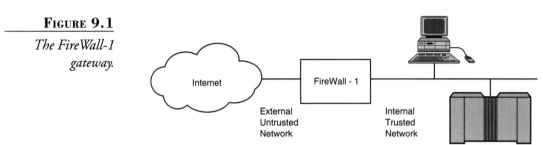

The FireWall-1 is composed of two major components, as follows:

✤ Packet-filter modules

✤ Control modules

A single control module can be used to control and monitor multiple packet filter modules. The packet filter module operates independently of the control module and can be placed on additional Internet gateways and servers to provide compartmentalized zones of risk. The control module is placed in the control workstation. The control module and packet filter module can reside on the same or different hosts. If they are placed on different hosts, communication between the control and packet filter modules are authenticated with a one-time password authentication.

The packet filter module implements the secure router functions between networks and is situated between the data link and network layers of the OSI model. Figures 9.2 and 9.3 show the packet filter operations implemented for incoming and outgoing packets, respectively. The data link layer is implemented by the network board, and the network layer is the IP protocol layer of the TCP/IP stack in the gateway.

For both incoming and outgoing packets, the packet headers are checked to see if they match a packet filtering rule. If no match takes place, the next rule is tried. For matched packets, a log/alert of the packet can optionally be done. After the log, a decision is made to pass the packet or drop it as specified in the packet filter rule.

If the packet cannot be matched, it is dropped in accordance with the security policy *That which is not expressly permitted is prohibited.*

A unique feature of FireWall-1's packet filtering is that it provides an effective way for filtering UDP and RPC traffic. This packet filtering is done by building context information for packets that are not part of a virtual circuit.

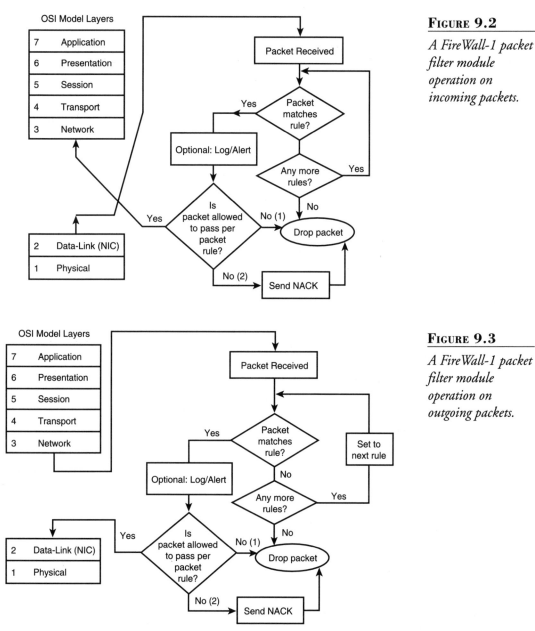

FIGURE 9.2

A FireWall-1 packet filter module operation on incoming packets.

FIGURE 9.3

A FireWall-1 packet filter module operation on outgoing packets.

Other capabilities of FireWall-1's packet filtering follow:

❖ **LISTS AND OBJECTS.** Networks and services are represented by objects, which can be grouped together and referenced in access lists, allowing filter rules to be specified at a higher level than most packet filters.

❖ **FULL DATA ACCESS.** The packet filtering rules can filter on addresses and header information for any of the layers 2 to 7 of the OSI model. Filtering on upper layer protocol information allows the specification of more intelligent rules based on more complete information. This allows the implementation of security policies based on application knowledge.

❖ **PROTOCOL INDEPENDENCE.** High-level definitions can be used to define new protocols and applications, making the packet filter module more generic and flexible.

❖ **AUDITING AND ALERTING.** Packets that are matched can be audited in a log or used to generate alerts. The log and alert formats and actions are user-configurable. The standard formats contain source and destination addresses, the protocol used, the service attempted, time and date, and the action carried out. Alerts can be programmed to run user-defined scripts to perform actions, such as triggering alarms and pager alerts, opening windows, and sending e-mail. Alerts can also be sent using SNMP to a SNMP Manager. The status report can be viewed using SNMP or through the Status System Monitor software.

❖ **STATUS REPORTING.** A summary of status information on network traffic is available in the System Status Monitor. This information is also available through an SNMP manager.

❖ **KERNEL MODULE.** The packet filter module is a dynamically loadable kernel module, meaning that upgrades are simple to implement. Because the packet filter operated inside the kernel, it is not hampered by context switching overheads, which would exist if the module existed as a user process. In general, running inside the kernel has the advantage of negligible processing overheads, and is more efficient.

❖ **OPTIMIZATION.** Packet filter optimizers are used to reduce the time spent processing packet filter rules. Techniques such as caching and hashing tables are used to unify multiple instances of objects and to access the data efficiently.

FireWall-1 Control Module

The Control Module is used to implement the network security policy and the control packet filter modules (also called communication gateways). The Control Module can also be used as a central facility to view logging and control information.

The control workstation uses the OpenLook X11R5 GUI. Alternatively, a set of command line utilities can be used that permit a simpler computer terminal to perform management functions. The command line tools also enable the writing of script files to perform specialized control functions.

The overall architecture of the control module is shown in figure 9.4.

You can use FireWall-1 to define a global security policy for the network. Figure 9.5 shows the user interface for setting the security policy parameters.

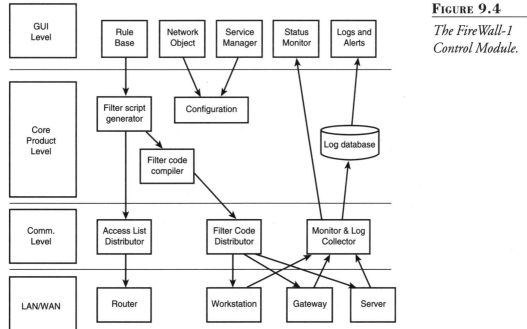

FIGURE 9.4

The FireWall-1 Control Module.

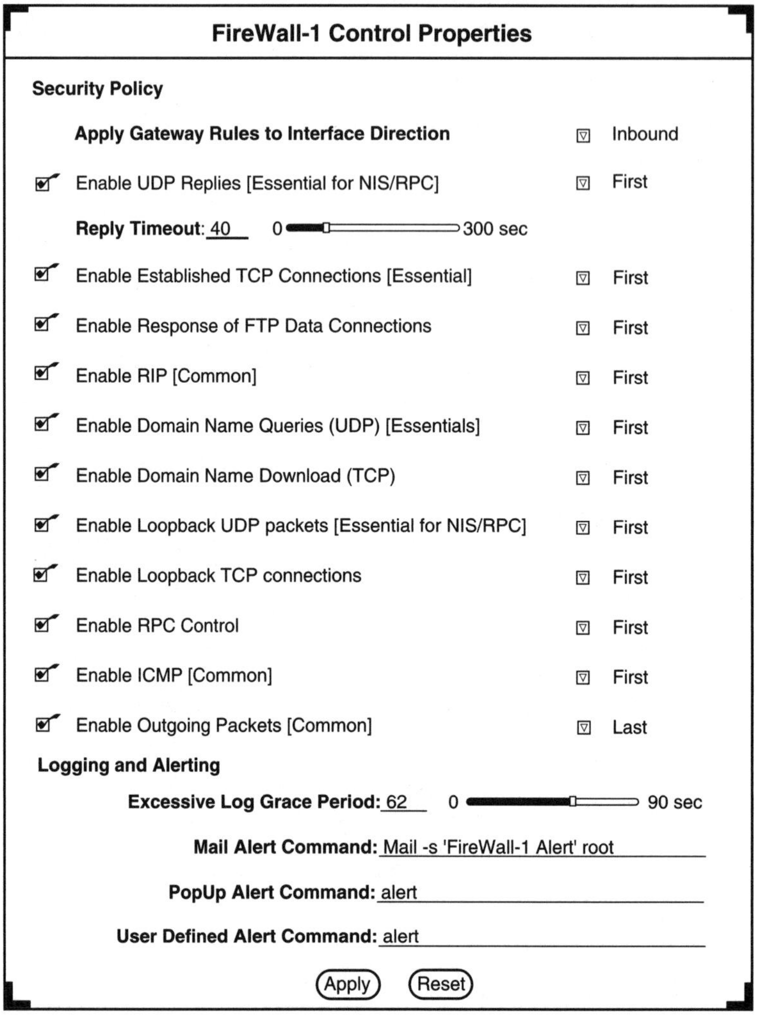

FIGURE 9.5

*The FireWall-1
control properties.*

FireWall-1 Control Properties

Security Policy

    Apply Gateway Rules to Interface Direction   ☑   Inbound

☑ Enable UDP Replies [Essential for NIS/RPC]   ☑   First

    Reply Timeout: _40_   0 ●━■▭▭▭▭▭▭▭▭➔300 sec

☑ Enable Established TCP Connections [Essential]   ☑   First

☑ Enable Response of FTP Data Connections   ☑   First

☑ Enable RIP [Common]   ☑   First

☑ Enable Domain Name Queries (UDP) [Essentials]   ☑   First

☑ Enable Domain Name Download (TCP)   ☑   First

☑ Enable Loopback UDP packets [Essential for NIS/RPC]   ☑   First

☑ Enable Loopback TCP connections   ☑   First

☑ Enable RPC Control   ☑   First

☑ Enable ICMP [Common]   ☑   First

☑ Enable Outgoing Packets [Common]   ☑   Last

Logging and Alerting

    Excessive Log Grace Period: _62_   0 ●━━━━━━■▭▭➔ 90 sec

    Mail Alert Command: _Mail -s 'FireWall-1 Alert' root_

    PopUp Alert Command: _alert_

    User Defined Alert Command: _alert_

      (Apply)   (Reset)

NETWORK OBJECTS MANAGER

The Network Objects Manager is used to define objects that are specified in the security policy. These include the following object types:

❖ Networks and sub-networks

❖ Servers and workstations

❖ FireWall-1 hosts and gateways

- ✤ Routers

- ✤ Internet daemon

Figure 9.6 shows the Network Object Manager screen that can be used to define objects of the type discussed in this section. You can view the networks by types (internal, external) and type of objects (host, network, router, gateway, domain, group). All the object types in this figure are selected.

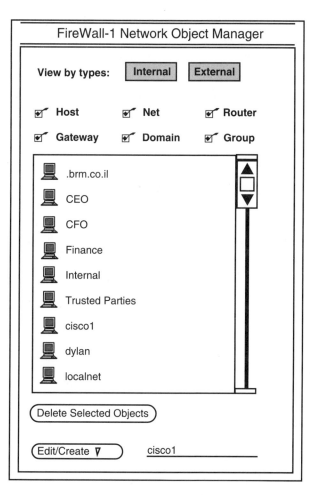

FIGURE 9.6

The FireWall-1 Network Object Manager screen.

Every network object has attributes, such as IP addressees and subnet masks, that define the characteristics of that object. These object attribute values are initialized from information stored in network databases. These network databases include files such as the /etc/hosts, /etc/networks, /etc/services, /etc/gateways. SUN-base networks may have the *Network Information Services* (NIS) databases. The information about various network objects can be extracted by polling SNMP (Simple Network Management) agents running on these devices. Objects can be combined in groups to create higher level object abstractions and hierarchies.

Figure 9.7 shows the attributes of a Host Object. This figure shows that some of the host properties are its IP address, location (internal or external), whether it is a host or gateway, whether FireWall-1 is installed on the host, and information on its network interface. The SNMP MIB (Management Information Base) variables for this host can be set, and you can define parameters such as the SNMP community name used to access the MIB variables in this host.

Host Properties

Name: monk

IP Addresss: 192.114.50.193   Get

Location: Internal   External

Type: Host   Gateway

FireWall-1:   Installed   Not Installed

Information: Sun SPARCstation, Ramat-Gan
ISRAEL, Shlomo Kramer +972-3-6131833   ▲▼   SNMP Info...

Comments:

Network Interfaces   SNMP Fetch
Add

Name	Connected To	Net Address	Net Mask
1. le0	Internal External	192.114.50.193	255.255.255.224
2. sl0	Internal External	128.139.250.2	255.255.255.0

Apply   Reset

SERVICES MANAGER

The Services Manager defines the services that are known to the system and that are specified in the network security policy. All network services are screened and controlled. FireWall-1 comes pre-loaded with definitions for over 40 TCP/IP and Internet services that include the following:

❖ Standard services: Telnet, FTP, SMTP, and so on

❖ Berkeley r* services: rlogin, rsh, rcp, rexec, rwho, ruptime, and so on

❖ SunRPC services: NIS, NFS

❖ Internet search tools: HTTP (Hyper Text Transfer Protocol), Gopher, Archie, WAIS (Wide Area Information Services)

❖ IP services: ICMP, RIP

❖ Management services: SNMP

The Services Manager can be used to define a new service by selecting the service type. The service types include the following choices:

❖ TCP

❖ UDP

❖ RPC

❖ Others: This enables definition of other services and protocols that are not standard.

Services can be grouped into families and hierarchies, such as the NFS group that includes NFS-server, Lock Manager, and Mount Program. Another example is Mosaic (WWW) that includes HTTP, Archie, Gopher, and others.

Figure 9.8 shows the Services Manager. You can use this screen to define new services or edit existing ones. Figure 9.9 shows the service properties of a standard service such as Telnet.

FireWall-1 Services Manager

View By Types:

☑ Tcp   ☑ Rpc   ☑ Group

☑ Udp   ☑ Other

🔲 nfsprog
🔲 nlockmgr
🔲 rstat
🔲 smtp
🔲 talk
🔲 telnet

(Delete Selected Objects)

(Edit/Create ▽)   telnet_____

TCP Service Properties

Name: telnet

Port Number: 23_____   (Get)

Source Port Range:_____-_____

Color: ▽ ■

(Apply) (Reset)

RULES-BASE MANAGER

The Rules-Base Manager is a software component that is used for managing the packet filter rules for FireWall-1. After you define the network objects and services, you can define the rules that make these services for implementing the security policy. When the rules are compiled and installed, they act as a packet filter. The Rules-Base editor is used for making changes to the packet filter rules. Figure 9.10 shows the Rules-Base editor for FireWall-1. This figure shows that rules can be entered in a table that has columns for source, destination, services, action, track, and "install on."

In figure 9.10, Rule 1 accepts an SMTP service packet from any source to a group of hosts defined by the group "mailservers." The action is to accept these SMTP services on the installed gateways.

Rule 2 allows any host on the network to access any service on any network. This rule is installed on the gateway. Additionally, a short log entry is created for matching packets.

Rule 3 blocks any attempt by any external source to the local network. This rule is implemented on the gateway. Additionally, alert messages are sent with the occurrence of such attempts.

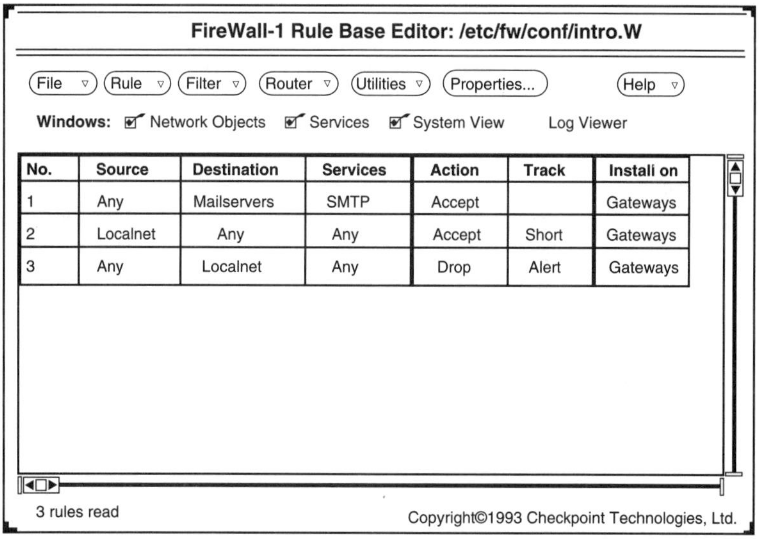

FireWall-1 Rule Base Editor: /etc/fw/conf/intro.W

File ▽ Rule ▽ Filter ▽ Router ▽ Utilities ▽ Properties... Help ▽

Windows: ☑ Network Objects ☑ Services ☑ System View Log Viewer

No.	Source	Destination	Services	Action	Track	Install on
1	Any	Mailservers	SMTP	Accept		Gateways
2	Localnet	Any	Any	Accept	Short	Gateways
3	Any	Localnet	Any	Drop	Alert	Gateways

3 rules read   Copyright©1993 Checkpoint Technologies, Ltd.

FIGURE 9.10

The FireWall-1 Rule Base Editor.

These rules are a high-level definition that consists of four parts: match, action, track, target. These parts are explained as follows:

✤ **MATCH.** Specifies the communication attempt in the rule. It includes the source and destination of the services involved in the communication.

✤ **ACTION.** Specifies how the communication attempt should be handled. Communication attempts can be accepted or rejected, and a negative-acknowledgment generated or simply dropped.

369

❖ **TRACK.** Specifies the type of auditing or alerting that should be performed, including the following:

No logging

Short format record

Long format record

Send e-mail message

Generate a SNMP trap

Activate a user defined procedure

Generate Alert message, such as a pop-up window on the system manager's workstation

❖ **TARGET.** Used to specify which packet filter module on the network should implement the filter rule. This mechanism can be used to implement enterprise-wide security rules. Rules can be enforced on all gateways, destination servers and gateways, and on source gateways and hosts.

Every communication attempt is matched against the Rules-Base. Rules are matched in the order they are specified, enabling predictable behavior of the packet filtering system. If no rules are matched, the packet is rejected, thus implementing the *That which is not expressly permitted is prohibited* security policy.

Rules are verified for correctness. This verification mechanism includes:

❖ Heuristic tests

❖ Definition inconsistencies

❖ Redundancy and order checking

The complete Rules-Base is used to generate a filter script. The *filter script* describes the objects and rules using the CheckPoint's filter definition language. These scripts can be used to implement sophisticated security policies.

You can view the filter scripts that are generated. Figure 9.11 shows an example of viewing a filter script generated from a Rules-Base.

FIGURE 9.11

The FireWall-1 Filter View.

```
                          Filter View

   ( File   ▽ )  ( Update View )

   // Filter Generated by marius@monk at 4Jan94 19:51:28 Rule-base intro
   // Prologue Begin

   // Define Log Preferences
   //
   #define LOG_TIMEOUT 62
   #define UDP_TIMEOUT 40
   #define LOG_MAILCMD       "![MaiL] -s 'FireWall -1 Alert' root"
   #define LOG_ALERTCMD      "![Alert] alert"

   #include "fwui_head.def

   // Default Filtering Code
   //
   eitherbound lo0@all { accept ;}
   ftpdata_code;
   accept_tcp_established;
   accept_rip;
   accept_icmp;
   rpc_code;
   udp_code;
   accept_domain_udp;
   accept_domain_tcp;
   // Prologue End

   // Filter Code Start

   ADDR_host(mailserver, 50.7.0.2)
   ADDR_net(localnet, 192.114.50.0, 255.255.255.0)

   intro.pf                              Copyright©1993 Checkpoint Technologies, Ltd.
```

ROUTER ACCESS LIST

The packet filter rules that are defined for routers are sometimes called router access lists by router vendors. The FireWall-1 supports both Cisco and Welfleet router access lists.

If Cisco routers with release level 9.1 (or higher) and Welfleet routers with release 8.0 (or higher) are used, they can be programmed with access lists that are generated from the Rules-Base. The rules for the routers are implemented using the router object definitions. The rules are verified and sent to the Access List Distributor module, which distributes it to the different routers.

Figure 9.12 shows an access list created from the filter script for a Cisco router. You might recognize these commands from the discussion of the access list commands for Cisco router in Chapter 6, "Packet Filters."

```
                              Cisco Access Lists


      ( File    ▽ )  ( Install.. )


      !
      ! Router cisco2
      ! Filter Generated by marius@monk at 15Feb94 15:01:56 Rule-base intro
      !
      no-access-list 101
      access-list 101 permit tcp  0.0.0.0  255.255.255.255  0.0.0.0  255.255.255.255
      established
      access-list 101 permit  udp 0.0.0.0  255.255.255.255  0.0.0.0  255.255.255.255  eq 520
      access-list 101 permit  icmp 0.0.0.0  255.255.255.255  0.0.0.0  255.255.255.255
      access-list 101 permit  udp 0.0.0.0  255.255.255.255  0.0.0.0  255.255.255.255  eq 53
      access-list 101 permit  tcp 0.0.0.0  255.255.255.255  0.0.0.0  255.255.255.255  eq 53
      access-list 101 permit  tcp 0.0.0.0  255.255.255.255  0.0.0.0  255.255.255.255  eq 25
      access-list 101 permit   ip  192.9.200. 0.0.0.0.127  0.0.0.  255.255.255.255
      access-list 101 deny  ip 0.0.0.0 255.255.255.255  192.9.200.  0.0.0.0.127
      ! Interface Bindings:
      !
      ! End of cisco2 filter code
      !
      !
      ! Router cisco3
      ! Filter Generated by marius@monk at 15Feb94 15:01:56 Rule-base intro
      !
      no access-list 101
      access-list 101 permit  tcp 0.0.0.0  255.255.255.255  0.0.0.0  255.255.255.255
      established
      access-list 101 permit udp 0.0.0.0  255.255.255.255  0.0.0.0  255.255.255.255  eq 520
      access-list 101 permit  icmp 0.0.0.0  255.255.255.255  0.0.0.0  255.255.255.255
      access-list 101 permit  udp 0.0.0.0  255.255.255.255  0.0.0.0  255.255.255.255  eq 53

      Intro.pf                                     Copyright©1993 Checkpoint Technologies, Ltd.
```

Most routers do not implement many of the capabilities required for secure packet filtering because they look at TCP/UDP/IP headers only. A protocol such as UDP is stateless, and the routers do not keep track of the context of previous packets.

STATUS MONITOR

The Status Monitor is a software component of FireWall-1 that is used to monitor the status of the FireWall-1 filter module. A system status window can be activated to display a snapshot of all the FireWall-1 filter modules at any time interval (see fig. 9.13). The status includes packet statistics such as the number of packets dropped, passed, logged, and so forth. The status of the filter modules is displayed as well.

The packet filtering modules support an SNMP agent that can be used for exporting information to other SNMP managers.

FIGURE 9.13

*The FireWall-1
System Status View.*

LOG VIEWER

The *Log Viewer* can display the events that have been logged, such as communication attempts, system shutdowns, firewall installations, and so on (see fig. 9.14). The event information includes date and time of event, originating machine, source and destination of communication, services attempted, action taken, and log alert types.

FIGURE 9.14

*The FireWall-1
Log Viewer.*

The Log Viewer can hide or display any of the information that has been logged (see fig. 9.15). A search facility enables you to locate rapidly any event of interest to you (see fig. 9.16). Reports are generated by applying selected criteria to the log fields. Reports can be viewed and exported to ASCII or PostScript. You can monitor communication activities and alerts in real-time. Nodes that appear in the log and that have SNMP agents can be probed from within the Log Viewer for SNMP information.

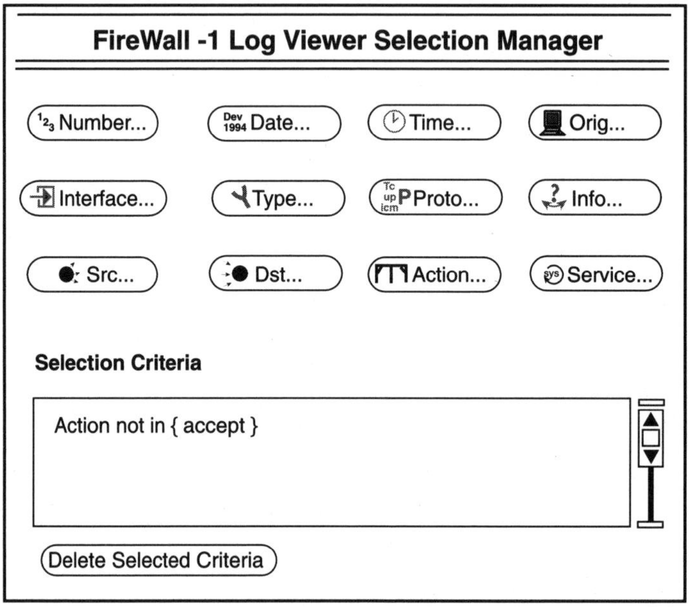

FIGURE **9.15**

The FireWall-1 Log Viewer Selection Manager.

FireWall -1 Log Viewer Selection Manager

¹₂₃ Number...	ᴰᵉᵛ₁₉₉₄ Date...	⏱ Time...	💻 Orig...
🔲 Interface...	↘ Type...	ᵀᶜ ᵤₚ ᵢcₘ P Proto...	❓ Info...
● Src...	● Dst...	🔲 Action...	ˢʸˢ Service...

Selection Criteria

Action not in { accept }

(Delete Selected Criteria)

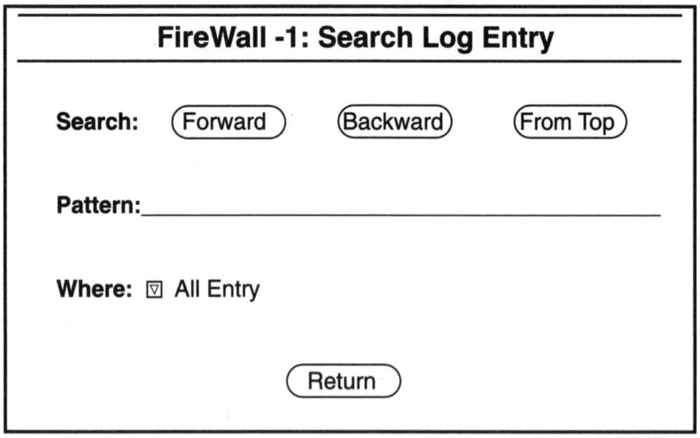

FIGURE **9.16**

The FireWall-1 Search Log Entry.

FireWall -1: Search Log Entry

Search: (Forward) (Backward) (From Top)

Pattern:_____

Where: ☑ All Entry

(Return)

EXAMPLES OF FIREWALL-1 APPLICATIONS

This section explains how FireWall-1 can be used to handle Internet Protocols and applications by performing secure packet filtering.

UDP APPLICATIONS

The problem of filtering UDP applications was discussed in detail in Chapter 6. Briefly, the problem with UDP, as it relates to packet filtering, is that it is a connection-less protocol. Unlike connections-oriented protocols such as TCP, there is no inherent distinction between the originator and request of the response. Because of this UDP source, port numbers can be easily "spoofed." UDP-based applications such as TFTP, DNS, and WAIS are difficult to filter in a secure manner. Some packet filtering solutions avoid this problem by not doing anything about it, thereby exposing the internal hosts to attacks through UDP ports, or by completely eliminating access to UDP ports.

FireWall-1 packet filtering solves the UDP packet filtering problem by maintaining context information on top of the UDP connection. You might think of this additional context information as representing an internal virtual-circuit in the firewall on top of the UDP connection. Every UDP request packet that is permitted to cross the firewall is recorded. Each incoming UDP packet is checked against a list of pending connections. Only when the packet is a response to a pending request is it delivered. Forged UDP packets pretend to be a response to a previous request. Because no such request is pending, the forged UDP packet is rejected.

OUTBOUND FTP CONNECTIONS

Although the FTP is a common application on the Internet, it still provides a level of complexity that can be difficult to handle. Briefly, the problem is that after the FTP client initiates a connection, the FTP server establishes a new back-connection (also called *call-back connection*) to the FTP client. The connection request originates from the FTP server, which may be outside the firewall boundary, to a dynamically allocated port on the FTP client. The dynamically allocated port is not known in advance. Many FTP clients specify new port numbers for each data transfer connection. Some older FTP clients open up the entire range of high-numbered ports, greater than 1,023, to back-connection requests. Unless a protection mechanism is implemented, the high-numbered ports are exposed to intruders.

> The call-back connection initiated by the FTP server exposes the entire range of high-numbered ports greater that 1,023 to "spoofed" back-connection requests.

N O T E

375

FireWall-1 handles FTP data connections by examining application level data. When the client generates a request for a back-connection (through the FTP PORT command), the firewall records this request. When the back-connection is attempted, it is checked against the pending FTP PORT command. Only the back-connection that specifies the port number in the pending FTP port command is allowed. All other attempts to connect from the FTP_DATA port number 20 are rejected. The list of pending connections is maintained dynamically, so only the required FTP ports are opened during an FTP session.

RPC-BASED PROBLEMS

RPC-based services, such as NFS, use dynamic port number assignments. The client program contacts, with the name of a service, the portmapper program that listens on UDP port 111. Other services register with the portmapper so that the portmapper has a record of all the services registered with it. The portmapper, on being contacted for an RPC-based service by a client, maps the service name to the registered port number and sends this information back to the client. Because of dynamic port assignments, you do not know which port numbers are in use, making it difficult to protect the port numbers.

FireWall-1 keeps track of RPC port numbers, and extracts application specific information from the packet. This information is used to identify the program and source using the service. It also keeps track of the UDP packets and builds context information for these circuits. By using a combination of these approaches, FireWall-1 protects the RPC-based services from attack.

MOSAIC, WWW, AND GOPHER

Clients, such as Gopher clients and Mosaic front-ends to the World Wide Web (WWW), pose a new set of problems for securing networks. Mosaic front-ends, in particular, can access a number of application services, such as HTTP, FTP, WAIS, Archie, and Gopher, through a unified front-end. These expose the network to the security risks of the underlying protocols, such as UDP, TCP, and FTP.

Because FireWall-1 can handle the underlying protocols, such as TCP, UDP, and FTP, it can be used for securing the network when used with Mosaic.

PERFORMANCE OF FIREWALL-1

Because FireWall-1 employs several optimization techniques, the performance degradation for most applications is negligible. These optimization techniques include the following:

❖ Running inside the operating system kernel reduces processing overhead and avoids context switching overheads.

✦ Packet filter optimization reduces the time spent performing filtering actions.

✦ Memory management techniques such as caching and hashing provide rapid access to network resource objects. These techniques can unify multiple instances of objects, which allows for more efficient sharing of memory.

The Internet Security Corporation reports that tests done on low-end Sparcstations showed negligible degradation over Ethernet at 10 Mbps. Performance degradation on lower speed links will be even less because WAN links operating at 56 Kbps or 1.544 Mbps (T1) are slower, and the bottleneck is the speed of the WAN link and not the packet filtering overhead.

FIREWALL-1 RULES LANGUAGE

You can use a text editor to write filter rules directly, using theFireWall-1 rules language. You might want to do this to have greater control over the packet filtering specifications. The following examples are presented to give you an overview of the FireWall-1 rules language.

The file std.def must be included in each rules set. This file contains definitions for standard macros, aliases, log formats and TCP packet structure.

EXAMPLE 1

The following rule checks inbound packets at all interfaces on ucs.xyz.com and allows any host to send smtp mail to ucs.xyz.com.

```
#include "std.def"
inbound all@ucs.xyz.com accept dst in ucs.xyz.com, smtp;
```

EXAMPLE 2

The following rule checks inbound packets at all interfaces on ucs.xyz.com and allows all hosts on the local net to do ftp or telnet sessions to ucs.xyz.com.

```
#include "std.def"
inbound all@ucs.xyz.com accept src in local_net, dst in ucs.xyz.com, (ftp or
telnet);
```

EXAMPLE 3

The following rule allows all hosts to access any other local host for services that are defined in the list locally_allowed. The list locally_allowed is user defined.

```
#include "std.def"
eitherbound all@all accept src in local_net, dst in local_net, service in
locally_allowed;
```

377

EXAMPLE 4

The following rule checks packets coming in through the sl0 serial interface of gateway GW1 and enables clients in TRUST.COM to send smtp mail to the local network.

```
#include "std.def"
inbound sl0@GW1 accept src in .trust.com, dst in local_net, smtp;
```

EXAMPLE 5

This rule checks outgoing packets on serial interface sl0 of the gateway GW1 and allows the local network to access services on hosts in the university BERKELEY.EDU.

```
#include "std.def"
outbound sl0@GW1 accept src in local_net, dst in .berkeley.edu;
```

EXAMPLE 6

The following rule checks incoming and outgoing packets on serial interface sl0 of the gateway GW1 and rejects all packets coming from .hacker.org to the local network. All such attempts that match the rule are logged and reported immediately to the systems manager.

```
#include "std.def"
eitherbound sl0@GW1 reject log <"! alert"> short src in .hacker.org and dst
in local_net
```

EXAMPLE 7

The first rule that follows logs the first packet of every attempt to establish a telnet connection through serial interface sl0 of gateway GW1, whether it succeeds or not. Clients must be in the user-defined list trusted_hosts to make the connection.

The second rule allows packets to travel in either direction once a TCP connection is established.

```
#include "std.def"
inbound sl0@GW1 accept src in trusted_hosts,  dst in local_net, telnet,
first. log short;
eitherbound sl0@GW1 accept tcp, established;
```

EXAMPLE 8

This rule checks incoming packets on serial interface sl0 of the gateway GW1 and blocks all packets coming from .hack.org to the hosts defined in the list protect_list. All such attempts that match the rule are logged and reported immediately to the systems manager though e-mail.

```
#include "std.def"
inbound sl0@GW1 drop src in .hack.org dst in protect_list log <"!mail -s FW-1
alert root"> short;
```

OBTAINING INFORMATION ON FIREWALL-1

Additional information on FireWall-1 can be obtained from the following:

Internet Security Corporation
Phone: (617)863-6400
Fax: (617)863-6464
Email: info@security.com

or

CheckPoint Software Technologies
Phone: (617)859-9051
Fax: (617)863-0524

ANS INTERLOCK

The FireWall-1 is a commercial gateway product, available from Advanced Network Services (ANS). The product currently runs on IBM AIX 3.2 (or higher) workstations or SparcStations (Solaris 2.3 or higher).

The ANS InterLock provides an application-level firewall gateway between an organization's internal network and an untrusted external network. The ANS InterLock can also be used to control access between segments of an internal TCP/IP network. This situation is shown in figure 9.17 where the InterLock service is deployed at the boundaries of the internal network. In this figure, the InterLock services running on host A is used to secure access to the Internet. The InterLock service running on host B limits access from a supplier (vendor) network. The InterLock service running on host C limits access from users of the Accounting department network, and the InterLock service running on host D limits access from users of the R&D department network.

The ANS InterLock gateway provides the following capabilities:

❖ Access control mechanisms

❖ Auditing and logging information

❖ Information hiding

❖ Mail Gateway services

379

FIGURE 9.17

Multiple ANS
InterLock
connections.

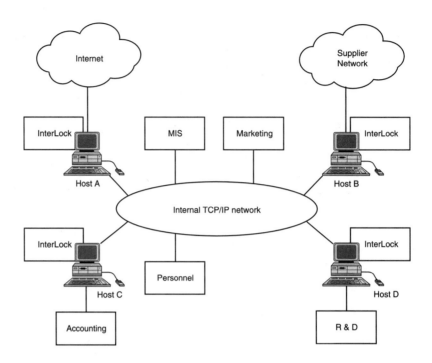

The Access control mechanism provides the ability to control access between any two networks based on a flexible criteria. Access control can be specified in terms of type of service, source, destination, and time of day the services are allowed. For example, one can specify that FTP access from external sites will be allowed from 9 a.m. to 5 p.m., Monday through Friday. You can also impose a requirement that users must authenticate themselves using a SecurID card (made by Security Dynamics Technologies, Inc.). This type of authentication can be used instead of the Unix user login, or to augment the Unix login.

The InterLock can be used to generate detailed logs and reports on authorized and unauthorized network connections. The logs accumulate usage statistics on a per user, per IP address, or per service basis. The data includes information on the duration of connection, bytes transferred, file names and sizes of files. Run-time data reduction tools are used to specify the level of detail and the amount of information logged for each service. Post run-time reporting tools can be used to generate usage statistics.

The InterLock does not reveal information about the internal network to the external network. The InterLock runs on a host with routing functions and IP forwarding disabled. As a result of this, information, such as host names, IP addresses, and network structure, is hidden from the external network. Although not recommended, it is possible to use non-NIC-assigned IP addresses to the internal network, because these addresses are hidden from the outside world.

RESOURCE REQUIREMENTS FOR INTERLOCK

Before investing resources in evaluating a product to see if it is suitable for your network environment, it is helpful to know details such as the hardware and software and training resources needed to implement the product. This information is provided for your reference.

The ANS InterLock runs on a dedicated platform based on R6000 IBM workstations or SUN SparcStations. The R6000 workstations run a modified version of the AIX operating system, and the SUN Sparcstations run a modified version Solaris. The modified workstations are pre-configured and can be purchased as a leased "turn-key." Alternatively, a leased software version (running on customer-provided hardware) and a software-only version can be purchased with an annual support contract.

The operating system modifications are done to prevent security holes that can exist because of improper configuration. Instead of turning off operating systems options that can be hazardous to security, ANS has completely removed these capabilities from the operating system to eliminate the possibility of an intruder gaining access to the system and enabling features that would bypass the firewall security.

The following operating system capabilities are removed from the operating system:

❖ No IP forwarding

❖ ICMP redirects are rejected

❖ No strict or loose source routing

With IP forwarding disabled, all connection requests are handled by application proxy daemons.

ICMP redirects can be used to create false entries in router tables, which can lead to denial of service or to network traffic being diverted to an unsecured host.

Source routing is removed to prevent packets from bypassing the firewall. On many systems, source routed packets are forwarded even if IP forwarding is disabled. By removing source routing and IP forwarding, packets can never be routed through the network layer.

OVERVIEW OF INTERLOCK

Typical tasks that need to be performed to set up the InterLock firewall are the following:

❖ Adding, deleting, and modifying user and groups

❖ Defining a security policy in the Access Control Rule Base

❖ Monitoring logs and generating reporting statistics

381

❖ Customizing prompts and system messages

❖ Executing the system backup scripts

❖ Editing mail mapping databases

❖ Establishing and managing password controls

All of the previously listed tasks can be performed by a single administrator or by a number of administrators. To ease system administration tasks, InterLock offers a flexible way of assigning different privileges to administrator accounts. A user account on the InterLock gateway can be assigned a combination of the following privileges:

❖ **MAIL.** Allows configuration and control over the mail system.

❖ **SECURITY.** Maintenance of security policies implemented by the Rules-Base.

❖ **ADMIN.** Creation and maintenance of user accounts.

❖ **AUDIT.** Monitoring and data reduction of log information.

❖ **SYSTEM.** Miscellaneous privileged operations.

Separation of the security privileges enables the organization to assign specific individuals to the different security functions. A specific privilege is assigned by making a user account a member of a group. This provides the organization with a flexible and familiar way of assigning privileges.

The access controls that govern the behavior of each application gateway are implemented in the *Access Control Rule Base* (ACRB). Rules to the ACRB can be specified using a menu-driven interface or a command interface. The organization's security policy is expressed as a set of rules. Explicit rules need to be provided to enable a service. Rules can be established for individual users, groups of users, or to an entire community of users using a wildcard entry.

> Because users have similar security needs, it is easier to define groups and establish rules for the groups. The individual users, then, inherit the rules because of membership in groups.

InterLock requires that all connections should be handled by application proxy daemons running on the InterLock gateway machine. Each application-layer daemon is responsible for reading its system configuration information and rules from the ACRB. If a proxy daemon is not provided, that service will be denied. InterLock provides proxy daemons for the following services:

❖ TELNET

❖ Login service

- ❖ FTP

- ❖ SMTP

- ❖ X Windows systems

- ❖ NNTP

- ❖ InterLock encryption service

- ❖ InterLock Generic Protocol Daemon (GPD)

- ❖ Network Time Protocol

CONFIGURING INTERLOCK

Before the InterLock gateway can be used, it must be configured with some site-specific information, which is defined in the file with the following path name:

/interlock/config/ILconfig

A sample ILconfig file follows:

```
#
# Interface names
#
     Public_Interface              en0
#    Private_Address               145.122.12.22
#    Public_Address                193.34.33.53
#Counters
#
     Max_TELNET_login failures     3
     Max_FTP_login failures        3
#
#Timers
#
     StartX_timeout_minutes               3
     X_Inactive_timeout_minutes           10
     Telnet_Inactivity_Timeout_minutes    20
     Telnet_Inactivity_Warning_minutes    5
#
#NNTP Configuration options
#
     NNTP_Public               server.pubcorp.net
     NNTP_Private              news.xyz.com
     NNTP_DomainName           disguise.com
     NNTP Post_Header_Mapping  On
     NNTP_Use_Mailmaps         Off
#
#Authentication options
#
     Authentication_List       unixpassword
```

The `Public_Interface` field is used to define which network interface is attached to the public network. The public network is the untrusted external network.

The `Private_Address` and `Public_Address` are commented out and are not configurable by the InterLock administrator.

The `Max_TELNET_Login_Failures` is the number of times a user will be allowed to attempt an unsuccessful TELNET login attempt before InterLock will close the connection.

The `Max_FTP_Login_Failures` is the number of times a user will be allowed to attempt an unsuccessful FTP login attempt before InterLock will close the connection.

There is currently no provision to lock-out an intruder for a period of time. Also, if specific TELNET and FTP connections are to be allowed or blocked, these must be specified by the Access Control Rule Base (ACRB).

The `StartX_timeout_minutes` defines the number of minutes the InterLock proxy X-daemon will listen for an X connection on the TCP port associated with the pseudo-terminal display number. If a connection does not occur in the specified time period, the InterLock X-daemon will close the connection and not accept any connections to the display number. When the value is set to zero, timeouts are disabled.

The `X_Inactive_timeout_minutes` defines the number of minutes that a X session can be inactive before the connection is closed. When the value is set to zero, timeouts are disabled.

The `Telnet_Inactivity_Timeout_minutes` is the number of minutes that a Telnet session can be inactive before the connection is closed. When the value is set to zero, timeouts are disabled.

The `Telnet_Inactivity_Warning_minutes` is the number of minutes that a Telnet session can be inactive before a warning message is issued. When the value is set to zero, warnings are not sent.

The `NNTP_Public` is used to define the host on the public (external) network that acts as a news server. If you have an internal news server that exchanges messages with the public news server, you must define this field.

The `NNTP_Private` is used to define the host on the private (internal) network that acts as a news server. This is the destination to which NNTP news originating from the external network will be directed.

The `NNTP Post_Header_Mapping` can be set to On or Off. When set to On, the NNTP proxy daemon will attempt to map the header portion of postings from internal users with the domain name specified in the `NNTP_DomainName` field. Remapping involves replacing the lines in the news header that contain references to internal hosts.

The NNTP Post_Use_Mailmaps can be set to On or Off. This field is defined only when the NNTP Post_Header_Mapping is On. When set to On, the NNTP proxy daemon will use the mail mapping database (/interlock/config/maild.mf derived dbm file) when changing the user part of the post headers. If Off, the user will query the database built from the file derived from /interlock/config/nntpd.mf.

Authentication_List is the list of available authentication types that are supported in a specific InterLock gateway. The default authentication type is Unix passwords (unixpasswd). You can use values of "securid" or "pinpad" to specify support for Security Dynamics' SecurID and Pinpad cards (optional services).

> The ILconfig file can be edited to change any of the parameter values just discussed. After editing this file, you can run the makeconfig command, which reads the entries in the configuration file and stores them in the binary database /interlock/config/config.bin.

THE INTERLOCK ACRB

The rules that govern the actions to be performed on packets, by an InterLock proxy application, are specified in the ACRB.

The first portion describes the situations in which the rule is to be enforced. Rules that do not match a particular situation (such as being outside the valid time range for which a service can be accessed) can be configured by the administrator to deny access or remain inactive.

The second part of the rule specifies what rule constraints should be enforced. You can define different levels of logging with each rule. For example, the logging levels could be low, medium, high, or debug, for each rule.

The rules can specify combinations of any of the following:

❖ **USER NAME OR GROUP.** This is the site-defined user name or group name. A wildcard (*) can represent any user. A special user name called "trust" can be used when the internal user's identity is not required from a specific host or network. This enables users on the internal network to use authenticated services TELNET and FTP without having to enter their user name and password.

❖ **PROTOCOL NAME.** This is the name of a service, such as LOGIN, TELNET, FTP, FTP-DATA SMTP, NNTP, X, or a customer-defined service. The port number can be used instead of the service name.

385

✦ **PRIVATE NETWORK OR HOST NAME.** This is the network or host on the inside (protected) network. The host's IP address or the network IP address (example: 144.19.0.0) can be used. A wildcard (*) matches all hosts on the internal network.

✦ **PRIVATE NETMASK.** This is the range of host IP addresses on the inside (protected) network. This mask value is not the subnet mask value.

✦ **PUBLIC NETWORK OR HOST NAME.** This is the network or host on the external (untrusted) network. The host's IP address or the network IP address (example: 144.19.0.0) can be used. A wildcard (*) matches all hosts on the external network.

✦ **PUBLIC NETMASK.** This is the range of host IP addresses on the external (untrusted) network. This mask value is not the subnet mask value.

✦ **START TIME.** This specifies the time when the rule will take effect, in a 24-hour format.

✦ **STOP TIME.** This specifies the time when the rule stops being in effect, in a 24-hour format. Existing connections are not shut down at the stop time; however, new connections are not allowed.

✦ **DAY-OF-THE-WEEK.** This specifies the day or range of days that the rule is in effect.

✦ **DIRECTION.** This defines in which directions the connections are allowed to flow.

✦ **ENCRYPTION.** This is defined only if encryption is provided as part of the package.

✦ **AUTHENTICATION TYPE.** This specifies the type of authentication mechanisms that are used. Valid authentication types are described in the ILconfig file described in the previous section.

The Username or group field and the Protocol name field cannot both be wildcards (*) in the same rule. The security policy of *That which is not expressly permitted is prohibited* is used. Therefore, at a minimum, there will be *N* rules if *N* applications are to be supported across the InterLock gateway.

To define the rules, a program called *rulebase* (located in the /interlock/security directory) is run. The user interface is simple to use, as shown in the following list. The subsequent list shows the choices (in bold) for adding a new rule. This rule defines that user ksiyan is allowed to telnet from any host on the private network to the host maclean.spy.com on the public (external) network. It also allows ksiyan to telnet from host MACLEAN.SPY.COM to any host on the private network. The user ksiyan is required to use the Unix password authentication. Telnet access is allowed only from 9 a.m. to 5 p.m., from Monday through Friday. Telnet access for this user is denied at all other times.

The following is the InterLock ACRB for Version 1.2:

```
<A>dd a new rule
<D>elete an existing rule
<M>odify an existing rule
<T>oggle remote login access for root
<S>how which rules apply
<C>heck user permissions
<W>rite text verson of rules base to a file
<Q>uit
```

This list shows the Add New Access Control Rule settings:

```
Group or username: ksiyan
Protcol name: telnet

Private network or host name: *

Public network or host name: maclean.spy.com
Is MACLEAN.SPY.COM a host name (y,n)? y

What direction is access permitted?
From MACLEAN.SPY.COM to ANY private host [y,n] ? y
From ANY private host to MACLEAN.SPY.COM [y,n] ? y

What type of user authentication is required on this connection?
Authentication type (unixpasswd,securid,pinpad,*): u

What type of encryption is required on this connection?
Encryption type (software,hardware,*,both,none): n

Should this rule be enforced all of the time (y,n) ? n
Days of week (su,m,tu,w,th,f,sa,*) [*]: m-f
Starting at time (00:00 - 23:59): 0900
Ending at time (00:00 - 23:59): 1700
Should KSIYANs TELNET access be DENIED all other times (y,n) ? y
```

INTERLOCK PROXY APPLICATION GATEWAY SERVICES

This section discusses some of the application gateway proxy services provided by the InterLock gateway. Examples are shown using the command line interface to these services.

INTERLOCK TELNET PROXY SERVICES

Figure 9.18 shows a typical deployment of the InterLock gateway. Users on either side of the InterLock gateway must first connect to the InterLock gateway and authenticate themselves.

387

FIGURE 9.18

Typical InterLock gateway deployment.

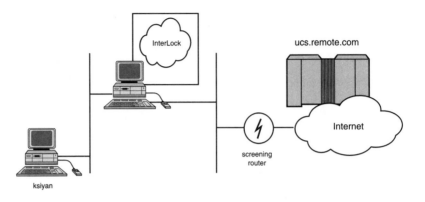

The InterLock gateway runs a telnet daemon that listens to well-known ports associated with these services. If desired, the organization can change the port associated with these services.

In this example, assume that the user ksiyan wants to establish a Telnet session from an internal host to a remote host on the Internet. The Telnet session must go through the InterLock gateway. The user must first initiate a telnet session to the InterLock gateway. The Telnet daemon on the InterLock receives this request and queries its ACRB to see if a Telnet session is allowed at the current time and day of week. If a connection is allowed, the user is prompted for a user name and password. If the InterLock service was configured with a SecurID option, prompts similar to that follow appear:

```
telnet interlock.kinetics.com
Trying...
Connected to interlock.kinetics.com
Escape character is ^[
InterLock login: ksiyan
ksiyans PIN: PIN entered is not displayed
ksiyans CARDCODE: cardcode entered is not displayed
```

After a successful login, you can see the InterLock gateway message. You must enter the remote destination to connect to.

```
InterLock Telnet Gateway N.0 (interlock.kinetics.com)
Destination: ucs.remote.com
```

The ACRB is queried again to determine if Telnet access to the specified destination is permitted. If access is allowed, connection is established by the proxy Telnet daemon to the remote host, and the user sees the login prompt for the remote host. If the ACRB checks fail (rules do not match), Telnet access is denied.

INTERLOCK FTP PROXY SERVICES

FTP works in a manner similar to Telnet. First an FTP connection to the InterLock gateway is established. The ACRB is consulted to see if a connection is allowed. The InterLock FTP server prompts the user for login name and authentication information. The user then issues the USER command to specify the user and host name for the desired destination. The InterLock FTP consults the ACRB to see if a connection is allowed.

If a connection is allowed, an FTP connection is established by InterLock FTP to the remote. The user is prompted for a password on the destination host. The following list shows a sample FTP session.

```
% ftp interlock.kinetics.com
Connected to interlock.kinetics.com
220 interlock.kinetics.com InterLock FTP Gateway N.0 ready at Wed Nov 16
12:34:33 1994
Name (interlock.kinetics.com:ksiyan): ksiyan
331 Password required for ksiyan
Password: password is not displayed
230- You are authorized as InterLock user ksiyan. Specify your remote user
230  and destination with the USER command (for example: USER
remoteuser@remotehost)
ftp> user anonymous@ucs.remote.com
331- ucs.remote.com  FTP server (Version 5.60) ready
331  Guest login ok, send ident as password
Password: password is not displayed
```

INTERLOCK SMTP GATEWAY SERVICES

The InterLock can act as a store-and-forward SMTP gateway. There is no password authentication of a user's SMTP session. The InterLock mailer, by default, consults a mapping database to determine where to deliver incoming mail from public hosts. This database also determines if the address in the FROM: line in the message header is allowed to send mail. An example mapping entry from this database follows:

```
ksiyan: karanjit@rama.kinetics.com, karan@shiv.kinetics.com
```

The entry before the colon defines the mailbox known to the outside network for this user. This is the user's external e-mail address. Mail to this user can be sent from the outside world to the address ksiyan@kinetics.com. The entries after the colon are valid sending internal e-mail addresses for the user. Mail sent to user ksiyan@kinetics.com is mapped to karanjit@rama.kinetics.com. Mail which arrives from karanjit@rama.kinetics.com or karan@shiv.kinetics.com is mapped as if it originated from the user ksiyan@kinetics.com. Therefore, the internal e-mail addresses are not known to the outside world. This is important for security reasons because internal e-mail addresses indicate the names of the hosts on the network.

An attempt made to send e-mail to the user at karanjit@rama.kinetics.com or karan@shiv.kinetics.com will fail because there is no such entry in the SMTP mapping database. A side benefit of this approach is that the remapping provides a common e-mail naming convention for the entire organization.

Rules can be specified to allow or block SMTP traffic between hosts or networks. Mail can also be configured to pass through the InterLock without requiring mapping. But in this case, replies will reveal the internal host names on the outbound headers.

INTERLOCK X SERVICES

The InterLock X daemon acts as a combination of a pseudo-X server and X-client. Suppose that an internal user wants to run an X-application that resides on a remote host (ucs.remote.com) on a local workstation (ws.kinetics.com). This situation is shown in figure 9.19. The user must telnet to the InterLock system where the user will receive the standard destination prompt after authentication. The user then runs the startX command and specifies the display number:

```
!startX ucs.kinetics.com:0
```

The exclamation mark (!) before the startX command tells the telnet daemon to run the command instead of specifying a destination host.

FIGURE 9.19

InterLock X services.

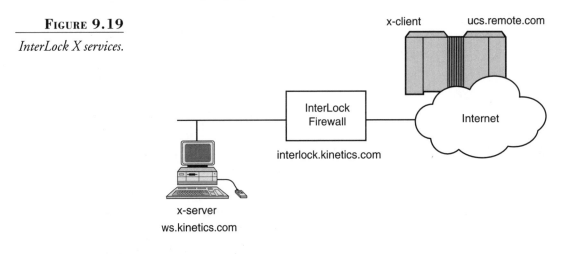

The following shows a typical X-session:

```
Destination [interlock.kinetics.com]: !startX ws.kinetics.com:0
interlock.kinetics.com will now accept X connections for screen 108.
```

```
Telnet to the machine which has your X client and use this host
and screen number in the display argument of your X client. e.g.:

        xterm -display interlock.kinetics.com:108
```

The server will shutdown if not used within the next 3 minutes.

The server will shutdown after 20 minutes of inactivity.

The user must then Telnet to the remote host on which the X client application resides by specifying the host name at the destination prompt. The user must then execute the xterm command at the remote host within the next three minutes, as follows:

```
Destination [interlock.kinetics.com]: ucs.remote.com
ucs% xterm -display interlock.kinetics.com:108
```

The InterLock X daemon then reads the X-packets from the host ucs.remote.com on port 6108 (X uses 6000 + *pseudo_screen_ number*), and display the graphics on ws.kinetics.com:0. The user must also give the InterLock gateway access permissions to his X-server, using the following command:

```
xhost +interlock.kinetics.com
```

Before establishing the X-sessions, the InterLock gateway checks its ACRB to see if the user has appropriate permissions for using Telnet and X-sessions to the remote host.

For security reasons, the InterLock gateway monitors the telnet session for inactivity. If there is no activity for 20 minutes, the session and the X-server shuts down. The time-out is configured in the ILconfig file discussed earlier.

INTERLOCK NNTP (NETWORK NEWS TRANSFER PROTOCOL) SERVICES

Under normal circumstances, when there is no InterLock firewall connecting to the external network, the news readers in the local network point to the local news servers, as shown in figure 9.20. On Unix systems, this is done by setting the NNTPSERVER environment variable to the news server host. A typical setting to run the news reader might be the following:

```
% setenv NNTPSERVER 194.23.34.5    # set the news environment variable
% xrn                              # Run the newsreader
```

With the InterLock gateway positioned between the internal hosts and the Internet, the news server must be contacted through the firewall (see fig. 9.21). The InterLock firewall does not allow direct news traffic between the internal and external networks. The internal users must, therefore, specify the InterLock gateway as their news server:

```
% setenv NNTPSERVER interlock.kinetics.com    # set the news environment
variable to point to firewall
% xrn                                          # Run the newsreader
```

FIGURE 9.20

*New Reader
configuration with
no InterLock
firewalls.*

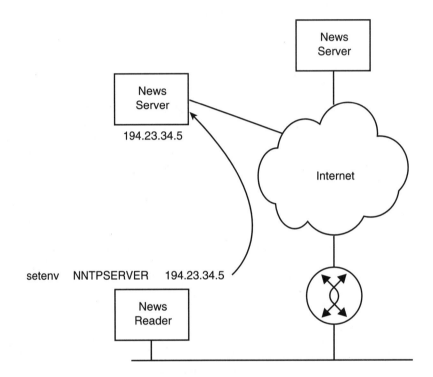

The InterLock gateway has a local application (/interlock/bin/nntpd) that listens for NNTP connection requests. When it gets a request, *nntpd* performs the following actions:

❖ It determines if the connection originated from the internal or external network.

❖ Checks the ACRB to see if the connection request is authorized. Unauthorized connection requests are logged in the file nntpd.log.

❖ If connection is authorized, nntpd opens a second connection request to the appropriate NNTP server. If the connection originated from the external network, and if an internal news server is defined, it will establish a connection to the internal news server defined by the field `NNTP_Private` in the ILconfig file. Similarly, if the connection originated from the internal network, nntpd will establish a connection to the external news server defined by the field `NNTP_Public` in the ILconfig file.

❖ nntpd reads data from one interface and copies it to the other interface, thus, acting as a circuit-gateway. If the Post_Heading_Remapping in the ILconfig file is set to On, it performs mapping operations in the posting header fields of the news messages. As a result of these mapping operations, it appears as if the news originated from the firewall, and all references to internal host names are remapped to the firewall host name. To perform this mapping, the nntpd can use a separate database (files nntpd.mf.dir, nntpd.mf.pag) or the same database used by SMTP mail (files smtpd.mf.dir, smtpd.mf.pag).

The InterLock gateway does not require password identification for users accessing the NNTP service because the NNTP protocol currently does not support any authentication. However, the InterLock can deny or allow access to services based on the value of the From: field in the news message post header.

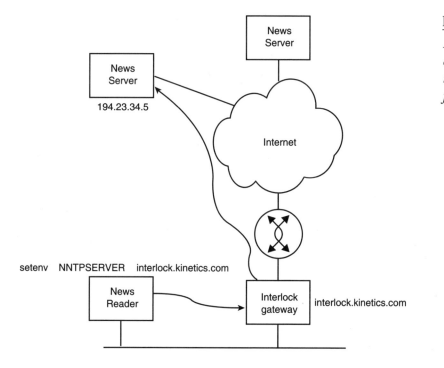

FIGURE 9.21

News Reader configuration through InterLock firewalls.

INTERLOCK HTTP (HYPER TEXT TRANSPORT PROTOCOL) SERVICES

The InterLock gateway can act as a HTTP forwarder by providing WWW proxy agents on the gateway. The InterLock forwarder can also work with WWW clients that support the

393

CERN proxy model (such as NCSA's Mosaic and University of Kansas' Lynx). By setting the http_proxy environment variable in the WWW clients, HTTP requests are directed to the InterLock gateway for resolution.

INTERLOCK GOPHER SERVICES

To access gopher services through the InterLock firewall, users must point their gopher clients to the InterLock gateway. The InterLock gateway can act as a data-less gopher server with menu entries but no associated data, or point to a real gopher server. The gopher protocol involves the exchange of selector information between the gopher client and server. The InterLock gateway forwarder replaces the returned selector with a *Uniform Resource Locator* (URL) containing the type, selector, and port associated with the real gopher server. The host field containing internal host names are replaced with the appropriate InterLock name. These translations occur transparently.

The user needs to know how to convert the URL advertised by external gopher servers to an appropriate InterLock format; otherwise, the InterLock gateway rejects the user's requests. Most gopher clients have mechanisms to specify information on the gopher servers to connect to. The gopher protocol sends information in four fields separated by the tab character and ending in a carriage-return/line-feed combination character (see RFC 1436). An example of the entries in these four fields that are needed to contact a remote gopher server is shown as follows:

```
Type = 0           # Gopher item is a file
Name = Remote Corp Gopher
Path = 0/gopher/recipes
Host = gopher.remote.com
Port = 70
```

Because the InterLock gateway hides knowledge of public hosts from the internal network, the gopher clients cannot directly connect to the host gopher.remote.com. This host name must be replaced by the InterLock gateway (interlock.kinetics.com in this example). The gopher client must access the external gopher using the following information:

```
Type = 0           # Gopher item is a file
Name = Remote Corp Gopher
Path = gopher://gopher.remote.com:70/0/gopher/recipes
Host = interlock.kinetics.com
Port = 70
```

For sites using the data-less model, a gopher root menu is constructed on the InterLock gateway for user connection from the internal network. A different root menu can be created for users attempting connections from the external network.

INTERLOCK GENERIC PROTOCOL DAEMON SERVICES

The *Generic Protocol Daemon* (GPD) implements a TCP and UDP forwarder and is meant for those applications that are not directly supported as InterLock application gateways. The TCP and UDP forwarders query the ACRB to determine if connection requests should be granted. Because no authentication is required, no user-level access controls, such as time-of-day, day-of-week, encryption required, and so on, can be specified.

To illustrate how the GPD works, consider the following example. The security policy requires that that organization's clients on the external networks access a special application on an internal host at TCP port 81. The TCP forwarder can specify a rule that consists of the IP address of the server, and the TCP port. Users on the external network can be informed to connect to port 81 on the InterLock gateway. When a request is received for port 81, the InterLock gateway queries the ACRB and checks if this connection is allowed. If the connection is authorized, it establishes a second connection from the InterLock gateway to port 81 on the internal host.

The GPD can be used to support services such as lpr, archie, nslookup, whois, traceroute, and dig.

ADDITIONAL SOURCE OF INFORMATION ON ANS INTERLOCK

For additional information on the ANS InterLock product and related services contact:

Advanced Network & Services, Inc.
1875 Campus Commons Drive
Suite 220
Reston, VA 22091
Phone: (703)758-7700
Fax: (703)758-7717
E-Mail: info@ans.com

TRUSTED INFORMATION SYSTEMS GAUNTLET

Gauntlet is a firewall product from Trusted Information Systems, Inc. (TIS). The product can run on the Intel-made *Classic-R* system. The base system consists of a board VGA adapter connected to a WYSE monochrome VGA monitor, two serial ports, and one parallel port.

An Adaptec SCSI controller is used to connect to a 440-MB SCSI drive. Additional SCSI devices can be added through the standard Centronics "D" connector on the Adaptec SCSI card. The CPU is an Intel 486 with a 66-MHz clock, 256 KB of cache memory, and 16 MB of main memory. The system board comes with a *zero insertion force* (ZIF) socket that can be used to upgrade to the Pentium processor.

The base operating system used for the Gauntlet product is BSD Unix from Berkeley Software Design, Inc (BSDI). The Gauntlet product comes pre-installed with BSD Unix. This pre-installed version is a subset of the binaries and utilities that normally come with BSD Unix from BSDI.

In the Gauntlet system, the kernel of BSD Unix has been modified to identify and log certain network-based threats. End users can reconfigure and rebuild the kernel, but care should be exercised to ensure that the custom networking utilities are linked into the kernel.

The Gauntlet system includes a single embedded license from BSDI. This is a special low-cost license restricted for using BSDI's BSD Unix for firewall processing. The license does not extend to general use of the system. The pre-installed BSD Unix system has, in itself, the capability to be used as a general-purpose computing platform, but this type of use is in violation of the licensing policy.

The Gauntlet system provides firewall-based proxy services for the following:

- ❖ TELNET
- ❖ rlogin
- ❖ FTP
- ❖ SMTP
- ❖ NNTP
- ❖ Gopher+
- ❖ HTTP
- ❖ X-Windows

For each service, there is a separate secure forwarding server that performs protocol-specific access control and auditing.

Configuration for the different application-level services is done through a screen-based systems interface. Operational tools include those for installing binary upgrades, checking digital signatures of system files against a database of cryptographic checksum (to detect alteration in these files), tools for audit log reduction and reporting, system alerts, and trouble monitoring.

Gauntlet's base policy is that all systems, other than Gauntlet itself, are initially untrusted. Configuration, therefore, involves explicitly adding trusted systems. In its initial default configuration mode, Gauntlet does not permit any data traffic through the firewall.

CONFIGURATION EXAMPLES USING GAUNTLET

The Gauntlet system has two Ethernet interfaces. Typically, these are Intel Express boards with both Thin Wire and 10BASE-T connectors. Figure 9.22 shows a typical use of the Gauntlet firewall. The Gauntlet network interfaces are labeled as ex0 and ex1. The *ex0* interface is connected to the outside network, and the *ex1* interface is connected to the inside network. The Gauntlet acts as a firewall between the inside and outside networks.

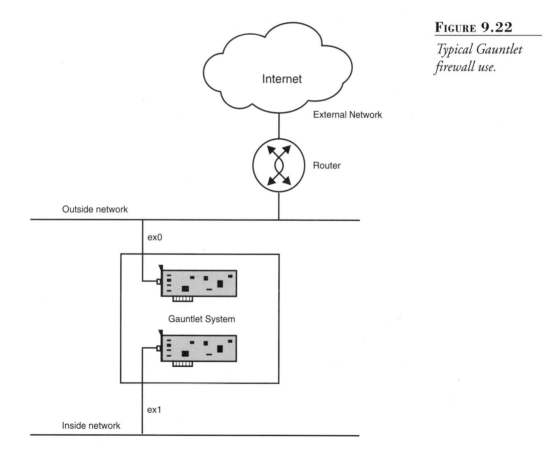

FIGURE 9.22

Typical Gauntlet firewall use.

397

Another possible use of the Gauntlet system is illustrated in figure 9.23. In this configuration, the Gauntlet system connects to the outside network through its network interface ex0 only. The network interface ex1 is not connected. A screening router is used to connect the outside network with the external network (Internet in this case), and another screening router is used to connect the outside and internal networks. The security of the network depends on a combined use of the screening routers and the Gauntlet system. If the screening routers are not set up correctly, the Gauntlet system could be completely bypassed.

FIGURE 9.23

The Gauntlet system using single network interface.

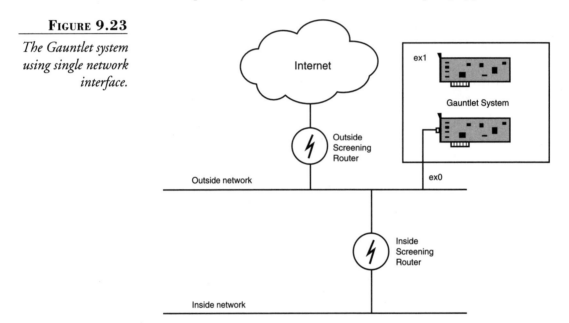

When setting up the routing tables for the screening routers, and the default route for the Gauntlet system, it is best to specify static routing to avoid accidental changes, and foil intruder attempts to change the routing tables. If your network policy requires that dynamic routes be used, the system can use the routed or gated daemons for providing dynamic routing.

CONFIGURING GAUNTLET

Configuration of the Gauntlet system can be done either through the menu interface or a command-line interface. A primary step is to configure the connected Ethernet interfaces with appropriate values for IP address, subnet mask, and broadcast address.

If the inside network interface, ex1, is not to be connected (refer to figure 9.23), it should not be configured. Additionally, you can specify the default route, which typically is the router used to connect to the Internet. A default DNS server can be specified initially to simplify testing while the system is being installed.

The following shows Gauntlet's main management menu. This list shows the type of administration options that are available through the menu interface. These options are performed using shell scripts that invoke the Gauntlet-specific utilities and commands.

```
                Gauntlet(tm) Main Management Menu
                --------------------------------

Select option: System Backups
               System Integrity Checks
               Install Software Upgrade
               System Event/Reporting Configuration
               Trusted Network Configuration
               System Access Configuration
               User Authentication Management
               IP Address Configuration
               DNS Configuration
               Electronic Mail Configuration
               NNTP Forwarder Configuration

                   Exit Configuration Menus
                           Help
                     Menuing System Help

              To navigate, use arrow keys and Tab
            To select a highlighted item, press Enter
```

The different Gauntlet options in the previous list are briefly explained so you can form an idea of the typical administration tasks needed to configure Gauntlet.

The *System Backup* option is used to configure and perform backups of the Gauntlet system. System backups are performed by using a SCSI tape drive. The BSD Unix *dump* utility is used for backups. The dump levels that are used are levels 0, 5, and 9. Level 0 represents the full-system backup. Level 5 represents backups of all data modified since dump level 5 or lower. Level 9 represents backups of all data modified since dump level 9 or lower. If a backup device is not available for the Gauntlet system, the backup can be performed on a network tape server. The configuration for this is also completed with this option.

The *System Integrity Checks* option is used to detect files that have been modified, deleted, or replaced. It can be used to alert the system administrator if accidental or deliberate changes (to lower the security, perhaps) have been done to the Gauntlet system. After making legitimate changes, this option can be used to update the integrity of the database. The System Integrity Checks' database can be copied to different devices to protect them for later use. Options exist to copy the systems integrity database to and from a floppy disk. You can also check the system integrity against databases stored on a floppy disk or network server. You can check the system release levels against an online database, a floppy disk, or a network server.

The *Install Software Upgrade* option is used to implement software patches and upgrades. Floppy disk upgrades are issued in the tar archive that contains multiple archives and the file "upgrade.cat," which lists the upgrade on the floppy disk.

The *System Event/Reporting Configuration* option is used to specify Gauntlet's report configuration and event reporting options. Reports can be generated on a daily or weekly basis. You can specify the e-mail address to which reports should be mailed. Unless you configure otherwise, the reports are mailed to the alias named "firewalladmin," defined in the file /etc/aliases. Even the daily and weekly reports are disabled; they are stored in the files /var/log/daily.out and /var/log/weekly.out so you can access them at a later time. The daily and weekly reports are run from the standard daily and weekly processing scripts /etc/daily and /etc/weekly. An alarm reporting option can be enabled, which allows you to specify the times at which the logs will be scanned for "noteworthy" events.

> Gauntlet uses an interesting approach to define that which is noteworthy. It does not attempt to list events that are noteworthy because this could leave out unexpected events that have not been defined. Instead, Gauntlet enables the administrator to define which events are ordinary. Noteworthy events are defined as those that are not ordinary. A file called /usr/local/etc/frequentcheck.ignore contains regular expression patterns defining ordinary events.

The *Trusted Network Configuration* enables you to define a list of trusted and untrusted networks, which are stored in /usr/local/etc/trusted-networks and /usr/local/etc/untrusted-networks. By default, the only network that Gauntlet trusts is its loopback interface (127.0.0.1)—that is, Gauntlet trusts only itself. The default untrusted network value is "*" (all other networks). The trusted and untrusted network files are used to build a copy of the firewall proxy permissions table file /usr/local/etc/netperm-table.

The *System Access Configuration* option is used to determine whether the administrator should be allowed to telnet or rlogin to the system. By default, these options are disabled, which means that the administrator must have physical access to the console.

The *User Authentication Management* is used to add, delete, or edit user configuration information. This screen can be used to specify the authentication mechanism that will be used for the user's login. The following authentication methods can be used with Gauntlet:

✦ **PLAIN PASSWORDS.** This is not recommended when logging in over an untrusted network.

✦ **SNK.** This is Digital Pathways Secure Net Key. Gauntlet supports the SNK authentication calculator.

✦ **S/KEY.** This is the freely available S/Key authentication system developed by Bellcore. Software for this is included, but TIS does not provide support for it.

The *IP Address Configuration* option is used to configure the network interfaces for the Gauntlet system. This option can be used to change the host name, domain name, IP address, subnet mask, broadcast address, default DNS server, and default router. If the internal network is subnetted and additional routes need to be defined for the Gauntlet system, the *route add* command can be used to add these routes in the /etc/netstart file. If the DNS software is to run on the Gauntlet system, the /etc/resolv.conf, which is used to list the DNS servers to contact for name resolution, must contain an entry for the Gauntlet system. This can be done by placing the following in the /etc/resolv.conf file:

```
nameserver 127.0.0.1
```

The *DNS Configuration* option is used to edit host tables (/etc/hosts), reload the DNS configuration from the host table, and configure DNS options. It can be used as a quick method for setting up a DNS server. For more complex configurations, you will have to edit and configure the DNS software directly, which would involve configuring the /etc/named.boot and the zone files referenced by this file.

The *Electronic Mail Configuration* option is used to specify if e-mail is to be forwarded to an internal mail hub, the postmaster for the Gauntlet system's e-mail address, or if mail headers should be modified to indicate that mail originated from the domain itself. This hides knowledge of hosts from the outside world. If there is no internal mail hub, you should not modify the mail headers; otherwise, return addresses might not be replyable.

The *NNTP Forwarder Configuration* is used to specify the internal and external NNTP servers between which news feed flows. Both internal and external news server should be configured to feed news to the Gauntlet system. The Gauntlet system uses proxy agents to forward the news.

USER'S VIEW OF USING THE GAUNTLET FIREWALL

Using a firewall such as Gauntlet changes the user's interaction for some standard services, such as Telnet, ftp, and rlogin. The user must first connect to the proxy server running on the firewall, then specify the destination to connect to. The application proxy on the firewall performs the requested action on behalf of the user. Sending e-mail does not require any change in the user interface, as long as the firewall is configured properly.

401

USING *FTP* WITH THE GAUNTLET FIREWALL

Assume that the user wants to do an anonymous FTP session to DS.INTERNIC.NET. The user must first connect to the FTP proxy server running in the firewall, as follows:

```
% ftp gauntlet.kinetics.com
```

Once connected to the server, the user is prompted for the user name and host name to connect to the remote FTP server. You have to format this in the following RFC-822 address syntax:

username@hostname

For the example in this section, you must specify this as the following:

anonymous@ds.internic.net

A typical session through the Gauntlet system from a host on the internal network follows:

```
ucs% ftp gauntlet.kinetics.com
Connected to gauntlet.kinetics.com
220 gauntlet FTP proxy (Version N stable) ready.
Name (gauntlet:you): anonymous@ds.internic.net
331-(----GATEWAY CONNECTED TO ds.internic.net----)
331-(220 ds.internic.net FTP server (Version 5.60 ready.)
331 Guest login ok, send ident as password.
Password: password not echoed
230 Guest login ok, access restrictions apply.
ftp> dir
200 PORT command successful.
```

When you see the message GATEWAY CONNECTED TO, it means that the FTP proxy server has established connection to the remote host. From then on, all commands you enter are forwarded to the remote host by the proxy. The proxy also returns all status messages for you.

The following shows the situation when you are using the FTP from an untrusted network and want to use an FTP server on an internal host. This sequence assumes that the SNK method of authentication has been enabled at the gauntlet firewall. Assume that the DNS name of the firewall from the outside is gatekeeper.kinetics.com.

```
% ftp gatekeeper.kinetics.com
Connected to gatekeeper.kinetics.com.
220-Before using the proxy you must first authenticate
220 gatekeeper FTP proxy (Version N stable) ready.
Name (gatekeeper.kinetics.com:you):
331 SNK Challenge "81416":
Password: password not echoed
230 User authenticated to proxy
ftp> user kss@ucs.kinetics.com
331-(----GATEWAY CONNECTED TO ucs.kinetics.com----)
```

```
331-(220 ucs.kinetics.com FTP server (Version 5.60 ready.)
331 Password required for you.
Password: password not echoed
ftp>
```

USING TELNET WITH THE GAUNTLET FIREWALL

The user must first connect to the Telnet proxy server running in the firewall, using the following line:

```
% telnet gauntlet.kinetics.com
```

After a short pause, the command prompt for the proxy server appears. Use **connect** *hostname* of the c *hostname* command to connect to the remote host. If the system is unreachable, the proxy informs you. You can then use the quit command to break the connection to the gateway. The following commands illustrate this sequence:

```
% telnet gatekeeper.kinetics.com
Trying 199.245.180.15 ...
Connected to gatekeeper.kinetics.com
Escape character is ^].
gatekeeper telnet proxy (Version N) ready:
tn-gw-> c ucs.siyan.com
ucs BSD 386/ v1.0 (ttys1)

login: enter loginname
Password: entered password not displayed
You have mail.
```

USING RLOGIN WITH THE GAUNTLET FIREWALL

The user must first connect to the rlogin proxy server running in the firewall, using the following line:

```
% rlogin  gauntlet.kinetics.com
```

After a short pause, the command prompt for the proxy server appears. Use the connect *hostname* or c *hostname* command to connect to the remote host. If the system is unreachable, the proxy informs you. Unlike Telnet, you do not have to authenticate the user twice.

Consider the following example where the rlogin server on ucs.siyan.com prompted for a password, because this firewall host was not in the user's .rhosts file.

```
% rlogin  gatekeeper.kinetics.com
rlogin-gw-> ?
Valid commands are: (unique abbreviations must be used)
   connect hostname
   help/?
   quit/exit
   password
```

403

```
rlogin-gw> c ucs.siyan.com
Password: entered password not displayed
Trying you@199.245.180.10
Last login: Wed Nov 16 17:45:23 from world.std.com
ucs BSD 386/ v1.0 (ttys1)

You have mail.
ucs%
```

If a user name and host name are specified, the rlogin proxy automatically reconnects to the specified remote system, as the following lines show:

```
% rlogin  gatekeeper.kinetics.com -l kss@rams.siyan.com
Trying you@199.245.180.12
Last login: Wed Nov 16 18:34:12 from world.std.com
ucs BSD 386/ v1.0 (ttys1)

You have mail.
ucs%
```

If you are logging in from an external site and the SNK authentication is used, you will see something similar to the following:

```
% rlogin gatekeeper.kinetics.com -l kss@si.kscs.com
Username: kss
SNK Challenge "23451": enter numeric code
Login Accepted
Trying you@193.25.10.3
Last login: Wed Nov 16 18:34:12 from world.std.com
ucs BSD 386/ v1.0 (ttys1)

You have mail.
ucs%
```

THE TIS FIREWALL TOOLKIT

Trusted Information Systems, Inc., the makers of the commercial Gauntlet product, also make available a free firewall package called the TIS Firewall Toolkit. Much of the functionality of the commercial Gauntlet product is built on top of this toolkit.

The TIS Firewall Toolkit is a collection of tools, from which you can pick and choose to implement the services that you need. The TIS Firewall Toolkit can be obtained by anonymous FTP from the following source:

    FTP server: FTP.TIS.COM

    Path: /pub/firewall/toolkit

> For a thorough presentation on the construction of a firewall using the TIS Firewall Toolkit, see Chapter 10 of this book.

N O T E

BUILDING THE TIS FIREWALL TOOLKIT

After you have downloaded the software package from the source mentioned in the previous section, you must compute and build the firewall toolkit on your system.

The firewall toolkit is a Unix compressed tar file. In this discussion, the name of this file shall be fwtk.tar.Z.

Copy this file into a working directory on your system and use the uncompress or gunzip commands to uncompress the file. You then must extract the files from the archive. An example of these commands for BSD Unix follows:

```
uncompress fwtk.tar.Z
tar -xvBf fwtk.tar
```

When the files are extracted, change the UID and GID on the extracted files to avoid any accidental access to these files. On BSD Unix systems, you can perform the following to assign the UID and GID for root and wheel.

chown -R root:wheel fwtk

Go to the fwtk directory under which the source files have been extracted. The file Makefile references the file Makefile.config. You should change some target definitions for this file. A listing of the Makefile.config follows:

```
#
# Copyright (c) 1993, Trusted Information Systems, Incorporated
# All rights reserved.
#
# Redistribution and use are governed by the terms detailed in the
# license document ("LICENSE") included with the toolkit.
#


#
#    Author: Marcus J. Ranum, Trusted Information Systems, Inc.
#
# RcsId: "$Header: Makefile.config,v 1.3 94/11/01 12:04:59 mjr rel $"
```

```
# Your C compiler (eg, "cc" or "gcc")
CC=     cc


# program to use for installation -- this may or may not preserve
# old versions (or whatever). assumes that it takes parameters:
# copy source dest
CP=     cp


# Options for your compiler (eg, "-g" for debugging, "-O" for
# optimizing, or "-g -O" for both under GCC)
#COPT=    -g -traditional
COPT=    -g
#COPT=    -O


# Version of "make" you want to use
#MAKE=    gnumake
MAKE=    make


# Your ranlib utility (use "touch" if you don't have ranlib)
RANLIB=   ranlib
#RANLIB=   touch


# Destination directory for installation of binaries
DEST=    /usr/local/etc


# Destination directory for installation of man pages
#DESTMAN=    $(DEST)/../man


# Names of any auxiliary libraries your system may require (e.g., -lsocket)
# If you want to link against a resolver library, specify it here.
AUXLIB= -lresolv
#AUXLIB= -lsocket


# DBM library should be specified if it is an external library or
# you with to use a different one than what is included in libc
#DBMLIB=    -lndbm
DBMLIB=
```

```
# Flags to pass to the linker (eg, -static for static binaries under GCC,
# or -Bstatic for static binaries under SunOS 4.1.x)
#LDFL=    -Bstatic
#LDFL=
LDFL= -g


# Location of the fwtk sources [For #include by any external tools needing
it]
FWTKSRCDIR=/u/b/mjr/firewall/fwtk
#FWTKSRCDIR=/usr/local/src/fwtk


# Location of X libraries for X-gw
#XLIBDIR=/usr/X11/lib
XLIBDIR=/usr/local/X11R5/lib


# Location of X include files
#XINCLUDE=/usr/X11/include
XINCLUDE=/usr/local/X11R5/include
```

You can change any of the variables defined in these configuration files, but pay special attention to the directories in which the files are referenced and installed. You should think about the settings of at least the following variables:

DEST, DESTMAN, AUXLIB, FWTKSRC, XLIBDIR, XINCLUDE

On BSDI Unix, you should change XLIBDIR to /usr/X11/lib and XINCLUDE to /usr/X11/include.

After making changes to the Makefile.config, execute the make command:

```
make
```

If you see compilation errors, make the appropriate fixes.

On BSD Unix, the author encountered the following error messages when trying to build the tools:

```
"Makefile", line 16: Need an operator
Fatal errors encountered -- cannot continue
```

This error message is caused by the fact that the "include" statements in the Makefiles in the fwtk directory and the subdirectories where the separate tools reside use a form of include that is incompatible with make on BSDI Unix. If you encounter the previous error, it is because the include statement in the Makefiles has the following syntax:

```
include name_of_file
```

You should change this to an include that uses the following syntax:

```
.include "name_of_file"
```

Another problem the author encountered was the conflict in getenv() and setenv() routines in the files in the fwtk/x-gw directory and the routines defined in the C-library. You can resolve this conflict by suitably renaming the functions that cause conflicts.

After you successfully compile and link the tools, you should run the following command from the fwtk directory:

```
make install
```

This command installs the tools in the directory specified in the DEST variable in the Makefile.config. To access these tools more conveniently, place the fwtk directory on your search path.

CONFIGURING THE BASTION HOST WITH MINIMAL SERVICES

You should configure the host on which you will be running the TIS Firewall Toolkit with only those services that are needed. This requires system-specific knowledge. The following is a partial list:

❖ Edit the system startup files, such as the /etc/rc, /etc/netstart, and /etc/rc.local (BSD Unix).

❖ Edit the operating system configuration and eliminate any undesirable kernel-based services, such as NFS, and rebuild the kernel.

❖ Edit the /etc/inetd.conf file, which specifies the internet daemon controlled services. Remove services that are not needed such as TFTP.

At each step, use the ps command to verify the services that are running. On a firewall, a reduced configuration should typically have the following processes:

```
% ps -aux
USER       PID %CPU %MEM   VSZ  RSS TT  STAT STARTED      TIME COMMAND
root         0  0.0  0.0     0    0 ??  DLs  2:35AM    0:00.00 (swapper)
root         1  0.0  0.0   652  116 ??  Is   2:35AM    0:00.11 init --
root         2  0.0  0.0     0   12 ??  DL   2:35AM    0:00.00 (pagedaemon)
```

```
root     29   0.0  0.0  608  112 ??  Ss   2:36AM   0:00.30 syslogd
root     46   0.0  0.0  520   28 ??  Ss   2:36AM   0:00.11 update
root     48   0.0  0.0  676  152 ??  I    2:36AM   0:00.38 cron
root     74   0.0  0.0  652  104 ??  Is   2:36AM   0:00.14 inetd
root     87   0.0  0.0  972  412 co  Is+  2:36AM   0:00.66 -tcsh (tcsh)
root    488   0.0  0.0  692  172 p0  R+   5:06PM   0:00.07 ps -aux
%
```

You can also use the netstat -a command to see a status of the network services that are running, as follows:

```
% netstat -a
Active Internet connections (including servers)
Proto Recv-Q Send-Q  Local Address          Foreign Address        (state)
tcp      0      0     *.time                 *.*                    LISTEN
tcp      0      0     *.daytime              *.*                    LISTEN
tcp      0      0     *.chargen              *.*                    LISTEN
tcp      0      0     *.discard              *.*                    LISTEN
tcp      0      0     *.echo                 *.*                    LISTEN
tcp      0      0     *.finger               *.*                    LISTEN
tcp      0      0     *.telnet               *.*                    LISTEN
tcp      0      0     *.ftp                  *.*                    LISTEN
tcp      0      0     *.smtp                 *.*                    LISTEN
tcp      0      0     *.sunrpc               *.*                    LISTEN
udp      0      0     *.time                 *.*
udp      0      0     *.daytime              *.*
udp      0      0     *.chargen              *.*
udp      0      0     *.discard              *.*
udp      0      0     *.echo                 *.*
udp      0      0     *.659                  *.*
udp      0      0     *.syslog               *.*
Active Unix domain sockets
Address  Type   Recv-Q Send-Q  Inode    Conn     Refs  Nextref Addr
fe46c400 dgram    0      0        0   fe396a94     0   fe3eea14
fe46c800 dgram    0      0        0   fe396a94     0   fe453994
%
```

You also can use the *portscan* tool that is in the fwtk directory under tools/admin/portscan to scan the ports on a host to see if any ports are active. You first will have to run make on the Makefile in the tools directory. Figure 9.24 shows the results of scanning ports 500 to 515 on host ucs.kinetics.com. The ports that are active on the host are displayed.

FIGURE 9.24

Using the FWTK portscan tool.

```
                          Telnet - bsd
 File  Edit  Disconnect  Settings  Script  Network  Help
ucs# portscan -l 500 -h 515 -v ucs.kinetics.com
ucs.kinetics.com: trying stream ports between 500 and 515
...........
512
.
513
.
shell
.
515
.
ucs# Nov 17 17:51:15 ucs rshd[840]: Connection from 199.245.180.15 on illega
Nov 17 17:51:15 ucs rlogind[839]: Connection from 199.245.180.15 on illegal

ucs# █


 Ready                                    VT100              16, 6
```

INSTALLING THE TOOLKIT COMPONENTS

When you run the make install command after successfully compiling the individual components, the binaries are installed in the directory specified by the DEST variable in the fwtk/Makefile.config file. The default is to install the tools in the /usr/local/etc directory.

Most of the toolkit components are invoked by the inetd daemon. The configuration for inetd is specified in the /etc/inetd.conf file. You must edit this file to invoke the firewall proxy components. The access control configuration information for the toolkit components is kept in the netperm-table file. By default, this file is found in the /usr/local/etc directory.

The following listing shows the partial contents of the /etc/inetd.conf file configured for the firewall.

```
#
# Internet server configuration database
#
#    @(#)inetd.conf    5.4 (Berkeley) 6/30/90
#
ftp        stream    tcp    nowait    root    /usr/local/etc/netacl
ftpd
ftp-gw     stream    tcp    nowait    root    /usr/local/etc/ftp-gw
ftp-gw
```

```
telnet     stream     tcp     nowait     root      /usr/local/etc/tn-gw
tn-gw
tn-admin   stream     tcp     nowait     root      /usr/local/etc/netacl
telnetd
login      stream     tcp     nowait     root      /usr/local/etc/rlogin-gw
rlogin-gw
finger     stream     tcp     nowait     nobody    /usr/local/etc/netacl
fingerd
smtp       stream     tcp     nowait     root      /usr/local/etc/smap
smap
echo       stream     tcp     nowait     root      internal
discard    stream     tcp     nowait     root      internal
chargen    stream     tcp     nowait     root      internal
daytime    stream     tcp     nowait     root      internal
time       stream     tcp     nowait     root      internal
echo       dgram      udp     wait       root      internal
discard    dgram      udp     wait       root      internal
chargen    dgram      udp     wait       root      internal
daytime    dgram      udp     wait       root      internal
time       dgram      udp     wait       root      internal
```

The netacl is a TIS firewall toolkit program that is invoked for standard ftp and administrative telnet sessions. It provides network access control for TCP-based services based on the network permissions table (/usr/local/etc/netperm-table). Usually, the netacl is configured to allow hosts on the internal network limited access to the gateway. The netacl is similar to the TCP Wrapper program discussed earlier in this chapter. This netacl program is designed to work with the network permissions table used by the TIS firewall toolkit.

If a telnet proxy gateway service has to be set up, it must be assigned the telnet standard port of 23 because the telnet program often disables options processing when connecting to a port that is different from this standard port. The telnet proxy service requires options processing so it must be connected to the standard telnet port. In the /etc/inetd.conf listing shown previously, this is done by the following entry:

```
telnet     stream     tcp     nowait     root      /usr/local/etc/tn-gw     tn-gw
```

The telnet gateway program can be found in /usr/local/etc/tn-gw . The tn-gw in the last column is the name of the service. When the /usr/local/etc/tn-gw program runs, it consults the permissions table to see if this access should be permitted or denied.

The meaning of the other fields are as follow: The *telnet* in the first column is the name of the service defined in the /etc/services file. The field *streams,* in the second column, refers to the TCP byte stream service. The field *tcp* in the third column refers to the protocol service which is TCP. The field *nowait* in the fourth column refers to the fact that when inetd receives a connection request, it does not have to wait, but can easily begin listening for additional connection requests. The field *root* in the fifth column is the user name under whose permissions the service runs.

If standard port 23 is used by the telnet gateway service and administrative access to the standard telnet service is required, the standard telnet service must be defined on another port. For example, you can define the standard telnet service on port 24, and make the following entry in the /etc/services file:

```
tn-admin      24/tcp
```

Then, in the /etc/inetd.conf file, you can make the following entry:

```
tn-admin stream tcp    nowait    root    /usr/local/etc/netacl    telnetd
```

When a connection attempt is made on port 24 of the firewall, the program /usr/local/etc/netacl executes, consulting the network permissions table file /usr/local/etc/netperm-table to determine if access is allowed or not.

The FTP gateway can be configured on any port. You might want to configure the FTP gateway on a different port, if you want internal users to have access to the standard FTP server. In any case, the standard FTP services should be under the control of the netacl wrapper program which can control access to this service.

```
ftp     stream    tcp    nowait    root    /usr/local/etc/netacl    ftpd
```

The FTP gateway service can be configured, as follows, in the inetd.conf file:

```
ftp-gw    stream    tcp    nowait    root    /usr/local/etc/ftp-gw    ftp-gw
```

The following are partial contents of a sample /etc/services file that define the firewall proxy services:

```
#
# Network services, Internet style
#
#     @(#)services    5.8 (Berkeley) 5/9/91
#
echo          7/tcp
echo          7/udp
discard       9/tcp        sink null
discard       9/udp        sink null
systat        11/tcp       users
daytime       13/tcp
daytime       13/udp
chargen       19/tcp       ttytst source
chargen       19/udp       ttytst source
ftp           21/tcp
ftp-gw        22/tcp
telnet        23/tcp
tn-admin      24/tcp
smtp          25/tcp       mail
time          37/tcp       timserver
```

```
time            37/udp        timserver
rlp             39/udp        resource      # resource location
nameserver      42/tcp        name          # IEN 116
whois           43/tcp        nicname
domain          53/tcp        nameserver    # name-domain server
domain          53/udp        nameserver
```

> When debugging the firewall toolkit configuration, you must restart inetd if you make changes to the /etc/inetd.conf file. You can restart inetd by using the ps command to determine its *process identifier* (PID) and then using kill -HUP on inetd's PID. For example:
>
> ```
> % ps -aux ¦ grep inetd
> root       76  0.0  0.0   652  128 ??  Is    5:27AM    0:00.99
> ↪inetd
> % kill -HUP 76
> ```

If rlogin proxy is to be installed, it must be installed on the firewall's rlogin service port (512). Rlogin requires binding to a privileged port, an operation that requires system permissions. Because of the permissive nature of rlogin security, you can set the rlogin proxy's directory option to ensure that it runs under chroot.

> The *chroot* is a mechanism under Unix where a process is confined to a single branch of the file system. After the chroot is performed, the root of the restricted branch of the file system is treated as the root directory, preventing the process from accessing critical parts of the file system, such as the /etc directory that contains the password files and other critical information, and the /dev directory that contains the device files.

THE NETWORK PERMISSIONS TABLE

The netacl and the firewall proxies read the network permissions table file to determine if access is permitted. A sample network permissions table file (/usr/local/etc/netperm-table) follows:

```
#
# Sample netperm configuration table
#
```

```
# To get a good sample working netperm-table, just globally
# substitute YOURNET for your network address (e.g.; 666.777.888)
#

# Example netacl rules:
# -------------------
# if the next 2 lines are uncommented, people can get a login prompt
# on the firewall machine through the telnet proxy
netacl-telnetd: permit-hosts 127.0.0.1 -exec /usr/libexec/telnetd
netacl-telnetd: permit-hosts 199.245.180.9 199.245.180.10 -exec /usr/libexec/
telnetd
#
netacl-ftpd: permit-hosts 199.245.180.9 199.245.180.10 -exec /usr/libexec/
ftpd
netacl-ftpd: permit-hosts unknown -exec /bin/cat /usr/local/etc/noftp.txt
netacl-ftpd: permit-hosts * -chroot /var/anon-ftp  -exec /usr/libexec/ftpd


#
# if the next line is uncommented, the telnet proxy is available
netacl-telnetd: permit-hosts * -exec /usr/local/etc/tn-gw
#
# if the next 2 lines are uncommented, people can get a login prompt
# on the firewall machine through the rlogin proxy
netacl-rlogind: permit-hosts 127.0.0.1 -exec /usr/libexec/rlogind -a
netacl-rlogind: permit-hosts 199.245.180.* -exec /usr/libexec/rlogind -a
#
# if the next line is uncommented, the rlogin proxy is available
#netacl-rlogind: permit-hosts * -exec /usr/local/etc/rlogin-gw


#
# to enable finger service uncomment these 2 lines
netacl-fingerd: permit-hosts 199.245.180.* -exec /usr/libexec/fingerd
netacl-fingerd: permit-hosts * -exec /bin/cat /usr/local/etc/finger.txt
# Example smap rules
# ----------------
smap, smapd:    userid
smap, smapd:    directory /var/spool/sma
smapd:          executable /usr/local/etc/smap
smapd:          sendmail /usr/sbin/sendmai
smap:        timeout 360


# Example ftp gateway rules
# ------------------------
ftp-gw:     denial-msg    /usr/local/etc/ftp-deny.tx
ftp-gw:     welcome-msg    /usr/local/etc/ftp-welcome.tx
ftp-gw:     help-msg    /usr/local/etc/ftp-help.tx
ftp-gw:          timeout 360

# uncomment the following line if you want internal users to be
# able to do FTP with the internet
ftp-gw:          permit-hosts 199.245.180.* -log {retr stor}
```

```
# uncomment the following line if you want external users to be
# able to do FTP with the internal network using authentication
ftp-gw:        permit-hosts * -authall -log { retr stor }

# Example telnet gateway rules:
# -------------------------
tn-gw:         denial-msg     /usr/local/etc/tn-deny.txt
tn-gw:         welcome-msg    /usr/local/etc/tn-welcome.txt
#tn-gw:        help-msg       /usr/local/etc/tn-help.txt
tn-gw:         timeout 3600
tn-gw:         permit-hosts 127.0.0.1 199.245.180.* -passok -xok
# if this line is uncommented incoming traffic is permitted WITH
# authentication required
#tn-gw:        permit-hosts * -auth
# Example rlogin gateway rules
# -------------------------
rlogin-gw:     denial-msg     /usr/local/etc/rlogin-deny.tx
rlogin-gw:     welcome-msg    /usr/local/etc/rlogin-welcome.tx
rlogin-gw:     help-msg       /usr/local/etc/rlogin-help.tx
rlogin-gw:     timeout 360
rlogin-gw:     permit-hosts 199.245.180.* -passok -xo
# if this line is uncommented incoming traffic is permitted WIT
# authentication require
rlogin-gw:     permit-hosts * -auth -xo


# Example auth server and client rule
# ---------------------------------
authsrv:       hosts 127.0.0.
authsrv:       database /usr/local/etc/fw-authd

authsrv:       badsleep 1200
authsrv:       nobogus true
# clients using the auth serve
*:             authserver 127.0.0.1 777


# X-forwarder rule
tn-gw, rlogin-gw:     xforwarder /usr/local/etc/x-g
```

Consider the following rules from this sample configuration file for the FTP proxy

```
ftp-gw:        denial-msg     /usr/local/etc/ftp-deny.tx
ftp-gw:        welcome-msg    /usr/local/etc/ftp-welcome.tx
ftp-gw:        help-msg       /usr/local/etc/ftp-help.tx
ftp-gw:          timeout 360
ftp-gw:          permit-hosts 199.245.180.* -log {retr stor
# uncomment the following line if you want external users to b
# able to do FTP with the internal network using authenticatio

ftp-gw:          permit-hosts * -authall -log { retr stor }
```

The meaning of the previous configurations statements is as follows: The hosts on the network 199.245.180.0 are permitted to use the FTP proxy. The "-log {retr stor}" indicates that logging actions for retrieval (GET) and storage (PUT) are enabled. The FTP proxy will timeout and shut the connection for a period of inactivity lasting 3,600 seconds. Also, external users can access the firewall FTP proxy if they are using authentication.

TELNET AND RLOGIN ACCESS

Normal telnet access to the firewall should generally be available to administrators only. To run the telnet/rlogin proxies, normal telnet/rlogin access cannot use the same port. You can use the following approaches for this problem:

❖ Permit administrative logins through the console of the firewall only.

❖ Run telnet/rlogin proxies on the standard service port. Run standard telnet/rlogin proxies on alternate ports, and protect them with netacl.

❖ Use netacl to switch services, depending on the origin of the request.

The first solution might be very restrictive to the administrators and might not always be possible.

The second solution might cause a problem with some telnet/rlogin implementations that do not work properly when connecting to a non-standard port.

The last solution is more convenient because users do not have to specify non-standard ports for standard telnet service. This solution, however, requires proper use of access controls. An example of the rules that provide this service follow:

```
#Telnet access
netacl-telnetd:    permit-hosts    127.0.0.1      -exec    /usr/libexec/telnetd
netacl-telnetd:    permit-hosts    199.245.180.10    -exec    /usr/libexec/
telnetd
netacl-telnetd:    permit-hosts    *         -exec    /usr/local/etc/tn-gw

#Rlogin access
netacl-rlogind:    permit-hosts    127.0.0.1      -exec    /usr/libexec/rlogind
netacl-rlogind:    permit-hosts    199.245.180.10    -exec    /usr/libexec/
rlogind
netacl-rlogind:    permit-hosts    *         -exec    /usr/local/etc/rlogin-gw
```

SETTING UP ANONYMOUS FTP ACCESS

Anonymous FTP user accounts have had their share of security problems, such as bugs in the FTP server implementation or misconfigurations. One approach to making Anonymous FTP more secure is to use the netacl program to "chroot" to a directory dedicated for anonymous FTP, before the FTP server is started. For example, the following lines from the sample network permissions table can be used for this purpose:

```
netacl-ftpd: permit-hosts 199.245.180.9 199.245.180.10 -exec /usr/libexec/
ftpd
netacl-ftpd: permit-hosts unknown -exec /bin/cat /usr/local/etc/noftp.txt
netacl-ftpd: permit-hosts * -chroot /var/anon-ftp  -exec /usr/libexec/ftpd
```

The first line permits only hosts 199.245.180.9 and 199.245.180.10 to connect to the FTP service. In the second line, hosts that are not known to DNS will have displayed the contents of the file /usr/local/etc/noftp.txt. Presumably, this text will have appropriate messages indicating that FTP service is not available to them. The third line permits access to any host, but it "chroots" to the /var/anon-ftp directory before executing the FTP service. When the FTP service starts, it will read the /etc/passwd file for user authentication. Because it has been chrooted to the FTP area, it will read the file /var/anon-ftp/etc/passwd, and not the main /etc/passwd file. This allows user accounts to be created and assigned that are for FTP only and that are independent of user accounts kept in the main /etc/passwd file.

SUPPORTING THE PROXY FTP SERVER AND STANDARD FTP SERVER ON THE SAME HOST

The proxy FTP gateway server can be invoked directly from the dedicated port 21 used for FTP service, or from inside a modified FTP daemon. If the proxy server is run on the standard FTP port, the standard FTP daemon cannot also run on this port, which means that standard FTP services are not available on the host that runs the FTP proxy. However, it is sometimes desirable to have both standard FTP and proxy FTP on the same host. For this reason, the toolkit supports a version of the FTP daemon that has knowledge about the FTP proxy, and invokes it when it recognizes an address in the form *user@host*. The source code for the modified daemon is in the fwtk/tools/server/ftpd directory. The Makefile in this directory defines a PROXY_PASSTHROUGH variable. The sample Makefile in this directory follows:

```
.include "../../../Makefile.config"

SRCS=    ftpd.c ftpcmd.c glob.c logwtmp.c popen.c vers.c
OBJS=    ftpd.o ftpcmd.o glob.o logwtmp.o popen.o vers.o
LIBS=      ../../../libauth.a ../../../libfwall.


# SETPROCTITLE sets the process title to something readabl
# PARANOID disables many internal FTP operation
# NOEXPORT enables TIS internal export control routine
# PROXY_PASSTHROUGH enables toolkit aware proxy switchin


#CFLAGS= $(COPT) -I../../.. -DNOEXPORT -DSETPROCTITLE
#CFLAGS= $(COPT) -I../../.. -DNOEXPORT -DSETPROCTITLE
CFLAGS= $(COPT) -I../../.. -DPARANOID -DSETPROCTITLE -DPROXY_PASSTHRU=\"/bin/
ftp-gw\"
```

```
all: ftpd
ftpd: $(OBJS
    $(CC) $(LDFL) -o $@ $(OBJS) $(LIBS) $(AUXLIB

install: al
    $(CP) ftpd $(DEST

clean
    rm -f ftpd $(OBJS
```

The PROXY_PASSTHROUGH should be set to the path name of the proxy executable, before you run make on the Makefile.

N O T E

If the modified FTP daemon is invoked after it has been chrooted to the FTP area, the PROXY_PASSTHROUGH must be relative to the FTP area, and not the root of the file system. A duplicate of the ftp-gw- and ftpd-specific rules from the netperm-table must also be installed in the ~anon-ftp/usr/local/etc/netperm-table file.

AUTHENTICATION MECHANISMS IN THE TOOLKIT

The TIS Firewall Toolkit has an optional authentication server, authsrv, that can be used to implement different types of authentication mechanisms in a mechanism-independent manner.

The authsrv program includes support for the following authentication mechanisms:

✦ Plaintext passwords

✦ Bellcore's S/Key

✦ Security Dynamics SecurID

✦ Enigma Logics Silver Card

✦ Digital Pathways SNK (Secure Net Key)

Plaintext passwords should not be used from untrusted networks. The authsrv should be run on a secure firewall. An administrative shell called the authmgr can be used from a remote location to manipulate the database information maintained by authsrv. The authmgr can optionally use encryption to protect its communication with the firewall.

When you compile the authsrv program, you must edit the authentication protocol bindings in the auth.h file for the authentication mechanisms specified in your network security policy.

The authsrv program supports authentication for all the interactive proxy servers used in the toolkit. Authentication can be done for both incoming and outgoing requests, and it consists of a simple challenge/response protocol that can be easily integrated in the software.

The authsrv maintains an internal user database that has a record for each user. This record contains the authentication mechanism to use for the user, user group, user full name, last successful authentication, and so on.

The users in the authsrv database can be organized in groups. Each group can have a separate administrator, who has administrative control of the group, including the ability to add and delete users to the group. Use of groups and a group administrator allows administrative responsibilities to be delegated in situations when a single firewall is shared by multiple departments in an organization.

The authsrv program is invoked for each authentication request. To configure authsrv, you must assign a free TCP port number and create entries in the /etc/services and /etc/inetd.conf files:

Use the following in the /etc/services file:

```
authsrv    7557/tcp    # Port 7557 was selected for authsrv
```

Use the following line in the /etc/inetd.conf file:

```
authsrv stream  tcp  nowait root /usr/local/etc/authsrv authsrv
```

It is not necessary to authenticate all services. You can authenticate selectively, based upon where the request originated and the type of requested operation. Consider the following example which shows the firewall gateway rules:

```
#
# FTP Firewall rules
#
ftp-gw:         authserver   127.0.0.1    7557
ftp-gw:         denial-msg   /usr/local/etc/ftp-deny.txt
ftp-gw:         welcome-msg   /usr/local/etc/ftp-welcome.txt
ftp-gw:         help-msg   /usr/local/etc/ftp-help.txt
ftp-gw:         permit-hosts   199.245.180.*    -log { retr stor } -auth
{stor}
ftp-gw:         permit-hosts    *    -authall
```

The first line identifies that the authsrv is running on the firewall (127.0.0.1 is the local host or loopback address).

The first permit-hosts statement identifies that hosts on the network 199.245.180.0 can access the FTP proxy. The file retrieval and storage options are logged. Of these, only file store operations are required to be authenticated. This is represented by the option:

```
-auth {stor}
```

The second permit-hosts statement says that all operations from external hosts will require authentication. This is represented by the following option:

```
-authall
```

To prevent intruders from probing the authentication server, the authsrv can be configured to specify which clients can connect to it. Typically, the authsrv and the proxy clients run on the same central firewall (bastion host). Because the clients and authsrv run on the same machine, it is only necessary to specify that the localhost (127.0.0.1) should be allowed to contact the authsrv. If administration is to be done from a remote workstation, the workstation's IP address should be listed. Following are some example rules for authsrv taken from the netperm-table configuration file:

```
#
# Example authsrv rules
#
authsrv:    database /var/adm/fwtk/authsrv.db
authsrv:    permit-hosts    127.0.0.1
authsrv:    permit-hosts    199.245.180.9 cipherkey
```

The database statement specifies the location of the authsrv database. This location should be secured from access by intruders. The clients on the host on which the authsrv runs are allowed access. The host at 199.245.180.9 is allowed access, presumably because this is a workstation used by the administrator. The keyword "cipherkey" indicates that communication between the workstation and authsrv is protected using DES encryption. The configuration file containing the cipher key should be protected from unauthorized access. To support encryption, two source code modules need to be replaced.

To import and export data from the authsrv database, two tools, authload and authdump, are included in the toolkit. The *authload* can be used to bulk-load the database from an ASCII text file. The *authdump* can be used to create an ASCII backup copy of the records in the database.

SUMMARY

In this chapter firewall solutions for several commercial products were discussed. These included Internet Security Corporation's FireWall-1, ANS's InterLock, and TIS's Gauntlet. The chapter also discussed how a firewall could be built using freely available toolkits such as the Trusted Information Systems (TIS), and the TCP Wrapper program tcpd.

## CHAPTER 10

THE TIS FIREWALL TOOLKIT

THE FIREWALL TOOLKIT produced by Trusted Information Systems, also known as TIS, is not a single integrated package, but a set of tools that are used to build a firewall. For this reason, it is not for everyone who intends to construct and operate a firewall. Consequently, it is difficult to produce documentation that can be used in all situations.

Remember that a firewall is intended to be the security policy your organization has chosen to develop and support. In this chapter, you will examine how to compile the TIS Toolkit, and configure the various components that make up the kit. By the end of the chapter, you will know the techniques and issues concerned with the construction of a firewall using this Toolkit.

UNDERSTANDING TIS

The TIS Firewall Toolkit is a collection of applications that, when properly assembled with a security policy, forms the basis of a firewall. This Toolkit is available as freeware to the Internet user community. As such, the Toolkit has gained a wide following and is in use worldwide.

The Toolkit is not a single integrated package like most commercial packages. Rather, it is a set of tools for building a number of different types of firewalls. Because of its inherent flexibility, a wide variety of combinations are possible regarding the installation and configuration of the TIS Toolkit. As such, this chapter explains what the Toolkit is and how the underlying technology works. With this knowledge in hand, and a copy of the Toolkit in another, you will be able to configure the Toolkit for your protection.

WHERE TO GET TIS TOOLKIT

The TIS Toolkit is available from the site `ftp.tis.com`, in the directory /pub/firewalls/toolkit. The filename is fwtk.tar.Z.

After you retrieve the file, it must be uncompressed and extracted from the tar archive. While you're at the TIS anonymous FTP site, you may want to examine its collection of firewall documentation and information. After uncompressing and extracting the archive, the directory structure illustrated in figure 10.1 is created.

FIGURE 10.1

The TIS Toolkit directory structure.

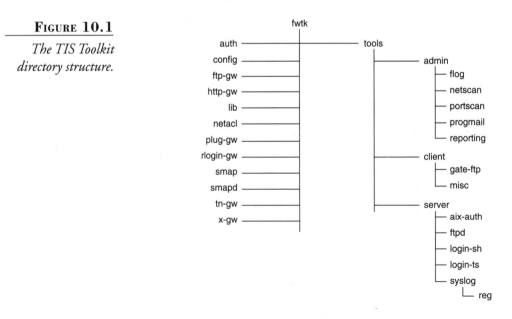

When the files are extracted from the tar archive, the next task is to compile them. Before compiling, any site-specific changes should be made to firewall.h and the Makefile.config files. Major issues that you need to consider are the installation location of the Toolkit—defaults to /usr/lcoal/etc—and how the library and compiler are to be configured.

> Most users experience difficulties compiling the X-gw proxy. The reason for this is the program's dependencies on the X Window System Athena Widget set. If you do not have this widget set, you will experience problems in getting this application to compile.

N O T E

COMPILING UNDER SunOS 4.1.3 AND 4.1.4

There should be little difficulty in compiling the TIS Toolkit under the SunOS 4.1.3 and 4.1.4 operating systems. There are no changes required from the base configuration to achieve a successful compile. After the archive is extracted, a successful compile can be achieved even without modifying the Toolkit configuration.

COMPILING UNDER BSDI

No significant surprises occur when you compile the Toolkit under BSD/OS Version 2.0 from BSD, Inc. A few changes do need to be made to ensure the compile is successful, however. First, the Makefiles are not in the correct format for the make command. In TIS, the Makefiles use the syntax:

```
include Makefile.config
```

This syntax is not understood by the make command that is shipped with BSD/OS. To resolve the problem you can edit each of the Makefiles by hand, or use the program fixmake. The include statement also requires a small change. The required format looks like this:

```
.include        <Makefile.config>
```

If you edit the Makefiles by hand, this is what the change looks like. However, you can also use the fixmake command to correct the syntax of the Makefile by removing the include statement and including all of the required instructions in one Makefile.

While you are tweaking, it is a good idea to make the following additional changes. No other changes are necessary.

```
CC=     gcc
COPT=   -g -traditional -DBSDI
```

CODE CHANGES

Several issues need to be considered when you compile the Toolkit components. These issues revolve primarily around the definition of sys_errlist. To resolve the problem, you must change the declaration of sys_errlist in all places where it is declared. For example, sys_errlist is defined in the code as:

```
extern char    *sys_errlist[];
```

Commenting out the line using the C comment symbols (/* */) results in a successful compile of the source code:

```
/* extern     char    *sys_errlist[]; */
```

INSTALLING THE TOOLKIT

After the compile process is completed successfully, you must install the files in the appropriate place. The easiest way to install these files is to use the command:

```
make install
```

This command uses information in the Makefile to place the objects in the correct place. The process is shown in the following command sequence:

```
pc# make install
if [ ! -d /usr/local/etc ]; then  mkdir /usr/local/etc;  fi
for a in config lib auth smap smapd netacl plug-gw ftp-gw tn-gw rlogin-gw
➥http-g
w; do  ( cd $a; echo install: 'pwd'; make install );  done
install: /usr/tis/fwtk/config
if [ ! -f /usr/local/etc/netperm-table ]; then  cp netperm-table /usr/local
/etc;  chmod 644 /usr/local/etc/netperm-table;  fi
install: /usr/tis/fwtk/lib
install: /usr/tis/fwtk/auth
if [ -f /usr/local/etc/authsrv ]; then  mv /usr/local/etc/authsrv /u
sr/local/etc/authsrv.old;  fi
cp authsrv /usr/local/etc
chmod 755 /usr/local/etc/authsrv
if [ -f /usr/local/etc/authmgr ]; then  mv /usr/local/etc/authmgr /u
```

```
sr/local/etc/authmgr.old;  fi
cp authmgr /usr/local/etc
chmod 755 /usr/local/etc/authmgr
if [ -f /usr/local/etc/authload ]; then  mv /usr/local/etc/authload
/usr/local/etc/authload.old;  fi
cp authload /usr/local/etc
chmod 755 /usr/local/etc/authload
if [ -f /usr/local/etc/authdump ]; then  mv /usr/local/etc/authdump
/usr/local/etc/authdump.old;  fi
cp authdump /usr/local/etc
chmod 755 /usr/local/etc/authdump
install: /usr/tis/fwtk/smap
if [ -f /usr/local/etc/smap ]; then  mv /usr/local/etc/smap /usr/local/etc/
➥smap.old; fi
cp smap /usr/local/etc
chmod 755 /usr/local/etc/smap
install: /usr/tis/fwtk/smapd
if [ -f /usr/local/etc/smapd ]; then  mv /usr/local/etc/smapd /usr/local/etc/
➥smapd.old;  fi
cp smapd /usr/local/etc
chmod 755 /usr/local/etc/smapd
install: /usr/tis/fwtk/netacl
if [ -f /usr/local/etc/netacl ]; then  mv /usr/local/etc/netacl /usr
/local/etc/netacl.old;  fi
cp netacl /usr/local/etc
chmod 755 /usr/local/etc/netacl
install: /usr/tis/fwtk/plug-gw
if [ -f /usr/local/etc/plug-gw ]; then  mv /usr/local/etc/plug-gw /u
sr/local/etc/plug-gw.old;  fi
cp plug-gw /usr/local/etc
chmod 755 /usr/local/etc/plug-gw
install: /usr/tis/fwtk/ftp-gw
if [ -f /usr/local/etc/ftp-gw ]; then  mv /usr/local/etc/ftp-gw /usr
/local/etc/ftp-gw.old;  fi
cp ftp-gw /usr/local/etc
chmod 755 /usr/local/etc/ftp-gw
install: /usr/tis/fwtk/tn-gw
if [ -f /usr/local/etc/tn-gw ]; then  mv /usr/local/etc/tn-gw /usr/local/etc/
➥tn-gw.old;  fi
cp tn-gw /usr/local/etc
chmod 755 /usr/local/etc/tn-gw
install: /usr/tis/fwtk/rlogin-gw
if [ -f /usr/local/etc/rlogin-gw ]; then  mv /usr/local/etc/rlogin-g
w /usr/local/etc/rlogin-gw.old;  fi
cp rlogin-gw /usr/local/etc
chmod 755 /usr/local/etc/rlogin-gw
install: /usr/tis/fwtk/http-gw
if [ -f /usr/local/etc/http-gw ]; then  mv /usr/local/etc/http-gw /usr/local/
➥etc
```

```
/http-gw.old;  fi
cp http-gw /usr/local/etc
chmod 755 /usr/local/etc/http-gw
```

With the Toolkit successfully installed and compiled, the next step is the security policy and the configuration of the Toolkit.

PREPARING FOR CONFIGURATION

When configuring the Toolkit, the first step is to turn off all unnecessary services that are running on the system that will affect your firewall. This requires that you have some level of Unix knowledge regarding the system startup procedure and services for your system. For example, you may have to:

❖ Edit the /etc/inetd.conf file

❖ Edit the system startup scripts such as /etc/rc /etc/rc2.d/* and others

❖ Edit the operating system configuration to disable unnecessary kernel-based services

You can use the ps command to see that a number of services are in operation. The following output shows such services on a sample system:

```
pc# ps -aux
USER       PID %CPU %MEM   VSZ  RSS  TT  STAT  STARTED   TIME    COMMAND
root       442  0.0  1.7   144  240  p0  R+    3:34AM    0:00.04 ps -aux
root         1  0.0  1.7   124  244  ??  Is    3:02AM    0:00.08 /sbin/init --
root         2  0.0  0.1     0   12  ??  DL    3:02AM    0:00.01 (pagedaemon)
root        15  0.0  6.0   816  888  ??  Is    3:03AM    0:00.47 mfs -o rw -s 1
root        36  0.0  1.5   124  220  ??  Ss    3:03AM    0:00.21 syslogd
root        40  0.0  1.2   116  176  ??  Ss    3:03AM    0:00.06 routed -q
root        77  0.0  0.5    72   72  ??  Ss    3:03AM    0:00.34 update
root        79  0.0  1.6   284  232  ??  Is    3:03AM    0:00.08 cron
root        85  0.0  0.3    72   36  ??  I     3:03AM    0:00.01 nfsiod 4
root        86  0.0  0.3    72   36  ??  I     3:03AM    0:00.01 nfsiod 4
root        87  0.0  0.3    72   36  ??  I     3:03AM    0:00.01 nfsiod 4
root        88  0.0  0.3    72   36  ??  I     3:03AM    0:00.01 nfsiod 4
root        91  0.0  1.0    96  144  ??  Is    3:03AM    0:00.07 rwhod
root        93  0.0  1.3   112  180  co- I     3:03AM    0:00.05 rstatd
root        95  0.0  1.3   128  192  ??  Is    3:03AM    0:00.07 lpd
root        97  0.0  1.3   104  184  ??  Ss    3:03AM    0:00.13 portmap
root       102  0.0  1.6   332  224  ??  Is    3:03AM    0:00.05 (sendmail)
root       108  0.0  1.4   144  200  ??  Is    3:03AM    0:00.11 inetd
root       117  0.0  2.1   228  300  co  Is+   3:03AM    0:00.90 -csh (csh)
root       425  0.0  2.0   156  292  ??  S     3:33AM    0:00.15 telnetd
chrish     426  0.0  2.1   280  304  p0  Ss    3:33AM    0:00.26 -ksh (ksh)
root       440  0.4  1.9   220  280  p0  S     3:34AM    0:00.17 -su (csh)
root         0  0.0  0.1     0    0  ??  DLs   3:02AM    0:00.01 (swapper)
pc#
```

By editing the /etc/inetd.conf file so that it resembles the following output, you can reduce the number of active processes. This reduces the load on the system and, more importantly, does not accept TCP connections on unnecessary ports.

```
#
# Internet server configuration database
#
#    BSDI    $Id: inetd.conf,v 2.1 1995/02/03 05:54:01 polk Exp $
#    @(#)inetd.conf  8.2 (Berkeley) 3/18/94
#
# ftp     stream   tcp    nowait   root     /usr/libexec/tcpd    ftpd -l -A
# telnet  stream   tcp    nowait   root     /usr/libexec/tcpd    telnetd
# shell   stream   tcp    nowait   root     /usr/libexec/tcpd    rshd
# login   stream   tcp    nowait   root     /usr/libexec/tcpd    rlogind -a
# exec    stream   tcp    nowait   root     /usr/libexec/tcpd    rexecd
# uucpd   stream   tcp    nowait   root     /usr/libexec/tcpd    uucpd
# finger  stream   tcp    nowait   nobody   /usr/libexec/tcpd    fingerd
# tftp    dgram    udp    wait     nobody   /usr/libexec/tcpd    tftpd
# comsat  dgram    udp    wait     root     /usr/libexec/tcpd    comsat
# ntalk   dgram    udp    wait     root     /usr/libexec/tcpd    ntalkd
# pop     stream   tcp    nowait   root     /usr/libexec/tcpd    popper
# ident   stream   tcp    nowait   sys      /usr/libexec/identd  identd -l
# #bootp  dgram    udp    wait     root     /usr/libexec/tcpd    bootpd -t 1
# echo    stream   tcp    nowait   root     internal
# discard stream   tcp    nowait   root     internal
# chargen stream   tcp    nowait   root     internal
# daytime stream   tcp    nowait   root     internal
# tcpmux  stream   tcp    nowait   root     internal
# time    stream   tcp    nowait   root     internal
# echo    dgram    udp    wait     root     internal
# discard dgram    udp    wait     root     internal
# chargen dgram    udp    wait     root     internal
# daytime dgram    udp    wait     root     internal
# time    dgram    udp    wait     root     internal
# Kerberos authenticated services
#klogin  stream   tcp    nowait   root     /usr/libexec/rlogind    rlogind
➥-k
#eklogin stream   tcp    nowait   root     /usr/libexec/rlogind    rlogind
➥-k -x
#kshell  stream   tcp    nowait   root     /usr/libexec/rshd       rshd -k
# Services run ONLY on the Kerberos server
#krbupdate stream tcp    nowait   root     /usr/libexec/registerd
➥registerd
#kpasswd stream   tcp    nowait   root     /usr/libexec/kpasswdd
➥kpasswdd
```

The reason for turning off all these services is to reduce the likelihood that your system will be compromised while the firewall is being installed and configured. You should also use the console to perform the initial setup and configuration of the firewall. With the /.etc/inetd.conf file updated, inetd must be signaled to know that some changes have been made. This signal is generated using the command:

```
kill -1 inetd.pid
```

The process identifier (PID) can be procured, and inetd restarted by using this command sequence:

```
pc# ps -aux ¦ grep inetd
root      108  0.0  1.4   144  200  ??  Is   3:03AM   0:00.11 inetd
pc# kill -1 108
```

To ensure that the services are turned off, you can attempt to connect to a service offered by inetd:

```
pc# telnet pc ftp
Trying 204.191.3.150...
telnet: Unable to connect to remote host: Connection refused
pc#
```

Now that the inetd services are disabled, disable other services that are part of the system startup files and the kernel. Some of these services are system-specific, which might require some exploration. Nevertheless, try to find the following services and processes and turn them off:

gated, cgd	pcnfsd	rwhod
mountd	portmap	sendmail
named	printer	timed
nfsd	rstatd	xntpd
nfsiod		

> **TIP**
>
> While timed, which is when the NTP time server process is turned off, you should configure your firewall to get time updates via an NTP server. This allows your firewall clock to have accurate time, which may prove invaluable should you take legal action.

After turning off these daemons, the process table on the sample system now looks like this:

```
pc.unilabs.org$ ps -aux
USER      PID %CPU %MEM  VSZ  RSS  TT  STAT  STARTED  TIME     COMMAND
chrish     89  2.3  2.1  280  304  p0  Ss    4:24AM   0:00.25 -ksh (ksh)
root        1  0.0  1.7  124  244  ??  Is    4:18AM   0:00.07 /sbin/init --
root        2  0.0  0.1    0   12  ??  DL    4:18AM   0:00.01 (pagedaemon)
root       15  0.0  3.2  816  464  ??  Is    4:19AM   0:00.08 mfs -o rw -s 1
root       36  0.0  1.5  124  220  ??  Ss    4:19AM   0:00.17 syslogd
root       71  0.0  0.5   72   72  ??  Ss    4:19AM   0:00.05 update
root       73  0.0  1.8  284  256  ??  Is    4:19AM   0:00.05 cron
root       75  0.0  1.3  140  192  ??  Ss    4:19AM   0:00.04 inetd
root       84  0.0  2.0  220  292  co  Is+   4:19AM   0:00.26 -csh (csh)
```

```
root          88  0.1  2.0   156  292  ??  S      4:24AM    0:00.13 telnetd
root           0  0.0  0.1     0    0  ??  DLs    4:18AM    0:00.00 (swapper)
chrish        95  0.0  1.6   136  232  p0  R+     4:24AM    0:00.02 ps -aux
pc.unilabs.org$
```

The ps command output shown now represents a quiet system. For clarification, the mfs command in the ps output is for a memory-based temporary file system on the BSDI Version 2.0 Operating System. However, this does not really list the actual services that are provided on this system. In the sample inetd.cof file presented earlier, virtually all the available network services were disabled. This is illustrated in the output of the netstat command:

```
pc# netstat -a
Active Internet connections (including servers)
Proto Recv-Q Send-Q  Local Address      Foreign Address        (state)
tcp        0      0  pc.telnet          stargazer.1037         ESTABLISHED
tcp        0      0  *.telnet           *.*                    LISTEN
udp        0      0  *.syslog           *.*
Active Unix domain sockets
Address  Type   Recv-Q Send-Q   Inode     Conn      Refs  Nextref Addr
f0764400 dgram       0      0       0  f0665c94         0  f0665214
f074e480 dgram       0      0       0  f0665c94         0         0
f0665c00 dgram       0      0  f0665780         0  f06d6194         0  /dev/log
pc#
```

The tools directory in the Toolkit distribution includes a utility called portscan, which probes a system to determine what TCP services are currently being offered. This program probes the ports on a system and prints a list of available port numbers, or service names. The output of the command is shown here:

```
pc# ./portscan pc
7
9
13
19
21
23
25
...
512
513
shell
1053
1054
1055
1056
1057
pc#
```

This command shows what ports were available prior to reducing the available services. After reducing those services by shutting off the entries in inetd.conf and the startup files, the system now offers the following ports:

```
pc# ./portscan pc
21
23
pc#
```

With the host almost completely shut down from the network, the next step is to configure TIS Toolkit components.

CONFIGURING TCP/IP

For TIS to be effective as a firewall, the system on which it is running must not perform routing. A system that has two or more network interfaces must be configured so that it does not automatically route packets from one interface to another. If this occurs, services that are being constructed with the TIS Toolkit will not be used.

IP FORWARDING

To receive any real benefits from a firewall installation, you need to make sure IP forwarding has been disabled. IP forwarding causes the packets received on one interface to be retransmitted on all other applicable interfaces. To help illustrate IP forwarding, suppose you are considering setting up a firewall on the system in figure 10.2.

FIGURE 10.2

Multihomed machines.

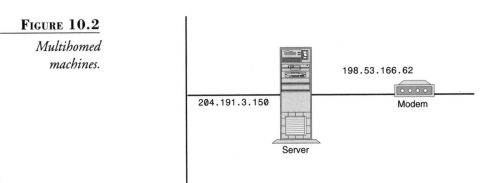

This machine has two interfaces: one is for the local area network, which has an IP address of 204.191.3.150. The other interface is for the wide area network, and is a PPP link using an IP address of 198.53.166.62. When IP forwarding is enabled, any packets received on the LAN interface of this machine that are destined for a different network are automatically forwarded to the PPP link. The same is true for packets on the PPP link. If the packets received on the PPP link are for the rnet, they will be transmitted on the Ethernet interface in the machine.

This type of arrangement is unsuitable for a firewall. The reason is that the firewall will still pass unlogged and unauthenticated traffic from either direction. Consequently, there is little or no point in going through this exercise if you leave IP forwarding enabled.

Disabling IP forwarding usually requires that a new kernel be configured. The reason for this is that the process of IP disabling involves changing some kernel parameters. Table 10.1 lists parameters that must be changed for the identified operating systems.

TABLE 10.1
Disabling IP Forwarding

Operating System	Parameter
BSDI Version 2.0	Make sure GATEWAY is commented out in the kernel configuration files.
SunOS 4.1.x	Run adb on the kernel to set IP_forwarding to -1, and save the modified kernel image. Alternatively, modify /usr/kvm/ sys/netinet/in_proto.c) to set the variable to -1 by default and rebuild the kernel.

After making the required changes to the kernel parameters, you need to build a new kernel, install it, and reboot. This removes any configured IP forwarding, and enables you to maximize the capabilities of the Toolkit. After IP forwarding is removed, all traffic requests either into or out of the private network need to be made through the proxy servers on the firewall.

THE NETPERM TABLE

The netperm table, found in /usr/local/etc/netperm-table, is the master configuration file for all the components in the Trusted Firewall Toolkit (netacl, smap, smapd, ftp-gw, tn-gw, and plug-gw). When an application in the Toolkit starts, it reads its configuration and permissions information from netperm-table and stores it in an in-memory database. Saving the information in an in-memory database allows the information to be preserved, even after a chroot system call is used to reset the directory structure.

The permissions/configuration file is organized into rules. Each rule is the name of the application that rule applies to, followed by a colon. Multiple applications can be targeted by a single rule by separating the names with commas, or wildcarding them with an asterisk. When an application extracts its configuration information, it only extracts the rules that apply to it, preserving the order in which they appeared in the file. The following sequence lists a sample set of rules for the smap and smapd application.

```
# sample rules for smap
        smap, smapd:  userid 4
        smap, smapd:  directory /mail/inspool
        smap:         timeout 3600
```

N O T E

> Comments regarding the rules can be inserted in the configuration file by starting the line with "#" as the first character. As with any configuration file or program, the more comments that are used, the easier it is later to maintain the rules.

When an application has matched a rule, the rule is translated into whitespace-delimited strings for later use. Typically, the application retrieves matching rules based on the first word in the rule; the remaining words serve as parameters for that particular clause. For the smap client and smapd server in the preceding example, the rules specify the userid to use when the application executes, the directory clause identifies the location of files, and the timeout clause indicates how long the server or client will wait before assuming that the remote end is "hung."

Special modifiers are available for each clause. For example, if the clause begins with a permit- or deny- modifier, the rule is internally flagged as granting or revoking permission for that clause. This means that if an application retrieves all of its configuration clauses for "hosts," the following will be returned:

```
netacl-in.ftpd: permit-hosts 192.33.112.117 -exec /usr/etc/in.ftpd
netacl-in.ftpd: permit-hosts 198.137.240.101 -exec /usr/etc/in.ftpd
netacl-in.ftpd: deny-hosts unknown
netacl-in.ftpd: deny-hosts *
```

Although this example may not seem clear, keep in mind that each application within the Toolkit has its own unique set of clauses. The default configuration for each of the application's clauses and examples are presented with the application's description.

When assembling your netperm-table file, you might want to consider a few conventions. These conventions promote consistency in the file, and help produce a more readable and maintainable rules list. When a hostname or host IP address is specified in the rule, matching is performed based on whether the pattern to which the address will be matched is all digits and decimal points, or other characters.

To better explain this process, consider this configuration rule:

```
netacl-in.ftpd: permit-hosts 192.33.112.117 -exec /usr/etc/in.ftpd
```

When a connection is received and this rule is applied, the IP address of the remote machine will be used to match this rule. If the pattern to match consists entirely of digits and decimals, matching is performed against the IP address; otherwise, it is performed against the hostname.

If the rule specifies a host or domain name, as in the following rule,

```
netacl-in.ftpd: permit-hosts *.istar.net -exec /usr/etc/in.ftpd
```

then the remote system's name is used to validate against the rule, not the IP address. To prevent any vulnerability from DNS spoofing, it is highly recommended that the configuration rules be bound to IP addresses. When matching, asterisk wildcards are supported, with syntax similar to the shell's, matching as many characters as possible.

When the application attempts to resolve an IP address to the domain name and the reverse lookup fails, the hostname is set to "unknown." Otherwise the real hostname of the remote system is returned. When the Domain Name resolution is performed by the firewall, a check is made to ensure that the IP address for the DNS name returned by the reverse lookup is the same.

This setup prevents DNS spoofing. If a hostname for this IP address cannot be located in the DNS system, the hostname is set to "unknown" and a warning is logged. This permits rules to operate on hosts that didn't have valid DNS mappings. This means that it is possible to allow any host in the Internet to pass through your firewall, or access certain services (or both) as long as reverse DNS, or IN-ADDR.ARPA addressing is properly configured.

CONFIGURING NETACL

netacl is a network access control program; it provides a degree of access control for various TCP-based services available on the server. For example, you may want to have Telnet access to the firewall for authorized users. The netacl program and the appropriate rules enable you to create this setup. The same capabilities are possible for any of the available services, including FTP and rlogin.

The netacl program is started through inetd; after inetd performs some checks, netacl allows or denies the request for service from the remote user/system. When configuring the inetd.conf file for netacl, it is important to know that netacl accepts only one argument: the name of the service to be started. Any other arguments that are intended for the service do not go in the inetd.conf file. Consider this example:

```
ftp      stream tcp    nowait root    /usr/local/etc/netacl    ftpd
```

In this situation, when a connection request is accepted by inetd for an FTP service, the netacl program is started with an argument of ftpd. Before the ftpd daemon is started, the request is validated using the rules found in the netperm-table. The rule name for netacl consists of the keyword netacl- followed by the name of the service. For example, if the named service is ftpd, the rule name consists of netacl-ftpd, as in the following:

```
netacl-ftpd: permit-hosts 204.191.3.147 -exec /usr/libexec/ftpd -A -l
```

When you examine these two lines—the first from inetd.conf and the second from netperm-table—you can see that the command-line arguments and other information required for the daemon are found in netperm-table.

As with all the TIS Toolkit components, arguments and descriptive keywords are permitted in the authentication clause. As seen in the preceding command output, only the host 204.191.3.147 is permitted access on the firewall to run the ftpd command. It does, however, mean that FTP requests can be sent through the firewall. Table 10.2 lists various keywords that are understood by the netacl program.

TABLE 10.2
The netacl Rules and Clauses

Service	Keyword	Description
netacl	permit-hosts IP Address or hostname	Specifies a permission rule to allow the named hosts. This is a list of IP addresses or hostnames.
	deny-hosts IP Address or hostname	Specifies a permission rule to deny the named hosts. This is a list of IP addresses or hostnames. The denial of service is logged via syslogd.
	-exec executable [args]	Specifies a program to invoke to handle the service. This option must be the final option in the rule. An -exec option must be present in every rule.

Service	Keyword	Description
	-user userid	userid is the numeric UID or the name from a login in /etc/passwd that the program should use when it is started.
	-chroot rootdir	Specifies a directory to which netacl should chroot(2) prior to invoking the service program. This requires that the service program be present, and the pathname for the executable be relative to the new root.

Acceptance or rejection of the service is logged by the syslog facility. The messages printed in the syslog files resemble those shown here:

```
Oct  4 00:56:12 pc netacl[339]: deny host=stargazer.unilabs.org/204.191.3.147
service=ftpd
Oct  4 01:00:20 pc netacl[354]: permit host=stargazer.unilabs.org/
➥204.191.3.147
service=ftpd execute=/usr/libexec/ftpd
```

The first line in the log report indicates that the host stargazer.unilabs.org was denied access to the FTP service through the netacl program. The second line of output indicates that the FTP request was accepted and allowed. Notice that the logging information only specifies the service that was originated, and from where it originated. It does not show who the user connected to. The sample netacl rules that follow illustrate the use of some of the parameters and clauses for netacl.

```
netacl-in.telnetd: permit-hosts 198.53.64.* -exec /usr/etc/in.telnetd
netacl-in.ftpd: permit-hosts unknown -exec /bin/cat /usr/local/etc/noftp.txt
netacl-in.ftpd: permit-hosts 204.191.3.* -exec /usr/etc/in.ftpd
netacl-in.ftpd: permit-hosts * -chroot /home/ftp -exec /bin/ftpd -f
```

In this example, netacl is configured to permit Telnet only for hosts in a particular subnet. netacl is configured to accept all FTP connections from systems that do not have a valid DNS name ("unknown") and to invoke cat to display a file when a connection is made. This provides an easy and flexible means of politely informing someone that they are not permitted to use a service. Hosts in the specified subnet are connected to the real FTP server in /usr/etc/in.ftpd but all connections from other networks are connected to a version of the FTP server that is already chrooted to the FTP area, effectively making all FTP activity "captive."

CONNECTING WITH NETACL

When netacl is configured for the service that you want to provide, you should test it to ensure that it is working. Testing requires verifying rules configured for that service to ensure that they are in fact operating as they should. Consider the following rules:

```
netacl-ftpd: permit-hosts 204.191.3.147 -exec /usr/libexec/ftpd -A -l
```

This rule says that FTP connections will be accepted only from the host 204.191.3.147. When this connection is received, the ftpd server with the appropriate arguments will be started. This can be evaluated by connecting to the FTP server from the authorized host, as illustrated here:

```
C:\ >ftp pc
Connected to pc.unilabs.org.
220 pc.unilabs.org FTP server (Version wu-2.4(1) Fri Feb 3 11:30:22 MST 1995)
➥ready.
User (pc.unilabs.org:(none)): chrish
331 Password required for chrish.
Password:
230 User chrish logged in.
ftp>
```

As you can see from this output, the connection from the authorized machine to the target system did in fact work. This could further be validated by examining the syslog records for the target system where any transfers may in fact be logged. The availability of this feature depends on the implementation of the ftpd that is in use at your site.

Another security breach you want to avoid is granting a non-authorized system a connection. To illustrate, consider the exchange:

```
pc# ftp pc
Connected to pc.unilabs.org.
421 Service not available, remote server has closed connection
ftp>
```

The connection is initially established, but after netacl has performed verification of the rules, it finds that the host is not permitted access, and the connection is closed. On the target system, a deny informational message is written to the syslog and to the console:

```
Oct  4 02:53:12 pc netacl[1775]: deny host=pc.unilabs.org/204.191.3.150
➥service=ftpd
```

In this case, the remote system received no information other than the connection has been closed. Meanwhile, the system administrator knows that the remote has been attempting to gain access. If this occurs enough, some other action may be required against the remote user.

Such a blunt response to an unauthorized attempt to gain access might not be the most appreciated. For this reason, you might be wise to consider a rule like the one that follows:

```
netacl-ftpd: permit-hosts 204.191.3.147 -exec /bin/cat /usr/local/etc/
➥noftp.txt
```

In this case, a user who attempts to connect from the site 204.191.3.147 will not be refused a connection; he or she will just not get what they want. With this configuration, you can log the connection, and tell the user that he or she is not permitted access to the requested service. For example, when you attempt to connect to your server, the /usr/local/etc/noftp.txt file displays this response:

```
C:\ >ftp pc
Connected to pc.unilabs.org.

**** ATTENTION ****

Your attempt to use this server's FTP facility is not permitted due to
organizational security policies.  Your connection attempt has been logged
and recorded.

Use of the FTP Services on this machine is restricted to specific sites.

If you believe that you are an authorized site, please contact Jon Smith
at 555-1212 ext 502, or e-mail to ftpadmin@org.com.

Connection closed by remote host.

C:\ >
```

Any type of message can be displayed here instead of allowing access to the requested service. This "denial" can be for system administration purposes, for example, or because of maintenance.

Restarting inetd

Remember that after each reconfiguration of the inetd.conf file, inetd must be restarted. To do this, you must find the Process ID or PID number for inetd and send a SIGHUP to it. The following commands are used in this process:

```
Signalling inetd

pc# ps -aux ¦ grep inetd
root      1898 0.0  0.2    120   28 p3 R+   10:46AM   0:00.02 grep inetd
root        75 0.0  1.5    140  220 ?? Is   11:19AM   0:00.25 inetd
pc# kill -1 75
pc#
```

When inetd has been signaled with the -1, or SIGHUP, it rereads the /etc/inetd.conf file and applies the new configuration immediately.

This is the most common problem that system administrators have when changing the configuration file. They make the change, but forget to restart inetd.

Configuring the Telnet Proxy

The Telnet proxy, tn-gw, provides passthrough Telnet services. In many circumstances, a system administrator may not want to allow Telnet access through the firewall and either into or out of the private network. The Telnet proxy does not provide the same type of access to the firewall host as the netacl program. The intent behind using Telnet with netacl is to allow access to the firewall host. With the proxy, the intent is to provide passthrough Telnet with logging control.

Because of the dilemma of allowing remote administrative access and establishing a proxy Telnet, it is common for the firewall administrator to run the real telnetd on a TCP port other than the default, and to place the proxy on the standard TCP port. This is accomplished by editing the /etc/services file and changing it to be something similar to the following:

```
telnet          23/tcp
telnet-a        2023/tcp
```

These changes are only effective after /etc/inetd.conf has been changed to reflect the configuration shown here:

```
telnet          stream  tcp     nowait  root    /usr/local/etc/tn-gw     tn-gw
telnet-a        stream  tcp     nowait  root    /usr/local/etc/netacl    telnetd
```

When an incoming connection is received on the Telnet port with this configuration, the tn-gw application is started. When tn-gw receives a request, it first verifies that the requesting host is permitted to connect to the proxy. Access to the proxy is determined by the rules established in the netperm-table. These rules resemble those seen previously for the netacl application. However, there are application-specific parameters. The rule clauses for tn-gw are listed in table 10.3.

TABLE 10.3
tn-gw Rules and Clauses

Option	Description
userid user	Specifies a numeric userid or the name of a password file entry. If this value is specified, tn-gw will set its userid before providing service.
directory pathname	Specifies a directory to which tn-gw will chroot(2) prior to providing service.
prompt string	Specifies a prompt for tn-gw to use while it is in command mode.
denial-msg filename	Specifies the name of a file to display to the remote user if he or she is denied permission to use the proxy. If this option is not set, a default message is generated.
timeout seconds	Specifies the number of seconds of idleness after which the proxy should disconnect. Default is no timeout.
welcome-msg filename	Specifies the name of a file to display as a welcome banner upon successful connection. If this option is not set, a default message is generated.
help-msg filename	Specifies the name of a file to display if the "help" command is issued. If this option is not set, a list of the internal commands is printed.
denydest-msg filename	Specifies the name of a file to display if a user attempts to connect to a remote server for which he or she is not authorized. If this option is not set, a default message is generated.
authserver hostname [portnumber [cipherkey]]	Specifies the name or address of a system to use for network authentication. If tn-gw is built with a compiled-in value for the server and port, these values will be used as defaults but can be overridden if specified in the authserver rule. If support for DES-encryption of traffic is present in the server, an optional cipherkey can be provided to secure communications with the server.

continues

439

TABLE 10.3, CONTINUED
tn-gw Rules and Clauses

Option	Description
hosts host-pattern [host-pattern2...] [options]	Specifies host and access permissions.

The initial configuration for the tn-gw application is shown here.

```
tn-gw:        denial-msg     /usr/local/etc/tn-deny.txt
tn-gw:        welcome-msg    /usr/local/etc/tn-welcome.txt
tn-gw:        help-msg       /usr/local/etc/tn-help.txt
tn-gw:        timeout 3600
tn-gw:        permit-hosts 204.191.3.* -dest *.fonorola.net -dest !* -
➥passok -xok
```

> **NOTE**
> If any of the files identified in the denial-msg, welcome-msg, help-msg, or denydest-msg clauses are missing, the connection will be dropped as soon as a request is made for that file.

This configuration informs users when they are or are not allowed to connect to the proxy server, and when connections are denied due to their destination. The timeout line indicates how long the Telnet connection can be idle before the firewall will terminate it. The last line establishes an access rule to the tn-gw application. This rule and the optional parameters are discussed shortly. A sample connection showing the host denial message is shown as follows:

```
$ telnet pc
Connecting to pc ...

**** ATTENTION ****

Your attempt to use this server's telnet proxy is not permitted due to
organizational security policies.  Your connection attempt has been logged
and recorded.

Use of the telnet proxy Service on this machine is restricted to specific
sites.

If you believe that you are an authorized site, please contact Jon Smith
at 555-1212 ext 502, or e-mail to ftpadmin@org.com.

Connection closed by foreign host
$
```

If the host is permitted to converse with the tn-gw application, tn-gw enters a command loop where it accepts commands to connect to remote hosts. The commands available within the tn-gw shell are listed in table 10.4.

TABLE 10.4

tn-gw Commands

Command	Description
c[onnect] hostname [port] telnet hostname [port] open	Connects to a remote host. Access to the remote host may be denied based on a host destination rule.
x[-gw] [display/hostname]	This command invokes the X Windows gateway for a connection to the user's display. By default, the display name is the connecting machine followed by :0.0, as in pc.myorg.com:0.0. The x-gw command is discussed later in this chapter.
help ?	Displays a user-definable help file.
quit exit close	Exits the gateway.

CONNECTING THROUGH THE TELNET PROXY

When a permitted host connects to the proxy, it is greeted by the contents of the welcome file—configured in the tn-gw options—and by a prompt. At the prompt, tn-gw expects to receive one of the commands listed in table 10.4. When the connect request is made, the access rules are applied to the destination host to confirm that a connection to that host is permitted. If the connection is permitted, the connection is made. A successful connection is shown as follows:

```
Welcome to the URG Firewall Telnet Proxy

Supported commands are
        c[onnect] hostname [port]
        x-gw
        help
        exit
```

441

```
To report problems, please contact Network Security Services at 555-1212 or
by e-mail at security@org.com

Enter Command>c sco.sco.com
Not permitted to connect to sco.sco.com
Enter Command>c nds.fonorola.net
Trying 204.191.124.252 port 23...


SunOS Unix (nds.fonorola.net)

login:
```

In this output you can see that a Telnet connection is established to the firewall, from which the tn-gw application is started. The user first attempts to contact sco.sco.com, which is denied. A second connection request to nds.fonorola.net is then permitted. This sequence begs the question, "What's the difference?" The answer is that host destination rules are in force. This means that a given system may be blocked through options on the host command in the tn-gw rules.

HOST ACCESS RULES

The host rules that permit and deny access to the Telnet proxy can be modified by a number of additional options, or rules that have other host access permissions. As seen in table 10.3, the host rules are stated:

```
tn-gw:    deny-hosts unknown
tn-gw:    hosts 192.33.112.* 192.94.214.*
```

These statements indicate that hosts that cannot be found in the DNS in-addr.arpa domain are unknown, and therefore denied, or that hosts connecting from the network 192.33.112 and 192.94.214 are allowed to connect to the proxy. Optional parameters, which begin with a hyphen, further restrict the hosts that can connect to the proxy, or where the remote host can connect to behind the firewall.

Earlier output showed that the connect request to sco.scolcom was denied by the proxy because the user was not permitted to connect to that host. This was configured by using the rule:

```
tn-gw:        permit-hosts 204.191.3.* -dest *.fonorola.net -dest !* -passok
➡ -xok
```

This rule states that any host from the 204.191.3 network is allowed to contact any machine in the fonorola.net domain, but no others. This example illustrates the -dest option, which restricts which hosts can be connected. The -dest parameter, described in table 10.5 with the other optional parameters, is used to specify a list of valid destinations. If no list is specified, then the user is not restricted to connecting to any host.

TABLE 10.5
Host Access Rules

Rule	Description
-dest pattern -dest { pattern1 pattern2 ... }	Specifies a list of valid destinations. If no list is specified, all destinations are considered valid. The -dest list is processed in order as it appears on the options line. -dest entries preceded with a "!" character are treated as negation entries.
-auth	Specifies that the proxy should require a user to authenticate with a valid userid prior to being permitted to use the gateway.
-passok	Specifies that the proxy should permit users to change their passwords if they are connected from the designated host. Only hosts on a trusted network should be permitted to change passwords, unless token-type authenticators are distributed to all users.

The -dest options are applied in the order that they appear in the line. Consequently, in the example used so far in this chapter, if the machine you are connecting to is sco.sco.com, then the first option describing a machine in the fonorola.net domain is not matched. This means that the second destination specification is matched, which is a denial. The "!" is a negation operator, and indicates that this is not permitted. The end result is that users on the 204.191.3 network can only connect to systems in the fonorola.net domain, and no others.

The use of an IP address instead of a domain name does not alter the rule. Before the connection is permitted, the tn-gw application attempts to validate the IP address. If the returned host matches one of the rules, then the rule is applied. Otherwise, the connection is dropped.

VERIFYING THE TELNET PROXY

The operation of the proxy rules can be determined by attempting a connection through each of the rules, and verifying whether the correct files are displayed when information is requested. For example, if a user connects to tn-gw and enters the help command, does the user get the requested information? Are the restricted sites in fact restricted?

This verification is accomplished by exercising each of the rules. For example, consider the following rule:

```
tn-gw:          permit-hosts 204.191.3.* -dest *.fonorola.net -dest !*
```

The operation of this rule can be easily verified, once it is clear what is being controlled. This rule says: "Permit any host in the 204.191.3 network to connect to any machine in the fonorola.net domain. All connections to machines outside that domain are denied."

This can be easily verified by using Telnet to contact tn-gw and attempting to connect to a site within the fonorola.net domain space, and then attempting to connect to any other site. If the fonorla.net site is accessible, but no other site is, then it is safe to say that the Telnet is working as it should.

For example, consider the following rules:

```
tn-gw:          permit-hosts 204.191.3.* -dest *.fonorola.net -dest !* -passok
➥-xok
tn-gw:          deny-hosts * -dest 204.191.3.150
```

If the connecting host is from the 204.191.3 network, access is granted to the proxy, but the user can only connect to the sites in the fonorola.net domain. The second line says that any host attempting to access 204.191.3.150 will be denied. Should the second line be first in the file, access to the proxy server itself would not be permitted.

> When entering the rules in the netperm-table, remember to write them from least to most specific. Or, write them in order of use, after conducting some traffic analysis to determine where the traffic is going. This can be difficult and time-consuming.

This type of configuration is advantageous because it ensures that the firewall cannot be accessed through the proxy, and leaves the Telnet server available through the netacl program, which has been configured to listen on a different port.

Even though the firewall host is not available through the proxy, it can still be accessed through the netacl program and the Telnet server running on the alternate port.

CONFIGURING THE RLOGIN GATEWAY

The rlogin proxy provides a service similar to the Telnet proxy with the exception of access being provided through the rlogin service rather than Telnet. Typically, access to the firewall using rlogin would not be allowed because of the large number of problems that can occur. Consequently, the only access to the firewall host is through Telnet.

Regardless, there are requirements that justify the need for an rlogin proxy service. For example, the rlogin service provides rules for additional authentication that allow the connection to be granted without the user logging in like Telnet. The process of configuring the rlogin-gw rules is similar to the tn-gw application; they both support the same options. The rules that are available for the rlogin-gw service are listed and explained in table 10.6.

TABLE 10.6
rlogin-gw Rules and Clauses

Option	Description
userid user	Specifies a numeric userid or the name of a password file entry. If this value is specified, tn-gw will set its userid before providing service.
directory pathname	Specifies a directory to which tn-gw will chroot(2) prior to providing service.
prompt *string*	Specifies a prompt for tn-gw to use while it is in command mode.
denial-msg *filename*	Specifies the name of a file to display to the remote user if he or she is denied permission to use the proxy. If this option is not set, a default message is generated.
timeout seconds	Specifies the number of seconds the system remains idle before the proxy disconnects. Default is no timeout.
welcome-msg *filename*	Specifies the name of a file to display as a welcome banner after the system successfully connects. If this option is not set, a default message is generated.
help-msg *filename*	Specifies the name of a file to display if the "help" command is issued. If this option is not set, a list of the internal commands is printed.

continues

TABLE 10.6, CONTINUED
rlogin-gw Rules and Clauses

Option	Description
denydest-msg *filename*	Specifies the name of a file to display if a user attempts to connect to a remote server from which he or she is restricted. If this option is not set, a default message is generated.
authserver hostname [*portnumber* [*cipherkey*]]	Specifies the name or address of a system to use for network authentication. If tn-gw is built with a compiled-in value for the server and port, these will be used as defaults but can be overridden if specified on this line. If support exists for DES-encryption of traffic in the server, an optional cipherkey can be provided to secure communication with the server.
hosts host-pattern [*host*-pattern2...] [*options*]	Specifies host and access permissions.

To illustrate the use of these rules to configure the rlogin-gw service, examine these sample rules from the netperm-table file:

```
rlogin-gw:    denial-msg     /usr/local/etc/rlogin-deny.txt
rlogin-gw:    welcome-msg    /usr/local/etc/rlogin-welcome.txt
rlogin-gw:    help-msg       /usr/local/etc/rlogin-help.txt
rlogin-gw:    denydest-msg   /usr/local/etc/rlogin-dest.txt
rlogin-gw:    timeout 3600
rlogin-gw:    prompt "Enter Command>"
rlogin-gw:    permit-hosts 204.191.3.* -dest *.fonorola.net -dest !* -passok
➥-xok
rlogin-gw:    deny-hosts * -dest 204.191.3.150
```

NOTE

If any of the files identified in the denial-msg, welcome-msg, help-msg, or denydest-msg clauses are missing, the connection will be dropped as soon as a request is made for that file.

These rules are virtually identical to the rules used to configure the tn-gw. One exception is that the rlogin-gw is configured to display a different message when a connection request is made for a restricted host. The following output shows the different message for rlogin:

```
pc# rlogin pc
Welcome to the URG Firewall Rlogin Proxy

Supported commands are
        c[onnect] hostname [port]
        x-gw
        help
        password
        exit

To report problems, please contact Network Security Services at 555-1212 or
by e-mail at security@org.com

Enter Command>c fox.nstn.ca

*** ATTENTION ***

You have attempted to contact a restricted host from this rlogin proxy.  Your
attempt has been recorded.

To report problems, please contact Network Security Services at 555-1212 or
by e-mail at security@org.com

Enter Command>
```

Now that the proxy configuration is finished, you can move on to establishing a connection.

CONNECTING THROUGH THE RLOGIN PROXY

Connecting through the rlogin proxy requires a process similar to the Telnet proxy. A connection is first established with the firewall host, and then the user requests a connection to the remote host. The commands supported by the rlogin proxy are the same as for the Telnet proxy. The following output illustrates a successful connection to a remote host using the rlogin proxy:

```
pc.unilabs.org$ rlogin pc
Welcome to the URG Firewall Rlogin Proxy

Supported commands are
        c[onnect] hostname [port]
        x-gw
        help
        password
        exit
```

```
To report problems, please contact Network Security Services at 555-1212 or
by e-mail at security@org.com

Enter Command>c nds.fonorola.net
Trying chrish@204.191.124.252...
Password:
Last login: Sun Oct  8 20:33:26 from pc.unilabs.org
SunOS Release 4.1.4 (GENERIC) #1: Wed Sep 13 19:50:02 EDT 1995
You have mail.
bash$
```

The user enters the name of the host he or she wants to connect to by using the c[onnect] command followed by the hostname. Before the connection request is made, the local username is added to the left of the requested hostname. Consequently,

```
nds.fonorola.net
```

becomes

```
chrish@nds.fonorola.net.
```

The establishment of the rlogin session to the remote host is then a matter of how the service is configured on that host. Remember that the name or IP address of the gateway must be in the .rhosts file because that is the machine where the connection is coming from, not the real originating host.

HOST ACCESS RULES

Host rules that permit and deny access to the rlogin proxy can be modified by a number of additional options, or rules. The host rules use the following format:

```
rlogin-gw:    deny-hosts unknown
rlogin-gw:    hosts 192.33.112.* 192.94.214.*
```

In this example, hosts that cannot be found in the DNS in-addr.arpa domain are unknown, and therefore denied; hosts connecting from the networks 192.33.112 and 192.94.214 are allowed to connect to the proxy. The optional parameters—each beginning with a hyphen— further restrict the hosts that can connect to the proxy by limiting where they can connect.

VERIFYING THE RLOGIN PROXY

Operation of the rlogin proxy is verified by attempting to circumvent the established rules, and checking to see that the text from each of the configured files displays when it should display. For example, if your security policy states that only certain hosts can connect to the rlogin proxy, you must test this from each of the permitted hosts, and also test the connection from a few hosts that are not permitted.

Each rule for rlogin-gw must be carefully evaluated to ensure that it is operating as it should.

CONFIGURING THE FTP GATEWAY

The FTP proxy allows FTP traffic through the firewall to either private or public networks. The FTP proxy executes when a connection is made to the FTP port on the firewall. From there a connection could be made to the firewall, although it is not a good idea to allow FTP traffic to the firewall on the default port. It is better to have an additional FTP server system running elsewhere. A more secure setup would be to run the FTP server processes when a connection is made to a different port. By not publishing this port number, it is harder to have an FTP session established directly on the firewall.

Remember that the FTP service is found on port 21 as stated in the /etc/services file. To change this, edit the /etc/services file and add a second ftp entry called ftp-a—like the telnet-a that was added earlier. Establish this ftp-a service to run on a different port, such as 2021. The new /etc/services file will look like this:

```
ftp         21/tcp
ftp-a       2021/tcp
```

This new ftp-a entry only addresses part of the problem. The /etc/inetd.conf file is where the actual specification is made regarding which service is executed when a connection is made. The trick here is to configure the inetd.conf file so that when a connection is made to the FTP port, the ftp-gw application is started. When a connection is made to the ftp-a port, the real FTP server is started through the netacl application:

```
# ftp    stream  tcp     nowait  root    /usr/libexec/tcpd       ftpd -l -A
ftp      stream  tcp     nowait  root    /usr/local/etc/ftp-gw   ftp-gw
ftp-a    stream  tcp     nowait  root    /usr/local/etc/netacl   ftpd
```

Three entries for the FTP service are included here to illustrate a point. The first entry is uncommented out and is provided to show you how the FTP service was originally started. The second entry establishes a connection to the FTP proxy. The third line allows FTP connections to the firewall itself. Examine the configuration of the ftp-gw proxy application first.

The ftp-gw proxy, like the other Toolkit applications, reads the lines in the netperm-table file that start with the application name, ftp-gw. Table 10.7 lists clauses that are understood by ftp-gw.

TABLE 10.7
The ftp-gw Program Rules

Rule	Description
userid user	Specifies a numeric userid or the name of a password file entry. If this value is specified, ftp-gw will set its userid before providing service.
directory pathname	Specifies a directory to which ftp-gw will chroot(2) prior to providing service.
denial-msg filename	Specifies the name of a file to display to the remote user if he or she is denied permission to use the proxy. If this option is not set, a default message is generated. When the denial-msg file is displayed to the remote user, each line is prefixed with the FTP codes for permission denied.
welcome-msg filename	Specifies the name of a file to display as a welcome banner upon successful connection. If this option is not set, a default message is generated.
help-msg filename	Specifies the name of a file to display if the help command is issued. If this option is not set, a list of the internal commands is printed.
denydest-msg filename	Specifies the name of a file to display if a user attempts to connect to a remote server from which he or she is restricted. If this option is not set, a default message is generated.
timeout secondsvalue	Specifies the idle timeout value in seconds. When the specified number of seconds elapses with no activity through the proxy server, it will disconnect. If this value is not set, no timeout is enforced.

If these options are not used, default values are used instead. When these options are used, however, the ftp-gw rules look like this:

```
ftp-gw: denial-msg    /usr/local/etc/ftp-deny.txt
ftp-gw: welcome-msg   /usr/local/etc/ftp-welcome.txt
ftp-gw: help-msg      /usr/local/etc/ftp-help.txt
ftp-gw:        timeout 3600
ftp-gw: denydest-msg  /usr/local/etc/ftp-badest.txt
```

By using the Host Access rules, you can control who has access to your private network using FTP, or to whom your internal users can connect.

HOST ACCESS RULES

The host rules that permit and deny access to the FTP proxy can be modified by a number of additional options. The host rules use the format:

```
ftp-gw:     deny-hosts unknown
ftp-gw:     hosts 192.33.112.* 192.94.214.*
```

In this example, hosts that cannot be found in the DNS in-addr.arpa domain are unknown, and therefore denied; hosts connecting from the network 192.33.112 and 192.94.214 are allowed to connect to the proxy. The optional parameters—each beginning with a hyphen—further restrict the hosts that can connect to the proxy by limiting where they can connect.

Like the other proxy agents, a number of options, listed in table 10.8, are available for controlling the proxy.

TABLE 10.8
Host Access Options

Option	Description
-dest pattern -dest { pattern1 pattern2 ... }	Specifies a list of valid destinations. If no list is specified, all -dest destinations are considered valid. The -dest list is processed in the order it appears on the options line. -dest entries preceded with a "!" character are treated as negation entries.
-auth	Specifies that the proxy should require a user to authenticate with a valid userid prior to being permitted to use the gateway.
-passok	Specifies that the proxy should permit users to change their passwords if they are connected from the designated host. Only hosts on a trusted network should be permitted to change passwords, unless token-type authenticators are distributed to all users.

The use of an IP address instead of a domain name does not alter the rule. Before the connection is permitted, the tn-gw application attempts to validate the IP address. If the returned host matches one of the rules, then the rule is applied. Otherwise, the connection is dropped.

VERIFYING THE FTP PROXY

Verifying the operation of the FTP proxy involves testing each of the rules and connection points. For example, if you are allowing FTP sessions to originate from the private network, but deny FTP access to hosts outside the private network, then the ftp-gw rules would look like this:

```
ftp-gw: permit-hosts   206.116.65.*   -log { retr stor }
```

This can only be verified by attempting to establish an FTP session from a host on the LAN and going out to the public network. To prove the proper operation of the proxy, a connection from the public network to a machine on the private network must be attempted. The following command sequence illustrates the use of Telnet to access the firewall from a host on the internal network:

```
C:\WINDOWS>ftp pc.unilabs.org
Connected to pc.unilabs.org.
220-Welcome to the URG Firewall FTP Proxy
220-
220-To report problems, please contact Network Security Services at 555-1212
or 220-by e-mail at security@org.com
220
User (pc.unilabs.org:(none)): chrish@nds.fonorola.net
331-(----GATEWAY CONNECTED TO nds.fonorola.net----)
331-(220 nds.fonorola.net FTP server (Version A) ready.)
331 Password required for chrish.
Password:
230 User chrish logged in.
ftp>
```

Notice that the user was allowed access to the FTP proxy, and an FTP session was established to the machine nds.fonorola.net. The converse for this rule then must also be true: Any host outside the private network is not permitted access to the FTP proxy. The following output illustrates this restriction:

```
bash$ ftp pc.unilabs.org
Connected to pc.unilabs.org.
500-
500-**** ATTENTION ****
500-
500-Your attempt to use this server's ftp proxy is not permitted due to
500-organizational security policies.  Your connection attempt has been
➡logged
```

```
500-and recorded.
500-
500-If you believe that you are an authorized site, please contact Jon Smith
500-at 555-1212 ext 502, or e-mail to ftpadmin@org.com.
500
ftp>
```

In this situation, the user on the system nds.fonorola.net attempted to connect to the firewall, but because its IP address [204.191.124.252] is not within the address space specified on the ftp-gw rule, the connection is denied, and the message shown here appears. Remember that this message is from the denial-msg rule in the configuration file.

CONNECTING THROUGH THE FTP PROXY

Establishing a connection through the proxy involves connecting to the FTP port and then specifying the host to connect to. The target specification, however, is not quite what you might expect:

```
$ ftp 204.191.3.150
Connected to 204.191.3.150.
220 pc.unilabs.org FTP proxy (Version V1.3) ready.
User (204.191.3.150:(none)): anonymous@ftp.fonorola.net
331-(----GATEWAY CONNECTED TO ftp.fonorola.net----)
331-(220 net FTP server (Version wu-2.4(1) Fri Apr 21 22:42:18 EDT 1995) ready.)

331 Guest login ok, send your complete e-mail address as password.
Password:
230-
230-                    Welcome to i*internet Inc.
230-                    Anonymous FTP Server
230-
230-We are currently in the process of deploying the Washington
230-University Anonymous FTP Server.
230-
230 Guest login ok, access restrictions apply.
ftp>
```

When establishing a connection through the proxy, you first run the ftp command and connect to the firewall, which serves as the host. After you are connected, you must specify the user name and the site to connect to. This is done using the syntax:

```
user@site
```

After validating that the site is indeed one that is allowed, the proxy connects to the FTP server on the remote system and starts to log in using the supplied username. The remote server then prompts for the user's password, and if it is correct, allows the connection.

ALLOWING FTP WITH NETACL

It is fairly common to restrict the proxy from connecting to the firewall for FTP services, but occasionally you may need to upgrade software or change text files and messages. For this reason, you may need to enable FTP access. This can be done using the services of netacl. With netacl, you can restrict what machines can connect to the firewall to specific machines within the local network. Consider the sample configuration entries in the following command:

```
netacl-ftpd: permit-hosts 204.191.3.* -exec /usr/libexec/ftpd -A -l
```

This entry for netacl allows systems on the 204.191.3 network to connect to the FTP server through netacl. The entry also locks out all other systems, as you can see when one of them tries to access the FTP server:

```
ftp> open 198.53.166.62 2021
Connected to 198.53.166.62.
421 Service not available, remote server has closed connection
ftp>
```

From this message it appears that there is no server listening on port 2021, when in fact there is. netacl does not allow the request because the IP address where the request originated does not match the rule established previously.

If you're not sure whether you will ever need access for FTP services to the firewall, the safest thing to do is to not allow this type of access except when absolutely necessary. This means that netacl can be set up in the netperm-table file, but commented out, thereby making it unavailable. Furthermore, the proxy must be configured to prevent connections to the firewall on the FTP port.

CONFIGURING THE SENDMAIL PROXY SMAP AND SMAPD

Two components are used for the successful delivery of mail through the firewall: smap and smapd. The smap agent is a client that implements a minimal version of SMTP. The smap program accepts messages from the network and writes them to disk for future delivery by smapd. smap is designed to run under chroot as a non-privileged process; this setup overcomes potential security risks from privileged mailers that can be accessed from over a network.

The smapd daemon periodically scans the mail spool area maintained by smap and delivers any messages that have been gathered and stored. Mail is delivered by sendmail, and the spool file is deleted. If the mail cannot be delivered normally, smapd can be configured to store spooled files to an area for later examination.

These two applications can share configuration information in the netperm-table file if desired. Some of the operations are different, so different steps need to be taken when configuring the two applications.

INSTALLING THE SMAP CLIENT

The smap client runs whenever a connection request is received on the smtp port of the firewall. This is done by adding an entry for smtp to the /etc/inetd.conf file:

```
smtp    stream tcp    nowait root    /usr/local/etc/smap    smap
```

After /etc/inetd.conf has been updated, the inetd process must be restarted so that smap accepts connections. This can be checked by connecting manually to the smtp port:

```
pc# telnet pc 25
Trying 206.116.65.3...
Connected to pc.unilabs.org.
Escape character is '^]'.
220 pc.unilabs.org SMTP/smap Ready.
helo
250 Charmed, Im sure.
help
214-Commands
214-HELO   MAIL    RCPT    DATA    RSET
214 NOOP   QUIT    HELP    VRFY    EXPN
quit
221 Closing connection
Connection closed by foreign host.
pc#
```

As you can see, smap implements a minimal SMTP implementation, and spools the mail into the specified spool area. In the spool directory, it may be required that an etc directory with system specific configuration files be installed. A recommended setup is to build smap so that it is completely stand-alone—it does not depend on other libraries and will run without fail.

CONFIGURING THE SMAP CLIENT

The smap client reads its configuration from the netperm-table file by looking for the lines beginning with smap. If the line applies to both smap and smapd, the two programs can be listed on the same line by separating them with a comma:

```
smap, smapd:    userid 6
```

The rules for smap are listed in table 10.9.

455

TABLE 10.9

smap Rules

Rule	Description
userid name	Specify the userid under which smap should run. The name can be either a name from the password database, or a numeric userid. This userid should be the same as that under which smapd runs, and should have write permission to the spool directory.
directory pathname	Specifies the spool directory where smap should store incoming messages. A chroot system call is used to irrevocably make the specified directory the root file system for the remainder of the process.
maxbytes value	Specifies the maximum size of messages to gather, in bytes. If no value is set, message sizes are limited by the amount of disk space in the spool area.
maxrecip value	Specifies the maximum number of recipients allowed for any message. This option is only for administrators who are worried about the more esoteric denial of service attacks.
timeout value	Specifies a timeout, after which smap should exit if it has not collected a message. If no timeout value is specified, smap will never time out a connection.

As you can see in table 10.9, some items are common between the smap and smapd applications. These similarities will be discussed later. For now, develop a configuration section for the smap application.

The userid, directory, and timeout values are self-explanatory. However, unlike the directory clauses for the other applications, the smap client also uses the directory to save incoming messages. Consequently, these form the basis of your configuration:

```
smap:    userid 6
smap:    directory /var/spool/smap
smap:    timeout 3600
```

The maxbytes value specifies the size of the largest email message. If the message is larger than the maxbytes value, the message size is truncated. If maxbytes is not included in the configuration information, then the maximum message size is the size of the available space in the spool area. The final clause specifies the maximum number of recipients that can be attached to the mail message. This is not a commonly used option. The completed entry for the netperm-table file looks like this:

```
smap:     userid 6
smap:     directory /var/spool/smap
smap:          timeout 3600
smap:          maxbytes        10000
smap:          maxrecip        20
```

If you set the value of maxbytes too small, users may not be able to receive some messages because of the message's size. This type of problem reveals itself in the log files. Lines that resemble the following indicate the incoming mail message is too large to process:

```
Oct 29 12:09:52 pc smap[868]: connect host=unknown/198.53.64.9
Oct 29 12:09:59 pc smap[868]: exiting too much data
```

No other warnings of this problem occur. This is the only way the firewall operator can check to see if large messages are the reason why mail isn't being sent.

At this point, you have installed and configured the smap application. It is not very difficult to complete its setup.

Installing the smapd Application

Unlike smap, which is started from inetd on a connection by connection basis, smapd is started from the /etc/rc.local script and runs the entire time the system is running. The daemon startup is added to the file /etc/rc.local and then the system is rebooted. The following shows the addition of the command to the rc.local file:

```
echo "Starting Firewall Mail Processor ..."
/usr/local/etc/smapd
```

Because sendmail is not running in daemon mode, messages that cannot be delivered and are queued must be delivered by periodically invoking sendmail to process the queue. To do this, add a line similar to the following to the crontab file:

```
0,30 * * * * /usr/sbin/sendmail -q > /dev/null 2>&1
```

This ensures that any messages that cannot be successfully delivered by the smapd application will be properly handled.

Configuring the smapd Application

The configuration of the smapd application is no more difficult than configuring smap. They generally run without a problem. Like smap, smapd reads its configuration from the netperm-table file; it accepts no command-line arguments. The smap application reads the mail queue on a periodic basis and delivers mail to the remote system. Rules that are available to build the smapd configuration file are listed in table 10.10.

TABLE 10.10
smapd Rules

Rule	Description
executable pathname	Specifies the pathname of the smapd executable. For historical reasons, smapd forks and execs copies of itself to handle delivering each individual message. THIS ENTRY IS MANDATORY.
sendmail pathname	Specifies an alternate pathname for the sendmail executable. smapd assumes the use of sendmail but does not require it. An alternate mail delivery system can replace sendmail, but it should be able to accept arguments in the form of executable -f fromname recip1 [recip2 ... recipN]. The exit code from the mailer is used to determine the status of delivery; for this reason, replacements for sendmail should use similar exit codes.
baddir pathname	Specifies a directory where smapd should move any spooled mail that cannot be delivered normally. This directory must be on the same device as the spool directory because the rename(2) system call is employed. The pathname specified should not contain a trailing "/".
userid name	Specifies the userid that smapd should run under. The name can be either a name from the password database, or a numeric userid. This userid should be the same as that under which smap runs, and should have write permission to the spool directory.
directory pathname	Specifies the spool directory in which smapd should search for files. smapd should have write permission to this directory.
wakeup value	Specifies the number of seconds smapd should sleep between scans of the spool directory. The default is 60 seconds.

Some options are common for smap and smapd. Nevertheless, you can build a separate configuration for smapd, such as the one shown here:

```
smapd:          executable /usr/local/etc/smapd
smapd:          sendmail /usr/sbin/sendmail
smapd:          userid 6
smapd:          directory /var/spool/smap
smapd:          baddir /var/spool/smap/bad
smapd:          wakeup 900
```

This configuration defines the operating parameters for smapd. The executable rule identifies the location of the smapd program. This rule is mandatory. The sendmail option specifies where the sendmail program is found. Alternate programs such as zmailer or smail can be used in place of sendmail, as long as they conform to the exit codes used within sendmail.

The userid and directory rules specify the user under which the smapd binary executes, and the home directory used for that configuration. The baddir value is related to directory. The value assigned to directory provides the name of the directory where the in transit mail messages are stored; a bad directory will be created there to save any undelivered or questionable messages.

The last value for smapd specifies how long the delay is between the processing of the queue. The default is 60 seconds; this example uses a 15 minute window.

CONFIGURING DNS FOR SMAP

For mail to be successfully and correctly routed through the firewall, MX records need to be published in the zone's DNS files to identify where SMTP mail is to be sent. This is done by adding MX, or mail exchanger, records to the DNS providers for the network domain, or zone. The zone information shown here provides some information regarding how this is configured.

```
Server:  nic.fonorola.net
Address:  198.53.64.7

unilabs.org     nameserver = nic.fonorola.net
unilabs.org     nameserver = fonsrv00.fonorola.com
unilabs.org     preference = 10, mail exchanger = mail.fonorola.net
unilabs.org     preference = 1, mail exchanger = pc2.unilabs.org
unilabs.org     preference = 5, mail exchanger = nis.fonorola.net
unilabs.org
        origin = nic.fonorola.net
        mail addr = chrish.fonorola.net
        serial = 95102902
        refresh = 10800 (3 hours)
        retry   = 1800 (30 mins)
        expire  = 3600000 (41 days 16 hours)
        minimum ttl = 86400 (1 day)
```

```
unilabs.org       nameserver = nic.fonorola.net
unilabs.org       nameserver = fonsrv00.fonorola.com
nic.fonorola.net          internet address = 198.53.64.7
fonsrv00.fonorola.com     internet address = 149.99.1.3
mail.fonorola.net         internet address = 198.53.64.8
pc2.unilabs.org           internet address = 198.53.166.62
nis.fonorola.net          internet address = 198.53.64.14
>
```

This output is from the nslookup command. Despite how this looks, you are in fact looking for the lines that contain the description mail exchanger, which are as follows:

```
unilabs.org       preference = 1, mail exchanger = pc2.unilabs.org
unilabs.org       preference = 5, mail exchanger = nis.fonorola.net
unilabs.org       preference = 10, mail exchanger = mail.fonorola.net
```

When mail for the domain unilabs.org is to be sent from a host, that host will first try to locate the unilabs.org domain itself. The rule determining which host will be contacted first is simple: The host that has the lowest preference value is the first to be contacted. In the sample setup you've watched develop throughout this chapter, the host pc2.unilabs.org, which is the firewall, will be contacted first to see if it can in fact accept the e-mail. A recommended setup is to give the firewall the lowest priority on the system, so that no other machines can be directly contacted by the outside world.

If the machine with the lowest preference value is not available, then the next system is contacted—in this case, nis.fonorola.net. If the mail is delivered to nis.fonorola.net, then the sendmail daemon on nis will now take responsibility for attempting to deliver it to the lowest preference value machine, pc2.unilabs.org. The same is true should the second mail system not be available and the mail server must then contact the third system. The behavior described here may not be what happens in all situations. For example, the system nis.fonorola.net could simply decide to attempt delivery itself and not use the next MX record. The operation of sendmail is controlled by the sendmail.cf file on the remote machine. Remember that when you make changes to your DNS, you must restart or reload the DNS so that the new information is integrated into the DNS.

CONFIGURING THE HTTP PROXY

The HTTP proxy, http-gw, does more than simply provide a mechanism for HTTP requests to be sent through the firewall. It also provides support for Gopher clients, so that Gopher, Gopher+, and FTP requests can originate from a Gopher client, and for HTPP, Gopher, Gopher+, and FTP requests to be passed through from a WWW client.

The HTTP proxy also supports "proxy-aware" clients, and supports clients that are not designed to work with these daemons. Before examining how to enable these services, first examine the steps required to place the proxy into operation, and also look at the configuration rules for this proxy.

By default, an HTTP or Gopher server usually runs on TCP/IP ports 80 and 70, respectively. These will not be running on the firewall, so it is necessary to configure inetd to accept connections on these ports and start the proxy agent. This is done by adding the following line to the /etc/services file:

```
gopher          70/tcp
httpd           80/tcp
```

With these lines added, inetd now knows on what ports to listen. inetd must then have the appropriate lines added to its configuration file, inetd.conf:

```
httpd    stream  tcp    nowait  root    /usr/local/etc/http-gw  http-gw
gopher   stream  tcp    nowait  root    /usr/local/etc/http-gw  http-gw
```

With the inetd configuration file now updated, inetd must be restarted, or instructed to read its configuration file using the kill -1 command. When these steps are completed, the http-gw proxy is ready to configure.

http-gw reads its configuration rules and permissions information from the firewall configuration table netperm-table, retrieving all rules specified for "http-gw." The "ftp-gw" rules are also retrieved and are evaluated when looking for host rules after all the http-gw rules have been applied. Table 10.11 lists configuration rules applicable to this proxy.

TABLE 10.11

http-gw Proxy Rules

Option	Description
userid user	Allows the system administrator to specify a numeric userid or the name of a password file entry. If this value is specified, http-gw will set its userid before providing service. Note that this option is included mostly for completeness; http-gw performs no local operations that are likely to introduce a security hole.
directory pathname	Specifies a directory to which http-gw will chroot prior to providing service.
timeout secondsvalue	Used as a dead-watch timer when the proxy is reading data from the Internet. Defaults to 60 minutes.
default-gopher server	Defines a Gopher server to which requests can be handed off.

continues   **461**

TABLE 10.11, CONTINUED
http-gw Proxy Rules

Option	Description
default-httpd server	Defines an HTTP server to which requests can be handed off if they came from a WWW client using the HTTP protocol.
ftp-proxy server	This defines an ftp-gw that should be used to access FTP servers. If not specified, the proxy will do the FTP transaction with the FTP server. The ftp-gw rules will be used if there are no relevant http-gw rules, so this is not a major problem.

The userid, directory, and timeout values serve the same functions as the other proxy agents in the Toolkit. However, you need to examine the rules that the default-httpd server, default-gopher server, and default-ftp server play. To understand their impact, you need to examine how a non–proxy-aware and a proxy-aware WWW client operate.

NON–PROXY-AWARE HTTP CLIENTS

A non–proxy -aware HTTP client, such as the Internet Explorer Version 1.0 from Microsoft, cannot communicate with a proxy. The user must configure the client to connect first to the firewall, and then to go to the desired site. To do this, the user must specify the URL in the format:

```
http://firewall_system/http://destination
```

as in

```
http://pc.unilabs.org/http://www.unilabs.org
```

The client will pass the request for `http://www.unilabs.org` to the firewall. The firewall then establishes the connections required to bring the requested information to the client.

Although a proxy-aware client can still use this format, this is the only format that can be used with non-proxy HTTP clients. World Wide Web clients are also capable of accessing FTP and Gopher services. Table 10.12 lists the URL formats used for each of these services.

TABLE 10.12
Supported URL Formats

Service	URL
HTTP	http://firewall_name/http://www_server
Gopher	http://firewall_name/gopher://gopher_server
FTP	http://firewall_name/ftp://FTP_server

Internet users who work with non–proxy-aware clients need to make changes to their WWW client if a firewall is installed after the users have developed and built their hotlists. In these situations, their WWW client hotlists will have to be edited to include the firewall in the URL.

USING A PROXY-AWARE HTTP CLIENT

A proxy-aware HTTP client such as Netscape Navigator or NCSA Mosaic does not have these problems. However, some application-specific configuration is required to make it work. Although nothing additional must be done on the HTTP proxy side, the client must be configured with the appropriate proxy information.

Aside from this application-specific customization, there are no other difficulties in using the proxy-aware client. When these WWW clients have been configured, they are much easier for the end user to handle because there is less confusion in accessing sites.

All World Wide Web clients can access Gopher (and FTP) sites. As you have seen, if the client is aware of the proxy, access to these different types of Internet sites is much simpler to set up. Accessing a Gopher server with a World Wide Web browser is much easier than with many Gopher clients, if the World Wide Web browser is proxy-aware. Connecting to the Gopher server is as simple as specifying an URL:

```
http://firewall_host_name/gopher://gopher_server_name
```

This syntax allows the connection to the external Gopher server through the firewall.

HOST ACCESS RULES

Up to this point in the chapter, you have seen how the user interacts with the proxy. Now examine how you can alter the operation of the proxy by applying some host access rules. Some of these rules have been examined already, and are important enough to mention

463

again. The host access rules may include optional parameters to further control the session. Some of these parameters include restricting the allowable functions. The rules and their parameters are included in table 10.13.

TABLE 10.13
Host Access Rules

Option	Descriptions
Hosts host-pattern [host-pattern ...] [options] Permit-hosts host-pattern [host-pattern ...] options] Deny-hosts host-pattern [host-pattern ...]	Rules specify host and access permissions. Typically, a host rule will be in the form of: http-gw: deny-hosts unknown http-gw: hosts 192.33.112.* 192.94.214.*
-permit function -permit { function [function ...] }	Only the specified functions are permitted. Other functions will be denied. If this option is not specified, then all functions are initially permitted.
-deny function -deny { function [function ...] }	Specifies a list of Gopher/HTTP functions to deny.
-gopher server	Makes server the default server for this transaction.
-httpd server	Makes server the default HTTP server for this transaction. This will be used if the request came in through the HTTP protocol.
-filter function -filter { function [function ...] }	Removes the specified functions when rewriting selectors and URLs. This rule does not stop the user from entering selectors that the client will execute locally, but this rule can be used to remove them from retrieved documents.

Several host patterns may follow the "hosts" keyword; the first optional parameter after these patterns begins with "-". Optional parameters permit the selective enabling or disabling of logging information.

Some basic configuration rules are shown here to help you understand how the options for host rules are used:

```
http-gw:        userid www
# http-gw:      directory /usr/local/secure/www
http-gw:        timeout 1800
http-gw:        default-httpd www.fonorola.net
http-gw:        default-gopher gopher.fonorola.net
http-gw:        permit-hosts 206.116.65.*
```

The permit-hosts line establishes what hosts or networks are allowed to pass through the firewall using the proxy. To deny access to specific hosts or networks, use a line similar to:

```
http-gw:    deny-hosts 206.116.65.2
```

When this type of setup is in operation, a user who is trying to use the proxy from this machine receives a `Sorry, access denied` error message.

The permit-host rules can include function definitions that are permitted or denied depending on the established criteria in the rule. The proxy characterizes each transaction as one of a number of functions. For the deny options the request is used; for filter options the returned selectors are used. These functions are listed in table 10.14.

TABLE 10.14
Function Definitions

Function	Description
dir	Fetching Gopher menus. Getting a directory listing via FTP. Fetching an HTML document.
read	Fetching a file of any type. HTML files are treated as read, even though they are also dir.
write	Putting a file of any type. Needs Gopher+ since only available to Gopher+ and HTTP/1.x.
ftp	Accessing an FTP server.
plus	Gopher+ operations. HTTP methods other than GET.
wais	WAIS index operations.
exec	Operations that require a program to be run; that is, Telnet.

Function controls enable the firewall administrator to specifically set up what will and will not be allowed to pass through the proxy. If no deny or permit functions are specified, every function is permitted. Consider, for example, a setup that would not allow file transfers using the -deny ftp command:

```
http-gw:        userid www
# http-gw:      directory /usr/local/secure/www
http-gw:        timeout 1800
http-gw:        default-httpd www.fonorola.net
http-gw:        default-gopher gopher.fonorola.net
http-gw:        permit-hosts 206.116.65.* -deny ftp
# http-gw:      deny-hosts 206.116.65.2
http-gw:        deny-hosts unknown
```

By using this deny request to restrict the use of the ftp command, users can no longer request an FTP session through the http-gw proxy. A sample error message would look like:

```
use file fig11.pcx
```

In this configuration, any attempt to establish an FTP session using either the following syntax or a WWW page will result in failure:

```
ftp://ftp.somewhere.com
```

> If you are concerned about FTP transfers, and you have disabled the ftp-gw proxy to prevent FTP transfers, you need to carefully consider the value of disabling the ftp commands in the HTTP protocol set. Closing one door but leaving a related one open is not wise.

Few of the current Gopher clients are capable of interacting as well as proxy-aware WWW clients. To use a Gopher client, you must configure the default Gopher server that is used to establish the connection to the firewall. From here you will have to configure jumping off points to different Gophers.

Because of the looming difficulty associated with Gopher clients, the use of Gopher via the World Wide Web interface is popular and widely accepted. Clearly, this capability indicates that there is more flexibility within the HTTP architecture.

CONFIGURING THE X WINDOWS PROXY

The x-gw X Windows proxy is provided to allow a user-level X Windows interface that operates under the tn-gw and rlogin-gw access control. Recall from the earlier discussion of the tn-gw command that this command enables an X session through the gateway.

The proxy operates by allowing clients to be started on arbitrary hosts outside the firewall, and then requesting a connection to the specified display. When the X connection request by the client is made, the x-gw proxy displays a window that is running on a virtual display on the firewall. Upon receiving the connection request, x-gw displays the window on the user's real display. This display prompts for confirmation before proceeding with the connection. If the user agrees to accept the connection, x-gw passes the data from the virtual display to the user's real display.

The x-gw proxy can be started from a telnet or rlogin sequence, as shown by this output:

```
% telnet pc
Trying 206.116.65.3...
Connected to pc.unilabs.org.
Escape character is '^]'.
pc.unilabs.org telnet proxy (Version V1.3) ready:
tn-gw-> x
tn-gw-> exit
Disconnecting...
Connection closed by foreign host.
```

At this point a window pops up on the user's display that shows the port number of the proxy to use; the window also serves as the control window. Choosing the Exit button will close all multiple X connections.

Although the x-gw proxy is advanced and user-friendly, some issues concerning this proxy need to be mentioned. The major issue is that this proxy relies on the X11 Athena Widget set. If your system does not have the X11 libraries or the Athena Widget set, this proxy will not compile, and you will be forced to live without it. Fortunately, very few people allow the use of X windows applications through their firewall.

UNDERSTANDING THE AUTHENTICATION SERVER

The TIS Firewall Toolkit includes extensive authentication mechanisms. The TIS authentication server consists of two components: the actual server itself, and a user authentication manager, which is used to interact with and configure the server.

The authentication server, known as authsrv, is designed to support multiple authentication processes independently. This server maintains an internal user database that contains a record for each user. The information stored for each user consists of:

- ❖ The user's name

- ❖ The user's group

- ❖ The user's full name

- ❖ The last successful authentication

Passwords may be plaintext for local users, or encrypted for all others. The only time plaintext passwords would be used is when the administrator wants to control access to firewall services by users on the protected network.

W A R N I N G

> Plaintext passwords should never be used for authentication by users on non-secure networks.

Users in the authsrv database can belong to different groups; a group administrator can be named who can only manage the users in that group. authsrv also contains support for multiple forms of authentication, including:

- ❖ Internal plaintext passwords

- ❖ Bellcore's S/Key

- ❖ Security Dynamics SecurID

- ❖ Enigma Logics Silver Card

- ❖ Digital Pathways SNK004 Secure Net Key

N O T E

> The Bellcore S/Key mechanism that is included with the Toolkit does not include the complete software. The entire S/Key distribution can be downloaded via FTP from thumper.bellcore.com.

When compiling authsrv, the administrator needs to decide which authentication forms will be supported locally. It is typical to find multiple forms in use by a single company depending on cost and availability. For each proxy in the Toolkit, authentication can be enabled or disabled, or fit certain criteria, such as incoming must authenticate, and outgoing requires no authentication.

Authsrv should be run on as secure a host as possible, which is generally the firewall itself. To configure the authentication server, you must find an unused TCP/IP port number and add it to /etc/services. For example, if you use port 7777 as the TCP port, the following line would be added to the /etc/services file.

```
authsrv          7777/tcp                # TIS Toolkit Authentication
```

Authsrv is not a daemon. It runs whenever a connection request is made on the specified TCP port. Consequently, it is necessary to add an entry to the /etc/inetd.conf file, such as this example:

```
authsrv stream  tcp     nowait  root    /usr/local/etc/authsrv  authsrv
```

After the required entries are placed in the /etc/services and /etc/inetd.conf files, inetd must be reloaded or restarted using the kill command. At this point, individual clients must be configured to use the authentication server when required. Keep in mind that not all operations need to require authentication.

To configure a given proxy, you must use the port number and the authserver keyword specifying the host to connect to for the authentication server. To see this in action, consider adding authentication to the FTP proxy. For the FTP proxy to be able to use the authentication server, you must tell it to use authserver rule:

```
# Use the following lines to use the authentication server
ftp-gw: authserver      localhost       7777
```

When the FTP proxy is activated, requests must be authenticated. The permit-hosts entry, however, has the flexibility to take advantage of the authentication system. For example, consider the permit-hosts entry in the following:

```
ftp-gw: permit-hosts    206.116.65.*    -log { retr stor } -auth { stor }
```

The permit-hosts entry says that all retrieve and store file requests to the FTP proxy are logged, and all store file requests are blocked until the user has authenticated. This process will be demonstrated later in this chapter after you learn how to configure the users in the authentication database.

THE AUTHENTICATION DATABASE

The authentication server must also be configured to accept connections from specific clients. This prevents unwanted attempts to probe the authentication server from hosts running software that needs no authentication. The authentication server reads its rules from the netperm-table, which can include rules listed in table 10.15.

TABLE 10.15
Authentication Server Rules

Rule	Description
database pathname	Specifies the pathname of the authsrv database. The database is stored as a dbm(3) file with a third file used for locking. If the software is built with a compiled-in database name, this option need not be set; otherwise, it is mandatory.
nobogus true	Indicates that authsrv should return "user-friendly" error messages when users attempt to authenticate and fail. The default message is to simply respond, "Permission Denied" or to return a bogus challenge. If nobogus is set, attempts to log on will return more explicit error messages. Sites that are concerned about attempts to probe the authentication server should leave this option disabled.
badsleep seconds	Establishes a "sleep time" for repeated bad logins. If a user attempts to authenticate five times and fails, his user record is marked as suspicious, and he cannot log on again. If the badsleep value is set, the user may attempt to log in again after the set number of seconds has expired. If the badsleep value is 0, users can attempt to log in as many times as they would like. The default value is to effectively disable the account until an administrator re-enables it manually.
userid name	Specifies the userid under which authsrv should run. The name can be either a name from the password database, or a numeric userid.
hosts host-pattern [key]	Specifies that authsrv should permit the named host or addresses to use the service. Hosts that do not have a matching entry are denied use of the service. If the optional key is specified, and the software is compiled with DES-encrypted communications, all traffic with that client will be encrypted and decrypted with the specified key.

Rule	Description
operation userid telnet-gw host	Operation rules are stored in operation userid ftp-gw host put netperm-table. For each user/group the name is specified followed by the service destination [optional tokens] [time start end]. The user/group field indicates whether the record is for a user or a group. The name is either the username or the group name. The service can be a service specified by the proxy (usually ftp-gw, tn-gw, or rlogin-gw). The destination can be any valid domain name. The optional tokens are checked for a match, permitting a proxy to send a specific operation check to the authentication server. The time field is optional and must be specified time start_time end_time; start_time and end_time can be in the range 00:00 to 23:59.

If no other systems on the private network require access to the authsrv, then clients and the server should be configured to accept connections only using the localhost name or IP address 127.0.0.1. The authentication server configuration rules shown earlier illustrate a sample configuration for the server.

The example shown here establishes the following rules for the authentication server:

```
authsrv:        hosts 127.0.0.1
authsrv:        database /usr/local/etc/fw-authdb
authsrv:        badsleep 1200
authsrv:        nobogus true
```

- ✤ Identifies that the localhost is allowed to access the server

- ✤ Specifies that the authentication database is found in /usr/local/etc/fw-authdb

- ✤ The user cannot attempt to authenticate after five bad logins until 1,200 seconds have expired

- ✤ Prints more verbose messages about authentication failures

The operation rule is essential to administrators who want to restrict the commands that can be executed by certain users at certain times. This is done by adding configuration rules consisting of the user, the operation, and the time restrictions to the netperm-table. These rules apply to the authsrv command and not to the individual proxies themselves. Consider the following example:

```
authsrv permit-operation user chrish telnet-gw relay.cdnnet.ca time 08:00
➡17:00
authsrv deny-operation user paulp telnet-gw mailserver.comewhere.com
➡time 17:01 07:59
authsrv permit-operation group admin telnet-gw * time 08:00 17:00
```

You can see that through careful consideration, the availability of various services can be tightly controlled depending on the environment and the organization's security policy. With the authentication server configured and ready, users must now be added so that they can be authenticated whenever necessary.

ADDING USERS

Before a user can be authenticated by the server, the user must be added to the database. This can be done by using the authsrv command. When invoking authsrv on the firewall with a userid of zero, authsrv grants administrative privileges for the database.

The authentication server has a number of commands, listed in table 10.16, for user administration.

TABLE 10.16

Administrator Commands for Authentication Setup

Command	Description
adduser username [longname]	Adds a user to the authentication database. Before the authentication server permits the use of this command, the administrator must first be authenticated to the server as an administrator or a group administrator. If the user is a group administrator, the newly created user is automatically initialized as a member of that group. When a user is added, the user is initially disabled. If a long name is provided, it will be stored in the database. Long names should be quoted if they contain whitespace.
deluser username	Deletes the specified user from the authentication database. Before an administrator can use this command, he or she must first be authenticated to the server as the administrator or group administrator of the group to which the user belongs.

Command	Description
display username	Displays the status, authentication protocol, and last login of the specified user. Before the authentication server permits the use of this command, the administrator must first be authenticated to the server as the administrator or as the group administrator of the group to which the user belongs.
enable username or disable username	Enables or disabled the specified user's account for login. Before this command can be used, the administrator must first be authenticated to the server as the administrator or group administrator of the group to which the user belongs.
group user groupname	Sets the specified user's group. To use this command, the administrator must first be authenticated to the server as the administrator. Group administrators do not have the power to "adopt" members.
list [group]	Lists all users that are known to the system, or the members of the specified group. Group administrators may list their own groups, but not the entire database. The list displays several fields, including: ✦ user. The login ID of the user. ✦ group. The group membership of the user. If none is listed, the user is in no group. ✦ longname. The user's full name. This may be left blank. ✦ status. Contains codes indicating the user's status.
password [username] text	Sets the password for the current user. If an optional user name is given and the authenticated user is the administrator or group administrator, the password for the specified user is changed. The password command is polymorphic depending on the user's specified authentication protocol. For example, if the user's authentication protocol is plaintext passwords, it will update the plaintext password. If the authentication protocol is SecurID with PINs, it will update the PIN.

continues

TABLE 10.16, CONTINUED
Administrator Commands for Authentication Setup

Command	Description
proto user protoname	Sets the authentication protocol for the specified user to the named protocol. Available protocols depend on the compiled-in support within authsrv. To change a user's authentication protocol, the administrator must be authenticated to the server either as the administrator or group administrator of the user's group.
quit or exit	Disconnects from the authentication server.
superwiz user	Sets the specified user as a global administrator. This command should only be used with deliberation; global administrative privileges are seldom used because the group mechanism is powerful enough.
wiz user	Sets or turns off the group or unwiz user administrator flag on the specified user. To issue this command, the administrator must be authenticated to the server as the administrator.
? or help	Lists a short synopsis of available commands.

To illustrate the use of these administrator commands, suppose you want to add a new user to the database. To do this, make sure you are logged in as root on the firewall, and run the authsrv command:

```
pc# pwd
/usr/local/etc
pc# ./authsrv
authsrv#
```

At this point, you can run any command shown in table 10.16. To add a user, use both the user name and the long name with the command:

```
authsrv# adduser chrish "Chris Hare"
ok - user added initially disabled
authsrv#
```

Notice that the user, although added, is initially disabled. No password is associated with the user. At this point, you need to set a password for the user, and specify the group to which the user belongs.

```
authsrv# password chrish whisper
Password for chrish changed.
authsrv# group chrish production
set group
authsrv#
```

Now that the password and group membership are changed, identify the authentication protocol that will be used for this user. Available protocols depend on the protocols that were compiled when authsrv was built.

```
authsrv# proto chrish plaintext
Unknown protocol "plaintext", use one of: none password
authsrv# proto chrish password
changed
authsrv# enable chrish
enabled
authsrv#
```

If an unknown protocol is used when you set the protocol type, authsrv lists the available authentication protocols. In this instance, the only options available are none and password. After the authentication protocol is set, the user chrish is enabled. At this point, the user chrish can authenticate him- or herself using the authentication server.

Before you give the user free rein, however, establish for this user the wizard for group administrator privileges, and superwiz, which grants global administrator privileges. Normally this wouldn't be done because global administrative privileges supersede the privileges of the group administrator.

```
authsrv# wiz chrish
set group-wizard
authsrv# superwiz chrish
set wizard
```

With these additional privileges set, you can list the information from the authsrv database using the list command.

```
authsrv# list
Report for users in database
user        group       longname        status proto    last
----        -----       --------        ------ -----    ----
chrish      production  Chris Hare         y G  passw    never
authsrv#
```

This output shows the user name, the group that the user belongs to, the long name, the status flags, authentication protocol, and when the user last authenticated. The status field includes the following information:

Letter	Description
b	Account locked due to too many failed logins
n	Account disabled
y	Account enabled
G	Group Wizard flag set
W	Global Wizard flag set

The list command displays information for all the users; the display command shows more information for a given user.

```
authsrv# display chrish
Report for user chrish, group production (Chris Hare)
Authentication protocol: password
Flags: WIZARD GROUP-WIZARD
authsrv#
```

As you can see, this command provides information similar to the list command, but includes a text explanation of the flags set for this user.

As many users as needed can be added in this manner, although you can see that this is a tedious job for even a small organization.

THE AUTHENTICATION SHELL—AUTHMGR

The authsrv command enables a local user access to the firewall host to manipulate the database; the authmgr program also allows users to manipulate the database such access, but from a trusted host on the network or through the local host. Unlike the authsrv command, the authmgr program requires that the user log in to authenticate him- or herself to the database. If the user is not enabled or in the database, the connection is refused. Here is a short authmgr session.

```
pc# ./authmgr
Connected to server
authmgr-> login
Username: admin
Password:
Logged in
authmgr-> list
```

```
Report for users in database
user        group       longname       status  proto    last
----        -----       --------       ------  -----    ----
paulp       copy                         n G   passw    never
chrish      production  Chris Hare       y W   passw    never
admin       manager     Auth DBA         y W   passw    Fri Oct 27 23:47:04 1995
authmgr-> quit
pc#
```

All the commands and functionality that are part of the authsrv command are also part of authmgr. This may be apparent, but keep in mind that the authmgr command actually established a TCP session to the authsrv program.

DATABASE MANAGEMENT

Two more commands are available for manipulating the authentication database: authload and authdump. The authload command manipulates individual records in the database; it does not truncate an existing database. It is useful when you need to add several new entries to the database, or when you need to share databases between sites. If you have users who share similar information between sites, the existing records will be overwritten with newer information when this information is loaded by the authload command.

The authdump command creates an ASCII backup copy of the information in the database. This ASCII copy contains all the information regarding the user account. The passwords however, are encrypted, so that they cannot be read and used to circumvent the security provided by the Toolkit.

The authdump command reads the contents of the authentication database and writes the ASCII text. A sample execution of the command is here:

```
pc# ./authdump

user=chrish
longname=Chris Hare
group=production
pass=cY8IDuONJDQRA
flags=2
bad_count=0
proto=p
last=0

user=admin
longname=Auth DBA
group=manager
pass=tx6mxx/1Uy2Mw
flags=2
```

If the command is executed and the output is redirected to a file, the program prints a dot for each record dumped, along with a report of the total records processed:

```
pc# ./authdump > /tmp/auth
...
3 records dumped
pc#
```

If you have this information stored somewhere else in a human-readable form (except for the passwords), you can re-create the user database if the firewall ever needs to be rebuilt.

The authload program can take the output of the authdump program and reload the database. The authload command is valuable if the user database was destroyed, or you have a large number of users to add at once. In this manner, new records can be added to the ASCII file and only the new records will be loaded into the authentication database. Consider the new entry added to this ASCII dump file:

```
user=terrih
longname=Terri Hare
group=production
pass=
flags=0
bad_count=0
proto=p
last=
```

Now you can load the records into the database, using input redirection because the information is in the ASCII dump file:

```
pc# ./authload < /tmp/auth
....
4 records loaded
pc#
```

This results in a report showing the number of records that have been loaded. You can then verify the status of the additional records using the authmgr "list" command:

```
pc# ./authmgr
Connected to server
authmgr-> login
Username: admin
Password:
Logged in
authmgr-> list
Report for users in database
user        group       longname      status proto    last
----        -----       --------      ------ -----    ----
paulp       copy                        n G  passw    never
terrih      production  Terri Hare      y    passw    never
chrish      production  Chris Hare      y W  passw    never
admin       manager     Auth DBA        y W  passw    Sat Oct 28 01:45:32 1995
authmgr->
```

At this point, it is important to note that the new account terrih is enabled, but there is no password. A password should be assigned as quickly as possible to prevent fraudulent use of the firewall, and potential loss of security of the network.

As an added measure of safety, it is advised to add a line to root's crontab to make "backups" of the authentication database. The following shows a sample entry:

```
0    1    *    *    *    /usr/local/etc/authdump > /usr/local/etc/auth.backup
```

The cron command will run the authdump command at 1:00 AM, every morning. This ensures a reliable backup of your database in ASCII format. If the information on your server does not change very often, you probably should adjust the timing of the cron execution of authdump.

AUTHENTICATION AT WORK

You might now be interested in seeing how the authentication server operates. Each of the proxies has the option of being configured to operate with the authentication server. The example shown here focuses on the FTP proxy. The FTP proxy's configuration can be found in the earlier section "Configuring the FTP Gateway."

```
ftp-gw: denial-msg      /usr/local/etc/ftp-deny.txt
ftp-gw: welcome-msg     /usr/local/etc/ftp-welcome.txt
ftp-gw: help-msg        /usr/local/etc/ftp-help.txt
ftp-gw: authserver      localhost       7777
ftp-gw: timeout         3600
ftp-gw: permit-hosts    206.116.65.*    -log { retr stor } -auth { stor }
```

Recall from earlier discussions that the last line of this configuration is actually what causes the authentication to be performed. In fact, it is fairly specific in that any request to retrieve a file from the remote, or to store a file on the remote results in that operation being logged by the proxy. In addition, the store command to save a file on the remote system is not permitted until the user authenticates him- or herself to the proxy. This process is illustrated here:

```
pc# ftp pc
Connected to pc.unilabs.org.
220-Welcome to the URG Firewall FTP Proxy
220-
220-To report problems, please contact Network Security Services at 555-1212
or 220-by e-mail at security@org.com
220
Name (pc.unilabs.org:chrish): chrish@nds.fonorola.net
331-(----GATEWAY CONNECTED TO nds.fonorola.net----)
331-(220 nds.fonorola.net FTP server (Version A) ready.)
331 Password required for chrish.
```

```
Password:
230 User chrish logged in.
Remote system type is Unix.
Using binary mode to transfer files.
ftp> put /tmp/trace
local: /tmp/trace remote: /tmp/trace
200 PORT command successful.
500 command requires user authentication
ftp> quote authorize chrish
331 Enter authentication password for chrish
ftp> quote response whisper
230 User authenticated to proxy
ftp> put /tmp/trace
local: /tmp/trace remote: /tmp/trace
200 PORT command successful.
150 Opening BINARY mode data connection for /tmp/trace.
226 Transfer complete.
2181 bytes sent in 0.0061 seconds (3.5e+02 Kbytes/s)
ftp> quit
221 Goodbye.
```

For FTP clients that do not know which proxy is used for authentication, the ftp quote command must be used to "speak" with the authentication server on the firewall. During this process, the password that is submitted by the user is echoed on-screen, and is therefore visible to anyone in the immediate vicinity.

This is just one example of authentication use with proxies; countless more examples could be used. Hopefully, the information and examples you have seen so far on proxies and the authentication server should help you design a secure firewall.

USING PLUG-GW FOR OTHER SERVICES

The applications you have read about so far cover about 80 percent of the network traffic. What about TIS Toolkit support for the Network News Transport Protocol (NNTP) or even the Post Office Protocol (POP)? Both of these services, and many others, are available through the plug-gw application. This application provides plugboard type connections; that is, it connects a TCP/IP port on the firewall to another host using the same or a different TCP port number. This functionality makes it easy to provide other services through the firewall. The next few sections examine the operation and configuration of plug-gw by looking specifically at their services.

CONFIGURING PLUG-GW

plug-gw reads the configuration lines that start with plug-gw: from the netperm-table file—just like the other Toolkit applications. The clauses listed in table 10.17 are used with the plug-gw application.

TABLE 10.17
plug-gw Rules and Clauses

Rule	Description
timeout seconds	Specifies a timeout value, after which inactive connections are disconnected. If no timeout is specified, the default is to remain connected until one side or the other closes its connection.
port portid host pattern [options]	Specifies a connection rule. When a connection is made, a match is searched for on the portid and calling host. The portid may be either a numeric value (such as 119) or a value from /etc/services (such as "nntp"). If the calling port matches, then the host pattern is checked for a match following the standard address matching rules employed by the firewall. If the rule matches, the connection will be made based on the remaining options in the rule, all of which begin with "-".
-plug-to host	Specifies the name or address of the host to connect to. This option is mandatory.
-privport	Indicates that a reserved port number should be used when connecting. Reserved port numbers must be specified for protocols, such as rlogin, which rely on them for "security."
-port portid	Specifies a different port. The default port is the same as the port used by the incoming connection.

The purpose of plug-gw is to allow for other services to be passed through the firewall with additional logging to track the use of these services. The availability of this service means that additional service-specific applications do not need to be created unless required. Some applications do not have extended authentication mechanisms in them; plug-gw makes their use with firewalls much less of a bother.

The rules available for plug-gw, when used on a POP connection, look like this:

```
plug-gw:      port 110 206.116.65.* -plug-to 198.53.64.14
```

This line indicates that any connection received on port 110 (Post Office Protocol) from the 206.116.65 network is to be connected to 198.53.64.14. Additional options for the rule allow for the specification of a priveleged port number. Few services actually require these. The final option allows for the specification of an alternate port number should the same service be running on a different port number at the remote end.

As with the other services, the host pattern that is specified with the port command allows for both the allowed and non-allowed network or host IP addresses to be specified.

PLUG-GW AND NNTP

The NNTP news protocol is used for reading Internet newsgroups. This protocol also performs news feeds and is often used to provide news reading services at the workstation level. The configuration of the plug-gw proxy for an Internet news feed is essentially the same as the configuration for a news reader.

In both cases, the NNTP port is defined in the etc/services file as 119. You must configure the plug-gw line as follows:

```
plug-gw:      port 119 206.116.65.* -plug-to 198.53.64.1
```

This means that any connections received on port 119 from the local LAN will be directed to the same port on the system at 198.53.64.1. The two major reasons for handling NNTP with plug-gw are to allow NNTP client access through the firewall, and to allow for a newsfeed.

For the firewall to accept news connections, inetd must be configured to start the plug-gw application whenever a connection request is made for the NNTP port. This is done by adding the following line to the /etc/inetd.conf file and restarting inetd:

```
nntp    stream tcp    nowait  root    /usr/local/etc/plug-gw plug-gw 119
```

If you configure plug-gw but forget this step, the TIS firewall Toolkit will seem to not operate—no log messages will print to the files or to the console.

To configure an NNTP client, such as WinVN for the PC-based architecture, you must set up WinVN so that it knows where to connect. Normally, this would be the actual NNTP server that you want to access, but in this case, it is the name or IP address of the firewall. On the firewall, the appropriate line in the netperm-table file must be included to specify where the NNTP client requests are to go. If several NNTP servers are available for reading news, you may want to separate them onto different network ports on the firewall, so that traffic can be sent to the different sites. Consider this sample part of the netperm-table file:

```
plug-gw:    port 2119 206.116.65.* -plug-to 198.53.64.1 -port 119
plug-gw:    port 2120 206.116.65.* -plug-to 198.53.64.5 -port 119
```

In this scenario, when users want to read news from the 198.53.64.5 server, they must connect to the firewall on port 2120. Figure 10.3 illustrates the configuration of the WinVN client for access to news through the firewall.

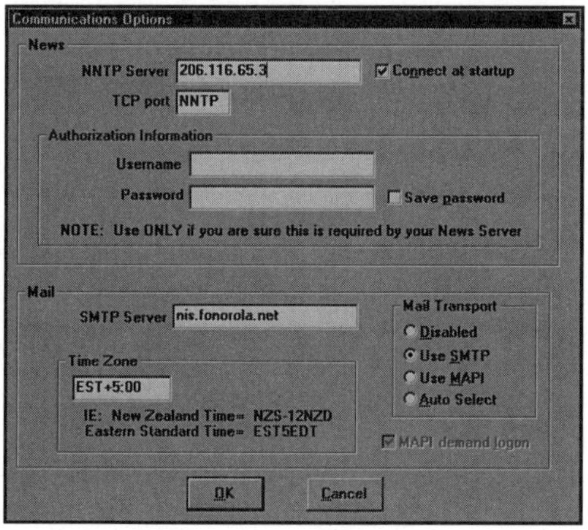

![Communications Options dialog box showing News section with NNTP Server 206.116.65.3, TCP port NNTP, Connect at startup checked; Authorization Information with Username and Password fields; Mail section with SMTP Server nis.fonorola.net, Time Zone EST+5:00, and Mail Transport options](dialog)

FIGURE 10.3

Configuring WinVN to use the NNTP proxy.

Regardless of the news reader client software that you use, it needs to be configured to use the firewall as the connection point or news host.

What if different news servers are available that your hosts are permitted to connect to? How does the system administrator configure multiple hosts at the same TCP/IP service port? The answer is to specify a different port on the firewall, and let plug-gw redirect to the correct port on the remote system. This is done by using a rule in the nbetperm-table file:

```
plug-gw:    port 2120 206.116.65.* -plug-to 198.53.64.5 -port 119
```

According to this command, if a connection on port 2120 is requested, redirect that request on port 119 or the host at 198.53.64.5. This is only part of the solution. The /etc/services file should also be edited to add a news NNTP service entry to show the new service port for this connection. For example, the following line specifies that the service nntp-a is on port 2120:

```
nntp-a     2120/tcp                readnews untp    # USENET News Transfer Protocol
```

The next step is to tell inetd that connections on this port are to be sent to the plug-gw application. This is done by adding the following line to the /etc/inetd.conf file and restarting inetd.

```
nntp-a  stream  tcp     nowait  root     /usr/local/etc/plug-gw  plug-gw 2120
```

When the user wants to use this alternate server, he or she must reconfigure the news client software, as shown in figure 10.4, to point to the new services port.

FIGURE 10.4

*Configuring
WinVN and
NNTP.*

Although you can set up your firewall so that NNTP clients can read news, this is generally not a popular setup. A much more realistic configuration would be for the clients to interact with a local news server. This configuration requires the firewall to allow for a news feed to be passed through to the internal news server.

To do this, the external news server and the internal news client must be set up so that they pass their information through the firewall. The trick is understanding what configuration information must be placed in the news server configuration files on both ends. For the purpose of this discussion, assume that the news server software in use is INN 1.4. The file hosts.nntp provides information regarding what hosts are permitted to connect to the INN NNTP server. Consider the news server and firewall configuration shown in figure 10.5.

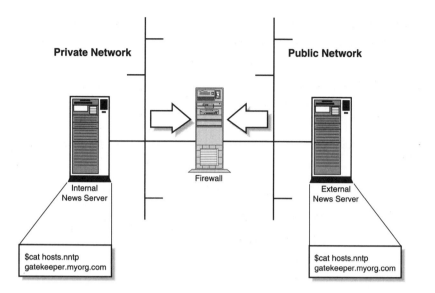

FIGURE 10.5

News client and server.

Normally, the hosts.nntp file on each news server contains the name or IP address of the other news server that is allowed to connect to it. In this case, the name of the machine that goes in both hosts.nntp files is in fact the name or IP address of the firewall. This is because the firewall actually establishes a connection from one network to the other, and from one server to the other using the correct service port. With the hosts.nntp file correctly configured, there will be no problems passing news through the firewall.

PLUG-GW AND POP

When you first think about using plug-gw with the TIS plug-gw application, the obvious question that comes to mind is "How do I configure things for authentication?" The trick is to remember which machine is actually performing the authentication. The firewall using plug-gw does no authentication. It merely accepts the incoming connection on the named port, and establishes a connection from itself to the named system on the same or different port.

To see this in operation, you can establish a Telnet connection to the POP port. Consider the sample output shown here:

```
$ telnet 206.116.65.3 110
+OK UCB Pop server (version 2.1.2-R3) at 198.53.64.14 starting.
USER chrish
+OK Password required for chrish.
PASS agdfer
```

485

```
+OK chrish has 0 message(s) (0 octets).
QUIT
Connection closed by foreign host.
$
```

Notice that the connection to the firewall was established at 206.116.65.3. The remote system [198.53.64.14] does not normally list its IP address in the output; a modified version of the POP server was used to show the IP instead of the name.

Unfortunately, simply adding the entries to the netpwrm-table file is not enough. Like NNTP, inetd must be configured to accept connections on the POP service port, 110. This is done by adding the following line to the /etc/inetd.conf file and restarting inetd:

```
pop      stream tcp      nowait root      /usr/local/etc/plug-gw plug-gw 110
```

With the firewall now accepting POP service requests, plug-gw must be configured to redirect those POP requests to the appropriate server. This is done by adding this next line to the netperm-table file:

```
plug-gw:      port 110 206.116.65.* -plug-to 198.53.64.14
```

After it is added, POP service requests received by the firewall are redirected to the specified server.

The preceding example shows the process of establishing a POP session using Telnet, but how do you configure a workstation that relies on POP to pass traffic through the firewall? Figure 10.6 shows a configuration screen from the Eudora 1.52 shareware e-mail package.

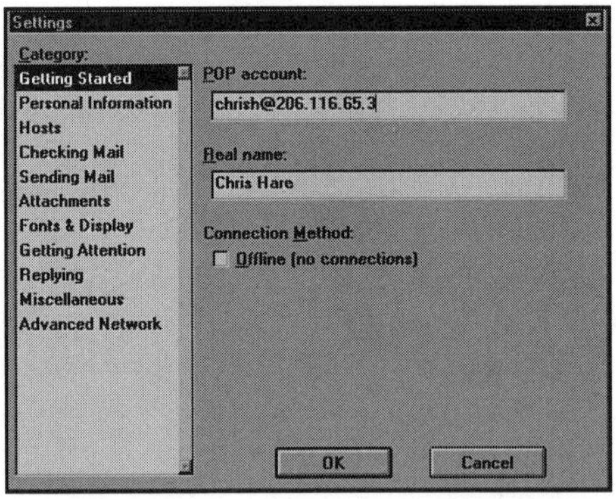

FIGURE 10.6

Setup for a POP e-mail package.

In this example, the user@hostname specification for the POP server identifies the real user name, but specifies the IP address for the firewall. The IP or name of the firewall can be used interchangeably in this field. The only reason for using the IP address rather than the name is if you have a DNS reliability problem, or to ensure that you connect to the correct host.

Consequently, when the incoming connection is received on port 110, plug-gw starts a session to the remote host specified in the plug-gw rule. This results in the mail being transferred from the remote end through the firewall to the workstation.

Incidentally, the POP mail client in use is irrelevant. The plug-gw configuration has been tested with Eudora, Microsoft Exchange, and Pegasus Mail; every package tested functions properly.

THE COMPANION ADMINISTRATIVE TOOLS

A set of support tools are included with the TIS Toolkit to assist in the setup and ongoing administration of the firewall. These include a port scanner, a network subnet ping manager, and log analysis and reporting tools.

> Depending upon the version and completeness of the Toolkit you downloaded, some services and programs may not be installed or compiled automatically. It is strongly suggested that you retrieve the lastest version and patches directly from the the TIS FTP site.

N O T E

PORTSCAN

The portscan program attempts to connect to every TCP port on a given machine. The default operation is to connect to each port in sequence on the named host/. The portscan program's scan of the machine pc.unilabs.org, for example, was answered by the following ports:

```
pc# ./portscan pc.unilabs.org
ftp
telnet
gopher
httpd
pop
nntp
who
2021
2023
2120
7777
pc#
```

You can see from the output of portscan that very few ports are in fact in operation on the machine that was contacted.

NETSCAN

This is a network ping program. It accepts as an argument a network address and starts to ping each address on the network. Its default output is a list of each of the addresses that responded to the ping, along with the host's name. The use of netscan in default mode is shown in this example:

```
pc# ./netscan 198.53.32
198.53.32.5
Vaxxine-GW.Toronto.fonorola.net (198.53.32.6)
198.53.32.9
Harte-Lyne-gw.Toronto.fonorola.net (198.53.32.10)
198.53.32.13
Globe-n-Mail-GW.Toronto.fonorola.net (198.53.32.14)
^C
pc#
```

This output shows that the first host that responded to a ping was 198.53.32.5. Notice that even though the program pings each address in turn, there is not always a response. This indicates that either no device exists, or netscan attempted to contact a device that does not respond to pings.

A verbose mode is also available with netscan. In verbose mode, addresses that respond to a ping are placed with their name or address flush left; addresses that did not respond are indented one tab space. This mode is enabled by using the -v option on the command line:

```
pc# ./netscan -v 198.53.32
trying subnet 198.53.32
    198.53.32.1
    198.53.32.2
    198.53.32.3
    198.53.32.4
198.53.32.5
Vaxxine-GW.Toronto.fonorola.net (198.53.32.6)
    198.53.32.7
    198.53.32.8
198.53.32.9
Harte-Lyne-gw.Toronto.fonorola.net (198.53.32.10)
    198.53.32.11
    198.53.32.12
198.53.32.13
^C
pc#
```

This tool helps determine what hosts are on a network, which may affect how you specify the configuration rules for your network.

REPORTING TOOLS

The TIS Toolkit, configured as a firewall, logs transactions and requests processed by Toolkit applications, and records the outcome of these requests. The log file messages are recorded through the syslog daemon. The files used to save the details are listed in /etc/syslog.conf, and vary from system to system. The TIS Toolkit applications all interact with the syslog service and send logging information and status messages for the lifetime of the connection.

You can periodically peruse the log files, or use the reporting programs included with the Toolkit to search out and report usage of the firewall. Because the logging is performed using the syslogd service, the log messages observe the standard format:

```
Date Time hostname program[PID]: message
```

This format appears in the log file looking like this:

```
Oct  4 02:42:14 pc ftp-gw[1763]: permit host=stargazer.unilabs.org/
➥204.191.3.147 use of gateway
```

A wide variety of log messages can be displayed in the syslog file. Some of these are illustrated in the following output:

```
cannot connect to server 198.53.64.14/110: No route to host
cannot connect to server 198.53.64.14/110: Operation timed out
cannot connect to server nis.fonorola.net/110: Connection refused
cannot connect to server nis.fonorola.net/110: Operation timed out
cannot get our port
connect host=stargazer.unilabs.org/206.116.65.2 destination=198.53.64.14/110
connect host=unknown/206.116.65.2 destination=198.53.64.14/110
connected host=pc.unilabs.org/204.191.3.150 to nds.fonorola.net
content-type= multipart/x-mixed-replace;boundary=ThisRandomString
content-type= text/html
deny host=204.191.3.150/pc.unilabs.org connect to fox.nstn.ca
deny host=pc.unilabs.org/204.191.3.150 service=ftpd
deny host=stargazer.unilabs.org/204.191.3.147 destination=sco.sco.com
deny host=unknown/206.116.65.2 service=110
disconnect host=stargazer.unilabs.org/206.116.65.2 destination=198.53.64.14/
➥110 in=3512 out=92 duration=8
disconnect host=unknown/206.116.65.2 destination=198.53.64.14/110 in=0 out=0
➥duration=75
exit host=pc.unilabs.org/204.191.3.150 dest= in=0 out=0
exit host=pc.unilabs.org/204.191.3.150 dest= in=0 out=0 user=unauth
➥duration=2
exit host=pc.unilabs.org/204.191.3.150 dest=nds.fonorola.net in=35 out=21
➥user=unauth duration=37
exit host=pc.unilabs.org/204.191.3.150 dest=none in=0 out=0 user=unauth
➥duration=14
```

```
exit host=stargazer.unilabs.org/204.191.3.147 cmds=1 in=0 out=0 user=unauth
➥duration=2
exit host=stargazer.unilabs.org/204.191.3.147 no auth
failed to append to file (null)
failed to connect to http server iback.gif (80)
fwtksyserr: cannot display denial-msg /usr/local/etc/tn-deny.txt: No such
➥file or directory
fwtksyserr: cannot display help file /usr/local/etc/tn-help.txt: No such file
➥or directory
fwtksyserr: cannot display help message /usr/local/etc/rlogin-help.txt: No
➥such file or directory
fwtksyserr: cannot display welcome /usr/local/etc/rlogin-welcome.txt: No such
➥file or directory
fwtksyserr: cannot display welcome /usr/local/etc/tn-welcome.txt: No such
➥file or directory
log host=stargazer.unilabs.org/206.116.65.2 protocol=HTTP cmd=dir
➥dest=www.istar.ca path=/
log host=stargazer.unilabs.org/206.116.65.2 protocol=HTTP cmd=dir
➥dest=iback.gif path=/
log host=stargazer.unilabs.org/206.116.65.2 protocol=HTTP cmd=get dest=
➥www.nstn.ca path=/cgi-bin/test/tide.cgi
Network connection closed during write
permit host=pc.unilabs.org/204.191.3.150 connect to 204.191.124.252
permit host=pc.unilabs.org/204.191.3.150 connect to chrish@nds.fonorola.net
permit host=pc.unilabs.org/204.191.3.150 use of gateway
permit host=stargazer.unilabs.org/204.191.3.147 connect to mail.fonorola.net
permit host=stargazer.unilabs.org/204.191.3.147 destination=204.191.3.150
permit host=stargazer.unilabs.org/204.191.3.147 service=ftpd execute=/usr/
➥libexec/ftpd
permit host=stargazer.unilabs.org/204.191.3.147 service=ftpd execute=/bin/cat
permit host=stargazer.unilabs.org/204.191.3.147 service=telnetdexecute=/usr/
libexec/telnetd
permit host=stargazer.unilabs.org/204.191.3.147 use of gateway
permit host=stargazer.unilabs.org/206.116.65.2 use of gateway (Ver p1.4 /  1)
```

These log messages do not represent a complete list. The only way to see a complete list of possible log messages and their exact meanings is to perform a line-by-line review of the TIS Toolkit code, and then document each item individually.

The Toolkit includes a number of reporting tools that can be used to analyze the log records saved by the syslog service. These shell scripts, listed in table 10.18, are in the fwtk/tool/admin/reporting directory.

TABLE 10.18
syslog Report Generating Scripts

Script Name	Description
authsrv-summ.sh	Summarizes auth server reports
daily-report.sh	Runs the report scripts on a daily basis
deny-sum.sh	Reports on denial of services
ftp-summ.sh	Summarizes ftp-gw traffic
http-summ.sh	Summarizes the http-gw traffic
netacl-summ.sh	Summarizes netacl accesses
smap-summ.sh	Summarizes smap email records
tn-gw-summ.sh	Summarizes tn-gw and rlogin-gw traffic
weekly-report.sh	Top-level driver that calls each summary report generator

The reporting tools included in the TIS Toolkit are not installed automatically when the Toolkit applications are compiled and installed. They must be installed later by changing to the directory tools.admin.reporting and running the make install command. This copies all the files to the same directory in which the Toolkit applications were copied.

THE AUTHENTICATION SERVER REPORT

The authentication server report identifies various authentication operations that are carried out on the server. A typical report of authsrv-summ.sh looks like this:

```
pc# ./authsrv-summ.sh < /var/log/messages.0

Top 100 permitted user authentications (total: 6)
Logins        User ID
------        -------
4             admin
2             chrish

Top 100 failed user authentications (total: 2)
Attempts      Username
--------      --------
1             paulp
1             chrish
```

```
Authentication Management Operations
----------------------------------------
administrator ADDED admin
administrator ADDED admin
administrator ADDED chrish
administrator ADDED chrish
administrator ADDED paulp
administrator DELETED admin
administrator DELETED chrish
administrator ENABLED admin
administrator ENABLED chrish
administrator GROUP admin manager
administrator GROUP chrish production
administrator GROUP paulp copy
administrator GWIZ chrish
administrator GWIZ chrish
administrator GWIZ paulp
administrator PASSWORD admin
administrator PASSWORD chrish
administrator PROTOCOL admin
administrator PROTOCOL chrish
administrator UN-GWIZ chrish
administrator WIZ admin
administrator WIZ chrish
```

Notice that this and all the other reporting tools expect to read their data from the standard input stream. These reporting tools can do this by using the cat command with a pipe, or by redirecting the input stream from the log file.

The authsrv summary report lists the total authentication requests made and by whom, the denied authentication, and the authentication database management operations. If you run this report after a heavy period of user administration, it will be quite verbose.

THE SERVICE DENIAL REPORT

The purpose of the service denial report is to identify hosts that attempted to connect through the firewall and were not permitted. The report reads through the specified log file and reports on:

- ✦ The top 100 network service users
- ✦ The top 100 denied service users
- ✦ The total service requests by service

A sample execution of deny-summ.sh looks like this:

```
pc# ./deny-summ.sh < /var/log/messages.0
```

```
Authentication Failures
Failures        Proxy: Host - ID
--------        ----------------
1               s: disable - paulp
1               ftp-gw: pc.unilabs.org/206.116.65.3 - chrish

Top 100 network service users (total: 152)
Connects        Host/Address
--------        ------------
120             stargazer.unilabs.org/206.116.65.2:
11              pc.unilabs.org/206.116.65.3:ftp
5               stargazer.unilabs.org/206.116.65.2:telnet
3               stargazer.unilabs.org/206.116.65.2:telnetd
3               stargazer.unilabs.org/206.116.65.2:ftpd
3               pc.unilabs.org/206.116.65.3:telnet
2               stargazer.unilabs.org/206.116.65.2:ftp
2               pc.unilabs.org/206.116.65.3:
1               unknown/206.116.65.2:
1               pc.unilabs.org/206.116.65.3:telnetd
1               pc.unilabs.org/206.116.65.3:ftpd

Top 100 Denied network service users (total: 12)
Connects        Host/Address
--------        ------------
2               stargazer.unilabs.org/206.116.65.2:telnet
2               pc.unilabs.org/206.116.65.3:ftp
1               unknown/206.116.65.2:110
1               stargazer.unilabs.org/206.116.65.2:telnetd
1               stargazer.unilabs.org/206.116.65.2:110
1               stargazer.unilabs.org/206.116.65.2:
1               pc.unilabs.org/206.116.65.3:2120
1               pc.unilabs.org/206.116.65.3:119
1               pc.unilabs.org/206.116.65.3:110
1               pc.unilabs.org/206.116.65.3:

Service Requests
Requests        Service
--------        -------
125
15              ftp
10              telnet
5               telnetd
4               ftpd
3               110
1               2120
1               119
```

The report can be used to highlight sites that have attempted unauthorized connections to the firewall; the report also highlights sites that are authorized to connect, but whose users do not know how, or have forgotten their passwords. All of these examples may be legitimate problems or potential security breaches.

THE FTP USAGE REPORT

The FTP usage report identifies sites that are connected to FTP services through the firewall. It identifies the number of connections, the origin of the connection, and the amount of data transferred. A sample execution of ftp-summ.sh looks like this:

```
pc# cat /var/log/messages* ¦ ./ftp-summ.sh
FTP service users (total: 23)
Connects      Host/Address
--------      ------------
13            stargazer. unilabs.org/204.191.3.147
5             pc.unilabs.org/206.116.65.3
3             pc.unilabs.org/204.191.3.150
2             stargazer.unilabs.org/206.116.65.2

Denied FTP service users (total: 4)
Connects      Host/Address
--------      ------------
2             pc.unilabs.org/206.116.65.3
2             nds.fonorola.net/204.191.124.252

FTP service output thruput (total Kbytes: 6)
KBytes        Host/Address
------        ------------
6             pc.unilabs.org/206.116.65.3

FTP service input thruput (total Kbytes: 4)
KBytes        Host/Address
------        ------------
3             pc.unilabs.org/206.116.65.3
0             stargazer.unilabs.org/206.116.65.2
0             stargazer.unilabs.org/204.191.3.147
pc#
```

As you can see in this report, several service denials occurred on this firewall. A couple came from an external site, but also an internal host attempted to access the site. Many sites choose to not allow FTP at all because of the potential problems associated with pirated software or virus-infected software.

THE HTTP USAGE REPORT

The HTTP usage report identifies traffic that has been passed through the http-gw application. The report covers connection requests, denied service requests, and input and output through the proxy. A sample HTTP usage report looks like this:

```
pc#   cat /var/log/messages* ¦ ./http-summ.sh
HTTP service users (total: 130)
Connects        Host/Address
--------        ------------
127             stargazer.unilabs.org/206.116.65.2
2               pc.unilabs.org/206.116.65.3
1               unknown/206.116.65.2
Denied HTTP service users (total: 1)
Connects        Host/Address
--------        ------------
1               stargazer.unilabs.org/206.116.65.2

HTTP service output thruput (total Kbytes: 1)
KBytes          Host/Address
------          ------------
1               stargazer.unilabs.org/206.116.65.2

HTTP service input thruput (total Kbytes: 315)
KBytes          Host/Address
------          ------------
315             stargazer.unilabs.org/206.116.65.2
pc#
```

A few requests out through the firewall may result in a much higher rate of information input to the firewall. You can see this in list 4; 1 KB of data out through the firewall resulted in 315 KB from the remote end.

THE NETACL REPORT

Recall that netacl is a method of allowing access to the services on the firewall itself, such as Telnet. This program enables administrators and other users to operate directly on the firewall without the need to be on the console.

The netacl report identifies the connects that have been made to the firewall and on what services, as well as the origin of the requests. A sample execution of the netacl-summ.sh command is shown here:

```
pc# cat /var/log/messages* ¦ ./netacl-summ.sh
Top 100 network service users (total: 40)
Connects        Host/Address
--------        ------------
19              stargazer.unilabs.org/204.191.3.147
13              stargazer.unilabs.org/206.116.65.2
4               unknown/206.116.65.2
2               unknown/204.191.3.147
2               pc.unilabs.org/206.116.65.3
```

```
Top 100 Denied network service users (total: 11)
Connects        Host/Address
--------        ------------
6               pc.unilabs.org/204.191.3.150
2               stargazer.unilabs.org/204.191.3.147
1               stargazer.unilabs.org/206.116.65.2
1               nds.fonorola.net/204.191.124.252
1               mail.fonorola.net/198.53.64.8

Service Requests
Requests        Service
--------        -------
32              ftpd
18              telnetd
```

In a previous section in this chapter, only Telnet and FTP services were configured to be available with netacl. This setup was chosen so that you, the network administrator, could update files and interact with the firewall from places other than the console. The denied requests result from other hosts attempting to connect to your netacl ports (Telnet was 2023, and FTP was 2021).

This report identifies sites that are attempting to log in or ftp directly to the firewall itself, rather than log in to a site behind the firewall.

THE MAIL USAGE REPORT

Another important piece of information for the administrator is knowing how much mail is flowing through the firewall. Many sites do not allow any traffic other than mail through the firewall; for this reason, knowledge of the amount of information available helps determine whether the chosen hardware platform is in fact doing the job. The mail usage report generator identifies for the administrator the number of messages received per user, and how many bytes in mail traffic were handled by the firewall.

The following sample execution of the mail report, smap-summ.sh, illustrates this script's importance:

```
pc# cat /var/log/messages* ¦ ./smap-summ.sh
Total messages: 10  (22 Kb)

Top 100 mail recipients (in messages)
Messages
  Count   Kb    Address
  -----   --    -------
      2   7.6   skhan@compmore.net
      2   7.6   chrish
      2   2.9   74507.3713@compuserve.com
```

```
    1      1.5    chrish@fonorola.net
    1      1.1    chrish@unilabs.org
    1      0.9    denny@nstn.ca
    1      0.9    chrish@nds.fonorola.net
```

```
Top 100 mail senders (in messages)
Messages
  Count     Kb     Address
  ----      --     -------
      9    21.4    chrish@unilabs.org
      1     1.1    news@news.compmore.net
```

```
Top 100 mail recipients (in kilobytes)
Messages
  Count     Kb     Address
  -----     --     -------
      2     7.6    skhan@compmore.net
      2     7.6    chrish
      2     2.9    74507.3713@compuserve.com
      1     1.5    chrish@fonorola.net
      1     1.1    chrish@unilabs.org
      1     0.9    denny@nstn.ca
      1     0.9    chrish@nds.fonorola.net
```

```
Top 100 mail senders (in kilobytes)
Messages
  Count     Kb     Address
  -----     --     -------
      9    21.4    chrish@unilabs.org
      1     1.1    news@news.compmore.net
```

THE TELNET AND RLOGIN USAGE REPORT

The Telnet and rlogin usage report (tn-gw-summ.sh) combines activity through the firewall of the Telnet and rlogin services. This report identifies the following:

❖ The number of connections

❖ The connecting host

❖ Characters input to the firewall for transmission to the public network

❖ Characters received by the firewall for the private network

❖ Denied connections

The following report provides a sample execution of tn-gw-summ.sh:

```
Top 100 telnet gateway clients (total: 43)
Connects      Host/Address            Input   Output    Total
--------      ------------            -----   ------    -----
     17       stargazer.unilabs.or      924      177     1101
     16       pc.unilabs.org/204.1    97325     1243    98568
      3       stargazer.unilabs.or      274        6      280
      3       mailhost.unilabs.org    26771      717    27488
      2       unknown/204.191.3.14    27271      710    27981
      1       unknown/206.116.65.4    10493      701    11194
      1       pc.unilabs.org/206.1        0        0        0


Top 100 telnet gateway clients in terms of traffic
Connects      Host/Address            Input   Output    Total
--------      ------------            -----   ------    -----
     16       pc.unilabs.org/204.1    97325     1243    98568
      3       mailhost.unilabs.org    26771      717    27488
      2       unknown/204.191.3.14    27271      710    27981
      1       unknown/206.116.65.4    10493      701    11194
     17       stargazer.unilabs.or      924      177     1101
      3       stargazer.unilabs.or      274        6      280
      1       pc.unilabs.org/206.1        0        0        0


Top 100 Denied telnet gateway clients (total: 20)
Connects      Host/Address
--------      ------------
     14       stargazer.unilabs.or
      2       stargazer.unilabs.or
      2       204.191.3.150/pc.uni
      1       unknown/204.191.3.14
      1       mail.fonorola.net/19
```

This report provides details on who is connecting through the firewall, how much traffic is being generated, and who is being denied. You can see, for example, that stargazer.unilabs.org is in both the connections and denied lists. This may indicate that at one point the site was denied, and then later authorized to use the Telnet or rlogin gateways.

WHERE TO GO FOR HELP

Help with the TIS Toolkit is easy to find. Discussions on general Internet security-related topics can be found in the Usenet newsgroups:

alt.2600

alt.security

comp.security

You can also find help by joining the mailing list concerned with a general discussion of firewalls and security technology:

firewalls@greatcircle.com

To subscribe to the mailing list, send a message to

majordomo@greatcircle.com

with the text

subscribe firewalls

in the body of the message.

To reach users familiar with the TIS Toolkit applications and their configuration, contact this mailing list:

fwall-users-request@tis.com

In addition, the TIS Toolkit includes a large amount of documentation on firewalls. If you plan to make significant use of the Toolkit you should join the TIS discussion lists first. Before you commit to an operating system and hardware platform, ask questions on this mailing list; probably many of the list's readers have had similar questions and experiences.

## CHAPTER 11

BLACK HOLE

FIREWALL IMPLEMENTATIONS are available today from a wide array of vendors. With the ever-increasing awareness of network security and the costs of lost information, many new firewall implementations continue to emerge. This chapter discusses Black Hole, which is the firewall produced by Milkyway Networks Corporation in Ottawa, Canada. This firewall is currently the only implementation certified at the AL-1 level (refer to Chapter 2, "Security") from the Canadian government's Department of National Defense Communications Security Establishment (DND-CSE).

Black Hole was developed to address the challenge of securing the private network from the public network, more commonly known as the Internet. Black Hole does this by providing the following:

❖ Full authentication for both incoming and outgoing traffic

❖ Mail relay services to eliminate the need for sendmail on the firewall for mail delivery

❖ Real-time alert messaging for faster administrative response

❖ Statistical traffic processing that logs intruder attempts

❖ Full network address translation to reduce administrative time and costs

❖ One-time password schemes that increase user and password security

❖ A flexible hardware platform and full GUI interface to provide ease of use and customization

This chapter discusses how to protect the systems and information on your private network using Black Hole as your firewall.

UNDERSTANDING BLACK HOLE

A black hole is by definition a void. Dr. Stephen Hawking describes a black hole in his book *A Brief History of Time* as a compact star with sufficient gravitational force as to prevent any light from escaping, and would therefore not be visible to us (paraphrased here for this book's purposes). This is in fact what Black Hole firewall does. It completely isolates the internal network from the external, blocking all knowledge of the internal network from the external network.

When this firewall is initially installed, it defaults to a totally secure policy of "that which is not explicitly permitted is prohibited." The security manager must determine how to configure Black Hole to satisfy the organization's security policy.

Black Hole is a secure application and circuit-level gateway that is installed between the public and private networks. It utilizes rule-based proxy servers and does not require nor use packet-filtering mechanisms of any kind. Black Hole also can be installed inside an organization if internal networks exist that must be protected against from the remainder of the organization. Black Hole's most common application is that of an Internet firewall; it is capable of offering Virtual Private Network services between multiple Internet-connected sites.

A Virtual Private Network can be constructed between two or more sites with Black Hole and an Internet connection. The Internet is used to provide the network connection, and the VPN capabilities of Black Hole are used to provide an encrypted and secure communications channel between the sites.

Figure 11.1 illustrates several different connection scenarios.

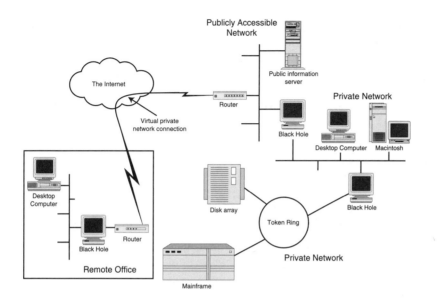

FIGURE 11.1

Sample Black Hole installation points.

Figure 11.1 presents Black Hole in several different configurations, such as providing services for a remote office using a Virtual Private Network scenario, protecting the corporate LAN from the public, and isolating the corporate accounting network from the remainder of the LAN. This variety of configurations demonstrates that Black Hole can be used in an interdepartmental role as well as the more common Internet security role. As an application-level firewall, Black Hole enables the security manager to restrict both inbound and outbound traffic based upon the following:

✦ Source and destination IP address

✦ Protocol or application

✦ User ID

✦ Time of day

In addition, for the allowed services, Black Hole's operation can be completely transparent to the user. This transparency distinguishes Black Hole from some other firewalls, such as the freely available TIS Firewall Toolkit. Having a transparent operation means that the firewall does not require the user to have special training to access the typical services, which decreases the training time and initial operational problems often associated with the installation of a firewall.

503

Transparency need not be applied in all cases, however. For example, it may be reasonable to allow certain users or types of traffic through the firewall without authentication. In this case, other types of traffic are restricted to users who can authenticate and are permitted for that service. The extensibility of Black Hole can rely upon the requirement for user authentication; this chapter also addresses the configuration of user accounts in the later section "Services, Users, and Rules."

The implementation of a security policy that makes it harder for the users to do their jobs and complete their assignments is an undesirable situation. Black Hole was designed to protect the systems, information, and users—not to inhibit them.

System Requirements

Black Hole comes in either a SPARC- or PC-based configuration. The SPARC-based configuration consists of a SPARC CPU such as a SPARC-2, SPARC-5, SPARC-10, or SPARC-20. The determining factor on the CPU size is the anticipated amount of traffic that will be running through the firewall. The configuration for the SPARC-based system is as follows:

- ✧ SPARC-based CPU (SPARC-2, SPARC-5, SPARC-10, SPARC-20)
- ✧ 16 MB of RAM (minimum)
- ✧ 500 MB of disk space (minimum)
- ✧ Two network interface cards, either Token-Ring or 10-MB Ethernet
- ✧ 17-inch or 20-inch high-resolution monitor

Sun Microsystems and other vendors produce other SPARC systems. At this time, however, only systems that are compliant with the previously mentioned SPARC architectures are supported. Although other forms of network interface cards are provided by manufacturers, Token-Ring and 10-MB Ethernet NICs are proven and do not cause network performance bottlenecks. Milkyway is working to support other network interfaces.

The PC-based implementation requires either a 486/66 MHz as a minimum, or a Pentium processor. The configuration for an Intel-based system is as follows:

- ✧ Intel 486/66 MHz or Pentium processor
- ✧ 16 MB of RAM (minimum)
- ✧ 500 MB of disk space (minimum)
- ✧ Two network interface cards, Token-Ring or 10-MB Ethernet
- ✧ 15-inch or 17-inch high-resolution monitor

If you have chosen to provide your PC-based hardware yourself, you need to remember that the system will be running a modified version of the BDSI implementation of BSD Unix. Consequently, any hardware selections should be verified through Milkyway as supported under the modified BSDI kernel before purchasing.

Black Hole is available in several different sizes depending on the needs of the organization. The determining factors as to which version of Black Hole you should consider are the following:

✤ The number of licensed users

✤ The hardware platform

✤ The number of simultaneous sessions

Table 11.1 illustrates the different configurations of Black Hole.

TABLE 11.1
Black Hole Software Configurations

Product Number	Product Name	Product Description	Simultaneous Sessions
M-BH-2001	Black Hole	Security-enhanced SUN OS	Unlimited
M-BH-2002	Mid-size Black Hole	Security-enhanced SUN OS	100
M-BH-2003	Entry level Black Hole	Security-enhanced SUN OS	40
M-BH-2006	Sub Entry Black Hole	Security-enhanced SUN OS	5
M-BH-2004	Mini Black Hole	Security-enhanced BSDI OS	Unlimited
M-BH-2005	Macro Black Hole	Security-enhanced BSDI OS	40
M-BH-2007	Sub Micro Black Hole	Security-enhanced BSDI OS	5

In table 11.1, the number of simultaneous sessions is defined as the number of currently active proxy processes. The current number of active proxies is determined by running a ps command on a running Black Hole implementation. Consequently, the selection of the product to use becomes a question of how many users are in the organization and how much external network traffic there will be. The more users, or the greater the amount of network traffic, the larger the number of simultaneous sessions that will be required for Black Hole to provide the requested services.

BLACK HOLE CORE MODULES

Both the SPARC- and PC-based implementations are based on secured versions of SunOS or BSDI Unix respectively. These kernel modifications include the following:

❖ Disabled source routing to ensure that unauthenticated source-routed packets are not forwarded

❖ Disabled ICMP redirect functions to ensure that the routing table cannot be modified

❖ Disabled IP forwarding so that Black Hole cannot be made to function as a router

❖ Forcing all IP packets arriving on the physical interface to be processed through the TCP/UDP layer for delivery to the proxies

❖ Monitoring all 64-KB TCP/UDP ports for connections

❖ Verifying IP packet direction to eliminate the possibility of IP spoofing of the internal network addresses

> IP address spoofing occurs when the source address of the packet is based on the internal network address protected by Black Hole. When Black Hole receives a packet on its external network interface with a source address of the internal network, the packet is discarded as being spoofed.

❖ Disabling X Window, Open Look, and syslog ports on Black Hole to prevent a vandal from using these network ports to make contact with Black Hole

The base Unix system also has been modified to remove as many of the potential threats as possible while still leaving the system in an operable state. The operating system modifications include the following:

❖ Removal of all redundant applications

❖ Establishment of static routing

❖ Removal of route listeners (routed and so on)

❖ Removal of all unnecessary user accounts

❖ Removal of all compilers and loaders, with the exception of PERL, which is used for application support

> One might question the existence of the PERL interpreter on a firewall with the capabilities of this language. However, the version of PERL provided has been secured and does not provide network sockets support.

NOTE

❖ Configuration of services to run in a chroot environment

Black Hole is composed of a collection of management programs that operate the system and apply the rules for each incoming or outgoing packet. The Guardian is the module that offers services similar to the standard inetd super-server. The Guardian performs some rudimentary checking of the incoming requests, examining the source and destination addresses and ports, at which point it either accepts or denies the requested connection.

The Oracle, or Authentication Server, is responsible for implementing the policies and rules configured by the security manager. The result of the Oracle's processing can be one of several scenarios:

❖ The client is properly authenticated and the connection is allowed to proceed.

❖ The client has not been properly authenticated.

❖ The client is not permitted to connect, in which case the connection is terminated.

Black Hole includes a series of proxy agents, or processes that relay information from one side of Black Hole to the other. The proxies are listed in table 11.2.

TABLE 11.2
Available Proxy Applications

Proxy Name	Description
Proxy-telnet	Handles all telnet requests and connections
Proxy-FTP	Handles FTP requests and connections

continues

507

TABLE 11.2, CONTINUED
Available Proxy Applications

Proxy Name	Description
Proxy-Gopher	Handles Gopher requests and connections
Proxy-HTTP	Handles all HTTP requests and connections
Proxy-TCP	A generic proxy handler that processes TCP traffic not handled by a specific proxy
UDP Relay	A generic proxy handler that establishes a virtual UDP session to the destination and waits for a response before relaying the answer to the requester
NetACL	Permits controlled access to Unix services, such as telnet and FTP on ports 23 and 21 respectively. These services can be used to provide for remote administration of Black Hole itself.

Mail on Black Hole is handled through a specialized mail handler known as DuhMail. DuhMail consists of two components: a mail receiver and a mail sender. The mail receiver is started by Guardian whenever a connection on port 25 is received. The message is collected and saved in a secure area on disk and then transmitted to the remote site by the mail sender.

Black Hole does not run sendmail; therefore, it is not prone to the typical sendmail attacks. Black Hole requires that an SMTP server running sendmail or another SMTP Message Transfer Agent be on the private network to handle the message delivery.

The Black Hole Alarm system constantly reviews the log messages being recorded and watches for patterns specified by the security manager. When a match is found, a predetermined action is taken, which can include sending e-mail messages, ringing the console bell, and calling a pager.

The final core module is the report generator. This module is used to construct statistical reports based on the log file and traffic flow analysis. Once generated, these reports are typically sent via e-mail to the security manager. A printer can be attached directly to the system to generate paper copies of the report if required. The reports available include the following:

❖ Traffic summary by hour

❖ Incoming traffic

❖ Outgoing traffic

❖ Connections per hour

✦ Traffic by port

✦ Top 10 destinations

The report generator is discussed later in this chapter in the section "Generating Reports."

BLACK HOLE EXTENSION MODULES

Black Hole supports Virtual Private Networks through additional software plug-in modules. These modules enable two more Black Hole systems to send information in an encrypted data stream over a public network such as the Internet. As of version 3.0, Black Hole supports Virtual Private Networking with public-key encryption. Although the previous version of Black Hole supported VPN using DES encryption, version 3.0 uses public-key encryption.

Public-key encryption is the most common form of encryption on the Internet today. This form of encryption uses a pair of mathematically related numeric keys. One key is private; the other can be known by anyone. When one key is used to encrypt data, only the other key can be used to decrypt the data. Because public-key encryption and decryption are slow (when compared to private-key encryption), Milkyway's VPN solution uses a mixture of public-key and private-key encryption. In this scheme, each Black Hole has a public key and a private key. Each participating Black Hole has the public keys of each of the other Black Holes in the VPN. When an initial connection is made between two Black Holes in the VPN, a private key (or session key) is created by Black Hole accepting the connection.

Black Hole 3.0 uses a VPN mechanism that will interoperate within a Nortel Entrust environment (Entrust encapsulates key management, encryption, and digital signature software).

> Entrust is a public-key encryption system developed by Northern Telecom (Nortel) Secure Networks division. This client/server application supports digital signatures and public-key encryption in an application-independent fashion.
>
> **N O T E**

With the 3.0 release, Black Hole became the only firewall gateway with strong key management using technology that meets the existing and emerging security standards, such as X.509 certificates, X.500 corporate directory, digital signatures, Diffie-Hellman key exchange, and public-key cryptography.

NETWORK DESIGN WITH BLACK HOLE

The design or redesign of your network is not complicated by Black Hole. Black Hole's easy integration is due to the transparent operation of which Black Hole is capable. With a transparent configuration, users do not even know that Black Hole is there. The principle of Black Hole is to divide the network into two portions: the external network and the private network.

WARNING

In an Internet situation, the external or public network has unrestricted access to only the servers that are on the public network, as shown previously in figure 11.1. This unrestricted access means that any machine outside Black Hole is visible and still open to attack. Consequently, extra caution and care should be taken when you're configuring these systems to ensure they are not compromised.

When a publicly accessible system may be compromised, it must be removed from the network immediately until an investigation is completed. The process of conducting an investigation must be designed into the security policy and not left until the time when you need it.

A system that has been compromised must be reinstalled. Do not attempt to surgically remove the affected components; you may miss something. Consider a compromised machine a cancer—you can't be sure that you got it all without radical action.

To Black Hole, the public information servers on the locally attached network have no preferred status; they are simply machines on the Internet. To protect these publicly accessible servers, the system administrator may want to place them on a third network known as the service network, which is illustrated in figure 11.2.

This service network configuration requires a third network interface on Black Hole. External users are allowed to access only the authorized services on the publicly available servers (FTP service on FTP server; HTTP service on HTTP server; and so on) found on the service network. Should an intruder gain privileged access to one of the servers, that intruder will have access only to the systems on the service network, which is simply a protected version of an external network.

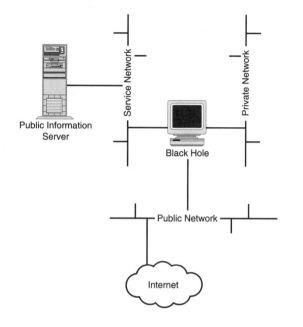

FIGURE 11.2

A Service Network configuration.

Public Information Server

Service Network

Private Network

Black Hole

Public Network

Internet

Because the service network must be visible to the Internet or external networks, you should configure this service network in a "White Hole" configuration. As was previously mentioned, Black Hole typically is configured in an environment where RFC 1597 private network addresses are used on the network behind Black Hole. In a White Hole configuration, the addresses behind the White Hole are registered and routable network addresses.

> White Hole uses the same software and configuration services of Black Hole, but does not render the internal network invisible. White Hole is used to provide external access to the internal network with the extended logging and alarm features of Black Hole.

N O T E

The White Hole configuration can be used in the Service Network approach or in the situation in which the organization primarily wants better logging capability, with the added features that Black Hole brings in this configuration.

By placing the public servers on a service network, the security manager prohibits an intruder from using a penetrated machine on the external network to monitor traffic between the Internet and the private network to collect passwords and to penetrate the internal private network.

Remembering the Security Policy

Black Hole is a tool used to enforce the security policy that the organization has developed. Attempting to use Black Hole without a security policy leads to inconsistent behavior among users and a poor understanding of the benefits within the organization. The organization must remember that as many threats come from within the organization as without. The security manager must therefore be aware of the organization's network design and how Black Hole is configured. If Black Hole is configured as a White Hole, an internal accomplice could assist the external intruder in accessing systems within the White Hole subnet, providing a way for the intruder to then move on through Black Hole using tunneling or a back door. The security policy must clearly delineate that this assistance is an unacceptable procedure and describe ways of discouraging its use.

Using the Black Hole Interface

The Black Hole interface is built around the X Windows System using X11 Release 6 technology. When you start Black Hole, you see a login screen, and you must log in through the X display Manager (XDM) interface. Along with the XDM login screen, nonmanaged windows showing the Console and Alarm Windows appear. When the screen is logging, it changes to that shown in figure 11.3, which displays the Log and Alarm Windows, and an xterm session, as managed by an X window display manager.

Figure 11.3

The Black Hole Alarm Window.

```
Alarm Window                                                                    _ □ ×
Apr 24 19:27:07 warn    Proxy-UDP child[110]: w35591 disallow IPv4[192.168.1.2:udp/177] => IPv4[204.191.124.252:udp/177]
Apr 24 20:27:15 warn    oracle[73]: w016K disallow IPv4[192.168.1.2:udp/177] -> IPv4[204.191.124.252:udp/177]
Apr 24 19:27:15 warn    Proxy-UDP child[111]: w35591 disallow IPv4[192.168.1.2:udp/177] => IPv4[204.191.124.252:udp/177]
Apr 24 20:27:31 warn    oracle[73]: w016K disallow IPv4[192.168.1.2:udp/177] -> IPv4[204.191.124.252:udp/177]
Apr 24 19:27:31 warn    Proxy-UDP child[118]: w35591 disallow IPv4[192.168.1.2:udp/177] => IPv4[204.191.124.252:udp/177]
Apr 24 20:28:03 warn    oracle[73]: w016K disallow IPv4[192.168.1.2:udp/177] -> IPv4[204.191.124.252:udp/177]
Apr 24 19:28:03 warn    Proxy-UDP child[126]: w35591 disallow IPv4[192.168.1.2:udp/177] => IPv4[204.191.124.252:udp/177]
Apr 24 20:28:35 warn    oracle[73]: w016K disallow IPv4[192.168.1.2:udp/177] -> IPv4[204.191.124.252:udp/177]
Apr 24 19:28:35 warn    Proxy-UDP child[134]: w35591 disallow IPv4[192.168.1.2:udp/177] => IPv4[204.191.124.252:udp/177]
```

As mentioned previously, the FTP and telnet services are also available for remote administration. The X Windows interface is intended for use on the console or from an X Windows display server somewhere on the private network. The FTP and telnet mechanism is used when administration must be performed without X Windows, such as over a modem.

To start a remote X windows session for managing the server, a telnet session to Black Hole must be started, and then the desired X windows clients can be initiated. The windows started are an xterm session, an alarm window, and a log window. The Alarm Window, as shown in figure 11.3, is a continuous listing of the contents of the file /var/log/swatch. Each record displays the time of the alarm, the alarm level (as listed in the upcoming minitable), the application initiating the alarm, and the message text.

Worth noting is that the alarm mechanism used in Black Hole is based on the publicly available tool, swatch. The Alarm Window displays the entries from the log file that are matches for the criteria established in the Alarms section of Black Hole.

The second window shown contains the actual Black Hole log file (see figure. 11.4). This file is /var/log/messages, and each record written to that file is also displayed in this window.

FIGURE 11.4

The Black Hole Log Window.

Like the Alarm Window, the Black Hole Log Window displays the date and time of the record, the level of the message, the service that generated the message, and any information for the record, such as source and destination IP addresses. Because DNS names can be spoofed, and Black Hole uses the IP source and destination IP addresses, no IP address to host name translation is performed. Several message levels define the severity of the message, as listed in the following minitable:

Reported Name	Expanded Name	Description
crit	Critical	Any message that could indicate a potential system failure.
Error	Error	An error has occurred, but a system failure is not imminent.
warn	Warning	A potential problem has occurred.
notice	Notice	Something out of the ordinary has occurred.

Actions that Black Hole takes may not always be logged. These situations are known by the security manager; they must be consciously configured. This configuration is achieved by changing the service flags for the rule applicable to the action. This is discussed further in the section entitled "Services, Users, and Rules" later in this chapter.

The main GUI interface for Black Hole is shown in figure 11.5. This screen allows the user to select the different configuration areas of the application: Users, Services, Alarms, and Reports.

513

FIGURE 11.5

*The Black Hole
main interface.*

The main interface allows the security manager to configure the users who are permitted to access services through Black Hole, the services or applications that are permitted to interact with Black Hole, and the Alarms that should be reported. The main interface also is used to generate reports.

As shown in figure 11.6, the File menu contains the selections Commit and Revert. The Revert selection cancels changes that have been made and reverts to the previous version of the policy database. If several changes have been made, and you want to cancel all those changes before Commit has been selected, you may select Revert. If you choose to revert to the previous version of the database and lose your changes, Black Hole prompts you to confirm that you want to revert to the previously saved version of the policy database.

FIGURE 11.6

The File menu.

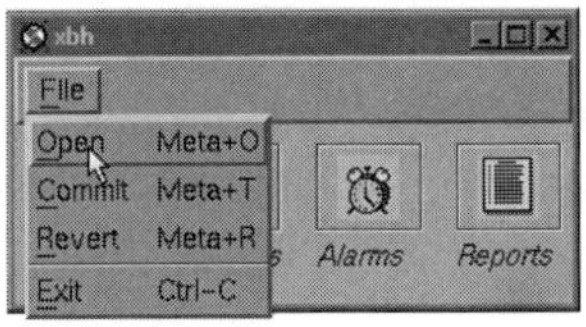

If you select Yes, then the changes you have made are lost. Conversely, if you choose Commit, then all changes you have made are written to the policy database and are placed immediately into operation.

The balance of the interfaces and windows are presented in the following discussion, but focus mainly on the services, users, and rules that enable Black Hole to enforce the corporate security policy.

UNDERSTANDING THE POLICY DATABASE

The policy database can be considered the heart and soul of Black Hole. The policy database contains the rule sets used to determine what action is taken when a connection is received by Black Hole. The security manager uses Black Hole policy database to implement the organizational security policy by developing rules for services and users.

The policy database is comprised of several tables that are assembled by a relational engine to produce rules. These tables are listed in table 11.3.

TABLE 11.3
Rule Tables

Table	Contents
Time	Start times/dates and duration
Service	Applications offered to the users
Address	IP addresses and address patterns
User	Black Hole user IDs, passwords, and minimum password clauses
Rule	Relationships to the four aforementioned tables

Black Hole comes with some predefined rules that allow it to be placed into operation with minimal effort on the part of the security manager. The advantage is that the security manager can immediately work to secure the organization and protect its assets in the short term.

N O T E

> To protect the security manager and the organization, Black Hole makes a copy of the policy database in ASCII format every hour. This copy is made to allow for easy recovery should some attempted action leave Black Hole in an inoperable or questionable state. The ASCII database can then be reloaded, and the previous database recovered.
>
> The ASCII copies are stored in the directory /usr/local/blackhole/oracledb/ dumps. If Black Hole crashes, and either the Oracle or Guardian processes stop functioning, no connections will be accepted from either the internal or external networks, making it extremely difficult for the hacker to violate the system.

As mentioned, the rule table defines a series of relationships that are used to determine what action is taken when a connection is received. Each record in the rule table, also known as a *rule*, consists of the components in table 11.4.

TABLE 11.4
Rule Components

Component	Description
Interval	A reference to an entry in the Time table.
Service	A reference to a service type from the Service table.
Source	A reference to the Address table. In this case the address supplied may act as the source address for the rule.
Destination	A reference to the Address table, supplying an address that may act as the destination address.
User	A reference to the User table. A user name is required if the user must authenticate before being permitted to use the service.
Transfer	The action performed when the rule is applied. There are four options, which are explained later in this section.
Password	Defines the minimum password class that can be used when authenticating for this rule. The options are discussed in the text.
Service Flag	Additional options specific to the individual service.
Connect	Additional options that modify the behavior of the rule as a connection is being established. These options are discussed later in this section.

As mentioned in table 11.4, the Transfer entry in the rule has four options. These options are the following:

❖ **ALLOW.** Connect to the request service transparently, meaning that no user authentication is required.

❖ **CHALLENGE.** Connect only after proper authentication has been performed.

❖ **DENY.** Do not connect, and provide a "deny" message to the user.

❖ **DROP.** Do not connect and do not provide any feedback to the user.

The rule entry contains two password-related options. One is Fixed, which means that a fixed password in the Unix style is the minimum password type permitted for this rule. An alternative method of describing this is a password that is set once and changed only when the user requests it. The second option is to use a one-time password, such as S/Key. This then becomes the minimum password level. Using this level means that using a fixed password for authentication is not permitted.

The Service flag options modify the FTP and UDP proxies provided with Black Hole. The UDP proxy operates in the same fashion as the other connection-based, or TCP, proxies by receiving the UDP packets, applying the rules for the service, and then relaying them to the internal or external host. Remember, if the service is not permitted, it is denied. The Service flag has four FTP options and three UDP options as follows:

Service	Option	Description
FTP	Put Permission	Allows the FTP put command
FTP	Get Permission	Allows the FTP get command
FTP	Delete/Rename Permission	Allows the FTP destructive administration commands
FTP	CD/DIR permission	Allows the FTP non-destructive administration commands
UDP	Multiple UDP Packets	Enables the receipt of multiple response packets, such as seen with Archie
UDP	Do not log	Prevents logging of certain activity (for example, DNS)
UDP	Use privileged port	Uses a port at 1024 or lower

The Connect options modify the behavior of the rule as a connection is being established. The modifications include the following:

❖ **TRANSPARENT PROMOTE.** If the Transfer option previously discussed is set to Challenge, and transparent mode was previously enabled on the source address, then the connection is prompted to transparent for this session only.

❖ **PLUG TO.** This is the IP address of the system to which connection requests should be sent. This IP address is used in the destination field when the packet is transmitted on the other network.

❖ **SOURCE FIREWALL.** This is the default configuration, and it means that the originating address is always Black Hole. This configuration causes the internal network and related routing to be invisible.

With these changes, the security manager can determine where the request will be sent. For example, incoming requests on port 80 would be sent to a specific system in the network. A specific example is discussed in this chapter in the later section "Configuring Application Services."

Transparent mode is a way for users to interact with the other network as if Black Hole were not even there. This seeming absence can be a great advantage sometimes. For example, all FTP requests for systems behind Black Hole from the external network can be denied. However, FTP requests originating from the internal network are permitted. Transparent mode can be enabled for individual addresses or for entire networks. Even if transparent mode is enabled for a specific address, the individual service rule must also be configured to Transparent-Allow; otherwise the connection will fail.

Transparent mode access is granted only if the connection rule uses a transfer type of Allow, in which case the connection proceeds, or a value of Challenge, in which case the user must authenticate first. For the Challenge transfer rule to succeed, the Transparent Promote flag in the Transfer options must also be selected.

When the Transfer type is set to Challenge, the user must authenticate before being able to access the requested service through the firewall. The challenge presented to the user is illustrated in figure 11.7.

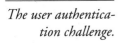

FIGURE 11.7

The user authentication challenge.

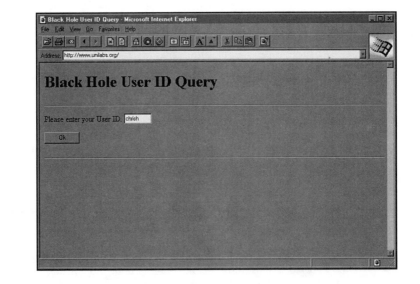

As shown in figure 11.7, the user enters his or her user name and chooses OK. If the user enters a valid user name, then the dialog box shown in figure 11.8 is displayed.

The user then enters his or her password and selects Enable Transparent mode. With this mode enabled, the user does not have to authenticate for services until the session ends.

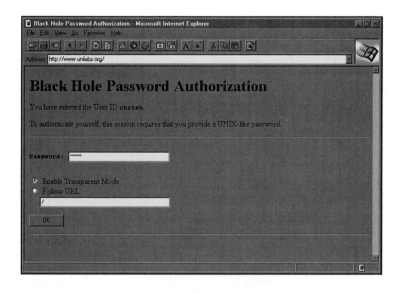

FIGURE 11.8

*The user authentica-
tion response.*

With the multitude of client software available, some implementations might not work when Black Hole prompts the user to authenticate. For example, if the FTP client does not implement the FTP protocol specification as documented, problems may occur during authentication. If the application uses extensions specific to its implementation, which is common for Windows programs, problems will likely occur.

If your client cannot authenticate and is not proxy-aware, then you must authenticate through the WWW and enable transparent access. This will enable your client to operate properly through the firewall.

N O T E

POLICY AND RULE RESOLUTION

As mentioned earlier, the rule table provides the information needed when a connection request is received. For each new request, a two-step process is carried out. The first step involves a comparison of the first request packet, the rules in the rule table. The comparison looks for matches between the following items:

✤ The current system time and the time in the rule

✤ The packet source address and the rule source address

❖ The packet destination address and the rule destination address

❖ The packet destination port and the rule service port

If all of these fields match within a certain range, then the rule is considered for the next step in the process. If no matches exist, the rule is dropped. If all the rules have been applied, and there is no corresponding match, then the connection is dropped.

> The default action is that no data is transferred through Black Hole unless specifically configured.

Any and all rules that match are then processed a second time to determine which rule is priority. This phase is called the *priority and challenge phase.* The values in each field of the packet and the rule are considered according to the following priorities:

❖ Service ID or port. A unique service port, like telnet, has a higher priority than the TCP wildcard rule.

❖ A specific user ID has a higher priority than the default (all users).

❖ The 32-bit source address in the packet is compared with the rule. The rule having the most matched bits from Most to Least Significant (MSB to LSB) has priority over the other rules.

❖ The 32-bit destination address in the packet is compared with the rule. The rule having the most matched bits from Most to Least Significant (MSB to LSB) has priority over the other rules.

❖ The transfer field is checked: a more restrictive action has priority over a less restrictive action in the Drop->Disallow->Challenge->Allow order.

This means that if you choose to disallow a service to all users except one, the service can be denied even for that user because of the transfer restrictions.

With some careful thought to how you will apply rules to implement your security policy, developing solutions to very complex access problems becomes possible.

SERVICES, USERS, AND RULES

Black Hole distinguishes between users and services, each of which has its own distinct rules. A *user* corresponds to a human who is accessing some resource and must be allowed access through the firewall to reach that resource. A *service* is equivalent to an application, such as SMTP, which must be configured in order to allow packets for that protocol, or application, to be handled and, if appropriate, passed through Black Hole.

RULES

The rules are the underlying infrastructure for Black Hole. Without them, all that would be left is a fancy interface. They provide the function and operational definition of what is permitted and denied through Black Hole. Rules are saved in the policy database and are applicable to either a user or a service. This section focuses on the rules' windows and how to interact with them. Specific issues relating to user or service rules are presented in the following section.

USERS AND USER MAINTENANCE

Users are equivalent to Unix accounts on a typical Unix machine. It is recommended that each user within the organization be provided with an account, unless you intend to provide unrestricted access to the commonly used services (such as the World Wide Web) and restrict other applications such as telnet and FTP to certain users. However, providing each user with his or her own distinct account makes identifying the user associated with an action easier because, if no authentication is done, log records do not include the name of the user who performed the action, as illustrated here:

```
Apr  8 20:15:09 notice  proxy-tcp[22706]: n3559 connection terminated:
➥user=unknown
transfered 0 bytes to IPv4[192.168.1.3:tcp/1146] and 0 bytes to
➥IPv4[198.53.144.31:tcp/110].
```

USER ACCOUNT MANAGEMENT

To create users' accounts, the security manager double-clicks on the Users icon, or selects it and chooses Open from the File menu. The user-management window is then displayed, with a selection of buttons and menu items (see fig 11.9). The buttons and menu choices enable the security manager to manipulate and manage the user population.

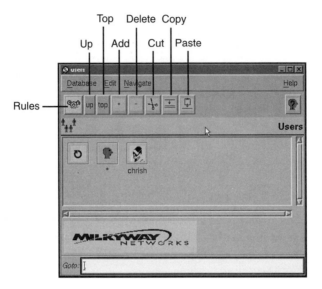

FIGURE 11.9

The user-management window.

The buttons are described in table 11.5.

TABLE 11.5
Icon Descriptions

Button Name	Action
Rules	Opens the Rules window for the selected user or group
Up	Moves view of users/groups up in the group hierarchy
Top	Moves view to the root group
Add	Adds a new user
Delete	Deletes a user
Cut	Removes the selected user or group to paste it in elsewhere
Copy	Copies the selected user or group
Paste	Pastes the information in the selected group

The buttons listed in table 11.5 are found in several places in Black Hole. The controls available to administer the users and groups are identified in table 11.6.

TABLE 11.6
User-Management Commands

To	*Action*
Add a new user	Select Add from the Edit menu, or press the Add (+) button
Delete a user	Select Delete from the Edit menu, or press the Delete (-) button
Modify a user	Select a user icon and choose modify from the Edit menu, or double-click on the User icon
Disable a user	Modify the user account and, in the Update User window, select the Disable user button
Open a group in the same window	Select the group and choose Follow from the Navigate menu
Open a group in another window	Select the group icon and choose Open from the Navigate menu
Add a group	Choose New from the Navigate menu
Modify a group	Select the group and choose Modify from the Edit menu
Move up a group	Choose Up from the Navigate menu or press the Up button
Go to the top group (root group)	Select the top button, or choose Top from the Navigate menu
Go to a specific group	Enter the group name in the Goto field and press Enter
Add or modify rules	Select a user icon and choose Rules from the Edit menu, or press the Rules button
Save changes	Select Commit from the File menu

CREATING USERS AND GROUPS

Before adding users, considering how to structure the users in your organization is wise. For example, are there specific departments in which people work? If so, arranging by department may be one method of organizing the user accounts. For example, say that Company

523

ABC Corporation makes widgets. It has administration, accounting, sales, operations, technical, and management groups. The security manager chooses to create the user groups according to the same structure. To do this, select New from the Navigate menu to display the Update Group window shown in figure 11.10.

FIGURE 11.10

Adding a new user group.

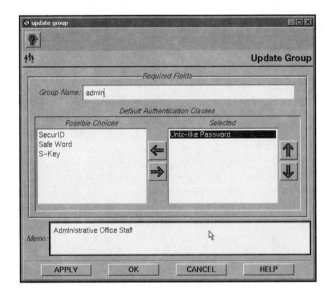

In this window, the security manager enters the name of the group, which is limited to eight characters despite the size of the text field in the window, and selects the password method.

USER AUTHENTICATION METHODS

The authentication types are used to determine how the users in this group will gain access to the firewall. The available options are the following:

✦ SecurID

✦ Safe Word

✦ Unix-like Password

✦ S/Key

The possible authentication methods are selected from the list and added as possible methods for users in this group. When users must authenticate a specific service, they may have to authenticate with something stronger than their user account. For example, users may require only Unix-like passwords when they are authenticating for FTP usage, but may require

SecurID authentication when they are using the telnet proxy. This is controlled not only by the user account but by the authentication established for the service.

The Memo field is simply a note for the security manager that describes the group. To save the group information, choose OK to save it temporarily and return to the Users window, with the new group created. To save these current changes permanently, select Commit from the File menu.

After establishing the possible password authentication methods for each user group, you can add users to the groups. To create a user in the admin group, first choose the group by selecting the admin group from the users window and open it by choosing Open from the Navigate menu. This creates another Users window with no entries in it. Then select the Add option from the Edit menu to open the Update User window (see fig. 11.11). The Update User window contains a series of buttons and fields to be completed before the user is added.

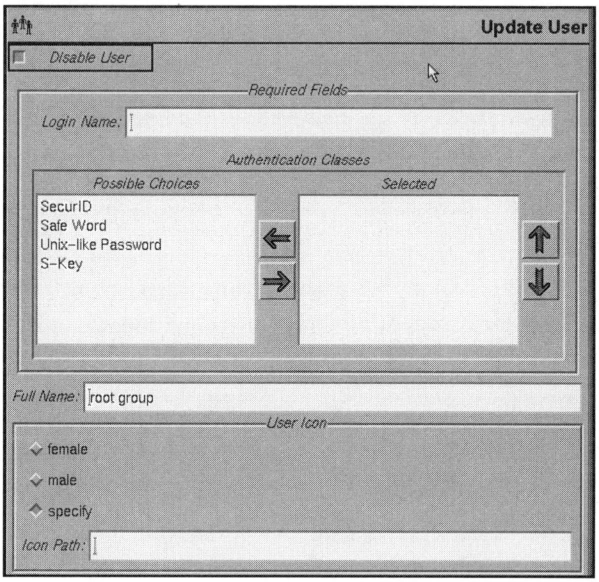

FIGURE 11.11

The Update User window.

The buttons found at the top of the Update User window (which are not visible in figure 11.11) are described in table 11.7.

TABLE 11.7
Update User Window Icons

Icon	Name	Description
	Password	Enables password management
	Icon Browser	Allows for the selection of a picture to identify the user
	Rules	Opens the rule management window

The Password button provides the security manager with the opportunity of establishing an initial password or changing a forgotten password. This button is used for the S/Key and Unix-like password schemes. Those users that utilize a hardware-type device such as SecurID and Safe Word do not require a password to be provided. When you click on the Password button, a message indicating that the password is not required, or a dialog box allowing the user to enter a password, is displayed. If the dialog box is displayed, then the user must correctly type the password twice before it is accepted.

NOTE

> Users can change the password for their accounts by establishing a telnet session to Black Hole. The telnet proxy enables them to connect to a remote host or to change their password. At this point they must provide their current password, and then if validated, can supply a new password.

WARNING

> Unfortunately, no mechanism is currently in place to verify that the password provided by the user is in fact a good one. Although a single carriage return may appear to be sufficient, in fact it is not. You should note that there is some basic password checking on the admin (root) password used to secure Black Hole.

THE USER ICON

The Icon browser is a tool that allows the security manager to select an icon for a user, group, or service. The browser displays the available icons and their names for inclusion in the Icon Path field. The User Icon window contains default icons for male and female users. The icon is simply a method of graphically depicting the user in the users window and has no significance beyond that.

> To add new icons for use in Black Hole, add them to the directory /usr/ X11R6/lib/X11/pixmaps. The only file format supported is XPM, which is the X Windows Pixmap.

The Memo section at the bottom of the Update User window is used for saving information about the user such as his or her full name, workstation location, phone number, and position.

THE USER RULES

The final issue is the rules for this user. Rules, as mentioned previously, are the mechanisms by which Black Hole actually operates. A set of predefined rules exists; making changes, however, to a Black Hole configuration—such as adding users—requires that rules be added.

The rules for users affect the following:

- ✦ What services they can use

- ✦ Source and destination addresses

- ✦ Whether users are allowed to use services, must authenticate in order to use services, or are denied services

- ✦ The type of password that users must use to authenticate

- ✦ Any connection-specific options

- ✦ When users are permitted to use services

Using the rules enables the security administrator to limit who has access to what, and when. For example, if certain Internet sites are receiving too much traffic during work hours for non–work-related material, then access to those destinations could be denied during work hours. This denial could apply to a specific user or to all users.

The rules window, which is the same for the administration of user or service rules, is discussed in the earlier section, "Understanding the Policy Database."

CONFIGURING BLACK HOLE

The preceding section discussed how to add a user to Black Hole. If you have a large number of users, this can be tedious work. However, Black Hole must also be configured to offer the applications that you require as part of your operations. This section discusses the available services and how to configure them. It also presents how to add support for a currently nonsupported application.

The initial configuration of Black Hole is not very difficult, but some thought must be given before you embark on the activation of Black Hole. For example, Black Hole relies on DNS for name lookups. The DNS configurations available include the following:

❖ Internal and external DNS

❖ Black Hole as internal DNS

❖ Black Hole as external DNS

The solution that offers the maximum protection is to use an internal and external DNS that is not operating on Black Hole. This is the recommended practice because the versions of BIND change very quickly due to new protocol enhancements and security-related problems. By adding these unknowns to the firewall, you may be creating a problem that is not obvious until the security of your firewall has been circumvented.

CONFIGURING AN INTERNAL AND EXTERNAL DNS

As you saw earlier, Black Hole is often used to completely hide the internal network from the Internet, or public network. When using an internal and external DNS, you can use the Private Network Number Addressing scheme presented in RFC 1597. To use this scheme, however, an external and internal nameserver must be in operation. The external DNS is used to point systems at the private network, and the internal DNS is used to resolve hostnames in the internal network. However, you must take some care in configuring both services. Figure 11.12 illustrates the internal and external DNS configuration.

FIGURE **11.12**

*The internal and
external DNS
configuration.*

The internal DNS is used to resolve hostnames within the private network. When a host outside the local enterprise is named, the internal nameserver sends the query to an external nameserver for resolution. If you have a valid root.cache file for your internal nameserver, providing a forwarder with Black Hole 2.0p3 is not necessary. Here is the named.boot file from the internal nameserver:

```
;
;    boot file for name server
;
directory /etc
cache         .                               root.cache
primary    unilabs.org         named.hosts
primary    0.0.127.IN-ADDR.ARPA              named.local
primary    1.168.192.IN-ADDR.ARPA            named.rev
```

In this file, the nameserver loads local names from the listed files. However, nonlocal names are sent to the nameservers listed in the root.cache file via Black Hole. This in itself does not mean that Black Hole is running a nameserver. Black Hole then retransmits the request on to the external nameserver for resolution and the answer.

The internal nameserver must be configured with the correct hostnames and IP addresses for the internal network, as follows:

```
ns:/etc# cat named.hosts
@       IN SOA  ns.unilabs.org. chrish.unilabs.org. (
                1996041001      ; Seria
                18000           ; Refresh
                3600            ; retry
                84600           ; expire
                84600           ; minimum
                )
IN      NS      ns.unilabs.org.
```

529

```
                  IN      MX      20 mail.unilabs.org.
internet          IN      A       192.168.1.1
blackhole         IN      A       192.168.1.1
stargazer         IN      A       192.168.1.2
ns                IN      A       192.168.1.3
mail              IN      A       192.168.1.4
ns:/etc#
```

The named.hosts file contains only addresses for the internal systems. With this minimal configuration, the internal nameserver is operational. However, to allow for external addresses to be resolved, including a valid root.cache file on your internal nameserver is essential. This means that the internal nameserver will be able to resolve unknown addresses by contacting the root nameservers listed in the cache file to provide the requested answer.

The external nameserver is configured to show that the external machines, or those in the public network space, are listed with their real IP Addresses. This means that no private hosts are listed in the external nameserver, as illustrated in the following zone file:

```
unilabs.org.     IN SOA  nic.fonorola.net.       chrish.fonorola.net. (
                         96040901      ; Serial
                         10800   ; Refresh
                         1800    ; Retry
                         3600000 ; Expire
                         86400 ) ; Minimum
@                IN NS   nic.fonorola.net.
                 IN NS   fonsrv00.fonorola.com.
                 MX      10 owl.nstn.ca.
nis.fonorola.net.        IN      A       198.53.64.14
www.unilabs.org.         IN      A       204.191.126.10
cisco.unilabs.org.       IN      A       206.116.65.1
stargazer.unilabs.org.   IN      A       206.116.65.10
reliant.unilabs.org.     IN      A       206.116.65.3
mailhost.unilabs.org.    IN      A       206.116.65.4
pc2.unilabs.org.         IN      A       198.53.166.62
stealth.unilabs.org.     IN      A       206.116.65.5
blackhole.unilabs.org.   IN      A       206.116.65.10
```

Those systems that are hidden behind Black Hole and must be visible to the public network, however, are configured with Black Hole external address. This allows Black Hole to accept the connection and forward it to the correct system on the internal network. This type of configuration is done on a case-by-case basis depending on the application and host involved. A specific example is illustrated in the next section, "Configuring Application Services."

The systems on the private network should be able to resolve internal and external hosts. This capability to resolve the hosts can be tested using the nslookup command. The operation and view of the DNS from Black Hole must be tested until it operates as expected before traffic handling commences.

CONFIGURING APPLICATION SERVICES

A series of specific proxy applications exist that govern how Black Hole accepts and handles connections for those services. Aside from the specific proxies, a generic proxy is available to handle applications for which no proxy is supplied.

The configuration for all these service is handled through the Services window in xbh. To add or modify a service, open the Services window and select Add from the Edit menu. This opens the Services window, where you specify the information required for the proxy. This window is illustrated in figure 11.13.

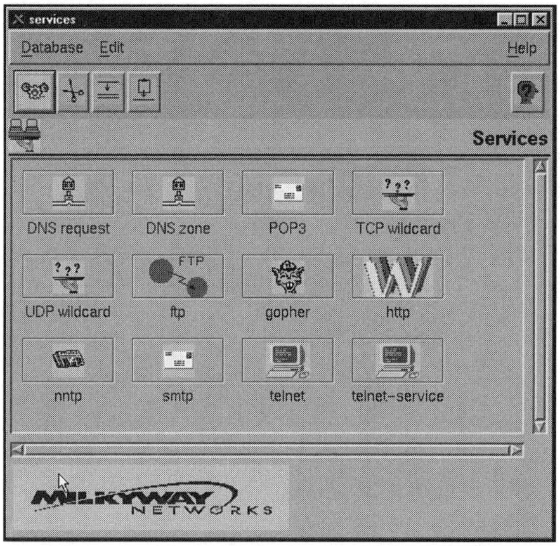

FIGURE 11.13

The Black Hole Services window.

From the Services window, you select the type of proxy, TCP or UDP; the port on which the service will listen; and the class of proxy. The class of proxy determines which of the proxy agents will be used to handle the traffic. If the specific service has no proxy agent, then the best idea is to try the generic class proxy first.

The following sections illustrate how to add services that are not initially defined on Black Hole, and what issues you must be aware of when configuring the other services for operation.

POP

The use of the Post Office Protocol (POP) through Black Hole is rather unusual; therefore, a POP proxy does not come preconfigured. It is, however, part of the rules database and can be easily added. This service makes use of the generic class proxy with no special rule configuration required. No special configuration is required because the host making the POP request will be attempting to contact a specific host on either side of Black Hole.

FTP

The FTP protocol is configured by default as part of Black Hole. When Black Hole initially arrives at your site, use of the FTP service will be denied. Allowing FTP services to transfer from the internal network to the external is accomplished by changing the rules to indicate the transfer. An example is shown in figure 11.14.

Figure 11.14

Configuring an FTP rule.

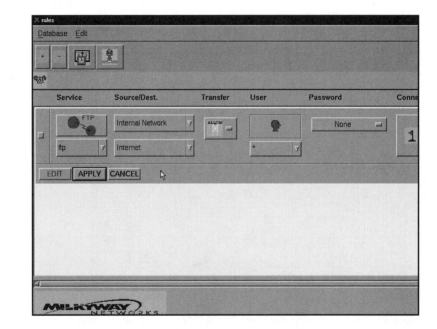

Figure 11.14 shows the rule allowing FTP transfers originating from the internal network. There is a corresponding rule that denies external FTP attempts. When configuring outgoing FTP services, it is important to configure the rule with a TCP service name of "FTP," and to use a class of FTP so that the FTP proxy is used. By doing so, the proper authentication will be used, and you will be able to configure which FTP commands are allowable for the connection.

When you are considering the need for incoming FTP services, determine whether you will have an FTP server outside the firewall as shown in the sample network in figure 11.15.

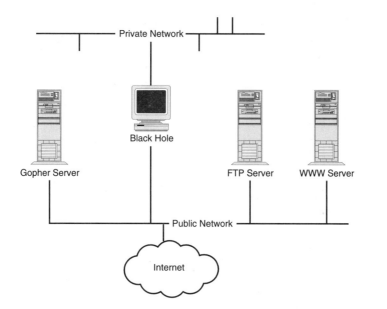

FIGURE 11.15

An information server network.

If you will have an FTP server outside the firewall, probably no one will ever need to download a file through Black Hole to your internal network. Not to worry, however: Even though outgoing FTP is permitted, incoming FTP from the Internet to the Private network is already denied; nothing is permitted unless specifically configured.

GOPHER

Although the services database has an entry for the Gopher service, no rules are defined in the rule table, so Gopher access will be denied. When you are considering a rule for outgoing Gopher access, you should note that even if the Gopher connection request is made from a WWW browser, the connection is made through the Gopher proxy, not the HTML proxy. The connection will therefore fail, as shown in figure 11.16.

The denial of this Gopher attempt also is supported by the log files:

```
May 15 22:12:28 notice  guardian[81]: n5136 ACL port=70
[/usr/local/blackhole/etc/sockperm/tcp/0/70:192.168.1.2] => disallow
May 15 22:12:28 warn  guardian[81]: w5132 ACL disallow IPv4[192.168.1.2:1480]=>
IPv4[204.191.126.2:70]
```

When you are configuring your Gopher proxy, you must use a TCP service named "Gopher," with a class of Gopher, using port 70. You can also set up another rule using the Gopher type and class with a port of "Any." This allows other services such as Veronica to operate properly.

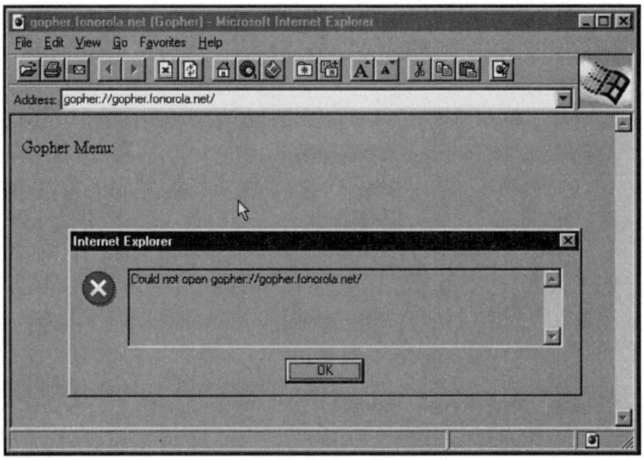

FIGURE 11.16

A failed Gopher via HTML.

When you are considering the need for incoming Gopher, you must determine whether you have a Gopher server on the network, as shown in figure 11.15. If so, you should disable incoming Gopher access through Black Hole using a rule similar to that shown in figure 11.16 for FTP.

HTTP

When you are configuring HTTP rules, you should use a service type of WWW, with a class of HTTP on port 80, or the other commonly used WWW port, 8080. To make sure that other facilities that can operate from a WWW browser are included, you may also create a rule that uses a port of "Any." If you want to restrict sites with material that the organization does not want to be available on its systems (such as pornography), you can restrict access to those sites by applying specific outgoing rules, as shown in figure 11.17, in which a rule to prevent access to www1.playboy.com is illustrated.

When you examine incoming HTTP, you must decide whether you will have a Web server on the outside of your firewall, as shown in figure 11.15. If so, consider blocking all incoming HTTP requests. If, however, you plan to run your HTTP server from behind your firewall, you should configure a rule to use the connection-specific plug-to address in order to indicate exactly where the HTTP will be sent, as shown in figure 11.18.

In figure 11.18, any attempts to contact Black Hole on port 80 are automatically sent to the address named in the plug-to field. To configure this rule, establish the source address as the Internet and the destination address as the public side of Black Hole in the rules window. For example, if the public address of Black Hole is 206.116.65.10, then the destination address for the rule is 206.116.65.10. Any connection requests on port 80 at this address will be redirected to the system identified in the Plug To field of the connection rules.

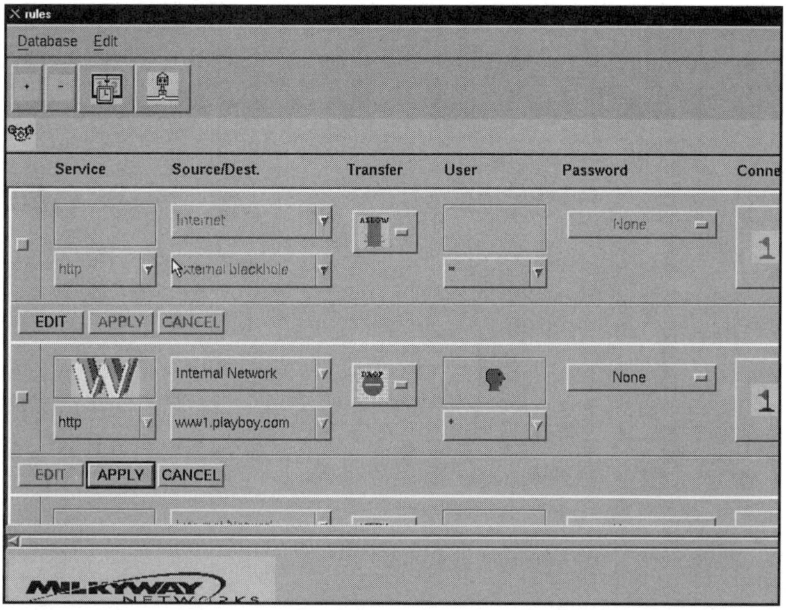

FIGURE 11.17

Denying host access.

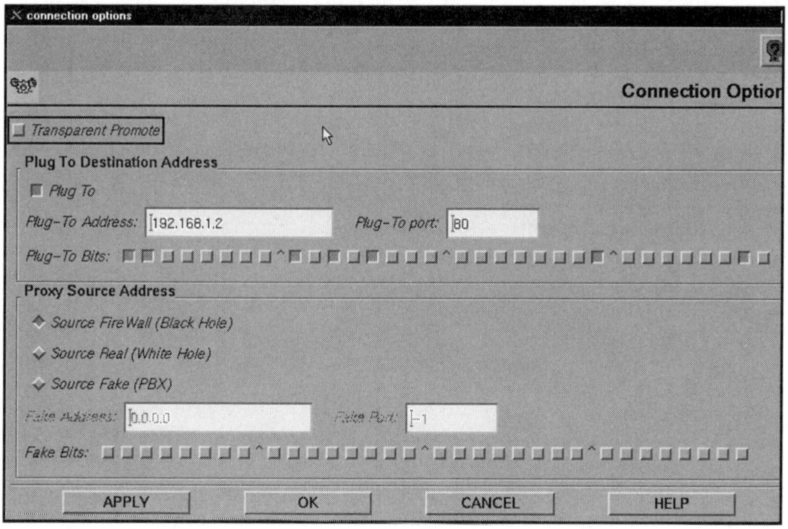

FIGURE 11.18

Using the plug-to address.

NNTP

Configuring Black Hole for Network News using the NNT protocol is done by configuring the external news server to transfer with an internal news server, as shown in figure 11.19.

535

FIGURE 11.19

The NNTP relay news configuration.

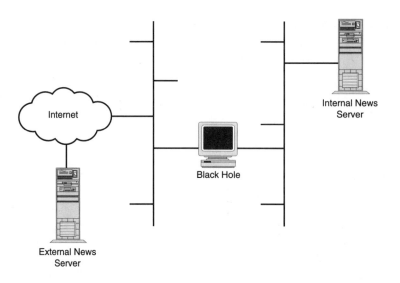

Figure 11.19 illustrates a relay news server configuration in which Black Hole accepts the connection from the external news server and then forwards the packets without processing for assembly on the internal news server. From there, the news clients in the organization access news through the internal news server. The benefit of this method is that it is easier to control what administrative commands can be done through the news protocols, which have been exploited from time to time.

When configuring Black Hole for NNTP support, remember to use a service name of "NNTP," the generic proxy, and a port of 119. The generic proxy is used because no proxy specific to NNTP services exists. To establish a trusted relationship between the internal and relay news server, the source address in the rule is configured as

❖ The internal news server address for outgoing connections

❖ The relay server for incoming connections

The destination address is configured as

❖ The relay news server for outgoing connections

❖ The Black Hole address for the incoming connections

In the last case, in which the incoming address on Black Hole is used for incoming news requests, the connection-specific options are used to specify a plug-to field to specify where the packet is to be routed within your LAN.

When you are completing the configuration for this service, remember that this service will be active 24 hours a day, so transfer access must be set to Allow, and the interval must be set to Daily. These settings mean that your NNTP news provider will use a connection address equal to the public address of Black Hole. Black Hole will then forward any received packets on the NNTP port to the internal news system. News packets for the external server are first sent to the NNTP port on Black Hole, which then redirects them to the external news server.

SMTP

When the initial installation of Black Hole is completed, the mail handler is configured, making Black Hole ready to receive mail from the external sites on port 25 and deliver it to the internal mail processing server. What remains to be completed, if it hasn't already been done, is an MX entry in the DNS for your domain indicating the name of the server IP address of Black Hole, which receives the mail and then forwards it internally. This DNS entry is to be made in the external server so that Internet sites know how and where to send their messages. This entry is made by adding the following lines to the nameserver records for your domain and reloading the nameserver:

```
IN MX blackhole.unilabs.org.
```

```
blackhole.unilabs.org IN A 192.168.1.1
```

GENERATING REPORTS

Black Hole also provides for a series of reports to be generated so that you can view the traffic through your Black Hole. The reports that are currently available are the following:

- ❖ Transactions Per Hour
- ❖ Total Bytes In
- ❖ Total Bytes Out
- ❖ Connections Per Host
- ❖ Bytes per Port
- ❖ Top Ten Destinations

To access the report generator, select Reports from the xbh menu. This displays the Reports window as shown in figure 11.20.

FIGURE 11.20

*The Black Hole
report generator.*

The Report window has two menu options, Operations and Reports, and one push-button. The push-button clears the Report window. The only menu choice under Operations is to close the Report window. The reports previously listed are found in the Report menu. The reports are based on the records found in the /var/log/messages file. Depending on the traffic on your system and how often this file is "rolled over," the file may include all information since the system was started.

The Transactions Per Hour report lists the transactions per hour over the previous 24 hours. A sample report follows:

```
TRAFFIC REPORT on Sun May  5 23:05:34 EDT 1996
   Traffic Summary by Hour
-------------------------------------------------------------
Time Interval                       Connections
        0:00 to  1:00                    83
        1:00 to  2:00                    84
        2:00 to  3:00                    83
        3:00 to  4:00                    79
        4:00 to  5:00                    85
        5:00 to  6:00                   169
        6:00 to  7:00                   134
        7:00 to  8:00                   104
        8:00 to  9:00                   198
        9:00 to 10:00                    97
       10:00 to 11:00                    86
       11:00 to 12:00                   164
       12:00 to 13:00                   178
       13:00 to 14:00                   123
```

```
       14:00 to 15:00                          119
       15:00 to 16:00                          212
       16:00 to 17:00                          135
       17:00 to 18:00                          175
       18:00 to 19:00                          125
       19:00 to 20:00                          230
       20:00 to 21:00                          186
       21:00 to 22:00                          238
       22:00 to 23:00                          211
       23:00 to 24:00                           90
Done.
```

This report lists the transactions made per hour through Black Hole. It does not identify the protocol or user, or the direction of the connection.

The Total Bytes In and Total Bytes Out reports identify the amount of traffic received from the internal and external hosts, respectively. The report identifies the total traffic received by each unique IP address in the internal network. The same is true for outgoing, where the total traffic to each external address is listed. A Total Bytes In report is shown here:

```
TRAFFIC REPORT on Sun May  5 23:10:25 EDT 1996
    Traffic Statistics by direction (Incoming)
-------------------------------------------------------------
station IP                          Incoming Bytes
192.168.1.2                             24603459
192.168.1.3                              1231037
204.101.157.18                            136882
204.101.157.20                             80597
128.100.177.220                            70673
204.191.39.9                               68528
198.53.212.63                              65829
205.150.42.41                              65681
199.185.131.63                             63063
206.172.244.95                             56835
204.191.141.216                            50266
198.53.212.104                             46751
206.172.228.113                            46751
142.78.43.65                               46751
Total incoming bytes = 26919911
Done.
```

The Connections Per Host report lists the number of connections made to each host identified in the report. A sample report resembles the following:

```
TRAFFIC REPORT on Sun May  5 23:16:37 EDT 1996
    Traffic Statistics by Station
-------------------------------------------------------------
Station IP                            Connections
192.168.1.2                              3016
204.101.157.18                             39
198.53.167.27                              34
206.172.244.95                             31
128.100.177.220                            26
```

539

```
199.45.70.109                                    23
204.191.39.9                                     22
Done.
```

The Bytes Per Port report lists the amount of traffic though each of a predetermined set of ports. The amount of traffic includes connections made from both sides of the firewall. The ports reported cannot be changed. You may notice that the report does not include the SMTP port. It is not included because the report is based on the log messages found in /var/log/messages. SMTP log messages are not written in that file and therefore are not reported. Because the reports are written in PERL, however, they can be extended and modified to suit your needs. The following is a sample Bytes Per Hour report:

```
TRAFFIC REPORT on Sun May  5 23:18:03 EDT 1996
   Packet Count by Port (Service)
- - - - - - - - - - - - - - - - - - - - - - - - - - - - - - - - - - - - - - - - -
Port                            Number of Bytes
    21                             14856854
    80                              8234632
   110                              3151985
   119                               662296
    23                                17048
    53                                   31
Done.
```

The last report available lists the top ten destinations for internal users, meaning the ten sites that internal users visit most often. A sample report is shown here:

```
TRAFFIC REPORT on Sun May  5 23:23:32 EDT 1996
   Most Popular Destinations
- - - - - - - - - - - - - - - - - - - - - - - - - - - - - - - - - - - - - - - - -
Rank  Station IP                        Connections
   1   198.53.144.31                        2077
   2   192.168.1.2                           358
   3   206.61.207.115                        104
   4   206.29.210.100                         94
   5   204.191.126.13                         78
   6   199.85.71.65                           61
   7   199.0.62.2                             40
   8   198.73.137.2                           39
   9   140.142.50.1                           37
  10   193.129.186.2                          31
Done.
```

Although no method currently exists for a user to easily generate on-the-fly reports, Black Hole reports are written in the PERL programming language. An experienced programmer could therefore easily develop some additional reports. However, adding them to the Reports menu is impossible at this time. According to Milkyway Networks, a new SQL-based report generator that will support on-the-fly and ad-hoc reporting is coming in Black Hole Version 3.0.

FOR MORE INFORMATION

For more Information on Black Hole, you can reach Milkyway Networks Corporation as follows:

Milkyway Networks Corp.
255-2650 Queensview Drive
Ottawa, Ontario K2B 8H6

Voice +1 (613) 596-5549
Fax: +1 (613) 596-5615

URL : `http://www.milkyway.com`

SUMMARY

The selection of the firewall that will be used to protect your organization is a choice that will follow you for many years. The decision must be based upon several questions:

✤ What features do I need within my firewall?

✤ Do I need an application gateway?

✤ How much effort will it take to maintain?

This chapter has presented the operation of the Black Hole firewall/application gateway from Milkyway Networks. It has covered how to design a network with Black Hole and how to operate and manage the system to implement the organizational security policy. Black Hole is a capable, application-level secure gateway that has many of the features that most security managers want. The success of Black Hole in the commercial marketplace is testimony to the value placed upon the product.

PART III

APPENDIXES

LIST OF WORKSHEETS

This book contains several worksheets designed to assist you in determining your own firewall and security needs. The list below is included to aid in quickly locating them.

SOURCES OF INFORMATION

A VAST COLLECTION OF tools and vendors offer software and security products and services. Even though the term and use of firewalls is relatively new, it is quickly becoming a major part of the network security business. The author recommends that you carefully examine any publicly available code before trusting it to protect your networks, computer systems, and data. This caution is not meant to insinuate that the code itself might be questionable, but to ensure that what you think you are getting is actually what you want. Furthermore, the tools and vendors listed here are not necessarily any better than those not mentioned.

> The path information supplied for each of these tools is the location of one source of the software. There might be other sources, some of which are more convenient to access from your location. Conduct a search with Archie or your favorite World Wide Web search tool to find other sources of these tools.

Most of the sites listed in this appendix also are a good source of other security-related information, so be sure to have a look around.

TOOLS

The list of publicly available tools is long, and the network administrator who is prepared to spend some time investigating each of them is wise. A list of some popular tools and where to get them is identified here.

Keep in mind that neither the authors of this book nor the authors of the software make any claims as to the software's usefulness. As the network administrator, you are responsible for verifying the usefulness and risks associated with any of the software listed here.

TCPWRAPPER AND PORTMAPPER

This is probably one of the best known tools for adding logging and filtering to most standard services. The tcpwrapper program supports only services that are invoked through inetd, whereas portmapper is used for RPC services that are invoked through the standard portmapper. The TCP Wrapper software also is included on the CD-ROM that accompanies this book.

Host: FTP.WIN.TUE.NL

Path: /pub/security/tcp_wrapper

Path: /pub/security/portmap

FIREWALL KIT

The TIS Firewall Toolkit is a collection of software components and system configuration practices that enable you to put together an Internet firewall. Included in the kit are application proxies for ftp, telnet, and rlogin as well as tools for securing SMTP mail.

Host: FTP.TIS.COM

Path: /pub/firewalls/toolkit

BELLCORE S/KEY

S/Key is a one-time password scheme that requires no extra hardware. The user can print a list of challenges and responses prior to traveling. S/Key is included on this book's CD-ROM.

Host: THUMPER.BELLCORE.COM

Path: /pub/nmh/skey

ONE-TIME PASSWORDS IN EVERYTHING (OPIE)

OPIE is an implementation of one-time passwords that was developed by the United States Naval Research Labs. The OPIE software is included on the CD-ROM that accompanies this book.

Host: FTP.NRL.NAVY.MIL

Path: /pub/security/nrl-opie

SWATCH LOGFILE MONITOR

Swatch is a tool that lets you associate actions with logfile entries. When logfile entries are found, the administrator can arrange for a command to be executed such as mail, finger, etc.

Host: FTP.STANFORD.EDU

Path: /general/security-tools/swatch

TCPDUMP

Tcpdump is a collection of tools that can be used to capture and examine the TCP/IP packets flowing on a network. It is considered by many to be one of the best network analysis tools available on the Internet.

Host: FTP.EE.LBL.GOV

Path: tcpdump-3.0.tar.Z

TAMU TIGER

The TAMU Tiger system is a collection of tools you can use to build a firewall or detect attack signatures. A collection of scripts are included that can be used to assess the security of the machines in your own network. Be advised that the anonymous FTP server at this site has some very tight restrictions governing the number of anonymous FTP users. It may take a while for you to get this code.

Host: NET.TAMU.EDU

Path: /pub/security/TAMU

COPS

COPS (Computer Oracle and Password Program) is another popular system auditing package. The COPS package is a collection of scripts and programs that can be used to evaluate the status of a system's security. It includes features to check passwords, SUID and SGID files, protected programs, and more. The COPS software also is included on the CD-ROM that accompanies this book.

Host: FTP.CERT.ORG

Path: /pub/tools/cops

CRACK

Chapter 2, "Security," discussed the use of a password-cracking program. This is one of the best known password-cracking programs, and it can be customized to use your own dictionaries.

Host: FTP.CERT.ORG

Path: /pub/tools/crack

A good set of alternative dictionaries can be found at the following:

Host: FTP.OX.AC.UK

Path: /pub/wordlists

SATAN

SATAN, also known as the Security Administrator's Tool for Analyzing Networks, was written by Dan Farmer and Wietse Venema. It is a collection of tools that run on Perl 5 and your HTML browser to analyze a machine or group of machines for common security problems. A copy of SATAN is included on the accompanying CD-ROM.

Host: FTP.WIN.TUE.NL

Path: /pub/security/satan-1.0.tar.Z

PASSWD+

The passwd+ program performs an analysis of the entered passwords based on the specific rules that your site specifies.

Host: FTP.DARTMOUTH.EDU

Path: /pub/security/passwd+.tar

NPASSWD

The npasswd program is a drop-in replacement for the passwd program. It can be extended to allow changes to other fields in the password file.

Host: FTP.UGA.EDU

Path: /pub/security/npasswd.tar.gz

TRIPWIRE

The Tripwire tools check the files stored on the system to determine whether any have been changed. It checks for damaged or tampered files in an effort to limit the damage.

Host: FTP.NORDU.NET

Path: /networking/security/tools/tripwire

FINDING COMMERCIAL FIREWALL VENDORS

Many commercial operations offer firewall software products and other security related services. Some of these vendors include the following:

✦ Advanced Network and Services (ANS) of Reston, Virginia

   URL: http://www.ans.net/InterLock

✦ Border Network Technologies of Mississaugua, Ontario, Canada

   URL: http://www. borderware.com

✦ Digital Equipment Corporation in Stow, Massachusetts

   URL: http://www. dec.com/info/security/products.htm

✦ Raptor Systems of Wilmington, Delaware

   URL: http://www.raptor.com

✦ Trusted Information Systems in Glenwood, Maryland

   URL: http://www.tis.com

✦ Milkyway Corporation in Ottawa, Canada

   URL: http://www.milkyway.com

EXPLORING FIREWALL AND SECURITY MAILING LISTS

A number of mailing lists and forums are available on the topics of firewalls and security in general. Some are distributed through e-mail, whereas others are part of the USENET News System.

FIREWALL MAILING LISTS

There are two major mailing lists for firewalls. One is hosted by GREATCIRCLE.COM, and the other is hosted by TIS.COM. To subscribe to the Great Circle mailing list, send a message to majordomo@greatcircle.com, with the body of the message reading as follows:

```
subscribe firewalls your-email-address
```

The TIS.COM firewall list, which focuses primarily on using the TIS firewall toolkit, can be subscribed to by sending a message to fwall-user-request@tis.com, with the body of the message reading as follows:

```
subscribe fwall-users your-email-address
```

In either case, the messages from each list will start flowing to your mailbox within a day or two.

Other discussion groups for security-related topics exist. For S/Key and one-time passwords, a mailing list is maintained by Bellcore. To be added to the list, send a request to skey-users-request@bellcore.com. This list is not automated, so it takes a day or two for requests to be completed.

SECURITY FORMS

Other forums are available for the discussion of security in general, not necessarily just firewalls. These forums are generally part of the USENET News system and include the following newsgroups:

> comp.security.announce
>
> comp.security.misc
>
> comp.security.unix
>
> alt.security

This is not meant to be an all-inclusive list, as security-related discussions arise in many other newsgroups as well.

APPENDIX **C**

VENDOR LIST

The following vendors and their products represent security packages or firewall implementations:

3COM   *LAN Security Architecture* is a randomly generated mask for Ethernet networks. 5400 Bayfront Plaza, Santa Clara, CA 95052; (800)638-3266. URL: http://www.3com.com.

ANS   *Interlock* provides gateway protection, encryption, and firewall implementation. 1875 Campus Commons Drive, Suite 200, Reston, VA 22091; (800)456-8267. URL: http://www.ans.net.

BASELINE SOFTWARE   Several products include *Password Coach, Information Security Policies Made Easy,* and *Password Genie*. P.O. Box 1219, Sausalito, CA 94966; (800)829-9955. URL: http://pomo.nbn.com/people/infosec/.

BAY NETWORKS   *Lattis Secure* is access control hardware. 4401 Great America Parkway, Santa Clara, CA 95052; (800)776-6895. URL: http://www.baynetworks.com.

BLUE LANCE LT   *Auditor* provides access control for DOS, Macs, and Windows. 1700 W. Loop S., Suite 1100, Houston, TX 77027; (713)680-1187.

BORDER NETWORK TECHNOLOGIES INC.   *Borderware* is a firewall implementation. 20 Toronto Street, Suite 400, Toronto, Canada M5C 2B8; (416)368-7157. URL: http://www.borderware.com.

COMPUTER ASSOCIATES *CA-Unicenter* offers encryption capabilities for a wide range of operating systems. 1 Computer Associates Plaza, Islandia, NY 11788; (800)225-5224. URL: http://www.cai.com.

CYBERSAFE *Challenger/Kerberos* offers access control encryption. 2443 152nd Avenue N.E., Redmond, WA 98052; (206)883-8721.

IC ENGINEERING *Modem Security Enforcer* provides call-back modem protection, as well as access encryption and several other features. P.O. Box 321, Owings Mills, MD 21117; (410)363-8748.

LIVINGSTON ENTERPRISES *Portmaster, IRX,* and *Firewall* packages. 6920 Koll Center Parkway, Suite 220, Pleasanton, CA 94566; (800)458-9966. URL: http://www.livingston.com/.

M&T TECHNOLOGIES *Microsafe* offers operating system independent virus protection. 1435 N. Hayden Road, Scottsdale, AZ 85257; (602)994-5131.

MILKYWAY NETWORKS *Black Hole* and other network security services. 255-2650 Queensview Drive, Ottawa, ON Canada K2B 8H6; (613)596-5549. URL: http://www.milkyway.com.

PARALON TECHNOLOGIES *Path Key* provides encryption, access control, and authentication. 3650 131st Avenue S.E., Suite 210, Bellevue, WA 98006; (206)641-8338.

RAPTOR SYSTEMS *Eagle* firewalls for Unix and Windows NT systems. 69 Hickory Drive, Waltham, MA 02154; (617)487-7700. URL: http://www.raptor.com.

THE ROOT GROUP *Sudo* provides access control with on-screen and email event notification. 4700 Walnut Street, Suite 110, Boulder, CO 80301; (303)447-3938. URL: http://www.rootgroup.com.

SEMAPHORE COMMUNICATIONS *Semaphore Network Security System* adds access control, encryption, and data integrity features. 2040 Martin Avenue, Santa Clara, CA 95050; (408)980-7750.

THE OPIE AND LOG DAEMON MANUAL PAGES

THIS APPENDIX CONTAINS the manual pages for the OPIE and Log Daemon packages. The manual pages are presented here to complement the text in Chapter 4, "The One-Time Password Authentication System."

THE OPIE MAN PAGES

This section presents the online man pages for the NRL OPIE distribution.

OPIEFTPD

opieftpd—File Transfer Protocol server that uses OPIE authentication

SYNOPSIS

opieftpd [-d] [-l] [-t *timeout*] [-T *maxtimeout*]

DESCRIPTION

opieftpd is the Internet File Transfer Protocol server process. The server uses the TCP protocol and listens at the port specified in the ftp service specification; see *services(5)*.

OPTIONS

-d	Debugging information is written to the system logs.
-l	Each ftp(1) session is logged in the system logs.
-t	The inactivity timeout period is set to *timeout* seconds (the default is 15 minutes).
-T	A client may also request a different timeout period; the maximum period allowed may be set to *maxtimeout* seconds with the **-T** option. The default limit is 2 hours.

COMMANDS

The ftp server currently supports the following ftp requests; case is not distinguished:

Request	Description
ABOR	Abort previous command
ACCT	Specify account (ignored)
ALLO	Allocate storage (vacuously)
APPE	Append to a file
CDUP	Change to parent of current working directory
CWD	Change working directory
DELE	Delete a file
HELP	Give help information

Request	Description
LIST	Give a list of files in a directory
MKD	Make a directory
MDTM	Show last modification time of file
MODE	Specify data transfer mode
NLST	Give name list of files in directory
NOOP	Do nothing
PASS	Specify password
PASV	Prepare for server-to-server transfer
PORT	Specify data connection port
PWD	Print the current working directory
QUIT	Terminate session
REST	Restart incomplete transfer
RETR	Retrieve a file
RMD	Remove a directory
RNFR	Specify rename-from file name
RNTO	Specify rename-to file name
SITE	Non-standard commands (see next section)
SIZE	Return size of file
STAT	Return status of server
STOR	Store a file
STOU	Store a file with a unique name
STRU	Specify data transfer structure
SYST	Show operating system type of server system
TYPE	Specify data transfer type
USER	Specify user name
XCUP	Change to parent of current working directory (deprecated)
XCWD	Change working directory (deprecated)
XMKD	Make a directory (deprecated)
XPWD	Print the current working directory (deprecated)
XRMD	Remove a directory (deprecated)

The following non-standard or Unix-specific commands are supported by the SITE request:

Request	Description
UMASK	Change umask (e.g., SITE UMASK 002)
IDLE	Set idle-timer (e.g., SITE IDLE 60)
CHMOD	Change mode of a file (e.g., SITE CHMOD 755 file)
HELP	Give help information (e.g., SITE HELP)

The remaining ftp requests specified in Internet RFC-959 are recognized, but not implemented. MDTM and SIZE are not specified in RFC-959, but will appear in the next updated FTP RFC.

The ftp server will abort an active file transfer only when the ABOR command is preceded by a Telnet "Interrupt Process" (IP) signal and a Telnet "Synch" signal in the command Telnet stream, as described in Internet RFC-959. If a STAT command is received during a data transfer, preceded by a Telnet IP and Synch, transfer status will be returned. *Opieftpd* interprets file names according to the globbing conventions used by *csh(1)*. This allows users to utilize the metacharacters \&*?[]{}~.

Opieftpd authenticates users according to three rules:

❖ The user name must be in the password database, */etc/passwd*, and not have a null password. In this case, a password must be provided by the client before any file operations may be performed.

❖ The user name must not appear in the file */etc/ftpusers*.

❖ The user must have a standard shell returned by *getusershell(3)*.

If the user name is *anonymous* or *ftp*, an anonymous ftp account must be present in the password file (user ftp). In this case, the user is allowed to log in by specifying any password (by convention, this is given as the client host's name). In the last case, *opieftpd* takes special measures to restrict the client's access privileges. The server performs a *chroot(2)* command to the home directory of the *ftp* user.

In order that system security is not breached, it is recommended that the *ftp* subtree be constructed with care; the following rules are recommended:

~ftp	Make the home directory owned by ftp and unwritable by anyone.
~ftp/bin	Make this directory owned by the super-user and unwritable by anyone. The program *ls(1)* must be present to support the LIST command. This program should have mode 111.

~ftp/etc   Make this directory owned by the super-user and unwritable by anyone. The files *passwd(5)* and *group(5)* must be present for the *ls(1)* command to be able to produce owner names rather than numbers. The password field in *passwd* is not used, and should not contain real encrypted passwords. These files should be mode 444.

~ftp/pub   Make this directory mode 777 and owned by *ftp*. Users should then place files which are to be accessible via the anonymous account in this directory.

SEE ALSO

ftpd(8), ftp(1), opie(4), opiekey(1), opiepasswd(1), opieinfo(1), opiesu(1), opieftpd(8), opiekeys(5), opieaccess(5)

BUGS

The anonymous account is inherently dangerous and should be avoided when possible. In *opieftpd*, it is a compile-time option that should be disabled if it is not being used. The server must run as the super-user to create sockets with privileged port numbers. It maintains an effective user id of the logged in user, reverting to the super-user only when binding addresses to sockets. The possible security holes have been scrutinized, but are possibly incomplete.

AUTHOR

Originally written for BSD, *ftpd* was modified at NRL by Randall Atkinson, Dan McDonald, and Craig Metz to support OTP authentication.

OPIEKEY

SYNOPSIS

opiekey | opie-des | opie-md4 | opie-md5 | otp-md4 | otp-md5 [-v] [-h] [-4|-5]

[-d] [-a] [-n *count*] *sequence_number seed*

.sp 0

DESCRIPTION

opiekey takes the optional count of the number of responses to print along with a (maximum) sequence number and seed as command-line arguments. It prompts for the user's secret password twice and produces an OPIE response as six words. The second password entry can be circumvented by entering only an end of line.

opiekey is downward compatible with the *key(1)* program from the Bellcore S/Key Version 1 distribution and several of its variants.

OPTIONS

-v Displays the version number and compile-time options, then exit.

-h Displays a brief help message and exit.

-4, -5 Selects MD4 or MD5, respectively, as the response generation algorithm. The default for opie-md4 and otp-md4 is MD4, and the default for opie-md5 and opie-md5 is MD5. The default for opie-des and opiekey depends on compile-time configuration, but should be MD5. MD4 is compatible with the Bellcore S/Key Version 1 distribution.

-d Selects DES-based key processing, if opiekey was built with this optional support. The default is not to use DES key munging.

-a Allows you to input an arbitrary secret pass phrase, instead of running checks against it. Arbitrary currently does not include '\0' or '\n' characters. This can be used for backwards compatibility with key generators that do not check passwords.

-n <count> The number of one-time access passwords to print. The default is one.

EXAMPLE

```
wintermute$ opiekey -5 -n 5 495 wi01309
Using MD5 algorithm to compute response.
Reminder: Don't use opiekey from telnet or dial-in sessions.
Enter secret password:
Again secret password:
491: HOST VET FOWL SEEK IOWA YAP
492: JOB ARTS WERE FEAT TILE IBIS
493: TRUE BRED JOEL USER HALT EBEN
494: HOOD WED MOLT PAN FED RUBY
495: SUB YAW BILE GLEE OWE NOR
wintermute$
```

BUGS

opiekey(1) can lull a user into revealing his/her password when remotely logged in, thus defeating the purpose of OPIE. This is especially a problem with xterm. opiekey(1) implements simple checks to reduce the risk of a user making this mistake. Better checks are needed.

SEE ALSO

opie(4), opiepasswd(1), opieinfo(1), opiesu(1), opielogin(1), opieftpd(8), opiekeys(5), opieaccess(5)

AUTHOR

Bellcore's S/Key was written by Phil Karn, Neil M. Haller, and John S. Walden of Bellcore. DES key crunching contributed by Marcus J. Ranum of TIS. OPIE was created at NRL by Randall Atkinson, Dan McDonald, and Craig Metz.

S/Key is a trademark of Bell Communications Research (Bellcore).

OPIEPASSWD

opiepasswd—Change or set a user's password for the OPIE authentication system

SYNOPSIS

opiepasswd [-v] [-h] [-c] [-n *inital_sequence_number*][-s *seed*] [*user_name*]

DESCRIPTION

opiepasswd will initialize the system information to allow one to use OPIE to login. *opiepasswd* is downward compatible with the keyinit(1) program from the Bellcore S/Key Version 1 distribution.

OPTIONS

-v   Display the version number and compile-time options, then exit.

-h   Display a brief help message and exit.

-c   Set console mode where the user is expected to have secure access to the system. In console mode, you will be asked to input your password directly instead of having to use an OPIE calculator. If you do not have secure access to the system (i.e., you are not on the system's console), you are volunteering your password to attackers by using this mode.

-n   Manually specify the initial sequence number. The default is 499.

-s   Specify a non-random seed. The default is to generate a "random" seed using the first two characters of the host name and five pseudo-random digits.

EXAMPLE

Using *opiepasswd* from the console:

```
wintermute$ opiepasswd -c
Updating kebe:
Reminder: Only use this method from the console; NEVER from remote. If you
are using telnet, xterm, or a dial-in, type ^C now or exit with no password.
Then run opiepasswd without the -c parameter.
Using MD5 to compute responses.
```

563

```
Old secret password:
New secret password:
New secret password (again):
ID kebe OPIE key is 499 be93564
CITE JAN GORY BELA GET ABED
wintermute$
```

Using *opiepasswd* from remote:

```
wintermute$ opiepasswd
Updating kebe:
Reminder: You need the response from your OPIE calculator.
Old secret password:
otp-md5 482 wi93563
Response: FIRM BERN THEE DUCK MANN AWAY
New secret password:
otp-md5 499 wi93564
Response: SKY FAN BUG HUFF GUS BEAT
ID kebe OPIE key is 499 wi93564
SKY FAN BUG HUFF GUS BEAT
wintermute$
```

FILES

/etc/opiekeys   database of key information for the OPIE system.

SEE ALSO

passwd(1), opie(4), opiekey(1), opieinfo(1), opiesu(1), opielogin(1), opieftpd(8), opiekeys(5), opieaccess(5)

AUTHOR

Bellcore's S/Key was written by Phil Karn, Neil M. Haller, and John S. Walden of Bellcore. DES key crunching contributed by Marcus J. Ranum of TIS. OPIE was created at NRL by Randall Atkinson, Dan McDonald, and Craig Metz.

S/Key is a trademark of Bell Communications Research (Bellcore).

OPEINFO

opieinfo—Extract sequence number and seed for future OPIE challenges

SYNOPSIS

opieinfo [-v] [-h] [*user_name*]

DESCRIPTION

opieinfo takes an optional user name and writes the current sequence number and seed found in the OPIE key database for either the current user or the user specified. opiekey is compatible with the *keyinfo(1)* program from Bellcore's S/Key Version 1 except that specification of a remote system name is not permitted.

opieinfo can be used to generate a listing of your future OPIE responses if you are going to be without an OPIE calculator and still need to log into the system. To do so, you would run something like:

opiekey -n 42 `opieinfo`

OPTIONS

-v	Display the version number and compile-time options, then exit.
-h	Display a brief help message and exit.
<user_name>	The name of a user whose key information you wish to display. The default is the user running opieinfo.

EXAMPLE

```
wintermute$ opieinfo
495 wi01309
wintermute$
```

FILES

/etc/opiekeys   Database of key information for the OPIE system.

SEE ALSO

opie(4), opiekey(1), opiepasswd(1), opiesu(1), opielogin(1), opieftpd(8), opiekeys(5) opieaccess(5)

AUTHOR

Bellcore's S/Key was written by Phil Karn, Neil M. Haller, and John S. Walden of Bellcore. DES key crunching contributed by Marcus J. Ranum of TIS. OPIE was created at NRL by Randall Atkinson, Dan McDonald, and Craig Metz.

S/Key is a trademark of Bell Communications Research (Bellcore).

OPIELOGIN

opielogin—Replacement for login(1) that issues OPIE challenges

SYNOPSIS

opielogin [-p] [-r *hostname*| -h *hostname*| -f *username*| *username*]

DESCRIPTION

opielogin provides a replacement for the *login(1)* program that provides OPIE challenges to users and accepts OPIE responses. It is downward compatible with the *keylogin(1)* program from the Bellcore S/Key Version 1 distribution, which, in turn, is downward compatible with the *login(1)* program from the 4.3BSD Net/2 distribution.

OPTIONS

-p	By default, login discards any previous environment. The -p option disables this behavior.
-r	Process remote login from hostname.
-h	The -h option specifies the host from which the connection was received. It is used by various daemons such as telnetd(8). This option may only be used by the super-user.
-f	The -f option is used when a user name is specified to indicate that proper authentication has already been done and that no password need be requested. This option may only be used by the super-user or when an already logged in user is logging in as themselves.
Username	The user name to log in as.

EXAMPLE

```
wintermute$ opielogin
login: kebe
otp-md5 499 wi43143
Password: (echo on)
Password: SLY BLOB TOUR POP BRED EDDY
            Welcome to wintermute.
wintermute$
```

FILES

/etc/opiekeys	Database of information for the OPIE system.
/etc/opieaccess	List of safe and unsafe networks and masks to go with them.
$HOME/.opiealways	Presence makes OPIE for logins mandatory for the user.

SEE ALSO

login(1), opie(4), opiekey(1), opiepasswd(1), opieinfo(1), opiesu(1), opieftpd(8), opiekeys(5), opieaccess(5)

AUTHOR

Bellcore's S/Key was written by Phil Karn, Neil M. Haller, and John S. Walden of Bellcore. DES key crunching contributed by Marcus J. Ranum of TIS. OPIE was created at NRL by Randall Atkinson, Dan McDonald, and Craig Metz.

S/Key is a trademark of Bell Communications Research (Bellcore).

OPIESU

opiesu—Replacement su(1) program that uses OPIE challenges

SYNOPSIS

opiesu [-f] [-c] [*user_name*]

DESCRIPTION

opiesu is a replacement for the su(1) program that issues OPIE challenges and uses OPIE responses. It is downward compatible with keysu(1) from the Bellcore S/Key Version 1 distribution and the su(1) program from the 4.3BSD Net/2 distribution.

Unlike other OPIE programs, *opiesu* always requires an OPIE response and will not accept a normal password.

OPTIONS

-f   If the invoked shell is csh(1), this option prevents it from reading the ".cshrc" file. (The [f] option may be passed as a shell argument after the login name, so this option is redundant and obsolescent.)

-c   Set console mode where the user is expected to have secure access to the system. In console mode, you will be asked to input your password directly instead of having to use an OPIE calculator. If you do not have secure access to the system (i.e., you are not on the system's console), you are volunteering your password to attackers by using this mode.

user_name   The name of the user to become. The default is root.

EXAMPLE

```
wintermute$ opiesu kebe
otp-md5 498 wi910502
(OTP response required)
kebe's password: (echo on)
kebe's password: RARE GLEN HUGH BOYD NECK MOLL
wintermute#
```

567

FILES

/etc/opiekeys Database of information for OPIE system

SEE ALSO

su(1), opie(4), opiekey(1), opieinfo(1), opiesu(1), opielogin(1), opieftpd(8), opiekeys(5), opieaccess(5)

AUTHOR

Bellcore's S/Key was written by Phil Karn, Neil M. Haller, and John S. Walden of Bellcore. DES key crunching contributed by Marcus J. Ranum of TIS. OPIE was created at NRL by Randall Atkinson, Dan McDonald, and Craig Metz.

S/Key is a trademark of Bell Communications Research (Bellcore).

THE LOG DAEMON MANUAL PAGES

The following section provides manual pages for the current implementation of the Log Daemon tools.

FTPD

ftpd—DARPA Internet File Transfer Protocol server

SYNOPSIS

/etc/ftpd [**-d**] [**-S**] [-t timeout] [-T maxtimeout]

DESCRIPTION

Ftpd is the DARPA Internet File Transfer Protocol server process. The server uses the TCP protocol and listens at the port specified in the "ftp" service specification; see services(5).

If the **-d** option is specified, debugging information is written to the syslog.

If the **-S** option is specified, each anonymous file transfer is logged in /var/adm/ftp-log.

The ftp server will timeout an inactive session after 15 minutes. If the **-t** option is specified, the inactivity timeout period will be set to timeout seconds. A client may also request a different timeout period; the maximum period allowed may be set to timeout seconds with the **-T** option. The default limit is 2 hours.

The ftp server currently supports the following ftp requests; case is not distinguished:

Request	Description
ABOR	Abort previous command
ACCT	Specify account (ignored)
ALLO	Allocate storage (vacuously)
APPE	Append to a file
CDUP	Change to parent of current working directory
CWD	Change working directory
DELE	Delete a file
HELP	Give help information
LIST	Give list files in a directory ("ls -lgA")
MKD	Make a directory
MDTM	Show last modification time of file
MODE	Specify data transfer \fImode\fP
NLST	Give name list of files in directory
NOOP	Do nothing
PASS	Specify password
PASV	Prepare for server-to-server transfer
PORT	Specify data connection port
PWD	Print the current working directory
QUIT	Terminate session
RETR	Retrieve a file
RMD	Remove a directory
RNFR	Specify rename-from file name
RNTO	Specify rename-to file name
SITE	Non-standard commands (see next section)
SIZE	Return size of file
STAT	Return status of server
STOR	Store a file
STOU	Store a file with a unique name
STRU	Specify data transfer \fIstructure\fP
SYST	Show operating system type of server system
TYPE	Specify data transfer \fItype\fP

continues

Request	Description
USER	Specify user name
XCUP	Change to parent of current working directory (deprecated)
XCWD	Change working directory (deprecated)
XMKD	Make a directory (deprecated)
XPWD	Print the current working directory (deprecated)
XRMD	Remove a directory (deprecated)

The following non-standard or Unix specific commands are supported by the SITE request:

Request	Description
UMASK	Change umask. \fIE.g.\fP SITE UMASK 002
IDLE	Set idle-timer. \fIE.g.\fP SITE IDLE 60
CHMOD	Change mode of a file. \fIE.g.\fP SITE CHMOD 755 filename
HELP	Give help information. \fIE.g.\fP SITE HELP

Note: SITE requests are disabled in case of anonymous logins.

The remaining ftp requests specified in Internet RFC 959 are recognized, but not implemented.

MDTM and SIZE are not specified in RFC 959, but will appear in the next updated FTP RFC.

The ftp server will abort an active file transfer only when the ABOR command is preceded by a Telnet "Interrupt Process" (IP) signal and a Telnet "Synch" signal in the command Telnet stream, as described in Internet RFC 959. If a STAT command is received during a data transfer, preceded by a Telnet IP and Synch, transfer status will be returned.

Ftpd interprets file names according to the "globbing" conventions used by csh(1). This allows users to utilize the metacharacters ``*?[]{}~''.

Ftpd authenticates users according to four rules.

1. The user name must be in the password database, /etc/passwd, and not have a null password. In this case a password must be provided by the client before any file operations may be performed.

2. The user name must not appear in the file/etc/ftpusers.

3. The user must have a standard shell returned by getusershell(3).

4. If the user name is "anonymous" or "ftp," an anonymous ftp account must be present in the password file (user "ftp"). In this case the user is allowed to log in by specifying any password (by convention this is given as the client host's name).

In the last case, ftpd takes special measures to restrict the client's access privileges. The server performs a chroot(2) command to the home directory of the "ftp" user. The process umask is changed so that files delivered by an anonymous user cannot be retrieved by an anonymous user. In order that system security is not breached, it is recommended that the "ftp" subtree be constructed with care; the following rules are recommended.

~ftp)   Make the home directory owned by the super-user (not "ftp") and unwritable by anyone. In fact, there is no need for any file or directory below ~ftp to be owned by "ftp."

~ftp/bin)   Make this directory owned by the super-user and unwritable by anyone. The program ls(1) must be present to support the list command. This program should have mode 111.

~ftp/etc)   Make this directory owned by the super-user and unwritable by anyone. The file motd is printed after successful login. The files passwd(5) and group(5) must be present for the ls command to be able to produce owner names rather than numbers. The password field in passwd is not used, and should not contain real encrypted passwords. These files should be mode 444, and should be owned by the super-user.

~ftp/pub)   If you make this directory world writable (mode 1777), it is recommended that you run a "cron" job to wipe files delivered after anonymous login.

SEE ALSO

ftp(1), getusershell(3), syslogd(8)

BUGS

The anonymous account is inherently dangerous and should be avoided when possible.

The server must run as the super-user to create sockets with privileged port numbers. It maintains an effective user id of the logged-in user, reverting to the super-user only when binding addresses to sockets. The possible security holes have been extensively scrutinized, but are possibly incomplete.

KEY

key—Compute responses to S/Key challenges

SYNOPSIS

key [-n count] sequence seed

DESCRIPTION

key takes an S/Key sequence number and seed as command-line arguments, prompts for the user's secret password, and formats the response as English words.

OPTIONS

-n   Count the number of one-time access passwords to print. The default is one.

EXAMPLE

```
>key -n 5 99 th91334
Enter password: <your secret password is entered here>
OMEN US HORN OMIT BACK AHOY
.... 4 more passwords.
```

SEE ALSO

skey(1), keyinit(1), keysu(1), keyinfo(1)

AUTHOR

Command by Phil Karn, Neil M. Haller, John S. Walden

KEYINFO

keyinfo—Display current S/Key sequence number and seed

SYNOPSIS

keyinfo [username]

DESCRIPTION

keyinfo takes an optional user name and displays the user's current sequence number and seed found in the S/Key database /etc/skeykeys.

The command can be useful when generating a list of passwords for use on a field trip, by combining with the command key in the form

```
>key -n  <number of passwords to print> `ke yinfo`llpr
```

EXAMPLE

```
Usage example:
>keyinfo
0098 ws91340
```

ARGUMENTS

username   The S/key user to display the information for. The default is to display S/Key information on the user who invokes the command.

SEE ALSO

keyinit(1), key(1)

AUTHOR

Command by Phil Karn, Neil M. Haller, John S. Walden

KEYINIT

keyinit—Change password or add user to S/Key authentication system

SYNOPSIS

keyinit [-s] [<user ID >]

DESCRIPTION

keyinit initializes the system so you can use S/Key one-time passwords to log in. The program will ask you to enter a secret pass phrase; enter a phrase of several words in response. After the S/Key database has been updated you can log in using either your regular Unix password or using S/Key one-time passwords.

flkeyinit requires you to type a secret password, so it should be used only on a secure terminal. For example, on the console of a workstation. If you are using \flkeyinit while logged in over an untrusted network, follow the instructions given below with the -s option.

REMOTE LOGIN PROCEDURE

When logging in from another machine you can avoid typing a real password over the network by typing your S/Key pass phrase to the key command on the local machine: the program will respond with the one-time password that you should use to log into the remote machine. This is most conveniently done with cut-and-paste operations using a mouse. Alternatively, you can pre-compute one-time passwords using the key command and carry them with you on a piece of paper.

KEYINIT OPTIONS

-s Set secure mode where the user is expected to have used a secure machine to generate the first one-time password. Without the -s the system will assume you are directly connected over secure communications and prompt you for your secret password. The -s option also allows one to set the seed and count for complete control of the parameters. You can use keyinit -s in combination with the key command to set the seed and count if you do not like the defaults. To do this run keyinit in one window and put in your count and seed, then run key in another window to generate the correct 6 English words for that count and seed. You can then "cut" and "paste" them or copy them into the keyinit window.

<user ID> The ID for the user to be changed/added

FILES

/etc/skeykeys, database of information for S/Key system

SEE ALSO

skey(1), key(1), keysu(1), keyinfo(1)

AUTHOR

Command by Phil Karn, Neil M. Haller, John S. Walden

REXECD

rexecd—Remote execution server

SYNOPSIS

/etc/rexecd

DESCRIPTION

Rexecd is the server for the rexec(3) routine. The server provides remote execution facilities with authentication based on user names and passwords.

Rexecd listens for service requests at the port indicated in the "exec" service specification; see services(5). When a service request is received the following protocol is initiated:

1. The server reads characters from the socket up to a null ('\e0') byte. The resultant string is interpreted as an ASCII number, base 10.

2. If the number received in step 1 is non-zero, it is interpreted as the port number of a secondary stream to be used for the stderr. A second connection is then created to the specified port on the client's machine.

3. A null terminated user name of at most 16 characters is retrieved on the initial socket.

4. A null terminated, unencrypted password of at most 16 characters is retrieved on the initial socket.

5. A null terminated command to be passed to a shell is retrieved on the initial socket. The length of the command is limited by the upper bound on the size of the system's argument list.

6. Rexecd then validates the user as is done at login time and, if the authentication was successful, changes to the user's home directory, and establishes the user and group protections of the user. If any of these steps fail the connection is aborted with a diagnostic message returned.

7. A null byte is returned on the initial socket, and the command line is passed to the normal login shell of the user. The shell inherits the network connections established by rexecd.

DIAGNOSTICS

Except for the last one listed below, all diagnostic messages are returned on the initial socket, after which any network connections are closed. An error is indicated by a leading byte with a value of 1 (0 is returned in step 7 above upon successful completion of all the steps prior to the command execution).

"username too long"	The name is longer than 16 characters.
"password too long"	The password is longer than 16 characters.
"command too long "	The command line passed exceeds the size of the argument list (as configured into the system).
"Login incorrect."	No password file entry for the user name existed.
"Password incorrect."	The wrong password was supplied.
"No remote directory."	The chdir command to the home directory failed.
"Try again."	A fork by the server failed.
"<shellname>: ..."	The user's login shell could not be started. This message is returned on the connection associated with the stderr, and is not preceded by a flag byte.

SEE ALSO

rexec(3)

BUGS

A facility to allow all data and password exchanges to be encrypted should be present.

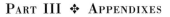

RLOGIND

rlogind—Remote login server

SYNOPSIS

/etc/rlogind [-ln]

DESCRIPTION

Rlogind is the server for the rlogin(1) program. The server provides a remote login facility with authentication based on privileged port numbers from trusted hosts.

Rlogind listens for service requests at the port indicated in the "login" service specification; see services(5). When a service request is received the following protocol is initiated:

1. The server checks the client's source port. If the port is not in the range 512–1023, the server aborts the connection.

2. The server checks the client's source address and requests the corresponding host name (see gethostbyaddr(3), hosts(5), and named(8)). If the hostname cannot be determined, the dot-notation representation of the host address is used.

Once the source port and address have been checked, rlogind proceeds with the authentication process described in rshd(8C). It then allocates a pseudo terminal (see pty(4)) and manipulates file descriptors so that the slave half of the pseudo terminal becomes the stdin, stdout, and stderr for a login process. The login process is an instance of the login(1) program, invoked with the -f option if authentication has succeeded. If automatic authentication fails, the user is prompted to log in as if on a standard terminal line. The -l option prevents any authentication based on the user's ".rhosts" file, unless the user is logging in as the super-user.

The parent of the login process manipulates the master side of the pseudo terminal, operating as an intermediary between the login process and the client instance of the rlogin program. In normal operation, the packet protocol described in pty(4) is invoked to provide ^S/^Q type facilities and propagate interrupt signals to the remote programs. The login process propagates the client terminal's baud rate and terminal type, as found in the environment variable, "TERM"; see environ(7).

The screen or window size of the terminal is requested from the client, and window size changes from the client are propagated to the pseudo terminal.

Transport-level keepalive messages are enabled unless the -n option is present. The use of keepalive messages allows sessions to be timed out if the client crashes or becomes unreachable.

DIAGNOSTICS

All diagnostic messages are returned on the connection associated with the stderr, after which any network connections are closed. An error is indicated by a leading byte with a value of 1.

"Try again."   A fork by the server failed.

"/bin/sh: ..."   The user's login shell could not be started.

SEE ALSO

ruserok(3), rshd(8)

BUGS

The authentication procedure used here assumes the integrity of each client machine and the connecting medium. This is insecure, but is useful in an "open" environment.

A facility to allow all data exchanges to be encrypted should be present.

A more extensible protocol should be used.

RSHD

rshd—Remote shell server

SYNOPSIS

/etc/rshd

DESCRIPTION

Rshd is the server for the rcmd(3X) routine and, consequently, for the rsh(1C) program. The server provides remote execution facilities with authentication based on privileged port numbers from trusted hosts.

Rshd listens for service requests at the port indicated in the "cmd" service specification; see services(5). When a service request is received the following protocol is initiated:

1. The server checks the client's source port. If the port is not in the range 0–1023, the server aborts the connection.

2. The server reads characters from the socket up to a null ('\e0') byte. The resultant string is interpreted as an ASCII number, base 10.

3. If the number received in step 2 is non-zero, it is interpreted as the port number of a secondary stream to be used for the stderr. A second connection is then created to the specified port on the client's machine. The source port of this second connection is also in the range 0–1023.

4. The server checks the client's source address and requests the corresponding host name (see gethostbyaddr(3N), hosts(5), and named(8)). If the hostname cannot be determined, the dot-notation representation of the host address is used.

5. A null terminated user name of at most 16 characters is retrieved on the initial socket. This user name is interpreted as the user identity on the client's machine.

6. A null terminated user name of at most 16 characters is retrieved on the initial socket. This user name is interpreted as a user identity to use on the server's machine.

7. A null terminated command to be passed to a shell is retrieved on the initial socket. The length of the command is limited by the upper bound on the size of the system's argument list.

8. Rshd then validates the user according to the following steps. The local (server-end) user name is looked up in the password file and a chdir is performed to the user's home directory. If either the lookup or chdir fail, the connection is terminated. If the user is not the super-user, (user id 0), the file /etc/hosts.equiv is consulted for a list of hosts considered "equivalent." If the client's host name is present in this file, the authentication is considered successful. If the lookup fails, or the user is the super-user, then the file .rhosts in the home directory of the remote user is checked for the machine name and identity of the user on the client's machine. If this lookup fails, the connection is terminated.

9. A null byte is returned on the initial socket, and the command line is passed to the normal login shell of the user. The shell inherits the network connections established by rshd.

DIAGNOSTICS

Except for the last one listed below, all diagnostic messages are returned on the initial socket, after which any network connections are closed. An error is indicated by a leading byte with a value of 1 (0 is returned in step 9 above upon successful completion of all the steps prior to the execution of the login shell).

"locuser too long"	The name of the user on the client's machine is longer than 16 characters.
"remuser too long"	The name of the user on the remote machine is longer than 16 characters.
"command too long "	The command line passed exceeds the size of the argument list (as configured into the system).
"Login incorrect."	No password file entry for the user name existed.
"No remote directory."	The chdir command to the home directory failed.
"Permission denied."	The authentication procedure described above failed.

"Can't make pipe."	The pipe needed for the stderr wasn't created.
"Try again."	A fork by the server failed.
"\<shellname>: ..."	The user's login shell could not be started. This message is returned on the connection associated with the stderr and is not preceded by a flag byte.

SEE ALSO

rsh(1), rcmd(3)

BUGS

The authentication procedure used here assumes the integrity of each client machine and the connecting medium. This is insecure, but is useful in an "open" environment.

A facility to allow all data exchanges to be encrypted should be present.

A more extensible protocol should be used.

SKEY.ACCESS

skey.access—S/Key password control table

DESCRIPTION

The S/Key password control table (/etc/skey.access) is used by login-like programs to determine when Unix passwords may be used to access the system. When the table does not exist, there are no password restrictions. The user may enter the Unix password or the S/Key one. When the table does exist, Unix passwords are permitted only when explicitly specified.

For the sake of sanity, Unix passwords are always permitted on the systems console.

TABLE FORMAT

The format of the table is one rule per line. Rules are matched in order. The search terminates when the first matching rule is found, or when the end of the table is reached.

Rules have the form:

permit condition condition...

deny condition condition...

where permit and deny may be followed by zero or more conditions. Comments begin with a '#\' character, and extend through the end of the line. Empty lines or lines with only comments are ignored. A rule is matched when all conditions are satisfied. A rule without conditions is always satisfied. For example, the last entry could be a line with just the word deny on it.

CONDITIONS

"hostname wzv.win.tue.nl"

True when the login comes from host wzv.win.tue.nl. See the WARNINGS section below.

"internet 131.155.210.0 255.255.255.0"

True when the remote host has an internet address in network 131.155.210. The general form of a net/mask rule is:

internet net mask

The expression is true when the host has an Internet address for which the bitwise and of address and mask equals net. See the WARNINGS section below.

"port ttya"

True when the login terminal is equal to /dev/ttya. Remember that Unix passwords are always permitted with logins on the system console.

"user uucp"

True when the user attempts to log in as uucp.

"group wheel"

True when the user's primary group is wheel, or when the user is explicitly listed in the group file under the wheel group.

COMPATIBILITY

For the sake of backwards compatibility, the Internet keyword may be omitted from net/mask patterns.

WARNINGS

Several rule types depend on host name or address information obtained through the network. What follows is a list of conceivable attacks to force the system to permit Unix passwords.

"Host address spoofing (source routing)"

An intruder configures a local interface to an address in a trusted network and connects to the victim using that source address. Given the wrong client address, the victim draws the wrong conclusion from rules based on host addresses or from rules based on host names derived from addresses.

Remedies: (1) do not permit Unix passwords with network logins; (2) use network software that discards source routing information (e.g., a tcp wrapper).

Almost every network server must look up the client host name using the client network address. The next obvious attack therefore is:

"Host name spoofing (bad PTR record)"

An intruder manipulates the name server system so that the client network address resolves to the name of a trusted host. Given the wrong host name, the victim draws the wrong conclusion from rules based on host names, or from rules based on addresses derived from host names.

Remedies: (1) do not permit Unix passwords with network logins; (2) use network software that verifies that the hostname resolves to the client network address (e.g., a tcp wrapper).

Some applications, such as the Unix login program, must look up the client network address using the client host name. In addition to the previous two attacks, this opens up yet another possibility:

"Host address spoofing (extra A record)"

An intruder manipulates the name server system so that the client host name (also) resolves to a trusted address.

Remedies: (1) do not permit Unix passwords with network logins; (2) the skeyaccess() routines ignore network addresses that appear to belong to someone else.

DIAGNOSTICS

Syntax errors are reported to the syslogd. When an error is found the rule is skipped.

FILES

/etc/skey.access, password control table

AUTHOR

Wietse Venema
Eindhoven University of Technology
The Netherlands

581

SKEYSH

skeysh—S/Key login shell

SYNOPSIS

/usr/etc/skeysh [username]

DESCRIPTION

skeysh is a solution for sites that cannot replace the login program. Instead, one sets up an unprivileged dummy account with skeysh as its login shell.

A user first logs into the S/Key dummy account. Skeysh then prompts for the user's real account name and presents the corresponding S/Key challenge. When the user produces the correct responses, the program invokes the user's login shell after performing user-specific activities: updating of environment variables; updating of the last login, wtmp, and utmp files; looking at the motd and mail files.

AUTHOR

Command by Wietse Venema, idea from *Hobbit*.

SU

su—substitute user identity

SYNOPSIS

su [-**Kflm**] [login]

DESCRIPTION

Su requests the Kerberos password for login (or for login.root, if no login is provided), and switches to that user and group ID after obtaining a Kerberos ticket-granting ticket. A shell is then executed. Su will resort to the local password file to find the password for login if there is a Kerberos error. If su is executed by root, no password is requested, and a shell with the appropriate user ID is executed; no additional Kerberos tickets are obtained.

By default, the environment is unmodified with the exception of USER, HOME, and SHELL. HOME and SHELL are set to the target login's default values. USER is set to the target login, unless the target login has a user ID of 0, in which case it is unmodified. The invoked shell is the target login's. This is the traditional behavior of su.

The options are as follows:

-K Do not attempt to use Kerberos to authenticate the user.

-f If the invoked shell is csh(1), this option prevents it from reading the '.cshrc' file.

-l Simulate a full login.

  The environment is discarded except for HOME, SHELL, PATH, TERM, and USER. HOME and SHELL are modified as above. USER is set to the target login. PATH is set to '/bin:/usr/bin' . TERM is imported from your current environment. The invoked shell is the target login's, and su will change the directory to the target login's home directory.

-m Leave the environment unmodified.

  The invoked shell is your login shell, and no directory changes are made. As a security precaution, if the target user's shell is a non-standard shell (as defined by getusershell(3)) and the caller's real uid is non-zero, su will fail.

The -l and -m options are mutually exclusive; the last one specified overrides any previous ones.

Only users in group 0 (normally 'wheel') can su to 'root' .

By default (unless the prompt is reset by a startup file) the super-user prompt is set to '#' to remind one of its awesome power.

SEE ALSO

csh(1), login(1), sh(1), kinit(1), kerberos(1), passwd(5), group(5), environ(7)

ENVIRONMENT

Environment variables used by su:

 HOME Default home directory of real user ID unless modified as specified above.

 PATH Default search path of real user ID unless modified as specified above.

 TERM Provides terminal type, which may be retained for the substituted user ID.

 USER The user ID is always the effective ID (the target user ID) after a su unless the user ID is 0 (root).

HISTORY

A su command appeared in Version 7 AT&T Unix. The version described here is an adaptation of the MIT Athena Kerberos command.

TELNETD

telnetd—DARPA TELNET protocol server

SYNOPSIS

/etc/telnetd

DESCRIPTION

Telnetd is a server which supports the DARPA standard TELNET virtual terminal protocol. Telnetd is invoked by the Internet server (see inetd(8)), normally for requests to connect to the TELNET port as indicated by the /etc/services file (see services(5)).

Telnetd operates by allocating a pseudo-terminal device (see pty(4)) for a client, then creating a login process which has the slave side of the pseudo-terminal as stdin, stdout, and stderr. Telnetd manipulates the master side of the pseudo-terminal, implementing the TELNET protocol and passing characters between the remote client and the login process.

When a TELNET session is started up, telnetd sends TELNET options to the client side indicating a willingness to do remote echo of characters, to suppress go ahead, and to receive terminal type information from the remote client. If the remote client is willing, the remote terminal type is propagated in the environment of the created login process. The pseudo-terminal allocated to the client is configured to operate in "cooked" mode, and with XTABS and CRMOD enabled (see tty(4)).

Telnetd is willing to do: echo, binary, suppress go ahead, window size, and timing mark. Telnetd is willing to have the remote client do: binary, terminal type, and suppress go ahead.

SEE ALSO

telnet(1)

BUGS

Some TELNET commands are only partially implemented.

Because of bugs in the original 4.2 BSD telnet(1), telnetd performs some dubious protocol exchanges to try to discover if the remote client is, in fact, a 4.2 BSD telnet(1).

Binary mode has no common interpretation except between similar operating systems (Unix in this case).

The terminal type name received from the remote client is converted to lowercase.

The packet interface to the pseudo-terminal (see pty(4)) should be used for more intelligent flushing of input and output queues.

Telnetd never sends TELNET go ahead commands.

INDEX

H

J-K

M

S

REGISTRATION CARD

Internet Firewalls and Network Security, Second Edition

Name _____ Title _____

Company_____ Type of business _____

Address _____

City/State/ZIP _____

Have you used these types of books before? ☐ yes   ☐ no

If yes, which ones? _____

_____

How many computer books do you purchase each year? ☐ 1–5   ☐ 6 or more

How did you learn about this book? _____

Where did you purchase this book? _____

Which applications do you currently use? _____

_____

Which computer magazines do you subscribe to? _____

_____

What trade shows do you attend? _____

_____

Comments: _____

_____

_____

Would you like to be placed on our preferred mailing list? ☐ yes   ☐ no

☐ **I would like to see my name in print!** You may use my name and quote me in future New Riders products and promotions. My daytime phone number is: _____

New Riders Publishing   201 West 103rd Street ◆ Indianapolis, Indiana 46290 USA

Fax to **317-581-4670**   Orders/Customer Service **1-800-653-6156**   Source Code **NRP95**

Fold Here

- -

**NEW RIDERS PUBLISHING
201 W 103RD ST
INDIANAPOLIS IN 46290-9058**

INFORMATION?

CHECK OUT THESE RELATED TOPICS OR SEE YOUR LOCAL BOOKSTORE

CAD

As the number one CAD publisher in the world, and as a Registered Publisher of Autodesk, New Riders Publishing provides unequaled content on this complex topic under the flagship *Inside AutoCAD*. Other titles include *AutoCAD for Beginners* and *New Riders' Reference Guide to AutoCAD Release 13*.

Networking

As the leading Novell NetWare publisher, New Riders Publishing delivers cutting-edge products for network professionals. We publish books for all levels of users, from those wanting to gain NetWare Certification, to those administering or installing a network. Leading books in this category include *Inside NetWare 3.12*, *Inside TCP/IP Second Edition*, *NetWare: The Professional Reference*, and *Managing the NetWare 3.x Server*.

Graphics and 3D Studio

New Riders provides readers with the most comprehensive product tutorials and references available for the graphics market. Best-sellers include *Inside Photoshop 3*, *3D Studio IPAS Plug In Reference*, *KPT's Filters and Effects*, and *Inside 3D Studio*.

Internet and Communications

As one of the fastest growing publishers in the communications market, New Riders provides unparalleled information and detail on this ever-changing topic area. We publish international best-sellers such as *New Riders' Official Internet Yellow Pages, 2nd Edition*, a directory of over 10,000 listings of Internet sites and resources from around the world, as well as *VRML: Browsing and Building Cyberspace, Actually Useful Internet Security Techniques, Internet Firewalls and Network Security*, and *New Riders' Official World Wide Web Yellow Pages*.

Operating Systems

Expanding off our expertise in technical markets, and driven by the needs of the computing and business professional, New Riders offers comprehensive references for experienced and advanced users of today's most popular operating systems, including *Inside Windows 95, Inside Unix, Inside OS/2 Warp Version 3*, and *Building a Unix Internet Server*.

Orders/Customer Service **1-800-653-6156**   Source Code **NRP95**

New Riders Publishing   201 West 103rd Street ◆ Indianapolis, Indiana 46290 USA